Business Cycles

Studies in Business Cycles
Volume 27

National Bureau of Economic Research
Conference on Research in Business Cycles

Business Cycles

Theory, History, Indicators, and Forecasting

Victor Zarnowitz

 The University of Chicago Press

Chicago and London

VICTOR ZARNOWITZ is professor emeritus of economics and finance at the University of Chicago Graduate School of Business and a research associate of the National Bureau of Economic Research.

The University of Chicago Press, Chicago 60637
The University of Chicago Press, Ltd., London
© 1992 by The University of Chicago
All rights reserved. Published 1992
Printed in the United States of America

01 00 99 98 97 96 95 94 93 92   1 2 3 4 5 6

ISBN (cloth): 0-226-97890-7

Library of Congress Cataloging-in-Publication Data

Zarnowitz, Victor
    Business cycles : theory, history, indicators, and forecasting/
Victor Zarnowitz.
        p.   cm.—(A National Bureau of Economic Research monograph)
    Includes bibliographical references and index.
    1. Business cycles.   2. Economic forecasting.   I. Title.
II. Series.
HB3711.Z37   1992
338.5'42—dc20   91-43392
                                                                CIP

Relation of the Directors to the
Work and Publications of the
National Bureau of Economic Research

1. The object of the National Bureau of Economic Research is to ascertain and to present to the public important economic facts and their interpretation in a scientific and impartial manner. The Board of Directors is charged with the responsibilityof ensuring that the work of the National Bureau is carried on in strict conformity with this object.

2. The President of the National Bureau shall submit to the Board of Directors, or to its Executive Committee, for their formal adoption all specific proposals for research to be instituted.

3. No research report shall be published by the National Bureau until the President has sent each member of the Board a notice that a manuscript is recommended for publication and that in the President's opinion it is suitable for publication in accordance with the principles of the National Bureau. Such notification will include an abstract or summary of the manuscript's content and a response form for use by those Directors who desire a copy of the manuscript for review. Each manuscript shall contain a summary drawing attention to the nature and treatment of the problem studied, the character of the data and their utilization in the report, and the main conclusions reached.

4. For each manuscript so submitted, a special committee of the Directors (including Directors Emeriti) shall be appointed by majority agreement of the President and Vice Presidents (or by the Executive Committee in case of inability to decide on the part of the President and Vice Presidents), consisting of the three Directors selected as nearly as may be one from each general division of the Board. The names of the special manuscript committee shall be stated to each Director when notice of the proposed publication is submitted to him. It shall be the duty of each member of the special manuscript committee to read the manuscript. If each member of the manuscript committee signifies his approval within thirty days of the traqnsmittal of the manuscript, the report may be published. If at the end of that period any member of the manuscript committee withholds his approval, the President shall then notify each member of the Board, requesting approval or disapproval of publication, and thirty days additional shall be granted for this purpose. The manuscript shall then not be published unless at least a majority of the entire Board who shall have voted on the proposal within the time fixed for the receipt of votes shall have approved.

5. No manuscript may be published, though approved by each member of the special manuscript committee, until forty-five days have elapsed from the transmittal of the report in manuscript form. The interval is allowed for the receipt of any memorandum of dissent or reservation, together with a brief statement of his reasons, that any member may wish to express; and such memorandum of dissent or reservation shall be published with the manuscript if he so desires. Publication does not, however, imply that each member of the Board has read the manuscript, or that either members of the Board in general or the special committee have passed on its validity in every detail.

6. Publications of the National Bureau issued for informational purposes concerning the work of the Bureau and its staff, or issued to inform the public of activities of Bureau staff, and volumes issued as a result of various conferences involving the National Bureau shall contain a specific disclaimer noting that such publication has not passed through the normal review procedures required in this resolution. The Executive Committee of the Board is charged with review of all such publications from time to time to ensure that they do not take on the character of formal research reports of the National Bureau, requiring formal Board approval.

7. Unless otherwise determined by the Board or exempted by the terms of paragraph 6, a copy of this resolution shall be printed in each National Bureau publication.

(Resolution adopted October 25, 1926, as revised through September 30, 1974)

To my colleagues
in the NBER program
of research on business cycles,
1952–1991

Contents

Acknowledgments

I am indebted for helpful comments and suggestions to J. Bradford De Long, Robert Gordon, Mark Watson, and two anonymous reviewers for the National Bureau of Economic Research and the University of Chicago Press. I am also grateful for encouragement and advice from Martin Feldstein and Geoffrey Carliner of the NBER. Special thanks are due to Julie McCarthy of the University of Chicago Press and Pamela Bruton for meticulous editorial work; to Mark Fitz-Patrick of the NBER for help with editing; and to Shirley Kessel for the preparation of the indexes. Most of the typing was done by Cynthia Davis.

Two of the essays are joint products of work with colleagues: Phillip Braun (chapter 12) and Louis A. Lambros (chapter 17). I thank them for the opportunity to collaborate in research and for permission to report the results.

My greatest debt is the one accumulated over many years of my work at the National Bureau to the many colleagues in the field of business cycle research. Much of the effort and accomplishment embodied in the long series of the NBER Studies in Business Cycles was and is cooperative and interactive in nature. I learned much from my colleagues and try to express my deep appreciation to them in the dedication of this book. I wish to thank in particular Moses Abramovitz, Jacob Mincer, and Geoffrey Moore, and, of those no longer with us, Charlotte Boschan, Arthur Burns, and Solomon Fabricant.

Acknowledgments to others who helped with particular papers are stated at the beginning of most of the chapters.

Preface

This book originated several years ago as a proposed collection of a few of my older articles and some more recent papers in the general area of business cycles, indicators, and forecasting. It ended up consisting largely of new chapters and some recently published and updated material. As happens so often, writing took more time than expected, in part because of the extension of my plans and in part because of delays caused by teaching and other research responsibilities.

How well scientific papers stand up to the test of time is a question that should always be faced when it comes to reprints. All research results exist to be challenged, tested, and either invalidated or tentatively confirmed. But the threat of obsolescence is much greater in some fields than elsewhere. Here the risk is made acute by the present highly unsettled and active state of the theory of business cycles (although the reasons for this situation are probably in large part inherent in the subject and shared with much other work in economics). New theories try to replace the old ones, in most instances unsuccessfully. This is common in subjects where models proliferate but few are systematically tested and many are not even testable at all.

Not only models but also data and techniques of economic analysis and forecasting continually evolve and multiply. Huge advances in research technology and the accumulation of new information favor new work. Yet the changes are not always for the better. For example, some useful time series have been discounted, forcing alterations in the composite indexes of leading indicators. The computer has enormously facilitated the calculation of economic data and model parameters, but ease of estimation often increases the quantity rather than the quality of the estimates; it certainly does not compensate for inadequate theory or erroneous measurement.

These considerations argue, not simply for the new and against the old, but rather in favor of selectivity and synthesizing what appears to be valuable or promising in both. I decided not to use several of the originally considered articles but use some of the material in updated form in five newly written chapters. My purpose was to reexamine some of my earlier research as well as introduce the themes of the book against the background of recent developments in the literature and history. Chapters 1, 6, 10, and 13 serve partly as previews or overviews to the four parts of the volume: I. Theories and Evidence; II. History and Measurement; III. Indicators; and IV. Forecasting.

As reworked in its final form, the book consists of 18 chapters, 8 of which (the 4 just listed and chapters 3, 4, 8, and 11) have not been published elsewhere. Most of these, whether addressing problems of theory, evidence, indicators, or prediction, are rather comprehensive in scope. This reflects a gradual expansion of my research interests from particular cyclical processes, events, and hypotheses to the long history and modern evolution of business cycles, the range of their theoretical interpretations, and the record and prospects of cyclical indicators and forecasts.

My work on business cycles started at the NBER in 1952, but the earliest two essays included here go back to 1972. One, on business cycle studies of NBER from 1920 to 1970 (chapter 5) will, I hope, be useful as an interpretation of a large and important body of literature in its relation to other concurrent work in the same area. It is a slightly revised and strongly abbreviated version of sections from my introductory chapter to volume 1 of the NBER 50th Anniversary Colloquium (*The Business Cycle Today*). The other (chapter 9), from the same volume, sums up the results of a large NBER project on econometric model simulations of cyclical behavior (reported in Hickman 1972 and followed by much related research; see Klein and Burmeister 1976). This study shows that random shocks failed to generate movements with observable cyclical characteristics in several well-reputed quarterly models. The evidence, confirmed elsewhere, contradicts the still often repeated assertion that macroeconometric estimates demonstrate the high likelihood of small random shocks alone being the source of business cycles.

The other published papers used in parts I and II are "Recent Work on Business Cycles in Historical Perspective" (1985) and "Business Cycles and Growth" (1981). The first of these is complemented by three new chapters dealing with aspects of continuity and change in cyclical behavior and analysis, the treatment of endogenous and exogenous elements, and the relation of movements in real and nominal variables. The second is accompanied by two new chapters on how trends and fluctuations are observed and modeled and how regular (or irregular) the historical business cycles have been.

Part III includes "Major Macroeconomic Variables and Leading Indexes: Some Estimates of Their Interrelations" (1990), a report on a study of vector autoregressive models using recent and historical data. The first of two unpublished chapters on cyclical indicators discusses the systematic aspects of their behavior, distinctions concerning economic process and timing, and analytical meaning and functions. The second is a comprehensive study of the composite indexes of leading, coincident, and lagging indicators: their objectives, standards, assessments, composition, performance records, and conventional as well as new uses in forecasting.

Part IV opens with a new introductory chapter on who forecasts what, when, how, and how well, that is, on sources, targets, methods, and accuracy of short-term, aggregative economic predictions. The next chapter is a comparative analysis of the properties and performance from 1947 to 1976 of annual and quarterly multiperiod forecasts of nominal and real GNP growth and inflation (1979). The remaining four chapters are all recent (1984–87). One compares the accuracy of a large number of individual forecasts with group average forecasts from the quarterly Economic Outlook Survey conducted jointly by the NBER and the American Statistical Association (ASA). I have reported on and evaluated the results of the NBER-ASA survey from its inception in 1968:4 through 1990:1. Another chapter looks at the hypothesis of rational expectations and applies tests for bias and serially correlated errors to diverse forecasts by survey participants and group means. The next presents and discusses measures of consensus and uncertainty based on point and probabilistic forecasts from the surveys. Finally, I offer a general assessment of the record and improvability of macroeconomic forecasting.

The findings of this work are reported in the introductory chapters and in concluding sections elsewhere. Here I will only outline some overall views that seem consistent with these results.

1. Growth in the United States (and other developed market-oriented economies) proceeded through nonperiodic but recurrent sequences of business expansions and contractions. The cycles moderated in recent times and now show up more regularly in growth rates than in levels of total output and employment. This is due to profound structural, institutional, and policy changes. However, on the presently available evidence, there are still no good reasons to assert or project the demise of the business cycle in its classical form (which needs to be distinguished from the growth cycle, i.e., a sequence of high and low positive growth phases).

2. Business cycles are characteristically persistent and pervasive, interact with the longer growth trends, and show many important regularities of comovement, relative timing, and relative amplitude of different economic variables. They are not mere transitory deviations from an independently determined long-term growth trend.

3. Although the economy is always exposed to and affected by a variety of external disturbances, its major fluctuations are not simply aberrations due to these random shocks. Instead, they are to a large extent of endogenous nature. Important interactions and cyclical movements occur among all of the following variables: output prices, input costs, and profits; productivity and investment; money, credit, and interest rates. These relationships are dynamic, involving distributed lags and probably also some essential nonlinearities.

4. Although they have some major elements in common, business cycles

are not all alike and cannot be ascribed to any single factor or mechanism. Real, financial, and expectational variables all participate and interact; no monocausal theory has explained these movements or is likely to succeed.

5. The comprehensive and evolutionary view of business cycles which I hold owes much to the thinking that prevailed in a long sequence of NBER studies directed first by Wesley Mitchell and then by his successors Arthur Burns, Solomon Fabricant, and Geoffrey Moore. Other pioneers in the field, such as Joseph Schumpeter and Gottfried Haberler, adopted a similar position, although differing in many other respects. It is important to note that this conception of business cycles does not by any means imply that contractions in general economy are inevitable or must recur with any frequency. In periods and countries with strong growth trends, recessions are typically short and mild; indeed, they are often replaced by retardations of real growth. Thus, it is possible (as well as obviously very desirable) for a market-oriented economy to achieve both higher and more stable growth.

6. More recent research, at the National Bureau and elsewhere, focused greater attention on the random elements in business cycles and the effects of government activities and policies. This can serve two major purposes. First, there is need to study what shocks impinge on the economy at various times, with what frequency, persistence, and repercussions. Second, it is critically important to learn which policies can reduce and which can aggravate the cyclical instability of the economy, and when and how they do so. But an overreliance on the stochastic approach runs the danger of *assuming* that business cycles are caused only by external disturbances about which little or nothing can be done. Thus the role of internal stresses and imbalances may be neglected or underrated; also, a latent bias may enter the consideration of procyclical and countercyclical policy effects.

7. The cyclically sensitive time series form a system of leading, coincident, and lagging indicators, consistent with long-established timing regularities. To aid macroeconomic analysis and forecasting, the cyclical indicators and indexes are best used in combination rather than individually; in a continual mode rather than sporadically; along with other approaches rather than in isolation. The reasons for the observed behavior of important indicators have significant links to business cycle theories. The leading index has a strong influence on output in equations that also include such major macroeconomic variables as money, fiscal policy, inflation rates, and interest rates.

8. Macroeconomic forecasts must rely on both model and judgment but vary strongly with regard to the relative roles of the two elements. Those based on explicit models are easier to replicate and assess, but they are not on average more accurate than the others as a set. There is no demonstrated superiority of forecasts of some particular theoretical or political orientation, but few professional forecasters follow any single and well-defined model or program consistently. Combining time series of corresponding predictions from different sources and of different types produces smaller overall errors than

those of large majorities of the component individual series. The biases apparent in some forecasts are probably due mainly to insufficient information or instability of the processes that generate the data.

9. The largest errors in forecasts of real and nominal GNP growth, inflation, and the unemployment rate are made in the vicinity of business cycle and growth cycle turning points, particularly peaks. Many forecasts are overly influenced by the most recent events or developments; they rely on the persistence of local trends and are insufficiently cyclical in the sense that they miss the turns and underestimate recessions and recoveries. Leading indicators rarely miss major turns in economic activity, but they now and then err in giving false signals of a recession or (less often) recovery. A forecaster is understandably anxious to avoid predicting a downturn spuriously or prematurely ahead of others, which explains why some indicator warnings are not heeded.

I Theories and Evidence

1   Macroeconomics and Business Cycles: An Overview

"Theories and Evidence" is a fitting general title but it conceals the variety of subjects covered in part I of this book. The purpose of this chapter is to introduce these themes, point out the connections between them, and provide some explanations and extensions. References and detail will be mostly left to chapters 2–5, for which this is to serve as a guide.

1.1   Early and Recent Theories

Theories of business cycles should presumably help us to understand the salient characteristics of the observed pervasive and persistent nonseasonal fluctuations of the economy. The next chapter first presents a summary of these "stylized facts." The discussion then proceeds from historical theories, which were largely endogenous, deterministic, multicausal, and descriptive, to contemporary theories, which are largely exogenous, stochastic, monocausal or limited to very few types of shocks, and based on small formal models.

The early authors emphasized the instability of investment in fixed capital and inventories as well as of the supply of credit used for the acquisition of real and financial assets. Changes in relative input and output prices, interest rates, and profits constituted another important area of interest. Uncertainty about the profitability of future business ventures and volatility of the associated expectations received much attention even before Keynes elevated these factors to particular importance. The investment accelerator was among the earliest discoveries of the theories of economic growth and instability.

The rise of mathematical analysis in the 1930s and 1940s was marked by a dichotomy between the endogenous accelerator-multiplier models driven by nonlinearities and lags and the exogenous models, often of similar content but driven by shocks. The shocks can be few and large or many and small, random or serially correlated. The macroeconometric models, which first became

1

prominent at about the same time, embraced the exogenous, stochastic approach, perhaps largely for reasons of technical convenience as nonlinearities are difficult to handle on a large scale. This did not change with the development of ever more sophisticated analytical and computational techniques and ever larger econometric models. The latter came under heavy criticism recently in the mainstream literature, which favors simple and stable but also linear and stochastic models. However, there is no conclusive evidence that nonlinearities are not very important or that identifiable random shocks do in fact drive business cycles.

Money and prices received little or no attention in the accelerator-multiplier interaction and other Keynesian disequilibrium models. In contrast, shocks to the stock of money, notably those due to shifts and errors in monetary policy, represent the principal source of instability in the monetarist theory. Monetary change has real effects, except in the long run where it influences prices only as in the classical Walrasian prototype theory. Any trade-off with unemployment can exist only for unanticipated changes in the price level; in equilibrium with fully anticipated inflation, the "expectations-augmented" Phillips curve is approximately vertical.

In the Keynesian literature of the 1960s and 1970s the role of money and monetary policy in business cycles was increasingly recognized, but other influences retained their importance as well, notably the variability of private investment and shifts in fiscal policy. The natural-rate hypothesis has been generally accepted, too, but the shifts in the Phillips curve due to changes in inflationary expectations are mostly viewed as slow. A common feature of these theories is that they are concerned mainly with changes in aggregate demand that are translated into fluctuations in output and employment because wages and prices are considerably less than fully flexible over the relevant time horizons. This view of the world has long prevailed in the work on business cycles, which thus sharply departed from the competitive market-clearing paradigm that dominated the theory of price and long-term growth.

It has only been in the last two decades that this contradiction has led to an important new-classical resurgence and new-Keynesian response in macroeconomics. Two strong motivations stirred up this ferment in the recent literature. The first is to build dynamic models consistent with what are viewed as the basic empirical characteristics of business cycles. The second is to ensure that these models have the desired microeconomic foundations, that is, that they are consistent with utility- and profit-maximizing behavior of individuals and firms. The task of achieving both of these objectives simultaneously is very ambitious, far from accomplishment, and indeed of uncertain feasibility. One reason for this is the complex and changing nature of business cycles, as discussed briefly below (and in more detail in chapters 2 and 3). Other reasons lie in problems of theory introduced in sections 1.4–1.6 below and examined more thoroughly in chapters 2 and 4.

1.2   The Diversity and Evolution of Business Cycles

The National Bureau of Economic Research, in its comprehensive studies of long time series for the United States, Britain, France, and Germany, documented the timing and amplitudes of recurrent nonseasonal fluctuations in numerous indexes and aggregates covering a variety of economic processes. Based on the strong elements of consensus in these movements, chronologies of peaks and troughs in macroeconomic activity were constructed for the four countries (see chapter 5 for a brief survey of this research). There is much evidence of the pervasiveness and persistence of business cycles. However, although individual cycles share important family characteristics, they are by no means all alike. The historical experience includes some violent swings of boom and bust, some extended depressions, and (especially in recent times) some long periods of relative tranquillity.

In short, the record shows much diversity of the so measured business cycles. Although most contractions were short and mild, some were long and/ or severe. Although most expansions were neither very long nor very vigorous, some had one or both of these attributes.

The long and widely held view that the U.S. economy tended to be less unstable after World War II than before has recently been challenged. A review of data and literature in chapter 3 upholds the earlier view, with some modifications. In particular, business contractions became somewhat shorter, and much milder and less frequent, whereas both real growth and inflation grew much more persistent. When the possible sources of the moderation of business cycles are considered, they are found to form a rather long list. Several of the examined hypotheses are affirmed, and the selection has some implications for the general analysis of business cycles.

The following factors have probably contributed significantly to the increased stability of the economy:

1. Shifts in employment to less cyclical, largely service-producing industries. This is consistent with the net destabilizing role of changes in business inventories and durable-goods purchases.
2. Increased size of the acyclical government sector.
3. Increased role of automatic (mainly fiscal) stabilizers. Points 2 and 3 are consonant with the idea that growth in normal government activities can, up to a point and given certain rules, offset some of the instability of aggregate private demand.
4. Reduced frequency and intensity of financial crises. Here the implication is simply that such crises can aggravate (if not necessarily cause) business cycles.
5. Some favorable fiscal (mainly tax) policies.
6. Reduced volatility of monetary growth (to the extent that money plays an independent role rather than merely adjusting to changes in income or

business activity). Points 5 and 6 imply that fiscal and monetary policy actions can add to or reduce macroeconomic instability.

7. Greater confidence of private economic agents, both induced by the observed business cycle moderation itself and inducing behavior favorable to more stable economic growth. This suggests a role for endogenous and self-validating expectations in reinforcing positive (or negative) macroeconomic trends.

1.3 Some Implications and Evidence: Problems with Monocausal Explanations

What theories can do justice to such diverse and evolving phenomena? It is doubtful that monocausal hypotheses can, whether the single factor to which they attribute business cycles be real, monetary, or expectational. Theories that rely on a simple interaction (such as that of the accelerator-multiplier) or a single type of shock (e.g., to the money supply, investment demand, or technology) are attractively simple and can be instructive. But they fare on the whole poorly when confronted with data, presumably because they are seriously incomplete.

Models that rely on cumulative propagation effects of small and frequent white-noise shocks from a single source produce fluctuations with common properties that may be fairly regular. They cannot account for any systematic variation or historical evolution of business cycles.

Although a model should be as simple as possible, the wider the range of the relevant facts it covers, the greater is its claim to validity. There is no way to discriminate effectively between the many models that address "the" business cycle on the sole basis of this or that of its selected aspects; one must ask of the models that they be reasonably consistent with all or most of the important stylized facts supplied by history.

Empirically implemented stochastic models suggest that the U.S. economy is exposed to a mixture of shocks, mostly small but occasionally large, with no one source being dominant. Small "structural" models using vector autoregressions (VAR) have aggregate demand disturbances accounting for the largest proportion of the variance of total output; aggregate supply, fiscal, money, and credit shocks exert smaller effects. As the forecast or simulation horizon grows longer, the relative importance of demand shocks tends to decline, that of supply shocks tends to rise.[1]

---

1. In the model of Blanchard and Watson 1986 (quarterly, 1947–82), demand shocks contributed 54% to the variance of the log of real GNP four quarters ahead; shocks to supply, fiscal operations, and the stock of money contributed 15%–16% each. One quarter ahead, the role of aggregate demand was much larger yet (74%); the fiscal and monetary influences were much smaller (3%–4%). For a model with bank loans and M1, Bernanke (1986) reports somewhat larger demand effects four quarters out and smaller supply effects; money and credit account for 11%–12% of GNP variance each.

Different and larger macroeconometric models detect different and more types of shock, which here affect the stochastic equations and the variables treated as exogenous. But the reported simulation results, when properly aggregated, are similar in that they assign the largest effects to demand shocks (mainly to durables consumption, housing, and business fixed and inventory investment). Fiscal, supply, and monetary shocks taken together explain statistically about 30%–40% of the variance of output (Fair 1988; also see Eckstein and Sinai 1986).

The numerical results of any such decomposition are questionable because of differential limitations of the applied econometric and VAR methods, the likely specification errors and identification problems, the reliance on linear relations with constant parameters, and the restriction to short time series covering only the moderate postwar fluctuations. Different models may well be required in application to different conditions, for example, the interwar depressions. But the consensus of a wide range of recent models on at least one point is telling: the theory of business cycles must recognize more than one critical factor and come to grips with the interaction of shifts in demand and supply, real and nominal variables, and changes originating in private behavior and government actions.

1.4 New Developments

Three trends are manifest in the contemporary literature: (1) the increased emphasis on the role of aggregate supply, its determinants and effects; (2) the new insistence on maintaining the assumption of competitive markets cleared by relative price changes; and (3) the adoption of the hypothesis of rational expectations (RE). All of these converged in the family of new-classical equilibrium theories of the business cycle.

The first generation of these models relied on imperfect information: prices outside one's own market are known only with a lag. Random monetary shocks induce changes in the price level that are temporarily mistaken for changes in relative prices, which gives rise to wrong production and investment decisions. The second generation, currently favored by equilibrium theorists, is the theory of real business cycle (RBC), which can be viewed as a stochastic version of the Walrasian prototype. It assumes full information, replaces perfect foresight by RE, and links fluctuations in output and employment to real disturbances only, not nominal disturbances misperceived as real ones.

The existing RBC models use shocks to technology and hence to the representative worker's productivity (other conceivable real shocks are to preferences, weather, government expenditures, and tax rules). Favorable impulses of this type raise the current return relative to the expected future return and so stimulate the present productive effort at the expense of the future effort; negative impulses have the opposite effect of inducing workers to substitute more leisure now for less later. A high degree of intertemporal substitution of labor is assumed in both the imperfect-information and the RBC equilibrium theories. Productivity of capital varies with that of labor, so positive shocks cause investment to rise. A long gestation lag spreads the effects of investment on output over the time needed to build the finished capital goods.

Although lacking clear support from the data, the hypothesis of RE was widely adopted as a maintained premise, with important implications for the analytical methods used. The hypothesis of price flexibility was not, but many of those economists who continued to treat wages and prices as "sticky" now embarked on a search for a reconciliation of this assumption with economic theory. The resulting work on the "microeconomic foundations" of macroeconomics gave particular impetus to studies of aspects of aggregate supply.

A sharp distinction has been drawn in some recent writings between new-classical (NC) and new-Keynesian (NK) macroeconomics (see especially R. J. Gordon 1990). The assumption that prices continuously clear the markets is common to both generations of NC but is not accepted by NK. The NK literature uses imperfections of competition, information, and capital markets in attempts to explain *why* prices and wages are to a large extent set and sticky. This is to provide the microtheoretic foundation for why a decline in nominal demand should be associated with a fall in aggregate output (recession) rather than a proportional downward adjustment in the price level. The new theories of cost and price rigidities are discussed in chapter 4 from the viewpoint of their contributions to our understanding of business cycles.

1.5   The New-Classical Single-Shock Models

Since monetary and price data increased greatly in availability, quality, and promptness, the theory of recurrent price misperceptions resulting from un-anticipated monetary disturbances should be less applicable now than in ear-lier times. Indeed, the main recognized defect of this theory is the implausi-bility of its informational assumptions. At the present, aggregate data on nominal variables are not so much stale as of uncertain dependability and subject to revisions over time. Moreover, output does not appear to be inde-pendent of that component of monetary growth which could have been ob-served or anticipated (and which should have been therefore met exclusively by price adjustments).

The hypothesis that has people confuse absolute with relative price changes also requires prices to be flexible in the short run. It is impaired by the evi-dence that the responsiveness of the price level to fluctuations in monetary growth and income has diminished. As discussed in chapters 3 and 4, indus-trial prices used to decline in cyclical slowdowns and contractions, but they no longer do so in the postwar era of continuing inflation.

Prices are flexible also in the RBC theory, now the more active class of equilibrium models. Here inside money and credit provide inputs into the production process in the form of transactions and financial services; they are driven by the economic activity and this explains their positive correlation with output. In reality, passive responses of money and credit are common, though they take different forms under different monetary regimes (chapter 3). But this is not the whole story: on occasions active money changes occur that are of paramount importance. Thus, monetary authorities can take actions that result in curtailment of monetary growth or even the stock of money. Under other conditions, banks may restrain the availability and raise the real cost of credit.

The aggregate RBC model postulates overall productivity shifts that have strong effects on the total demand for labor. This requires that the diffusion of the shocks to technology across the economy be wide and prompt, but actually technical changes are likely to be localized and gradual. Thus, most of the interest in the dynamics of Schumpeterian innovations—new products, new technologies, new markets—centers on their role in "long waves," not business cycles (cf. van Duijn 1983, ch. 6; Tichy 1983, esp. pp. 80–81). For five major innovations in the United States, 1953–74, the estimated average half-life of the diffusion process was about eight years (Mansfield 1980, pp. 578–80).

The shocks to productivity must be sufficiently large in either direction to result in general business expansions and contractions in the absence of multiplier effects. (The RBC model makes no distinction between the actual and the potential output and so has no multipliers.) It is difficult to think of what would cause such recurrent disturbances and particularly of a technical regress that could account for a major depression. The only supply shocks with demonstrably large power that have been identified so far are the oil cartel's explosive price increases in the middle and late 1970s, which were associated with unique inflationary recessions. These are important cases that the RBC model can help explain but no other similar examples come to mind. Historically, the predominant relationship between the cyclical movements in output and the price level (or its deviations from long trends) was positive, not inverse.

1.6 Technical Change, Productivity, and Investment

The rate of neutral technical change has been estimated residually from an aggregate production function under the assumptions of perfect competition and constant returns to scale (Solow 1957). Updating such calculations confirms that the "Solow residual," an indirect measure of the rate of change in total factor productivity, is positively correlated with the rate of growth in output (see, e.g., Mankiw 1989, p. 84). When interpreted as a proxy for exogenous shifts in the technology of production, these estimates show that such shocks fall to negative values (technical regress) in the years of recessions and rise and are positive in the years of business recoveries and expansions.

Whether the shocks derived from this model are viewed as highly persistent (Prescott 1986, pp. 25–27) or as random (Plosser 1989, p. 63), this reading supports the RBC theory.

It is very unlikely, however, that any nationwide technological decline occurred in the recessions of 1949, 1954, 1958, 1960, 1979, or 1980–82 without anyone having noted it at the time (the OPEC shocks in 1974 and 1979, of course, aroused great public concern). It is far more plausible that the productivities of both labor and capital fall in business slowdowns and contractions because workers and machines have less work to do as demand declines. Skilled and specialized labor is "hoarded" since dismissing and reacquiring it is costly, and speedy capacity adjustments are costly as well. It is important to make investment in human capital pay and difficult to predict the occurrence and duration of demand fluctuations; hence uncertainty impedes the proper timing of input changes.

Labor hoarding can be added to a model of RBC with indivisible labor (i.e., a fixed shift length in hours, as in Hansen 1985) by making firms vary the effort required from their workers in response to exogenous shocks. The work effort is then procyclical and positively correlated with the Solow residual and government consumption or military expenditures used as proxy for demand shocks. In this model, which has perfectly competitive and complete markets, the ability of technology shocks to account for fluctuations in aggregate output is drastically reduced (Burnside, Eichenbaum, and Rebelo 1990). The model shows some improvement on the standard RBC analysis in that it approximates better the observed leading cyclical behavior of the average productivity of labor (which is here positively correlated with future, and negatively correlated with lagged, total hours worked).

Still another interpretation of the procyclical movement of the Solow residual is that it reflects market power and excess capacity (Hall 1986). The markup ratio of price over marginal cost (P/MC) exceeds 1 (its value under competition) and firms often operate in the region of decreasing average cost or increasing returns. This would impart a procyclical bias to the residual estimate even if the true factor productivity were constant (neither influenced by nor causing business cycles). This approach represents the opposite extreme to the aggregate RBC model; it also conflicts with the alternative explanation of procyclical productivity based on labor hoarding, constant returns, and sticky prices (Rotemberg and Summers 1988).[2]

"Autonomous" investment in fixed capital driven by innovations that require more capital per worker has long been recognized as an important force

---

2. Finally, one should mention a strong statistical argument against the reliability of the method of residual estimation of total factor productivity with the available data. In this approach, technical change accounts for more than 50% of real GNP growth in the United States between 1909 and 1949. Alternative calculations suggest that this makes "technical change" a catchall for omitted factors and measurement errors, much of it a "measure of our ignorance" (Denison 1974, 1980; Jorgenson, Griliches, and Denison 1972).

in both economic development and business cycles (e.g., in such diverse theories as those of Schumpeter and Hansen). In Keynesian models the autonomous investment is volatile, and its unpredicted shifts have important multiplier effects on consumption and income. But the desired stock of capital increases with output (more strictly, the expected demand for output), so investment is also in part induced by real growth through a "flexible accelerator" relation. Accelerator-multiplier interaction processes play a central role in various dynamic models. Depending on the parameters involved, they can give rise to explosive, maintained, or damped fluctuations, that is, either to endogenous nonlinear theories or to exogenous stochastic theories of business cycles.

The NC equilibrium models have no multiplier mechanisms, and compensatory combinations of large shocks to technology and a strong instantaneous accelerator lack credibility. The models also fail to produce the sizable positive autocorrelation of investment that is observed.

1.7   Cyclical Movements in Prices, Cost, and Profits

Indexes of U.S. wholesale (and to a lesser extent consumer) prices tended to fluctuate procyclically around alternating upward and downward trends between 1789 and 1932 (Zarnowitz and Moore 1986, pp. 525–31). These movements canceled each other to a large extent over the long stretch covered by historical statistics, even when the inflationary war periods are included. The last half-century, however, witnessed the longest, largest, and most continuous inflation on record. The recent recessions and major slowdowns were no longer associated with any general deflation, only and at most with some disinflation. (Indeed, inflation accelerated during the contractions in 1974 and 1980, in part as a result of the novel supply shocks—the huge increases in oil prices imposed by the OPEC cartel.) The variability of quarterly log differences in prices was much smaller after World War II than in the earlier periods.

A review of the evidence suggests that in recent times money wages as well as prices have become less sensitive to retardations and declines in aggregate demand, even while the cyclical instability of the economy has decreased (chapter 4). This seems inconsistent with the principle of the market-clearing role of prices but it really is not. Depending on the underlying conditions and sources of the shifts in the economy, departures from price flexibility may or may not be destabilizing. The main contrast is between the stabilizing potential of flexible relative prices and the destabilizing potential of large movements in the general price level.

Major deflations of the past had strong adverse expectational and distributional effects, and their nonoccurrence after the Great Contraction of 1929–33 was salutary. But the long persistent inflation of the postwar era could not stay moderate or unanticipated and became itself a major source of instability. It accelerated in the 1970s, grew increasingly volatile, and gave rise to varying inflationary expectations, much uncertainty, and popular discontent. It led to oscillating, tardy, and excessive policy interventions that had disturbing consequences of their own.

The effects on the economy of changes in expected inflation depend on the adjustments of nominal interest rates. The latter have become prompter and stronger in the last two decades than they had been before. They can be stabilizing, up to a point, if permitted by the monetary authorities.

Relative price adjustments work best when the general price level is reasonably stable. Moderate fluctuations in the price level or the rate of inflation are not necessarily detrimental to real growth. In contrast, protracted and anticipated declines in wages and prices have aggravated demand contractions and accompanied the worst depressions in the history of U.S. business cycles. Long and rapid inflations can also be associated with very depressed economic conditions, as illustrated by recent developments in several Latin American countries. (The United States has avoided such inflations in peacetime.)

The structural changes that have contributed to the relative stabilization of the economy in recent times are probably also responsible in part for the reduction in the cyclicality of wages and prices. Not only quantities but prices as well tend to be cyclically less sensitive for services than for goods. Hence, the large rise in the overall weight of services should have made the comprehensive cost and price indexes more sticky.

Another factor working in the same direction was the spread of long and staggered wage contracts prompted by the growth of labor unions (which peaked in the first half of the postwar period). More generally, technical progress and competition require large investments in human capital that pay off best when employment relations are long term, maintaining stably rising levels of productivity and real compensation. Implicit contracts designed to produce such conditions would favor, and might be inferred from, the observed growth of career employment in the corporate sector, professions, and government.

A rise in confidence and the perceived probability that business contractions and slowdowns will remain brief and mild would help to keep up spending and hence firm up prices in general. So expectations of prosperity may also counteract price declines or cuts.

Procyclical movements in delivery lags help absorb changes in demand. The frequency of price changes is reduced by nonprice market clearing. An increase in the role of production to order and adjustments in delivery periods would have made the measured price level more sticky.

Prices of finished industrial products generally move less than average production costs, which tend to rise *relative* to their trends in slowdowns and downswings and decline late in recessions and particularly in early and high expansions. (These lagging cost changes reflect mainly the sensitive behavior of labor productivity—output per hour—and the sluggish behavior of wages.) As a result, the markups on unit labor costs and profit margins have strong cyclical movements that typically lead at peaks and troughs by long intervals, responding directly to changes in productivity and inversely to changes in cost. Total profits have similar large fluctuations with somewhat shorter leads. These patterns of relative movements in prices and costs, productivity and profitability, are well documented in recent data, but they may have a long history and do not imply that prices in general are necessarily very sticky.

Certain NK hypotheses on why wages and prices are rigid assume monopolistic competition or oligopoly. Labor productivity is taken to be a rising function of real or relative wages, which are therefore kept high ("efficiency wages"). Small deviations from the equilibrium price affect profits only slightly and are therefore not worth correcting, as the individual firm sees it ("menu cost"). These are interesting ideas but their applicability is still to be established. They would gain support from the data if it could be shown that market power has increased in recent times, but it is not clear that it has.

1.8   Elements of Business Cycle Dynamics: Some Illustrations

Lags and nonlinearities provide the essential ingredients of endogenous business cycle models, which are valued for not being dependent on the theoretically unexplained and empirically unobserved outside shocks. There is a strong presumption that these elements are indeed important in the immanent dynamics of the economy. Some simple examples are presented in figure 1.1 and the text below; they draw on theories discussed in more detail in the chapters that follow. But it should be noted at the outset that the available formal and fully articulated models of self-sustaining cycles are generally small, abstract, and of uncertain value in interpreting the world. The main probable reason lies in the limitations imposed by the mathematical complexity of constructing larger models of this type. In any event, what we have is a number of ingenious but fragmentary constructs and a larger number of interesting ideas that may serve as building blocks for a more general theory. My purpose here is merely to introduce some such notions that seem to fit the facts at least some of the time.

One old idea is that near, at, and above full employment the demand for labor and materials tends to outrun supplies, driving up wages and other input costs. At the same time, growth of capital and output may deter comparably large rises in prices of final goods and services. At low employment and capacity utilization, however, prices rise faster than wages and other costs. In other words, the rate of change in costs (c) leads the rate of change in prices (p), as shown by the upper pair of curves in figure 1.1. When the increase in p exceeds the increase in c, profits per unit of sales rise; when the reverse obtains, they fall (see curve Π/S).

As depicted, p and c would rise in booms, decline in slumps, and remain

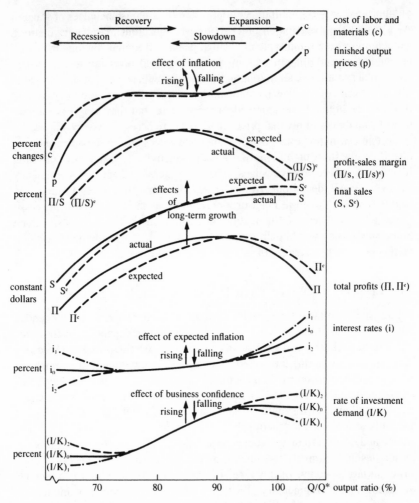

Fig. 1.1   Selected nonlinear relationships used in business cycle models

stable during the intervening periods of moderate growth. The long-term average rate of inflation is assumed to be low (perhaps close to 0) and highly stable. History offers examples of a prevalence of such conditions of long-period monetary and price stability in peacetime, notably during the pre–World War I gold standard era (which presumably explains the good overall fit of the original Phillips curve). But in an age of secular inflation, the expected rates of price and wage changes will not indefinitely lag behind the actual rates, unless the latter continually accelerate. Hence, the simple Phillips relationship between inflation and unemployment (or the ratio of actual to natural output, Q/Q^*) will be destabilized as it was in the late 1960s and

1970s. In such times, then, the c and p curves would steepen (i.e., tilt counterclockwise) and shift upward with anticipations of rising inflation, as indicated by arrows in figure 1.1).[3] It seems plausible that the hypothesized cyclical effects on, and differential behavior of, the relative prices (c. vs. p) could well persist as long as the inflation remained moderate, but one can certainly think of disabling conditions in this context as well (e.g., rapid inflation with c lagging behind p; the two curves tending to common verticality).

In various theories of the business cycle, demand rises less than output as the expansion unfolds; that is, final sales flatten or "lag," as shown by the S curve in the chart. One possible source is the short-run consumption function, whose slope is positive but less than 1 and perhaps getting gradually smaller. The accelerator effects on fixed investment and inventory investment of the declining growth in consumption must also be considered. The growth in output itself is thought of as decelerating as full employment is approached and bottlenecks are increasingly encountered. Meanwhile, the accumulation of the real capital stock (K) is picking up steam at high levels of capacity utilization, which according to the flexible accelerator hypothesis has a negative effect on net investment in business plant and equipment.

Given the Π/S and S function, the total profits curve (Π/S) $\times$ S will have an inverted-U shape, like Π/S but lagging and steeper on the downgrade (see fig. 1.1). Since K is a slow-moving stock variable dominated by an upward trend, the profit rate Π/K would reflect mainly the leading cyclical pattern of Π, with an even sharper decline. Expected profits should be influenced by past and present realized profits and have a similar profile of cyclical movement. This supposition is indeed generally consistent with the observed tendencies of both corporate profits and stock price indexes to lead at business cycle turns, particularly peaks.

The decline in profit expectations is likely to dampen the rate of real investment demand, I/K, where I represents investment plans and commitments (appropriations, contracts, and orders) rather than the lagging realizations (outlays and completions of capital projects). The sigmoid function $(I/K)_0$ in figure 1.1 assumes that I responds positively to Q, given K, in the midrange of perceived positive profit opportunities. When expected profits are poor, dI/dQ is low or 0, however, and this is the case at both very low and very high capacity utilization levels. Given Q, net investment should depend inversely on K, but gross investment need not, since depreciation and replacement investment are positively related to the volume of the capital stock. A sufficiently large expansion of K can nevertheless depress the total investment rate temporarily as a result of "overbuilding."

Investment is clearly an inverse function of the level of interest rates (i) to the extent that higher i represents in real terms both higher financing costs and

---

3. The alternative curves are not shown to avoid cluttering figure 1.1, which tries to reduce complex dynamic situations to their simplest common elements.

higher returns on nominal assets. This relationship too may be nonlinear, as in the case when I is more interest sensitive at high than at low levels of i. In the course of a business expansion, i will often start rising because of any or all of the following: (1) the demand for credit outruns the supply of credit, (2) the real rate of return on physical capital rises, and (3) expectations of inflation increase (note that this last effect relates directly to the nominal, rather than real, interest rates and can occur during business contractions as well). In figure 1.1, this type of behavior is illustrated by the curve i_0. But other developments are just as possible, since interest rates depend not only on the demand for credit and its determinants, notably Q as the measure of aggregate economic activity, but also on the supply of credit and its determinants, notably the role of banking and monetary policy. For example, increasing the money supply growth rate at low levels of Q/Q^* and reducing it at high levels may produce such curves as i_1 and, in response, $(I/K)_1$. The opposite combination of a relatively restrictive (stimulative) policy when Q/Q^* is low (high) can be represented by curves i_2 and $(I/K)_2$.

Movements to the right along the hypothesized curves occur in recoveries and expansions; movements to the left occur in slowdowns and recessions, as indicated by the arrows at the top of figure 1.1. But no simple schematic representation can do justice to business cycle dynamics that include elements of trends, irreversibilities, and shifts over time in some of the depicted functions. As already noted, inflationary trends and expectations tend to shift the c, p, and i curves. Also, long-term real growth will gradually pull upward the aggregate sales and profits (S, Π) curves at any Q/Q^* ratio. The direction of these effects is shown by arrows on the figure.

1.9   Extensions and Qualifications

Business cycles are diversified largely because they are propelled by a number of endogenous forces whose relative intensity varies over time. A major source of differences between the historical explanations of business cycles is that one author places the main stress on factor A, another on B, etc. But the selective emphasis is excessive, and the interaction of A and B may not be given due attention. As is well known, the same observed relationship is frequently predicted by several quite different theories. (Another reason for the diversity of both business cycles and their explanations is that various outside shocks impinge on the system.) Consider the following examples:

1. One of the theories which predict that costs typically rise faster than prices in expansion combines the accelerator principle and differential supply elasticities. The rise of final demand at high levels of capacity utilization stimulates investment in new productive facilities. This drives up further the demand for labor, raw materials, and other producer goods at the very time their supplies are becoming more scarce and less elastic. The unit labor costs increase sharply as the availability of skilled workers is reduced and higher

wages must be paid but growth of average productivity (output per hour) slackens. It takes more time to plan and build capital goods—producers' durable equipment and plant. Many materials are of agricultural origin and have long and rather rigid production periods (e.g., industrial crops, cattle hides).[4] The supply of standardized finished products can be expanded much more readily.

2. Nonmonetary overinvestment theory argues that the rise in consumer demand causes larger percentage rises in the demands for plant and equipment and, a fortiori, materials processed by industry. Hence, again, c increases relative to p. Investment, financed by the initially easy bank credit, is overextended relative to consumer saving, and must eventually be curtailed as profits fall, banks retrench, and interest rates rise. Thus early analysts of the business cycle as different in their outlook and procedure as Mitchell and Hayek (see 2.3.1 and 2.3.6) had similar views on the role of the price-cost-profit movement.[5]

3. That p is reduced relative to c in contraction is due mainly to wages being more resistant than prices of finished products to downward recessionary pressures. Prices of crude materials tend to soften more than prices of finished goods and services during general business slowdowns and recessions. The strongly procyclical and leading behavior of the profit margin Π/S is implied by the assumed behavior of p and c, and well documented in the data, and so is the downturn of total profits later in expansion, which results not only from the decrease in Π/S but also from the reduced growth of S. The "profit squeeze" is therefore as much a demand as a supply phenomenon. It too features in various business cycle theories emphasizing changes in cost, overinvestment, and other maladjustments, but most notably in the early work of Mitchell (see Haberler [1937] 1964, ch. 4).

4. The deceleration of final demand in the latter stages of expansion has been given explanations varying from full-employment ceiling and accelerator effects to cyclical changes in functional income distribution and consumption. The share of labor in national income has a mildly countercyclical pattern because real hourly wages increase somewhat less than output per hour (labor productivity) in expansion, whereas the opposite prevails in contraction. The proportion of consumption is larger in labor income than in property income, which is consistent with the finding that the ratio of total consump-

---

4. It should be noted that a large proportion of raw materials is imported, which at times can strongly influence their relative prices. Thus, a change in the terms of trade against materials and in favor of finished products occurred in the 1950s and 1960s, tending to reduce the rise in c vs. p.

5. Still other early business cycle theorists with widely varying views agreed on the strong procyclical fluctuation of the relative price of capital goods, including Marx and Kalecki, as shown in Sherman 1991, esp. chs. 10 and 11. This new monograph offers a very accessible treatment of many theories, particularly the endogenous historical ones, plus interesting illustrations of the average behavior of many time series during the post–World War II business cycles in the United States.

tion to national income (the average propensity to consume) is also mildly countercyclical (Sherman 1991, chs. 5 and 8). Theories of underconsumption span a long era from some early classics and social reformers (Lauderdale, Malthus, Sismondi, Rodbertus) to Hobson 1922, Neisser 1934, A. H. Hansen 1939, and others. Keynes's idea that in an ex ante sense saving outruns investment at full employment has an underconsumptionist flavor.[6] But, unlike investment in producer and consumer durable goods, consumption properly defined is not very sensitive cyclically. Except perhaps in some past episodes of deflation and stagnation, examples of a systematic tendency for underconsumption seem hard to find.[7]

5. Errors of expectations play a critical role in several otherwise quite different theories. Thus, Lavington, Pigou, and Keynes all see a spread of overoptimism in expansion and disappointment and overpessimism in contraction. Business people form their expectations adaptively by learning gradually from the past, but they also share in pervasive moods and opinions, seeking safety in numbers, especially in times of high uncertainty. The assumption made in figure 1.1 is very simply that the prevailing expectations of sales and profits (S^*, $(\Pi/S)^*$, and Π^*) are lagged versions of the corresponding actual values (S, Π/S, and Π). At high levels of economic activity, as measured by Q/Q^*, expectations exceed realizations; at low levels, the reverse is the case (compare the paired solid and broken curves). An overcorrection of errors of optimism generates errors of pessimism. This depresses business confidence and the demand for investment I/K, contributing to the economy's downturn. Similarly, the shift from pessimistic to optimistic forecasts would raise confidence and investment, aiding the recovery.

6. To make the model of expectations less crude and more convincing, one would have to show what causes many agents to commit similar errors simultaneously, and why such errors are not avoided or at least not discovered and corrected more promptly. This leads to a study of how competition works under conditions of uncertainty, that is, deficient knowledge, fragmentary and partly wrong information, and very limited foresight. Economists have only begun to explore this difficult subject (see 2.4.5). Empirical studies show that economic forecasts tend to have much in common with extrapolations from the recent past and so make large errors around turning points.[8] The above

6. Note the long quotation from and sympathetic references to Hobson and Mummery 1889 in Keynes 1936, ch. 23.

7. According to Haberler, "The under-consumption theory is a theory of the crisis and depression rather than a theory of the cycle" ([1937] 1964, ch. 5, pp. 119ff.). Sherman argues against this view, though recognizing the serious incompleteness of the theory (1991, ch. 9). He presents an "underconsumptionist cycle model," which reduces to a second-order difference equation in the national income, but that model treats as constant several parameters that are unlikely to be so (the same applies to his models for some other endogenous theories that are probably essentially nonlinear).

8. For evidence, see part IV; also, Lovell 1986. This argues against the hypothesis that expectations are based immediately on the correct model of how the economy works. Insisting on superrationality in this sense often seems equivalent to the fallacy of *petitio principii*. But this is not to

error model, though primitive, still has some useful implications. Investment in new plant and equipment is often associated with investment in new products, markets, and technologies; as such, it typically requires a considerable degree of confidence in the future. Confidence is an intangible but important and clearly procyclical factor. Its influence on business capital investment can be very strong at times, especially near and after cyclical turning points.

7. Expected sales are presumably the major determinant of business inventories. If total inventory depends on S^e as assumed in figure 1.1, then it should be increasingly perceived as too large relative to S in late expansion when S^e rises above S. By the same token, inventory should be increasingly perceived as too small relative to S in contraction when S^e falls below S. The data indicate that total stocks of goods held in manufacturing and trade tend to increase less than sales in recoveries (when S typically grows fast) and more than sales in late stages of expansion and in contraction (when growth of S declines and becomes negative). The inventory-sales ratio is mainly countercyclical and lagging; inventory investment is procyclical and leading, but very volatile and irregular. These patterns reflect a mixture of intended and unintended investment.

1.10   Approaches to Diversity

Because business cycles are not all alike and are subject to historical changes along with the structure and institutions of the economy, it is not surprising that the numerous efforts to model them as a uniform by-product of one type of random shock or another have failed. Endogenous nonlinear models can capture important aspects of the economy's motion, but they are very underdeveloped at present and far from the stage of empirical usefulness. Whether they can reach that stage without the aid of various shocks is uncertain.

It is difficult but necessary to explain not only why business cycles occur but also why they are diverse and changing. One possible approach is to look for identifiable major events that might have "caused" the fluctuations with the observed differential features. This view is widely adopted in popular discussions of current developments, where market reactions to economic and political, domestic and foreign news receive much continuing attention. There is certainly a great deal to be learned from keen observation of the contemporary scene aided by good economics and intuition. But the large-shock view in itself is very limited and potentially misleading because it neglects the common core of business cycles and inclines to a barren episodic treatment of the subject that ignores important lessons of both theory and history. Still, major disturbances can help to allow for the diversity of cyclical experience.

---

deny that expectations which drive forward-looking behavior are likely to be rational in the more limited sense of attempting to make the best use of the information deemed worth collecting.

With regard to the moderation of business cycles, it is not at all clear that the last 40 years had fewer major shocks than the periods 1894–1914 and 1919–39. Wars cause strong perturbations, and recent times witnessed the wars in Korea and Vietnam as well as the high tensions of the cold war, all of which produced a rising but very unsteady flow of defense expenditures. In 1989–90 the cold war was effectively won by the United States and its allies, and in 1990–91 the conflict and war with Iraq ended in a quick and low-cost victory, so military spending may be reduced. In contrast, peace prevailed in the earlier periods, though it was increasingly threatened. When the wartime cycles are excluded, recent contractions still turn out to be on average shorter and milder than their historical counterparts, and recent expansions longer, if not more vigorous.

The great advance in the production of comprehensive economic information may have contributed to the reduction in general business fluctuations by enabling both the policymakers and the public to monitor and react to macroeconomic developments in a much more informed and therefore potentially more efficient manner. It is only after World War II that quarterly data for national income and product accounts, monthly data on the money stock, and monthly data on new investment commitments and other leading indicators, among others, became publicly and relatively promptly and freely available. However, this is a neglected factor and little is known about its effects.

Another possible way of dealing with diversity is through disaggregation. In systems with many goods and markets, information is always incomplete and partly private as people must be selective and economical about what data they acquire. The resulting gaps and asymmetries, especially when combined with temporary price rigidities in many markets, can give rise to recurrent maladjustments of relative prices and quantities. Although varying by sectoral origin, such imbalances can, if sufficiently large and widespread, contribute significantly to the instability of total output and employment. They are reflected in the cyclical patterns of inventory-sales ratios, price-cost markups, and profit margins. These imbalances have been noted in early NBER studies but they appear to be important in the present moderate business cycles and mild growth cycles as well (for references, see chapters 2 and 5 and Boehm 1990). There is still much to be learned about the sources and dynamics of these diffusion processes.

In the disaggregate and extended versions of the RBC theory, random local shocks to technology and tastes are propagated across markets. Although prices are flexible, complex lags may arise because sectoral shifts are not recognized promptly and correctly, and specialized labor and capital require time to be reallocated (Black 1982; Lilien 1982). Conceivably the shifts and transfers could be concentrated during recessions because the value of the forgone output is then relatively low, but the idea encounters some serious problems.[9]

---

9. In particular, this hypothesis (Darby, Haltiwanger, and Plant 1985; S. Davis 1987) is difficult to reconcile with the observed strong inverse correlation between cyclical movement in the un-

Diversified market economies appear to be very resilient with respect to even large and persistent shifts in the composition of demand, relative prices, and technological advances. For example, in 1980–85 important parts of U.S. manufacturing suffered strong setbacks from intensive foreign competition aided by a massive appreciation of the dollar. Yet the expansion that began in 1982 endured because of the prevalence of gains elsewhere in the economy. Most sectoral disturbances are much smaller, more varied, and localized, and it is reasonable to think of their effects as canceling each other out across markets within fairly short periods of time. But this argument is not entirely compelling, and there is certainly much more scope for useful research in studying disaggregate systems than in dealing with "representative agent" models.

What generally matters more than industry detail, however, is the coverage of the main variables and specification of their interactions in the cyclical process. A theory relevant to both the major and minor cycles experienced over long time periods by the industrialized market economies will probably have to be eclectic and accommodative in the spirit of Mitchell (see chapter 5, sec. 5.2 below). It will combine tested elements from early and recent business cycle studies and from ongoing work but avoid excessive generalization and spurious rigorism.

---

employment rate and the job vacancy (or help wanted) rate. In contrast, fluctuations in aggregate demand can readily account for this relationship as well as for the clearly procyclical movements in the quit rate (Abraham and Katz 1986).

2   Recent Work on Business Cycles in Historical Perspective

2.1   Introduction

Interest in business cycles is itself subject to a wavelike movement, waxing during and after periods of turbulence and depression, waning in periods of substantial stability and continuing growth.[1] At time, confidence in government institutions and actions persuaded many that cyclical instability had ceased to be a serious problem. Thus in the early heyday of the Federal Reserve System, 1922–29, monetary policies were expected to help maintain prosperity. In the 1960s, the late heyday of Keynesian economics, fiscal fine-tuning evoked similar hopes.

The present is another time of disillusionment—now extending to both types of stabilization policy. The sequence of serious worldwide recessions in the last decade soon refuted the perennially attractive idea that business cycles had become obsolete. Beyond that, the credibility of both Keynesian and monetarist explanations has diminished. Once again, the apparent failure of old solutions prompts the profession to pay more attention to the continued existence of business cycles.

Reprinted from the *Journal of Economic Literature* 23 (June 1985): 523–80.

The author thanks Alan Blinder, William Fellner, Stanley Fischer, Milton Friedman, Robert Gordon, Robert Hall, Bert Hickman, Wilhelm Krelle, David Laidler, Ronald McKinnon, John Taylor, and two anonymous referees for many helpful suggestions and criticisms of the first outline and earlier drafts of this paper. Also gratefully acknowledged is the financial and intellectual support received from the National Bureau of Economic Research and the Graduate School of Business of the University of Chicago. Naturally, responsibility for the expressed opinions and any remaining errors is exclusively the author's.

1. This is well illustrated in the early literature, which focused on the episodes of commercial crises, but it is also reflected in the timing of later, classical studies of the nature and causes of business cycles at large. There is little doubt about the impetus provided in this context by the major depressions of the late 1830s, 1870s, 1890s, 1907–8, 1920–21, and most strikingly the 1930s.

The rediscovery of an important subject is always welcome, even if long overdue. However, much of the recent work has neglected the long history of both the phenomena of major economic fluctuations and their interpretations, concentrating instead on contemporary theoretical and policy controversies, mainly in the United States. An overview of selected literature will attempt to demonstrate that this myopia is costly and needs to be corrected.

The study of business cycles is almost coextensive with short-term macro-dynamics and it has a large interface with the economics of growth, money, inflation, and expectations. The literature is huge; its level of difficulty is in general high. This survey attempts to provide a historical background and outline the evolution of thought leading to the recent developments in theory and related evidence. The coverage is extensive, yet of necessity much is left out, including theories that are largely concerned with unemployment and inflation, much less with business cycles directly. [2]

In particular, no attempt can be made here to discuss in any detail the statistical and historical work on the observed regularities and idiosyncrasies of business cycles and their possible long-term changes. This empirical literature is rich and important: it deserves a separate review. After all, it is the "stylized facts" which it provides that ought to be explained by the theory. Those main facts are summarized in section 2.2, but with a minimum of references and commentary.

Section 2.3 discusses the main elements of older theories, before and after the Great Depression, and proceeds to more recent models driven by changes in investment, credit, and price-cost-profit relations. Most of these theories and models are primarily endogenous and deterministic. Exogenous factors and stochastic elements are introduced early in section 2.4.

The sections that follow deal, first, with the monetarist interpretation of business cycles, then with the newer equilibrium models with price misper-ceptions and intertemporal substitution. The route leads generally from "adaptive" to "rational" expectations. The approach is generally monetarist in the sense of relying on monetary shocks, but the emphasis shifts from nominal demand changes and lagged price adjustments to informational lags and sup-ply reactions. Various problems and complications arise, revealed in large part by intensive testing and criticism. This leads to new attempts to explain the persistence of cyclical movements, the role of uncertainty and financial insta-bility, real shocks, gradual price adjustments, etc. Conclusions are drawn in the last section, which stresses the need for a realistic synthesis.

---

2. Two sets of writings should be mentioned in this context, namely, the theories of the new radical economists and those embodied in some of the recent "disequilibrium" models. For sum-maries or surveys, see Sherman 1976; Malinvaud 1977; and Drazen 1980.

  Also, the early mathematical models and the more recent theories of the "political business cycle" receive little attention in the present paper; monographs surveying this literature are Rau 1974; Gapinski 1982; and Mullineux 1984.

2.2 Stylized Facts

2.2.1 The Overall Aspects and Varying Dimensions of Business Cycles

The term "business cycle," is a misnomer insofar as no unique periodicities are involved, but its wide acceptance reflects the recognition of important regularities of long standing. The observed fluctuations vary greatly in amplitude and scope as well as duration, yet they also have much in common. First, they are national, indeed often international, in scope, showing up in a multitude of processes, not just in total output, employment, and unemployment. Second, they are persistent—lasting, as a rule several years, that is, long enough to permit the development of cumulative movements in the downward as well as upward direction. This is well established by the historical chronologies of business cycles in the United States, Great Britain, France, and Germany, a product of a long series of studies by the National Bureau of Economic Research (Burns and Mitchell 1946; Moore 1961, 1983; Moore and Zarnowitz 1986; see also chapter 5). For all their differences, business expansions and contractions consist of patterns of recurrent, serially correlated and cross-correlated movements in many economic (and even other) activities.

Seasonal movements, which are periodic but often variable in size and pattern, may obscure the cyclical developments from an observer of current changes in individual time series. The same applies to short, erratic movements, which are similarly ubiquitous. But, looking back across monthly or quarterly data representing many different variables, business cycles can be clearly distinguished from the other fluctuations in that they are as a rule larger, longer, and more widely diffused. They dominate changes in the economy over spans of several years, in contrast to the seasonal and other variations which spend themselves over spans of a year or less. They reflect, and interact with, long growth trends which dominate developments across decades.

Peacetime expansions in the United States averaged about 3 years in the last half-century, 2 years in the earlier periods containing 10 cycles each (table 2.1). Each of the wartime expansions was much longer. Contractions have averaged close to 1 year since 1933, almost twice as long in the earlier periods. This suggests a strong shift toward longer and more variable expansions and shorter and more uniform contractions since the Great Contraction of the early 1930s. However, the NBER dates for the early business cycles are based on limited information and may overstate the length of some of the recessions (see note to the table). The mean duration of full peacetime cycles has remained approximately stable at 4 years.

The individual phase and cycle durations show considerable variability over time, as shown by the standard deviations in table 2.1. However, when the relatively rare outliers are discounted, fairly clear central tendencies emerge. Thus the ranges of 1.5–3 years, 1–2 years, and 2.5–5 years account for three

Table 2.1   **Average Duration of Business Cycles in the United States, 1854–1982**

Period (years, T to T)	No. of Business Cycles Covered (1)	Average Measures of Phase and Cycle Durations					
		Expansion		Contraction		Full Cycle (T to T)	
		Mean (2)	S.D. (3)	Mean (4)	S.D. (5)	Mean (6)	S.D. (7)
1854–97	10	27	9	24	17	51	24
1897–1933	10	23	10	20	10	43	10
1933–82	10	49	27	11	3	60	26
1933–82, excl. wars	7	37	15	11	4	48	14
1854–1982	30	33	20	18	12	51	22
1854–1982, excl. wars	25	27	11	19	13	46	16

Note: All means and standard deviations (S.D.) are rounded to full months. Expansions are measured from troughs (T) to peaks (P), contractions from P to T, the full cycles from T to T. Figures in line 4 exclude the expansions during World War II, the Korean War, and the Vietnam War and the immediately following contractions. Figures in line 6 exclude also the expansions during the Civil War and World War I and the immediately followng contractions. For references and underlying detail see Moore and Zarnowitz 1986.

It should be noted that the data available for identifying and measuring the historical business cycles are fragmentary and often weak. Much of the evidence relates to cyclically sensitive sectors and processes. Hence some of the early fluctuations may have involved only slowdowns rather than absolute declines in total output and employment. If so, the averages in lines 1 and 2 should be somewhat larger for expansions and smaller for contractions. This would only moderately reduce the contrast with the entries in line 3 and would not significantly alter the overall conclusions drawn in the text (see chapter 7).

fourths or more of the peacetime expansions, contractions, and full cycles in the United States, respectively.

The amplitudes of cyclical expansions vary as much as their durations, with which they tend to be well correlated. The rates of change (velocities) and diffusion show less variability across the cycles. Table 2.2 provides some evidence in support of these generalizations.

In the 20 years between the two world wars three major depressions occurred, including the uniquely deep one of 1929–33. Since then no general declines of comparable magnitude have occurred, notwithstanding the gravity of recent conditions of rising and high unemployment in some countries, such as the United Kingdom. On the whole recessions have become not only much shorter but also shallower and less diffused. Table 2.3, using a sampling of measures for the U.S. business contractions of 1920–82, illustrates the contrasting dimensions of major depressions versus other declines and the much smaller but consistent differences between the "severe" and "mild" recessions.

2.2.2   Main Features of Cyclical Behavior

Most industries and sectors of the economy participate in the general business cycles with substantial regularity (i.e., they exhibit high conformity or

Table 2.2   **Selected Characteristics of Seven Expansions, United States, 1949–82**

Line	Statistic	Largest Value (1)	Smallest Value (2)	Mean (3)	Standard Deviation (4)
	Real GNP:				
1	Duration (months)	106	12	46	30
2	Total increases (%)	49.2	4.4	21.1	14.7
3	Rate of increase (% per year)	6.4	3.5	4.7	1.0
	Unemployment rate:				
4	Total decline (% points)	−5.3	−0.6	−2.7	1.5
	Nonfarm employment:				
5	Percent of industries expanding	100	73	89	9

Source: Moore and Zarnowitz 1986, table 6.
Note: The entries in col. 1 refer to the expansion of 2/1961–12/1969 (lines 1–3) and 10/1948–7/1953 (lines 4 and 5). The entries in col. 2 refer to the expansion of 7/1980–7/1981. The entries in col. 3 and 4 cover all seven expansions. Line 5 shows the maximum percentage of nonagricultural industries with rising employment, based on changes over 6-month spans.

Table 2.3   **Average Duration, Depth, and Diffusion of Thirteen Contractions, United States, 1920–82**

Line	Statistic	Great Depression (1)	Two Major Depressions (2)	Six Severe Recessions (3)	Four Mild Recessions (4)
1	Average duration (months)	43	16	12	10
	Percentage decline:				
2	Real GNP	−32.6	−13.4	−3.3	−1.7
3	Industrial production	−53.4	−32.4	−13.1	−7.8
4	Nonfarm employment	−31.6	−10.6	−3.8	−1.7
	Unemployment rate:				
5	Total increase (% points)	21.7	9.6	3.8	2.3
	Nonfarm employment:				
6	Percent of industries contracting	100	97	88	77

Source: Moore and Zarnowitz 1986, table 7.
Note: The contraction of 8/1929–3/1933 is referred to as the Great Depression; the contractions of 1/1920–7/1921 and 5/1937–6/1938 are the major depressions. The dates of the six severe recessions are 5/1923–7/1924, 11/1948–10/1949, 7/1953–5/1954, 8/1957–4/1958, 11/1973–3/1975, and 7/1981–11/1982. The dates of the four mild recessions are 10/1926–11/1927, 4/1960–2/1961, 12/1969–11/1970; and 1/1980–7/1980.

coherence), but some do not (e.g., agriculture, which depends heavily on the weather, and production of naturally scarce resources).[3] Durable producer and consumer goods tend to have high conformity and large amplitudes of cyclical movements in production, employment, and inventories. The amplitudes are

3. This section is based primarily on studies of U.S. economic history, but many of the *qualitative* features of cyclical behavior summarized here are found as well in the data for other major industrialized countries with private enterprise and free markets: Mitchell 1913, 1927; Schumpe-

much smaller for nondurable goods, and still smaller for most of the (nonstorable) services. Manufacturers' sales move with greater amplitudes than wholesalers' sales, and the latter with greater amplitudes than retailers' sales. In many industries, particularly manufacturing of durables, production is, in large measure, guided by advance orders, which show large fluctuations followed, with variable lags, by much smaller fluctuations in outputs and shipments. The resulting changes in backlogs of unfilled orders and average delivery lags are themselves procyclical.

Private investment expenditures, although much smaller in the aggregate than consumer spending, have much larger cycles in percentage terms. Aggregate production typically fluctuates more widely than aggregate sales, which implies a procyclical behavior of inventory investment. Business profits show very high conformity and much greater amplitude of cyclical movements than wages and salaries, dividends, net interest, and rental income.

The level of industrial prices tends to have wider fluctuations than the levels of retail prices and wages. Virtually all U.S. business contractions before World War II were associated with declines in wholesale prices.[4] However, the last recession to be accompanied by a significant deflation was that of 1948–49. Since then the price level never fell cyclically, but each of the seven U.S. recessions of 1953–82 resulted in a temporary reduction of the rate at which prices rose, that is, in some disinflation. But, in contrast to the general price indexes for consumer and producer goods, prices of industrial commodities and raw materials traded in organized auction markets continued to show high sensitivity to business cycles, often turning down early in slowdowns as well as contractions.

Narrowly and broadly defined monetary aggregates usually experience only reduced growth rates, not absolute declines, in connection with ordinary recessions. Only in cycles with severe contractions do substantial downward movements interrupt the pronounced upward trends in these series. The income velocity of money (i.e., ratio of income to the stock of currency and commercial bank deposits held by the public) tends to move procyclically (up in expansions and down in contractions), allowing for its long trends (downward before World War II, then upward for some time).

Short-term interest rates display high positive conformity and generally large amplitudes of movements relative to their average level in each cycle. However, when measured in basis points, cyclical changes in these series are typically small when the interest-rate levels are low. Long-term rates usually

---

ter 1939; Frickey 1942; Burns and Mitchell 1946; Abramovitz 1950; Mitchell 1951; Gayer, Rostow, and Schwartz 1953; Matthews, 1959; Moore 1961, 1983; R. A. Gordon 1961; M. Friedman and Schwartz 1963a; Hultgren 1965; Zarnowitz 1972a, 1973; Zarnowitz and Moore 1984; P. Klein and Moore 1985.

4. This is true both for the periods of long-term inflationary trends (1843–64, 1896–1920) and for those of long-term deflationary trends (1864–96, 1920–32).

lag behind the short-term rates and have much lower conformity and much smaller amplitudes. The relative movements in both short-term market rates and bond yields increased significantly in the recent past compared with their historical averages. Near cyclical peaks, short rates tend to come close to or exceed the long rates; near cyclical troughs, they tend to be much lower.

Along with these conformity and amplitude characteristics, the recurring features of business cycles include an array of timing sequences. Months before total employment, output, and real income turn down, activities marking the early stages of investment process begin to decline. These include the formation of new business enterprises, corporate appropriations for capital expenditure, contracts for commercial and industrial construction, new orders of machinery and equipment, and new bond and equity issues. Investment realizations—construction put in place, deliveries and installations of equipment—keep increasing long after the decline in these investment commitments as work continues on the backlog of orders accumulated during the busiest stages of expansion. Indeed, business expenditures for new plant and equipment often peak when the overall economic contraction is already well under way. At business cycle troughs, with lower levels of capacity utilization, the delivery lags are generally shorter, but investment commitments still tend to lead and expenditures coincide or lag.

Long before the downturn in total sales, profits per unit of sales decline. Total profits (a product of margins times sales) also lead, but by shorter intervals. Stock prices move early as well, reflecting expected changes in corporate earnings. Bond prices tend to turn earlier yet (bond yields are generally lagging).

Labor productivity (output per hour) fluctuates procyclically around a secularly rising trend, generally with leads. Money wages often rise less than prices in recoveries and more than prices in late expansion stages. This combines with the marked and persistent productivity changes to induce a procyclical and lagging movement in labor costs per unit of output.

Net changes in consumer installment credit and in mortgage credit outstanding have similar procyclical, leading behavior patterns. So has the net change in bank loans to business, but here the leads tend to be shorter and less consistent. Compared with the overall credit flows, the rates of growth in monetary aggregates show, in general, lower cyclical conformities and amplitudes and more random variations. They have historically led at business cycle turns by highly variable but mostly long intervals. Indeed, these leads are often so long as to produce strong elements of inverted behavior in the monetary growth rates: that is, extended declines during expansions and rises during short recessions.

Consumers' "sentiment," that is, anticipations concerning their economic and financial fortunes, also has a predominantly leading pattern. Recent recessions in the United States have been preceded, more often than not, by downturns, and recoveries by upturns, in consumer buying plans and actual expenditures on automobiles, housing, and related durable goods. Residential construction commitments, such as new-building permits and housing starts, have particularly long leads at peaks and often also at troughs of the business cycle. Here the gestation periods are fairly short so that the expenditures themselves show sizable leads.

Change in business inventories not only conforms positively to cycles in general economic activity but is highly sensitive and volatile, often leading, albeit by variable and, on the average, short intervals. Total manufacturing and trade inventories, on the other hand, are dominated by long trends and tend to lag. Inventory investment plays a very important role in short and mild cycles, whereas fluctuations in fixed investment acquire a greater weight in the longer and larger cycles.

Table 2.4 provides a conspectus of the timing relationships found to be typical of business cycles.

2.2.3   Some International Aspects and Recent Developments

Business cycles have tended to be shorter in the United States than in Europe (e.g., the 1854–1938 period witnessed 21 U.S. cycles averaging 4 years and only 16 British cycles averaging 5⅓ years). However, before World War II, more than 60% of the cyclical turning points can be matched for all four countries covered by the NBER chronologies, and only 10% cannot be matched at all (Moore and Zarnowitz 1986). After World War II, an era of great reconstruction in Western Europe and Japan set in, which witnessed, first, a restoration of sound currencies and free markets, then rapid growth. For some time cyclical setbacks in these countries assumed the form of retardations of growth rather than absolute declines. However, these slowdowns and the intervening speedup phases continued to show a high degree of international diffusion. Then growth slackened and the "classical" business cycles (with absolute declines in total output and employment) reappeared everywhere in the 1970s. The tendency for these cycles to be roughly synchronized across the major trading countries became visible again, even without allowances for discrepancies in the longer growth trends.[5]

In a large economy dominated by production for domestic markets, business cycles are likely to be induced primarily by internal mechanisms (e.g., fluctuations in spending on durable goods endogenously and elastically financed) but they are then transmitted abroad through the movements in imports that are a positive function of production and income. For small and, particularly, less developed countries, fluctuations in exports usually call the tune. Of course, foreign influences can be critical, at times, for even the largest and relatively least open economy. This is well illustrated by the adverse effects on the United States of the OPEC oil price boosts in 1973–74 and

---

5. These events rekindled interest in business cycles of larger dimensions and essentially endogenous nature; see Volcker 1978.

Table 2.4   **Typical Leads and Lags among Major Economic Indicators**

Leading	Roughly Coincident	Lagging
I. Investment in Fixed Capital and Inventories		
New building permits; housing starts; residential fixed investment	Production of business equipment	Backlog of capital appropriations, mfg.*
New business formation	Machinery and equipment sales*	Business expenditures for new plant and equipment*
New capital appropriations, mfg.*; contracts and orders for plant and equipment		Mfg. and trade inventories
Change in business inventories		
II. Consumption, Trade, Orders, and Deliveries		
New orders for consumer goods and materials	Production of consumer goods	
Change in unfilled orders, durable goods*	Mfg. and trade sales	
Vendor performance (speed of deliveries)		
Index of consumer sentiment		
III. Employment, Production, and Income		
Average workweek; overtime hours (mfg.)	Nonagricultural employment	Average duration of unemployment
Accession rate; layoff rate (mfg.)	Unemployment rate	Long-term unemployment
New unemployment insurance claims	GNP; personal income	
Productivity (output per hour)	Industrial production, total	
Rate of capacity utilization (mfg. mtls.)		
IV. Prices, Costs, and Profits		
Bond prices*		Unit labor costs
Stock prices*		Labor share in national income
Sensitive materials prices*		
Profit margins		
Total corporate profits; net cash flows		
V. Money, Credit, and Interest		
Monetary growth rates*	Velocity of money	Short-term interest rates*
Change in liquid assets*		Bond yields*
Change in consumer credit*		Consumer credit outstanding*
Total private borrowing*		Commercial and industrial loans outstanding
Real money supply		

Note: Series marked * are in nominal terms (some have the same average timing properties when deflated). All other series are in real terms (constant dollars, physical units) or related indexes and ratio numbers. The selection is based on U.S. indicators published in *Business Conditions Digest*, a monthly report by the Bureau of Economic Analysis, U.S. Department of Commerce. The timing relations among corresponding series for other countries are in many respects similar (Moore 1983, ch. 6).

Abbreviations: mfg. = manufacturing; mtls. = materials.

1979–80 through increased costs and prices (leftward shifts in the aggregate supply schedule) and reduced real disposable income (hence, presumably also, some leftward shifts in the aggregate demand schedule). Such world-wide supply shocks, although clearly of major importance in the context of contemporary problems of productivity, growth, and development, are new and rare phenomena whose role in business cycles generally is modest but in danger of being overemphasized.[6] The more persistent effects come from changes on the demand side. Thus the volume, prices, and value of U.S. exports show fluctuations that correspond well to cycles in the dollar value of imports by the outside world (Mintz 1967). The demand changes are power-fully reinforced when the links among the major countries convert their independent cyclical tendencies into fluctuations that are roughly synchronized.

These links result not only from international trade (current-account transactions in goods and services) but also from international lending and investment (capital-account transactions in assets). The latter factor became particularly important in recent times when asset markets became highly integrated worldwide. Interest rates (adjusted for the anticipated exchange-rate movements) are now linked across the open economies, and capital flows are extremely sensitive to the risk-adjusted differentials in expected rates of return.

Partly because of the increased capital mobility, the shift from fixed to flexible exchange rates in the early 1970s provided much less insulation against foreign disturbances than was hoped for, and also much less autonomy for effective national macroeconomic policies. The price levels adjusted for exchange rates (i.e., the "real exchange rates") show large and persistent movements over time: the purchasing power parity does not hold over time spans relevant for the study of business cycles. The recent fluctuations in real economic activity show a very considerable degree of international convergence, which presumably reflects not only the exposure to common disturbances but also the increased interdependence among (openness of) nations (Whitman 1976; P. A. Klein 1976; Moore 1983, ch. 6).

In the 1960s, when it appeared that business contractions in Europe and Japan were being replaced by mere retardations, there was a revival of interest in cycles defined in terms of deviations from long trends rather than levels of economic aggregates. For lack of a better term, the alternations of above-trend and below-trend growth phases came to be called growth cycles. These short fluctuations are defined by the consensus of detrended indicators just as business cycles are defined by the consensus of the same time series with no allowance for their long-term trends. The trends are estimated only to be eliminated from each series separately. Growth cycles in this sense are thus sharply dif-

---

6. James Hamilton (1983), writes about the role of changes in crude oil prices in the U.S. recessions after World War II. It should be noted that many recessions are preceded by upward cost pressures and supply restrictions associated with the boom-and-slowdown sequence of middle and late expansion stages. On the developments during 1973–76, see Zarnowitz and Moore, 1977.

ferent from, and should not be confused with, any fluctuations in the long-term growth rates themselves.

They also need to be clearly distinguished from business cycles. Most persistent and pervasive economic slowdowns begin with much reduced but still positive growth rates and then develop into actual declines—recessions. Thus the high-growth phase typically coincides with the business cycle recovery and middle-expansion, and the low-growth phase with late expansion and contraction. But some slowdowns stay in the range of positive growth rates and result in renewed expansion, not recession. Thus growth cycles are more numerous than business cycles and more symmetrical, being measured from rising trends.

One can imagine a lengthy period of low, positive growth that would be associated with as much deterioration in business conditions and rise in unemployment as a short and moderate recession—and more. But it is also possible for a slowdown mainly to reduce inflationary excess demand created in the preceding boom, without causing much surplus capacity and real hardship. The policy implications of such a deceleration in economic growth are entirely different from those of a recession, which always depresses real incomes and spending, outputs, and employment.

In actual experience, those decelerations in growth that have *not* led to absolute declines in aggregate economic activity (in recent U.S. history: 1951–52, 1962–64, and 1966–67) occupy an intermediate position between the two hypothetical cases considered above. Their adverse effects were felt primarily in areas of particular sensitivity, notably as declines in housing activity and stock prices. Unemployment would cease falling rather than rise substantially, and profits would weaken rather than tumble. Thus the overall impact of each of these slowdowns on economic activity was definitely less than even the mildest of recent recessions.

Some economists focus on the nature and sources of expansions and contractions, that is, on the business cycles. Others, by abstracting from the long-run trend, actually address growth cycle phenomena while aiming at an analysis of business cycles; that is, they fail to differentiate between the two categories. The latter treatment, frequently implicit in the theoretical literature of recent years, may not be a good practice. General business contractions need to be distinguished from periods of low but positive growth. However, mild recessions and severe depressions are also quite different. Also, many important regularities described in the previous section are observed, to a large extent, in the context of growth cycles as well. Thus, when the series that tend to lead at business cycle turns are adjusted for their own long trends, the resulting detrended series are generally found to be leading at growth cycle turns. An analogous statement can be made for the roughly coincident and lagging indicators. Systematic differences among the series with respect to their conformity and amplitude characteristics are likewise largely retained after the necessary transformations.

2.3   Theories of Self-Sustaining Cycles

2.3.1   Disparities and Common Elements in Some Early Theories

The classics of business cycle literature made lasting contributions to the description and analysis of the motion of industrialized market economies. They addressed the cumulative processes of inflationary expansions and deflationary contractions induced by bank credit fluctuations constrained by the availability of reserves under the gold standard (Hawtrey 1913). The role of discrepancies between the market and the "natural" interest rates in this process was much explored following Knut Wicksell ([1898] 1936). At below-equilibrium market rates, excessive bank credit creation produces overinvestment in capital-goods industries and imposes "forced saving" on those whose incomes lag behind inflation (Hayek 1933). But banks will have to curtail the supply of credit, and individuals will tend to restore their old consumption standards. As the demand and resources shift back to consumer-goods industries, undersaving—real capital shortage and losses to the producers of capital goods—results, causing a decline in these industries which cannot be compensated elsewhere in the short run. A deflationary downturn cannot be avoided. Here the monetary changes are linked to real "vertical maladjustments": that is, imbalances between production of capital and consumer goods or between aggregates of investment plans and savings decisions (Tugan-Baranovskii [1894] 1913; Spiethoff [1925] 1953).

Other writers worked out the importance of long gestation and life periods of capital goods and developed some cyclical aspects of the acceleration principle (Aftalion 1913; J. M. Clark 1917, 1934). Schumpeter (1939) saw economic growth itself as a cyclical process, reflecting technological progress and spurts of innovations—opening up and temporary exhaustion of opportunities for new, profitable investment. Related factors include the failure of foresight, intersectoral shifts, and changes in relative prices. Thus, under uncertainty, interdependent expectations of business people generate widespread errors of optimism in expansions and pessimism in contractions (Pigou 1927). Unpredictable shifts in demand or supply lead to "horizontal maladjustments"—say, overinvestment in a particular sector, which involves indivisible and durable fixed capital, high costs of adjustments, and temporary but cumulative depressant effects (Robertson [1915] 1948). Unit costs of labor and production tend to rise relative to output prices before and after the downturn, and they tend to fall before and after the upturn, reflecting changes in capacity utilization and productivity; as a result, business profits show large fluctuations, which help explain the cyclical movements in investment and output (Mitchell 1913, 1927).

This capsule summary can merely illustrate the broad range of views held by these early students of business cycles. It is clear that there are important disagreements among their theories, particularly with respect to the relative importance of monetary and real factors, long a major point of contention. But the dominant tone is one of awareness that what matters most is the *interaction* of changes in money and credit with changes in economic activity, particularly those connected with business investment. Most of the writers considered business cycles to be caused and conditioned by a number of factors and circumstances, and so their theories typically overlap and vary mainly in the emphasis accorded the different elements (Haberler [1937] 1964).

Not surprisingly, there is much in these individual theories that is unsatisfactory, unduly restrictive, or out-of-date. Here we must abstract from the detail and note that it is the high degree of consensus and achievement that is much more remarkable from the present point of view.

The first aspect of essential agreement is that the theories are mainly endogenous. That is, they purposely concentrate on internal dynamics of the system (interrelations and lagged reactions among its components). The authors generally held that contemporary industrial economies are, as a result of such dynamics, subject to recurrent fluctuations with major regularities that can be explained economically. They believed that "the cyclical movement has a strong tendency to persist, even where there are no outstanding extraneous influences at work which can plausibly be held responsible." Hence they viewed the role of the exogenous forces as secondary, even though acknowledging that the latter continually act "as the originators or disturbers of endogenous processes, with power to accelerate, retard, interrupt, or reverse the endogenous movement of the economic system."[7]

Second, these economists all basically adhered to the standard economic theory of their times, which is what Keynes later labeled the "classical school"; indeed, the latter is well personified by some of them. At the same time, they generally appreciated the seriousness of the problem of economic instability. The business cycles of their principal concern were major fluctuations measured in years of cumulative expansions and contractions. The recurrent phases of widespread unemployment and underutilization of productive capacities did (and still do) present a deep puzzle to the classical doctrine, according to which the economy is always in, or at least tending closely to, the general equilibrium. Thus, for a long time, business cycles were simply ignored by most economic theorists or, at best, were viewed as merely temporary "frictional" interference with, and departure from, equilibrium. But students of the subject, including those who were themselves committed to the equilibrium theory, have done much to counteract this evasive and untenable position.

---

7. Both quotations are from Haberler (1937) 1964, p. 10. This characterization is strongly confirmed by numerous passages in works by Robertson (1915, in particular pt. II, ch. 4); Mitchell (1927, esp. chs. 1 and 5), Hayek (1933, esp. ch. 4), and Pigou (1927, chs. 6–8, 21). For Schumpeter, the basic mechanism of credit-financed innovations is of much greater intrinsic interest than the multitude of diverse "external factors," no matter how important the latter may be on any particular occasion (1935–1939, vol. 1, chs. 1–4).

Third, in the historical periods addressed by these studies the level of prices tended to move up during the general business expansions and down during contractions. The positive correlation between cyclical movements in broad price indexes and real activity measures implied that fluctuations in total nominal expenditures parallel the fluctuations in the aggregates of real income, employment, and output. This was generally accepted as a central characteristic of business cycles by the early theories, in which the fluctuations in aggregate money flows of income and spending play a large, proximately "causal" role. Of course, for these fluctuations to produce cyclical movements in real variables, it is necessary that wages and prices adjust with some sufficient lags rather than being highly flexible. Sometimes this condition was assumed explicitly but it was not much discussed and often only implied (Haberler [1937] 1964, pp. 459–61).[8]

2.3.2   Uncertain Expectations, Unstable Investment, and Long Depression Cycles

Keynes (1936, ch. 22, esp. pp. 314–15) attributed to the trade cycle a sudden, sharp downturn, a protracted decline, and a gradual, sluggish upturn. These are all characteristics of the 1929 peaks and the depressions and recoveries of the 1930s in Great Britain and the United States; also, in part, of the British experience in the depressed early 1920s. They are not typical of most cycles in these countries and elsewhere.

The sharp downturn, or "crisis," is explained mainly by "a sudden collapse in the marginal efficiency of capital." During a boom, the supply of new capital goods and the cost of their production and financing rise, with growing adverse effects on the current returns on investment. The inducement to invest is further weakened if the current costs come to be viewed as higher than the probable future costs. Optimism about the always uncertain future returns lingers for some time, but sooner or later doubts arise about the reliability of the hopeful expectations engendered by the boom.

Investment expectations are highly volatile because even those forecasts of long-term profitability of specific business projects which are viewed as most probable inspire little confidence. Observable frequencies of past outcomes are not generally a source of predictive knowledge in these matters. Keynes's world is thus one of pervasive uncertainty which is sharply distinguished from calculable and insurable risk (as in Knight 1921).

It is easier and more rewarding to predict the short-term movements in the stock market, which are strongly affected by "mass psychology," than to divine the long-term prospects for individual business concerns. The market reacts promptly to news of fluctuating business profits with revaluations which

---

8. In terms of the present-day conventional macroeconomic model, let us add, the positive correlation of fluctuations in prices and real variables would indicate that shifts in aggregate demand dominate the shifts in aggregate supply over the business cycle. If this sounds rather alien to the early theories, it is because the latter are typically more disaggregate.

inevitably exert a decisive influence on the rate of current investment. A new business will not attract investors if a similar existing one can be acquired on the exchange at lower costs (Keynes 1936, p. 151).

This last insight gave rise to an influential theory of James Tobin (1969), which makes investment in new plant and equipment an increasing function of q, the ratio of the value placed by the security markets on the existing firm to the replacement cost of its capital. This approach has several advantages: it is relatively simple, uses observable variables, and provides an analytically attractive linkage between investment and the expectations of the financial asset markets. Implicitly, it also relates the expected profit rate to the required rate of return on capital in the stock market and, hence, to the interest rate. However, the hypothesis has not fared well in empirical tests (Von Furstenberg 1977; P. K. Clark 1979; Blanchard and Wyplosz 1981; Abel and Blanchard 1983; R. J. Gordon and Veitch 1984). This is perhaps partly because of the use of average q instead of the theoretically more appropriate marginal q[9] but more likely because of various simplifying restrictions used in this work: homogeneous capital and perfect financial markets with no liquidity constraints on firms. These idealizations are poorly suited for an analysis of cyclical movements in investment and they certainly clash with the Keynesian views on the instability of financial markets (sect. 2.4.6).[10]

Once aroused, the doubts about profitability of planned and current investment projects spread rapidly, bringing down in "disillusion" the stock market, which is revealed to have been overoptimistic and overbought. As the pendulum swings to overpessimism, the demand for broadly defined money will increase, raising the rate of interest and hence seriously aggravating the crisis. The revival of investment will require a "return of confidence . . . an aspect of the slump which bankers and businessmen have been right in emphasizing" (Keynes 1936, p. 317). But confidence, once severely shaken, takes time to mend. Also, the propensity to consume is adversely affected by the fall in the value of equities.

Only as the downswing develops will it bring the level of interest rates down. This decline will not be as prompt and large as would be necessary to counter the "collapse" of investment. The demand for money is interest elastic, highly so at low levels of the rates, because of bearish speculation in the face of basic uncertainty as to future changes in the rate of interest. The con-

9. This is the ratio of the increase in the value of the firm from acquiring an additional unit of capital to the marginal cost of that unit (which, in contrast to the measured average q, is an ex ante and not directly observable quantity).

10. The same observations apply a fortiori to the "neoclassical" investment theory dating from Jorgenson 1963, which concentrates on the average long-term behavior as determined by the requirement that the expected returns over the life of a project exceed its costs. The short-run deterrent effect on investment of the rising flow supply price of capital goods (stressed in Keynes 1936, ch. 11) is not well captured in this approach, and the expectational lags are not distinguishable from the gestation periods or delivery lags (Abel 1980). For recent tests of this and other investment theories, see also Bischoff 1971; and Kopcke 1977.

clusion here is that a recovery from a severe slump is possible only after the capital stock of business has been reduced sufficiently to restore its profitability. This may take several years, through use, wear and tear, or obsolescence (Keynes 1936, p. 151).

It might appear that overbuilding is the cause of the downturn and long slump but Keynes insists that it is not. Rather, the effective private demand fails to sustain full employment because investment is too unstable and the propensity to consume is stable but too low. It is only relative to the deficient demand that "overinvestment" can occur; there is no saturation of profitable investment opportunities at full employment.

Keynes's concern was with long and severe depressions characterized by very large declines to low levels of both real investment and stock market values. Such major depressions have occurred at intervals of a few decades through the 1930s but most business contractions were much milder and shorter. Even in long contractions the stock of capital usually continues to increase, although at much reduced rates; also, an *abrupt* collapse of investment is rare.[11] Consumer spending is much less stable in the short run than Keynes assumed (but also much more stable and supportive of growth in the long run). As for the demand for money, there is a mass of evidence that its interest-elasticity tends to be relatively low (Laidler 1969). These observations raise serious questions about some elements of Keynes's theory.

2.3.3   Wage and Price Dynamics in Business Cycles

Despite the great rise and persistence of unemployment, real wages *increased* throughout the 1930s, thereby failing to provide one classical cure for the apparent disequilibrium in the labor market.[12] Keynes (1936, chs. 19 and 21) did not argue that money wages are entirely rigid downward but rather that they adjust but sluggishly to excess supplies of labor. Such slow wage declines are apt to reduce incomes, consumption, and prices before they begin to improve profitability and stimulate investment. When the resulting gradual deflation becomes widely anticipated, people repeatedly postpone purchases, mainly of durable goods, while waiting for prices to fall further. The demand for money increases at the expense of the demand for goods and equities.

Moreover, unexpected deflation increases the burden of accumulated debt, which falls most heavily on businesses and individuals with high propensities to borrow, invest, and spend. The activities of these units are severely curtailed as their bank credit lines are cut. Business failures and personal bankruptcies rise in numbers and size. Irving Fisher (1932, 1933) ascribed the

11. These points were made early by Burns (in his collected essays, 1954, pp. 3–25, 207–35). On the dispersion of peaks in various categories of investment commitments and expenditures, see Zarnowitz 1973, ch. 4.

12. In the United States, average hourly earnings in manufacturing divided either by the consumer price index or by the wholesale price index rose approximately 20% between 1929 and 1934, for example. Money wage rates declined less than prices. Hours of work fell along with the number of the employed workers (Temin 1976, pp. 138–41).

depth of the Depression to the confluence and mutual reinforcement of deflation and "overindebtedness" inherited from the boom. (This suggests overinvestment as the cause of the downturn.) His policy prescription was monetary
reflation, a reversal of the price decline.

A one-time large drop in the general wage level is a theoretical but hardly a
practical alternative in a large decentralized economy with numerous,
strongly differentiated labor markets and a complicated structure of relative
wages. A spreading depression in an open system is more likely to result in
competitive devaluations and various protectionist "beggar my neighbor"
measures, with deeply damaging overall consequences.

The actual and expected changes in the *rates of change* in wages and prices
can certainly be of great importance in business cycle dynamics. The effects
on aggregate demand of changes in the *levels* of wages and prices, on the other
hand, are believed to have their main roles in comparative statics and the long
run.[13] The static and dynamic elements were never clearly distinguished by
Keynes and his immediate critics; the debate proceeded for a long time in the
framework of comparative statics, which obscured the essentially dynamic
disequilibrium nature of Keynes's theory (Leijonhufvud 1968).

After World War II inflation became, for the first time, a chronic condition
in peacetime, drawing attention away from the concurrent, relatively mild
recessions and at the same time making their understanding apparently much
more difficult. The old problem of depression-cum-deflation was replaced by
the new problem of unemployment-cum-inflation. The famous Phillips curve
emerged first as a nonlinear and inverse dependence of the rate of change in
nominal wages (w) on the rate of unemployment (U) and was rationalized by
relating U to the excess supply of labor (Phillips 1958; Lipsey 1960). Soon
the rate of inflation (p) was similarly related to U, on the ground that p and w
normally differ by a steady rate of growth in labor productivity (Samuelson
and Solow 1960).[14]

The classical view of an aggregated labor market posits the existence at any
time of a unique equilibrium, or "natural," unemployment rate (U^N) as a function of *real* wages (M. Friedman 1968). An inflation that has lasted for some
significant time will be expected to persist at some positive average rate (p^e).
Changes in the price level that are generally and correctly anticipated are

13. The reference here is, first, to the "Keynes effect" (at lower prices, a given quantity of
money represents a larger real quantity) and the "Pigou effect" (at lower prices, a given quantity
of net nominal private wealth represents a larger real quantity). The former would raise investment
through lower interest rates; the latter would raise consumption. To stimulate the economy in the
short run both require downward flexibility of prices generally. The Keynes effect depends inversely on the interest-elasticity of the demand for money. The Pigou effect depends positively on
the magnitude of *net* private wealth, which is probably small in relative terms. Deflationary expectations and distributional shifts may also greatly weaken this process (Pigou 1947; Patinkin
1948).

14. It should be noted that from the cyclical perspective it is far from innocuous to substitute
price for wage inflation. As will be shown in section 2.3.6, labor productivity and the related price
and cost variables undergo partly systematic changes over the cycle.

matched by wage changes and hence cannot cause deviations of U from U^N. Only unanticipated inflation, that is, forecast errors ($p^e - p$), can cause such deviations. Equilibrium requires that $p^e = p$, hence a stable long-run tradeoff between p and U cannot exist (the natural-rate hypothesis—NRH: Friedman 1966, 1968; Phelps 1967). A short-run Phillips curve, associated with unanticipated or disequilibrium inflation, stays in place only as long as p^e remains unchanged.[15]

The initial reaction of most economists to the Friedman-Phelps critique was to embrace the NRH without questioning the existence of an inverse relationship between inflation and unemployment *in the short run*. This was because they assumed expectations to be "adaptive," that is, backward looking and involving only partial and lagging corrections of past errors.[16] Indeed, it was frequently assumed that the errors of inflation forecasts are fully eliminated only on the average over the business cycle. On this permissive interpretation of a "long run," the NRH is entirely consistent with continuing parallel fluctuations in inflation and real economic activity around their (uncorrelated) long-trend movements.

The expectations-augmented but only slowly shifting Phillips curve appears in Tobin's 1975 analysis of Keynesian models of cyclical contractions, with the qualification that this does not imply a full acceptance of the NRH. In this dynamic model, output (Q) moves in reaction to changes in aggregate real demand (E). In the short run the two variables can differ: say, $E<Q$ when Q is rising because of lags in consumption and unintended inventory changes. E depends positively on Q and the expected price change p^e and negatively on the price level P. Actual inflation p (= rate of change in P) adjusts to changes in p^e and in Q relative to Q^N (the full-employment output). Finally p^e reacts to the divergencies of p from p^e. The equilibrium conditions are $E = Q$, $Q = Q^N$, and $p = p^e$. The main inference from the model is that "a strong negative price-level effect on aggregate demand, a weak price-expectations effect, and a slow response of price expectations to experience are conducive to stability" (Tobin 1975, pp. 199–200). Large adverse shocks to E can push the economy into a depression, and market price adjustments will provide no reasonably prompt and effective remedy under conditions where the price-change effects on E are stronger than the price-level effects.[17]

2.3.4 Disequilibrium Models with Capital Accumulation

Keynes's analysis is only implicitly and partially dynamic. Since net investment varies, so does total capital, which influences output, investment,

---

15. The general form for the original equation is $w_t = f(U_t)$; for the "expectations-augmented" equation satisfying the NRH it is $w_t = f(U_t) + p_t^e$.

16. A simple model of this type if $p_t^e - p_{t-1}^e = k(p_{t-1} - p_{t-1}^e)$, where $0<k<1$.

The early *locus classicus* for adaptive expectations is Cagan 1956; also Muth 1960; Nerlove and Wage 1964; and Mincer 1969a.

17. Tobin, 1980, ch. 1, has a more recent reassessment, with similar conclusions concerning the cyclical effects of deflation.

and savings. But these effects are ignored and the stocks of production factors and technology are treated as constant. The older acceleration principle has no role in the *General Theory,* and indeed is not even mentioned. But the 1930s and 1940s saw a proliferation of formal models of essentially endogenous cycles in aggregate output, which use various versions of the investment accelerator and the consumption multiplier and let the two interact (Harrod 1936; Kalecki 1937; Samuelson 1939; Metzler 1941; Hicks 1950).

In most of these formulations, net investment is a function of *changes* in output, which implies that fluctuations in consumption are transmitted with increasing amplitudes to the higher stages of production—the derived demand for intermediate and producer goods. This contrast in amplitudes is broadly consistent with the evidence (sec. 2.2.2), which has long made the acceleration principle attractive to business cycle theorists. Yet it is clear from the data that investment series have much higher persistence or serial correlations than the series of first differences in output or sales. The simultaneous relationship between these variables over short unit periods is weak, not surprisingly, since investment depends on expectational and financial factors as well as on changes in technology, cost of labor, etc. [18]

With consumption lagging behind income and induced investment behind change in output, the multiplier-accelerator interaction can produce a model of fluctuating output in the form of a second-order difference equation. Small values of the coefficient of acceleration result in damped cycles, large values in explosive cycles. When a trend is added reflecting continuous technological change embodied in "autonomous" investment, the cycles are slanted upward around a line whose slope represents the equilibrium rate of the economy's real growth. In the potentially explosive case, fluctuations in actual output are constrained between a "ceiling" along which the (growing) resources are fully utilized and a "floor" set by the non-negativeness of gross investment (Hicks 1950). This model uses distributed lags in consumption and investment functions and suspends the accelerator during a steep downswing, with the result that the slump is both cushioned and prolonged as the excess stocks of capital depreciate but slowly down to the levels required by the low production at the floor.

A closely related but more general class of models is based on the capital stock adjustment (or "flexible accelerator") principle: current investment equals some fraction of the gap between the desired and the actual capital. The desired stock varies directly with output (taken, questionably, as a proxy for the expected demand for output that the capital is to help produce). Net

18. The theory of the production function of the firm includes the acceleration effect but also, in the general case of variable factor proportions and prices, a substitution effect (e.g., Gapinski 1982, chs. 2 and 4). Net investment cannot decline in any period by more than the capital stock can be worn out, which suggests asymmetrical behavior between upswings and downswings. In principle, it is in the long run, along the rising trend of capacity output, that the simple accelerator making net investment proportional to the change in output should work best, not in the short run of cyclical analysis.

investment therefore depends positively on output and inversely on the initially available stock of capital. This formulation (used early in Kalecki 1935; Kaldor 1940; Goodwin 1951) is capable of being improved, with some significant advantages. Since profitability should depend positively on the output-capital ratio, the role of profits in the investment function (stressed by many authors, particularly after Tinbergen 1938–39) is given at least an indirect consideration. The fraction of the capital gap closed in the short unit period (the speed of adjustment) may be made a function of the interest rate and, more generally, the costs of capital. The costlier the speed, the more gradual will be the optimal adjustment; this opens the way to a potentially useful dynamic analysis. On the other hand, the cyclical changes in capital stock, being relatively small (and rarely negative), have probably rather weak short-term effects on investment and output.

The dynamics in the models under review come from lags, nonlinearities, or both. Nonlinearities are likely to be very common in economic relationships, in part because the numerical values of certain important parameters should vary with the phases of business cycles, which cover a wide variety of macroeconomic conditions. Yet, few theoretical models of the cycle make important use of nonlinearities. In Kaldor 1940, investment (I) is a sigmoid function of output (Q), with much lower positive slopes at both extremes than in the broad middle range of the Q scale. I is deterred by both surplus capacity in slumps and rising construction and financial costs in booms. Saving (S) has a converse shape, with higher positive slopes at both extremes than in the middle range of Q: people stabilize consumption over time by temporarily reducing (raising) the average rate of savings when their incomes are unusually low (high).[19] Given Q, I depends inversely and S depends positively on the capital stock K. There are three possible equilibria; two of which are stable. The result is a self-sustained cycle in the real aggregates, from stable to unstable to another stable equilibrium.[20]

The substantive uses of nonlinearities in the theory of business cycles are yet to be systematically explored. There are, to be sure, various nonlinearities in mathematical and econometric models but they are, on the whole, scattered and treated mainly as technical detail. The early models by Kaldor, Hicks, and Goodwin remain influential in this literature.[21]

19. The argument seems to anticipate the more recent theories of consumption if one adds the assumption that people perceive larger proportions of their incomes as being transitory in booms and slumps than in the more "normal" times closer to the trend. Transitory income is taken to be largely saved; permanent income consumed.

20. The path of output is $dQ/dt = \alpha[I(Q,K) - S(Q,K)]$, with $\alpha > 0$ denoting the speed of adjustment. The equilibria are defined by $I(\cdot) = S(\cdot)$; they are stable when $\delta S/\delta Q > \delta I/\delta Q$, which occurs at both low and high levels of Q, and unstable when $\delta S/\delta Q < \delta I/\delta Q$, which occurs in an intermediate position. The responses of Q, that is, movements along the I or S curves, are speedier than the shifts of these curves caused by the changes in K.

21. A list of some references must suffice: Ichimura 1954; Rose 1967; Bober 1968; Chang and Smyth 1971; Kosobud and O'Neil 1972; Torre 1977; Scarfe 1977, ch. 4; Gapinski 1982, chs. 4–6, Schinasi 1981, 1982.

Recently, some methods of the "singularity" and "catastrophe" theories, new branches of applied mathematics, began to be applied to the analysis of large economic fluctuations involving crises, depressions, and rapid recoveries. The theory is concerned with the interaction of "fast" and "slow" variables in dynamic systems described by differential equations, where the short-run equilibrium may jump from one region of the state space to another. For example, the rate of change in output may depend on the level of output, a "fast" variable, and physical capital and financial assets, "slow" variables (expectations or other parameters may also be treated as slow variables). An illustration using a modified Kaldor model is offered by Varian (1979). This is an interesting approach, though still in its infancy.

Although innovative in their dynamics, the models discussed here are severely limited in their contents. They slight or ignore the monetary, financial, and expectational factors which, theory and evidence suggest, are particularly important in major cycles, crises, and depressions. Most of these models, too, neglect the role of new technology as a determinant of investment (Goodwin 1951 is a notable exception). These criticisms were made early in the heyday of the endogenous investment theories of the cycle (Burns 1952a; Haberler 1956; Lundberg 1958). A. Hansen (1964) viewed the accelerator as relatively weak and stressed the driving force of autonomous investment related to innovations which require more capital per worker.

However, it is also clear that the models in question contain important elements and are capable of being expanded and improved, in particular by incorporating monetary factors. Indeed, Hicks (1950, chs. 11 and 12), added to his main real model a monetary subsystem which could aggravate some downturns.[22] Tobin's 1955 model has similar cycles but also explicit roles for the supply of monetary assets and the inflexibility of money wages. More recently, Laidler (1973b) makes the desired capital stock depend on the lagged real interest rate as well as the lagged output, thereby modifying Hicks's equation for induced investment so that it includes monetary effects. Inflation expectations, formed adaptively, appear in a Phillips-type relationship which complies with the NRH but permits gradual price adjustments. This model retains an accelerator-multiplier mechanism and can generate fluctuations in output and prices. However, unlike in Hicks, the cycles are here damped, and exogenous changes in either the nominal interest rate or autonomous expenditures may be required to move the economy off either the floor or the ceiling.[23]

22. The "monetary complication" takes the form of a cobweb cycle in the IS-LM space, with rather complex lags and nonlinearities. A quarter-century later, Hicks (1974) revised his views, stressing the need for greater reliance on monetary factors and autonomous investment.

23. Laidler considers, alternatively, the nominal rate of interest and the money stock as exogenous. Output is systematically related not to inflation or deflation but to the rate of change in either.

2.3.5   On Causes and Consequences of Fluctuations in Inventory Investment

Inventories have a much shorter expected life span than fixed capital and can be adjusted much more quickly to the desired levels. Nevertheless, the success of attempts at such adjustment is by no means assured as it depends partly on accurate sales forecasts and partly on how promptly production reacts to unanticipated sales changes. Some of the observed inventory investment is planned, and some is unintended.

It is difficult to use stocks as a buffer protecting output from the variation in sales, except when the changes in demand are small and short, calling for no alteration in production. In the more persistent business cycle movements, inventory investment tends to be, on the contrary, *de*stabilizing, as shown by the already noted fact that aggregate output fluctuates more widely than final sales.

An early and influential theory of inventory cycles was developed in Metzler's (1941, 1947) multiplier-accelerator models. Here the desired level of stocks of consumer goods varies with anticipated sales to consumers, which reflect sales observed in the recent past. Output lags behind consumption, which is proportional to contemporaneous income. An initial rise in the level of noninventory investment, which is treated as autonomous, depletes inventories; hence business people attempt to increase them. But inventory investment has the feedback effect of raising income and consumption, which reduces the stocks still more. This causes further rounds of increase in inventory investment, output, and sales. However, at some point during the expansion, the rates of increase in sales, and hence also in inventory investment, will start falling. Declines in income and consumption will ultimately result, reducing the desired stock levels. Again, the very efforts to get rid of the unwanted stocks depress income and consumption further and are thus temporarily self-defeating, but eventually the rate of decline in sales and the disinvestment in stocks will begin to diminish, and an upturn in income and consumption will initiate a new cycle.

Several papers report generally favorable tests of Metzler's model based on annual and quarterly data, mainly for the United States in the first two decades after World War II (Coppock 1959, 1962, 1965; Hillinger 1966, 1979). The periodicities are heavily concentrated in the 3–4 year range and are not seriously disturbed by inclusion of random error terms, but there is substantial damping. Anticipated values are derived from distributed lags (adaptive expectations). The techniques include cyclical (NBER) measures, regression, and spectral analyses. The hypothesis that fluctuations in nonfarm business inventory investment and nonresidential fixed investment are essentially periodic, with cycles of about 3–5 and 7–10 years, respectively, has been recently revived by Hillinger (1982, 1983). However, the unconventional methods used in this work are subject to serious doubts and the results are yet to be fully described and evaluated.[24]

Metzler's hypothesis, like other cyclical investment models of the multiplier-accelerator type, runs entirely in real terms and pays no attention to price adjustments and monetary and financial factors. Also, it fits best the finished-goods inventories subject to changes reflecting errors in sales forecasts. But studies which disaggregate inventories by stage of fabrication and type of production (Abramovitz 1950; Stanback 1962; Lovell 1964; Mack 1967; Zarnowitz 1973; Popkin 1984) show that for good reasons the behavior of stocks varies systematically between these categories. Thus finished-goods inventories are important primarily in production to stock; in production to order, which plays a very large role in durable-goods and particularly capital-goods industries, inventories consist mainly of goods-in-process, which depend positively on the rate of output, and materials, which are strongly influenced by cyclical changes in supply conditions (delivery periods, availability). The stocks of materials can be promptly adjusted in the ordering stage. Of course, it is difficult to allow for such details in aggregate models but an important lesson here is that desired inventories depend importantly on other variables in addition to sales.

2.3.6   The Role of Changes in Prices, Costs, and Profits

In his 1913 volume, Mitchell linked the major changes in business activity to the outlook for profits or (in time of crisis) the quest for solvency. Prospective profits depend on sales experience and expectations and on the price-cost relation, which is itself changing with the rate of employment and capacity utilization. Business costs tend to rise faster than product prices in the late stages of expansion, which depresses profit margins and expectations. Accordingly, new investment commitments are curtailed well before sales flatten. Income receipts and consumption expenditures weaken, inventories pile up, and production cuts multiply, particularly in durable-goods industries. Pessimistic expectations spread and are confirmed and worsened when output and employment turn down. In the contraction that follows, similarly, price-cost margins and profits first deteriorate and then improve, excess stocks and other imbalances are gradually liquidated, and new investment orders, sales, and output eventually revive.

When Mitchell first proposed a theoretical account of these developments, he had little empirical knowledge of them from the very inadequate data then in existence. By now, however, there is much evidence that the relations he stressed are generally consistent with the stylized facts discussed in section 2 above. (On their validity, see Fabricant 1959; Hultgren 1950, 1965; Kuh

---

24. Cycles are estimated by cosine functions applied to residuals from polynomial trends. The latter lack a theoretical rationale and are limited to the period of estimation. The paucity of annual observations presents another grave problem of statistical nature.

1960; Moore 1962, 1975a; Zarnowitz, 1973; Moore and Cullity 1983; Boehm 1990.) What is particularly well established and important is the typically procyclical but lagging pattern in labor costs per unit of output, which reflects primarily the positive conformity and lead times of labor productivity (output per hour of work). Real wages, on the other hand, normally do not show large deviations from trend that are consistently associated with business cycles.[25]

In a 1967 model of Rose, employment and labor supply fluctuate relative to the stock of capital, which grows with net investment. The rates of change in wages (w) and prices (p) are equal in the long-run equilibrium but differ in the short run, reflecting these fluctuations. During a recession, the ratio of labor supply to capital increases, the rate of employment falls, and prices start rising faster than wages. The improvement in profitability leads to an upturn in the rate of employment. During the recovery, the condition $p > w$, persists, but gradually investment revives and growth of capital accelerates. First employment and then capital start growing faster than the labor supply. The upswing eventually causes wages to overtake prices. In the new phase, where $p < w$, the profit rate and the employment-capital ratio turn down. Investment is reduced, the rate of employment declines, and a new recession begins.

The model has debatable implications for the real-wage movements and its shortcomings are apparent, given the lessons of the recent inflationary era.[26] But all formal models are heavily restricted and the aspect covered here, namely, the cyclical role of changes in the relative input/output prices, is important enough to make the attempt interesting. Earlier theories of this type, although not worked out mathematically, are in some respects broader and more satisfactory.[27]

The price-cost-profit nexus can and should be combined with monetary elements, since, as stressed by Mitchell, business cycles arise only in a "money economy" in its late stage of development and are incompatible with pure barter. (For one interesting attempt in this direction, see Rose 1969.) In mod-

---

25. Countercyclical movements in real wages are implied by the classical marginal productivity theory of the demand for labor, which was accepted by Keynes, and they are also suggested by the view that prices generally are more flexible and procyclical than money wages. However, the evidence is mixed and not conclusive. It varies with the choice of the deflator, the characteristics of the period covered, methods and data (e.g., the intracycle changes may not show up well in regressions with annual series). A few studies favor the countercyclical hypothesis (Neftçi 1978; Sargent 1978), but there is more support for both procyclical behavior (Dunlop 1938; Tarshis 1939; Modigliani 1977; Stockman 1983; Bils 1985) and no significant relationship between real wages and employment (Kuh 1960; Bodkin 1969; Geary and Kennan 1982).

26. Under perfect competition, Rose's hypothesis has real wages increasing in the boom and early contraction, decreasing in late contraction and recovery. Under imperfect competition, however, real wages could be either invariant or procyclical, depending on the elasticities of demand and marginal costs. A single nonlinear Phillips wage-employment curve is involved; shifts in it would have to be introduced, lest the model be applicable at best to a short period before any endogenous expectations of inflation changes develop and take effect.

27. Krelle (1981) demonstrates the similarity of Rose's theory to that of Erich Preiser (1933). The main difference is that Preiser had a two-sector (consumer-goods, producer-goods) model, whereas Rose has a simpler, one-sector model.

erate cycles, the effective limit on the volume of transactions is set by demand, whereas in "intense booms" a higher limit of monetary nature is reached. [28]

2.4   Theories of Cyclical Response to Monetary and Real Disturbances

2.4.1   Exogenous Factors, Stochastic Elements, and Types of Theory

Section 2.3 discussed mainly the work of economists who attribute business cycles to the modus operandi of industrialized private-enterprise economies. Here the cycle itself is the principal source of the stresses and imbalances that keep it going. A nonlinear model that requires only a single initial disturbance to produce self-sustaining cycles has maximum endogeneity. [29]

In reality, of course, the economy is always influenced by outside factors (e.g., weather) so that a comprehensive explanation of its motion cannot be purely endogenous. But no outside influences can by themselves produce the recurrent sequences of expansions and contractions; in the first place, this presumably requires the particular dynamics of an interdependent economic system. A really satisfactory theory, therefore, should explain how business cycles are generated by the internal mechanism of an economy exposed to the impact of a great many potentially relevant external events. What matters, then, is the relative role of the inside and outside factors, not the extreme cases. Nevertheless, a *mainly* endogenous model of business cycles differs in principle sharply from a *mainly* exogenous one.

The specific events and variables that are usually treated as exogenous include wars and changes in population, technology, weather, government spending, tax laws, etc. They clearly can and often do have major economic consequences that affect cyclical behavior. In addition to these factors, which usually show considerable persistence over time (are serially correlated), there are also the random shocks—uncorrelated disturbances of various kinds which impinge upon the structure of economic relationships. Both the white-noise and the identifiable exogenous factors play important roles in the linear and dynamically stable model of Frisch (1933). Here a low value for the accelerator is assumed but also a sufficiently close succession of erratic impulses which keep the system fluctuating. That is, the response of the economy to

---

28. For example, an expansion can be halted by the constraint on a further rise in bank credit imposed by the gold standard, as in Hawtrey (Mitchell 1927, ch. 2). On Mitchell's efforts to synthesize real, monetary, and expectational factors in viewing both the causes and effects of business cycles, see M. Friedman 1952; Zarnowitz 1968a, and ch. 5 this volume.

29. Fluctuations that are neither damped nor explosive but self-sustaining are simply not credible in linear models. It would be extremely unlikely, for example, for the accelerator always to assume that precise middle value which is needed to keep the system in a constant cycle. With random shocks imposed upon such a model, the cycles would increase over time (Samuelson 1947, pp. 268–69). This does not apply to nonlinear models, which can produce recurrent cycles with bounded variances, as shown for a Kaldor-type model by L. Klein and R. S. Preston (1969).

random but continual disturbances is such that what would otherwise be damped (fading) oscillations are converted into the recurrent business cycles. This hypothesis (which was suggested earlier by Wicksell and Slutsky) gained much recognition in recent theoretical writings and it particularly influenced the work of macroeconometric model builders.

Several econometric models of the U.S. economy in the post–world War II period have been found generally noncyclical in the absence of outside disturbances, as shown by simulation studies (I. Adelman and F. Adelman 1959; Hickman 1972). But random shocks applied to the more recent quarterly models proved to be insufficient to generate movements with the observed cyclical properties; to induce fluctuations in these models, it was necessary to use serially correlated disturbances (Zarnowitz, Boschan, and Moore 1972; Howrey 1972). Moreover, even the best simulations show only residual cyclical elements, much weaker than those found in the historical series used in the estimation of the models. This could be due to errors in either the structure of the models or the estimates of the disturbances or both. [30]

It should be noted that the large macroeconometric models used primarily for short-term forecasting are frequently and extensively revised, and the more recent versions of them may well be substantially more cyclical. Simulation of one commercially successful model suggests that random noise from equation errors accounts for only 7% of an overall measure of "cyclicality" and that some two thirds of the latter would remain even with stable monetary policy, no financial disintermediation "crunches," and no oil price shocks (Eckstein and Sinai 1986).

The validity of the evidence from macroeconometric models which appear to refute the endogenous cycle and favor the random shock theory is, for these and other reasons, open to doubts. Thus Blatt (1978) constructed artificial time series on income, consumption, and investment based on Hicks's model with a high accelerator, implying unstable behavior. An econometric analysis of these data shows that they are seemingly well explained by a linear model with random shocks, which has a low accelerator yielding stable conditions. The problem is attributed to the limitations of linear models (Hicks's theory is essentially nonlinear). [31]

Business cycles interact with long-term trends in varied and subtle ways, so the separation of the two is difficult conceptually and empirically (see chapter

---

30. Parameters that may well vary with changes in policy regimes (Lucas 1976), the structure of the economy, and major departures from average cyclical patterns are estimated as constant by the models. Models estimated with data from periods with mild business cycles such as those of the 1950s and 1960s are known to be unable to reproduce much more violent fluctuations such as those of the 1930s (Zellner and Peck 1973).

31. Further, Blatt (1980) argues that the random shock theory is inconsistent with the evidence that deviations of many economic time series from smooth long-term trends show a pronounced asymmetry: the rises tend to be longer than the declines and also smaller per unit period. The measures are based on long monthly time series examined in trend-adjusted form by Burns and Mitchell (1946, ch. 7).

7). Decompositions using purely deterministic (say, log-linear) trends ignore such interactions, for example, the imprint that major cycles leave on the growth rates for some considerable time. Cyclical analyses based on deviations from such trends are suspect on statistical grounds (Nelson and Plosser 1982). The proposed alternative is to use stochastic trends approximated by random walks, but this means in practice that most of the contractions as well as expansions are included in such trend constructs, whereas the residual components labeled the "cycle" are largely pure noise (Beveridge and Nelson 1981). There is no good *economic* theory to justify this way of looking at the world.

The regularities reviewed in section 2.2 of this paper cannot be reconciled with the suggestion made by Fisher in 1925 and reviewed by McCulloch (1975, p. 303) that business cycles resemble "the cycles superstitious gamblers believe they can discern in their luck at casinos like the one at Monte Carlo." As shown by McCulloch, once an expansion or contraction has exceeded its minimum historical duration, the probability of its being reversed in a given month is independent of its age. But that is merely a proof of nonperiodicity, not of randomness, of the fluctuations called "business cycles." Endogenous processes can still bring about the downturns and upturns, but they interact with all types of random and serially correlated outside events, which makes the timing of the reversals unpredictable (cf. Matthews 1959, pp. 199–205).[32]

Certainly, the processes and relations economists study are in general stochastic, and purely deterministic explanations of macroeconomic movements cannot be sufficient. But purely stochastic explanations have no theoretical content, and it is the factors which can be integrated in an economic theory that are naturally of primary interest to any economist who attempts to understand the nature and causes of business cycles.

In the generally prosperous times after World War II, however, business cycles slipped way down in the public and professional interest. The weight of the public sector increased greatly throughout the industrialized world, and government actions and policies attracted growing attention as a likely source of large macroeconomic effects, notably the rising inflation. The idea that business contractions are also policy induced and episodic rather than a part of self-sustaining cycles seemed increasingly plausible.

Even while the style of macroeconomic analysis and policy remained predominantly Keynesian, the theory soon veered sharply away from the unstable accelerator-multiplier models to concepts that imputed much more stability to the private sector. This evolution shows up strongly in Duesenberry

---

32. Such processes include those arising from particular historical and institutional developments, for example, the "misintermediation" practice of banks and thrift institutions which McCulloch elsewhere (1977, 1981) asserts are a cause of financial instability and recurrent, if nonperiodic, business fluctuations. Similarly, Irving Fisher's debt-deflation hypothesis of the 1930s treats the business cycle problem much more seriously than his writings in the 1920s.

1958.[33] The notion of strong cyclical effects from high values of the accelerator and multiplier was further deflated by new theoretical developments: the permanent income and life-cycle hypotheses of consumption and the "neoclassical" models of investment. Used along with adaptive expectations reacting only gradually to past events, these formulations suggested relatively stable trends in private demands. The rise of monetarism (see next section) worked in the same direction.

Historically, the main substantive differences among the theories centered on the relative importance of real versus monetary factors. This can be linked to the distinction between the impulses and the propagation mechanism, introduced formally by Frisch in 1933. There can be models with monetary shocks and real propagation, models with real shocks and monetary propagation, and various mixtures of the two. Even in the largely endogenous theories it is sometimes possible to differentiate in a somewhat similar manner between the mainly originating factors and the mainly conditioning or response factors.[34]

In sum, the several dichotomies encountered in modern business cycle dynamics intersect in various ways, and the extant theories actually represent many of the possible resulting combinations. They generally resist being neatly characterized by these categories, but even attempts at approximations can be instructive. A few illustrations for some theories, lightly treated above, are given in table 2.5. (See the first four cases; the others refer to materials to be discussed later.)

2.4.2   The Monetarist Interpretation of Business Fluctuations

In the 1960s, the rise of monetarism mounted a frontal challenge to Keynesian economics, starting from the simple quantity-theoretic proposition: changes in the stock of money are the main determinant of changes in nominal income. The demand for money is a relatively stable function linking real balances to wealth or permanent income and to expected rates of return on money and alternative assets. Given significant lags in wage and price adjustments, sequences of alternating phases of high and low growth rates in the quantity of money lead to corresponding fluctuations in aggregate demand and real economic activity relative to the secular trends. Sufficiently long periods of low but predominantly positive monetary growth rates are likely to produce business slowdowns or recessions; sufficiently long periods of negative monetary growth rates lead to depressions (Friedman and Schwartz 1963a, 1963b).[35]

33. In this relatively disaggregate and complex theory, growth is explained by the interaction of a capital-adjustment process with autonomous investment, downturns by the operation of various exogenous factors, and upturns by the corrective forces inherent in the basically stable system.

34. The idea is found in Pigou 1927, p. 8, A. M. Hansen (1964, chs. 17 and 18) applies it to the work by Wicksell, Aftalion, Pigou, and J. M. Clark.

35. Of course, monetarism (like Keynesianism) has come to denote a broad assortment of theoretical concepts and empirical propositions attributed to economists who agree in some respects and disagree in others. Here there is need only for a selective treatment of these character-

The lags of output behind the monetary changes are seen as variable but, on the average, lengthy. This is so because, say, an accelerated increase in the quantity of money must first alter the relative prices or yields on a broad range of assets. The resulting discrepancies between the actual and the desired portfolios prompt the banks and the public to take corrective actions. The stimulus would eventually spread to product markets, causing rises in payments for services of, and the investments in, nonfinancial assets. As spending, income, and prices rise, interest rates will snap back from their earlier decline. If price expectations are adaptive, that is, subject to lagged error corrections, people will tend to underestimate the rising prices; hence they will overestimate their real money balances for some time. This will induce more transitory spending to liquidate the extra amounts of "redundant" money, and in the process, the rates of rise in prices and nominal income will overshoot the new equilibrium paths for these variables.[36] Thus, even in the case of a single shock, some cyclical (presumably damped) reaction may well occur.

The rate of growth of output or real income corresponding to full employment (or the "natural unemployment rate") is exogenous in this model, being determined by real factors. The monetarist theory of macroeconomic fluctuations deals with deviations of output from this trend, that is, with "growth cycles."[37]

The early and still influential versions of this theory, due largely to Friedman, treat monetary changes—growth rates or deviations from trend of the quantity of money—as if they were predominantly autonomous, that is, having strong one-way effects on movements in total spending, income, and output. The reverse effects, from business activity to money, are recognized to exist but only as secondary "feedbacks." The main source of critical monetary disturbances is thus located outside the private economy, in policy actions and institutional changes. Private expenditures, including business investment, are viewed as essentially stable, except when affected by the money shocks: when undisturbed, they tend to be consistent, in real terms, with the natural rates of employment and output.

This is a new emphasis. Earlier monetary theories generally gave most attention to private-sector instabilities, particularly credit fluctuations. The differences are highlighted in table 2.5 above (see also, section 2.3.1).

This brings us to the subject of the determinants of money supply. Under

istics inasmuch as they bear on the evolution of the work on business cycles. (For comprehensive surveys, see R. J. Gordon 1974; Stein 1976; Mayer et al. 1978.)

36. These paths would run parallel but higher than the new equilibrium path for the money stock, because at a higher rate of price rise less money in real terms would be demanded relative to wealth and income (Friedman and Schwartz 1963b; Friedman 1970b).

37. The equilibrium or trend level of output in this sense is associated with less than full utilization of resources; hence, it can be either higher or lower than the actual level of output at any time. This is unlike the concept of a "ceiling" imposed on output by full employment (as in Hicks 1950).

the present fiduciary standard, money consists of currency and, mainly, deposits in private banks. Monetary authorities can affect the quantity of money only indirectly and over time, by trying to control the monetary base (bank reserves plus currency). Subject to legal or regulatory constraints, banks vary their reserve-to-deposits ratios and the public their currency-to-deposits ratios in response to actual and expected changes in interest rates, real income, and probably some other indicators, (e.g., those of business and consumer confidence). In principle, then, a supply function for money in nominal units can be derived, involving the policy-related base and a few endogenous determinants of the money multiplier (ratio of the money stock to the base). The stability of this function is an empirical question on which there is significant disagreement.[38] However, there is a substantial consensus, not only among monetarists, that any effects that interest rates, wealth, or income may have on the nominal money supply are much weaker and less consistent than the effects of these variables on the demand for real balances. Moreover, monetarist studies argue that central banks have the power and tools to exercise the dominant influence upon the money stock, except in the very short run.

The potential for an autonomous monetary policy is generally overestimated by analysts who concentrate on the United States, the only large market economy in which balance-of-payments considerations could long be treated as secondary even under fixed exchange rates. For any small economy under this regime, the nominal money supply depends on changes in the available foreign exchange reserves; it must tend to be consistent with prices and incomes that will balance the country's international payments and hence cannot be determined independently by domestic authorities. Under the gold standard, a business expansion would come to a halt when the drain of cash and shortage of gold reserves forced the banking system to curtail credit on a sufficiently large scale. This was the ultimate source of the relatively large and regular British cycles in the nineteenth century for Marshall, Hawtrey, and Lavington.

An early expectation that the monetarist approach may ultimately produce a theory of "a partly self-generating cyclical mechanism . . . including a feedback in the rate of change in money itself" (Friedman and Schwartz 1963b, p. 64) has remained unfulfilled. The feedback, or "reflex influence," running from business activity to monetary growth has not been analytically developed and integrated into a theory of how money, prices, and real factors interact in the short run. The approach produced instead an essentially

---

38. Cagan (1965) shows that high-powered money fluctuated more erratically than, and often opposite to, the currency and reserve ratios. One source of the interrelation is indirect—common response to business cycles; another is direct—central-bank operations designed to stabilize the economy. He finds that "the dependence of the money stock on prices and business activity, as well as on other variables, is strong but is neither rigid, uniform, nor immediate" (p. 16). Friedman and Schwartz stress that "neither interest rates nor real income have a consistent and sizable influence on the nominal quantity of money supplied" (1982, p. 35). On the other hand, Brunner and Meltzer argue that an empirically stable money supply function exists (1968, 1972).

Table 2.5   A Synopsis of Selected Business Cycle Theories

Type of Theory (1)	Main Factors		Most Sensitive Processes (4)	Are Cycles Linked to Growth? (5)	Special Features (6)	Author and Dates (7)
	Originating (2)	Responsive (3)				
I. Some Largely Endogenous Theories						
Monetary disequilibrium	Unstable flow of money (bank credit)	Interest rate changes; cycles of inflation and deflation	Investment in traders' inventories	No	Cycles tend to be periodic under the gold standard	Hawtrey 1913–37
Monetary overinvestment	Unstable supply of bank credit	Discrepancy between the natural and money interest rates	Capital investment, lengthening and shortening of production processes	No or weakly	Real vertical maladjustments result from monetary disequilibria	Hayek 1931–39
Cyclical real growth	Bursts of innovation (new products, markets, etc.) contested by imitators	Credit financing; excesses of speculation and misjudgment	Business capital investment booms and readjustments in contractions	Yes	Simultaneous interacting long, intermediate, and short cycles	Schumpeter 1912–39
II. Some Theories with Major Exogenous and Stochastic Elements						
Impulse and propagation in a real model	Undefined erratic shocks and discontinuous Schumpeterian innovations	Investment accelerator, lags in output of capital goods, money demand, and imperfectly elastic supply	Capital-goods production, but the system as a whole is damped (dynamically stable)	Yes (through innovations)	Random shocks or innovations bunched in expansions needed to maintain oscillations	Frisch 1933

The original monetarist theory	Sequential shocks: high monetary growth rates followed by low rates, etc.	Relative prices and asset yields, then spending flows	Both consumption and investment react to monetary changes	No	Monetary policies destabilize the private sector	Friedman and Schwartz 1963a, 1963b
Market clearing with rational expectations and incomplete information	Random monetary shocks causing price-level variations	General price changes misperceived for relative price changes; intertemporal substitution of labor and leisure	Prompt and strong reactions to perceived changes in relative prices or real rates of return on the supply side	No	Flexible prices and wages clear markets continuously; money and price surprises cause fluctuations in output and investment	Lucas 1977
A disequilibrium theory of investment and financial instability (largely endogenous)	Unstable expected profits drive business investment, which generates fluctuations in realized profits	Money created by bank lending to business; short-term financing of long-term investment	Relative prices of capital assets set in financial markets under uncertainty about future returns, costs of capital, and cash flows	Yes	Long expansions produce overconfidence, unsound financing practices, a growing debt burden and illiquidity . . . sources of contractions and crises	Minsky 1982

exogenous and monetary model of the business cycle. Yet the same studies that show an important, independent role of money, particularly in major inflationary booms and severe deflationary slumps, also find much evidence that fluctuations in the monetary variables reflect those in real aggregates, particularly in mild cycles (summarized by Cagan 1965, p. 294). The primacy of the monetary effects cannot be established by the less-than-compelling argument that since money plays a key role in the major cycles, it should also be important in the minor cycles, which are just "less virulent members of the same species" (Friedman and Schwartz 1963b, p. 55).

The idea that cyclical instability is mainly policy induced is not an integral part of, or a necessary inference from, the monetarist theory. It is an empirical judgment held by some monetarists as well as other economists.[39] The popularity of this view rose in the late 1960s and 1970s, when both inflation and unemployment drifted upward, the Phillips curve moved north-to-northeast through a series of clockwise cycle-related loops, and failures of attempted stabilization policies were evident. Rather paradoxically, the 1970s also witnessed the culmination of belief in the power of macroeconomic policies that took the conceptual form of a "political business cycle," which is not of monetarist origin.[40]

Monetarist models can acquire some cyclical dynamics by combining an expectations-augmented Phillips curve with the quantity-theoretic demand for money function. Laidler (1973a) presents an intentionally simple model of this type, with exogenous monetary growth, the full-employment output rate, and adaptive expectations of inflation. The causation runs from lagged and current money growth rates and current inflation to the change in output, then back to inflation, and so on, recursively. The model generates a cyclical movement in output and inflation (relative to their natural and expected values, respectively) in response to a single shift in the rate of monetary expansion. Laidler notes that its simulations leave much to be desired, probably in large part because of the missing variables, particularly the interest rate.[41]

39. Consider the following statement by authors who contributed much to the development of the money supply function: "Our version of monetarism does not deny that if exogenous shocks take the form of government policies, including fiscal policies, the system may oscillate or even explode into inflation or cumulative deflation. Our proposition asserts that cyclical instability is mainly the product of government policies that are imposed on a stabilizing private sector" (Brunner and Meltzer in J. Stein 1976, p. 180).

40. The political models of business cycles maintain several strong and questionable assumptions. (1) Policymakers know the structure of the economy; the public does not. (2) The inflation-unemployment short-run trade-off can be exploited effectively by the party in power. (3) Voters are myopic and concerned with the current electoral period only. Thus the government is capable of fine-tuning the economy periodically. It is not surprising that these models, though ingenious, find little support in facts. The related evidence is mixed and generally inconclusive: Nordhaus 1975; Lindbeck 1976; MacRae 1977; also Fels 1977; Moore 1977a; Tufte 1978. A very useful, balanced overview is given in Alt and Chrystal 1983, esp., ch. 5.

41. For a corresponding theoretical analysis of a model for a small open economy under fixed exchange rates, see Laidler 1975, ch. 9.

2.4.3   Price Misperceptions and Intertemporal Substitution of Labor

Adaptive expectations often imply long lags of adjustment and persistence of apparently systematic errors. Critics regard models that yield such results as ad hoc and inconsistent with optimizing behavior. They accept instead the view that "expectations are essentially the same as the predictions of the relevant economic theory" (Muth 1961, p. 316). Application of this rational expectations hypothesis (REH) to macroeconomics was part of a new, ambitious program of work undertaken in the 1970s by several economists following the initiative of Lucas (1972). The objective was to develop a general business cycle theory in strict adherence to the basic principles of the analysis of economic equilibrium: consistent pursuit of self-interest by individuals and continuous clearing of all markets by relative prices. [42]

Under REH, the route of the older monetarist theory which used adaptive expectations to help explain the duration of cyclical movements is closed. Expectations are now taken to be free of any bias and subject to random errors only. All persistent monetary changes, inasmuch as they are predictable, will be correctly anticipated and met directly by proportional changes in prices and related nominal variables. Only random monetary impulses can lead to price surprises and miscalculations, which, in this view, are necessary to explain any cyclical movements in real variables.

The short-run aggregate supply function for labor (Lucas and Rapping 1969) is upward sloping relative to the deviations of the current level of real wages from their expected (discounted future) level. It is seen as typically elastic, reflecting strong competitive incentives to take advantage of temporarily higher rates of real return. Since the substitutability of leisure over time is high, a small change in the return on the current work effort can induce a large change, in the same direction, in the amount of work done. This intertemporal substitution hypothesis (ISH) plays a central role in the recent attempts to explain employment fluctuations as an aggregate result of individual choices on the supply side of the labor market.

By an analogous argument, firms are expected to vary their output positively in response to transitory changes in their selling prices, provided that these are seen as relative or real price changes and not equated with general inflation. But they would likewise vary their output inversely in response to transitory changes in the relative prices of their inputs, particularly labor. The basic equilibrium model of business cycles disregards this complication by

---

42. See Lucas 1973, 1975, 1977; Sargent and Wallace 1975, 1976; Sargent 1976a; Barro 1976, 1980; Lucas and Sargent 1978. Lucas (1977, p. 7) cites Hayek (1933) as an "intellectual ancestor" who posed the problem of explaining the business cycle as part, not a contradiction, of the equilibrium theory. This was indeed Hayek's intent, but it is also correct to characterize his solution as a theory of monetary disequilibrium and an unstable cumulative process, with excessive credit creation causing distortions of relative prices and the structure of production (as Hayek 1933 and 1939 are commonly interpreted).

simply combining workers and firms into a single group. The representative worker-entrepreneur then generally supplies more (less) of both labor and output when faced with an unanticipated rise (fall) in selling prices.

This approach, by eliminating other prime suspects of earlier business cycle theories (including real disturbances, which are viewed as dispersed and localized), places a heavy explanatory burden on a single causal chain: random monetary shocks induce price misperceptions, which induce wrong production decisions. By assumption, prices other than those in one's own market are known to anyone only with a lag of one unit period of unspecified length. Agents have complete and timely local information but only incomplete and lagging information about other "island" markets (Phelps 1970) and about economy-wide aggregates such as the money stock and the overall price level. Suppose now that an unanticipated acceleration in monetary growth occurs, raising prices in general; then the representative worker-entrepreneur first observes a higher selling price than he expected, takes it to be in some part a temporary increase in his relative price or real rate of return, and raises his output in accordance with the ISH. These reactions prevail whenever the observed prices turn out to be higher than the level most producers had expected on the basis of previous information. In the opposite situation of prices having proved lower than expected, output is, on the average, reduced. The random forecasting errors are unavoidable and can be recognized only after the outside price data become available. However, by then many erroneous decisions will already have been made, and the necessary revisions and corrections will also involve time and costs.

The model of the "representative producer," with its fusion of worker and employer, assumes that labor and business recognize that their interests generally coincide, or at least act as if they did. This is not consistent with the strong evidence of significant patterns of cyclical behavior in cost-price-profit relationships (secs. 2.2 and 2.3.5). These observations can best be interpreted with the commonsense assumption that firms and workers pursue their own interests in reacting rationally to changing business and labor market conditions.[43]

The issue of the relative timing of output prices versus input costs can be reduced to an informational problem in a number of ways. It might be assumed that firms have more immediate knowledge of price changes than workers or, more generally, that the representative producer unit (firm or worker) knows the prices of things it sells better than the prices of things it buys (Friedman 1968). If so, then inflation will be stimulative because it is largely unanticipated by workers or buyers (or, which is much the same, because it is recognized sooner in output prices than in input costs). Some critics

---

43. To be sure, the interests of workers and employers may coincide in some respects and are reconciled in negotiated or implicit contracts (sec. 2.4.7).

view these assumed informational asymmetries as arbitrary specifications (B. Friedman, comment on Lucas and Sargent 1978, p. 76; Tobin 1980, p. 42).

The equilibrium approach to business cycles can be explained well in general terms (Lucas 1977) and restated simply. (See the text above and the capsule description in table 2.5.) The individual models based on the REH and the ISH, however, are much too diverse, experimental, and complex to lend themselves to such verbal summarization. Some of them use changes in current prices relative to the next period's expected price level to induce intertemporal substitution on the supply side (Lucas 1972, 1973; Sargent and Wallace 1975). Others allow for the existence of assets that earn a nominal interest rate and add that rate to the above price surprise term to obtain a measure of anticipated one-period real rate of return. This relative price variable then appears with a positive sign as a determinant of supply and with a negative sign as a determinant of demand (Barro 1980).[44]

The general criticism of the price misperception hypothesis is that it requires long informational lags, which are even less likely under rational than under adaptive expectations. Ample, frequent, and low-cost monetary and price statistics are now available, so informational confusion of the type here hypothesized can only be short lived and associated with random changes, not persistent cyclical fluctuations, in output and employment (Hall 1975, 1980b; Tobin 1977; Modigliani 1977). True, this argument is partly countered by the observation that there are indeed serious deficiencies in these and other important data on the economy, which in many cases are reduced only through a time-consuming sequence of revisions. This can distort initial expectations and delay successful signal detection for several months (Zarnowitz 1982c). Still, informational lags are surely much shorter than the average cyclical movements, so they alone cannot account for the duration of the observed fluctuations (Okun 1980) or, one may add, for the large size of procyclical fluctuations in corporate profits and stock prices. Beginning with an economy at full employment,[45] most errors caused by temporary misperceptions of monetary and price changes would be detected and corrected before they could give rise to large cumulative income movements in either direction. Finally, the knowledge of the nominal interest rates, a set of timely and global variables, may convey information about the unobserved part of money growth (King 1983; Barro 1980).[46]

44. The net effect of a rise in this composite variable, then, will be to stimulate output if on the aggregate across the markets, the induced increase in supply is larger than the induced decrease in demand. This formulation takes into account the debate about the direction of informational asymmetries noted in the preceding paragraph of the text.

45. It is against the spirit of the new equilibrium theory (and some older scholars such as Hayek and other Austrians) to start an attempted explanation of business cycles by postulating an initial state of recession.

46. This prompts Barro (1981a, p. 51) to observe that the "stress on confusions between temporary and permanent monetary shocks has been overdone. The real effects of temporary, but

The criticism of the ISH centers on observations said to be inconsistent with continuous equilibrium in the labor market (e.g., Okun 1980). Thus during recessions and depressions, indefinite layoffs and involuntary separations account for most of the rise in unemployment. More people are looking for work at current (or even lower) wages over longer average time periods. Fewer people quit their jobs as vacancies drop.

General critiques, however, have limited power of persuasion, particularly against strong priors of the economic equilibrium theory. It is therefore particularly important that the hypotheses under consideration have been subjected to various tests, in large part by their proponents.

In one set of tests, the reaction function of monetary authorities was estimated by regressing the rate of growth in money on its own past values and selected lagged variables, and identifying the *residuals* from this regression with the "unanticipated" component of monetary change (Barro 1977b, 1978; Barro and Rush 1980). These tests could not reject the joint hypotheses of rationality and neutrality of money, but many doubts were raised about the specification and identifiability of Barro's reaction function as well as its consistency with private *and* public rational behavior.[47]

The neutrality hypothesis that anticipated money growth has no real effects is strongly rejected by tests reported by Mishkin (1982). Here, anticipated as well unanticipated money growth influences output and unemployment, with lags of up to 20 quarters.[48]

Data on monetary aggregates are available promptly and often (now weekly) but they are also repeatedly revised. The revisions are frequently large relative to the average rates of money growth, but on the whole, they appear to be random. They are interpreted as "components of unperceived monetary movements" and found to have no significant real effects (Barro and Hercovitz 1980). Economic agents should not be assumed to be ignorant of the current monetary values for which they do have usable approximations. And, contrary to the RE-IS models, in which prices are fully flexible, output is in fact positively associated with these measured and knowable values of the money stock (King 1981; Boschen and Grossman 1982; McCallum 1982).

The early tests by Lucas and Rapping (1969) favor the ISH but they are based on adaptive expectations. When reestimated by Altonji (1982) under

---

perceived, money shocks would be eliminated by the appropriate adjustment in the nominal rate of return."

47. See the comments by Blinder, R. J. Gordon, Weintraub, and Fischer in S. Fischer, ed. 1980, pp. 49–72 and 219–21. On the related basic problems of "observational equivalence" and testability, see also Sargent 1976b; and Sims 1980b.

48. It is these longer lags that are primarily responsible for Mishkin's conclusion being the opposite of that reached in the Barro papers, where lags of 2 years or 10 quarters are used. No attempts to rationalize the persistence of such long distributed lags under the REH are made in any of these reports. See also Nelson 1981 on the dependence of unemployment on lagged values of nominal GNP.

rational expectations and a variety of alternative assumptions about agents' information sets, the results generally fail to support the ISH. [49] Weak negative effects of a price surprise term on the unemployment rate are reported by Sargent (1976a) but disputed by Fair (1979); there are simultaneity problems with these estimates, as shown by Barro (1980). These and other tests (Hall 1979) are admitted to be rudimentary and on the whole inconclusive; all participants in this work stress that it presents great difficulties. Still, for the most part, other recent tests addressed to certain manageable aspects of the problem have produced negative results (K. Clark and Summers 1982; Mankiw, Rotemberg and Summers 1982).

To sum up, the evidence can be fairly described, on balance, as unfavorable to the theories here considered. This has led to some reassessments on the part of their authors. Thus, Barro (1981a, p. 74) expresses "doubts about the explanatory value for business cycles of currently available equilibrium theories." [50] McCallum (1982, p. 4.) argues that the evidence requires abandonment of "flexible-price equilibrium models" but not of the "*equilibrium approach* to macroeconomic analysis," which can rationalize sticky or slowly adjusting wages and prices.

2.4.4 Cyclical Persistence and Extensions of the Equilibrium Models

Can random monetary shocks produce *persistent* fluctuations of real aggregates in an economy with market clearing and incomplete information? Those who deny it attack mainly the ISH as leading to misguided attempts to represent business cycles as a "moving equilibrium" (Modigliani 1977; Tobin 1977, 1980; Solow 1980). Some expect that the postulate of continuous market clearing will have to be abandoned in the RE models (Okun 1980; R. J. Gordon 1981).

Equilibrium theorists recognize that the basic ingredients of their models are not sufficient to produce the persistent movements in output and employment which occur during the business cycle. However, they point out that random shocks to aggregate demand can be converted into persistent movements by suitable propagation mechanisms, as in Frisch 1933. Further, Lucas and Sargent (1978, pp. 65–67) argue that some devices of this type have already been incorporated in the equilibrium models, and others are likely to be developed.

The first of these propagation mechanisms relates to the familiar observation that rapid adjustments of employment and production rates are costly.

---

49. "For most specifications, the current real wage, the expected future real wage, and the expected real rate of interest are either insignificantly related to unemployment and labour supply or have the wrong sign" (Altonji 1982, p. 784; Altonji and Ashenfelter 1980).

50. He hastens to add that these doubts "do not constitute support for Keynesian disequilibrium analysis," which is incomplete and even more questionable. His argument implies that there are only two sides to the debate, the "new classical macroeconomics" and "Keynesian macroeconomics." This is a widespread but mistaken and, in my opinion, much too restrictive point of view.

Accordingly, firms respond with lags to the relative price signals they perceive.[51] In practice, modeling the cost-of-adjustment effects takes the form of making the demands for factors of production depend partly on their own lagged values. It is important to note that this mechanism is entirely different from and extraneous to that of the random price misperception effects. The latter should not be spread over time by the old device of distributed lags. The unit period here is defined by the lag of data on the nominal aggregates which was already shown to be relatively short. The logic of this approach seems to leave no good reasons for extending the lag to more than one period and so opening up the possibility of autocorrelated forecast errors. Cost-of-adjustment models may provide a rationale for more complex and longer lags. However, in a world without uncertainty about the probability distributions governing the future (see next section), where markets clear continuously, leaving no unexploited opportunities for gain, there should be little ground for any sizable distributed lags in economic decision making (Poole 1976).

Another propagation device incorporates a form of an investment accelerator (Lucas 1975). Positive price surprises induce not only increases in current employment and output but also acquisition of additional capital. Capacity is supposed to increase promptly during a period when the nature of the shock is not yet recognized. This increment to the stock of capacity raises labor productivity and temporarily increases the demand for labor and the supply of commodities; it also retards the general price increase, thereby delaying the recognition of, or adjustment to, the initial shock. Thus a persistence effect is created.

This formulation also poses some major problems. Many capital investment projects involve indivisibilities, high costs and risks, and gestation periods measured in years and quarters, not months. Decisions to initiate them are unlikely to depend on isolated signals that could well prove false after a short information lag (R. J. Gordon 1981, p. 510). Not surprisingly, random monetary disturbances and price misperceptions have not attracted much attention in the literature as potentially important determinants of investment; instead, expectations have—based on systematic changes in demand, profits, credit, and cost of capital. In this class of models neglect of these factors deprives the treatment of business capital investment of much interest.

Furthermore, because of the relatively long ordering and construction lags, investment will tend to add to demand before it adds to capacity. The effects of increased capacity on supply, prices, and the anticipated real rate of return on capital are delayed. It must be recalled, too, that capacity itself normally continues to increase during recessions; it is investment and the rate of capacity utilization that are highly sensitive, cyclically. In models that concentrate

---

51. It should be noted that such lags could also rationalize a dynamic model of fluctuations in employment and output that is purely "real", that is, independent of the behavior of money and prices (Sargent 1979, pp. 370–79).

on monetary and price effects on the stock of capital, which is presumably optimally utilized throughout (as is the stock of labor), the role of the reformulated "accelerator" would seem to be quite limited.

In models with lagging information, the effects of purely random monetary-price shocks do not cumulate: the responses peak in the first period and decline gradually thereafter (Lucas 1975, p. 202). This feature is not changed by the introduction of investment as long as new capital is installed with a lag of one period only. But these timing specifications are very unrealistic. There is strong evidence that investment in plant and equipment requires, on the average, about seven quarters to complete, with few projects taking less than 1 year (Mayer 1960; Zarnowitz 1973, pp. 505–19; Hall, 1977).

Kydland and Prescott (1980, 1982) use the "time to build" new capital stocks as a feature of technology which dictates the number of periods needed to produce durable producer and consumer goods. These lags are treated as policy invariant and constant for a given type of capital. (This is unlike the observed delivery lags on these goods, which vary procyclically with backlogs of orders: Popkin 1965; Zarnowitz 1973, pt. 3; Carlton 1979.) Time to build contributes to the persistence of output movements over the multiple periods required to produce the finished capital goods (unfinished goods are not part of the productive stocks). The models used in this work rely on an intertemporal labor supply function and are driven basically by real shocks that affect technology and the productivity of the representative worker.[52]

Investment realizations are a distributed-lag function of investment plans. But the series of new capital appropriations and contracts and orders for plant and equipment that proxy for investment plans are also serially correlated like the expenditures that follow them, only less so (e.g., Zarnowitz 1973). Hence they lack the random shock property which the equilibrium theorists look for in "an essential propagator of business cycle fluctuations" (John Taylor in Fischer 1980, p. 192). Nevertheless they are an important link in the cyclical process. The lag of investment expenditures behind investment decisions is an essential element in several otherwise quite different theories of business cycles (Mitchell 1913; Kalecki 1935; Hicks 1950).

Inventory investment provides still another potential channel for persistence effects in equilibrium models. In Blinder and Fischer (1981), an unanticipated rise in money and prices leads firms to sell out of inventories at the same time as they increase output. In subsequent periods, production is gradually raised to restock the depleted inventories. More specifically, inventory investment depends positively on the excess of the desired stock ($N_t^* - N_t$) and inversely on the price surprise term ($p_t - p_{t-1}^e$). The aggregate supply function

---

52. The real shocks have permanent (autocorrelated) and transitory components; the former also contribute to the cumulative movements or "momentum" in employment and output. The 1980 paper by Kydland and Prescott includes random shocks to nominal wages as well, but these monetary disturbances are secondary. The 1982 model contains real shocks only.

has Q_t vary positively with Q_t^N and the same price surprise (as in Lucas 1972, 1973) but now also with $(N_t^* - N_t)$. The desired inventory N_t^* will stimulate activity, but a rise in N_t relative to N_t^* will discourage it. Even with N^* a constant, this model can account for some serial correlation of output. With interest-sensitive N_t^*, larger fluctuations would result since even fully anticipated changes in money would have some real effects (Blinder and Fischer 1981, sec. 5).

This approach draws on some old ideas about the aggregate sales-inventory-income nexus in business cycles (sec. 2.3.5) and combines them with elements of the new equilibrium models for a rather uneasy match. It needs to be recalled, too, that the role of inventory adjustments is large during mild recessions and slowdowns, such as prevailed in the post–World War II period, but is otherwise supporting rather than central (Blinder and Holtz-Eakin 1984).

Summing up, the cost-motivated adjustments lags, durability and long gestation periods of capital goods, and desired inventory effects have all been long recognized as important in studies of business cycles. These elements, however, do not exactly mesh with the basic core of the equilibrium model. The random monetary shocks and price surprises have smaller and less intelligible parts to play, while the real factors in the "propagation" processes move to the center of the stage. These extensions, indeed, "may undermine the quantitative role of the underlying intertemporal substitution mechanism as the basis for fluctuations in output and employment" (Barro 1981a, p. 49).

2.4.5   Rationality, Knowledge, and Uncertainty

To be "rational" in a technical sense, expectations must be consistent with the structure of the given model. Unless they are self-fulfilling, on the whole, the model of behavior assumed to be ruled by them is vitiated. Given the relevant information set, it may be possible to solve a RE model for its equilibrium path over all futures. As new information becomes available, the forecast-solution is updated. Used as a principle of modeling dynamic stochastic equilibria, RE gained wide popularity and produced important new insights.[53]

However, even in relatively simple linear models, the computational problems posed by this radically logical approach are often formidable. Using RE as a model of actual behavior cannot mean imputing to economic agents generally the ability to solve such problems. Rather it is the markets that are supposed to work as if they somehow approximated this capacity. This could

---

53. These include the criticism of some aspects of macroeconometric models, the analysis of competitive markets with imperfect information, and work on the consequences of endogenous expectations for the effectiveness of economic policies (Lucas 1976; Poole 1976). These matters lie outside the scope of this chapter. Assessments of the RE models abound (Shiller 1978; Kantor 1979; Fischer 1980; McCallum 1980b). For surveys of the literature and references, see Begg 1982; Sheffrin 1983; and Frydman and Phelps 1983.

be interpreted along the lines of what may be called a weak version of the REH: market incentives and penalties favor the dominance of optimal or cost-efficient predictions. Firms and individuals whose forecasts are consistently poor will not be able to survive economically. The anticipations of those who do survive will tend to come true. This implies that predictively valuable information, on which such anticipations are based, is scarce so that collecting it is a profitable activity (Grossman and Stiglitz 1980).

Such propositions, when applied to well-functioning individual markets, seem simply good, standard economics. In the aggregate, they need not imply more than a long-run tendency toward equilibrium, promoted by learning from experience but inhibited by limited opportunities for controlled experiments. Thus no firm link is established between the type of model and the expectational hypothesis used. In particular, RE models have been built without the property of continuous market clearing. In principle, various types of disequilibria could be expected by people and modeled with the aid of RE methodology; or, if expectational confusions prevail, no unique solutions should be found.

The REH of the macroeconomic literature in the 1970s, however, is a strong version which adds to the reasonable premise of rational use of costly information another assumption—namely, that the available data and models provide sufficient knowledge about the future such that the prevailing expectations are free of any systematic errors and consistent with *continuous* aggregate equilibrium. Economic behavior is guided by subjective probabilities which agree, on the average, with the true frequencies of the events in question. Unlike in Knight 1921 and Keynes 1936 there is no uncertainty as to what these objective probabilities are.[54]

Now there seem to be no good a priori reasons why this should generally be so; indeed, the belief that it is not accounts for most objections to the REH. It is evident that there is no agreement on what is the "objective" probability distribution of future outcomes for the economy at any time, since different theories and models coexist. Another reason why forecasts differ across people, firms, etc., is that skills to acquire and use information are not evenly distributed.

Attempts to form rational predictions of any macrovariable that depends on anticipatory actions of many or all agents in the economy involve adjustments through a learning process in which not only the individual forecaster's own beliefs but also those of others are continually evaluated. Each agent, then, tries to predict the average forecast, or what others are likely to predict that average will be, and so on. This is the difficult "infinite regress" problem, well known from the "beauty contest" example of Keynes (1936, p. 156). Al-

54. Indeed, Lucas (1977, p. 15), argues that "in cases of uncertainty, economic reasoning will be of no value." For the REH to apply, business cycles must represent "repeated instances of essentially similar events."

though increasingly and ingeniously attacked, this problem is still far from being fully tractable or understood. However, an important result that is strongly suggested by this work is that a unique, stable RE equilibrium path, along which prices continually clear all markets, entails the collective consistency of individual plans. But individual rationality (the cornerstone of modern microeconomic analysis) does not necessarily imply such a consistency.[55]

In a stochastically stationary environment that has persisted long enough to be familiar, agents are assumed to have learned all they can about the probability distributions they face.[56] In the economy as it is, however, change is to a large extent unanticipated and learning is perpetual. In models with learning and disparate expectations, convergence to the RE equilibrium requires that agents know no less than the laws governing the change in the key parameters of the economy and the effects of exogenous shocks. Learning itself can act as a cyclical propagator mechanism by including serial and cross-correlations in forecasts (Townsend 1978, 1983a, 1983b).

The strong assumptions of prior knowledge are implausible but there seems to be no alternative to them that would be satisfactory from the RE point of view.[57] Some simple but flexible rules of adaptive expectations (AE) may be consistent with optimal learning (Taylor 1975; B. Friedman 1979) and some models with a common, simple rule converge to an equilibrium solution (e.g., Bray 1983). But the collective adherence to a rule which, if individually followed, would yield biased forecasts is in conflict with the idea of the optimizing representative agent in a decentralized market economy.

It is important to distinguish between the critique of the RE and the critique of the particular market-clearing models with RE (e.g., Fair 1978). Many critics agree that the pre-RE treatments of expectations are generally arbitrary and, at least in principle, inferior (Tobin 1980, pp. 28–29; Meltzer 1982, p. 3). Further advances in the intensely used and studied RE methodology are to be expected (as argued, e.g., in Lucas and Sargent 1978; Lucas 1981; Grossman 1981). Still, the claim to general validity of the strong form of the REH as applied to market-clearing macromodels is now rejected by a wide range of economists (Arrow 1978; Tobin 1980, 1981; Laidler 1981, pp. 11–15; Friedman and Schwartz 1982, p. 630).

In the present context, the critical questions concern the stationarity and predictability of the processes observed during business cycles. Their recurrent and sequential nature is indeed well established, but so is their lack of periodicity and the large intercycle differences in durations and amplitudes (sec. 2.2). The separability of business cycles from the long trends can by no

55. See the several essays and the introductory chapter by the editors in Frydman and Phelps 1983.
56. Most of the early basic RE models, constructed on this premise, simply contain no learning processes.
57. Without some such assumptions, convergence may not occur even in single-market contexts (Cyert and DeGroot 1974; B. Friedman 1979; DeCanio 1979).

means be taken for granted. These are arguments against the applicability of the RE methods. In a nonstationary world with a mixture of random and serially correlated disturbances, uncertainty in the sense of Knight and Keynes is pervasive, even under the (empirically dubious) premises of no structural change and stable policy regimes.

The monetarist models with AE may be interpreted to contain uncertainty.[58] Meltzer (1982) distinguishes between uncertainty, which is associated with variations in nonstationary means resulting from "permanent" changes in levels or growth rates, and risk, which is associated with transitory, random deviations around stable trends. He argues that the current RE models err in ignoring uncertainty, which is essential to an explanation of the persistence of cyclical contractions. Models of business cycles should allow permanent changes to occur but not to be identified immediately. Stochastic shocks, whether monetary or real, have permanent and transitory components which cannot be reliably separated (new information reduces but does not eliminate the confusion). The rational response to the shocks is adaptive, taking the form of gradual adjustments of beliefs about the permanent values of the endogenous variables.[59]

What is the evidence on how people actually form their expectations? Recent work using survey data has been preoccupied with tests for the rationality of inflation forecasts. Typically, actual values are regressed on predicted values, and the forecasts fail the tests when (1) the sample intercept and slope estimates are significantly different from 0 and 1, respectively, and/or (2) the residual errors are significantly autocorrelated. Data from the semiannual surveys of economic forecasters conducted since 1947 by Joseph A. Livingston, a syndicated financial columnist, reject the REH according to most of these and related tests (Pesando 1975; Carlson 1977; Wachtel 1977; Moore 1977b; Pearce 1979; Gramlich 1983; more favorable results are reported in Mullineaux 1978). Tests of individual forecasts confirm those of the group average forecasts, and the results from the quarterly NBER-ASA economic outlook surveys are consistent with those obtained for the Livingston surveys (Figlewski and Wachtel 1981; see also chapter 16).[60]

Studies of consumer survey data from the Survey Research Center of the University of Michigan show mixed but, in large measure, negative results

58. See M. Friedman 1972, pp. 923–24, on uncertainty; Muth 1960; Frenkel 1975; Mussa 1975; Brunner, Cukierman, and Meltzer 1980; Friedman and Schwartz 1982, pp. 415 and 447, on the rationality and empirical usefulness of AE.

59. Note that this is a general approach, compatible with Keynesian, monetarist, and other theories. It is used in the 1980 model of Brunner et al., in which monetary shocks affect only the price level and the rate of interest, while unemployment is caused by errors due to the inability of workers to distinguish between permanent and transitory real productivity shocks. This model is subject to all doubts concerning the hypotheses of complete neutrality of money and intertemporal substitution in labor supply.

60. The relevant literature on the properties of expectational data is voluminous and can be only briefly summarized here. For a more comprehensive review of the evidence, see Zarnowitz 1984b.

(Juster 1979; Huizinga 1980; Curtin 1982; Gramlich 1983). The same applies to surveys of business executives (de Leeuw and McKelvey 1981) and European and Japanese surveys (Aiginger 1981; Papadia 1982; Visco 1984).[61]

Few authors have tested data on anticipations for variables other than inflation. U.S. manufacturers' sales expectations have been on the whole negatively assessed in a comprehensive study by Hirsch and Lovell (1969), more positively by Pashigian (1964) and Irvine (1981). For professional economic forecasters, including econometric service bureaus, there is strong evidence that predictions of inflation in the 1970s have been generally biased, while those of other important aggregates (growth in nominal and real GNP, the unemployment rate) pass the rationality tests much more frequently and better (see chapter 16; also McNees 1978).[62]

The REH finds the strongest support in the "efficient markets" literature (Fama 1970; Poole 1976). This is readily understandable since financial assets and commodities are traded in well-organized and informed competitive auction markets. However, some tests of forecasts by active participants in these markets reject the REH, as shown in the survey of Wall Street predictions of interest rates by B. Friedman (1980). This could merely mean that this survey was not adequately representative of the most successful traders and hence of the market.[63]

Expectations which fail the rationality criteria in ex post tests may well prove entirely consistent with optimizing ex ante behavior once the consequences of uncertainty, unique events, defective models, and fragmentary or costly information are taken into account (Zarnowitz 1982c). Also, they need not be adaptive or otherwise backward looking only. In fact, it appears that time-series models rarely explain statistically much more than half of the variance of expectational data. (See several papers in Mincer 1969a; Aiginger 1979). The evidence suggests that economic expectations are neither mere projections of the past nor flashes of intuition about the future but combinations of both extrapolative and autonomous components. Predictions of real growth and inflation are usually diversified and uncertain, seldom demonstrably self-fulfilling. Anticipatory action is often inhibited by prior commitments incurred in part to reduce uncertainty. Thus not all past is bygones and expec-

61. All these surveys collect largely qualitative responses (on the direction and in some cases range, rather than the precise size, of the expected price movements). The conversion of these data to the quantitative form required for the tests presents some difficult problems.

62. For many early forecasts of U.S. aggregate series, there is evidence of significant bias (Mincer and Zarnowitz 1969). The most common pattern is underestimation of growth and, less frequently, of cyclical changes (Theil 1958; Zarnowitz 1967). There are indications of adaptive learning behavior (Mincer 1969b).

63. Indeed, Mishkin (1981a) constructs forecasts from the bond market data which fail to reject the rationality tests for interest-rate expectations. But the concurrent bond market predictions of inflation fail the tests. The argument that this reflects the unusual character of the 1960s, a period of rising inflation, is not really persuasive. The inflation forecasts in the perhaps even more "unusual" 1970s seem generally worse yet. Long periods of tranquillity are hard to find.

tations are not all-important. Yet they matter a great deal and are a proper subject for empirical as well as theoretical studies.[64]

2.4.6 Models of Financial Instability

Speculative excesses or "manias" have attracted the attention of contemporaries and economic historians at least since the Dutch Tulip Bubble of 1625–37. Financed by credit expansion and characterized by "overtrading" in real or financial assets (e.g., gold, land, or securities) they have been associated with more than two dozen major booms in business activity, often involving many countries (Kindleberger 1978). Historically, they tended to be followed by "panics," that is, distress selling of the same assets to reacquire money and repay debt, and crashes in the prices of the now illiquid objects of the speculation. The resulting financial crises accompanied or aggravated downturns in the business cycle.

In asset markets, as a rule, the current price depends positively on its own *expected* rate of change. Expectations are influenced by outside events as well as the "market fundamentals"—economic determinants of the rates of return. The markets may react to the events by adopting such price anticipations as would drive the actual prices away from the path consistent with the fundamentals. In this view, accepted much more readily by practitioners than theorists, anticipations of a strong market trend are occasionally capable of causing speculative "bubbles"—cumulative, even explosive, fluctuations in prices of selected assets.

Very recently, these ideas, long mistrusted by most contemporary economists, began to receive support from writers using rigorous techniques of equilibrium analysis. Shiller (1981a, 1981b) concludes that stock price movements are too large to be explained by an efficient-markets model which incorporates future dividends, capital gains, and inflation. Blanchard and Watson (1982) argue that bubbles can occur in efficient markets with new entry and no unexploited arbitrage opportunities; also, that they have potentially strong real effects on relative asset prices, wealth, and aggregate demand.[65]

Much of the recent work in this area uses the overlapping-generations ap-

---

64. The evidence from surveys has certain important limitations and must be assessed with caution, but the consensus of careful independent tests based on such data should be taken seriously; indeed, the materials now available are rich and in need of much further exploration (Tobin 1980, p. 29). Lessons from such work can usefully counter and correct the freely speculative analysis that treats expectations as being inevitably "unobservable."

65. The problems of indeterminacy and instability of RE equilibria are now well recognized and much studied. Conditions under which bubbles may be excluded from the RE paths of the price level have been specified for some monetary models (e.g., Brock 1975). Tests for the German hyperinflation of the early 1920s reported by Flood and Garber (1980) give no support to the hypothesis that a price-level bubble occurred in that extreme episode. But it is easy to see that expectations alone cannot account for a long or rapid inflation in the absence of persistent or very high rates of money creation. Clearly, bubbles are much more likely in speculative markets for financial assets.

proach due to Samuelson (1958; Kareken and Wallace 1980). Models of this type, with markets continuously cleared by price movements, typically have a multiplicity of RE solutions, a large proportion of which may involve fluctuations prompted by arbitrary but self-fulfilling shifts in anticipations (Azariadis 1981). Thus, if the belief that sunspots predict future prices were widely held, many individuals would act on it so as to bear out their expectations. Cass and Shell (1983) argue that RE equilibria generally can be influenced by extrinsic uncertainty, that is, random phenomena such as "animal spirits" or "market psychology," which do not affect the basic parameters of the economy (endowments, preferences, technologies). The conditions under which this would *not* be the case are so unrealistic as to be devoid of any empirical interest.[66]

These abstract treatments rationalize the role in financial crises of "sunspots," but they do not tell us how much these interacting and self-fulfilling expectations matter. The crises are seldom isolated phenomena; rather they form a part of some business cycles and are thus related to the monetary, institutional, and real factors involved in these cycles. Market psychology plays a large role in some crises, mainly the major ones.

Mild financial crises of recent U.S. history, called "credit crunches," are associated by some observers primarily with reduced availability of credit, not high interest rates (Wojnilower 1980). Credit rationing by banks is linked to imperfect information about the borrowers' default risk (Stiglitz and Weiss 1981; Blinder and Stiglitz 1983). When banks refuse to renew their loans, the high-risk borrowers and many small firms are unable to secure credit elsewhere and are forced to curtail investment and perhaps current operations. The retrenchment may or may not be caused by restrictive open-market policies of the central bank. Under fractional banking, loans and deposits are highly collinear, so it is difficult to use the data to distinguish between this "credit" hypothesis and a "money supply" hypothesis of a downturn. Since the early 1950s, broad credit aggregates such as the total debt of U.S. nonfinancial sectors have been closely and stably related to GNP—better or not worse than the money stock and monetary base series (B. Friedman 1983).

In several collected papers, Minsky (1982) argues that long periods of prosperity interrupted only by mild recessions or slowdowns breed overconfidence, excessive short-term financing by banks of long-term business projects, investment booms interacting with stock market booms, and growing indebtedness and illiquidity. Innovative practices and new instruments are used to increase the availability of investment finance: money should be broadly defined and is endogenously determined. Its supply, however, becomes at some point inelastic as uncertainty grows and banks increasingly

66. They include (1) strong RE—unanimity of beliefs, (2) complete markets—there are markets for all types of contingent claims, and (3) unrestricted access to these markets for all agents at all times—across the "generations." Conditions (1) and (2) are merely improbable; (3) is altogether impossible.

deem it prudent to retrench (or monetary authorities act to constrain inflation). The demand for credit to finance planned and progressing investment projects nevertheless continues to rise. It takes sharp increases in interest rates and declines in the present value of expected net returns on capital assets to check and reverse the expansion in new investment. Business cash flows and profits decline and eventually so do total sales, output, and employment. The resulting losses force many industrial concerns and financial intermediaries into refinancing of debt and liquidation of assets to raise cash. Many retrench; some fail. When a sufficiently large number of these units experience inadequate cash flows from current operations and declining ability to sustain debt, a financial crisis must occur, unless the central bank intervenes, injecting sufficient money into the system and preventing large bank defaults and business failures. If a crisis is averted and stimulative monetary and fiscal policies continue, a mild recession may ensue but another inflationary and eventually destabilizing investment boom will soon follow.

This is a disequilibrium theory with strong endogenous elements. The originating factors are real, but monetary and credit changes have much to do with the propagation of the cycle and are primarily responsible for its worst manifestations (see also the summary in table 2.5). This is the opposite of some recent theories (such as that of Lucas) which have monetary shocks and real propagation mechanisms. Minsky's hypothesis predicts the recurrence of financial crises and business depressions, which invites controversy. It deserves to be carefully evaluated, but it is difficult to test (in part inevitably so since financial crises and depressions are rare and complex events). In general terms, however, the account provided by Minsky tends to be consistent with the history of speculative investment booms, financial crises, and deep depressions in the United States (Burns and Mitchell 1946, ch. 11, sec. 6; Kindleberger 1978; Hoyt [1933] 1970). It also has interesting connections with several diverse business cycle theories.[67]

2.4.7 Demand and Supply Shocks and Responses: A Search for New Concepts

Dissatisfaction with the results obtained by using random money supply shocks and price misperceptions prompted some economists to experiment with different models (while retaining the basic RE methodology in most cases). Abstracting from numerous detail, one can distinguish the following approaches.

---

67. Minsky credits primarily Keynes, whom he interprets as having a dynamic analysis that does not rely on price rigidities, but his emphasis on the instability of credit flows and business debt relative to income recalls the Austrians and draws on Fisher. Some complementarity may even exist between elements of the Kindleberger-Minsky hypothesis and the monetarist approach, particularly with respect to accounting for financial crises on an international scale (Bordo 1984). Another linkage is to the "corridor effects" suggested by Leijonhufvud: deflationary shocks large enough to produce financial crises and waves of bankruptcies may throw a normally stable system into a deep depression in which disequilibrating forces prevail for some time (Howitt 1978).

Focus on Interest Rates and Related Factors

These received much attention in the literature from Wicksell and the Austrians to Keynes. Monetary intervention or excesses of credit creation were seen as causing interest rates to deviate from their equilibrium levels so that they fail to coordinate saving and investment decisions. Inconsistencies arise in the aggregate between the expectations of those who make these decisions and the expectations of the financial intermediaries. Monetarists opposed these ideas on the ground that investment and savings depend on the *real* interest rates, which cannot be affected by the banking system, except transitorily. In the early RE models, too, interest rates had no important roles to play. However, fluctuations in credit and interest, which have been so pronounced in recent years, are receiving renewed attention in the literature since the late 1970s (Leijonhufvud 1981, ch. 7; Frydman and Phelps 1983, ch. 10).

This includes some new departures along the incomplete-information line of approach. McCulloch (1977, 1981) argues that business fluctuations are associated with unanticipated changes in interest rates that misdirect real investment decisions toward a wrong mix of capital goods and so distort the intertemporal production process (as in the real part of the theories of Hayek and Mises).[68] In an equilibrium model by Grossman and Weiss (1982), random real shocks affect productivity and the real interest rate, causing investment and output to fluctuate. Random monetary shocks affect inflation and the nominal interest rate, with the effect of amplifying the cycle. Agents make errors in trying to infer the ex ante values of the real rate and inflation from the nominal rate (which includes the two) because the latter's movements contain much random noise. The critical gap in information concerns the relative rates of real return (on own compared with other investments). The model involves only supply decisions, with the role of demand being purely passive.[69]

Recent empirical work suggests that output (real GNP or industrial production) interacts with price-level indexes, comprehensive credit aggregates, interest rates, and narrow money aggregates. None of these variables is definitely exogenous relative to all the others; in particular, money adds to the

68. The novel element is the stress on "misintermediation" rather than on the money-creating function of the banks (the two are closely connected). Banks and other intermediaries, by borrowing short and lending long, are said to mismatch asset and liability maturities and to add to the uncertainty about interest rates by creating imbalances in their term structure. This hypothesis and the related estimates deal only with nominal, not with real, rates, besides posing other problems that cannot be discussed here in the available space; but the hypothesis does address an important and long-recognized institutional aspect of financial instability (to which the previous section also briefly referred).

69. Investment here is equated with the process of transforming labor input into next period's output. No durable goods are produced. The nominal shocks take the form of disturbances to money demand. These simplifications are made to allow some difficult problems in the dynamic equilibrium theory to be rigorously analyzed, but they also deprive the model of some highly relevant characteristics of the modern capitalist economies, which experience business cycles. This is, to be sure, not uncommon in the recent theoretical literature.

incremental prediction of the real variables along with credit and interest rates, but it is not predetermined or predominant (Sims 1980a; B. Friedman 1983; see also chapter 12).[70]

These results are interesting and may prove robust, but they should be interpreted with much caution. Nominal interest rates may matter because their changes are read as signals of changes in the stock of money and inflation. But they may also be important in their own right as the major part of the true costs of credit. Historically, their adjustments to inflation (and deflation) were sufficiently sluggish and incomplete to suggest that people treated the nominal rates as if they were adequate proxies for the real ones. Evidence going back to the 1860s shows that this condition continued to prevail at least well into the 1950s; only thereafter did the relationship between interest and inflation strengthen to become rather close in the 1960s and 1970s. More recently, it weakened again considerably.[71]

The ex post real interest rates, pre- and post-tax, have small cyclical variations, which makes it difficult to detect how they are correlated with movements in real variables, but this is rightly seen as a problem in measurement rather than evidence of no significant relationships (Mishkin 1981b). Real rates rose sharply to unusually high levels in the early years of the Great Depression and again in 1980–82, a period of severe recession and strong disinflation. It is only reasonable to view these changes as mainly unanticipated and their probable net effects as seriously adverse.[72] The measured real rates are inversely correlated with lagged inflation. Increased money growth, then, by raising inflation, lowers the real rate; but the evidence for a short-term effect of monetary policy, independent of inflation, is mixed and weak (Shiller 1980; Mishkin 1981b).

Focus on Real Factors

Consider two polar models. (1) Exogenous fluctuations in real investment cause the business cycle. Banks meet the borrowers' demand for money and the depositors' demand for money because the monetary authority provides

70. These exogeneity tests ask whether, say, the lagged values of money help explain or predict output in a regression equation containing the lagged values of output itself and of the other variables. This question is answered for each variable in the system in terms of all variables included. This method of variance decomposition or accounting for the interactions among the "innovations" (serially uncorrelated residuals) of the series in question avoids some major shortcomings of simple distributed-lag regressions but encounters some difficult problems of its own (see the following paragraph and chapter 12).

71. These findings refer to the United States; for the United Kingdom the corresponding relation was much weaker throughout (see Friedman and Schwartz 1982, ch. 10). According to Summers (1983) the impact of inflation on interest rates has been much smaller throughout the post–World War II period than a general equilibrium model would predict on classical assumptions, particularly when properly allowing for the effective tax rates (see also Feldstein 1976a).

72. But note that the real rates stayed relatively high in 1983–84 without visibly obstructing a vigorous recovery. Presumably, once the economy adjusted to the large changes, the smaller ones had only weak effects.

them with the necessary reserves at any given level of interest rates. (2) Exogenous fluctuations in money supply cause the business cycle. The demand for money adjusts continuously to the supply through changes in permanent income associated with much larger changes in measured real income or output.

Tobin (1970) sets the two models up so that model (1) implies a consistent pattern of early cyclical timing for monetary growth rates or deviations from trend, whereas (2) does not. Friedman denies that these examples cast doubt on his views. The two debaters agree that evidence on leads and lags alone cannot prove any hypothesis about causation (though it can disprove some); also, that both of the above models are far from adequate. Indeed, (1) is an oversimplification and partial distortion of Keynes, (2) of Friedman. The widely used general IS/LM-AD/AS framework can accommodate some of the ideas of some of the Keynesians and monetarists with respect to the effects and interactions of both autonomous expenditure and monetary changes.[73] But this long-ruling paradigm was designed for comparative statics of exogenous interventions with a stationary environment; its adaptation to dynamic and expectational processes confronts a host of difficult and unresolved problems.

Earlier sections contain several diverse illustrations of recent work oriented toward nonmonetary (real, psychological, institutional) explanations of macroeconomic instability. Other such efforts relate to the old idea (preceding Keynes, though often associated with him) that both money and real activity respond to the common factor of fluctuations in aggregate demand and the corresponding changes in interest rates and the value of existing assets. Sims (1980a), referring to Tobin (1970), urges the development of a stochastic version of this theory. Some new historical studies also emphasize the importance of factors other than the independent influence on business conditions of changes in the stock of money.[74]

---

73. IS and LM relate output and interest rates; AD and AS (aggregate demand and supply functions) relate output and the price level. It is assumed that the IS and AD curves slope downward; the LM and AS curves upward. The Keynesian view is often associated with relatively steep IS and flat LM; the monetarist view with relatively flat IS and steep LM curves. But this interpretation is by no means universally acceptable; even if accepted, it leaves open other important issues in the controversy. The IS/LM-AD/AS model evolved from Hicks 1935, 1937, through a long series of writings including, notably, Patinkin [1954] 1965.

74. Thus Temin (1976) attributes the 1929 downturn to a decline in "autonomous" spending (interestingly, mainly in consumption and exports rather than investment). For monetarist counterarguments, see the essays by Schwartz and Brunner (Brunner 1981); for a view that both money and investment (and other spending) mattered, see R. J. Gordon and J. Wilcox in the same volume.

King and Plosser (1984) examine the possibility that the positive correlation between the rates of growth in output and monetary aggregates reflects, in large part, the causal chain running from business activity to "inside money," that is, bank deposits.

Bernanke (1983) produces evidence linking the sharp drop in output during the early 1930s to the reduced quality and higher real costs of credit intermediation services, a result of the institutional weakness and crises of banking.

It remains to take note of the most radical reactions against monetarist and monetary shock theories by some strong believers in general-equilibrium modeling and the neutrality of money. Here the main idea is that unanticipated changes in tastes and technology cause intersectoral shifts of human and physical capital associated with much friction and temporary idleness. Unemployment generated by a large number of partly independent shocks to different sectors will persist for considerable time because rapid transfers of resources are costly, the more so the greater the specialization of the production factors (Black 1982).[75] But changes in tastes and technology will tend to penalize some sectors and benefit others, causing numerous shifts in relative prices and outputs; they may occasionally have significant net favorable or adverse effects on growth but can hardly be responsible for *recurrent sequences* of expansions and contractions in aggregate economic activity.

The most restrictive formal model of purely real "business cycles" (Long and Plosser 1983) abstracts not only from money and government but also from technological change, durable goods, and adjustment costs; it assumes RE, complete information, and stable preferences. There are random shocks to outputs of the many commodities, each of which can be either consumed or used as input in the production of any other commodity during each unit period. The optimal allocation rule is such that when the ith output is unexpectedly high (low), the simultaneous inputs of i in all its productive uses are increased (reduced). It is shown that this works to propagate the effects of the output shocks both forward in time and across the sectors of the economy. The model is intended to serve as a benchmark for evaluating the importance in actual business cycles of the many factors it omits, but it admittedly presents serious problems and the approach itself is questionable.[76]

Focus on the Causes and Effects of Contractual Wage and Price Setting

Recent literature is much concerned with the specification of economic reasons for the existence of explicit or implicit multiperiod contracts that limit the flexibility of wages and prices in response to unanticipated shifts in demand and supply.[77] The "contract-theoretic" models based on this work drop

---

75. This recalls the "horizontal maladjustments," which were treated as a potentially important aggravating factor, but not a prime cause, in classical writings (see sec. 2.3.1).

76. In particular, the model has constant employment of labor while the commodity outputs fluctuate. Simulations based on a 1967 input-output table for six major industry divisions result in output series that show considerable comovements and two complete quasi cycles in runs of 100-unit periods of undefined length. It is not clear whether the fluctuations due to the output shocks are separable from those due to other factors.

77. One hypothesis is that fixed-wage, variable employment contracts sell risk-averse workers partial insurance against the variability of their incomes (Baily 1974; D. F. Gordon 1974; Azariadis 1975). Another is that labor contracts or understandings treat incomes as normal returns on the loyalty and efficiency of long-term employees and protect large investments in firm-specific human capital (Hall 1980a; Okun 1981, chs. 2 and 3). Steady pricing policies are used to reduce the costs of shopping and attract steady customers (Okun 1981, ch. 4). In sum, contracts are attempts to deal economically with a variety of "transaction" (information, negotiation, adjust-

the assumption of market clearing and the reliance on price errors and inter-temporal substitution effects. They restore the changes in aggregate demand to their old role as a direct determinant of fluctuations in the real aggregates by delaying the adjustments in the contractually predetermined wages and the wage-related prices.

The main models of this type are monetarist in the original sense of relating short-run fluctuations in output to monetary policy operating via changes in demand. This is so even where the policy is based on a fixed feedback rule known to the public, because the money stock can be changed more fre-quently than the wage is renegotiated (Phelps and Taylor 1977; Fischer 1977a; Taylor 1980a). The authors work with staggered contracts in which wages are linked to expectations that are rational (i.e., model-consistent; sec. 2.4.5). Fischer relates wages to price-level forecasts; his contracts are (frustrated) at-tempts to keep real wages from falling in the face of inflationary policy. Taylor relates wages to other past and anticipated wage settlements; the degree of inertia in these interrelations helps explain the persistence of unemployment. These models have attracted much attention and criticism.[78]

According to the "credibility" hypothesis (Fellner 1976, 1980), a *consistent* policy of adhering to preannounced moderate money growth targets can deter inflationary wage and price setting and reduce instability in the long run. A correlate is that unions will push for higher wages in labor contract negotia-tions and business will respond by raising prices if both parties expect the monetary authorities to "ratify" their decisions through accommodative poli-cies. This view differs in some important respects from monetarism and the newer RE and contract theories, but it also incorporates some of their ele-ments. It recognizes that, in practice, systematic policy components are often weak and only belatedly detectable (Sims 1982). It is related to the idea of "coordination failures" (Leijonhufvud 1981) in a game-theoretic form: it is possible for expectational impasses to develop, that is, a recession-cum-inflation may continue while the central bank waits for wage demands to mod-erate and business and labor wait for a resumption of monetary expansion (Phelps 1981). All this certainly raises issues that are very important in deal-ing with inflation; how much bearing it has here depends on how strongly policy-induced changes in monetary growth and inflation influence business cycles. The notion that such changes are the principal *cause* of the cycles (which many now accept as if it were self-evident) is not supported by the

---

ment) costs in the face of price instability and general uncertainty. For surveys, see R. J. Gordon 1976; Barro 1981a.

78. The issues include the consistency of the assumed contract features with rational behavior (Barro 1977a; Fischer 1977b) and the reasons why wages are not fully indexed under anticipated inflation (Brunner and Meltzer 1977). For a detailed critique of Fischer and Taylor and a proposed improved model, see McCallum 1982. For some evidence and further discussion, see Taylor 1980b and 1983.

long record of cyclical instability coexisting with alternating extended periods of inflations and deflations. It is also countered by the argument that business contractions, whatever their causes, have deflationary or disinflationary *effects*.[79]

Most recent RE models, including those of the contract-theoretic type, consider only one determinant of aggregate demand, the real money balances, and concentrate on the effects of monetary policy. But shifts in aggregate demand may be due to real and expectational as well as monetary factors. They may reflect the instability of any of the major expenditure components of real GNP. Neither theory nor evidence supports the focus on nominal demand shocks and real supply shocks alone. In recent times, at least, consumer capital outlays have been no less cyclical than business investment (R. J. Gordon and Veitch 1986). Indeed, new models of consumption which embrace RE have consumers respond promptly and strongly to any new information that revises their forecasts of future income. This in itself would tend to increase the sensitivity of consumption, and hence of income, to unanticipated changes in aggregate demand or "autonomous expenditures" (compared with the earlier models which used adaptive rather than rational expectations in the calculation of permanent income). The increased instability on the demand side is offset only when the REH is combined with speedy clearing of the markets and a highly stable and inelastic aggregate supply curve, that is, in the new-classical equilibrium models (Bilson 1980, pp. 279–83; and comment by Hall, p. 301).[80]

2.5 Conclusion: The Needed Synthesis

Business cycles belong to the history of modern economies with interdependent markets, free enterprise, and private ownership of financial assets and capital goods. They developed in the era of great growth of industry, banking, and credit. They are varied and changing, even while retaining their general characteristics of persistence and pervasiveness as well as specific regularities of amplitude and timing. All this was long recognized by serious scholars and careful observers with abiding interest in the subject.

For a long time, too, there was a substantial consensus among these economists that business cycles have mainly endogenous explanations involving recurrent fluctuations in interrelated monetary and real variables, prices and quantities, expectations and realizations. The theories tended to agree on the

---

79. None of this, of course, is to deny that the inflationary bias of government actions and the reactions to it have economic consequences of great importance; what is questioned is the view (going far beyond the credibility hypothesis) that these consequences include the business cycle.

80. Many interesting theoretical and empirical studies of the consumption function have appeared in recent years, but the implications of this work for business cycles remain to be worked out (Hall 1978; Davidson and Hendry 1981; Blanchard and Wyplosz 1981; Flavin 1981; Bernanke 1982).

cast and setting, disagreeing principally on which factors should play star and which supporting roles. Chance and outside disturbances were left behind the stage, interfering with and modifying the action but not determining its main course. The cycle had plural causes and effects; it produced and resolved its own stresses and resources, nationally and internationally. Few attributed it to any single factor or defect, and few believed that it can be eliminated by any single, low-cost type of policy intervention or institutional reform.

The 1930s convinced many that the economy is not merely cyclical but depression prone. The instability of profits, investment, and credit (old concerns) attracted renewed attention. In the 1940s and 1950s, however, there was a rise of interest in the dynamics of multiplier-accelerator interaction which yielded highly aggregative and purely endogenous models of potentially unstable output fluctuations. The monetary, financial, and expectational aspects of the cycle were largely neglected. Soon, strong reactions developed against this one-sided conception. One took the form of stochastic, dynamically stable mathematical models. This greatly influenced macroeconometric models which emphasized the destabilizing role of random shocks and exogenous factors.

The other reaction against theories of endogenous instability was monetarism. Its targets included not only the Keynesian models of aggregate demand, with fluctuating but often weak investment and a major role for fiscal policies to combat unemployment, but also the older models with unstable credit-investment interactions. Fluctuations in monetary growth attributed to erratic or misguided policies were made primarily responsible for disturbing the basically stable private economy and creating "business cycles." The real, financial, and expectational factors received little attention.

The natural-rate and rational expectations hypotheses, plus the discouraging record of the 1970s, led to new hopes for a program of study with a grand design: to reconcile business cycles with the postulates of the competitive general-equilibrium theory in its modern dynamic form. The initial approach relied upon random monetary shocks, price misperceptions, and intertemporal substitution of labor. However, critical analyses and tests soon cast serious doubts on this construction and thereby on the underlying premises, mainly that of flexible prices continuously clearing all markets. No convincing remedy could be provided by adaptation of familiar elements of older disequilibrium theories such as the accelerator and lags due to costs of adjustments in the stocks of production factors.

Some equilibrium theorists questioned the importance of the disturbances to money supply and tried to explain business cycles in real terms only. Their RE models are more restrictive yet. They consist of supply reactions of a "representative" producer-consumer to productivity or input-output shocks. The environment is purely competitive or of a Robinson Crusoe type. There is little or no evidence to support these models.

Contract theories, designed to explain why most wages and prices are temporarily "sticky," formed the basis of very different models in which aggregate demand fluctuations are restored to their usual prominence. Other work, also using the currently favored RE methodology, turned to factors with a long history of service in business cycle models: uncertainty and shifts in "market psychology," interest-rate misperceptions or maladjustments, and long investment gestation periods.

There is not much empirical validation that random shocks of all kinds play as large a role in business cycles as has been attributed to them in recent literature. The weight of exogenous policy factors, too, seems more often than not overstated. The theoretical interest in self-sustaining cycles, or elements thereof, declined in times when economic events and thought favored a revival of the faith in the private sector's capacity for stable growth. New work in this area, therefore, has been limited, but it still produced some interesting and significant results.

The most disturbing aspect of what must be viewed as the new mainstream literature (the RE models) is its increasing fragmentation in the face of various theoretical problems and recalcitrant facts. The ruling research strategy in these studies is to demonstrate for each particular model that one or more of the selected factors can contribute to fluctuations in total output or employment, while recognizing that others can do so as well. The authors are mainly concerned with theoretical possibilities rather than with explanations of what actually happens. There is in general little regard for how the pieces fit each other or the "real world." The variety of the models is only loosely limited by the ingenuity of the theorists, but many of the offered hypotheses are not tested and some are not testable. Small linear models are favored because of their mathematical tractability in the equilibrium RE framework, but this certainly does not mean that larger and/or nonlinear systems are somehow inferior. The criterion of conformity to stylized facts would, in fact, suggest the opposite.

As a matter of simple logic, if each of a number of models is indeed valid, then it should in principle be possible to integrate them and improve the theory. Of course, this is easier said than done, but when each model is treated in isolation, there is little chance for the job to be ever seriously attacked. The conclusion reached here, then, is that a movement toward a synthesis of the tested and nonfalsified hypotheses is urgently needed if real progress is to be made in our understanding of business cycles.

In this view, research in this area will profit most from the confrontation of testable hypotheses with a broad range of evidence on stylized facts and from efforts to combine those hypotheses that survive the tests. This assigns high priorities to the work on (1) the consolidation and updating of findings from the historical and statistical business cycle studies and (2) using the results to eliminate those elements of the extant theories that are definitely inconsistent with the evidence and to improve the modeling of the other elements. This strategy could lead us away from the proliferation of models which give lopsided stress to either the monetary or the real factors, either the supply or the demand behavior, either random shocks or purely endogenous movements; instead, we would be working toward a better comprehension of how these forces interact. As was recognized early by the "classics," the sharp dichotomies and monocausal theories tend to be invalidated by experience.

Also, the hypothesis that business cycles are all alike would itself be tested in the course of this research. It is important to know not only what the common core of the cyclical process has been for the U.S. economy in recent times but also how it may have changed historically and how it differs from similar processes elsewhere. The knowledge is necessary for an assessment of the temporal and spatial reference points of business cycle theory. (For the most recent work on these problems, see R. J. Gordon, 1986a).

We have witnessed a period of great intellectual ferment, activity, and controversy in the theory of macroeconomic fluctuations and policies, but the debate seems to be growing less heated lately, and some signs of a future rapprochement can be discerned. The present may be a good time to ponder the needed synthesis.

3 Facts and Factors in the Modern Evolution of U.S. Economic Fluctuations

In the 1970s and the 1980s the old problem of the business cycle once again moved to the forefront of the economic profession's active interest. Among the most intensely debated issues is that of continuity versus change in cyclical behavior. Are business cycles all alike? Have they changed in any systematic way and, if so, why?

The purpose of this chapter is to review in a selective and critical way the recent developments and literature bearing on these questions. I examine the hypothesis that the U.S. economy was cyclically less unstable after World War II than before and concentrate on the role of structural, institutional, and policy changes.

3.1 Have Business Cycles Moderated?

3.1.1 Problems with Old and New Data

The main novelties in the post–World War II business cycles include a shift toward longer expansions and shorter as well as shallower contractions in aggregate output and employment, combined with a persistence of inflation during peacetime recessions (see chapter 2, sec. 2.2.1; and Zarnowitz and Moore 1986). How well documented are these developments? What are their principal sources, consequences, and implications? Substantial work on these questions has been done in the last few years, much of it published in voluminous proceedings from a 1984 NBER conference (Gordon 1986a).

The earliest influential statement that a significant "progress towards economic stability" is under way was made by Burns (1960). Later data confirmed in large measure Burns's analysis and projections, according to the new NBER studies (Gordon 1986b).

However, Romer (1986a, 1986b, 1986c, 1986d, and 1987a) presents new annual series for GNP, 1869–1918, and the unemployment rate, 1890–1930, and argues that the greater stability of the U.S. economy in the postwar era compared with the pre-1930 era is mainly a "figment of the data." She constructs estimates for the postwar period imitating the procedures used by the creators of the historical estimates (Kuznets 1946, 1961; Shaw 1947; Lebergott 1964) and shows that her artificial data are about as volatile as their series. She then produces her own series for selected periods before the Great Depression, using regression index methods that in effect force the prewar data to reflect certain postwar relationships. Not surprisingly, these rearranged series are considerably smoother and have smaller cyclical amplitudes than the corresponding original estimates, being in both respects more similar to the postwar data.

It is certainly true, and well known, that the information-gathering and measurement techniques available to the pioneers in U.S. historical statistics were inferior to those that we have now. Yet it does not necessarily follow that simply imposing the recent patterns on the old data will improve the latter. Just to mention some of the assumptions that must hold true for Romer's methods to be applicable; her unemployment revisions require that the output-employment relations in each sector, the cyclicality of labor force participation rates, and the sectoral composition of employment all be the same in both the pre-1930 and post-1948 periods (Weir 1986). Yet at least some of these assumptions have already been falsified by the data. The same goes for the Romer GNP series where, for example, the elasticity of GNP to commodity output in terms of deviations from trend is taken to be the same before 1918 as after 1948. The implicit theorizing behind these calculations ignores the structural and other changes that occurred in the economy over the past century (see sec. 3.3). More fundamentally still, Romer's estimation procedure precludes any possibility of stabilization, thus making her conclusion inevitable and prejudging the issue in question (Lebergott 1986).

In support of Romer's position (but not her approach), it can be said that much of the direct historical evidence consists of cyclically sensitive series, which would indeed exaggerate the fluctuations in the economy at large, as noted in chapter 7 (Zarnowitz 1981). Although not overlooked by Kuznets and others who created the basic macroeconomic series for the United States, this problem of a possible bias results just from lack of data and so has no real solution short of introducing new pertinent historical information.

Regrettably, no one can create comprehensive historical time series where the required data simply do not exist. But several considerations suggest that the problem is less critical that it appears. (1) Monthly indexes of commercial and industrial activity exist for the United States in trend-adjusted form since 1834, without trend adjustments since 1882. They have a broad coverage in terms of the industries and processes important at the time: manufacturing, mining, agricultural marketings, construction, railway freight ton-miles, electric power, foreign-trade volume. The sectors worst represented, notably private and government services, played a much smaller role in earlier times than in the last four decades. (2) Historically, business contractions used to be accompanied by declines in financial and nominal aggregates or indexes: security prices, bonds and shares traded, interest rates, business failures (inverted), bank clearings, and commodity and wholesale prices. The evidence from these series tends to confirm the evidence from indexes of real activity with regard to the identification and dating of business cycles. (3) Further support for the historical chronology of business expansions and contractions created by the NBER comes from accounts of contemporary observers (business annals), the directional consensus of series on real and financial activity and prices (diffusion indexes), and chronologies independently derived by others (Burns and Mitchell 1946, ch. 4; see also chapter 7). All of this information also helps to compare business cycles and rank expansions by their vigor and contractions by their severity.

3.1.2.   Evidence for Changes in Volatility

Figures 3.1–3.3 help us compare the variability of real GNP, the wholesale price index, and money supply, M2, over three subperiods of the last century: 1875–1918, 1919–45, and 1946–83. To concentrate on short-run relative changes and counteract heteroscedasticity, series of log differences are used.

The graphs and the associated descriptive statistics (table 3.1) provide strong indications that the rates of change in output, prices, and money (q, p, and m, respectively) all tended to be much less volatile after 1945 than in either of the two earlier eras. Thus, the standard deviations for 1875–1918 are about 1.5–2 times larger and those for 1919–45 are 2–3 times larger than their counterparts for 1946–83 (table 3.1, col. 4, lines 1–12). The coefficients of variation (ratios of standard deviations to means) yield identical rankings of the subperiods (cols. 4, 5, and 9). The interquartile ranges give similar results.

The averages of q and m do not differ strongly across the subperiods, whereas the averages of p do, reflecting the mixture of inflation and deflation in 1875–1918, the prevalence of deflation in the interwar period, and the persistent inflation of recent times. For q, the medians exceed the means, and the skewness measures (not shown) are negative throughout. For m and p, the distributions are skewed negatively in the 1920s and 1930s only (cf. cols. 3 and 6.)

Besides having generally larger fluctuations, q, p, and m also show higher proportions of negative signs in the first decades covered than in the last four. The curves in figures 3.1–3.3 fall much more often and further below the zero level in 1875–1945 than in 1945–83. In the latter period, aggregate level declines were relatively infrequent for real GNP and rare indeed for the broad indexes of producer (and consumer) prices and measures of the stock of money.

The quarterly changes in the rate on prime commercial paper (i) show great

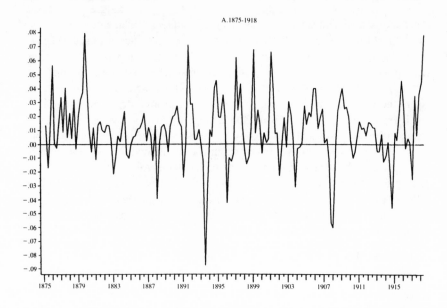

A.1875-1918

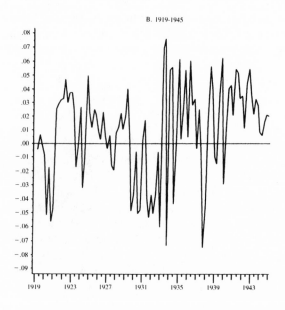

B. 1919-1945

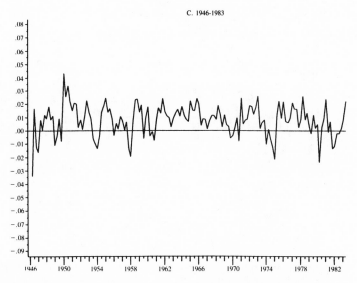

Fig. 3.1 **Quarterly changes in real gross national product, log differences, 1875–1983**

volatility in 1875–1918 and more persistence in the two later periods (fig. 3.4).[1] A very conspicuous feature here is the sharp contrast between the amplitudes of *i* in 1933–53 and thereafter. This reflects the strong heteroscedasticity of interest rates: the higher their levels, the larger their changes. Clearly, too, the very high variability of the nominal interest rates in the second half of the post–1945 period is closely related to rising inflation, recurrent attempts to disinflate, and the resulting instability of inflationary expectations. In 1875–1945 inflation did not persist in peacetime but alternated with deflation. Indeed, it is only in the last quarter-century or so that expectations of a "secular" inflation developed, driving up interest. The short-term sensitivity of the price level declined, but recessions and major slowdowns typically induced temporary reductions in the rate of inflation, which helped to make the recent movements in the general level of interest rates decidedly procyclical.

According to standard deviations of *i*, the variability of short-term rates was somewhat greater in 1946–83 than in 1875–1918 and was lowest in 1919–45 (table 3.1, col. 4, lines 13–16). The corresponding measures for log differences show a nearly perfect tie between the three subperiods, with standard deviations of about 0.13 for each of them. Thus, logarithmic transformations remove virtually all of the observed heteroscedasticity.

1. This is probably due to the effects of the dissolution of the gold standard and/or the founding and activities of the Federal Reserve System (Barsky et al. 1988). The series on the 4- to 6-month paper is used here because of its homogeneity over the entire period 1890–1980 (Gordon 1982a, p. 1114). The data for 1875–89 are for the commercial paper rate in New York City (Macaulay 1938, pp. A141–61); the data for 1981–83 are for the 6-month paper (*Federal Reserve Bulletin*).

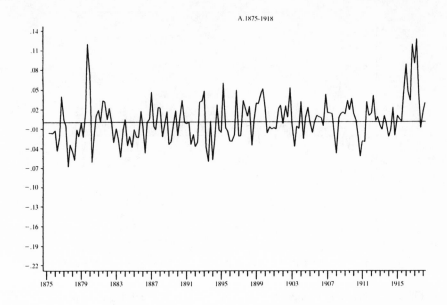

A. 1875-1918

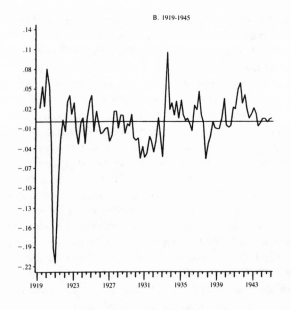

B. 1919-1945

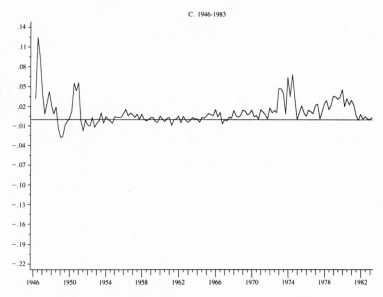

Fig. 3.2   Quarterly changes in wholesale (producer) price index, log differences, 1875–1983

3.1.3   Evidence for Changes in Cyclical Behavior

The measures discussed in the previous section are based on variations over short unit periods such as quarters or years, not on variations over intermediate periods of varying length that are characteristic of business cycles. They therefore reflect strongly the influence of short erratic movements and are probably better viewed as estimates of volatility than of cyclicality. Moreover, they do not distinguish between expansions and contractions in economic activity. To examine changes in the durations and magnitudes of cyclical fluctuations, there is still no alternative to the reference cycle method applied in the historical NBER studies.

No *systematic* changes over time can be detected in the total duration of business cycles, which averaged about 4 years, give or take a few months, before and after World War II. But the relative length of cycle phases changed dramatically: in 1885–1945, for example, business expansions were less than twice as long as contractions; in 1945–82 they were 3–4 times as long (see Zarnowitz and Moore 1986, tables 9.1 and 9.4). Or to put it differently, the proportions of time in contractions averaged more than 30%–40% in the six decades beginning in 1885 but only 20%–25% in the four decades following 1945. This finding does not depend significantly on the incidence of wars or the few doubtful links in the chronology that may represent slowdowns, rather than absolute declines, in macroeconomic activity.

Judging from the average percentage amplitudes of cyclical declines (*C*)

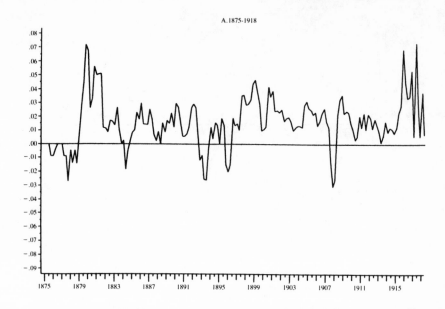

A. 1875-1918

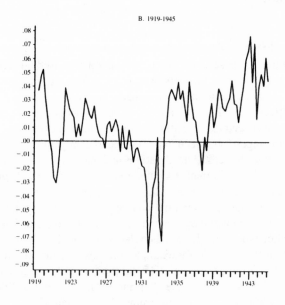

B. 1919-1945

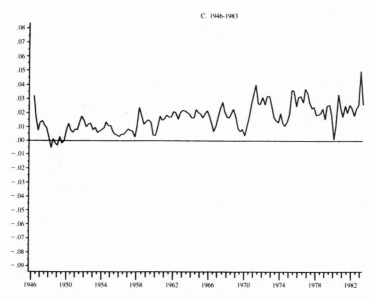

Fig. 3.3   Quarterly changes in money supply (M2), log differences, 1875–1983

and rises (E) in industrial activity and employment, contractions became not only much shorter but also much milder in the post–World War II cycles. Expansions also moderated greatly but less than contractions, so the E/C amplitude ratios increased. The employment ratios for 1885–1912, 1912–45, and 2.3, 1.8, and 5.0, respectively.[2] These changes are large and quite unlikely to be statistical artifacts, although they may well be overstated because of the differences between the historical and recent data.

Table 3.2 lists the average durations and amplitudes of fluctuations in the levels of the four variables whose quarter-to-quarter variability was examined above with the aid of figures 3.1–3.4. Also included here is the series of current-dollar GNP estimates, which helps to document that prices and values were historically no less cyclical than quantities. However, GNP had no declines after 1960, nor did the wholesale price index after 1967 (lines 3, 6, and 9).

The shift toward longer expansions and shorter contractions can be seen clearly by comparing the post–1945 duration measures for nominal and real GNP, prices, and interest rates with their counterparts for the pre–World War I and interwar periods (col. 5–6). History shows that monetary aggregates had declines associated with major business contractions, which are few and far between, and only slowdowns marking the milder recessions. Indeed, M2

2. Excluding marginal recessions and wartime, the corresponding average E/C ratios are 2.2, 1.2, and 3.7.

Table 3.1   Estimated Variabilities of Changes in Output, Prices, Money, and Interest: Selected Statistics for 1875–1983 and Three Subperiods

Line (1)	Period[a] (2)	Mean[b] (3)	Standard Deviation[b] (4)	Coefficient of Variation[c] (5)	Median[b] (6)	Interquartile Range[b] (7)	Range[b] (8)	Rank of Subperiod[d] (9)
				Real GNP (log differences)				
1	1875–1918	.99	2.37	2.40	1.04	2.40	16.72	2
2	1919–1945	.75	3.56	4.76	1.19	4.38	15.09	1
3	1946–1983	.78	1.18	1.52	.87	1.47	7.71	3
4	1875–1983	.85	2.42	2.83	.91	2.27	16.72	
				Wholesale (Producer) Price Index (log differences)				
5	1875–1918	.28	3.28	11.59	0	4.28	19.49	2
6	1919–1945	−.20	4.11	20.53	.33	3.60	32.13	1
7	1946–1983	1.13	1.96	1.74	.58	1.43	15.24	3
8	1875–1983	.46	3.18	6.92	.46	2.78	34.18	
				Money Stock, M2 (log differences)				
9	1875–1918	1.60	1.84	1.15	1.45	1.99	10.40	2
10	1919–1945	1.42	2.77	1.95	1.63	3.10	15.76	1
11	1946–1983	1.64	.96	.59	1.67	1.40	5.53	3
12	1875–1983	1.57	1.89	1.21	1.62	1.90	15.76	
				Commercial Paper Rate (changes)				
13	1875–1918	−.00	.82	n.a.[e]	0	1.02	5.64	2
14	1919–1945	−.04	.40	n.a.	0	.16	2.80	3
15	1946–1983	.06	.92	n.a.	.09	.46	8.49	1
16	1875–1983	.01	.78	n.a.	.01	.60	8.49	

Source: See text and fig. 3.2.

[a]Year dates of the first and last turning points of the series during each period.

[b]Identified according to specific cycle peaks and troughs dated by inspection of the charts of the series. Only complete upward and downward movements (called "rise" and "fall," respectively) are counted.

[c]Measured from trough to peak for rises and from peak to trough for falls.

[d]Col. 9 = col. 7 ÷ col. 5. Col. 10 = col. 8 ÷ col. 6.

[e]Only one cyclical decline in the level of M2 occurred in the period 1946–83, dated 1948:1 (peak) to 1949:1 (trough).

[f]The entries in cols. 7–10 are average amplitudes of absolute (not percentage) changes.

(and M1) had no declines of any cyclical persistence at all after the 1948–49 recession (lines 10–12). The period 1918–38 featured the longest and the post–World War II era the shortest and least frequent cyclical downswings in all cases (as well as for several other related variables that were examined).

For all but one of these series, too, the declines were on average the largest in the interwar and the smallest in the post-1945 era (col. 8). The exception is the commercial paper rate, where these ranks are reversed. The same relationship applies to the per-quarter amplitudes of fall (col. 10). The differences in size among the average rises are relatively smaller and less systematic across the variables (cols. 7 and 9). Worth noting, however, are the large percentage amplitudes of expansions in income, output, and prices during the interwar period and in interest rates during 1946–83.

3.1.4   Qualifying and Interpreting the Results

The main point emerging from this examination of the data is that the hypothesis of reduced cyclical instability in the last 40 years receives broad support from independently compiled series on several principal aggregative variables. The underlying historical data come from well-known sources: for real income, Gallman and Kuznets; wholesale prices, Bureau of Labor Statistics; money, Friedman and Schwartz; interest rates, Macaulay and the *Commercial and Financial Chronicle*. Balke and Gordon (1986a) present quarterly series on levels of these (and other related) variables.

The least dependable of the historical estimates under review are probably those for quarterly real GNP. Balke and Gordon obtained them by interpolating the annual series with the index of industrial production and trade from Persons (1931) for the period 1875–1930 and the Federal Reserve industrial production index for 1931–45. The method of interpolation is state of the art and well employed, but the quarterly series used as interpolators have, inevitably, limited and selected coverage.[3] However, comparisons of more reliable annual output series produce qualitatively similar conclusions (Baily 1978, esp. pp. 13–18).

The detrended real GNP series had standard deviations of 2.1 in 1950–80, according to current Department of Commerce data, and 3.4–4.5 in 1872–

---

3. The interpolation procedure follows that of Chow and Lin (1971), assumes that the quarterly errors are subject to an AR(1) process, and allows for a constant and a linear time trend (Gordon and Veitch 1986, pp. 328–35). The index of industrial production and trade is based on bank clearings outside New York City, 1875–1914; pig iron production, 1877–1918; imports of merchandise, 1903–14; gross earnings of leading railroads, 1903–14; employment, 1903–18; cotton consumption, 1915–18; net ton-miles of freight, 1915–18; electric power production, 1919–30; index of volume of manufacturing, 1919–30; railroad car loadings, 1919–30; construction contracts, deflated, 1919–30; and index of volume of mining, 1919–30 (Persons 1931, chs. 7–10, passim). The uneven and spotty nature of the compilation, especially before 1903, is beyond question, yet there is no way to quantify the errors of the resulting estimates. Other available indexes of business activity have similar shortcomings and none is demonstrably superior to others (see also chapter 7).

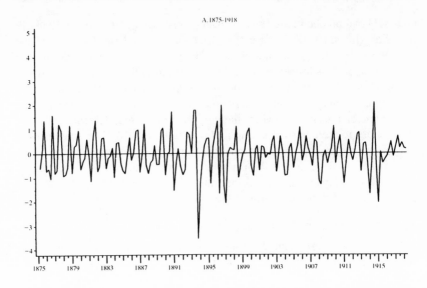

A. 1875-1918

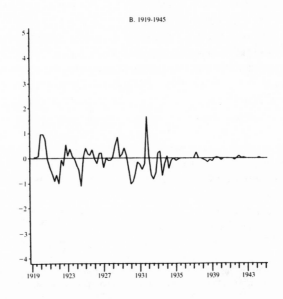

B. 1919-1945

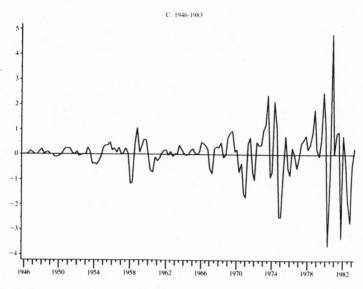

Fig. 3.4   Quarterly changes in commercial paper rate, 1875–1983

1928, according to the Gallman-Kuznets-Commerce estimates (Balke and Gordon 1986b). The corresponding Romer figure for 1872–1928 is 2.8, much smaller than the others but still significantly above that for 1950–80. Standard deviations of annual changes in real and nominal GNP, business fixed investment, and civilian employment were 2.1–2.4 times larger in 1891–1914 than in the post–World War II period, according to a list of estimates in Schultze 1986 (p. 61). For nonfarm aggregate hours worked, manufacturing production, steel production, and money supply (M2), the corresponding ratios are 1.7–1.8. These comparisons are based on relatively reliable data and they exclude the perhaps uniquely volatile interval between 1914 and 1945.

It is also useful to examine changes in long and reasonably consistent series on individual production series in physical units, as did Romer (1987b). Here standard deviations of first differences in the logarithms of data on 11 agricultural goods, 14 mineral products, and 13 manufactured commodities are presented for the prewar (1889–1914), interwar (1922–39), and postwar (1947–84) periods.[4] The prewar-to-postwar ratios for these measures average 1.2, 1.1, 1.5, and 1.2 for farming, mining, manufacturing, and all products, respectively. The corresponding statistics for the interwar-to-postwar ratios are 1.8, 2.0, 1.4, and 1.8. I interpret these results to indicate a tendency for these series to show less volatility in the post-World War II era than in the quarter century before World War I and the highest volatility in the interwar years. In

4. Data on refined sugar production are not available for the interwar period, and data on beer and distilled spirits production are influenced by the end of Prohibition in 1933–34. Hence, the measures reported in the text exclude these three series from the manufacturing group.

Table 3.2   Durations and Amplitudes of Cyclical Movements in Estimates of Nominal and Real GNP, the Price Level, Money Stock, and Short-Term Interest Rates: Pre–World War I, Interwar, and Post–World War II Periods

Line (1)	Period[a] (2)	No. of Cyclical Movements[b] Rise (3)	Fall (4)	Average Duration in Quarters[c] Rise (5)	Fall (6)	Average Percentage Amplitude[c] Rise (7)	Fall (8)	Average Percentage Amplitude per Quarter[d] Rise (9)	Fall (10)
				GNP in Current Dollars					
1	1878–1914	10	10	10.0	4.6	24.4	− 8.1	2.4	−1.8
2	1920–1938	4	5	10.5	6.0	37.2	−21.2	3.4	−3.5
3	1948–1960	3	4	12.3	2.8	28.0	− 2.2	2.3	−0.8
				GNP in Constant Dollars					
4	1878–1914	12	12	8.9	3.2	17.3	− 5.1	1.9	−1.6
5	1919–1938	4	5	11.0	6.0	30.1	−14.1	2.7	−2.4
6	1948–1982	7	8	16.3	2.6	20.9	− 2.5	1.3	−1.0
				Wholesale Price Index					
7	1876–1914	11	10	6.6	6.9	12.1	−11.8	1.8	−1.7
8	1920–1939	4	5	8.2	8.6	15.4	−21.6	1.9	−2.5
9	1948–1967	4	5	12.5	5.0	8.7	− 4.8	0.7	−1.0
				Money Stock (M2)					
10	1878–1908	4	4	26.0	3.2	82.3	− 5.9	3.2	−1.8
11	1920–1938	2	3	22.5	8.7	48.3	−14.4	2.1	−1.8
12	1948–1949[e]	...	1	...	4	...	− 0.9	...	−0.2
				Commercial Paper Rate[f]					
13	1875–1913	10	10	9.1	6.0	2.7	− 2.8	0.3	−0.5
14	1918–1937	5	6	5.6	7.7	1.8	− 2.4	0.3	−0.3
15	1946–1983	9	9	11.2	5.1	4.3	− 3.4	0.4	−0.7

Source: See text and fig. 3.2.

[a] Year dates of the first and last turning points of the series during each period.

[b] Identified according to specific cycle peaks and troughs dated by inspection of the charts of the series. Only complete upward and downward movements (called "rise" and "fall," respectively) are counted.

[c] Measured from trough to peak for rises and from peak to trough for falls.

[d] Col. 9 = col. 7 ÷ col. 5. Col. 10 = col. 8 ÷ col. 6.

[e] Only one cyclical decline in the level of M2 occurred in the period 1946–83, dated 1948:1 (peak) to 1949:1 (trough).

[f] The entries in cols. 7–10 are average amplitudes of absolute (not percentage) changes.

my view, the overall evidence clearly supports this ranking,[5] even though Romer herself prefers to stress that the prewar-postwar differences are small.

Moreover, it is important to recognize that moderation of business cycles does not necessarily require a diminution over time in fluctuations of individual products or even industries. Even with no change in the dimensions of these movements, a shift in the relative importance from sectors characterized by large fluctuations (such as manufactured goods) to sectors characterized by small fluctuations (such as services) would reduce the overall instability of the economy. As shown elsewhere and below, the structure of the economy has indeed undergone a major shift of this nature (Zarnowitz and Moore 1986).

Other developed economies have followed similar historical trends. In Sheffrin 1988, estimates of the dispersion of annual growth rates in output for six European countries are all larger for 1871–1914 than for 1951–84, but generally not by much. Backus and Kehoe (1988) add several countries for which relatively good annual data on national income for the period are available. They find that the standard deviations of detrended long output series were 1.1–2.5 times larger in the pre–World War I years than in the post–World War II years for Australia, Canada, Norway, Sweden, and the United Kingdom. Comparable ratios for series of log differences tend to be somewhat larger. The corresponding estimates for the United States are 1.8–2.1. The variability of output in most countries was much higher in the interwar period than in the postwar period, with ratios ranging from 1.2 to 3.6 for log differences. (For the United States, the figure is 3.1.)

In sum, there are good reasons to agree with Weir (1986, p. 365), whose conclusion from comprehensive tests and a critique of Romer's results is that "to the simple question of whether cyclical fluctuations around trend in GNP and unemployment have become smaller since World War II the data are more than adequate to deliver a definitive answer: yes." Similarly, Balke and Gordon (1986b, p. 3), after presenting a new regression index for real GNP, 1869–1908, based on Romer's "backcasting" method but using in part different and additional data, find "not a shred of evidence to support the view that the greater volatility of real GNP before 1929 is 'spurious.' " My own view is that the historical series are indeed more likely to err in the direction of too much than too little volatility. But this bias is (1) not all necessarily "cyclical"; (2) partly offset by shifts in weights that tend to favor the cyclically more stable sectors; and (3) almost certainly too small overall to refute the hypothesis of a significant stabilization in the postwar period (relative not only to the interwar but also to the pre–World War I era).

5. For example, when medians are used, the prewar-postwar ratio for all comparable 35 series is still 1.2, and the interwar-postwar ratio is 1.5.

3.2   What May Have Caused the Changes in Cyclical Behavior?

3.2.1   A List of Hypotheses

In section 3.1, I argued that the hypothesis of reduced economic instability is supported by a comparative analysis of a variety of pre– and post–World War II data for the United States. What are the possible sources of the observed moderation of the business cycles?

Several explanations have been proposed or are possible. They can be identified briefly and grouped broadly, as follows.

I. Structural changes in the private economy
   A. Shifts toward cyclically more stable components of demand
   B. Shifts toward cyclically more stable industries, occupations, and incomes
II. Increase in the size of government, a sector that does not decline in recessions
III. Institutional changes
   A. Rise of the fiscal "automatic stabilizers"—procyclical income taxes, countercyclical transfer payments and welfare benefits
   B. Postdepression financial reforms such as federal insurance programs for bank deposits (combined with discretionary lender-of-last-resort actions), savings and loan accounts, and mortgages
   C. Private stabilizing arrangements—pension plans, maintained corporate dividends
IV. Discretionary policies (fiscal or monetary or both) resulting in the following effects (which can be interpreted as a change in the propagation mechanism [see factor V below] or smaller shocks to the economy [see factor VIA below]):
   A. Reductions in the variability of aggregate demand (nominal GNP)
   B. Reductions in the variability of aggregate supply in response to the greater stability of demand
V. Gains in learning and confidence:
   A. Consumers and entrepreneurs learn from history (which reflects the operation of factors I–IV above) to expect less cyclical instability in the future
   B. Their greater confidence leads them to modify their behavior in ways that help stabilize the economy
VI. Smaller shocks to the economy
   A. Decreased shifts to aggregate demand (nominal GNP) due to countercyclical and counterinflationary discretionary policies, institutional and structural changes, and gains in confidence (factors I–V above)
   B. Decreased shifts in aggregate private demand (consumption, invest-

ment, exports) due to greater stability in preferences and/or accumulation of wealth and capital
  C. Decreased shifts in aggregate supply due to greater stability in technical progress and/or in expectations of profits
VII. Gains in technology, information, and knowledge
  A. Reduced inventory fluctuations through better management techniques (using advances in economic models and data production and analysis)
  B. Fewer major policy errors and better guidance from economic advisers and forecasters
VIII. Changes in the flexibility of wages and prices
  A. Past business contractions aggravated by deflation and deflationary expectations
  B. Stickier money wages and prices in the postwar era
  C. On balance, the greater stickiness makes for more stability

3.2.2 Some Observations and Plan of Procedure

The above list is purposely inclusive and there are some overlaps, as indicated. Some of the hypotheses are widely accepted (notably III), some are much discussed and very controversial (II, IV, and VIII), and still others are mere possibilities, little explored and perhaps remote (VIB, VIC, and VII). All are at best partial, more than one may be valid, and none need be dominant. Hence the proper strategy is not to test them against each other but rather to consider that they may apply in some combination. Ideally, one would wish to quantify the contributions of all factors that prove relevant, but this very ambitious goal is well beyond our present reach.

The last set of hypotheses in the list (VIII) concerns matters of great analytical importance and difficulty. They are treated separately in chapter 4.

The next section of this chapter deals with the first two topics in our list, that is, structural changes and the expansion of government. In section 3.4 I examine the third set of hypotheses, and in section 3.5 I look at the role of macroeconomic policies and related changes in the behavior of private agents (hypotheses IV and V). I shall have little to say about the other possibilities listed under VI and VII. The last section of the chapter sums up the results.

3.3 Structural Changes and the Size of Government

3.3.1 Components of Expenditures

Real consumer expenditures on durable goods have large fluctuations, most of which correspond well to business cycles, allowing for some tendency to lead (see table 3.3, lines 1 and 7, for a summary of the interwar and postwar evidence). In contrast, consumption of nondurable goods and services shows

Table 3.3 **Summary Measures of Cyclical Conformity, Timing, and Amplitude for Selected Components of Private Consumption and Investment, 1919–41 and 1947–83**

Series (1)	No. of Business Cycle Turns Matched (Missed)[a]		No. of Specific Cycle Turns Matched (Extra)[a]		Average Lead (−) or Lag (+) (in quarters)		Average Amplitude[b] (%)	
	Peaks (2)	Troughs (3)	Peaks (4)	Troughs (5)	Peaks (6)	Troughs (7)	Rise (8)	Fall (9)
1919–41								
1. Consumption, durable goods	5(0)	5(0)	5(3)	5(3)	−0.4	−0.4	+63	−32
2. Consumption, nondurable goods, and services	4(1)	4(1)	4(1)	4(1)	−0.5	−0.2	+24	−9
3. Residential structures	5(0)	5(0)	5(3)	5(3)	−0.2	−0.8	+101	−33
4. Producers' durable equipment	5(0)	5(0)	5(2)	5(2)	0.2	0.4	+121	−41
5. Nonresidential structures	4(1)	4(1)	4(2)	4(2)	−1.2	−0.2	+172	−44
6. Change in business inventories	5(0)	5(0)	5(4)	5(4)	+1.0	−0.4	+19[c]	−15[c]
1947–83								
7. Consumption, durable goods	7(1)	7(1)	7(3)	7(3)	−2.3	−1.3	+33	−10
8. Residential structures	7(1)	7(1)	7(5)	7(5)	−2.9	−0.9	+36	−21
9. Producers' durable equipment	7(1)	7(1)	7(3)	7(3)	−0.4	0.6	+30	−12
10. Nonresidential structures	6(2)	6(2)	6(4)	6(4)	−1.0	1.2	+22	−9
11. Change in business inventories	8(0)	8(0)	8(2)	8(2)	−4.4	−0.2	+45[c]	−47[c]

Sources: Balke and Gordon 1986b; Economic Report 1988.

[a]The following dates from the quarterly NBER reference cycle chronology are covered: *1919–41*: peaks, 1920:1, 1923:2, 1926:3, 1929:3, 1937:2 (five), and troughs, 1921:3, 1924:3, 1927:4, 1933:1, 1938:2 (five); *1947–83*: peaks, 1948:4, 1953:2, 1957:3, 1960:2, 1969:4, 1973:4, 1980:1, 1981:3 (eight), and troughs, 1949:4, 1954:2, 1958:2, 1961:1, 1970:4, 1975:1, 1980:3, 1982:4 (eight). Entries not in parentheses are numbers of those business cycle peaks or troughs (cols. 2 and 3) that are matched by like cyclical turning points in the quarterly series listed in col. 1 (cols. 4 and 5). Entries within parentheses are numbers of those business cycle turning points (cols. 2 and 3) or specific cycle turning points (cols. 4 and 5) that could not be matched.

[b]Measured from trough to peak for rises and from peak to trough for falls.

[c]Average amplitudes of absolute (not percentage) changes.

relatively small cyclical movements even in the turbulent interwar period, rising and falling on the average about one third as much as the durables (cf. lines 1 and 2). In 1947–83, nondurable goods had only a few declines, none longer than 1 quarter, and services rose continuously at growth rates substantially exceeding those of goods consumption.[6]

The main reason for the observed sharp differences is simple: durable goods are accumulated, render services, and depreciate over time, and their purchases are postponable. Hence, the sensitivity to business cycles of these purchases is typically high. There is no reason why this relationship should have varied over time or should not persist in the future. The demand for services is relatively stable in part because services cannot be stored. The nondurables fall in between.

Of course, major depressions would be associated with larger declines extending to nondurable goods and services as well. Even a lengthy stagnation of growth in real wages and disposable personal income can substantially reduce the consumer and business demand for many short-lived goods and services, particularly in the face of weak labor market conditions and persistent uncertainty about the economic outlook. This is what happened as a result of the protracted period of subnormal growth since early 1989, although the recession in 1990–91 was relatively mild.

New and replacement demands for plant and equipment and housing give rise to outputs of durable capital goods and structures, which, like the consumer durables, have large fluctuations and high conformity to business cycles. In 1919–41, the cyclical swings in business investment (producers' durable equipment and nonresidential structures) were huge, exceeding those in household investment (consumer durables and housing). In 1947–83, movements in all these aggregates were on the average more nearly equal in percentage terms (compare the corresponding entries in cols. 8 and 9).

The cyclical conformity of the investment series was high both before and after World War II (cols 2–5). Inventory investment, though always very volatile, also moved in both periods in a basically procyclical fashion.[7] Timing shifted to longer leads at peaks in the postwar era (cols. 6–7).

Studies that employ variance-analytic methods produce further information, with generally similar results. When total fixed investment is defined to include consumer durables as well as producers' durable equipment and residential and nonresidential structures, its variance accounts for about one quarter of the variance of real GNP in the interwar and postwar periods alike (Gordon and Veitch 1986, pp. 299–300). However, the components of this broad

6. Measures of the type used in table 3.3 are not available for the levels of these aggregates in the postwar period (to show any cyclical movements, the series have to be differenced).

7. Note the change from short lags to long leads at peaks (lines 6 and 11, col. 6). As for the frequencies of the "extra" turns (cols. 4 and 5), they relate to specific cycle movements that are generally at least 2 quarters long; had I counted all directional reversals, their number would have been much larger, especially for inventory investment with its frequent short oscillations.

concept of private investment show much larger covariance in 1919–41 than in the recent era. The contribution of nonresidential structures fell and that of consumer durables rose strongly. Further, the covariance between total investment and the rest of output was large and positive in 1919–41 and small and negative in 1947–83. This is consistent with the notion that government spending crowded out some investment in postwar years.

Inventory investment continued to play a major role in the recent business cycles, especially at turning points and in contractions. Indeed, properly measured in comparison to 1929–41, the variance of inventory investment increased after World War II, whereas that of final sales decreased strongly (Blinder and Holtz-Eakin 1986). These findings are not surprising, since the recent era was one of relatively short and mild aggregate fluctuations, and it has long been known that inventory changes are particularly important in just this type of cycle (Abramovitz 1950). Compared with the mostly moderate cycles of 1919–29, the share of inventory investment was larger in the postwar GNP contractions but smaller in expansions.

The variability of output tends to exceed that of final sales in all periods, which is difficult to reconcile with the popular buffer stock model, in which inventory adjustments are supposed to smooth production in the face of random shocks to demand.[8] Presumably, inventories are held in large part for other reasons, such as to facilitate production at all its stages and counteract the procyclical delivery lags and uncertainties of vendor performance.

The hypothesis that better inventory control reduced instability (see factor VIIA on our list) receives only weak support from these results. Nevertheless, it is premature to dismiss it. The variability of real inventory investment tended to decline in 1948–65 (Brooks and Gigante 1979); it increased later through 1983 but remained relatively low during the following 6 years. Surely in this area the promise of progress through computerized information technology looms large.

Has the structure of GNP by type of expenditure changed so as to contribute to the observed moderation of the business cycle in the postwar period? Such a change could take the form of a shift form the highly variable investment to the relatively stable comparison components. But the average share in real GNP of consumption of nondurables and services actually declined from about 65% to 54% between 1919–41 and 1947–83. Half of the resulting gap was offset by the rise from 18% to 24% in the combined share of consumer durable goods and gross private domestic investment. The other half was taken up by the increase in government purchases of goods and services, a generally acyclical GNP component, from 17% to 22%. In the private sphere,

---

8. Evidence from other countries supports that for the United States in this regard (West 1988). On the issues in the current debate concerning the sources of inventory fluctuations and the role of inventories as a cyclical propagation mechanism, see Maccini 1987 and chapter 2, sec. 2.3.5 and pp. 59–60 above.

then, the shift would appear to have been in the destabilizing, rather than stabilizing, direction (the role of increased government is considered below).[9]

It seems safe to eliminate the changes in the consumption-investment mix of the private demands on output as a major source of the reduction in cyclical instability.

3.3.2   Shifts in the Structure of Employment

The industrial composition of employment shifted in the long run from the categories that are highly recession prone to those that are not.[10] The set of major industries that are generally cyclical or volatile includes manufacturing, mining, construction, transportation, communications, and public utilities; they produce mostly goods but also some important capital-intensive services. The combined share of these industries in total employment increased from 29% in 1869 to 41% in 1948–53 and then declined to 32% in 1979–81. The rest of the private nonfarm sector—that is, trade, finance, insurance, real estate, and services in a narrow sense (professional, personal, business, and repair services)—is on the whole not very cyclical. The employment share of these industries gained steadily from about 19% in 1869 to 45% in 1979–81. The proportion of government employment, which does not vary systematically with the business cycle, rose approximately from 4% to 20% between 1869 and 1979–81.[11] The total of the acyclical services and government accounted for about 23% of national employment in 1869, 44% in 1929–37, and 64% in 1979–81.

The share of agriculture, measured in the same terms, dropped enormously from an estimated 48% in 1869 to little more than 3% in 1979–81. Farm output is not very sensitive to fluctuations in aggregate demand, but farm prices are sufficiently so that alternations of financial prosperity and distress in agriculture played a considerable role in the historical record of business cycles. Rough estimates based on historical data of Shaw, Goldsmith, and Kuznets suggest that the standard deviations of annual log differences declined between 1893–1915/1923–40 and 1947–82 by 67% for total output, 65% for nonfarm output, 57% for private output, and 56% for private nonfarm output (De Long and Summers 1986a, p. 686). These reductions are all very

9. It is true that the GNP shares themselves show some cyclical variation, which affects our comparisons. During business contractions the percentage of consumption usually increases and that of investment decreases; and the postwar contractions were short and mild in contrast to the interwar ones. However, these differences are mostly small and irregular. For example, the share of gross private nonresidential fixed investment in GNP averaged 10.2% in the 7 trough years and 10.7% in the 7 peak years of the 1953–83 period (with standard deviations of 1.1% in both cases).

10. Employment is defined in terms of "persons engaged in production," which includes full-time workers, part-time workers converted to full-time equivalents, and self-employed workers.

11. This covers general government at all levels, including the armed forces, plus a relatively small component of "government enterprise" (only the latter may be more appropriately thought of as producing goods rather than services).

large and they may well be overstated, but what matters here are the differences between them, which are negligible for the total versus nonfarm and
sizable for the total versus private comparisons. This implies that the changing
role of agriculture was of little significance in this context, and the changing
role of government had a stabilizing influence.

De Long and Summers, using only three measurements, in effect dismiss
summarily all "accounting explanations" (i.e., the linking of the change in
cyclical variability to structural shifts) as being of little importance. But their
method and estimates are open to serious criticism, particularly because they
consider only the changing roles of agriculture and government and ignore the
great increase in the weight of private service industries.[12]

A strong argument can be made that the shift in the employment structure
had much to do with the moderation of cyclical fluctuations of total employment in the post–World War II period. However, this factor was increasingly
important after 1950, when the combined weight of the more cyclical sector
fell below 50% and 40%; though of long standing, it probably played a much
lesser role in earlier times.

Also, it is noteworthy that public and private services, as a broadly defined
category, although scoring great gains in terms of employment, grew much
more slowly in terms of output. Average labor productivity, as measured, increased far less in services industries than in the production of goods ((Fuchs
1968). According to recent Department of Commerce statistics in 1982 dollars, services already accounted for 41% of real GNP in 1929, with the share
of goods being 43% and that of structures 16%. In 1985, the corresponding
estimates are 46% for services, again 43% for goods, and 11% for structures.

In sum, the hypothesis that structural shifts contributed to the moderation
of postwar business cycles should be neither rejected nor viewed as self-
sufficient. It is a valid but partial explanation that leaves much room for the
other hypotheses.

3.3.3   The Effects of Increased Government

For the government to be able to raise the average level of real economic
activity merely by growing itself and thus adding to total employment, two
conditions are necessary. First, the private economy must suffer from deficient
aggregate demand much of the time, and second, government and private activities must be on the whole complementary. That this should be so seems
inconsistent with the idea shared by mainstream economists of various persua-
sions that the steady state or long-run condition of the market economy is one
of full-employment equilibrium. But in the real world the economies are

---

12. The approach does not distinguish between cyclical and other short-term movements and
between expansions and contractions (see comment by Eisner 1986, pp. 721–22). Also, the estimates before 1929 are based on several major assumptions about the proportion of farm output in
GNP and the composition of government expenditures.

mixed, involving governments as well as markets, and their equilibrium properties should depend on the relative size (and also on the quality of financing and functioning) of their public sectors. Government growth may be beneficial when proceeding from suboptimal size but may be detrimental when carried too far.

In fact, the massive unemployment of the 1930s in the United States, whatever its cause, was finally eliminated only by the rapid defense buildup associated with the outbreak of the war in Europe. After World War II, the government remained much larger than it had been before, and the growth of its spending not only stimulated consumption but also kept up business profits and investment. U.S. foreign aid was a major factor in the recovery of the recipient countries and the reinvigoration of world trade. It is now widely acknowledged that the 1950s and 1960s constituted a golden era of relatively high and stable real growth in the then increasingly "mixed" economies of the Western world. [13]

However, the high wave of confidently expanding, activist government crested before long, perhaps already in the late 1960s, amidst growing worries about the course of the unpopular Vietnam War. In the 1970s the public became increasingly aware of the rising trends in inflation, interest rates, unemployment, and tax burdens. The oil price hikes hurt and so did the intermittent policy efforts to disinflate, which added to the cyclical instability in the mid-1970s and the early 1980s. For all this, the blame fell on what seemed the heavy and clumsy hand of government.

These developments helped promote antistatist ideas. The larger the government, the greater its capacity to interfere with efficient markets and be itself a source of major disturbances. Some government activities compete with or preempt business activities, sufficiently high tax rates diminish private initiatives, and some policy actions have large adverse effects on the economy. Inflationary policies, in particular, are a major source of macroeconomic instability. [14] The long-proposed remedies involve fiscal and monetary conservatism, deregulation, and privatization, that is, generally a reduction of the relative size and power of the government. Political programs along these lines gained much support in recent years, spreading from the United States and Britain to many countries. [15]

It is difficult to define the "size" of the government and distinguish the di-

---

13. See Eisner 1986 for a recent formulation of the argument that higher real government expenditures raised both the Hicksian "floor" and "ceiling" levels of real GNP during the business cycles of the postwar era in the United States.

14. The extreme case is that of the inflation tax used by a government that is too large and too costly, unable to raise much revenue by regular tax collection, and hence trying to finance itself by issuing new money. The results, as in most Latin American countries in the 1980s, are disastrously high inflations and attempts to disinflate and reduce foreign-debt burdens, often accompanied by business stagnation or depression.

15. Including, after the 1989 debacle of communist regimes, the nations of Central and Eastern Europe.

rect consequences of its growth from the related effectiveness of fiscal built-in stabilizers and the potential (for good or bad) for discretionary policies; still, these are in principle distinct matters. One of the relevant measures is the ratio of total real government purchases of goods and services (G) to total real GNP (Q). The acyclical behavior of the upward trending G translates into a mildly countercyclical behavior of G/Q. That is, the ratio tends to be higher at troughs than at peaks of business cycles, and this can be seen just as clearly before as after World War II. By this criterion, any stabilizing effects from the growth of G were only moderate between the interwar and the postwar periods and nonexistent between the pre- and post-1970 parts of the latter era. This is suggested by the following average value of G/Q, in percentages at the quarterly dates of business cycle peaks (P) and troughs (T):[16]

5P, 1920–37:14   8P, 1948–81:19   4P, 1953–69:20   3P, 1973–81:19
5T, 1921–38:17   8T, 1949–82:20   4T, 1954–70:21   3T, 1975–82:20

Since the large reduction of the federal income rates in 1981, the federal budget deficits, as conventionally measured, ran consistently high. Public spending responded weakly and was maintained at an approximately stable proportion of GNP. State and local governments had to assume a larger share of taxing the public and providing programmed services. Pressures against expanding total government expenditures intensified and became generally more effective. As a result, the tax system grew more regressive, government interest payments rose sharply, and complaints about the neglect of public spending, especially on the infrastructure, multiplied. The government may have ceased growing in relative size but the expected gains in efficiency never materialized.

In the Western world, governments vary substantially in size relative to the private economies, judging by the conventional criteria of comparing their budgets with the respective GNP or GDP figures. Several European countries with good records of macroeconomic growth and stability have proportionally larger public sectors than the United States has. But the shift from the prevailing optimism about the growing governments and their economic performance in the 1950s and 1960s to the increasing concern about excessive government expansion and economic powers in the 1970s and 1980s was a widespread, international phenomenon. The initial gains from the process may have become exhausted, while its negative aspects have gradually become apparent.

16. Note that G/Q at P in 1948:4 was 14 and at T in 1949:4 was 15. These values, relating to the period between the demobilization after World War II and the Korean War, are atypically low.

The data on G and Q come from Balke and Gordon 1986b for 1920–38 (in 1972 dollars) and the Economic Report 1988 for 1948–82 (in 1982 dollars). Recall that G covers state and local as well as federal government purchases; for the latter alone, a much larger and longer upward trend and much more pronounced countercyclical movements in the ratio to GNP can plausibly be estimated (see n. 17 and text below).

3.4 Institutional Changes and Financial Instability

3.4.1 Federal Budget since 1869: Growth and Cyclicality

Persistently large federal budget deficits occurred in the period 1879–1945 only during the two world wars and in the depressed 1930s (Firestone 1960). A balanced budget was viewed as a requirement of sound fiscal policy. Surpluses rose during expansions when the tax base broadened; they declined and occasionally yielded to deficits contractions when the tax base narrowed. These stabilizing elements of fiscal response to cyclical change played a minor role as long as the federal budget balances were very small and mostly positive.

Table 3.4 documents the huge growth of the federal budget from 2%-3% of GNP in 1869–1914 to 5%-6% in 1920–38 and 17%-23% in 1948–82.[17] Receipts differed from expenditures on the average by less than 1% of GNP in both the peak and trough years of the twelve business cycles of 1869–1914. Small surpluses prevailed in 1920–27 and larger deficits in the depressed 1930s. In 1948–61, the budget was in the red during recessions and in the aftermath of the Korean War but still in the black at other times. However, the surpluses were relatively small even at the top of the cycle, except for 3.2% in 1948. During the long expansion of the 1960s, there were only two years of balanced budgets and one of a surplus, but there were five of much larger deficits. Since 1970, deficits have occurred every year, ranging from less than 1% of GNP in the peak years 1973 and 1979 to more than 4% in the trough years 1975 and 1982.

The peak-trough differences reflect the cyclical or "passive" component of the measured deficit, which is closely associated with changes in the relationship between personal disposable income and GNP. In recessions, taxes fall more than proportionately with income, and transfer payments rise as more people collect unemployment insurance and benefits from welfare programs and social security. Hence disposable income declines much less than GNP. In expansions, disposable income rises less than GNP because of the faster growth of taxes and the decline in transfers.

Regressions of annual changes in real aggregates suggest that each $1 rise (fall) in GNP raised (lowered) disposable income by 76 cents in 1898–1926, 95 cents in 1923–40, but only 39 cents in 1949–82 (De Long and Summers 1986a, p. 694). These are rough estimates owing to the weakness in the early data, but there are no good reasons to doubt the existence of a major change of this sort between the pre- and post–World War II periods.[18]

17. The percentage increase in federal expenditures between 1929 and 1986 was more than 5 times as large as that in state and local expenditures. Federal transfer payments, small before World War II, grew more than twice as fast as federal purchases of goods and services between 1948 and 1982.

18. Some recent results relying on neoclassical models of intertemporal substitution of labor, production, and consumption suggest that output response to temporary changes in real military

Table 3.4   **Federal Government Receipts, Expenditures, and Surplus or Deficit in Percentages of GNP at Business Cycle Peaks and Troughs: Selected Subperiods from 1869 to 1982**

	1869–1894		1895–1914		1920–1927		1929–1938		1948–1961		1969–1982	
Statistic[a]	P(6) (1)	T(6) (2)	P(6) (3)	T(6) (4)	P(3) (5)	T(3) (6)	P(2) (7)	T(2) (8)	P(4) (0)	T(4) (10)	P(4) (11)	T(4) (12)
						Receipts							
Mean	3.3	3.2	2.2	2.3	5.4	5.7	4.7	5.0	18.2	17.0	20.3	19.5
S.D.[a]	0.8	1.0	0.4	0.4	1.7	2.1	1.1	2.3	1.0	1.4	0.7	0.9
						Expenditures							
Mean	2.6	2.7	2.3	2.3	4.7	4.7	5.8	8.0	17.6	18.5	20.8	22.6
S.D.	0.8	0.7	0.6	0.3	2.0	2.4	3.8	0.0	3.0	1.6	1.5	1.7
						Surplus or Deficit (−)							
Mean	0.6	0.4	−0.0	−0.0	0.7	1.0	−1.2	−3.0	0.6	−1.4	−0.6	−3.1
S.D.	0.3	0.6	0.3	0.2	0.4	0.3	2.7	2.3	2.1	0.7	1.2	1.6

Sources: 1869–1938: U.S. Bureau of the Census, *Historical Statistics of the United States, Colonial Times to 1957*, p. 711 (data from *Annual Report of the Secretary of the Treasury*, 1958). For GNP, Balke and Gordon 1986b, pp. 781–82. 1948–82: *Economic Report of the President*, 1988, p. 341 (receipts, expenditures, and surplus or deficit) and p. 248 (GNP).

Note: P refers to business cycle peak years, T to business cycle trough years, according to the annual reference cycle chronology of the NBER. The dates refer to the first and last business cycle turns (P and T, respectively) in each of the six subperiods. Receipts, 1869–1938: excludes receipts from borrowing. Prior to 1931, total receipts; thereafter, net receipts (excluding refunds for overpayment of taxes, transfers to federal trust funds, and capital transfers to the Treasury from government corporations). Expenditures, 1869–1938: excludes debt repayment. Prior to 1931, total expenditures; thereafter, net expenditures (net of refunds paid and of capital transfers). Surplus or deficit: receipts minus expenditures. Data for 1948–82 are from the national income and product accounts. Federal expenditures include grants-in-aid to state and local governments.

[a]S.D. = standard deviation.

3.4.2   Automatic Stabilizers

The cyclical changes in tax receipts and transfer payments represent the "automatic stabilizers" that rose to prominence in the first two decades of the postwar era. The term sums up what is probably the most familiar and widely accepted of the hypotheses that attempt to explain the moderation of business cycles in this period. The personal income tax emerged as the largest source of federal revenue with a progressive rate structure, hence as the main stabilizer. The corporate income tax, though much smaller and more nearly proportional, is more elastic cyclically because corporate profits rise and fall much more than any other type of income when the economy expands and contracts. At the same time, the flow of dividend payouts to stockholders tends to be generally well maintained. Large stabilizing effects on disposable income of changes in corporate and personal taxes and unemployment benefits were found early by econometricians (Duesenberry, Eckstein, and Fromm 1960).

Insofar as households' earnings effectively limit their expenditures, the diminution of the response of disposable income to cyclical changes in GNP implies a dampening of fluctuations in consumption. Although the liquidity constraints must have declined as consumers' wealth and creditworthiness rose, it is not surprising that they still appear to affect aggregate consumption substantially (as shown in Flavin 1981). Presumably many households of modest means and uncertain prospects simply cannot save enough during expansions or borrow enough during contractions to make their outlays as smooth and independent of current incomes as envisaged by the basic versions of the permanent-income and life-cycle theories.

According to estimates from an annual macroeconomic model, the multiplier effects on real GNP of an exogenous increase in real government expenditures fell from 3.2–5.1 in 1926–40 to 1.6–2.5 (Hickman and Coen 1976, p. 194). This is based on a simulation of high-employment conditions in the prewar period: data unadjusted for the massive unemployment and excess capacity in the 1930s produce much higher prewar multipliers. The strong decline in the multipliers is attributed entirely to the built-in stabilizers of the tax-transfer system. The consumption function itself was not a source of the observed stabilization.

The active and passive components of the budget deficit are of course unobserved, and it is an important caveat that the distinction between the two is difficult to define and implement statistically. The active component is identified with the full-employment or structural surplus (deficit). That is, estimates

expenditures (viewed as truly exogenous) was stable before and after 1945 and dampened rather than multiplicative. However, work along these lines (Hall 1980b; Barro 1981b) yields estimates with very high standard errors for total government spending and does not necessarily contradict the view that built-in stabilizers improve macroeconomic performance.

of how taxes and expenditures react to macroeconomic change are used to calculate what the budget balance would be if the entire labor force was employed at the prevailing incentives to work and all existing capital was in use. Then the cyclical component is taken to equal the difference: full-employment deficit minus actual deficit. But the basic assumptions of this approach, that the trend of the economy is one of full employment and separable from business cycles, have been questioned. Measures of the economy's potential, whether in terms of output or employment, are of uncertain quality, hence so are the related fiscal variables, probably a fortiori.

Despite these problems, the fiscal decomposition calculus yields interesting uniformities. Table 3.5 is a summary of changes in the real federal budget balance and its estimated active and passive components during the cyclical contractions and expansions in real GNP, 1948–86. Negative (positive) entries in the budget columns represent shifts in the direction of deficit (surplus). The early postwar recessions were associated with shifts from surplus to deficit; the later ones with rising deficit. Opposite changes occurred during expansions, except that the deficit rose in the Korean War period and, on an exceptionally large scale, in the 1980s. Also note that the fiscal changes were generally large relative to the cyclical declines but small relative to cyclical rises in real GNP.

The changes in the passive component of the federal surplus were all negative during recessions and almost all positive during expansions.[19] These estimates suggest a strong prevalence of automatic stabilizing effects. The active component declined in all contractions except 1953–54, but generally much less than the passive component. In expansions, rises and declines in the active component nearly canceled each other out, apart from a large negative shift in the expansion that began in late 1982.[20] On the whole, then, the active component contributed much less than the passive component to the movement in the total surplus/deficit.

Estimates of this type may overstate the benefits from automatic stabilizers because they fail to pay explicit attention to the role of inflation. Government tax receipts, expenditures, and budget balances all depend not only on real economic activity but also on prices and nominal incomes. Thus, according to the Holloway (1986) estimates scaled to the size of the economy and the budget in the early 1980s, the deficit rose by $25-$30 billion when the unemployment rate increased by 1 percentage point and fell by $7-$9 billion when the inflation increased by 1 percentage point; each $100 billion increase in current-dollar GNP lowered the deficit by about $34-$38 billion. These results

19. A small negative shift occurred in the short recovery of real GNP in 1980:2–1981:3.

20. In this incomplete phase, 1982:3–1986:1, the changes in the total real federal budget balance and its active and passive components were − 136, − 152, and + 16, respectively. Excluding this phase, the mean changes for seven expansions, 1949–81, are real GNP, + 357; total balance, + 23, active, − 4; passive, + 27.

Table 3.5   **Changes in the Real Federal Budget Balance, 1948–86 (mean change in billions of 1982 dollars)**

	Real GNP	Real Federal Budget Balance		
		Total	Active	Passive
Eight contractions, 1948–82	− 59	−41	− 9	−32
Eight expansions, 1949–86	+361	+ 3	−22	+25

Sources: Quarterly data on real GNP and the federal government budget surplus are from the U.S. Department of Commerce (1986 revision). The corresponding data on the active component of the surplus are based on Federal Reserve Bank of St. Louis estimates of high-employment surplus (1948–54) and Holloway 1986 estimates of cyclically adjusted surplus (1955–86) as modified in Gordon 1987 (see pp. 589–90). For the detail underlying these averages, see Zarnowitz 1989a, table 10.

imply automatic stabilization, given a procyclical movement of inflation. But when inflation accelerates during a recession, as exemplified in 1974, there is less of a shift toward a greater deficit and therefore less of a stabilizing (or more of a destabilizing) effect.

During each of the four business recessions of 1970–82, nominal GNP typically continued to rise while real GNP declined. In these years, the progressivity of personal taxes geared to current-dollar incomes acquired the perverse effect of pushing people into higher tax brackets even though their real incomes had fallen. In 1981, large reductions in marginal tax rates were enacted and tax indexation was introduced to begin in 1985. Deficits still moved countercyclically through the recession of 1981–82 but they remained unprecedentedly high during the business expansion of 1983–87, averaging 4.6% of GNP (equal to the trough year 1982 and much higher than in any previous postwar recession).

In sum, the stabilizing effects of cyclical changes in the budget appear to have been very important in the 1950s and 1960s, as recognized at the time. They were probably significantly reduced by inflation and the "bracket creep" in the 1970s and by an accelerated, long rise in deficits and the attendant worries about the long-term consequences of this new trend in the 1980s.

3.4.3   Financial Crises, Banking Panics, and Deposit Insurance

No systematic relationship exists between the dates of speculative peaks and financial crises on the one hand and the chronology of business cycle peaks and troughs in the United States on the other (cf. lines 1–2 and 6–7 in table 3.6A). The speculative "manias" (Kindleberger 1978) usually occurred late in business expansions, but 1818, 1836, and 1920 represent apparent exceptions. They culminated in "crashes," that is, sharp declines in asset prices, abrupt curtailment of credit, and scrambles to liquidate the speculative assets to obtain money. These events followed the business cycle peaks in 1857,

Table 3.6   Selected Chronologies and Measures of Financial Crises in the United States

A. 1818–1933

	1818–19 (1)	1836–37 (2)	1856–57 (3)	1873 (4)	1884 (5)	1890 (6)	1892–93 (7)	1907 (8)	1920–21 (9)	1929 (10)	1930 (11)	1931 (12)	1933 (13)
Speculative Peaks and Financial Crises[a]													
1. Speculative peaks	8/18	11/36	End of 56	3/73	...	...	12/92	Early 1907	Summer 1920	9/29	...	...	3/33
2. Crises	11/18–6/19	9/37	8/57	9/73	...	...	5/93	10/07	Spring 1921	10/29	...	...	3/33
Stock Exchange Panics: High and Low Months[b]													
3. High	...	...	...	2/73	2/84	5/90	2/93	1/07	10/19	9/29	4/30	3/31	...
4. Low	...	...	...	11/73	12/84	12/90	8/93	11/07	8/21	11/29	12/30	12/31	...
Banking Crises and Panics[c]													
5. Date	1818+	1837+	1857+	9/73	5/84	1890	6/93+	10/07+	...	...	10/30*	3/31*	1933+
Business Cycle Expansions (E) or Contractions (C)[d]													
6. Type of phase	C	C	E	E	C	C	C	C	C	C	C	C	Trough
7. Date	1815–21	1836–38	12/54–6/57	12/70–10/73	3/82–5/85	7/90–5/91	1/93–6/94	5/07–6/08	1/20–7/21	8/29–3/33	8/29–3/33	8/29–3/33	1933
Change in Liabilities of Business Failures[e]													
8. Percentage	...	...	...	...	174	143	425	169	508	41	33	23	*f*
Change in the Common Stock Price Index[g]													
9. Percentage	...	...	...	–22	–19	–17	–26	–35	–32	–33	–40	–52	*h*
Change in the Deposit-Currency Ratio[i]													
10. Percentage	...	...	...	+1	0	–1	–15	–20	–7	–4	–10	–32	–24

B. 1957–82

	1957–58 (1)	1959–60 (2)	1966 (3)	1969–70 (4)	1973–75 (5)	1980 (6)	1981–82 (7)
Precrunch Period/Credit Crunch[k]							
1. Period	55:4–57:4	59:2–60:2	66:1–66:3	69:1–70:1	73:1–74:3	78:2–80:1	81:1–81:4

			Bear Markets[k]				
2. Period	7/56–12/57	7/59–10/60	1/66–10/66	12/68–6/70	1/73–12/74	2/80–4/80	11/80–7/82
			Financial Crises[l]				
3. Month	…	…	8/66	6/70	5/74	3/80	6–8/82
			Business Cycle Expansions (E) or Contractions (C)[d]				
4. Type of phase	C	C	E	C	C	C	C
5. Dates	8/57–4/58	4/60–2/61	2/61–12/69	12/69–11/70	11/73–3/75	1/80–7/80	7/81–11/82
			Change in Liabilities of Business Failures[e]				
6. Percentage	51	68	25	163	139	153	279
			Change in the Common Stock Price Index[g]				
7. Percentage	–19	–10	–17	–29	–43	–11	–19
			Change in the Deposit-Currency Ratio[m]				
8. Percentage	+9	+4	–2	+7	–6	+2	+5

[a]Based on the entries for the United States in Kindleberger 1978, following p. 251.

[b]Compiled from the international chronologies and data in Morgenstern 1959, pp. 546–47 and 552 (tables 139 and 140), except for the 1919–21 and 1930 dates, which are additional declines in the S&P index.

[c]Based on Friedman and Schwartz 1963, chs. 2–5 and 7, passim. A + denotes a restriction on cash payments instituted in the given year, including the nationwide banking holiday of March 1933. A * denotes the onset of a banking crisis (pp. 308–15).

[d]Based on the NBER business cycles chronology.

[e]Computed from Dun and Bradstreet data, seasonally adjusted (quarterly 1875–94, monthly 1894–1982). Low-to-high percentage change in each period, defined in years (see column headings). Based on quarterly data.

[f]Liabilities reached a peak in 1932:2, 113% above their level at the beginning of the Depression in 1929:3, then declined 72% through 1933:4.

[g]Computed from S&P common stock price index; industrials, rails, and utilities, monthly, 1871–1939 (prior to 1918, the index is converted from that of the Cowles Commission). High-to-low percentage change in each period, based on the dates in lines 3 and 4 above.

[h]Index reached the Depression trough in 3/1933, 12% below 1/1933 and 81% below the pre-Depression peak of 9/1929.

[i]Based on data in Friedman and Schwartz 1963, pp. 799–804, table B-3, col. 3. High-to-low percentage change in each period (annual February or June dates used for 1890–93, monthly dates thereafter).

[j]From Eckstein and Sinai 1986, p. 49 (one of the "Stages of Postwar Business Cycles" in table 1.3).

[k]Based on the monthly index of stock prices of S&P Corp. (500 common stocks).

[l]From Wolfson 1986, p. 133, table 11.1.

[m]Computed from ratios of currency to demand and time deposits (components of the monetary stock M2). Based on seasonally adjusted monthly data compiled by the Board of Governors of the Federal Reserve System.

1893, 1907, 1921, and 1929 by intervals of 2–5 months. In 1873, the crisis preceded the NBER peak date by a month; the 1819 and 1837 episodes fall in years of contraction.

Morgenstern (1959, pp. 541–55) presents and discusses an annual chronology of international stock exchange panics, which involved massive and rapid sales of stocks at falling prices. The high and low dates for seven Wall Street debacles on Morgenstern's list are shown in table 3.6A, lines 3 and 4, along with two additional declines, in 1920–21 and 1930. In each of these cases, the market dropped sharply (line 9). Four of the nine declines have no counterparts among the financial crises (cf. lines 1–2 and 3–4). The stock market peaks in 1873, 1890, and 1907 led business cycle downturns by 8, 2, and 4 months, respectively, those in 1893 and 1929 lagged by 1 month each, and those in 1884 and 1931 occurred in midcontraction (cf. lines 3 and 7).[21]

A number of severe business contractions were associated with banking panics, that is, great surges in bank failures, runs on banks, fears of further failures, and often widespread suspensions of convertibility of deposits into currency. For the period covered by their monetary history, M. Friedman and Schwartz (1963a, chs. 2–5 and 7) identify and discuss eight such panics, from that in 1873 to the "great" one that ended in the nationwide banking holiday in March 1933 (table 3.6A, line 5). But cumulative bank failures, panics, and restrictions on cash payments can be traced back as far as 1814 and 1818, before and during the long depression of 1815–21. They also occurred in 1837, after a downturn that followed the curbing of a monetary expansion, inflationary boom, and speculation in public lands; and in 1857, when a boom in commodities, railroad shares, and building sites broke down sharply in midyear, to be followed by a business downswing through 1858.

No financial crises occurred for one third of a century after 1933, despite the tumultuous nature of this period. Federal insurance of bank deposits, effective since the beginning of 1934, prevented bank panics by radically reducing both bank failures and the depositors' fears for the safety of their money. Most ailing banks, particularly the large ones, were reorganized or merged with sound banks to avert failure. Commercial bank suspensions averaged 635 per year in 1921–29, 2,274 in 1930–33, 54 in 1934–42, and 4 in 1943–60 (M. Friedman and Schwartz 1963a, p. 438). Total losses to depositors fell 95% between 1930–33 and 1934–42 and melted further to negligible amounts in 1943–60.

Small depositors soon learned that they no longer bore the losses of those insolvent banks for which the Federal Deposit Insurance Corporation is responsible. The costs to the government, and hence to the public as taxpayers, were very small for several decades. So it was generally accepted that the

21. Numerous studies indicate that stock price indexes are highly sensitive to changes in aggregate economic activity, prospects for profits, and credit costs and availability. They tend to lead at business cycle peaks and troughs, but not very regularly, and they have frequent "extra" movements of their own as well (Moore 1983; Fischer and Merton 1984; Zarnowitz 1987).

FDIC is the rare example of a clearly and promptly successful reform measure. Only in the 1980s did a new wave of failures of financial (mainly thrift) institutions reveal how large the costs to taxpayers of the federal deposit insurance could be. The system greatly reduced the need of bankers to be careful with other people's money and the incentives of the depositors to be watchful. Overindebtedness, undercapitalization, poor management, and fraud became widespread and serious problems. Risks that look acceptable in good times often turn out to be excessive when conditions deteriorate, and there is little that government supervision can do about it.

3.4.4 Financial Instability after the Great Depression

The depression of the 1930s produced a large reduction in private debt and a temporary rise in financial conservatism. Fears of an imminent depression were widespread and persistent in the commentaries and forecasts of the late 1940s. World War II financing left the economy awash in Treasury securities, that is, high-quality liquid assets. Gradually the liquidity ratios of banks declined as the proportion of business and consumer loans held rose at the expense of government securities; but in the 1950s and the early 1960s liquidity was still high overall and the level of debt was still relatively low.

It is this prevalence of favorable balance-sheet conditions in the private economy that is credited with the absence of financial crises in the first two decades of the postwar era (Minsky 1980; Wolfson 1986, pp. 190–92). In addition, presumably the strong growth of government and aggregate demand, output, and profits helped, as did the fact that inflation was still restrained. The financial disturbances that did occur were brief and mild.[22]

The first post-Depression financial crisis widely recognized as such occurred in 1966 and involved a high degree of disintermediation—withdrawals of funds from savings and loan associations and banks for direct investment in the money market. The flow of credit to nonfinancial corporations fell as much as 40% in the second half of the year. Monetary policy turned very tight in May and eased only in late August and September, after banks were forced to liquidate large amounts of their investments in government and municipal securities. Yet no general business contraction developed, only a slowdown in output and employment that became known as the "minirecession" of 1966–67.

22. There was a disturbance in March 1953 when the Treasury issued new 3.25%, 30-year obligations and prices of outstanding bonds with 2.5% coupons fell sharply, but the Fed eased promptly, which may have helped to keep the 1953–54 recession mild and brief (M. Friedman and Schwartz 1963a, pp. 612–14; Wojnilower 1980, pp. 281–82). Eckstein and Sinai (1986) define a "credit crunch" as a "crisis stemming from the collision of an expanding economy with a financial system that has been depleted of liquidity" and place the first such postwar episode in 1957 (pp. 49 and 61). But this was hardly a "crisis," only a short phase of tighter nonprice credit rationing. In the fall of 1959, there was a more severe credit stringency and the first disintermediation as rates on government securities rose above the regulated ceiling rates on time deposits (Wojnilower 1980, pp. 282–84). The two crunches were associated with the recessions in 1957–58 and 1960–61, both brief, the second one very mild (see table 3.6B, lines 3–5).

Each of the next four crises (or crunches) did occur during a business contraction, as shown in table 3.6B (lines 1–5). Each was triggered by a particular shock: the bankruptcy of the Penn Central Railroad in June 1970; news about the effective insolvency of the Franklin National Bank in May 1974; troubles with the First Pennsylvania Bank and crisis in the silver futures market in March 1980; the Penn Square Bank failure and the confidence crisis connected with large bank losses on loans to government security dealers, energy producers, and some less developed countries in May–August 1982.

Although the disruptive events varied, the economic and financial developments that preceded and followed them had some important common characteristics. The precrunch periods (table 3.6B, line 1) witnessed high levels of real investment and inventories but declining corporate cash flows: hence the demand for credit would increase. In addition, corporations had to borrow funds to meet payments on increasingly burdensome debts. Banks suffered growing losses on their business loans and tightened their lending, particularly to new customers. Stock prices typically fell in sympathy but with no clear pattern of relative timing (line 2). Curtailment of credit supply was associated with each of the more serious financial crises (line 3), and in each case the crunch was followed by a phase of gradual debt reduction and restoration of liquidity.

3.4.5 Business Cycles and Crises

There is no consensus on the nature of financial crises and their role in business cycles. A good reason for this, I believe, is that there is in fact much variety in the sources of these disorders and also in the policy reactions to them.

An old view recently formalized in modern terms attributes financial crises to speculative bubbles in selected asset prices driven by fads, that is, temporarily self-fulfilling mass expectations that diverge from fundamentals.[23] Here no causal role is given to changes in macroeconomic conditions, but the financial booms and busts are seen as a potential source of significant shocks to the real economy.

Other theories relate financial instability to exogenously induced monetary instability or endogenous economic fluctuations. A monetarist interpretation links banking panics to prior monetary disturbances, whose real effects they aggravate (M. Friedman and Schwartz 1963a, 1963b; Cagan 1965). Another approach, which combines elements of early and Keynesian ideas, argues that crises result from long expansions in real investment characterized by overconfidence and overaccumulation of (to a large extent, short-term) debt. Such expansions are terminated by cutbacks in credit supply, debt deflation, and debt liquidation (Minsky 1977, 1980; Sinai 1976; Eckstein and Sinai 1986). A still different emphasis is on the real effects of changes in the cost of supply-

---

23. See chapter 2, section 2.4.6, for more detail and references for some of the theories mentioned below.

ing credit that occur during financial crises (Bernanke 1981, 1983; Hamilton 1987).

Partial evidence in support of each of these theories exists, but it is typically limited to particular conditions or episodes. The bubble hypothesis is considered to be consistent with the occurrence of sharp and rapid fluctuations in the level of financial asset prices that bear no intelligible relationship to movements in the economy. To give just one classic example, the record collapse of common stock prices in October 1987 followed upon a 3-year boom that exceeded to an extraordinary degree the concurrent expansion in output and profits and eventually could not be justified by any reasonable prospects of further gains in the foreseeable future. The business expansion itself was not seriously disrupted.[24]

The monetarist hypothesis relies on the effects on aggregate demand and output of shifts in the money supply and the money multiplier. Its assumptions agree well with the regime of exogenous money changes and sticky prices, but not with that of endogenous short-run monetary adjustments and flexible prices. Under the latter, which is perhaps approximated by the gold standard, the advantage may lie with the hypotheses that stress the role of deflationary shocks and changes in the availability and cost of credit (Calomiris and Hubbard 1989).

How much a financial crisis matters depends in part on policy factors. Prior restrictive actions of monetary authorities added substantially to the pressure on banks in some instances (1966 and 1980) but not in others (1974). A prompt intervention by the central bank as the lender of last resort and provider of the needed bank reserves is the one recognized way to end the immediate crises and cut the losses. The Federal Reserve neglected this function in 1930–33 but not in the mid-1980s.

The relationship between financial crises and business contractions was never as central and close as some theories would have it and should not be overstated (see De Long and Summers 1986a, pp. 686–90). Many contractions, including some of great severity, were not associated with either massive sellouts of illiquid assets for cash assets or even just an imposition of tight rationing on bank loans (some examples are found in table 3.6). Moreover, some expansions weathered financial problems no less grave than those that occurred in recessions.[25]

24. Although some warnings of an impending global disaster appeared in the press right after the crash, most professional forecasters only reduced their positive growth forecasts for the year ahead (Zarnowitz 1987). The actual outcome was merely small dips in the more sensitive components of real consumption and investment around the end of 1987. In contrast, the previous record panic in the market, that of October 1929, occurred in what turned out to be the initial stage of the Great Depression.

25. Recent examples include the drain of uninsured deposits from the Continental Illinois National Bank in May 1984 and the run on state-insured savings banks in Ohio in March 1985. These incidents show (1) that the system remains sensitive to confidence crises and (2) that the latter can be prevented from spreading into major panics by credible insurance of deposits and, when needed, lender-of-last-resort actions of supplying additional reserves to banks.

These caveats notwithstanding, a reduction in the frequency or intensity of financial disturbances could certainly have a significant impact on the economy (points IIIB and VIA in section 3.2.1). Table 3.6 lists percentage changes in (1) liabilities of business failures, (2) the stock price index, and (3) the ratio of deposits to currency, for each of the periods covered. These are all sensitive measures of the effects of financial or banking crises, with long records.[26] Each indicates that the disorders in speculative asset and credit markets were much more severe historically than in recent times.

Thus, total-failure liabilities more than doubled in each of the six crises of 1884–1932 (counting 1929–32 as one episode) and more than quadrupled on two of these occasions (table 3.6A, line 8). The mean amplitude of these movements was 189%, or 27% per month. The postwar rises in liabilities were on average longer but smaller (table 3.6B, line 6). Here the total mean amplitude was 126%, which is about ⅔ of the figure for the financial crisis years of 1884–1932. The postwar per-month amplitude was 11%, which is about 4/10 of its historical counterpart.

The declines in stock prices averaged 31% for the panics of 1873–1931 and 21% for the bear markets of 1957–82 (for the individual measures, see table 3.6A, line 9, and 3.6B, line 7). The postwar-to-prewar average ratio total amplitudes is here again close to ⅔, that of the mean per-month amplitudes close to 4/10. In sum, the recent market contractions were longer but smaller and gentler than those associated with the historical crises or panics.

Finally, declines in the deposit-currency ratio (D/C) occurred in each of the banking crises or panics of 1890–1933 as well as in 1920–21 and 1929, whereas 1873 and 1884 witnessed at least slowdowns in the rising trend of D/C (table 3.6A, lines 5 and 10). On the other hand, D/C increased in each of the postwar credit crunches except 1966 and 1973–75 (table 3.6B, lines 1 and 8). The contrast between the historical and recent behavior of D/C is clear from the following mean-amplitude measures: 1873–1933, −11%; 1957–82, +3%. Evidently, the FDIC reform succeeded in eliminating the massive runs on the banks caused by widespread fears of losses on uninsured deposits.

---

26. The liabilities act as an early leading indicator whose countercyclical movements reflect more the changes in size than the number of business failures (Zarnowitz and Lerner 1961). They tend to rise only modestly during mild contractions but explosively during severe contractions accompanied by much financial strain.

Stock prices are an important expectational or symptomatic, rather than causal, factor in relation to aggregate economic activity, despite their presumed effects on real investment (Fischer and Merton 1984). Their variability was exceptionally high during the 1930s but not significantly different in the periods before the First and after the Second World War (Officer 1973; Schwert 1988). The argument that this indicates a lack of stabilization in real activity in the postwar era (Shapiro 1988) is not persuasive. First, it overstates the closeness of the relationship between the market and the economy. Second, it ignores the likelihood that the market has grown more sensitive to movements in cyclical and policy indicators as the volume, quality, and currency of the data all increased greatly in the last half-century.

The D/C ratio is an indicator of changes in the confidence depositors have in the safety of their "money in the bank." For banks, large drops in D/C mean losses of both deposits and reserves, transitory rises in the deposit-reserve ratio, and an urgent need to acquire liquidity.

3.5   Macroeconomic Policies and the Business Cycle

3.5.1   Fiscal Policy: Motivations, Potential, and Record

The idea that government policies should be used to offset fluctuations in aggregate private demand was inspired by attempts to combat the depressions of the interwar period.[27] Although the Employment Act of 1946 called for promotion of "maximum employment, production, and purchasing power," many years elapsed before the objective of macroeconomic stabilization gained practical acceptance in the political process. Thus, not until the first half of the 1960s was tax policy deliberately used to increase employment.

The effective use of discretionary countercyclical policies is impeded by the variability of lags with which they operate and the limitations of economic forecasting. The difficulty of predicting the timing of a downturn is such that it is usually late during or after a recession that the administration may decide to ask for a tax cut or a program of increased expenditures. Congressional action will require more time. Hence, even if the taxpayers and beneficiaries of federal expenditures responded promptly with more spending, which is uncertain, the total lag is often apt to be so long as to make the policy ineffective or even destabilizing. This would be so especially for short and mild contractions.[28]

The federal budget is the focus of conflict about the distribution of income and wealth as various interest groups attempt to influence its structure. Political pressures and perceptions of public interest interact with partisan interest and self-interest of elected and appointed officials. The net effect of this clash of different motivations and pressures must surely be to impede consensus and impair the effectiveness of fiscal action as a tool for a discretionary stabilization policy. Although the *potential* of fiscal policy to influence the economy has grown greatly in the last half-century with the vast expansion of the budget, the *ability* of the government to use this power for the public good has not. This is attributable partly to deficient knowledge, partly to conflicting interests, and partly to the increasing complexity of the government and its interactions with the private economy.

The historical record is consistent with this argument. The label "too much too late" often applies to changes in federal expenditures, notably to the public works programs that operated with long lags, peaking in midexpansions (Zarnowitz and Moore 1982). The cessation of Korean hostilities in 1953 was followed by an unnecessarily abrupt and sharp cutback in defense spending that aggravated the 1953–54 recession. The budgetary policy of 1959–60 was excessively tight because of mistimed fears of inflation and high interest rates,

27. On the early advocacy of countercyclical monetary policy, see Keynes 1923; on the shift to fiscal stimulation, Keynes 1936; on the contemporaneous evolution of "classical" economists' views on unemployment and policies, Friedman 1967; Mayer 1988; Haberler 1988.
28. Moves to raise tax rates or to reduce or discontinue expenditures on social programs or public works, being politically unpopular, would likely involve even longer delays.

plus overoptimistic forecasts of real growth. In retrospect, it is tempting to relate this to the weakness and shortness of the recovery of 1958–60 (see Lewis 1962). Federal expenditures on goods and services fell in real terms between mid-1968 and mid-1973, particularly during fiscal 1970. This may have contributed to the recession of 1970 (Gordon 1980, p. 145), although it did not appear to retard the expansion of 1971–73.

Tax policies fare better in postmortem appraisals, but only partially.[29] The prompt raising of taxes in mid-1950 to finance the Korean War was a commendable move. In contrast, during the Vietnam War taxes were increased too late and inefficiently. The surcharge on the personal income tax, passed by Congress in 1968, was temporary and recognized as such; hence its main effect was to reduce saving rather than spending, in broad agreement with the forward-looking theories of consumption. The expiration of the surcharge in 1970 also affected primarily the saving ratio.

An activist "new economics" strategy was pursued in the 1960s to counter the "fiscal drag" attributed to overly high levels of the high employment surplus. New tax incentives to stimulate investment were legislated in 1962; large reductions in the personal income and excise taxes in 1964 and 1965. The result was that the initially sluggish business expansion was strengthened and probably prolonged but also that the active component of real federal surplus fell strongly to remain negative ever since. After 1965, the federal budget was in deficit each year but one (1969), that is, during expansion and contraction alike. Had fiscal policies been guided by considerations of either macroeconomic stabilization or growth, they could hardly have produced this result.[30]

The tax cut of March 1975 was enacted into law at the very end of the 1973–75 recession. It was followed by further reductions in 1975–76, but the March rebate was explicitly temporary and probably again not very effective. Altogether, repeated errors of fiscal policy added much to the woes of the 1970s (Blinder 1979 and 1981).

3.5.2   Readings of the Federal Reserve Performance

Historical assessments of monetary policy often implicitly proceed from the premise that changes in monetary aggregates strongly influence real activity in the short run and are controllable by the Federal Reserve. So the Fed is blamed for causing cyclical instability by *allowing* recurrent accelerations and

29. Some tax reductions were fortuitously well-timed. This applies to the tax cut that was enacted (over a presidential veto) in April 1948 and to the expiration of the Korean War taxes in January 1954.

30. Critics often blame the "Keynesian consensus" for helping to legitimize deficit spending intellectually, which is certainly not without some historical justification (Mayer 1988). But Keynes favored deficits during depressions, not during prosperity. Also, the deficits persisted under different administrations, legislatures, and ideologies. To a large extent, the explanation is simply that fiscal actions were taken in response to immediate political concerns, which notably include vocal demands for lower taxes or currently needed government services.

decelerations in the trend of the money stock. Drops in the money growth rates are viewed as leading to major slowdowns, as in 1966, or recessions, as in 1957, 1960, 1970, and 1980–81; sharp rises, to "overheated" expansions, as in 1967–68 and 1972–73 (see, e.g., Gordon 1980). Larger and more persistent errors of monetary policy are held accountable for the greater cyclical instability of the past (Friedman and Schwartz 1963a, 1963b).

Monetary policy is clearly more focused on short-term stabilization than fiscal policy is, for several reasons. The governing bodies of the Federal Reserve System being relatively small and the influence of the chairperson often strong, their decisions can be reached much more quickly than those of the Congress. The Fed is presumably less subject to diverse political pressures. Conflicts between bureaucratic self-interest and public interest are probably less frequent and sharp here than in the fiscal area (Willett 1988). Yet, great obstacles to effective monetary control remain as a result of deficient knowledge, uncertainty, and indecisiveness in the face of costly alternatives.

There is much that is simply not well understood about the role of money—most important, to what extent it is active rather than passive. Even economists who believe money matters a great deal disagree on how best to define it and agree that monetary policy operates with long and variable lags. There are always alternative forecasts with nonnegligible probabilities of occurrence, and alternative courses of policy, each of which imposes different costs on different classes of people. Hence, monetary policymakers will often differ on when to do what, seek more evidence and consensus, delay hard decisions, or proceed piecemeal. They may be *unable* to "take charge" in time, so their actions may be too weak to prevail or have too slow and hence unintended effects. Such outcomes have received less attention than they deserve.[31]

Another possibility is that the Federal Reserve is *unwilling* to assert active control over money. If its main concern is with the stability of interest rates and if the cyclical shifts in income and money demand are caused by fluctuations in the quantities of goods and services people want to buy, then money supply will simply accommodate these shifts.[32] In fact, these conditions were probably often closely approximated in recent times. Interest rates were pegged low during the war-dominated 1940s and early 1950s, after which the Fed used money market indicators in operating procedures that let money supply behave procyclically and were consistently attacked by monetarist critics. In the 1970s, the Fed set monetary aggregate targets as well as a federal funds target but observed mainly the latter. After October 1979, nonborrowed re-

31. The early monetarists' emphasis on the interrelated problems of uncertainty, ignorance, and lags led them only to reject activist policies, not to question whether, under discretionary policies, monetary changes have dominant short-term effects on economic activity (see, e.g., Laidler 1981, esp. p. 19).

32. In terms of the still widely used macroeconomic model of Hicks 1937, this is the case where the demand for goods fluctuates more than the demand for money (the IS curve is more unstable than the LM curve) and the Federal Reserve pursues the policy of targeting interest rates by open-market operations in government securities (Poole 1970).

serves were used for three years as the main target, and interest rates began to swing widely, but the fluctuations in monetary growth also increased greatly. In effect, much of the time, changes in the credit extended by banks determined the changes in the money supply.

Figure 3.3 shows that monetary growth rates have been on average larger and more volatile in the second than in the first half of the post-1945 era, but also that the relative changes in M2 were much more variable yet before World War I and, especially, in the interwar period. Was it the ineptness of the Federal Reserve System that caused the apparent rise in monetary instability in the early 1920s and then, a fortiori, in the 1930s? And was it the improved Fed policy that caused the apparent post–World War II stabilization? The notion that the monetary authorities performed first so poorly and then so much better almost continuously over such long periods of time seems rather farfetched. It seems easier to explain the record by recognizing that monetary change is in large measure endogenous (see sec. 3.5.3). But this does not by any means imply that Federal Reserve actions were unimportant. In particular, the fact that no significant periods of negative monetary growth rates occurred after 1948–49 is very probably related to successful preventive actions by the Fed. By the same token, the Fed must also bear the primary responsibility for the inflationary upward tilt in money growth during the last 30 years. Changes in the monetary regime can have strong effects on the economy's structure and responsiveness (see sec. 3.5.4).

3.5.3   Money and Economic Activity: Some Short-Run Dynamics

For the effects of money on income to dominate the reverse effects, the demand function for money must be reasonably stable over time and the supply function must include at least one critical factor independent of the determinants of demand. It is the central bank that is seen as providing that factor through its control over the monetary base.

Evidence available through 1973 favored a simple and stable money demand function of the form

$$(1)\qquad M_t - P_t = a_0 + a_1 Q_t - a_2 i_t + a_3(M_{t-1} - P_{t-1}) + u_t^d,$$

where all variables are in logs and M, P, Q, and i denote the money stock, the price level, output, and the interest rate, respectively.[33] However, after 1974 equation (1) went astray by systematically overpredicting demand deposits. This prompted an intensive but on the whole frustrating search for improved specifications (Judd and Scadding 1982.) After 1981 the apparent shortfall of

---

33. This is a short-run formulation in which portfolio adjustment costs are assumed to cause a given lag pattern in the reaction of real balances to changes in either Q or i (Goldfeld 1973). Somewhat different dynamic specifications are obtained when the gradual adjustment is assumed to occur instead in nominal balances (Goldfeld 1976), the price level (Laidler 1980), or both (Gordon 1984b). Q is usually represented by real GNP, P by the implicit price deflator, and M by M1, that is, currency plus checkable deposits.

the demand for M1 was replaced by an excess. The velocity ratio, GNP/M1, instead of following a long upward trend, started drifting downward. The probable sources of the observed instability of money demand are diverse and time specific: financial deregulation and innovations, changes in the Fed's targets, and the shift from rising to declining inflation.[34]

Money supply can be viewed as the product of the money multiplier, μ (which depends on the reserve-deposit, R/D, ratios chosen by banks and on the C/D ratios chosen by households and firms), and the base, B (which depends mainly on Federal Reserve dynamic and defensive operations). The theory predicts that money supply is positively related to i, the level of market interest rates (apart from any influence of i on the conduct of monetary policy).[35]

Attempts to estimate separately money demand and money supply functions encounter grave problems of simultaneity and identification (Cooley and LeRoy 1981). Suppose the Fed follows an interest-rate stabilization strategy with the target value i_t^*. Then

$$(2) \qquad\qquad i_t - i_t^* = \alpha B_t + \varepsilon_t^i,$$

where $\alpha > 0$. If, as suggested by the earlier discussion,

$$(3) \qquad\qquad \mu_t = \beta i_t + \varepsilon_t^m,$$

then

$$(4) \qquad\qquad M_t = \mu_t + B_t = b_1 i_t - b_2 i_t^* + v_t ,$$

where $b_1 = \beta + 1/\alpha$, $b_2 = 1/\alpha$, and $v_t = \varepsilon_t^i - \varepsilon_t^m$. Although i_t^* does not appear in equation (1), one cannot reasonably assume it to be independent of the unobserved determinants of money demand. If, say, money demand increases, exerting an upward pressure on i_t, then according to equation (2) the Fed will either accommodate the shift or revise i_t^* or use some balanced combination of the two moves. As this indicates, correlations are likely to exist between u_t^d and B_t, i_t and i_t^*, and u_t^d and v_t.

Monetary policy is more complicated than equation (2) implies: although often accommodative, it has at times attempted to be countercyclical. To approximate the latter case, allow for partial responses to B_t to output, Q_t, and

---

34. See Gordon 1984b for a comprehensive and discerning analysis of the dynamics of money demand. Our derivations in the text below resemble some of his. Gordon's empirical work proceeds by successive approximations that yield statistically significant improvements but at a considerable loss of simplicity.

35. A rise in i creates incentives for the banks to increase their borrowing from the Fed and to decrease their excess reserves; it may also cause the public to reduce their holdings of time deposits relative to checkable deposits. In practice, however, most of these effects (which would raise either B or μ and hence M) are likely to be weak most of the time because they rely on changes in interest differentials (i relative to the discount rate or deposit rates) that will be small and short lived, at least without certain working regulatory restraints. Also, excess reserves are apt to be small and mostly random, except in depressions following financial crises.

inflation, $P_t - P_{t-1}$, both with negative signs. Incorporating equation (3) as well, the result is a money supply function of the following type:

$$(5) \qquad M_t = c_0 + c_1 i_t - c_2 Q_t - c_3 (P_t - P_{t-1}) + u_t^s.$$

This equation resembles equation (1) closely. In fact, the two include the same variables, except for lags that probably belong in both functions.[36] A reasonable inference is that shifts in the demand for money are apt to be related to shifts in the policy reaction functions, or "monetary regimes," so that the two are difficult to separate (Gordon 1984b).

The most probable explanation of the historical correlation of short-term changes in money and real activity is a composite one. First, much of the time both money and output respond to the common influence of whatever forces drive the prevailing movement of the economy. For example, an investment boom is financed by credit expansion. Second, changes in output and income may affect monetary growth directly. The volume of inside money can adjust to the level of real activity, and it is inside money in the form of various deposits that constitutes the bulk of the total stock of money. The composition of monetary aggregates changes endogenously, and the stability of money demand is not assured. Third, as noted before, the Fed may target interest rates; if it aims at stabilizing the dollar under a fixed exchange rate or a "dirty float" system, the results will be similar. All these cases require an accommodative central-bank policy, and they are in practice very difficult to distinguish from each other.

Fourth, at least some of the time monetary authorities take the initiative in altering the course of money targets and the economy for better or worse. These actions may be episodic but they tend to be of great practical and theoretical interest. Here, unlike in the other cases, it is the aggregate activity that adjusts to the monetary change instead of the other way around.

3.5.4 Monetary Regime Changes

Monetary institutions and rules of conduct evolve historically and at times undergo major episodic shifts that result in different monetary regimes. There are related changes in the organization of the foreign-exchange market, banking and investment finance, and government fiscal operations. If the way economic policies are carried out is altered, and a new monetary or fiscal or exchange regime is established, the informed public will adjust its expectations and behavior accordingly over time (Lucas 1976). This raises the question of what relationship can be found between such regime shifts and the differences between business cycles in the prewar, interwar, and postwar periods.

---

36. The distinction between real and nominal balances is not very helpful in dealing with short-run changes, given the sluggishness of price reactions in countries with relatively low and not very volatile inflation. Under these conditions, too, expected inflation will not be an important additional factor in the money demand function.

Before World War I

From 1879 to 1914, the United States was on the gold standard: the dollar was convertible into gold at a fixed legal ratio, and the money stock and price level had to be consistent with an approximate balance in international payments maintained without abnormally large gold movements. So money was basically endogenous. Central banks influenced the international capital markets through interest-rate manipulations to keep the exchange rates fixed. Their role as monetary authorities was thus limited and so was the role of the U.S. Treasury. Variations in gold supply and demand (discoveries and changes in technology of production and use) resulted in changing trends in money supply and prices.

The rate of growth in the stock of M2 dropped below zero on five occasions between 1875 and 1918, each time during a severe business contraction (fig. 3.3A). Milder recessions were marked by smaller declines in positive rates of money growth. The data leave no doubt about the predominantly procyclical behavior of this variable (see also table 3.1, line 9, and table 3.2, line 10). But this pattern of movement in the rate of change in M2 can be attributed to procyclical fluctuations in the currency-money (C/M) ratio and the R/D ratio, not to the behavior of the monetary base (B), which under the gold standard was on the whole acyclical (see Cagan 1965, chs. 2 and 3). Changes in B (the "high-powered" money, which in this period included the public's holdings of gold coin or certificates, Treasury currency, and national bank notes) reflected mainly the changes in gold stock dominated by long trends. According to the vector autoregression (VAR) equations for rates of change in output (q), money (m_2), and base (b) in 1886–1914, q was influenced significantly by lagged values by m_2 but not b (see chapter 12).

The business cycles of the four decades before World War I were relatively frequent and characterized by several serious depressions and financial panics; they were much discussed by contemporaries with reference to the instability of bank credit rather than money supply, of commodity and asset prices as much as of output. Business expansions were seen as phases of rising demand for both credit (as investment rose) and currency (as wages and consumer spending rose). They would be curtailed by shortages of bank reserves and high real costs or low availability of credit. These ideas (elements or variants of which are found, e.g., in Sprague 1910; Hawtrey 1913; and Mitchell 1913) can help explain the cyclical behavior of the C/M (or C/D) and R/D ratios.

The wholesale price index tended to move procyclically around a downward trend in 1875–96 and around an upward trend in 1896–1914. Over the period as a whole, positive and negative rates of change in the index nearly offset each other, according to the average amplitudes of both quarterly and cyclical measures (see table 3.1, line 5, and table 3.2, line 7). Commodity prices generally had a high degree of cyclical flexibility, and deflations interacted with restrictions on credit supply in contributing to major business downturns.[37]

Short-term interest rates moved up in business expansions and down in contractions, with lags at turning points, but the quarterly changes in them were very volatile and almost symmetrically distributed between rises and declines (table 3.1, line 13, and table 3.2, line 13; fig. 3.4A). As there was no persistent inflation in this period, there was no reason to expect such an inflation to arise, and none did.

Between the World Wars

The interwar period saw a great weakening of the international gold standard and the link between U.S. money and international trade. In 1933 the dollar ceased to be freely convertible into gold, which was eliminated from circulation. The Federal Reserve System began operations in 1914 but came into its own only in the 1920s (during both world wars the financing needs of the Treasury were dominant). The two decades after 1919 include a period of relatively high economic and monetary stability in 1922–29, but they also provide two examples of major errors of monetary policy followed by severe business contractions: the sharp rises in the discount rates in January and June 1920 and the doubling of legal reserve requirements in 1936–37. The huge decline in the money stock during the depression of the early 1930s was driven mainly by the increases in the C/D and R/D ratios caused by the banking crises; the monetary base actually increased.[38]

On the whole, the fluctuations in monetary growth rates were clearly largest in the interwar period and smallest in the postwar period, and much the same applies to the fluctuations in the rates of change in output and prices (cf. figs. 3.1, 3.2, and 3.3). In contrast, changes in interest rates were not particularly large in 1919–33, and they then became very small and mostly negative, even during the cyclical expansion of 1933–37. They were on average smaller in the interwar period than in the earlier and later eras (fig. 3.4; tables 3.1 and 3.2, lines 13–15).

The interwar estimates in chapter 12 of this volume suggest that q was significantly affected by lagged growth rates in base and monetary growth but not by interest rates. This is unlike the estimates for both 1886–1914 and 1949–82, which show strong net effects of interest rates on output.

37. A very special episode is the long business contraction of 1873–79, which witnessed a persistent and sharp decline in prices but apparently, much of the time, rising output (see figs. 3.1A and 3.2A; and Friedman and Schwartz 1963a, chart 3 and text in ch. 2). This was the end of the "greenback period," characterized by political controversy over the resumption of specie payments, rather mild and vacillating movements in monetary aggregates and great financial instability (the 1873 crisis, rises in the R/D and C/D ratios, and bank failures).

38. Between the business cycle peak in August 1929 and the banking crisis in October 1930, the base declined 4.7% while M2 slipped 2.6%; between October 1930 and the business cycle trough in March 1933, the base rose 23.4% while M2 dropped 35.2% (data from Friedman and Schwartz 1963a, table A-1, col. 8, pp. 712–13, and table B-3, col. 1, pp. 803–4). To be sure, the Federal Reserve policy could and should have been more expansionist.

After World War II

The adherence to a program of strict support of government bond prices reduced the Federal Reserve to the passive role of an adjunct to the Treasury Department in the 1940s and until the March 1951 Accord: a time of war-induced expansion and inflation, a brief war-end contraction, and the last deflationary recession in 1948–49. The United States became the dominant economic power and the trading world was effectively on a dollar standard before and after the main European currencies returned to convertibility in 1958. The 1950s and 1960s saw great economic recoveries in Western Europe and Japan, and a remarkably high and stable real growth in the United States by historical standards, despite the shocks of the Korean and Vietnam wars and three recessions between 1953 and 1961. The stock of money grew at stable and moderate rates, which however began to show a rising trend in the 1960s. After the Korean inflation and disinflation, prices generally displayed stability, rising very little before 1960 and still slowly for several years thereafter. Interest rates resumed their cyclical pattern but remained low until the later 1960s, when inflationary expectations began to be clearly reflected in the data (see figs. 3.1–3.4).

In the face of past setbacks and expected difficulties of monetary policy-making, the Federal Reserve authorities, not surprisingly, showed much uncertainty and caution in the early postwar period, paying most attention to interest and credit changes and often yielding to the growing fiscal activism. The public availability of frequent monetary data, though helpful, may have also had some intimidating effects (see Friedman and Schwartz 1963a, pp. 637–38). It would be incorrect to credit the successes of this period to monetary activism, which was largely absent. But the caution and passivity seem to have worked well much of the time under the highly favorable conditions then prevailing, which merits recognition.

The environment deteriorated rapidly in the late 1960s and 1970s for several familiar reasons: the decline in U.S. comparative international advantage and the dollar, the breakdown of the Bretton Woods system, the experimentation with price and wage controls, the supply shocks, the reduced productivity growth, and rising financial instability. But the main factor underlying the problems of this period was the rising trend and volatility of inflation, which resulted in persistent inflationary expectations and heightened uncertainty about the general economic outlook. For this, much of the blame was naturally laid on the purportedly countercyclical and oscillating but mostly too expansionary monetary policy actions. The turn to a policy of reducing money growth in 1979–82 contributed to the business contractions of 1980–82 but also helped to produce the major disinflation of the first half of the 1980s.

The test statistics for the VAR model in chapter 12 indicate that in 1949–82 output (q) was strongly influenced by interest rates as well as by a leading index reflecting mainly real investment and related production and employment decisions. The direct effects of changes in monetary aggregates were significant but comparatively weak.

3.5.5   Gains in Confidence

There are good reasons to believe that the generally favorable trend of events between the late 1940s and the late 1960s has gradually produced a rise in public optimism that economic growth and prosperity can be maintained and recessions can be kept mild and short. In the spirit of self-fulfilling expectations, such a rise in optimism would be apt to encourage productive activity and enterprise.

Thus, the Standard and Poor's index of common stock prices moved strongly upward throughout this period, and its cyclical declines were short and relatively mild despite its high sensitivity.[39] The Survey Research Center index of consumer sentiment, available since 1952, averaged as high as 91 (1966:1 = 100) in its first 10 years and 96 in 1962–68, even though it too fell significantly in each recession and in the minirecession of 1966, leading at the business cycle turns. This index depends inversely on unemployment and inflation, positively on stock prices and its own lagged value (Lovell 1975).

By the same measures, investor and consumer confidence suffered serious setbacks during the years 1969–80. The S&P index had no trend but early and long recession-bound declines in 1969–70 and 1973–74 (also a lengthy extra one in 1977). The SRC index, similarly, had long and large contractions in 1969–70 and 1972–75; moreover, its expansions in this period were relatively weak and short (1971–72, 1975–77). Presumably, the public's perceptions and expectations were depressed because of a succession of bad economic, financial, and energy news. Inflation was not only rising but also becoming more volatile, which increases uncertainty (see chapter 17). Interest rates had a steepening upward trend and large fluctuations around it, in contrast to their earlier restraint.

However, considering its length and severity, the 1981–82 recession was associated with a relatively mild decline in stock prices and a remarkably short and small decline in consumer sentiment. The bull market came back to stay in the 1980s, surviving even the debacle of August–October 1987. The consumer sentiment index recovered quickly in 1982–83 and remained very high during 1984–88. There is little doubt about the reasons for the new rise in optimistic attitudes and expectations: disinflation and downward movements in interest rates and unemployment. Despite the depressant effects from news of high budget and trade deficits, and a rising debt, another wave of pessimism arose only after a long period of sluggish growth and recession in 1989–91.

---

39. The downturns in the index anticipated each of the four recessions, and the upturns anticipated each of the four recoveries of 1948–61, plus two episodes of slowdown-speedup sequences beginning in 1962 and 1966.

In sum, persistent changes in the economy's performance can have important effects on the confidence of consumers, investors, and business executives. The process of recognition and reaction to the changes involves lags of uncertain but probably substantial length. All this seems entirely consistent with rational behavior, without requiring an implausibly high degree of foresight.

According to the hypothesis V in section 3.2.1, if recessions are *expected* to be shorter and milder, they *will* be so because people will see less reason to curtail or postpone spending; hence consumption will slow less and investment will decline less. Baily (1978) argues that private behavior has indeed changed in this direction during the 1950s and 1960s as people learned to *believe* that monetary and fiscal policies are capable of keeping the economy close to the full-employment targets. He shows the employment reactions to changes in output and inventory reactions to changes in final sales were weaker in 1962–71 than in 1948–61. But these results are also consistent with the broader hypothesis stated above. Private economic behavior may have changed in response to the general climate of greater stability rather than because of confidence in the efficacy of government policies. When the climate deteriorated in the 1970s and public interest shifted to the seemingly unyielding problem of inflation, private confidence and supportive behavior seem to have decreased markedly. The rising budget deficits have probably undermined the belief in flexible countercyclical uses of fiscal policy. The popular credibility of monetary policy was at least temporarily restored in the 1980s, after what was widely viewed as the success of the Federal Reserve in reducing inflation and managing the long business expansion.

3.6 Conclusions

1. A review of data and results reported in the literature reveals great diversity of cyclical experience both in more distant and in recent U.S. economic history. The postwar period as a whole, however, has been one of distinctly reduced instability when compared with earlier times.

2. Significant net stabilizing effects can be attributed to shifts in the structure of employment to less cyclical industries, which produce mainly services, and, up to a point, to the increased size of the acyclical government sector.

3. The fiscal automatic stabilizers played an important positive role, mainly in the 1950s and 1960s, before the rise in inflation and the consequent distortions.

4. The smoother functioning of the financial system helped reduce overall instability. Most of the credit here goes to federal deposit insurance and prevention of general banking panics.

5. Discretionary fiscal policies rose to prominence in the course of the postwar era, but their record is very mixed. It is generally more favorable before

the mid-1960s than afterward, and also more favorable for tax policies than expenditure policies.

6. Quarterly rates of change in money supply were more volatile in 1875–1914 and, particularly, in 1919–39 than in 1946–83, although monetary growth increased and became more variable in the second half of the postwar period. These differences parallel those in output variability. The active and passive elements in monetary (as well as fiscal) policy are both important and intermingled, which makes it difficult to assess their effects. On balance, however, monetary policy probably made a modest contribution to the greater stability of real economic activity in the last 40 years.

7. Economic agents have gradually realized that business recessions have become shorter and milder, which has strengthened their confidence and induced behavior that promotes more stable growth. But expectations change with the trend of events; for example, the rise in inflation and unemployment during the 1970s had the opposite effects.

4   Cyclical Aspects of Cost and Price Movements

4.1   Background and Concepts

4.1.1   Introduction

As argued in chapter 3, there is sufficient evidence to establish that business contractions were on the whole shorter and milder after 1948 than before World Wars I and II. A comparison of standard historical estimates and recent data also suggests that the general price changes were more volatile and more cyclical in the earlier periods.[1] Inflation has prevailed since 1950, and generally procyclical movements in the rate of inflation have replaced the earlier procyclical fluctuations in the price level. Thus, the age of *reduced* cyclical instability was also an age of *increased* downward rigidity of prices (and, it will be shown, money wages). This presents a problem because the classical and still prevailing view in the profession is that stickier wages and prices make the real economy *more* unstable.

In large part, the voluminous and rapidly expanding literature on "microfoundations" of macroeconomics consists of attempts to rationalize why wages do not adjust promptly and fully to changes in the demand for labor, and prices to changes in the demand for output. But great differences in the degree of price and wage flexibility (or stickiness) are found in historical studies and cross-sectional and cross-country comparisons (see, e.g., Sachs 1979,

---

1. This is strongly supported by the available long wholesale price series (Zarnowitz and Moore 1986, sec. 9.10; chapter 3, fig. 3.2 and table 3.1, in this volume). Consumer prices have always been much less variable, and here the change in behavior is subject to doubt. The standard estimates for the GNP deflator may have greatly overstated the historical price volatility by using only wholesale and not consumer prices (Balke and Gordon 1989, pp. 71–75). However, even consumer prices responded with significant declines to some of the business contractions of the past (see, e.g., Zarnowitz and Moore 1986, fig. 1), whereas after 1949 neither producer nor consumer price levels did.

1980; Branson and Rotemberg 1980; Gordon 1982a, 1983; Bruno and Sachs 1985; P. Andersen 1989). Apparently, business cycles coexist with a broad range of behavior in labor and product markets, though they may influence, and be influenced by, changes in that behavior. It is these interactions that should ultimately be of primary interest to students of macroeconomic performance and policy, not a postulated dichotomy of flexprice and fixprice models.

For good reasons, however, little is known as yet about what causes what here. Macroeconomics deals with a limited number of aggregate variables and potential sources of overall growth and instability; it finds it exceedingly difficult to deal with an evolving economy and heterogeneity of market firms and participants. Yet it is useful to ask how the main contemporary hypotheses bearing on business cycles and broadly defined price flexibility are related to each other. I will attempt to answer this question by selectively reviewing work in this area and assessing its major implications and problems in the light of statistical and historical evidence.

4.1.2 Hypotheses of Wage and Price Inertia

For a long time Keynesian macroeconomics focused on the inflexibility of nominal wages rather than prices as the main link between fluctuations in demand and output. But if it were typically the case that prices fall or rise less in business contractions while money wages continue to rise faster than prices, then real wages should tend to be countercyclical. This is simply not consistent with the evidence, as reviewed below.

Further, labor compensation is the largest component of both total income and cost of output, so high rigidity of wages would induce high rigidity of prices, which would at some point be inconsistent with the degree of efficiency in resource allocation expected of the market economy. The premise that nominal wages are unresponsive to cyclical demand fluctuations must be examined rather than maintained. It would seem more plausible to expect that money wage rates will on the average rise faster than the value of the marginal product of labor in periods of high employment and will rise more slowly or even decline in periods of low employment. The tendency for real wage changes to reflect productivity changes would then manifest itself mainly in the long run.

To be sure, a competitive firm will not knowingly pay real product wages in excess of the employee's marginal product, except transitionally and when it expects to recoup its short-term loss in the longer run. Similarly, the worker will not knowingly accept less than his or her marginal product, except under analogous circumstances. So any discrepancies between wages and productivity must be due to any or all of the following: (1) lack of knowledge by the firm, the worker, or both of what the relevant marginal products currently are; (2) uncertainty about the economic conditions facing the firm and the workers;

and (3) departures from competition, mainly in the direction of bargaining between large oligopolistic companies and large labor unions.

Conditions (1) and (2) are probably of long standing. However, productivity is particularly difficult to assess in various service industries, such as finance, insurance, trade, health, and education, and also in professions and sales, clerical, technical, and managerial occupations. Many of these areas have gained greatly in relative importance in recent times. Some large shifts of type (3) certainly occurred as well, but so did important countermovements in the direction of more global competition.

Research confirms the common observation that few labor markets are of the competitive auction type, where nominal wage adjustments clear the market continuously. Explicit contracts negotiated by unions and corporations determine wages of organized labor over staggered periods of 1–3 years. Implicit contracts whose durations run over years fix wages and salaries of career job holders. Here current compensation is an installment payment on a long-term employment relationship. It is often in the best interest of both employer and employee to maintain such an association on multivariate terms that are not very responsive to changes in general economic conditions considered transitory.[2]

Contractual arrangements between buyer and seller also exist in product markets, at least for limited time periods, and they tend to be associated with low frequency and small average size of price changes. But some prices remain unchanged over long time periods even where no such contracts exist (e.g., newstand prices of magazines; see Cecchetti 1986). There is evidence that product prices in many industries, particularly those that are more concentrated, change only infrequently.[3]

All this explains why the emphasis on wage rigidity gave way to more attention to price rigidity in recent years. The shift suggests the general notion that the main reason why workers lose jobs in recessions is not that real wages rise but that prices do not fall even though sales do. Also, it recognizes that, up to a point, prices can decline despite temporarily sticky wages when allowed by some combination of gains in productivity and reductions in nonlabor costs and profit margins.

4.1.3 Real and Nominal Rigidities

In the business cycle context, it is particularly important to ask how changes in the aggregate demand for real output (Q) influence the levels of

2. For a critical review of the writings on implicit contracts, see Rosen 1985. On the "stylized facts" and theories of the labor market, see Parsons 1986; Stiglitz 1986; and Kniesner and Goldsmith 1987.

3. See Carlton 1986. Other comprehensive studies of price adjustment and surveys of the large and growing literature include R. J. Gordon 1981, 1983; Blanchard 1987a and 1987b; Rotemberg 1987; Ball, Mankiw, and Romer 1988.

nominal prices and wages (P, W). If P does not react promptly or fully to a change in Q, at any given level of W, there is some real price rigidity. Analogously, if W does not react promptly or fully to a change in Q, at any P, there is some real wage rigidity. These partial adjustments involve changes in price-over-wage markups or real wages. They are complemented by interactions between changes in P and W, given Q. If P does not react promptly or fully to a change in W, there is some nominal price rigidity; in the opposite case, there is some nominal wage rigidity.

One way to formalize this double dichotomy and isolate the parameters that embody each of these rigidities, as implemented in Blanchard 1987a, is to estimate and analyze equations of the type

$$(1) \qquad p = \mu w + \alpha q,$$

and

$$(2) \qquad w = \eta p + \beta q.$$

Here q might be represented by output in equation (1) and by employment in equation (2). Each variable (p, w, and q) involves a lag polynomial applied to the logarithms of levels, or alternatively to log differences (e.g., $p = a(L)P$ or $p = a'(L)DP$). The smaller the values of μ and η, the greater the nominal price and wage rigidities, and the smaller the values of α and β, the greater the real price and wage rigidities. Unless $\mu = 1$, p does not adjust fully to changes in w, and the same applies, mutatis mutandis, to η, α, and β. Depending on the time frame and type of analysis, the adjustments can differ with respect to both how complete (or partial) and how fast (or slow) they are.[4]

To close this simple model, it is necessary to make q a function of some exogenous factors. Keynes attributed business cycles to shifts in *real* aggregate demand, due mainly to instability of investment. In contrast, contemporary models that bear the broad Keynesian label relate the cycles to shifts in *nominal* aggregate demand, due mainly to instability of money supply. Given this orientation, q is often taken to be proportional to real balances $(m - p)$, where m is the log of the nominal money stock. Realistically, however, q should be thought of as depending on both monetary factors and nonmonetary ones (e.g., shifts in government spending and taxes, exports).

There are many good reasons for some degree of inertia in the response of relative wages and prices to changes in real demand. Some but not all of these explanations require major deviations from the basic competitive model. On the other hand, the problem of nominal rigidities simply does not arise under perfect competition. Suppose a sudden tightening of monetary policy causes

---

4. Blanchard (1987a) constrains the estimates so that p and w react to each other fully in the long run, but this restriction may not be appropriate (see comment by Sims on his paper).

a fall in aggregate demand, while no change occurs in technology or preferences. Under the classical competitive paradigm, since the equilibrium structure of prices remains unaltered, all nominal prices must decline proportionately. It is only in this way that the previous equilibrium levels of real money balances and real economic activity can be restored (or, rather, maintained: the process is executed promptly and smoothly by continuous price changes directed from open auction markets at atomistic agents).

4.2 Why Are Wages Not More Responsive to Declines in Demand?

4.2.1 Relative Wages and Efficiency Wages

For Keynes (1936, chs. 2 and 19), the idea that marks a key departure from "classical economics" is that labor is an aggregate consisting of groups that, whether or not formally organized, have as their main objective the protection of their *relative* real wages. Each group watches the others it compares itself with and bargains to obtain a possible advantage but at least not to fall behind. Thus, in a depression any group will resist an attempt to reduce its money wage. Although a uniform across-the-board wage cut may then be acceptable to labor, there is no practical way to engineer it in a diversified economy in which there is some dispersion of market power. The stickiness of relative earnings thus translates into a stickiness of nominal wage rates in general. Moreover, such partial reductions in these rates as come about are apt to do more harm than good, because they contribute to the spread of deflationary expectations and inhibit spending. In contrast, reflationary policies, by raising the price level and so lowering real wages overall, can provide the needed adjustments without disturbing the wage structure in ways to which labor objects.

If relative wages are what matters to groups of workers, then the net productivity of labor should be a positive function of these wages. In a sufficiently strong form, this relationship implies that a decline of real wages below a certain norm is associated with higher, not lower, unit labor costs. Here the old emphasis on the dependence of wages on productivity is replaced by a new emphasis on the reverse causation, the dependence of productivity on wages. Stiglitz (1986, pp. 182–92; 1987) provides the model for this analysis; for criticisms and references, see Katz 1986 and Murphy and Topel 1989.

Suppose that as the real wage of the ith labor group, ω_i, increases up to ω_i^*, the productivity of the group, λ_i, rises more than proportionately, while a further increase in ω_i is associated with less than proportionate gains in λ_i. Hence the cost per effective unit of labor service is U-shaped with a minimum at ω_i^*. The firm that employs ith labor will pay the "efficiency wage" ω_i^* with the intention of minimizing unit labor costs; it will not extend employment to people who offer their services at a lower wage, because it believes that this would reduce productivity and raise costs. The unemployed cannot underbid the "insiders" if they are viewed as sufficiently less productive or likely to raise the effective costs of labor to the firm.

Efficiency wages could be paid for any or all of several reasons, but problems arise for each of these variants

1. Let the perceived relative wage determine each employee's effort and indeed willingness to work. This may be viewed as an individualistic version of Keynes's notion that any labor group is averse to a reduction in its nominal wage, which is inevitably a relative wage cut. A self-validating convention of this kind could in principle generate a pervasive downward stickiness of wages in a decentralized market economy. But historically money wages fell in depressions, and wage concessions are not uncommon even during shorter and less severe contractions (as in the early 1980s). Considerations of fairness may well be very important, but economic self-interest should be stronger still. High unemployment will increase the value of holding a job and the incentive to work hard. Should prices fall more than wages, as they did in the early 1930s, these motivations will be further enhanced, and the role of relative wages could well be greatly diminished.

2. In the modern versions of the theory, it is not labor's resistance to lower wages that is stressed but rather management's strategy to give workers incentives in the form of relatively high earnings and benefits. The idea is that this is required to attract and keep high-quality employees and have them work at high levels of effort. Well-paid workers are less prone to search, quit, or join a union and exercise more bargaining power collectively. As a result, the firm will benefit from lower labor turnover costs. But the high-wage option is not the only one that is available here, and it need not be optimal; for example, offers of greater training and promotion opportunities or greater job security may be more attractive to some firms and workers.

3. The efficiency wages ω_i^* are set by firms with some (perhaps only informationally based and short-run) monopsony or oligopsony powers in the labor markets. It is not clear how important empirically such conditions are. In the resulting interior solution, small deviations of wages from long-term equilibrium cause only second-order losses to the firm, so that nonadjustment of wages to minor shocks is "near-rational" (Akerlof and Yellen 1985). Here the effect of efficiency wages is to decrease the fluctuations in wages and increase those in employment.

4. Shirking and negligence can cause large damages to firms, particularly where many workers perform sensitive tasks using complex machinery and equipment (so can fraud and stealing, which may be more diffuse). The detection of such misconduct is taken to be costly in the so-called primary (high-wage) sector of the labor market, but not in the secondary (low-wage) sector. Hence, the primary jobs pay a premium above the market-clearing wage for secondary jobs, so as to deter shirking, even if the workers are all alike in

ability (Shapiro and Stiglitz 1984; Bulow and Summers 1986). Critics point out that superior market-clearing solutions for the shirking problem exist in the form of explicit or implicit contracts that involve performance bonds posted by employees.[5]

4.2.2 Implications for Unemployment and Some Evidence

To rationalize involuntary unemployment in the sense of excess supply of labor, a theory must rule out the existence of a sufficiently attractive and expandable flexible-wage sector. In the model with dual labor markets, workers in the secondary market have menial jobs with low prospects and high turnover. This acts as a reputational barrier against the employment of these workers in the primary market. The unemployment in this scenario is mainly frictional and long term, due to the high incidence of quits and separations in the secondary sector and to the job rationing and queues in the primary sector. Static models of this type provide no explanation of cyclical unemployment. They generally produce an overall tendency for real wages to be sticky or even constant (Solow 1979).

Efficiency wages, like the market-clearing wages they exceed, are unobservable; hence there is, understandably, no direct knowledge of their empirical importance. It is also difficult to define the primary and secondary sectors, since industries and occupations generally overlap both. The level of wages paid perhaps constitutes the main measurable distinction between the two sectors (Doeringer and Piore 1971; Lang and Leonard 1987).

Consequently, the evidence bearing on these theories is indirect; it is also limited and mixed. The observed relatively large and stable interindustry wage differentials may provide support for the efficient wage models (as argued in Krueger and Summers 1987, 1988) or they may be due to unobserved quality differences across workers (Murphy and Topel 1987, 1989).[6] Some labor market statistics appear to contradict the hypothesis that hiring from a queue of long-waiting jobless searchers is particularly important in the primary as distinct from the secondary labor market.[7] Also, it is commonly observed that people look for better jobs while employed and do not deem it

5. Direct and complete bonding is apparently rare, perhaps because of limited ability or willingness to borrow, mistrust between the parties, etc., but there are practical alternatives observed in long-term employment relationships. Workers may in effect buy responsible high-paying jobs gradually, by initially accepting low wages for simple, easily monitored tasks and then proving themselves and advancing along the job ladders within the firm. Participation in costs of specific training programs and nonvested pension plans can also be interpreted as forms of bonding. On the role of seniority wages to solve the incentive problem, see Lazear 1981.

6. It is agreed that heterogeneity of labor, differentials compensating for nonwage aspects of the industry, and institutional factors such as unionization account for a substantial part of the wage structure, but the unexplained remainder appears to be large.

7 According to data for men who changed employers and industry or occupation between any successive years in 1977–83, 23.7% of new hires in high-wage industries and 29.5% in low-wage industries experienced unemployment spells (averaging 3.0 and 3.6 weeks, respectively) between jobs (see Murphy and Topel 1988, table 2 and text).

necessary to quit in order to search more efficiently. It is unsatisfactory for a theory to rely on assuming the opposite.

Shifts in the aggregate demand for output and in the derived demand for labor presumably have less effect on the efficiency wage than on the completely flexible market-clearing wage. This suggests that employment and unemployment should be more demand sensitive, and probably more cyclical, in the primary than in the secondary sector. Other considerations point in the same direction. Primary workers have large amounts of human capital, much of it firm specific; their spells of joblessness are likely to be infrequent, concentrated in bad times, but also long because they are motivated and financially able to search extensively. Secondary workers have less human capital and are less attached to their jobs, which have relatively low pay and promise; hence they are unemployed much more often in both good and bad times, but generally over shorter periods because their incentives and opportunities to search are limited.

It is difficult to test for such dichotomies because well-matched and sufficiently detailed time-series data on unemployment and wages are lacking. What is readily established is that both unemployment and average hourly earnings tend to be relatively high in some major industries (durable manufactures, mining, construction, transportation, and public utilities) and low in others (finance, insurance, and real estate; trade; and services). In industries where unemployment is on average higher, it also tends to fluctuate more between business cycle turns and be more volatile. Where earnings are on average higher, they also tend to be more variable over time. Measures of cyclicality and volatility of unemployment numbers and rates are positively correlated with both the average levels and standard deviations of earnings by industry.[8]

These findings are broadly consistent with the notion that the high-wage sectors should display high cyclical sensitivity, but they also point to several problems and ambiguities. Should the positive relationship between the level and variability of average hourly earnings be confirmed by a detailed analysis, this would be difficult to reconcile with the hypothesis that higher wages are the sticky efficiency wages. The high-wage industries may be associated with more cyclical unemployment for reasons other than those advanced by the sticky-wage theory, including the reverse-causation argument that higher wages are paid in part because of the greater instability of employment. Moreover, there are some well-known factors that help explain the interindustry

---

8. For data on unemployment and average hourly earnings in private nonagricultural industries, 1964–82 (from U.S. Bureau of Labor Statistics, various bulletins), the correlations between the mean levels and standard deviations are .94 for earnings and .82 for the unemployment rates. The correlations across these measures between earnings and unemployment rates and also between cyclical amplitudes of unemployment and the average levels or variability of earnings have a range of .62–.75. For the underlying detailed measures, see Zarnowitz 1989a, table 2.

differences in sensitivity to business cycles, notably the durability and storability of products.

4.2.3   The Role of Long-Term Labor Contracts

Explicit employment arrangements or contracts cover a large proportion of workers who stay on the job, particularly those organized in labor unions. Presumably much more widespread, however, are implicit contracts that benefit the firm and its work force and are therefore, as long as they are so perceived, complied with by both, despite the absence of express, legally enforceable agreements. For example, firms routinely extend employment and grant raises from year to year, especially to employees on salaries. There is evidence that long-tenure career jobs are indeed very important in the U.S. labor markets today; for example, as shown in Hall 1982, about 40% of workers aged 30 and above are likely to hold jobs that will last twenty years or more. Current compensation for work of this type may be viewed as an installment payment on a long-term employer-employee association, and as such its influence on current employment is apt to be small.

If workers are generally more risk averse than businessmen and have less access to capital markets, they may in effect wish to buy from firms insurance against income decreases in bad times in return for smaller increases in good times (Baily 1974; Azariadis 1975). In the same implicit bargain, the firm is conceded much latitude in varying the volume of employment over time (not surprisingly, given the normal functions and requirements of business and the realization that fluctuations in the demand for the firm's output must be accepted as exogenous). Both the firm and labor gain if hours and effort rise (decline) when there is more (less) work to be done. Convincing arguments attribute considerable efficiency at the microlevel to contracts that include a variety of risk-sharing arrangements and such devices as temporary layoffs, overtime pay, and cost-of-living adjustments (see in particular Hall 1980b).

But even optimal contracts are constrained by inevitable gaps and inaccuracies of information and cannot allow for all contingencies that are hidden from foresight in the world of uncertainty. Thus, the early implicit contract models noted above can account for sticky real wages but not cyclical unemployment. It is not clear why workers should be so strongly concerned about wage fluctuations but not about the risk of job losses during a recession. The contract theories face various problems related to the observability and verifiability of the events covered, the complexity and enforcement of the contracts, moral hazard, and adverse selection. In particular, the more complicated models with asymmetric information depend on special assumptions on how firms and workers differ with respect to what they know and what their attitudes to risk are (Grossman and Hart 1983). Some of the more questionable premises are that *generally* firms are risk averse, workers are uninformed about the state of the economy, and contracts are effectively explicit but of short duration.

Coordination or externality problems are inherent in systems with imperfect information and incomplete markets. The reason is simple: any change determined by decentralized decisions of parties to a contract or transaction concerns a relative or real price, since it is made given other prices. Thus nominal rigidities can arise from real rigidities, no matter what degree of microefficiency in real terms the implicit contracting may achieve.

It might seem that institutional means or contractual contingency provisions are readily available to reduce the nominal stickiness, at least in wages, by indexation. But informational lags and errors do not allow a complete wage indexation in practice. Moreover, to the extent that indexation does produce an approximately fixed real wage, it aggravates the effects of real shocks even as it reduces those of nominal shocks, so that, for example, the economy may suffer less from demand disturbances but more from supply disturbances (Gray 1976; Fischer 1977c). Also, if indexation is believed to reduce government's interest in pursuing consistent counterinflationary policies, the case for it is at least politically weakened (Fischer and Summers 1989).[9]

I conclude that the theory of optimal contracting cannot explain cyclical fluctuations in employment and unemployment. Indeed logically, the more efficient the contracts are in foreseeing or providing for contingencies, the less room they should leave for persistent departures from full employment. But inefficient labor contracts that incorporate informational asymmetries imply underemployment or work sharing rather than more layoffs than hires during business contractions. Simpler models with relative wage contracting (Taylor 1983; Summers 1988) may prove more helpful on nominal rigidities and unemployment but their consistency with rational expectations and optimizing behavior continues to be questioned.

4.2.4   A Summary of Wage Hypotheses

Table 4.1 provides for the reader's convenience a synopsis of the attempts to explain why wages are or appear to be sticky. After the preceding discussion, only two additional points remain to be made.

The first hypothesis is that real wage movements clear the labor market but are small because the supply of labor is highly elastic. This is consistent with the simple competitive model and assumed as a part of the recent theoretical framework of "real business cycles." It is contradicted by most tests of intertemporal substitution of leisure see (chapter 2, sec. 2.4.3) and generally by microestimates of labor supply elasticities (Pencavel 1986). Some reported results based on aggregate data show large elasticities (Kennan 1988) but they depend critically on prior assumptions and are very imprecise (Taylor 1988).[10]

---

9. General indexation extending to prices as well as wages presents still other difficult problems such as the choice of a commodity standard or numeraire in proposed monetary reforms (Blanchard 1987b).

10. Long time series reflecting the decrease in hours also indicate an inelastic or slightly negatively sloped supply, but postwar time series show substantially higher elasticities, especially for countries other than the United States (see Greenwald and Stiglitz 1988, pp. 223–29). In part,

Table 4.1   An Outline of Hypotheses about the Apparent Stickiness of Wages

Hypothesis	Critique
1. Supply of labor is highly elastic to transitory changes in the current and expected real return on work effort.	Tests do not support the idea that labor supply responds sensitively to current and expected changes in real wages and real interest rates. Evidence from panel data suggests that total labor supply elasticities are small.
2. Long-term implicit labor contracts ensure flexibility of employment for firms and stable real wages for workers.	Whether motivated by workers' risk aversion or informational asymmetries, the contract theory contributes to an explanation of sticky wages but not unemployment. Efficiency of the contracts is questioned.
3. Unions gain for their members wages above the competitive equilibrium, which results in unemployment among nonmembers.	The ability of unions to obtain and keep high wages depends on the degree of control they have over the entry into the work force. The hypothesis attracts more interest in Europe than in the United States because of the greater power of European unions, or "insiders."
4. Each labor group (unionized or not) protects, and in particular resists reductions in, its relative wage. This induces stickiness in wages generally.	A wage cut for any individual group may be resented as unfair and depress worker morale. Coordinated wage cuts across a decentralied economy are not practicable. A possible reason for nominal as well as real wage inertia. Criticized mainly for lack of roots in optimizing behavior.
5. Efficiency wages above the competitive equilibrium are paid by firms to attract and keep high-quality, high-effort workers and so minimize unit labor costs.	There are good reasons for productivity to rise with real wages, but the validity of the assumed form of this relation is uncertain. The links to relative wages and menu cost of wage change have some implications for cyclical unemployment, but most versions and elements of this hypothesis have none.

Note: See text for more detail and references.

Bargaining between a labor union with a fixed number of members and a sectoral monopolist can produce a sticky negotiated real wage in the presence of fluctuations in demand and employment, assuming that the unemployed members have an alternative source of income and that there is little variation over the cycle in the wage elasticity of labor demand. Let this situation prevail in the primary sector, while the competitive secondary sector offers much poorer jobs at a much lower flexible wage. Then unemployment will consist of those on temporary layoffs from the primary sector and those who wait for jobs in that sector. A fall in demand during a recession will widen the intersectoral wage differential. The models that give these results are worked out in McDonald and Solow 1981, 1985. Hypothesis 3 in table 4.1 states the relationship between unions and relative wage rigidity in general terms.

---

these differences are reconciled by the finding that the supply of labor for secondary workers is very elastic.

4.3   Why Prices Are Sticky; or, How Markets Clear

4.3.1   Competition and Costs

A combination of highly elastic supply and fluctuating demand produces a condition of relative price stability in equilibrium, which could be mistaken for a disequilibrium phenomenon of real price rigidity. This apparently simple and attractive theoretical possibility deserves to be considered.

The competitive firm's short-run supply function is horizontal at the minimum of its average variable cost (the threshold of profitable production) but elsewhere equals the firm's marginal cost (MC) curve, which slopes upward because of diminishing returns. The firm has strong incentives to operate as close to the capacity output (where MC rises steeply) as the price will allow. The supply curve for a competitive industry as a whole will tend to be still steeper because an expansion of industry output is apt to raise input prices and so shift upward the MC curves of all firms concerned. This argues against the hypothesis suggested.

However, it is not only the short-run supply responses that matter here. Since business cycles consist of movements measured in quarters and years, during which all factors of production eventually become variable, the analysis should include longer-run responses as well, where the supply elasticities will tend to be greater. Moreover, even over short periods of time firms will see some price changes as more "permanent" than others, and may differ in these assessments, so that what is being observed represents a changing mix of short-run and longer adjustments. On simple assumptions, notably of open access to given technology, the intermediate-run industry supply curves would probably be relatively flat in the middle output region and increasingly upward sloping at higher rates of production, which drive up MC.

It follows that the simple microeconomics of a competitive industry is not necessarily inconsistent with the story that high supply elasticities prevail for medium time horizons relevant for the analysis of business cycles. What is inconsistent with this hypothesis is the notion that sufficiently large demand-induced fluctuations in output can coexist with stable prices. When high levels of production are reached in a business expansion, overtime hours of work at extra pay rates become common and prices of many inputs rise sharply; at low output rates in a business contraction, the average workweek is cut and some input prices fall. These prices largely originate in competitive markets. They include the spot market prices of raw industrial materials known as "sensitive" and also wages of some categories of unskilled and unorganized workers.

The microeconomic argument in this section abstracts from changes in money and the general price level. It cannot explain why comprehensive price indexes seem to have responded less to decreases than to increases in demand during the recent predominantly inflationary period, in contrast to a more symmetric cyclical behavior in earlier times. The issue of the source of any upward or downward price inertia is still open (Cagan 1979; Okun 1981). Indeed, studies of micro data sets on transaction prices find no support so far for the existence of either bias (Stigler and Kindahl 1970; Carlton 1986).[11] What they do find, however, is that many industrial product prices remain unchanged over long time intervals that must overlap business cycle phases. Thus the evidence in Carlton 1986, 1987 shows average durations of price rigidity exceeding one year in most cases and two or even three years in some.

4.3.2 Nonprice Market Clearing

Evidence of *long* periods of rigidity in prices of numerous diverse products cannot be reconciled with a competitive model in which price always adjusts promptly to equate supply to demand. It is simply improbable that both demand and supply schedules do not move or that their shifts persistently offset each other so as to leave the price unchanged. Some common observations are also inconsistent with the model of market clearing through price change only: at times there is unintended inventory accumulation of goods held for sale, and at times there are queues for goods that are in short supply (so either sellers or buyers are unsatisfied). These considerations lead naturally to the question of what mechanisms may help clear markets in addition to price, and how they are related to the competitive model.

I suggested a long time ago that the endogenously determined delivery period variable (k) is an important equilibrating device (Zarnowitz 1962). Prompter delivery enhances the value of the product and so raises the quantity demanded (ordered) per unit of time; it also raises the average cost of the quantity supplied. This implies, as a condition for profit maximization by the firm, that

$$(3) \qquad dP - dc = -[(D_k/D_p) - C_k]dk = 0,$$

where $D_p = \partial D/\partial P < 0$, $D_k = \partial D/\partial k < 0$, and $C_k = \partial C/\partial k < 0$ based on the demand function $q^d = D(P, k)$ and the cost function $c = C(q^s, k)$. For any quantity demanded, say q_1^d, there is an indifference curve in the price/delivery period (P, k) space; and for the same quantity supplied, q_1^s, there is an indifference curve in the cost/delivery period (c, k) space. Joint optimization of P and k requires that the slopes of these loci be equal, so that

$$(4) \qquad dP/dk = dc/dk \qquad \text{and} \qquad C_k = -(D_k/D_p)$$

in conformity to equation (3).

In this simple model, as long as there is some substitutability between P

---

11. Surprisingly little price-theoretic work seems to have been done in this area. It includes some studies which show that the asymmetry can result from the pricing behavior of profit-maximizing firms with some market power, nondecreasing MC functions, and nonincreasing demand elasticity (Kuran 1983, 1986) or from differential effects of inventory and backlog adjustments (see secs. 4.3.2 and 4.3.3 below).

and k, the fluctuations of demand will in general be met partly by changes in price and partly by changes in delivery period, inducing a positive correlation between the two variables. Any responsiveness of k should make P more stable over time, but a variety of outcomes is possible, reflecting the characteristics of the product and the state of the market.

Even a physically identical commodity differs economically to the user depending on the date of its availability. An impatient buyer will pay a little more for an earlier purchase but a sufficiently large differential over the expected or stated future price will cause postponement or placement of an order for future delivery. If cost or demand changes today affect both present and future prices, intertemporal substitution in the use of producer and consumer goods may increase the equilibrating role of delivery lags and reduce that of current prices. Thus when demand is elastic with respect to P but inelastic with respect to k, more of the market clearing will be accomplished by variations over time in k and less by variations in P.

Some industries take or solicit orders in advance of production and hold large backlogs of unfilled orders and small or no inventories of finished goods. Other industries make goods and hold them in finished-goods inventories for sale. Products that are customized and particularly costly or risky to store tend to be made to order. There is much evidence that production to order is very important, especially in manufacturing, and that it is associated with large fluctuations in backlog-shipment ratios (a measure of k) and relatively small variability of prices (Zarnowitz 1973). Large procyclical movements are also observed in the index of "vendor performance" based on data on delivery lags reported by purchasing managers.

Market-determined changes in delivery periods and unfilled orders need not be indicative of noncompetitive behavior causing excess rigidities in P. Instead, their principal explanation, consistent with a high degree of competition, may be simply that when buyers choose or consent to wait, smaller or slower price fluctuations are needed to clear the markets (Zarnowitz 1973; Carlton 1979, 1983, 1987). Demand is often more likely to be sensitive to changes in P than to changes in k.[12]

Where inventories of finished goods are held, they absorb the impact of temporary shifts in demand at least partly, thereby permitting avoidance, reduction, or deferral of price changes. However, the production-smoothing (buffer) role of inventories seems to be in the main limited to short unexpected demand shocks. For inventory investment to act as a strong buffer against longer fluctuations, it would have to be countercyclical, but instead it is on the whole procyclical and destabilizing as demonstrated, for instance, by the fact that GNP varies more over the cycle than final sales.

12. However, there is some evidence that unfilled orders tend to be larger relative to shipments in highly concentrated industries than in less concentrated industries (Zarnowitz 1962). This suggests to Scherer (1980, pp. 195–96) that variations in order backlogs are particularly important in oligopolistic industries.

4.3.3   Some Implications of Market Power

The conventional analysis of imperfect or monopolistic competition is limited to price-quantity solutions for given cost functions: the firm faces a downward-sloping demand curve and sets P above MC according to the optimal markup $P/MC = \eta/(1 + \eta)$, where $\eta =$ elasticity of demand. This is a static theory that assumes full knowledge of demand and cost functions that firms in dynamic environments do not possess. Reliably estimating the current and future values of η is difficult and may not be feasible when demand is subject to unpredictable fluctuations or when uncertainty obscures the effects of the firm's own price adjustments on the behavior of other market participants. If the firm knows that $P > MC$, it will always wish to sell more at the current price but it may be reluctant to reduce price lest this should fail to stimulate sales sufficiently and so result in lower profits.[13]

Suppose the firm sees the uncertainty associated with price variations as greater than the uncertainty associated with output variations, which are to some degree reduced by changes in delivery lags and order backlogs or by changes in inventories. Then its preferred strategy would be to use price adjustments sparingly and conservatively and to rely more on quantity adjustments in response to fluctuations in demand that may prove transitory.[14]

Several recent studies (Hall 1986, 1988; Shapiro 1987; Domowitz, Hubbard, and Petersen 1988) present estimates of markup ratios P/MC that, for many diverse industries, substantially exceed the competitive benchmark of unity. Hall argues that spatial separation and product differentiation result in a wide dispersion of market power but not of extra profit opportunities. This is so because high setup, advertising, and fixed costs create much persistent extra capacity, absorb excess profits, and discourage new entry. In this view, firms operate most of the time above their (large) minimum efficient scales of production but below the maximum efficient scales, that is, where their MC curves are perhaps just slightly rising or nearly horizontal. So the observed stickiness of prices is seen as reflecting the hypothesized stability of costs under a regime of monopolistic competition. If both MC and η were (approximately) constant, firms would have little to gain from active pricing policies.

---

13. For a firm with some market power, linear demand and cost functions, and a homogeneous product, there will be more downward than upward price rigidity if the cost of shortages and stockouts exceeds the cost of inventory holding, and vice versa (see Amihud and Mendelson 1983; also Reagan 1982). This is an interesting notion but it remains to be seen how it would fare under less restrictive assumptions and with recognition of variable delivery periods and the distinction between made-to-stock and made-to-order goods. Thus, since backlogs always exist in production to order, they are not just an excess-demand phenomenon, and so their treatment as "negative inventories" is much too limited and potentially misleading.

14. For a development of this argument, see Zarnowitz 1962, p. 390; and 1973, pp. 301–5. For a recent formulation of the hypothesis that managers tend to be more uncertain about the consequences of their pricing and wage decisions than about those of their output and employment decisions, see Greenwald and Stiglitz 1989 (where inventory changes are considered but variable delivery lags are not). Even when quantity adjustments are otherwise costlier than price adjustments, the uncertainty differential may cause firms to prefer the former to the latter.

Data for manufacturing indicate that plant capacities are indeed designed to meet peak demands and are often much underutilized in cyclical slowdowns and recessions, even though the minimum efficient scales of operation are typically not so large. Early postwar and interwar estimates generally showed short-run MC to be declining or constant and long-run average cost functions to be falling and hence suggestive of economies of scale. But these regressions, being based to a large extent on observations of low levels of output, do not rule out rising costs in higher operational ranges, except probably for public utilities and railroads—industries long regulated as "natural monopolies."[15] Such microstudies can be informative mainly about long-run tendencies in the selected industries. About general dynamics of the behavior of costs and related variables, there is more to be learned from work on cyclical movements of monthly and quarterly aggregate time series.

4.3.4 Cyclical Changes in Cost, Productivity, and Profits

Several stylized facts established by studies in business cycles can be interpreted to favor the idea that MC is rising. In addition to the already noted cyclical sensitivity of the average workweek in manufacturing, there are the short but persistent lags of employment and the longer lags of inventories and unfilled orders, which suggest the presence of important costs of adjustment in labor input and production, respectively.

Indexes compiled and analyzed by Hultgren (1960, 1965) show that labor cost per unit of output and total unit cost in manufacturing, 1947–61, often declined in the late stages of contractions and regularly declined during recoveries and then rose as expansions matured and at times also rose well after a downturn.[16] This observed pattern is in a general sense consistent with the theory of U-shaped curves, since it implies that unit costs fall in the lower range of output and rise in the higher range, at least near the capacity levels. But it suggests additional dynamic elements in that the costs appear to depend on the rates of change as well as levels of production.

A decline in unit labor cost takes place when output per hour of work rises faster than the average hourly compensation; a rise occurs when the opposite happens. The former condition tends to prevail toward the end of a recession and notably during a recovery and high expansion; the latter condition tends to prevail in slowdowns and downswings. Labor productivity is basically procyclical and leading; its largest gains come at cyclical upturns and in recoveries when real growth rates are usually very high. On the other hand, wages

15. The verdict of a comprehensive survey paper by Walters (1963) was that this literature fails to convincingly refute the classical hypothesis of U-shaped cost curves; for an opposite view, see Simon 1979. Critics also charged that the techniques used had a bias toward linearity, which was disputed by the authors (Johnston 1960). Outside the regulated industries, the results are in fact rather meager and mixed. However, one should also note the findings from estimated production functions, which tend to provide broader support for constant returns to scale (Jorgenson 1974).

16. For railroads, a much longer record studied by Hultgren showed a stronger tendency for cost to be inversely related to output (in units of passenger and freight traffic).

often increase most in late stages of expansion and near cyclical downturns when labor markets become tight and output growth slackens. It is then that unit labor costs (ULC) begin to increase faster than the level of prices of industrial products. Total unit costs (UC) usually rise even more because of the developing shortages of raw and intermediate materials—inputs whose prices are known as particularly sensitive. As a result, markups on ULC and UC (P/ULC and P/UC), tend to turn down even while sales and output continue to grow. Profit margins, as inferred from aggregate accounting data, turn down with a similar early timing.

Figure 4.1 shows the average movements of ULC, the P/ULC ratio, output per hour, and the corporate profit margin before and during the recessions and recoveries of 1948–80.[17] Rates of change rather than levels are used for labor productivity and unit costs so as to eliminate the large but uneven upward trends in these variables. The resulting patterns demonstrate the strong inverse relationship between the cyclical change in average productivity of labor and the concurrent change in average costs of labor (see the left-hand half of the chart). The markup and profit margin variables are approximately stationary and here level data are used. The two series show nearly parallel cyclical movements most of the time, but the relative amplitudes are greater for the corporate profit margin than for the P/ULC ratio. Profitability responds directly to changes in productivity and inversely to changes in cost.

For the pre-1948 period, comparable data are not available but there is a strong presumption that the underlying relationships have a long history. In 1913 Mitchell predicted the sequence of changes in these variables without the benefit of data (see chapter 2, sec. 2.3.6 above). Hultgren (1950, 1960) documented with monthly series for 1932–58 that labor productivity led and ULC lagged in their procyclical movements. Consistent evidence is presented by Bernanke and Powell (1986) for 1923–29 and 1954–82 and by Klein and Moore (1985) for several major industrial countries.[18] An old and widely accepted explanation of why employment varies less than output is that firms hoard labor in sluggish times to preserve their human capital investments and because capacity and input adjustments take time and speeding them up is costly, particularly under uncertainty about demand. This hypothesis can also account for the tendency of output per hour to lead at business cycle turns.

The support that Mitchell's theory gets from the data, including the

17. The data are quarterly, mostly for the nonfarm business sector, from the U.S. Bureau of Labor Statistics. The BLS series, published since 1972, begin in 1948; they cover costs and profits per unit of output and also comparable prices received.

The series used in figure 4.1 contain 132 observations each. The mean duration of the six recessions in 1948–80 was 11 months, the distance between the vertical peak and trough lines in the graphs. For each recession-recovery sequence, each of the series was indexed to its level in the quarter of the business cycle peak and expressed in terms of two-quarter smoothed changes (following Moore and Cullity 1983, pp. 255–61 and fig. 16–5). The graphs in figure 4.1 represent averages of the resulting patterns. Measures of intercycle dispersion and inspection of the individual patterns indicate that these averages are fairly representative.

18. See also Fair 1969 and previous references in this section and chapter 2, sec. 2.3.6.

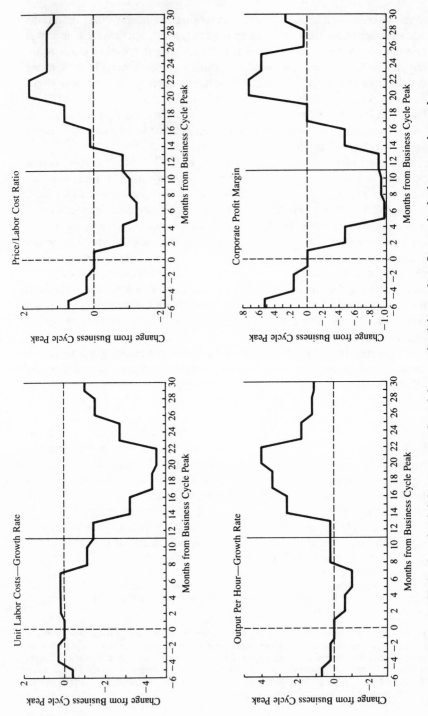

Fig. 4.1 Patterns of behavior of unit labor cost, markup, labor productivity, and profit margin during recession and recovery, 1948–80

evidence for the prewar periods, when prices were relatively flexible, suggests that cyclical variations in costs, margins, and profits deserve much more attention than they have received in recent literature and that the stickiness of prices perhaps deserves much less. It should also be promising to reexamine Mitchell's approach in light of current ideas (and vice versa). [19]

4.3.5 A Summary of Price Hypotheses

The attempts to explain price inertia are summarized in table 4.2. Two of the five listed hypotheses require some additional discussion. I then close this section with a summary of a recent appraisal of the theories of price stickiness by business executives.

In oligopoly (hypothesis point 3 in the table), the few sellers know that their pricing decisions are interdependent and act accordingly. Suppose each firm expects its rivals to match any price cut it would make but not a price hike, which means that each firm faces a demand curve that is kinked at the current price. This describes a situation in which the price would not change in response to moderate shifts in cost; it does not explain what the price is or how it was determined. Much of the time oligopolists may simply play it safe and settle for the implicit collusive outcome of the game. For example, it pays them to raise their prices simultaneously as soon as they recognize shared increases in cost or demand. Undercutting the collusive price can be individually rewarding, but the risks of a price war are large (see Green and Porter 1984; Porter 1985). If each firm is reluctant to move first on the price front, long periods of price rigidity are likely; if price leadership emerges, intermittent industry-wide price changes would be the expected result. The argument, then, reduces to the already familiar theme that commitments to maintain relative prices produce nominal rigidities as firms refrain from initiating price changes. Empirically, the macroeconomic importance of the oligopoly case is at least uncertain (for an attempt at a generalization, see Woglom 1982).

A hypothesis that gained more attention recently relies on monopolistic competition where firms produce differentiated products and have some market power in price setting. Firms have profit functions that are flat at the top,

---

19. Mitchell viewed business cycles as sustained by self-generated stresses and imbalances (as did other prominent scholars of his era), whereas most contemporary writers assume that macroeconomic fluctuations are caused by exogenous shocks. Thus, Mitchell would agree with the modern "real business cycle" theorists that changes in productivity are procyclical and very important, but not that they are exogenous, generalized shocks to technology that on their own "drive" business cycles. He would clearly disagree with the treatment of the average price-cost margin as close to constant (which is often found in recent models of wage and price rigidities). Recent regression estimates of industry P/MC markups find mostly procyclical behavior but yield mixed results (Domowitz, Hubbard, and Petersen 1986, 1988; Morrison 1988). This suggests that different market structures can produce different cyclical behavior, which may well be true (e.g., if η fluctuated procyclically, P/MC should be countercyclical—but there is no evidence that either this condition or its opposite prevails). However, these studies use short annual series, which cannot reveal leads and lags of less than a year's duration and may not be adequate to determine the cyclicality of the markups.

Table 4.2   An Outline of Hypotheses about the Apparent Stickiness of Prices

Hypothesis	Critique
1. Marginal cost (MC) tends to be flat and stable over time; hence so is the competitive price P = MC.	Competitive auction markets cleared only by price are costly to organize and maintain. Most markets deviate from this model. MC should be rising for the firm in competitive equilibrium.
2. $P >$ MC by a stable margin because of monopolistic competition with flat and stable MC and constant elasticity of demand.	MC should be rising at least near capacity (where overtime payments are common) and is unlikely to be constant over the large range of output covered by business cycles (BC). Average cost and profit margins vary during BCs, in part in offsetting patterns.
3. Sticky oligopoly prices reflect kinked demand curves and/or desire to avoid costly price warfare.	Oligopoly prices may be sticky in response to *moderate* cost and demand changes, given the uncertainty about rivals' reactions, but large changes can induce the few sellers to alter price simultaneously.
4. Nonprice market-clearing mechanisms reduce the frequency of price changes under various types of market structure.	Procyclical movements in delivery lags demonstrably help absorb changes in demand, but the price-smoothing role of changes in inventory is not clear. Factors that may favor nonprice instruments: intertemporal substitution, product heterogeneity, advertising, search costs, and steady customer relations.
5. Each price change has a fixed menu cost, which is not worth incurring because the loss of profit from nonadjustment of price is second-order small.	The direct menu costs are probably very small and unlikely to prevent price adjustments in response to *large* changes in demand. The less elastic MC and the more elastic demand, the larger are the costs required to be effective. Results are uncertain if prices are initially not in equilibrium. Indirect costs, such as customer goodwill, may matter more.

Note: See text for more detail and references.

with zero derivatives with respect to price at the optimum; hence small deviations from the equilibrium price involve only small (second-order) reductions in realized profits. A firm that believes its price is set about right in relative terms has little incentive to change it, even when the "menu cost" of doing so is small. Yet the aggregate result of the individually rational decisions to keep prices unchanged is price-level stickiness, which can have large (first-order) macroeconomic costs. Suppose reduced monetary growth lowers aggregate demand: if all firms reduced their prices even slightly, they would collectively benefit from an increase in real money balances and a decrease in the level of interest rates.[20]

20. On the other hand, a small increase in monetary growth that would leave prices unchanged (because of menu costs) would have a positive welfare effect in this model by raising output. The reason for this is that equilibrium output in this imperfectly competitive economy is suboptimal compared with the competitive model because of an aggregate demand externality (Blanchard and Kiyotaki 1987).

The last model in table 4.2 sums up the menu cost hypothesis in its simplest form. In short, this model raises the possibility that weak price rigidities (and wage rigidities; see Akerlof and Yellen 1985) may be associated with strong fluctuations in output and employment (Mankiw 1985; Parkin 1986). But the applicability of the idea is still to be established. The costs of producing new menus or price tags seem trivial, but it is worth noting that price changes, unlike quantity (output, inventory, backlog) changes, must be publicized. The costs of calculational inconvenience to customers and possible goodwill losses may be much more important (Okun 1981; McCallum 1986). If the total menu costs are small, they may not prevent price adjustments in response to large shifts in aggregate demand. The less elastic the labor supply and MC, and the more elastic the demand curves, the larger are the required menu costs. Finally, the dynamics of the process, about which little is known, depends on whether prices are initially in equilibrium, on the timing and staggering of pricing decisions, and on potentially important nonprice adjustments. Multiple equilibria are possible, which reflects how individual prices interact and react to changes in the price level (Rotemberg 1987; Blanchard 1987b).

In a very recent study (Blinder 1991), business executives were carefully interviewed about (1) the extent of the observed price stickiness and (2) the perceived validity of different theories of infrequent price changes. According to the preliminary results of this well-designed research project, 55% of the 72 companies interviewed so far "repriced no more often than once a year" (p. 93). Thus, many prices are indeed "sticky" in the sense of showing relatively infrequent changes. They respond to shifts in demand and cost conditions with lags averaging 3–4 months.

When ranked by the firms, the hypothesis of variable delivery lags (nonprice market clearing) scored best. "Coordination failure"—the idea that firms wait for others to alter price first—ranked second, cost-based pricing, implicit contracts, and explicit nominal contracts ranked third, fourth, and fifth, respectively. The menu costs hypothesis (cost of the price adjustment) scored still lower, followed by the notion of procyclical demand elasticity. Five other hypotheses received more rejections than support. They include the theory that inventories rather than prices are adjusted in response to demand changes and the theory that both marginal costs and markups are constant over the business cycle.

4.4 Historical Evidence and Current Theories

The presently popular "rigidity" theories pay little if any attention to historical changes in the behavior of wages and prices. This section takes a look at these changes and asks what lessons history holds for a comparative appraisal of the extant hypotheses. Some international differences are also considered.

4.4.1   Nominal and Real Wages in Business Cycles

Measures of aspects of cyclical movements in several historical time series of wage earnings and rates in the prewar, interwar, and postwar periods are presented in table 4.3. The average annual money earnings from wages declined in about half of the business contractions of 1860–1914 and in all of those of 1920–38, according to the data compiled in Phelps Brown 1968 (lines 1–2). In contrast, they kept rising through the period 1945–60, which witnessed four moderate or mild recessions (line 3). Data for 1889–1914 from Rees 1961 show that peaks and troughs in annual earnings matched nearly two thirds of the like business cycle turns of the period, but those in hourly earnings fewer than half (lines 7 and 8). However, hourly earnings score high on cyclical conformity in the interwar period, according to both the annual series from Rees 1960 and the monthly series from Creamer 1956 (lines 9 and 11). The same applies to an index of money wage rates presented in Creamer 1950 (line 12).

The conclusion is that most of the major business downturns and some of the minor ones have historically been associated with declines in nominal wage earnings.[21] The comprehensive study by Phelps Brown, which goes back to 1860 and also covers France, Germany, Sweden, and the United Kingdom, supplies much additional evidence that money wages basically followed a procyclical pattern of movement in the eight decades preceding World War II, though skipping many smaller fluctuations.

However, it is clear from all available data that no cyclical declines at all occurred in any of the comprehensive money wage indicators for the United States after 1945. Such long and sustained expansions in wage rates and incomes, hitherto unprecedented, prevailed concurrently in other major industrialized and market-oriented countries as well, reflecting both the generally rising prosperity and inflation of the postwar era.

The real wage series used in Table 4.3 are estimated by dividing the money wage series by cost of living or consumer price indexes. Before 1914, more business cycle turns were matched by like turns in deflated annual and hourly earnings than in the corresponding nominal data, but the real series had more irregular timing and smaller amplitudes (cf. lines 1 and 4, and lines 8 and 10). In 1920–38, deflated annual earnings moved in sympathy with all major business contractions and recoveries but skipped the smaller cycles, which the money earnings did not (cf. lines 2 and 5).

In 1945–60 the real series declined only between 1945 and 1947, lagging behind the business contraction of 1944–46, which marked the reconversion

21. For example, the annual Rees series on hourly earnings shows downward movements in 1893–95, 1896–98, 1903–4, 1907–8, 1913–14, 1920–22, 1924–25, 1929–33, and 1937–39 (see Rees 1961, pp. 33–34; 1960, pp. 2–3). Earlier data in Douglas 1930 are broadly consistent with these results. The monthly series declined strongly but with long lags in response to the depressions of 1920–21 and 1929–33 and very mildly and sluggishly during and/or after the other business contractions of the interwar period (Creamer 1950, 1956, ch. 5).

from the war to the peacetime economy (cf. lines 3 and 6). The currently available quarterly Bureau of Labor Statistics (BLS) data on the real hourly compensation of production (nonsupervisory) workers on private nonagricultural payrolls provide strong, consistent evidence that these real wages did in fact keep rising throughout the 1947–60 period with its four recessions (line 13). However, the same series shows much less growth and more cyclicality in recent times; it flattened in 1969–70 and declined mildly but with considerable persistence in 1973–74, 1978–81, and 1983–84, matching five of the eight business cycle turns of the period since 1961 (line 14).

No detrending or differencing operations are needed to answer the question whether wages had declines corresponding to the contractions as dated by the NBER. Questions about the degree of responsiveness of real wages to changes in employment require more subtle analytic techniques. Studies of this problem, which are generally restricted by the data to very recent and short segments of time, produced mixed results. One reason is that the composition of the work force varies, in part systematically, over the business cycle. Expansions generate more overtime income, and those who change jobs and new entrants have more procyclical and on the average lower wages than those who stay on the same job. Hence the net effect of aggregation is a countercyclical bias, as shown in Bils 1985.

Note also that real wages as discussed so far are money wages deflated by the consumer price index (CPI), not by the producer price index (PPI) of the current output of labor. The wage in terms of consumables is of prime interest to workers, whereas the wage in terms of the products of work (product wage rate) is of prime interest to firms. Producer prices tend to vary more than consumer prices; if money wages are less flexible than PPI but more flexible than CPI, then the PPI-deflated real wages could turn out to be countercyclical or acyclical and the CPI-deflated real wages procyclical.[22]

Bernanke and Powell (1986) find that real wages (CPI-deflated) were weakly procyclical, lagged output significantly in the prewar (1923–39) period, and more nearly coincided with output or even led it in some industries in the postwar (1954–82) period. Product wages (PPI-deflated) led more often, particularly in the recent era, and had larger and more erratic variations and some countercyclical tendencies.[23] Both real and product wages were more serially persistent and less cyclically variable in the postwar than in the prewar period.

Money wages show long and pronounced upward trends, so an analysis of

22. See also Tsiang 1947 for an early analysis of the U.S. interwar data that suggests a similar distinction between the behavior of real wages and that of product wages.
23. The results for product wages presented in Sachs 1980 are generally similar. Geary and Kennan (1982) report that product wages are not significantly associated with employment in the United States and other OECD countries, but this may be due to the noisiness of these relationships in the time domain (as noted by Bernanke and Powell, who find stronger indications of cyclicality from the frequency domain).

Table 4.3 Money and Real Wage Earnings and Rates: Measures of Cyclical Conformity, Timing, and Amplitudes, 1860–1987

	Period (1)	No. of B.C. Turns[a]		No. of Timing Observations[b]			Average Lead (−) or Lag (+)[c]		Average Percentage Amplitude[d]	
		Covered (2)	Matched (3)	Leads (4)	Coincidences (5)	Lags (6)	Peaks (7)	Troughs (8)	Expansions (9)	Contractions (10)
				Average Annual Money Wage Earnings (Phelps Brown)[e]						
1	1860–1914	28	14	0	11	3	0.7(1.2)	0.1(0.4)	26(12)	−9(6)
2	1920–1938	10	10	0	8	2	0(0)	0.4(0.6)	18(20)	−13(13)
3	1945–1960	8	0	0	0	0	n.o.	n.o.	n.o.	n.o.
				Average Annual Real Wage Earnings (Phelps Brown)[f]						
4	1860–1914	28	15	5	7	3	0.5(1.9)	−0.4(0.8)	22(17)	−9(12)
5	1920–1938	10	6	0	6	0	0(0)	0(0)	33(17)	−6(5)
6	1945–1960	8	2	0	0	2	+1	+1	44	−8
				Average Annual Money Earnings, Manufacturing (Rees)[g]						
7	1889–1914	16	10	0	10	0	0(0)	0(0)	16(8)	−5(6)
				Average Hourly Money Earnings, Manufacturing (Rees)[h]						
8	1889–1914	16	6	0	6	0	0(0)	0(0)	15(9)	−4(3)
9	1920–1939	10	8	0	3	5	0.2(0.5)	+1(0)	19(18)	−9(10)
				Average Hourly Real Earnings, Manufacturing (Rees)[i]						
10	1890–1914	16	10	1	6	3	0.2(1.0)	0.5(1.0)	10(5)	−2(1)
				Average Hourly Money Earnings, Manufacturing (Creamer)[j]						
11	1921–1938	9	9	0	0	9	0.9(0.4)	0.6(0.5)	13(18)	−5(12)

Index of Money Wage Rates, Manufacturing (Creamer)[k]

| 12 | 1920–1935 | 8 | 8 | 0 | 0 | 8 | 0.6(0.2) | 0.9(0.6) | 4(6) | –7(8) |

Index of Real Average Hourly Compensation, Nonfarm Business Sector (BLS)[l]

| 13 | 1947–1960 | 8 | 0 | 5 | 3 | 0 | n.o. | n.o. | n.o. | n.o. |
| 14 | 1947–1987 | 16 | 0 | 5 | 3 | 2 | –0.8(1.1) | 0(0.4) | 4(2) | –3(3) |

Note: n.o. = no observations.

[a]Business cycle turns (peaks and troughs) as dated by the NBER.

[b]Lines 1–10: Based on the annual business cycle (reference) chronology of NBER because each of these series is annual. Lines 11–12: Based on monthly series and the monthly NBER reference chronology. Line 13: Based on a quarterly series and the quarterly NBER reference chronology.

[c]Expressed in (fractions of) years. Entries not in parentheses are means; entries in parentheses are standard deviations.

[d]Based on specific cycle movements (expansions and contractions) in the series covered. All such movements are included, regardless of whether or not they correspond to the business cycle phases in the NBER chronology. The averages refer to the total expansion and contraction amplitudes in percentages. Entries not in parentheses are means; entries in parentheses are standard deviations.

[e]Based on the current-dollar data in Phelps Brown 1968, app. 3, tables on the last five pages (corresponding to pp. 448–52), col. 1 in each case. Coverage: 1860–1914, manufacturing; 1920–38, bituminous coal mines, class I steam railroads; 1945–60, manufacturing, mining, communications, contract construction, railroads and bus lines, gas and electric utilities. Computed from hourly and weekly earnings by taking into account changes in the average numbers of working hours and weeks per year. Sources include Long 1960 and Rees 1961 (see Phelps Brown 1968, app. 2).

[f]Based on the "index of wage-earnings in composite units of consumables" in the tables referred to in n. *e*. Money wages deflated with the cost-of-living or consumer price indexes. The entries in line 6, cols. 7–10, are single observations.

[g]Based on data in current dollars, per full-time equivalent worker, in Rees 1961, p. 33 (table 10, col. 1).

[h]Line 8: Based on data in current dollars in Rees 1961, p. 33 (table 10, col. 5). Line 9: Based on data in current dollars in Rees 1960, p. 3 (table 1, col. 1).

[i]Based on data in 1914 dollars in Rees 1961, p. 120 (table 44, col. 1).

[j]Based on data in Creamer 1956, p. 40 (table 8, col. 2) and p. 48 (table 11, col. 2) for the entries in columns 3–8 and 9–10, respectively.

[k]Based on data in Creamer 1950, p. 7 (table 1, cols. 3 and 7) and pp. 43–45 (table A) for the entries in columns 3–8 and 9–10, respectively. Creamer used monthly data on changes in wage rates compiled by the U.S. Bureau of Labor Statistics (BLS) from reports in its establishment and payroll sample for 1919–35.

[l]Based on monthly BLS data taken from *Business Conditions Digest*, October 1987, p. 104, and other issues.

the cyclical behavior of their first differences or deviations from trend must complement the level analysis. Looking at differences between rates of change (last year of expansion minus contraction) in the average hourly compensation in manufacturing, Sachs (1980) finds that they were negative in 13 of 17 business cycles between 1890 and 1975.[24] Thus a deceleration of growth or disinflation in wages marked most of the business cycle downturns. Absolute declines in wages, however, occurred only on five of these occasions, all of them before World War II. According to these annual data, wage inflation actually accelerated in the recessions of 1969–70 and 1973–75.

In sum, the study of historical data makes it clear that the inflexibility of money wages is not a universal law (as some of the recent literature would suggest) but is essentially a phenomenon of the post–World War II period. (Much the same statement can be made about the stickiness of the price level in the face of aggregate demand changes, as demonstrated below.) Real wages do not conform closely to business cycles but do fluctuate in a predominantly procyclical fashion. Before 1914 and between the world wars, these movements tended to be somewhat less frequent and smaller than those of nominal wages, but the situation has been reversed in the recent era of persistent price and wage inflation.

4.4.2   Trends and Cycles in Producer and Consumer Price Indexes

The main fact about the recent evolution of both wages and prices is that they ceased declining during the postwar business recessions; that is, disinflation replaced deflation. The evidence is substantial and uncontradicted (Cagan 1975, 1979; Zarnowitz and Moore 1986; chapter 3, this volume). The following is a brief qualitative summary of the findings that are relevant here (for numerical detail, see Zarnowitz 1989b, table 2).

The first 150 years of U.S. history can be divided into three periods marked by inflation (associated to a large extent with wars) alternating with three periods of deflation. The cyclical conformity of prices, as indicated by the percentage of business cycle peaks and troughs matched by like turns in the wholesale price index (WPI), was considerable throughout and, interestingly, on average higher in the deflationary than in the inflationary periods. When the trend in WPI was up, the index rose strongly in expansions and fell weakly in contractions; when the trend was down, the movements in the index were likewise procyclical, only tilted in the opposite direction. Also, in the former periods the year-to-year increases in the index were more frequent than the decreases, whereas in the latter periods the opposite was the case. For the era 1789–1932 as a whole, the decreases were nearly as frequent as the increases.

---

24. The Great Depression and World War II years are excluded from these measures. Prices and wages fell in 1929–33 but rose strongly through the rest of the 1930s despite high unemployment. This is widely viewed as anomalous and attributable to special factors, namely the New Deal legislation, the support and growth of unions, and later the wartime administrative controls.

The record for the CPI is somewhat shorter but it too leaves no doubt about the basically procyclical behavior of prices between 1820 and 1932, even on an annual basis. Again, the distinction between the inflationary and deflationary periods shows up clearly in the data. The frequency of decreases in somewhat less here than for WPI.

In 1932–52, a very turbulent age of depression and wars, prices embarked on a long upward trend but they still declined in two of the three business contractions, the exception being the recession of 1945, which marked the economy's reconversion to peacetime. However, in the three following decades the annual price indexes ceased altogether to decline in response to recessions. Indeed, in 1952–82 for the first time both WPI and CPI rose on average more in the years of contraction than in those of expansion.

Monthly data contain more noise than the annual data but also more information, particularly on persistence and timing. In 1953–64, 35% of the monthly changes in WPI were effectively zero; in 1964–76, 19%; and in 1976–88, only 5%.[25] Of course, as inflation intensified, there was a steady rise in the share of index increases (from 39% of the time in 1953–64 to 74% in 1976–88), but the share of decreases exceeded 20% in both 1953–64 and 1976–88 (it fell to 12% in 1964–76). However, these decreases were sporadic and did not amount to cyclical movements matching the business contractions after the mid-1950s. Indeed, in the 1970s the largest rises in the WPI occurred during the recessions associated with the huge oil price shocks. The recessions did cause some reductions in the rate of inflation but only with considerable lags. The monthly CPI series shows an even greater preponderance of increases and generally higher inflation rates.

4.4.3   Trends in Unionization and Competition

Wage and price rigidities are by no means universal but they are treated as such in most contemporary models that try to explain them. We should favor any theory that can account not simply for the existence of the rigidities but also for their apparent increase in recent times.

Several of the relevant hypotheses assume deviations from the competitive model in the form of negotiated wages and price setting by firms. Did the degree of monopoly—of market power of labor and business—rise historically and produce reductions in wage and price flexibility? There is no clear and established answer to this broad question, but the issue cannot be avoided. My reading of the literature and evidence suggests that (*a*) unionization probably did contribute to the changed behavior of wages after the Great Contraction of 1929–33 and in the first two or three post–World II decades and (*b*) it is rather doubtful that a general increase in the degree of monopoly occurred,

---

25. It should be noted that the early annual index series carry no decimals. The monthly series for both WPI and CPI carry one decimal each.

although this probably does not rule out the possibility that noncompetitive practices or conduct became more common.

Unionization

The sensitivity of wages to cyclical changes in unemployment and related labor market conditions is smaller in the union than in the nonunion sector so that recessions generally increase the pay advantage of union workers (Rees 1973, chs. 10 and 16; D. J. B. Mitchell 1980, chs. 4 and 6). The rapid growth in unionization, from 6% of the labor force in 1933 to 27% in 1953, was naturally associated with large increases in the role, scale, and costs of collective bargaining. Impasses and strikes can be particularly costly to both parties in a dispute; therefore, long, often 3-year, union contracts became common in the postwar period.

However, union membership in the United States has fallen as a share of the total labor force since the mid-1950s and in absolute numbers since the mid-1970s, despite a rise in the public sector. Employer resistance to unions stiffened as growth rates of output and labor productivity declined and competition intensified internationally (Freeman 1988; Reder 1988). Wages and benefits negotiated by major unions grew in 1968–79 at annual rates averaging nearly 10% for the first year and 7.5% for the second and third contract years, according to BLS data. During the recession year of 1982, these rates fell rapidly to about 3% over the life of the contracts, and they remained there (occasionally even lower) in the ensuing expansion. Correspondingly, real average hourly earnings and compensation of production workers on private payrolls grew only weakly and discontinuously in the 1980s.

This remarkable development surely reflected the loss of economic and political power of the unions but also other, partly related and temporary factors: disinflation, import penetration, and declines or slow growth of some of the older domestic industries. At the same time, the civilian unemployment rate in the United States fell from 10.8% in December 1982 to 5.0% in March 1989. In contrast, unemployment rose and remained high in Europe, where unions are generally much more powerful, despite the concurrent business expansion. Theories that blame insiders for high real wage rigidity and persistent unemployment gained considerable popularity there, and they are indeed consistent with many, though by no means all, of the relevant facts.[26]

---

26. Lindbeck and Snower (1986) argue that current employees ("insiders") have the power to make it unprofitable for the firm to hire potential employees ("outsiders") at lower wages. Thus the burden of unemployment falls on the outsiders, while the insiders, who may be protected by union membership, enjoy both the stability of indexed incomes and a high degree of job security. A more general theory of hysteresis or high persistence of unemployment is developed in Blanchard and Summers 1986, 1987b; for a different view, see Gordon 1987. As noted in Andersen 1989, the union wage theory does not explain why some of the Nordic countries, where the share of unionized labor is very high, had relatively low unemployment.

Concentration and Market Power

Formidable conceptual, measurement, and aggregation problems beset all attempts to estimate the extent (and, even more, the trend) of competition versus monopoly in the economy. Most of the evidence comes from concentration ratios, particularly for manufacturing, but the relationship between these measures and the degree of monopoly depends on the size of the domestic market, the importance of foreign competition, the availability of substitutes, and the extent of collusion. Views on the issue have long ranged from the popular but undocumented belief that competition is steadily and perhaps strongly declining to the more cautious and supportable suggestion that there is much stability over time in the aggregate concentration and no clear unidirectional trend.[27] The share of the 100 largest corporations in total manufacturing assets moved up from 34% to 42% in 1927–33, down to 38% in 1941, up from 37% to 46% in 1947–57, and up again from near 45% to 48% in 1966–71 (Scherer 1980, fig. 3.1, p. 48). There is much agreement that close approaches to both pure competition and pure monopoly are rare, but some authors stress the prevalence of broadly defined or "workable" competition, and others stress that of monopolistic competition and oligopoly (cf. Nutter 1951, p. 44, and Scherer 1980, p. 67).

If it were well established that market power increased and competitive price taking gave way to price setting under conditions of imperfect competition, models that rely on monopolistic competition and oligopoly should have a better chance to explain the apparent rise in price inertia. (As shown in Carlton 1986, the average length of spells of price rigidity is an increasing function of industry concentration.) But there is no convincing evidence that greater monopoly power is what actually distinguishes the last 40 years from the earlier era. Large corporations setting prices have been around for a long time. The increasing globalization of markets is an important postwar trend that presumably has the net effect of raising the levels of competition and the importance of changes in relative prices and wages.

4.4.4   How to Explain the Observed Changes

The expected consequence of labor's experience in the depressed 1930s would be an increase in workers' aversion to the risk of job losses. This should have given rise to greater demand for employment insurance than for wage stabilization. But labor contracts commonly specify basic income to be paid

---

27. For an early study that encouraged the former thesis, see Berle and Means 1932; for the latter position, see Stigler 1949 and Nutter 1951. Stigler's judgment was that "competition declined moderately from the Civil War to the end of the nineteenth century, and thereafter increased moderately" (p. 54). Nutter's estimate of the share of manufacturing output accounted for by monopolistic industries (those with four-firm concentration ratios of 50 and higher) was 33% for 1895–1904, and Scherer (1980, p. 68) obtains approximately the same figure for 1963 (the corresponding proportions were 24% in 1947, 30% in 1954 and 1958, and 29% in 1972).

for work and fringe benefits; they do not ensure tenure. In the postwar era, the cyclical variability of money wages has practically vanished, but real wages have stagnated recently for many workers. Moreover, unemployment continues to have large cyclical swings and it even has a definite upward trend. It is difficult to see how the implicit contract theory can explain these phenomena.

The idea that above-equilibrium real wages are required to attract productive and loyal workers should apply better to prosperous than depressed times, to large established companies with internal labor markets than small firms with uncertain prospects, and to high-paying career jobs than low-paying menial jobs. It is possible that the applicability of the efficiency wage theory increased during the postwar ear, which was one of long phases of expansion, with strong growth of career employment in the corporate sector and elsewhere (government, professions). But this is presently only a vague speculation; in fact, there is as yet little tested knowledge to bear on the validity of models of this type.

Much the same applies to the menu cost theory of pricing. The overall costs of changing prices not having been measured, we simply do not know what they are, how they vary across time and space, and how they compare with the costs of changing quantities (of output, inventories, backlogs). We do know that stable prices reduce communication costs to sellers and shopping costs to buyers, which is conducive to long-term associations between the transacting parties. Perhaps the importance of such associations in the economy has increased in recent times but, again, the facts of the matter are yet to be established.

Long and staggered union contracts probably played an important role in reducing the cyclical variability and increasing the persistence of wages during the post-Depression era when the unions were on the rise. Such contracts can generate complex distributed lags in wages and prices (see chapter 2, section 2.4.7). But in the second half of the postwar period the share of organized labor in the United States, never very high, was falling. And outside North America, including countries where unions are very strong, wage negotiations are mostly annual and/or are centralized or simultaneous (Andersen 1989, pp. 43–44).

A comprehensive theory that can explain the reasons for both the persistence and the evolution of cycles remains a major unaccomplished task. But when the observed changes that are likely to have contributed to the relative stabilization of the economy in recent times are taken as given, it can be seen that they are probably also responsible in part for the reduction in the cyclicality of wages and prices. Prices as well as quantities tend to be cyclically less sensitive for services than for goods (Moore 1983, ch. 12). Hence the large rise in the relative importance of services will have had the effect of making the overall cost and price indexes more sticky. As the needs and preferences of consumers and producers grew more diversified and technologies to satisfy them were being developed, the share of output made to order may well have increased, too. If so, the result would be a greater role for delivery lag adjustments and a smaller one for price adjustments (perhaps also some reductions in the overall levels of manufacturers' finished inventories and short-term demand uncertainty).

The persistence of inflation in the last four decades should have rationally promoted indexation of incomes and increased the frequency of individual prices rises; that is, it probably worked to reduce nominal wage and price rigidities on the upward side but may have raised them on the downward side. But all this was apparently consistent with much inertia in the micro price data.

Concerning relative price adjustments, the effects of government policies were partly stabilizing and partly interfering and destabilizing. To the extent that the experience of greater macroeconomic stability generates expectations of more of the same, the probability that business recessions will remain relatively short and mild increases. Because buyers see less reason to reduce spending, sellers see less reason to reduce prices of inputs and outputs. But the optimism can be reversed by shocks or side developments such as the accelerated inflation in the 1970s, and both positive and negative expectations can be temporarily self-fulfilling.

In sum, it is not coincidental that the cyclicality of wages and prices declined during the last half-century even while business cycles moderated and inflation prevailed. But it is still possible that more flexibility would have helped. Between 1966 and 1980 ULC in manufacturing, which used to fall during business contractions, experienced only retardations as money wages rose strongly despite the adverse supply shocks and a decline in the growth rates of gross productivity of labor (whose procyclical and leading behavior pattern, however, remained unchanged). So new concern was expressed about the stickiness of wages, which was linked by some authors to the stagflation of the 1970s (Moore and Cullity 1983; Haberler 1988).

Yet the classical view that more flexibility is always desirable is not universally accepted. In what follows an opposite hypothesis will be considered.

4.5 Price Expectations and Interest Rates

4.5.1 Expectational and Distributional Effects of Deflations and Inflations

A macroeconomic model represents flexible prices by a steep, and sticky prices by a flat, aggregate supply (AS) curve. If the short-term fluctuations in aggregate demand (AD) are treated as given, the flatter the AS curve is, the more real activity will fluctuate. Hence, by this simple argument, price flexibility is necessarily stabilizing.

It is possible, however, that the variation of AD itself is not independent of the flexibility of wages and prices in general but rather is an increasing function of that flexibility. For this to be so, the expected rate of price change (p^e)

must have a strong positive effect on AD, and the actual price level (P) must have a weak negative effect. If P declines in a recession, this raises the real values of the money stock and net wealth of the public and hence acts to reverse the decline. But if at the same time p^e turns negative (i.e., a deflation is widely expected), then this would tend to depress AD by causing postponement of purchases.[28]

A similar distinction between level and expected-change effects applies to nominal wages. A reduction in the current wage level relative to the prospective future wage level would mean lower production costs now and hence encourage employment and investment, but the anticipation that wage rates generally will continue to decline would depress expected incomes, demand, and profitability and result in deferment of consumption and investment.[29]

A point-counterpoint discussion of these arguments led Keynes (1936, ch. 19) to the conclusion that on balance, there is little to recommend gradual reductions in money wages as a cure against depression. If prices fell in step with wages, no advantage of lower real costs would accrue to the employers; if prices were destabilized and fell more, conditions would deteriorate further. Decentralized wage bargaining can alter the relative money wages, not the overall level of real wages.

Moreover, it has long been recognized that when debt contracts are set in nominal terms, deflation worsens the financial position of debtors by raising the real value of their liabilities (Fisher 1933; Keynes 1936; Hart 1938; Minsky 1975, 1977). Such contracts certainly exist on a large scale in the United States and many other countries. True, the assets of creditors increase in real value at the same time, but the two effects need not and probably do not offset each other completely (Tobin 1975, 1980). Debtors spend more than creditors relative to their respective incomes and wealth (this is why the former borrow and the latter lend in the first place). Debtors who face increasing threats of insolvency are apt to curtail their spending sharply, and those who actually go bankrupt directly cause losses to creditors. In the 1930s, the results probably included a sharp rise in the real costs of financial intermediation, impeding the functioning of credit markets and depressing macroeconomic activity (Bernanke 1981, 1983). Simulations in Caskey and Fazzari 1987 suggest that a large real-debt effect can make greater wage and price flexibility seriously destabilizing.[30]

28. In the early statement, Patinkin (1948) contrasted the roles of P and p^e under the headings of static and dynamic analysis, respectively, and noted that the expectational effect, though presumably temporary, could well prove the stronger in the short run (see also Tobin 1975).

29. Other possible consequences of wage cuts include, on the positive side, lower interest rates (through reduced money demand), higher net exports (through reduced costs and greater competitiveness in an open economy), and possibly more business optimism. On the negative side, redistributional effects detrimental to workers and debtors would be likely to diminish aggregate demand.

30. Note that the argument about the depressant effect of a rise in the real burden of nominal debt and the attendant redistribution of wealth relies on the current movement of P and not p^e. A

In the absence of a general deflation, relative price movements combined with nominal debt contracting can seriously hurt some industries, occupations, or sectors, but these are partial difficulties that normally remain contained. The case in point is the experience of debt-burdened farmers after the 1981–82 recession when prices of their products and land stopped rising or fell.[31]

Jut as unanticipated deflation shifts income from debtors to creditors, unanticipated inflation does the opposite. The associated wealth redistribution effects are probably substantial, but individual losses and gains largely offset each other so that the costs to society vary and are difficult to determine (Fischer and Modigliani 1978). If money wages are sticky, unexpected price-level rises would reduce real wages and increase output. If there are no nominal rigidities but people misperceive the absolute for relative price rises, then unanticipated inflation would also increase output by raising labor supply.[32]

Large inflations or deflations of monetary origin are likely to obstruct, rather than promote, the flexibility of relative prices that is instrumental to the proper functioning of the market economy. Actual wage and price flexibility being always limited, deflations often aggravated the severe depressions of the past, and inflations (such as the long and uneven one of the 1970s) often contributed stresses and imbalances to expansions.

History suggests that what matters is not so much the direction but rather the size and variability of the general price movement. Large and volatile changes in the price level are difficult to predict, generate uncertainty, and adversely affect real economic activity. Evidence for the 1970s, when both inflation and unemployment rates were rising and inflation was increasingly variable, is consistent with this hypothesis (see, e.g., M. Friedman 1977; Makin 1982; also chapter 17). So are, a fortiori, the data for the short but severe depression of 1920–21, which was preceded by a large inflation and accompanied for a year by the most conspicuously rapid deflation on record for the United States (Friedman and Schwartz 1963b, ch. 5). On the other hand, one can find examples of moderate deflation or inflation coexisting with either high or low real growth rates.[33]

---

failure of foresight is still required, but only one that occurred earlier, at the time when the debts had been contracted for. The debtors must have failed to anticipate the downturn and decline in P, which is easy to explain if these were rare events.

31. The industry and regional troubles associated with the oil price decline of 1986 constitute another example.

32. Analogously, surprise deflation has negative effects on real aggregate economic activity in both those Keynesian theories that have nominal contracts with limited or delayed wage adjustments and those neoclassical theories that assume flexible wages and prices but also incomplete information.

33. M. Friedman and Schwartz (1963a, pp. 41–42) describe the post–Civil War period 1865–73 as one of deflation in product prices but not money wages, a mild rise in the stock of money, and a high average rate of increases in real income. Zarnowitz and Moore (1986, p. 553) compare some periods of low or negative inflation and relatively high real growth (e.g., 1923–29) with

4.5.2   Models with Potentially Destabilizing Price and Interest Expectations

Taylor (1986a) holds that the postwar improvement in economic stability occurred *despite* the greater rigidity of wages and prices, mainly due to policy-induced reductions in nominal GNP shocks. Monetary authorities react to rising inflation with tighter policies; this depresses output growth, which in time reduces inflation. The result has been smaller variances of the growth rates of output and prices but also greater persistence (serial correlation) of the fluctuations in both variables.

In contrast, De Long and Summers (1986a, 1986b) argue that at least some of the postwar moderation of the cycle is due precisely to the fact that money wages and prices have become more sticky and persistent. They assume that the short-run nominal interest rate (i) enters the LM equation, and the real rate ($r^e = i - p^e$) enters the IS equation. IS and LM together determine aggregate demand, while Taylor's model of overlapping wage contracts is used on the supply side. There is a serially correlated demand shift term but no wage or price shock. The model implies that increased price flexibility is destabilizing at the margin over a considerable range of assumed parameter values. Again, the reason is that output reacts more elastically to p^e than to P, but the channel is r^e.[34]

However, as shown by Driskill and Sheffrin (1986), increasing price flexibility is stabilizing at the margin in systems where fluctuations are driven by supply shocks (as in contract models with shocks to nominal wages; see Taylor 1979, 1980a). Hence greater price flexibility may simultaneously increase the output variance generated by demand shocks and reduce the output variance generated by supply shocks. The former effect will prevail over the latter in a model in which demand shocks are serially correlated and supply shocks are not. But the postwar era witnessed some large supply (or price adjustment) shocks of considerable persistence. It is clear that generally the results will depend on the mix and correlations of the demand and supply shifts.

Further, the assumption of a policy rule that links money supply to the interest rate leaves no room for any stabilizing role of monetary policy. Yet, as shown in chapter 3, monetary growth was much less volatile in the post–World War II era than in the earlier periods and was, moreover, free of the previously experienced phases of negative values. Policy may deserve some credit for this development, even if it is to a large extent endogenous (cf. H.

---

others of high inflation and lower growth (e.g., 1969–81). When inflationary trends prevail, business expansions tend to be longer but not necessarily stronger (Zarnowitz and Moore 1986, pp. 525–31).

34. If people expect disinflation or deflation (i.e., p^e falls or becomes negative), then so long as i does not adjust fully, r^e will increase, lowering real investment and output. Correspondingly, when p^e rises, r^e will fall, which raises economic activity. Hence, more price variability causes more output instability.

Grossman 1986). The stabilizing potential of flexible prices would be much enhanced under conditions of stable growth of nominal demand in the will-o'-the-wisp model with optimal monetary policy (S. King 1988).

In basic analytical terms, the short-run relationship between i and p (two endogenous, simultaneously determined variables) is unstable because it depends on the nature of the shifts in, or disturbances to, the system as a whole. This argument is sufficient to show that there is no simple and definite way to relate changes in r^e to economic fluctuations. Still, even a highly stylized attempt at some quantifiable linkage should be worthwhile. In times when persistent inflation is recognized and expected to continue undiminished, the simple price adjustment equation

(5)
$$p = p_{-1} + \frac{b(Q - Q^*)}{Q^*},$$

may not be a bad assumption.[35] (Here Q is actual and Q^* is potential output; subscripts t are omitted.) A dynamic version of the demand function for money is approximately

(6)
$$m - p = kq - \frac{h\Delta i}{i},$$

where $\Delta i = i - i_{-1}$. Following the derivation in Baily 1978 (pp. 42–45), consider an AD shock that raises Q above Q^* by a fraction q as money and prices increase at the equilibrium rate $\bar{m} = \bar{p}$. Then, from equation (5),

(7)
$$p = \bar{p} + bq,$$

and equations (6) and (7) imply that

(8)
$$\frac{\Delta i}{i} = q\left(\frac{k + b}{h}\right).$$

Suppose that the deviation of p from $\bar{p}$ in equation (7) is anticipated. Then, differencing the definitional equation $r^e = i - p^e$ and using equation (8) results in

(9)
$$\Delta r^e = \Delta i - bq.$$

And combining equations (8) and (9) gives

(10)
$$\Delta r^e = q\left(\frac{ik + ib - bh}{h}\right).$$

When equation (10) is solved for alternative values of the parameters (table 4.4), several relationships emerge. First, when inflation accelerates strongly

---

35. Survey data for 1959–76 indicate that forecasts of inflation have been on the average closely related to the most recent observed values of inflation (Zarnowitz 1979).

Table 4.4   Hypothetical Responses of the Real Interest Rate to a Demand Disturbance

A. $i = .06$, $k = 0.7$, $h = 0.2$		B. $i = .06$, $b = 0.2$			C. $k = 0.7$, $b = 0.2$, $h = 0.2$	
b	Δr^e	k	h	Δr^e	i	Δr^e
0	.21	0.7	0.2	.07	.02	−.11
0.2	.07	1.0	0.2	.16	.04	−.02
0.4	−.07	1.5	0.2	.31	.06	.07
0.6	−.21	0.7	0.1	.34	.08	.16
0.8	−.35	0.7	0.2	.07	.10	.25
1.0	−.49	0.7	0.5	−.09	.12	.54

Note: Based on the formula $\Delta r^e/q = i\,(k/h + b/h - b)$; see Baily 1978 and text for the derivation. A disturbance to AD is assumed to raise output from equilibrium by 1% ($q = 1$). Δr^e = change in real interest; k = income elasticity of the demand for money; h = interest elasticity of the demand for money; b = coefficient of the GNP gap in the price adjustment equation; i = nominal interest rate.

in response to excess demand as measured by the GNP gap (i.e., b in eq. [5] is large), Δr^e falls, given the values of i, k, and h. So in this sense greater price flexibility can be destabilizing in the short run (see pt. A of the table). Second, given i and b, Δr^e increases for higher values of the income elasticity of the demand for money (k) and decreases for higher values of the income elasticity of the demand for money (h). When h is as large as 0.5, changes in r^e are destabilizing (table 4.4, pt. B). Third, at values of k, b, and h that seem reasonable (0.7, 0.2, and 0.2, respectively), Δr^e is negative at relatively low values of the nominal interest rate (i) (pt. C). The meaning of this is not clear. The presence of i in equation (10) makes Δr^e dependent on money growth even in the long run, but the proper focus of this analysis is certainly on moderate short-run movements.

The examples suggest that r^e will change only by small amounts in response to a rise or fall of 1% in total output: for plausible parameter readings, perhaps at most by 30 or 40 basis points, most likely less.[36] This seems to be a sensible result that is consistent with much that is known about the behavior of interest rates and price expectations.

On the other hand, the De Long–Summers hypothesis implies that changes in r^e strongly influence aggregate economic activity, presumably through their effects on real private investment broadly defined (I). Since these changes are generally small, this requires a high elasticity of I with respect to r^e. Although such a major role for r^e is consistent with theory, it has not found much systematic support in the data. Most tests show relatively weak effects of cost of

36. Baily's own preferred figures correspond to line 2 in part A of table 4.4.

capital or the real interest rate on business and household real capital outlays, and some show no significant net effects at all.[37]

4.5.3 Interest and Inflation in History

What the *expected* inflation rates and real interest rates are at any time is always very uncertain, as indicated by the diversity of estimates of p^e obtained from different sources or by different methods (surveys of consumers and forecasters; inferences from financial and commodity market data; statistical implementation of the rational expectations model). Historically, the response of nominal interest rates to movements in the rate of price change has been quite varied and mostly weak.

Before World War II, inflation and deflation alternated in peacetime expansions and contractions, allowing for longer trends; short-term interest rates moved procyclically, like wholesale prices but with longer lags, and long-term rates had much smaller fluctuations (Zarnowitz and Moore 1986, pp. 553–65). Short rates moved in broad sympathy to the very large waves of inflation and deflation during World War I and thereafter through the slump of 1929–33, but even then their adjustment was lagged and incomplete. The ex post, observable real rate, $r = i - p$, was dominated much of the time by short erratic variations; it shows little association with output and other cyclical variables but a strong negative correlation with inflation (Mishkin 1981b).

The evidence is consistent with the hypothesis that most of the time people viewed the price movement at transitory and limited, so that their expectations smoothed out much of it. Hence, the changes in p^e tended to be small and not persistent so that the r^e and i values were on the whole close.[38]

A markedly tighter relation between i and p arises only in the second half of the 1960s and through the 1970s, a period during which the persistence of inflation must have become public knowledge. This is shown clearly by the graphs and correlations in M. Friedman and Schwartz 1982 (pp. 527–46; see also Summers 1983, pp. 216–25). The real rate rose from negative to high positive values during the great inflation of this period, which must have largely reflected the expectational adjustments of i to p. It should be noted, however, that the relationship weakened again during the following years of disinflation: r remained high in 1981–85 as i declined much less than p did.

The De Long–Summers hypothesis relies on the "nonadjustment" of nominal interest rates; that is, it requires that i respond only sluggishly and incom-

---

37. The literature is voluminous. For surveys and references see Jorgenson 1971; P. K. Clark 1979; Chirinko 1988. See also the estimates and critique of investment equations in Gordon and Veitch 1986.

38. That this was so looks particularly plausible for the pre–World War I era of the gold standard, when the long-term rate of price change was near zero (which, incidentally, helps explain the shape and relatively good fit of the original Phillips curve for the United Kingdom; see Phillips 1958 and Barro 1987, ch. 16).

pletely to changes in p^e. If the response is sufficiently strong, the change in r^e will be too small to have much of a destabilizing effect. Thus, the increase in the promptness and size of interest adjustments during the period of accelerated inflation in the late 1960s and the 1970s should have reduced the applicability of the hypothesis. And, according to the theoretical argument already noted, the same applies to the effects of the supply shocks, which also occurred in the 1970s.

To conclude, the validity of the hypothesis that stickier wages and prices had a moderating influence on postwar business cycles remains open. It was neither shown to draw much support from the data nor invalidated. The theoretical possibility of price flexibility being destabilizing clearly exists, but the historical importance of such a condition is uncertain.

A more limited hypothesis, which I think is favored by general considerations and evidence, is that only large changes in p^e and r^e associated with major deflations, inflations, and disinflations have much destabilizing potential; small and moderate changes, which are far more common, matter little.

4.6   Concluding Observations

The sensitivity of wage and price levels to cyclical declines was generally greater before than after World War II. The recent era was also one of more moderate fluctuations in real economic activity and more persistent inflation. Important structural, institutional, and policy changes contributed to all three of these concurrent developments. These linkages elude the current analytical models, which either disregard the evidence on the stickiness of industrial input and output prices or treat this stickiness as invariable, ubiquitous, and necessarily symmetrical.

Considerations of lesser risk and cost to long-term transaction partners may favor nonprice market-clearing devices even under conditions of substantial competition, as illustrated by the importance of changes in delivery periods and quality and availability of products. Relative wage cuts are disliked by nonunionized as well as unionized workers. Uncertainties about the consequences of price changes can deter them even if the direct costs involved are small.

Imperfections of competition, information, and markets make some wage and price rigidities inevitable. The departures from flexibility need not always be destabilizing; indeed, protracted and anticipated wage declines can aggravate demand contractions. But large wage or other cost increases outrunning productivity gains can also worsen the economy's condition. The strong hypothesis that the increased rigidities actually reduced the instability throughout the postwar era does not score convincingly against alternatives. The counterarguments draw support from the increased responsiveness of interest rates to changes in expected inflation and the importance of supply shocks in the 1970s.

The destabilizing potential of general price movements is probably nonlinear: great for large and rapid changes and negligible for small and slow changes. Major deflations of the past had demonstrably strong and adverse expectational and distributional effects. As the recent inflation accelerated, it grew increasingly volatile, generated much uncertainty and popular discontent, and led to policy interventions that had disturbing consequences of their own. Moderate fluctuations in the price level or the rate of inflation have not been shown to be necessarily detrimental to reasonably steady growth in real activity.

5   Research during the First 50 Years of the National Bureau

Research on the nature and causes, and later also on the indicators and forecasting, of business cycles has been a major part of the work of the National Bureau of Economic Research almost from its beginning in 1920. This reflected the need of the times and continued under the administration of each of the six NBER directors of research or presidents: Wesley Mitchell, Arthur Burns, Solomon Fabricant, Geoffrey Moore, John Meyer, and Martin Feldstein. Business cycles, viewed broadly as the major problem of economic instability, constituted a central scientific interest of three of these men— Mitchell, Burns, and Moore. Many research staff members and associates at the National Bureau devoted major parts of their working lives to studies of this subject.

5.1   A Wide Range of Interrelated Studies

I think that most students of the subject would accept, though agreeing it is difficult to prove, that the development of modern economic theory contributed importantly to the potential of economic policy by teaching the profession about the probable directional effects of different policy measures. Such lessons are usually applied with lengthy lags, but publicly minded people showed rather more receptiveness to them than many would have expected. Beyond that, great advances in economic statistics and econometrics gave increasingly powerful analytical tools to those concerned with quantitative economic research and its applications to questions of policy. Both the quantity

This chapter is a slightly revised and heavily abbreviated version of an essay written in 1970 to introduce the first in a series of colloquia celebrating the National Bureau's 50th anniversary ("The Business Cycle Today: An Introduction," in *The Business Cycle Today,* edited by V. Zarnowitz [New York: NBER, 1972]). In this form, the chapter is limited to a review of the NBER studies of business cycles in the years 1920–70 as related to some other concurrent work in the same area.

and quality of economic data have increased immensely in what has been termed "the statistical revolution" that in most countries started during the Second World War.

No attempt can be made here to trace all these lines of progress, of course, but this is an appropriate occasion for recalling at least some of the more important contributions of the National Bureau. These are by no means limited to the research classified specifically (and somewhat narrowly) as "studies in business cycles." At the Bureau, and elsewhere, inquiries in various fields have resulted in new materials and knowledge that proved helpful in dealing with the problem of economic instability.

That this is so can be seen most readily in the case of the massive studies that have led to the development of systematic national income accounting and its worldwide diffusion. Thanks in a large measure to these time-series data, "there now exists in all Western countries a relatively well-organized statistical universe to which our notions of development and stability refer. . . . Economic reality is a product of systematic statistical observations in a more serious sense today than it was during earlier decades (Lundberg 1968, p. 16). The pioneering National Bureau work in this area goes back to the earliest NBER publication, by Mitchell, W. I. King, F. R. Macaulay, and O. W. Knauth, but the main contributions here are those by Simon Kuznets and his associates, which appeared in the years 1937–46 (Mitchell et al. 1921; Mitchell 1922; Kuznets 1937, 1945; Kuznets, Epstein, and Jenks 1941, 1946). The great influence this research had on the development of economics since the 1930s is today generally recognized.[1]

Other basic measures developed in National Bureau studies concern business and household capital formation, consumption, and financing (Kuznets, Fabricant, Goldsmith, Lipsey, Becker, Juster, and Shay); output, employment, labor force, productivity, prices, and wages (Fabricant, Kendrick, Wolman, Long, Easterlin, Mincer, Mills, Stigler, Rees, Kravis, and Lipsey); money flows, interest rates, and the stock of money (Copeland, Macaulay, Durand, Braddock Hickman, Conard, Guttentag, Cagan, Friedman, and Schwartz); government, business, and consumer financing (Seltzer, Holland, Kahn, Saulnier, Haberler, Moore); etc.[2] Without the groundwork laid by these investigations, much of the recent economic research, particularly of a quantitative nature, would have been seriously impaired if not frustrated. This includes studies dealing with business cycle problems, some of them undertaken by the authors who developed the materials just listed (e.g., Friedman and Schwartz 1963a; Cagan 1965, 1966).

1. For example, Johnson (1967, p. 86) observes that Keynes's "original concept of the propensity to consume was very strongly influenced by national income accounting (in fact, the development of the Keynesian theory can be related fairly closely to the development of national income accounting)."

2. This recital, though long, is very incomplete; for references see any catalog of NBER publications.

Of course, in large part the Bureau's efforts in data collection and measurement originated directly in the program of research on business cycles initiated by Wesley Mitchell. Gradually, a uniquely rich library of well over two thousand time series on almost every aspect of economic activity was built up, with full annotations, seasonal adjustments, measures of cyclical timing, amplitude, conformity, etc. These data were assembled and used in the course of many studies, including, in addition to those mentioned above, the massive investigations by Mitchell and Burns of how to define, measure, and analyze business cycles; research on cyclical movements in transportation by Hultgren, in inventories by Abramovitz and Stanback, in personal income by Creamer, in consumption by Mack, in exports by Mintz; and studies of business cycle indicators by Moore, Shiskin, Hultgren, Bry, and Zarnowitz.[3] I believe it is fair to say that the materials assembled and analyzed in all these reports add up to a large proportion of our factual knowledge of how the various economic activities and aggregates behaved during the historically observed sequence of business expansion, downturn, contraction, and upturn— that is, in each phase of the uneven but pervasive fluctuations that marked the process of the economy's growth. To be valid, the theoretical explanations of economic growth and fluctuations must conform to the major facts disclosed by these largely empirical studies; to be useful, they will also have to incorporate the more important and durable of the findings of this research.

Those engaged in the study of economic fluctuations at the National Bureau placed their hope in the cumulation of economic knowledge: that their "quest of the lessons of experience will aid other students, as well as laymen who must wrestle practically with business cycles" (Burns [1946] 1954, p. 24).[4] Their work has been primarily in the nature of basic research—on how business cycles come about, vary, and interact with structural and operational changes in the economy—because this strategy promised to contribute most in the long run to the improvement of the analysis of current business conditions, economic forecasting, and policies. There is evidence in support of this strategy in the wide use made of various tools and results of this research, for example, the reference chronology of business cycle peaks and troughs, the identification of mild and severe contractions, systematic amplitude differences among individual economic processes, and the classification of the lat-

3. Let me add to this sentence an abbreviated list of references (all are volumes in the NBER series of Studies in Business Cycles: Mitchell 1927, 1951; Burns and Mitchell 1946; Hultgren 1948; Abramovitz 1950; Stanback 1962; Creamer and Bernstein 1956; Mack 1956; Moore 1961; Mintz 1967.

4. Having illustrated some problems in business cycle research that are of great importance to those concerned with economic policy ("Whether a cyclical downturn can be recognized promptly enough to permit immediate governmental intervention, whether cost-price relations are of slight consequence in the termination of a boom, whether inflationary tendencies become important only as 'full employment' is approached"), Burns continues: "True, the most painstaking studies of experience will not always lead to conclusive answers; but they should at least narrow the margins of uncertainty, and thus furnish a better basis than now exists for dealing with grave issues of business cycle theory and policy" ([1946] 1954, p. 24).

ter by characteristic cyclical timing. Serious criticism also appeared, but it centered on the methodology of the Bureau's cyclical analysis rather than on the substantive findings of this analysis.[5]

Recent literature on the behavior, determinants, and influence of such key economic variables as consumption, types of investment, prices, and money shows continuing concern with a number of economic relationships explored in the National Bureau reports. For example, fixed-investment functions in most of the major aggregate econometric models employ profit variables that have long been stressed in these reports.[6] The accelerator variables appear to be working with rather long distributed lags in these functions, which is consistent with the view that they explain long-run tendencies much better than short-run behavior.[7] In the determination of inventory investment, the accelerator has a role to play, and an important nexus exists involving new and unfilled orders, shipments, production, and price changes; this theme has received much attention in the work of Abramovitz, Stanback, Mack, and Zarnowitz and increasing recognition in more recent econometric studies.[8]

In the theory of consumption, formulations that are consistent with observation of both the short-term instability and the long-term stability and higher values of the proportion of income consumed have in effect superseded Keynes's simpler concept of a stable relationship between consumer expenditures and current income. The failure of early postwar forecasts and Kuznets's data (1946, pp. 52–54) showing a rough constancy of the share of capital formation in U.S. output led to doubts about the validity of Keynes's concept, at least as an explanation of the long-run savings-income relation, and to the emergence of the "relative income," "permanent income," and "lifetime income" hypotheses of Duesenberry (1949), M. Friedman (1957), Modigliani and Brumberg (1954), and Ando and Modigliani (1963). In empirical work, lagged consumption or income terms and measures of assets or wealth are now commonly included in the consumption equations. The National Bureau

5. Koopmans 1947, 1949; Vining 1949a, 1949b. This debate, with an "Additional Comment" by Koopmans 1957, is reprinted in Gordon and Klein 1965, pp. 196–231.
6. Cyclical changes in actual and prospective profits have a strategic part in Mitchell's *Business Cycles* (1913). Mitchell viewed the encroachment of unit costs on prices as one of the main factors limiting the boom and, correspondingly, the improvement in the price-cost ratios and profit margins as one of the main factors limiting the contraction and stimulating the revival.
7. This view is well represented in the literature on the determinants of investment in capital goods. See Burns 1952a, where tests by Kuznets, Tinbergen, and Hultgren are cited in support of this position. (These tests, however, refer to the simple old version of the "accelerator principle," which is now in disuse; recent and current studies employ instead the "flexible," or distributed, lag forms of the accelerator.) The econometric models of Tinbergen, Klein and associates, and Suits primarily use profits in their investment equations; some newer efforts such as the massive Brookings–Social Science Research Council (SSRC) model rely more on the modern stock adjustment (accelerator) formulations. For references, see two survey articles: Nerlove 1966 and Hickman 1969.
8. The Bureau reports include (in addition to the studies by Abramovitz, Stanback, and Mack listed in n. 3), Zarnowitz 1961, 1962; and Mack 1967. Other studies include Darling, Lovell, and Fromm 1961–62; Lovell 1964; Eckstein and Fromm 1968; Courchene 1967, 1969.

was actively involved in these developments (NBER publications include Brady and Friedman 1947; Modigliani 1949; Ferber 1953; M. Friedman 1957; see Burns 1952b for a critical review of the pre-1952 contributions).

Studies of business cycle indicators, diffusion indexes, anticipations data, and short-term economic forecasting all grew out of the Bureau's basic program of cyclical research, but their results are much more directly applicable to the practical problems of decision makers in government and business. The selection of the indicators was based on studies of hundreds of economic time series and successive reviews of the results by Mitchell, Burns, Moore, Shiskin, and associates (see chaps. 10 and 11 for references and detail). Since 1961, up-to-date charts, tabulations, and various analytical measures for these data have been published monthly by the U.S. Department of Commerce. The literature and the data on economic forecasts collected from a variety of sources indicate clearly that the materials and techniques developed in these studies have become important and widely used tools in the analysis and prediction of business conditions.[9] Here the story of the Bureau's efforts has a linkage with the broader subject of the development and present state of economic forecasting, which has recently become something of a "growth industry," reflecting the growth of both the economy and the concern with economic instability.

5.2 Direction of the NBER Research in Business Cycles

Theories of business cycles deal with the effects and interaction of two sets of factors, the exogenous disturbances (e.g., variation in weather, inventions, wars, political and perhaps economic policy changes) and the endogenous components of the economic system (quantities demanded and supplied, prices, etc., usually collected in large aggregates by major categories of markets or spending). There are some hypotheses that rely primarily on the first set, attributing the cyclical movements of the economy to cycles in the external disturbances (such as weather-induced harvest cycles). More common are theories that stress the second set, trying to identify endogenous causes of instability in the economic system:

> With very few exceptions, all serious explanations are neither purely exogenous nor purely endogenous. . . . Even if one assumes a weather cycle, the peculiar response of the business system, which converts harvest variations into a general alternation of prosperity and depression, has still to be explained. On the other hand, a purely endogenous theory is hardly satisfactory. It is not likely that, without outside shocks, a cyclical movement would go on forever: and, even if it did go on, its course would certainly be

9. Thus, most forecasts of the economy's course in the near future use the framework of the national income accounts, but business cycle indicators are consulted by a large majority of the forecasters in the samples we have reviewed and are listed along with the informal "GNP models" as the principal approaches actually employed (see Zarnowitz 1971).

profoundly influenced by outside shocks—that is, by changes in the data (however these may be defined and delimited by economically explained variables). [10]

Most business cycle theories, old and new, are dynamic in the sense of being designed to "explain how one situation grows out of the foregoing" (Frisch 1933). Dynamic models incorporate lags in response, that is, relationships among variables whose magnitudes pertain to different points of time. [11] Such models with lags can generate growth and cycles endogenously, that is, even without changes in the parameters, in the exogenous variables, or in the disturbances. More generally, however, changes in these outside "data," which may be either random or systematic-autonomous, are included in the analysis, and the models are then used to show how the cyclical response system in the economy converts such changes into recurrent, pervasive fluctuations. In this view, external impulses as well as the internal propagation mechanism are required for the cyclical movements in economic activity to persist; nevertheless, some writers who accept this type of theory still interpret business cycles as "self-generating," that is, having their essential traits determined primarily by the economy's organization and modus operandi, not by the nature of any disturbing causes "outside" the economic system.

It is probably this broad conception of self-generating cyclical fluctuations that best describes the core of the theory accepted by Wesley Mitchell, although his comprehensive "analytic description" of business cycles includes some very different elements as well, in subsidiary roles (see M. Friedman 1952). Exogenous forces and accidental events can accelerate or retard an expansion, alleviate or aggravate a contraction. These movements, which are basically endogenous, may also sometimes run into barriers; for example, an expansion may be halted by the upper limit on the supply of money under the gold standard. But there is no evidence that the business cycle peaks (troughs) are typically caused by a concentration of unfavorable (favorable) external disturbances. Also, the expansionary and contractionary processes, while "cumulative," are usually self-limiting due to the stresses and imbalances that they themselves create; they are rarely terminated by any identifiable barriers. Thus, the economy is definitely not viewed as fundamentally unstable in the sense of generating potentially "explosive" fluctuations which are constrained by some limiting factors. [12]

The National Bureau studies in business cycles show no commitment to any particular cyclical theory but rather deal with aspects of various theories and

10. Haberler 1964, p. 9. It may be added, however, that Haberler suggests that methodologically "[f]or various reasons, it seems desirable, in the explanation of the business cycle, to attach as little importance as possible to the influence of external disturbances" (1964, p. 10).

11. Other dynamic devices closely related to lags include uses of differences or derivatives, expressing rates of change over time, and of cumulated variables (see Christ 1956).

12. The best known theory of such fluctuations, based on a strong accelerator-multiplier interaction, was advanced much later by Hicks (1950). For a critique of this theory, with particular reference to the related evidence from the business cycle studies of the NBER, see Burns 1952a.

their empirical validity. This is probably to a large extent a reflection of the strong influence of Mitchell's work, in which business cycles are treated as a set of complex phenomena with a plurality of causes and which is itself in effect a synthesis of elements of several theories, old and new. There are distinctive concepts here, notably of the differential responses in the price system, the lag of selling prices behind buying prices or costs, and the effects of the consequent changes in profit margins (and the totals and diffusion of profits) on investment and business activity in general. But there are also other important components such as the lags of induced expenditures behind receipts and of investment outlays and deliveries behind investment decisions and orders, the responses of the monetary and banking system, the resulting changes in the cost and availability of credit, in expectations, etc. [13] Evidence collected and evaluated by the National Bureau indicates that these processes, despite their diversity and complexity, displayed a substantial degree of consistency over the successive cycles. This is shown by the diffusion indexes that reveal the pervasiveness and early timing of the fluctuations in the *scope* of expansions and contractions, which are hidden behind the movements of economic aggregates. It is seen, too, in the persistence of timing sequences of different activities: orders, production, shipments, inventory change; investment commitments, expenditures, and realizations; labor market adjustments; interest rates, bond and stock prices; industrial prices, costs, and profit margins. [14]

It seems fair to say that research of this kind and scope directly serves the purpose of analyzing the complex system of processes that are involved in business cycles rather than the purpose of constructing the simplest acceptable theory that could account for the basic features of business cycles. It works toward the latter objective but indirectly, in ways resembling a "roundabout" method of production, which seeks to be more efficient at the cost of being very time-consuming. Substantial contributions to the "tested knowledge of business cycles" have thus been made, but they do not add up to an integrated theory with demonstrated capacity to explain the past and predict the future phenomena in question. To be sure, this ultimate scientific goal may seem rather elusive in the context of dealing with complex processes of economic change which are themselves subject to subtle historical alterations as are,

---

13. In his essay on Mitchell, M. Friedman writes (1952, p. 271): "The business-cycle theory I have constructed from Part III of Mitchell's 1913 volume contains practically every element that is significant in the business-cycle theories that are currently prominent. Here are the multiplier process, the acceleration principle, the Pigovian cycles of optimism and pessimism, the Marshallian and Hawtreyan drain of cash from the banking system and the resultant tightening of the money market, a decline in the expected yield from new investment at the peak that is the counterpart of the Keynesian 'collapse of the marginal efficiency of capital' except that it is a continuous decline rather than a discontinuous 'collapse,' the Keynesian changes in liquidity preference. Here, too, is an attempt at a reasoned explanation and integration of these phenomena."

14. See Moore 1962 for a report on the early work of the National Bureau on the diffusion indexes, timing sequences, and other aspects of business cycles.

also, the structure and institutions of the economy and the targets and tools of economic policy.

5.3   The Concurrent Developments in Theory and Econometrics

More direct attempts to formulate "the" theory of business cycles, mainly by means of speculative thinking, deductive logic, and more or less abstract models, account for a large part of the literature on the economics of cyclical change and growth. There are intellectually attractive problems in economic dynamics, and some ingenious cyclical models have been constructed. It is, however, primarily by being confronted with historical evidence that such models can contribute to our understanding of the business cycles, and not all of the models are testable. When the work of testing and synthesizing is outdistanced by model construction, this tends to result in a proliferation of different (but typically overlapping) theoretical constructs, not in progress toward a unified, validated theory. The latter clearly requires that both empirical and theoretical studies be pursued so as to profit from the quasi-symbiotic interaction of selective fact and disciplined thought (Burns 1969, pp. 12–13).

The decade of the 1930s saw the beginning of three important developments: (1) the formulation and interpretation of explicit and complete mathematical models of business cycles in highly aggregative form (Frisch 1933; Kalecki 1935; Samuelson 1939); (2) the reformulation of macroeconomic theory (Keynes 1936); and (3) the construction of econometric models of business cycles (Tinbergen 1938–39). These were originally rather distinct approaches to the study of the economy and its movements, but their evolution soon came to be shaped by strong cross-influences, both between the theoretical and the econometric models and between either type of models and the post- or neo-Keynesian analysis.

The mathematical models include a system in which a given disturbance sets off fluctuations of an ever smaller amplitude, that is, a *damped* movement toward a new equilibrium. Frisch presents a linear model of this type, where external shocks keep alive the fluctuations in spite of dampening. He notes that the shocks need not be entirely or necessarily random and sees one of their sources in technological innovations, whose role in the economic process of growth and cycles was stressed by Schumpeter (see Frisch 1933; sec. VI; Schumpeter 1934, 1939). Another source of such autonomous impulses, which may be of increasing importance, is the public sector of the economy, whose rapid growth in recent times is a well-known matter of record.

Several early trade cycle theories have a basically Keynesian orientation but different dynamic features. Thus, Harrod (1936) stressed the acceleration principle; Kalecki (1937), the lag between investment decisions and realizations; and Kaldor (1940), investment and saving as nonlinear functions of the levels of output and capital. Samuelson (1939) has shown how combining the multiplier with the accelerator results in a model which can produce cycles that are either damped or constant or explosive, depending on the numerical values of the two interacting parameters. An endogenous model by Hicks (1950) specifies the values that would produce explosive fluctuations but uses nonlinear constraints to generate cycles around an upward equilibrium trend in national output.

These and other accelerator-multiplier and nonlinear models illustrate a variety of interesting problems in economic dynamics (see Kalecki 1935, 1937; Harrod 1936; Kaldor 1940; Metzler 1941, 1946; Goodwin 1951). They are, however, likely to be more useful for the (somewhat circular) purpose of studying the essential elements and causes of the observed fluctuations of the economy. Their explanatory or predictive power has not been demonstrated. The heavy emphasis on induced investment, with high values for the accelerator, makes these models highly unstable, a feature others found difficult to reconcile with the historical (particularly, recent) course of the economy.

Reactions against the limitations of the endogenous accelerator models can be found, in various explicit or implicit forms, in both theoretical and applied work (see notably Duesenberry 1958). The result is a new emphasis on the plurality of causes and diversity of elements in the individual business cycles, which will remind the reader of Mitchell's analysis and the evidence presented in the National Bureau studies. The similarities extend to several important components of the theory, notably the role of construction costs and profits in the explanation of investment.[15] There is certainly much less affinity between the Bureau's approach and those endogenous models that depend principally and rather rigidly on the acceleration principle.[16]

The construction of aggregate econometric models was originally (as in the pioneering work by Tinbergen 1938–39, 1940) strongly oriented toward business cycle research. In the postwar period, work on such models intensified and broadened, and its results are now being widely used for various purposes, including forecasting, tests of macroeconomic hypotheses, and simulation of the likely effects of alternative policies. The models for the U.S. economy progressed from annual to quarterly units; they vary greatly in size and complexity; but the evolution so far appears to be in the direction of ever larger systems. The models, for the United States as well as for the other countries, generally utilize the structure of national income accounts and are

15. See Duesenberry 1958, chs. 5 and 7. Important antecedent models featuring profits in the investment functions are found in Tinbergen 1938–39; L. R. Klein 1951; L. R. Klein and Goldberger 1955; and Meyer and Kuh 1957.

16. See Burns 1950 for a critique of the Hicks trade cycle theory. It is true that self-generating cycles are the central concepts in the work of Mitchell and others at the National Bureau and that the role of exogenous factors, though by no means disregarded, is treated as secondary. But the argument seems persuasive that the main ideas in the NBER approach (that the nature of the cycle is determined primarily by the structure and institutions of the economy and that both prediction and control of the cycle must be sought in the understanding of the "processes which run regularly within the world of business itself") would not be substantively changed even if the role of the "disturbing causes" were more explicitly involved (see M. Friedman 1952, pp. 253–54).

for the most part of Keynesian persuasion. Many have similar features. This similarity in part reflects the importance and influence in this area of the work by Lawrence R. Klein and his associates.[17]

Since the views about the nature and causes of business cycles are quite diverse, as illustrated by the preceding brief survey of the different theories and models, it is important to ask what light the econometric studies throw upon the relation of the exogenous and endogenous factors that may be involved. The question must be raised in the context of two developments: (1) the increasing emphasis on exogenous factors, among which are included political and economic policy changes, and (2) the challenge to certain tenets and applications of Keynesian theory raised in writings of several monetary economists, particularly Milton Friedman. In what follows, attention will be given to these topics.

5.4 Business-Cycle Simulations

In a study of the Klein-Goldberger econometric model of the U.S. economy, Irma Adelman and Frank Adelman (1959) concluded that nonstochastic simulations based on smooth extrapolations of the exogenous variables do not enable that model to generate cyclical movements resembling the historically observed fluctuations, nor do "type I" stochastic simulations, with random shocks superimposed upon the extrapolated values of the exogenous variables. They found, however, that "type II" stochastic simulations, with random shocks introduced into each of the fitted equations, do result in cycles whose average duration, conformity, and timing characteristics agree broadly with the measures developed by the National Bureau. They interpreted these results as consistent with the Frisch hypothesis that highly developed capitalistic economies react to random impulses so as to convert them into the pervasive and recurrent fluctuations described as the business cycle. Similarly, in his survey of 16 U.S. and foreign aggregate econometric models, Hickman (1969, p. 429) reported that "the weight of their evidence suggests strongly that modern mixed enterprise systems are characterized by stable response mechanisms and small dynamic multipliers. If that be so, then the cycles of experience must be kept alive by exogenous stimuli."

In a comprehensive investigation of econometric model simulations, a team of National Bureau researchers, aided by the active cooperation of the builders of several quarterly U.S. models, found that nonstochastic sample-period simulations produce strongly damped cyclical movements (Zarnowitz, Boschan, and Moore 1972). Only the first one or two recessions covered are, in some attenuated form, reproduced in such simulations; beyond that, the declines in

17. See L. R. Klein 1950, 1964; L. R. Klein and Goldberger 1955; Evans and Klein 1967. See the survey articles by Nerlove (1966) and Hickman (1969) for references to other U.S. and foreign econometric models.

the overall aggregates tend to disappear. In simulations extending for a hundred quarters into the future, the projected series are in general smooth and trend dominated, indicating that these models do not generate cyclical movement endogenously. When shocks are applied to these long ex ante simulations, many fluctuations do occur, but they are in large part too short to qualify as cyclical, according to comparisons with the NBER reference cycle measurements. The simulations based on autocorrelated shocks are much smoother and often appear more plausible than those with serially uncorrelated shocks.

The models examined in these simulation studies are in general stable. If it could be assumed that they are correctly specified, these experiments would provide some support for the Wicksell-Slutsky-Frisch theory of a dynamically stable (damped) response mechanism, with fluctuations being renewed and "kept alive" by erratic shocks. The support would appear strong in the case of the Adelmans' study and some of the models examined by Hickman. It must be viewed as much more limited and qualified, however, as far as the more recent and comprehensive reports of the 1969 NBER conference at Harvard are concerned.[18] Here the evidence suggests that random disturbances alone produce only weak fluctuations, visible in deviations from trends rather than in the stochastically simulated series proper. Smoother and longer (but similarly weak) fluctuations appear when the shocks to the equations are serially correlated. The cyclical aspects of the simulations would probably be strengthened by application of autocorrelated shocks not only to the equations with endogenous variables but also to the exogenous variables.[19] There are reasons to expect that wars, policy actions, technological change (innovations), etc., would indeed frequently result in autocorrelated "autonomous" shocks to the economy.

However, the econometric models in question may not be correctly specified. If so, then the autocorrelations observed in the sample residuals for many equations in these models may in the main reflect these misspecifications. Frequent caveats on this score are expressed in the work on econometric model simulations (Adelman and Adelman 1959; p. 301; Hickman 1969, pp. 428–29; and remarks by de Leeuw, Hickman, and Zarnowitz et al. in Hickman 1969).

It is not easy to document specification errors in the models; economic theory provides broad guidelines, but it does not prevent arguments among economists with different views about what the correct formulations ought to

18. These include, in addition to the NBER study by Zarnowitz, Boschan, and Moore (1972), Evans, Klein, and Saito 1972; Green, Liebenberg, and Hirsch 1972; Howrey 1972. See also the introduction in Hickman 1972.

19. A few such simulations were run for the Office of Business Economics (OBE) model by Green, Liebenberg, and Hirsch (1972), with the result that cycle declines were increased in amplitude and duration. But the effects of shocks in exogenous variables were not given adequate attention in the 1969 NBER conference studies.

be. Large-scale, complex models, in particular, pose many detailed specification problems that theory and empirical research have not yet been able to resolve with the existing information. The best tests available here are indirect, based on the predictive value of the model (see Christ 1968).

5.5   The Role of Money

According to many critics, a major source of specification errors in recent econometric models is the neglect or inadequate handling of the monetary and financial factors. This view is stressed particularly by those economists who take a "monetarist" approach to macroeconomics (e.g., M. Friedman 1959, 1968, 1970b; M. Friedman and Meiselman 1964; M. Friedman and Schwartz 1963a, 1963b, 1970; Cagan 1965, 1966). However, some economists basically sympathetic to the so-called neo-Keynesian concepts have also urged that greater attention be given to the monetary and financial sectors in econometric models, and efforts in this direction are apparent in the latest models.[20]

Evidence assembled by Friedman and Schwartz leads them to conclude (1963b, p. 63) that "there is an extremely strong case for the proposition that sizable changes in the rate of change in the money stock are a necessary and sufficient condition for sizable changes in the rate of change in the money income." For the minor U.S. economic fluctuations, "the case for a monetary explanation is not nearly so strong," but "it is plausible to suppose that changes in the stock of money played an important independent role, though certainly the evidence for these minor movements does not rule out other interpretations" (Friedman and Schwartz, 1963b, pp. 55, 63). The mechanism whereby monetary changes are transmitted in ways that can produce cyclical fluctuations in income is viewed as a series of reciprocal adjustments of stocks to flows, which involve variable but often lengthy lags. Absorption of newly injected money, for example, requires alteration of yields and prices of different assets, which creates discrepancies between the actual and desired portfolios and prompts the banks and the public to reshuffle their balance sheets in the effort to reduce such discrepancies. The first impact of an increase in the monetary growth that usually occurs early in contraction is on the financial markets (bonds, then equities), but eventually the stimulus spreads to the markets for goods and services, causing rises in investment and in payments for real resources at large. In the process, interest rates first decline and then rise, the reversal being due to the increase in spending, income, and prices. The process will tend to overshoot and involve cyclical, presumably damped, adjustments to each monetary "shock."

20. See Minsky 1963, pp. 65–66. The increased concern about the role of the monetary-financial factors and their interaction with the "real" factors can also be seen in the reports on the structure and performance of the large-scale Brookings-SSRC model and especially of the more recent FRB-MIT-Penn model (de Leeuw 1965; de Leeuw and Gramlich 1968; and Ando and Modigliani 1969).

This hypothesis envisages disturbances in the growth of money supply that induce cyclical adjustments and recur frequently enough to prevent the fluctuations from dying out. The stock of money is subject to large changes that are autonomous, that is, not directly attributable to contemporary changes in income and prices. Thus, the monetary changes are here treated as a mainly exogenous and "causal" factor in a narrow but important sense.

Formally, the model of the economy that is conveyed by these studies is dynamically stable, converting random or systematic disturbances into cyclical fluctuations in major economic variables. Substantively, it is the monetary factor that is the major source of these disturbances. In particular, this factor is regarded as basically responsible for the major economic fluctuations; the evidence for the minor ones, taken alone, would not be inconsistent with the alternative view "that the close relation between money and business reflected primarily the influence of business on money" (Friedman and Schwartz, 1963b, p. 55). In most applications, however, especially by other monetarists, the distinction between the major and minor fluctuations plays no operational role, and monetary changes are treated generally as the main independent force determining the movements in money income that are associated (sometimes identified) with business cycles. The main rival theory, namely, that "real" rather than monetary factors are critical, with investment being the main motive force in business cycles, is explicitly rejected, but the monetary hypothesis is also sharply distinguished from the earlier "credit" theories of the cycle. This conception of business cycles as essentially a monetary phenomenon (resembling the "dance of the dollar" view of Irving Fisher) is also clearly different from the much broader conception of Mitchell.[21]

5.6   Assessing Policies and Understanding Business Cycles

There is a marked tendency in recent discussions of problems of inflation and recession to emphasize the power of economic policy to do both good and evil—to stabilize and disturb. According to a view held by many Keynesians, the economy is rather unstable, in need of being stimulated by fiscal policies at some times and of being restrained by fiscal and perhaps monetary policies at other times. According to the monetarist view, the economy is fundamentally stable, and major business cycle movements are primarily attributable to "inappropriate movements in the money stock"; economic instability can therefore be minimized by controlling the rate of monetary expansion (Andersen and Carlson 1970, p. 8). These are opposite positions, yet they have one important point in common, namely, that economic policy is potent enough to be, if correct, a major force working to promote or restore economic stability; and also to be, if erroneous, a major cause of, or at least contributor to, eco-

21. This statement is, of course, entirely consistent with the fact that Mitchell attached great importance to the role of money in the structure and cyclical movements of contemporary industrial economies in the Western world.

nomic instability. It all depends only on the choice of the right policies at the right time, provided that the choice is defined broadly to include self-imposed institutional rules and automatic stabilizers as well as discretionary policies.

As usual, such positions are often exaggerated and vulgarized in popular debate. Also, extreme views on the powers of stabilization policies are not new.[22] But the increasing emphasis on exogenous and particularly policy factors in the analysis of business fluctuations is so manifest in recent professional writing as to merit serious attention. Is this emphasis based on new evidence or a revival of some old beliefs? Has it increased too much or too little or just about right?

The evidence from econometric models and related simulation studies tends to support the view that exogenous factors play a major role.[23] Policy changes are generally treated as exogenous in these models. But it must again be recognized that all these models represent only different ways of combining fragments of uncertain knowledge and outright hunches; they certainly contain serious errors of commission and omission, are implemented with very imperfect data, and are valuable primarily as vehicles of a continuing search for more and firmer understanding of the economy in motion. The models differ not only with respect to the underlying theories or intuitions, that is, in specification, but also in size and complexity, sample periods, and methods of estimation and application to forecasting. With so many sources of incomparability, which cannot be eliminated, neutralized, or fully allowed for (without removing the distinctive properties of the models), conclusive discrimination among the models is very difficult. However, predictive and dynamic simulation tests, which are probably more convincing than the others, suggest at least a few broad propositions, as follows: (1) Both monetary and fiscal policy variables have significant effects on aggregate spending; neither set should be treated as dominant at all times or as negligible, and improvements in dealing with both sets pay off in better performance of the model.[24] (2) The combined influence of both sets of policy variables is far from sufficient to account for the systematic component of changes in total spending (let alone for other

22. Thus M. Friedman (1968, pp. 1, 5) reminds us that in the 1920s "it came to be widely believed that a new era had arrived in which business cycles had been rendered obsolete by advances in monetary technology. . . . The Great Contraction destroyed this naive attitude. Opinion swung to the other extreme." He expresses the fear that "now as then, the pendulum may have swung too far, that, now as then, we are in danger of assigning to monetary policy a larger role than it can perform."

23. As noted by Hickman (1972, p. 11), "Some classes of shocks may generate cycles when acting upon the models studied in this Conference. It should be emphasized, however, that broadening the class of shocks to include perturbations in exogenous variables—and to allow for serial correlation in the disturbances to equations and exogenous variables—diminishes the role of model structure as a cycle maker."

24. See Andersen and Carlson 1970; Andersen and Jordan 1968, 1969; and de Leeuw and Kalchbrenner 1969. The St. Louis model in its present version (April 1970) indicates that the fiscal effects, though weaker and more temporary than the monetary effects, are significant. See also the references to the analysis of the FRB-MIT-Penn model in n. 20; in this larger and more elaborate model, both monetary and fiscal policy variables have pronounced effects on GNP.

important elements in economic fluctuations).[25] (3) Business cycle analysis and forecasting can benefit from econometric studies of structural models of various degrees of complexity, but inadequate knowledge and data, and perhaps also problems of coordinating the work of a large group of experts, impose definite limits upon the size of potentially useful models at the present time.[26]

There are, of course, good and easily understandable reasons why changes in economic policies attract much greater and more general attention now than in times past, when both the weight of the government and the extent of its intervention in the economy were much smaller. But precisely because this is so, the chances have also increased for overestimation of the potency of governmental policies. Policy changes tend to become a matter of public record, whereas the changes wrought by forces within the economy are more diffuse and subtle, hence often difficult to discern. Moreover, policy changes interact with other "outside disturbances" and endogenous forces so that the task of isolating and evaluating the effects of these factors on the movement of national income and other aggregates is very arduous, even conceptually and a fortiori in empirical applications. The policy variables can be exogenous only in the sense that they do not respond to *current* movements in the endogenous variables. They certainly do respond to earlier developments in the economy as policymakers try to counteract undesirable trends due to either internal causes or external disturbances (including the influence of past policies). These corrective efforts must frequently concur with the more "autonomous" policy initiatives, and both affect aggregate spending, income, etc., only with lags that may be substantial and variable. When these lagged effects are cumulated and attributed fully to policy changes, the influence of these changes may often be significantly overestimated.

This way of looking at economic policies has however, other implications as well, namely, that the governmental actions may at times tend to cancel each other or have net destabilizing effects.[27] One explanation of the latter centers on the difference between the immediate and the delayed conse-

25. For example, the St. Louis equation "explains" nearly two thirds of the variance of changes in GNP with changes in money stock and high-employment federal expenditures alone. This is a rather high R^2 considering the first-difference form of the model, but contemporaneous values of the policy variables as well as short-lag values are included, and there can be little doubt that there is some bias in this single-equation approach: the influence is not entirely from money to GNP but also in the opposite direction. Other formulations designed to reduce this basic and much-debated problem have led to lower correlations (de Leeuw and Kalchbrenner 1969).

26. These limitations are stressed by several reviewers of the Brookings-SSRC model, which contains several hundred equations (see Mosbaek 1968, pp. 194–96; Griliches 1968, pp. 215–34). On the other hand, the single-equation or reduced-form models such as the St. Louis model may be used to study the influence of certain exogenous policy factors, but they are much too "underdeveloped" and structurally undetermined to be helpful in business cycle research.

27. This includes the "policy cycles" as an extreme case of destabilizing action. Maddison (1960) and Gilbert (1962) argue that in Western Europe government intervention in the postwar years succeeded in limiting fluctuations in output to a narrower range at higher levels but also induced setbacks through restrictive anti-inflationary measures.

quences of a policy, as in M. Friedman's (1968) analysis of the monetary authority's attempts to peg either interest rates or the rate of unemployment. Another explanation would have policies alternate between the immediate goals of fighting inflation and of fighting unemployment, with the efforts to contain the rise in prices leading to a business recession or slowdown and efforts to reduce unemployment leading to renewed inflationary pressures, as in some analyses based on the Phillips curve (Bronfenbrenner and Holzman 1963). The two hypotheses are not logically inconsistent and could both be valid. There is evidence to support the view that reactions to discretionary policy shifts involve patterns of lengthy and varying lags, although measurements of the distributed lags in the effect of monetary policy vary considerably and are far from conclusive. There is also evidence to support the relationship between wage changes and unemployment as summarized by the Phillips curve, although it is plausible that in the long run no stable trade-off would exist between unemployment and *anticipated* inflation (M. Friedman 1968; Phelps 1968).

In trying to evaluate any advance in economics, it is proper to take a broad view. We are dealing essentially with gradual processes of increased understanding that cannot avoid occasional setbacks. Thus seen in this brief and very incomplete survey, the work of the National Bureau has resulted in many important and potentially useful contributions.

It is much more difficult to achieve and demonstrate definite progress directly measurable in terms of the resulting improvements in dealing with current economic problems. It is clear that we know much less about the working of economic stabilization policies than we need for both an objective appraisal of the past and as a guide to such conduct of current affairs as would command wide professional agreement. It is certainly difficult, even with the benefit of hindsight, to decide such questions as whether any of the postwar U.S. recessions could have been avoided by better policies and, if so, how and at what alternative costs. But underlying such questions is the central problem of business cycle theory to which frequent reference was made here: What are the relative roles of exogenous factors and endogenous processes in determining the course of the economy? There is great need for well-designed research on this subject, the eventual results of which could contribute greatly to a better understanding of current policy issues.

II   History and Measurement

6 How Trends and Fluctuations Are Observed, Modeled, and Simulated: An Introduction

Part I of this book included many excursions into the history of business cycles, but its focus was on theories and their assessment in light of "stylized facts" broadly defined. Part II concentrates on problems of history and measurement: How are long-term trends and short-term fluctuations of the economy related in the available records? What lessons can be learned about the regularity or irregularity of business cycles? Can macroeconometric models simulate cyclical behavior of major economic variables, and if so, how and how well? These questions are addressed in chapters 7, 8, and 9. What follows is a guide to this set of topics, again with some extensions.

6.1 Trend-Cycle Decompositions

A frequently used univariate approach to modeling growth and fluctuations in rising macroeconomic series is to adjust each for seasonal variations, if relevant, and then represent the nonseasonal series as a sum of a deterministic trend and the residual "cyclical" component. For example, the postwar real GNP would be treated as consisting of an exponential trend and stochastic deviations arising from cumulation of random shocks.[1] But it is very unlikely that a given type of a deterministic trend would persist and prove projectable over long stretches of historical time, that is, across periods of great technical and structural changes, wars, booms and depressions, inflation and deflation.

---

1. Let $Q = \log$ real GNP; $L^n Q_t = Q_{t-n}$, where L is the lag (backshift) operator; $AL = 1 - \Theta_1 L - Q_2 L^2 - \ldots - Q_K L^K$; and ε_t is white noise. Then

(1) $$Q_t = a + bt + A(L)\varepsilon_t,$$

where the trend $(a + bt)$ is purely deterministic and the shocks affect only the cyclical component. The effects of each shock would persist but decline and die out after k periods (the polynomial $A(L)$ must satisfy the stationarity and invertibility conditions).

This is a strong argument against the applicability of this trend-stationary (TS) representation.

In contrast, consider the autoregressive integrated moving-average (ARIMA) modeling, in which the time series are reduced to stationarity by differencing and then their autoregressive and moving-average components are analyzed (Box and Jenkins 1976). Here a purely stochastic difference-stationary (DS) process is obtained in the presence of an autoregressive (AR) unit root.[2] In this case, the shocks affect the *change* in the series in the short run or transitorily but the *level* of the series in the long run or permanently. There is evidence that real GNP and other important economic aggregates resemble DS processes much more than TS processes (Nelson and Plosser 1982). This was interpreted as lending support to the real business cycle (RBC) theory on the ground that only real, not monetary, shocks can have permanent effects. But economic activity is most likely affected by more than one type of disturbance, and some shocks may have long effects, others short effects.[3]

The empirical estimates of the DS process are unsatisfactory in that they confuse the trend and cyclical movements in series such as real GNP. The "trends" include not only the secular growth but also most of what is generally viewed as the "cycle," including major declines. Series that look like DS could alternatively originate in TS processes with AR roots close to but distinct from 1.0, and no finite-sample tests can conclusively distinguish between DS and TS series in such cases. Hence the RBC hypothesis cannot be validated statistically along these lines (McCallum 1986).

Much more satisfactory trend and cycle estimates have been obtained recently by using unobserved components (UC) models, in which the trend is a random walk with drift and the cycle consists of deviations from trend that represent a covariance stationary process (Watson 1986).[4] The UC model for

2. This model replaces $(a + bt)$ in equation (1) with a constant and adds to it a stationary and invertible ARMA term. A simple example is

(2) $$(1 - L)Q_t = \Delta Q_t = b + (1 - \Theta L)\varepsilon_t,$$

which is *DS* for $|\Theta| < 1$. (For $\Theta = 1$, however, the process is TS; in the case of $b = 0$, Q_t would just equal ε_t.)

3. A frequent assumption in modern macroeconomics is that demand disturbances have transitory effects that dominate business cycles, whereas supply disturbances have cumulative effects that dominate the long trends. For estimated decompositions of output and unemployment based on this premise, see Blanchard and Quah 1989.

4. For example, let T and C denote the trend and cyclical components of output Q, and let e^T and e^C be white-noise shocks to T and C. Then the model consists of

(3a) $$Q_t = T_t + C_t;$$

(3b) $$T_t = a + T_{t-1} + e_t^T;$$

and

(3c) $$C_t = \Theta(L)e_t^C.$$

In the version used for estimation, e_t^T and e_{t-k}^C are uncorrelated for all k. A more general but also more difficult to implement version would allow for some correlation between T_t and C_t.

real GNP produced a cyclical component with one-to-one correspondence with the NBER chronology for 1951–83 (Watson 1986, p. 64). Harvey (1985), too, presents a general argument and supporting evidence in favor of "structural" UC modeling.

What emerges from these and other recent studies (Beveridge and Nelson 1981; Stulz and Wasserfallen 1985; Campbell and Mankiw 1987a, 1987b; Clark 1987) is that changes in macroeconomic activity measured by real GNP, employment, and industrial production have exhibited a high degree of persistence, not prompt reversals to deterministic time trends, in the United States and other developed economies. The cyclical component was relatively strong before World War II and after 1970, and was weak in the early postwar period of mild fluctuations, when stochastic trend models performed very well (but, it is important to note, this is limited evidence coming from annual estimates only).

I interpret these results to mean that trends and cycles interact and cannot be clearly separated. This agrees with the view that "the business-cycle theorist . . . cannot imitate the business-cycle statistician in merely eliminating secular trends" (Mitchell 1927, p. 233; see also Burns and Mitchell 1946, p. 270). The interdependence of growth and fluctuations (discussed from the historical point of view in chapter 7) is consistent with a number of theories, endogenous and exogenous, and does not necessarily preclude an active role for money and credit or favor supply over demand factors in the origination of business cycles.

6.2   An Illustration: Trends and Cycles in Real GNP

Even though the trend-cycle decompositions thus appear to be basically problematic, working with detrended series is considered necessary for some analytical purposes. This includes in particular the study of "growth cycles," that is, sequences of significant retardations and accelerations, or phases of below-average and above-average growth rates in indicators of aggregate economic activity. In the initial stages of the development of growth cycle measures and chronologies, long-term moving averages were experimentally used as estimates of flexible but rising trends, with a fixed span of 75 months being favored (Mintz 1969, 1972). Later, improved results were found to be provided by phase-average trend technique (Boschan and Ebanks 1978; Klein and Moore 1985, ch. 2). Another alternative is the Whittaker-Henderson type of trend curve used as a low-frequency filter in Hodrick and Prescott 1980. Detrending in this form has been applied in several RBC studies, despite the claim of the underlying theory to explain growth along with cycles (for a criticism along these lines, see King and Rebelo 1989).

Figure 6.1 compares three different trend estimates for quarterly data on GNP in constant dollars, 1948–90, plotted separately but to the same logarithmic scales. The trends are shown as solid curves; the underlying RGNP data as dotted curves. The first trend is log-linear, that is, a straight line sloping

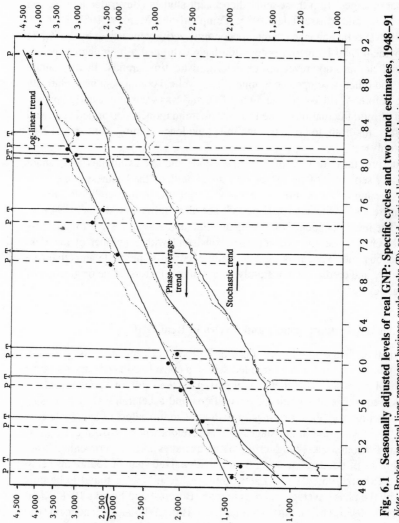

Fig. 6.1 Seasonally adjusted levels of real GNP: Specific cycles and two trend estimates, 1948–91

Note: Broken vertical lines represent business cycle peaks (P); solid vertical lines represent business cycle troughs (T). Dotted curves represent RGNP; solid curves represent trends in RGNP. Dots identify peaks and troughs of specific cycles in RGNP (shown for the top curve only).

upward at a constant rate of growth equal to 0.84% per quarter (or 3.42% per year). The second trend is nonlinear, based on the phase-average method of combining moving averages and interpolations between mean values of the series in its successive business cycle phases. The third trend, introduced and discussed in Watson 1986, is stochastic and based on an unobserved components representation of the process describing the RGNP data. Here log RGNP is treated as a sum of the trend, modeled as a random walk with drift, and a residual, modeled as a covariance stationary process and labeled the cyclical component. In the general case, the two components are partially correlated.[5]

The deterministic log-linear trend is, of course, free of any cyclical or other short-term movements. The phase-average trend is clearly much more flexible and fits the same data much more clearly; it too is designed so as not to contain any cyclical elements. In contrast, the stochastic trend flattens in several recessions (1953–54, 1973–75, 1981–82) and even declines in some (1957–58, 1960).

The specific-cycle peaks and troughs in the level of real GNP are identified by filled dots in figure 6.1. There is a one-to-one correspondence between the cyclical declines in the total output of the economy so measured and the business contractions as dated by NBER, which are represented by the grid of the vertical broken lines (peaks, P) and solid lines (troughs, T). But on a few occasions timing discrepancies can be observed, where the center month of the real GNP turning quarter precedes the monthly NBER reference date. The latter, it should be recalled, is based on the consensus of roughly coincident indicators, monthly and quarterly, including measures of real income, sales, production, and employment. The figure also shows that the recognized chronology of U.S. business cycles does not validate the popular rule of thumb according to which two consecutive quarterly declines in real GNP denote a recession. For example, according to the current data, no decline of two or more quarters occurred in either of the two recession years, 1960 and 1980.

Figure 6.2 shows deviations from each of the three trends, again plotted separately but to the same arithmetic scales, with each trend level equated to 100. The deviations of the data from the log-linear trend are very large much of the time, especially downward in the late 1940s and on and off in the last decade, upward in the middle 1960s and early 1970s. It is evident that the assumption of log-linearity produces a poor trend estimate. The economy grew much faster in 1948–52 (one recession) than in 1953–60 (three recessions), and again much faster in the 1960s (one long expansion) than in the 1970s and early 1980s (four recessions). The phase-average trend takes these variations into account, and the deviations from it are relatively small. The stochastic trend includes many small random movements, so here the deviations are remarkably smooth. They appear to be much more "cyclical" and

5. I am very much indebted to Mark Watson for letting me have his data and programs for both this univariate trend and also an interesting multivariate trend estimate from King, Plosser, Stock, and Watson 1991. (The latter is annual and not used here.)

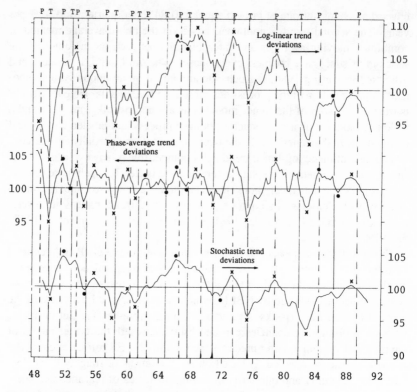

Fig. 6.2   Real GNP: Deviations from log-linear trend (A) and from phase-average trend (B), 1948–85

Note: Trend level = 100. Broken vertical lines represent growth cycle peaks (P); solid vertical lines represent growth cycle troughs (T). Dots identify peaks and troughs of specific cycles; crosses identify those turning points that match growth cycle peaks or troughs.

less "irregular" than the deviations from the phase-average trend and, though smaller, show more similarity to the deviations from the log-linear trend.

The deviations from trend follow a pattern of growth cycles represented in figure 6.2 by a grid of vertical broken and solid lines, which are respectively peaks and troughs separating phases of above-normal and below-normal growth. A comparison of figures 6.1 and 6.2 confirms that five of nine postwar business cycle peaks (in 1957, 1969, 1973, 1980, and 1990) were preceded by growth retardations that lasted from 6 to 17 months. On four occasions, in 1951–52, 1962–64, 1966–67, and 1984–86, the nation's output decelerated markedly without becoming negative. These are slowdowns that did not turn into recessions; that is, they belong to those growth cycles that did not become growth cycles.

The series of deviations from both the log-linear trend and the stochastic trend show three large waves each, with troughs in the recession years 1949,

1957, 1975, and 1982. The deviations from the better fitting phase-average trend do not have this configuration.

6.3 How Growth and Fluctuations Interact

The reference cycle analysis of Burns and Mitchell (1946) describes the movements of each time series of interest during each business cycle covered. The average standing of the series in each of nine successive stages of a cycle (the initial trough, three successive thirds of the expansion, the peak, three successive thirds of the contraction, and the terminal trough) is expressed as a percentage of the average level of the series during the entire cycle. That average level is always equated to 100, so the method eliminates the intercycle trend but retains the intracycle trend. The historical studies of the National Bureau analyzed such reference cycle patterns for hundreds of time series in efforts to identify the prevailing behavior of the variables covered and any systematic changes in it. This helped to build up our knowledge of the stylized facts, some of which are summarized in chapter 2, section 2.2, and elsewhere in part I of this book. The patterns for upward-trending series, which include most of the data on incomes, output, and employment, show strong effects of secular growth: terminal troughs tend to be higher than the initial troughs, and the peak and average levels as a rule increase from one cycle to the next. The few exceptions have occurred in connection with the most severe contractions and the shortest and mildest expansions.

Since business expansions and contractions vary in length across the different cycles, so will the stages into which they are divided. In effect, then, the NBER analysis proceeds in two units of measurement: business cycle time and calendar time. The latter is more familiar and probably preferable for many purposes, including studies of contemporary developments and forecasting (the calendar-time lengths of the current phase and cycle are unknown). But many historical regularities may be better articulated in business cycle time, for example, leads and lags may vary less across cycles when expressed in stages and their fractions rather than months. More generally, business cycle time may be more closely related to "psychological time" (Allais 1966, 1972). If events are perceived to move more slowly in long than in short cycle phases, then expectations may cover longer chronological time spans in the former and adjustments may be slower (Friedman and Schwartz 1982, p. 358).

This argument would apply best to a world in which qualitatively much the same train of events would occur in each business cycle, only stretched out in long phases and compressed in short ones. This is probably often a fair approximation to reality but far from being a firm rule. Occasionally an expansion is aborted: short *and* slow, with little net growth; or a contraction is aggravated: long *and* fast, that is, a severe depression. A long expansion may also be vigorous much of the time, though seldom continuously so.

Some RBC models explicitly predict a trade-off between growth and stability: when people opt for higher expected returns and accept higher risks, the result will be faster but also more volatile growth in profits, income, and output (see Black 1987, p. 76). But analogies between individuals and societies can be misleading, and rules of personal finance need not apply to processes of aggregate economic activity. Historical data indicate that in periods when the annual growth rates in U.S. output were on average high (low), their standard deviations were low (high). Thus in 1903–13, 1923–29, and 1948–69 (37-year, nine peak-to-peak cycles) mean growth per annum was 3.7%, with a standard deviation of 3.7; in 1913–23, 1929–48, and 1969–81 (41-year, nine peak-to-peak cycles) mean growth p.a. was 2.6%, with a standard deviation of 7.2.[6] In short, relatively *high* growth was apparently associated with relatively *low* instability.

The relationship between long-term growth and cyclical variability is apt to vary depending on their sources. No correspondence exists, for example, between the average growth rates and the relative duration of contractions. The latter was historically lower on average in periods of long inflationary trends than in periods of long deflationary trends (Zarnowitz and Moore 1986, pp. 525–31), but real growth was often weak in times of high inflation, as in 1913–23 and 1969–81.

6.4   Some International Comparisons

The evidence for the United States and other countries in the postwar period is consistent with the hypothesis that business cycles are less frequent and milder when and where long-term real growth is higher. First, growth was generally lower and cyclical instability greater in the second than in the first half of the postwar era. Second, economies that grew fast (notably Japan and West Germany) had milder fluctuations than economies that grew more slowly (notably the United States and United Kingdom).

In the 1950s and 1960s, France, Italy, West Germany, Japan, and a number of smaller countries enjoyed extraordinarily high rates of economic growth. World War II devastated the physical capital and wealth of these nations and their initial postwar activity levels were very low, but their human capital was much better preserved and hence their productive potential was high. Monetary and fiscal reforms restored sound currencies and free markets, and political reforms restored democratic values and institutions. The transitions from closed, regimented, and inept systems to open, free, and efficient ones were relatively smooth. Foreign aid helped in this historically unique process, and foreign trade helped even more.

During this period, real growth in continental Europe and the Far East was

6. See chapter 7, table 7.1 and text, and Zarnowitz and Moore 1986, table 9.11 and text, pp. 551–53, for detail.

interrupted infrequently and mostly by slowdowns rather than absolute declines in overall economic activity. Thus, the benefits of high growth were augmented by those of high cyclical stability.

Figure 6.3 presents the evidence, based on composite indexes of coincident indicators for eight countries. These indexes combine monthly and quarterly measures of total output, industrial production, employment, real sales, and inverted unemployment, and have trends equal to those of the corresponding series for real GNP or GDP. The data are collected and processed by the Center for International Business Cycle Research (CIBCR) at Columbia University Business School.

The black dots mark peaks and troughs of specific cycles in the indexes. The so-identified declines last several (as a rule, 6 or more) months and have amplitudes of several or more percentage points (as a rule, at least 1%). They presumably reflect business contractions.[7] The unfilled dots mark shorter and/ or smaller declines that do not qualify as recessions but may be associated with significant retardations in general economic activity. However, substantial business slowdowns can occur without any noticeable decreases in the levels of the coincident indexes, particularly in places and times of very high overall growth (e.g., West Germany, 1956–57, and Japan, 1957 and 1964).

The charts show some important similarities between the country indexes, notably the concentration of long expansions in the 1960s and 1980s, of mild recessions or slowdowns in the middle or later 1960s, and of more severe contractions in the mid-1970s and early 1980s. But there are also pronounced differences, which are clearly related in the main to longer growth trends. The central point here is that high growth helps to reduce the frequency and depth of business contractions.

Thus, according to these data (which for some countries begin only in the mid-1950s), France had its first postwar recession in 1958–59, Italy in 1963–65, West Germany in 1966–67, and Japan in 1973–75. Meanwhile, Canada, United Kingdom, United States, and Australia, all countries that suffered much smaller direct wartime damages, had less need of domestic reconstruction, lower growth rates, and earlier and more frequent recessions (fig. 6.3).

Economic growth slowed considerably everywhere during the 1970s and 1980s, and simultaneously business contractions became both more common and more severe. They spread worldwide in 1974–75, after the first oil price shock, and in 1980–82, after new OPEC cartel price hikes and strong counterinflationary policy moves in the United States. In 1990–91, recessions spread mainly in the English-speaking countries, following new tight-money actions, the conflict over Kuwait, and the war with Iraq.

The economies of the United States and United Kingdom had relatively low

7. There is no NBER-type international reference chronology of business cycle peaks and troughs for the post–World War II period.

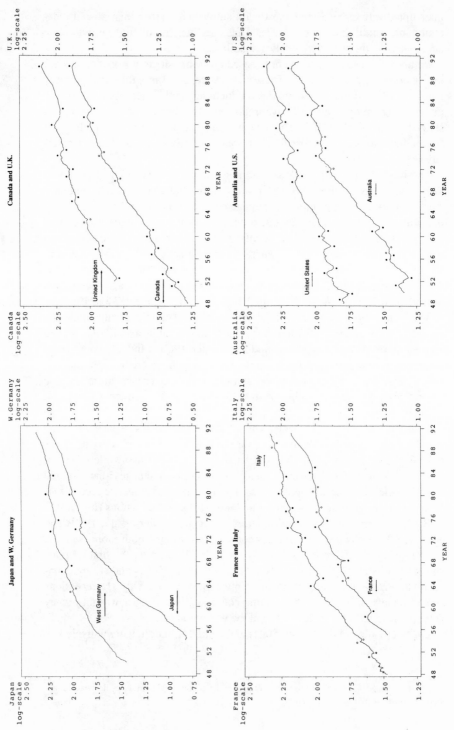

Fig. 6.3 Trend-adjusted indexes of coincident indicators

rates of real growth and most cyclical variability. In sharp contrast, West Germany and, particularly, Japan had both the highest growth rates and least cyclicality. Indeed, one can say that in Japan business cycles as we know them were essentially absent. Although Japan's growth was much slower after the mid-1970s than before, it still continued to be remarkably steady. The index for France shows frequent but short and shallow declines, except in 1958–59 and 1974–75 (its sharp decline in the spring of 1968 reflects largely the concurrent political unrest).

In 1955–90, the longest common period covered, the number of complete peak-to-peak cycles in the indexes were as follows: United States, six; United Kingdom and Italy, five each; France and Australia, four each; Canada and West Germany, three each; Japan, two. In all, the postwar business cycles were shorter and more numerous in the United States than in any of the other countries. An inspection of the charts suggests that this was mainly due to the shorter durations of U.S. expansions. More generally, expansions differed much more than contractions across the countries, in both length and amplitude.

It is widely recognized that higher rates of saving-cum-investment in real terms favor higher rates of growth. The most successful economies are those that achieve the highest average long-term rates of investment in productive capital, human and physical. Even though investment as measured in national income accounts (i.e., investment in the physical capital of the business sector) has been much more cyclical than consumption, it is not necessarily true that a larger share of this or a more comprehensive investment aggregate will increase the fluctuations of the economy, along with its growth. Investment can be both high and stable, provided it is a part of, and a response to, growth in aggregate demand that is sufficient to keep the economy near full employment.[8]

6.5   Are There Periodicities in Cyclical Behavior?

There is little evidence of regularity in the durations of business expansions and contractions inferred from the NBER studies of historical annals and data for the United States, Britain, France, and Germany. These numbers vary greatly without suggesting any particular pattern. But they synthesize measures for a wide range of conditions: major and minor cycles in times of peace and war, different monetary regimes, and long inflationary and deflationary trends. Some fluctuations are well documented in the data; others, mainly for the more distant past, are not. So the apparent lack of periodicity could be an artifact due to the aggregation over the different categories of observed cycles.

Moreover, it is possible for unobserved cycles of different durations to co-

---

8. Investment, broadly interpreted, is in the end only justified by growth in the demand for the product of the new capital. Equally true, growth itself depends positively on prior rates of investment that enhances productivity and improves competitiveness. See Zarnowitz 1991.

exist: there could be several of them, concurrent and interacting, each with its own characteristic frequency. The observed movements would then be composites of short and small subcycles, business cycles of larger and intermediate dimensions, and possibly "long waves" measured in decades rather than years. To isolate the multiple periodicities hidden in the data, careful distinctions and decomposition methods need to be applied.

However, this hypothesis is not supported by the data in any clear and consistent way (chapter 8). Excluding the wartime episodes (which consist of expansions of above-average length followed by contractions of below-average length) reduces the variance of durations of cyclical phases but not by much. The few cycles with deep depressions typically followed by long and large but not always vigorous expansions were certainly very different from all others. Of course, a separate treatment of such outliers would produce smaller variances for each of the resulting groups. But most of the NBER-designated business cycles do not lend themselves to a clear-cut classification into major and minor cycles. The longer cycles are not simply combinations of the short ones, nor do the large and small fluctuations occur in any particular sequence over time. Durations and amplitudes of cyclical movements are likely to be correlated positively but not strongly. Convincing evidence of the existence of long waves in economic growth is essentially lacking (Kondratieff 1926 [1935]; Burns and Mitchell 1946, pp. 431–40; Garvy 1943; chapter 8, sec. 8.2.2, this volume). This is so not just because it is very difficult to elicit the necessary information from time series that cover at most the two and a half cycles dated by Kondratieff between 1790 and 1920 (most cover only one or one and a half cycles). Support for the long-wave hypothesis comes mainly from series on wholesale prices; it is very fragmentary and weak for indicators of real economic activity.

The historical sequence of inflationary trends (1789–1814, 1843–64, 1896–1920) alternating with deflationary trends (1814–43, 1864–96, 1920–32) reflects mainly the parallel long movements in the growth of money and credit as related to gold discoveries, wars, and monetary regimes and policies. Expansions tended to be longer relative to contractions in the periods of rising trends in prices than they were in periods of falling trends, but there is no correlation between the long-term rates of growth and inflation, and none is expected on theoretical grounds.

Some elements of limited and temporary periodicities emerge between the 1870s and 1930s, when major cycles are defined as being marked off by troughs in severe contractions for both the United States and Britain. But no deep depressions occurred after World War II, and the long-wave theory predicted a deflationary downswing at least since the later 1960s or early 1970s, but none has materialized so far.

There are good reasons why no close and persistent periodicities exist in the recurrent macroeconomic fluctuations. If they did, the turning points of business cycles would presumably be easy to predict, but they are certainly not. Downturns in particular are poorly forecast (as demonstrated in part III below). If they could be correctly anticipated with sufficient lead times, successful actions might be undertaken to prevent or at least reduce socially costly declines in total output and employment.

6.6 Does Detrending Reveal Regularities?

Chronologies of growth cycles, based on the consensus of fluctuations in trend-adjusted series on aggregate output, employment, and other measures of real economic activity, were first developed by Mintz (1969, 1972, 1974) at the National Bureau. They were soon improved and extended to more countries by Moore and his associates at the CIBCR, where the international indicators used in this analysis are kept up to date (Klein and Moore 1985; Moore and Moore 1985). The basic methodology of identifying and dating cyclical movements remains the same as in the traditional NBER analysis, with the important difference that here it is applied to detrended series. However, as already noted, trend and cycles influence each other in such ways that it is impossible to separate the two without error, and the danger to guard against is that the procedure may hide or distort more than it reveals.

Some major results of comparing business cycles and growth cycles are clear and simple, however. Some slowdowns that interrupt long business cycle expansions are sufficiently long and diffuse to give rise to additional cyclical declines in the detrended aggregates when compared with the original ones. Also, most postwar recessions were preceded by marked retardations. Hence, growth cycles are on the whole shorter, more frequent, and more nearly symmetrical than business cycles; they are less differentiated by duration but still quite variable. There is considerable correspondence between the dates of postwar growth cycles in the principal industrialized economies of North America, Europe, and the Far East (see chapter 7, sec. 7.4; chapter 8, sec. 8.2.4; also Moore and Zarnowitz 1986, sec. 8).

As shown in section 6.4, slowdowns rather than recessions interrupted the sharp growth trends during the early part of the postwar era in continental Europe and Japan. Recessions reappeared there only in the mid-1960s or later as the rebuilding was completed and the growth rates came down to their normal levels. Meanwhile the more slowly growing economies of the United States, Canada, and the United Kingdom continued to experience recurrent recessions, though they were generally mild. Detrending reduces all these episodes to comparable growth cycles, but the international differences between the trends are important and should not be obscured, and the same applies to the differences between cyclical slowdowns and contractions.

In short, growth cycles recur with greater frequency than business cycles and are a feature of even those economies that expand at high rates and rarely contract. They seem to be more alike—that is, more regular—than business cycles. This is presumably because of the elimination of trends that vary over time and across the different variables and countries. Even so, growth cycles exhibit much variability in durations and amplitudes. When figure 7.1 in chapter 7 is updated, the following numbers are obtained, which indicate that slowdowns without recession prevailed in Japan, West Germany, and Canada, while slowdowns with recession prevailed in the United States, United Kingdom, and (slightly) France.[9]

	U.S.	Canada	U.K.	Germany	France	Japan
Slowdown, no recession	4	7	3	5	3	6
Slowdown and recession	7	5	5	3	4	2
Total	11	12	8	8	7	8

One reason why our knowledge of how trends and cycles interact is meager is that much empirical work in macrodynamics uses methods that apply to stationary series obtained by trend adjustment or differencing. Spectral analysis reveals periodicities at cyclical and shorter frequencies in all types of U.S. fixed investment (log differences) and inventory investment (levels) in both the interwar and the postwar periods. This does not support well the old idea that fixed investment is the source of major cycles, and inventory investment of minor cycles. Rather, the results suggest the limitations of the method but also, again, the likely diversity of cyclical experience (chapter 8, figs. 8.1–8.4).

6.7   Implications of Nonlinear Models

The fact that business cycles show no regularity in the durations of their phases constitutes a strong argument against those models which, on the contrary, imply periodic fluctuations. A simple and strict example is provided by the deterministic theory limited to a high accelerator-multiplier combination and a constant rate of autonomous real investment. With constant parameters, this nonlinear or piecewise-linear model (the accelerator is suspended in the downswing) will generate a periodic limit cycle. But it is in principle easy to enlarge such a model and produce more diversity, for example, by allowing for monetary influences and/or fluctuations in autonomous investment (Hicks 1950).

Other diverse examples of repetitive behavior include nonlinear models of income-investment or profit-investment dynamics in a stationary economy (Kaldor 1940; Kalecki 1971); a limit cycle in the labor market (Rose 1967); and the "predator-prey" model of interacting fluctuations in employment, wages, capital accumulation, and profits around an equilibrium path of growth (Goodwin 1967; Samuelson 1971). These models, too, are essentially illus-

9. This count does not include the 1990–91 recessions in the United States, Canada, and the United Kingdom.

trative of certain particular ideas or mechanisms, and they remain fragmentary and untested, though much explored mathematically. But extensions to include relationships with nominal and policy variables and stochastic elements are likely to receive future attention, along with efforts at empirical implementation (from calibration to econometric tests). Nonlinear models are attractive because they can generate undamped cyclical solutions, asymmetries, discontinuities, and irreversibilities. In fact, as discussed in chapter 8, section 8.3, this area of study has recently been very active. In addition to many papers elaborating on the earlier ideas, monographs surveying the old and new theories and techniques have appeared (Gabisch and Lorenz 1987; Ferri and Greenberg 1989).

Some of the above models are locally (piecewise) linear, and their overall nonlinearity arises because of constraints (ceilings, floors, or both) or regime switches at which changes in parameters or initial conditions are activated. Others are explicitly nonlinear throughout and use mathematical tools of classical nonlinear analysis. Both approaches produced endogenous models of periodic cycles. The ability to generate business cycles without having to rely on the deus ex machina of outside shocks was long viewed as a major advantage by many theorists, whereas the need to move away from models of periodic replication was not sufficiently appreciated. And it seemed that the only alternative to the elegant self-contained dynamics would indeed be the introduction of some unexplained disturbances, time variation or shifts of some parameters, and the like.

New analytical possibilities opened up with the discovery (in meteorology: Lorenz 1963) of "deterministic chaos," that is, for certain nonlinear difference equations changes in parameters can result in erratic, nonperiodic fluctuations that need not converge to a cycle of any order. Phases of sharp oscillations can follow upon or alternate irregularly with phases of relatively smooth growth in ways that are completely unpredictable. Thus a model without any random shocks is capable of generating behavior that "looks" stochastic. A small cause (difference or error in initial conditions) may be associated eventually with very large effects. In macroeconomic dynamics, examples of the emergence of chaotic fluctuations are provided in the context of the Goodwin model (Pohjola 1981), the classical and neoclassical growth models (Day 1982, 1983), and Keynesian models (Day and Shafer 1985).

The prospect of new lessons from new analytical approaches is generally exciting, but as stated by Samuelson (1990, p. 57), "It will take very large samples of time-series data to enable the scientist to refute the hypothesis of chaos or to provisionally accept it. History—relevant history—is what we economists are short on." The studies here considered are breaking new ground, and it is impossible to predict where they will lead (the same applies to the related exercises in "catastrophe theory" (see chapter 2, sec. 2.3.4). Still, it is important to note the problems that are already apparent. The available, dimensionally restricted illustrations of chaotic trajectories due to nonlinear feedbacks show hypothetical time series dominated by sharp saw-toothed movements. Few economic time series look like that, and hardly any comprehensive aggregates or indexes do. Business cycles are nonperiodic but they consist of fluctuations that are far more persistent and smooth. Economic rationalizations for the shapes of the functions underlying the models of chaotic behavior seem to be lacking. It is safe to conclude that the new paradigm and techniques will influence economic theorizing about business cycles and growth but represent no immediate threat to the prevailing type of stochastic modeling and econometric work.

6.8   Types of Theory and the Regularity of Business Cycles

One can conceive of fluctuations caused by regularly recurring outside events; such fluctuations would belong in the deterministic-exogenous class. In such "forced oscillations" the driving factor is itself cyclical and the system responds passively. But it is hard to think of any external force that could possibly dominate economic life to the point of being responsible for business cycles. Seasonal movements come to mind but they depend not only on the more or less regular changes in weather but also on custom, economic decisions, and random influences. Natural causes were invoked early to explain business cycles but it soon became clear that such theories fail: whatever drives the general expansions and contractions is almost certainly man-made in the socioeconomic sense. This practically rules out theories that are both deterministic and exogenous.

A counterargument might point to the possibility of government actions designed to win elections that would somehow cause business cycles without being themselves significantly affected by the recent or current changes in the economy. But this is hardly a serious possibility, because policymakers both react to the observed and expected changes and try to influence future macroeconomic conditions, whereas private individuals and organizations respond to the past and anticipated government operations. Unanticipated policy actions themselves act as shocks to the public, although a good deal of what is going on in the private economy is undoubtedly surprising to the government as well. Models of "political business cycles" are useful to the extent that they absorb these endogenous and stochastic elements.

The deterministic-endogenous class of theories is well represented. In the early and mathematically well-articulated models of this type, nonlinearities are required to keep the trajectories from exploding, because the moving equilibrium or "steady state" is here intrinsically unstable; also, as already noted, the cycles produced by these models are periodic-regular. These are not attractive features. The new chaos models are free of them but they are as yet short on economic motivation and long on output that, though not explosive, shows excessive volatility.

Stochastic theories can be either exogenous or endogenous. The latter include the models with multiple rational expectations equilibria, in which random events trigger generalized changes in expectations that become self-fulfilling. The "sunspot" events need not effect any changes in economic fundamentals. These theories increasingly center on financial market imperfections and crises and use techniques of nonlinear dynamics (see collections of essays in Barnett, Geweke, and Shell 1989; and Semmler 1989).

Stochastic and exogenous theories are currently the best known and most dominant in the literature. In this case, the equilibrium is intrinsically stable, and continuing outside shocks are needed to produce recurrent fluctuations. The prototype for linear business cycle models of this type is Frisch 1933, a pre-Keynesian dynamic model of cyclical motion (not growth). Frisch's idea that random "impulses" keep fluctuations alive even though the undisturbed economy (his "propagation mechanism") is highly dampened established a tradition for many subsequent theoretical and almost all active macroeconometric models.[10]

The magnitude of the white-noise shocks impinging on the so-represented economy is the main determinant of the amplitude of the resulting fluctuations, whereas the length of the latter and the tendency toward dampening depend primarily on the parameters of the propagation mechanism (Frisch 1933, p. 171). Other things equal, the less dampened the system, the more distinct will be the periodicity of the generated cycles. This is the case of "free oscillations," which arise in a system that responds cyclically to impulses that are themselves noncyclical.

The original stochastic-exogenous cycle analysis worked with white-noise shocks only. Serially correlated disturbances would result in smoother and more markedly periodic movements. Sufficiently large sporadic or clustered shocks could affect the timing of turning points and the duration of a business cycle.

It is instructive to think of the pure types of theory but they are not all mutually preclusive, and it stands to reason that the business cycles of the real world include elements of these theories in various combinations. For the central phenomenon to exist, a set of relationships possessing considerable regularity is necessary; but for the manifestations in time of this phenomenon to be variable, the balance of forces acting on and within the system must be changing. The more endogenously business cycles can be explained, the better in principle; but some parts of the big picture must be left exogenous if the

---

10. In the Frisch model, output of capital goods is a distributed-lag function of orders that depend on the change in consumption, which is inversely related to a weighted total output of both consumption and capital goods. Thus technology, the acceleration principle, and an equation based on the notion that consumption yields to cash pressure as money supply lags behind money demand are all linked to production and income. Recent simulations confirm that random shocks can produce considerable fluctuations in this model but not excessive periodicity for parameter values that Frisch favored, that is, for a relatively high degree of dampening. See Thalberg 1990, where it is shown that adding a multiplier relation improves the results of the model qualitatively while introducing a potential for instability.

explanation is to be economic and comprehensible. Some influences that are identifiably important are external to the economy, and some of these may be essentially random. Linear approximations will do well locally in many cases but not globally everywhere. The general fluctuations may be "free" but some particular relations within the economy probably reflect "forced" cyclical movements.

6.9   Simulations with Macroeconometric Models

The 1955 Klein-Goldberger model of the U.S. economy estimated on annual data for 1929–52 was intensively studied by Adelman and Adelman (1959), who found it to be essentially noncyclical in the absence of shocks. Stochastic simulations with random shocks to extrapolated values of the exogenous variables also did not generate significant fluctuations, but simulations with random shocks to the fitted equations of the model did. Adelman and Adelman compared the time paths of the latter with the NBER reference cycle patterns for the variables in question and found considerable similarities. They concluded that these results are consistent with the concept of an economy that is a dynamically stable system that propagates outside disturbances into business cycles (the Wicksell-Slutsky-Frisch hypothesis). Despite caveats by the authors about limitations of the model and method used, their findings have at times been taken as a *proof* that the origin of business cycles is truly stochastic.

However, detailed tests of an array of much more elaborate quarterly macroeconomic models reject the classical version of the Frisch theory, namely, that purely random shocks are necessary and sufficient to cause cyclical fluctuations in the estimated systems. A comprehensive study of three large-scale models (Wharton, Commerce Department, and FRB-MIT-Penn) found that they were all noncyclical in deterministic forms and also did not reproduce continuous cyclical developments when subjected to random disturbances (Zarnowitz, Boschan, and Moore 1972). In chapter 9, which is a brief summary of that study, some similar results for a fourth model (Brookings) are also included. When correlated shocks were used, smoother and more distinct fluctuations resulted, but even these were much weaker than those observed in the historical series used in the estimation of the models. Consistent evidence comes from several other contributions to the NBER conference that produced these simulation studies (Hickman 1972).

It is possible that a combination of random shocks to both the exogenous and the behavioral variables would perform better than either kind of shock alone and, also, that mixing correlated and uncorrelated disturbances would help (Adelman 1972, p. 535). Wars, strikes, technological innovations, government policy, and political developments, etc., are potential sources of temporal persistence in exogenous factors; they will inevitably impart some serial correlation to some of the shocks to the model equations as well. But the situation is unfortunately blurred by the very real possibility that the results of the simulations reflect in significant measure misspecification errors in the models. For example, the inadequate cyclicality of the long stochastically simulated trajectories could be partly due to insufficient nonlinear elements in the models.

The Hickman (1972) volume was followed by comparative studies of econometric model performance that were concerned more with forecasting accuracy and multiplier analysis but added some evidence on the cyclical problem under examination here (Klein and Burmeister 1976). The Michigan quarterly model is described as one that "will not produce a sustained cyclical path in non-stochastic simulations with 'smooth' exogenous variables" (Hymans and Shapiro 1976, p. 268). The mechanism of response to outside shocks is highly dampened, and dynamic simulations show generally smaller amplitudes than the corresponding actual series. The authors argue that this is as it should be, to the extent that recessions, booms, high inflation, etc., represent unique or abberrant behavior patterns.

Similarly, in the Data Resources, Inc. (DRI), model relatively smooth paths characterize simulations that removed many exogenous and random influences by holding constant the growth rates of fiscal variables, nonborrowed reserves, etc. (Eckstein, Green, and Sinai 1976). It is asserted that "the model's endogenous structure *should* display the strongly damped oscillatory character that the economy seems to possess" (p. 212; emphasis added). But "noise" defined narrowly to include only the (presumably random) equation errors accounted for very little (only 7.4%) of the total "cyclicality" (an index of relative deviations from trend) in the more recent version of the DRI model (Eckstein and Sinai 1986, pp. 70–73, 81). This may be largely attributable to the use of many special, or dummy, variables in the very large and difficult-to-evaluate DRI model. Be that as it may, the macroeconometric evidence lends more support to the hypothesis of the importance of exogenous variables than to the hypothesis of pure random shocks.

6.10   A Note on the Recent History of These Models

The late 1960s and early 1970s represent the heyday of the application of comprehensive econometric models to macroeconomic analysis and forecasting. Since then, the econometricians and their models came to be criticized for not dealing well with the short-term effects and future implications of commodity and oil price shocks (which were, understandably, unanticipated). More important, they were seen as unprepared for the concurrence of rising inflation and severe recessions that materialized in 1972–80. This failure has been widely shared in the profession and attributed to Keynesian theory and policy generally, but the ambitiously large and complex models presented a particularly visible target for criticism. Moreover, with the advent of the rational expectations hypothesis, the models came under attack on the ground that changes in policy regimes alter private expectations and behavior so as to invalidate certain key equations in the models that are wrongly treated as fixed (Lucas 1976).

These developments led to a sharp decline in the interest of academic economists in the existing and commercially active macroeconometric models. The influential Lucas critique met with the valid counterclaim that shifts in policy rules are very rare and normal policy actions have no disruptive effects on important macrorelationships (Sims 1982). Whether and how rational expectations apply is itself a matter of dispute (see chapter 2). Some of the defense of the models by their builders (Eckstein 1981) finds support in the data and some of the criticism does not. But the large-scale models no longer inspire the confidence and hopes they once did, their limitations are widely recognized, and even many friendly critics view them as overdeveloped and underexplained.

It is also true, however, that the models continue to be used with commercial success for practical purposes of forecasting and consulting. As such they are being almost continuously reexamined and repaired, but little is known about precisely how and with what effects. The estrangement between the academic economists and the practitioners in the econometric bureaus persists. This can hardly be a healthy state of affairs, since it is likely that the two sides have much to learn from each other.

Alternative simulations and forecasts with different macroeconometric models are useful devices in the search for good questions and answers on what is expected and unexpected and what is self-produced and externally caused in the economy's motion. Yet, to my knowledge, little work of the type discussed here and in chapter 9 has been done more recently. No major new models have been developed, and the documentation on the revisions of the commercial models is not publicly available. The lessons from the reported simulations and tests are worthwhile and need to be extended.

7 Business Cycles and Growth

7.1 Introduction

Is the long-term trend of the economy—growth—substantially influenced by the short-term movements—business cycles—and, if so, how? Are business cycles subject to major secular changes? Are these fluctuations the natural way growth takes in private-enterprise economies or are they mainly due to some outside shocks that could be avoided or reduced? Should their analysis be based on trend-unadjusted or on trend-adjusted time-series data?

These are major questions that have received considerable attention in economic literature, but they are difficult and still debated. In this chapter I shall attempt to contribute to the discussion of some aspects of how business cycles and growth are related. [1]

It is generally agreed that the process of long-term economic growth is "real" in nature: driven by increases in the quantity and productivity of human and physical resources (capital in the most general sense) and measured by the advances in output and wealth per capita. Business cycle theories, on the other hand, disagree on the relative roles of real and monetary factors. Those who emphasize the latter (changes in money supply, bank reserves and credits, the price level, and interest rates) have logically good reasons to assert that

Reprinted from *Wirtschaftstheorie und Wirtschaftspolitik: Gedenkschrift für Erich Preiser*, eds. W. J. Mückl and A. E. Ott, pp. 475–508 (Passau, Germany: Passavia Universitätsverlag, 1981).

Financial support from the National Science Foundation and aid of the Graduate School of Business of the University of Chicago and NBER are gratefully acknowledged. Any opinions expressed are those of the author and not those of the National Bureau of Economic Research.

The author is grateful to Stanley Lebergott and Geoffrey Moore for their helpful comments.

1. The volume in which what follows was first published commemorated my esteemed teacher, Erich Preiser. Preiser's first book (1933) contains a characteristically concise and lucid analysis of the process of capital accumulation, which he considered central to the understanding of both the long trend and business cycles. For other contributions to the study of growth, fluctuations, and their interface, see Preiser 1959, 1961, 1967a, and 1967b.

secular growth is not much affected by short-run fluctuations in nominal demand. Hence, they raise no objections in principle to the idea that trends and cycles are separable.

In practice, this conception leads to the measurement and analysis of "growth cycles"—movements in aggregate economic activity defined by the consensus of fluctuations in comprehensive indicators adjusted for their long-term trends. This view of business cycles as movements in the deviations from trend has a long history. However, the approach did not escape considerable difficulties and criticism in the past. Now growth cycles have come to enjoy a new popularity. This paper looks at this development from a historical perspective and examines its sources and chances to endure.

7.2 Trend-Cycle Interactions

The trend-cycle interactions are varied and in part subtle. Measures of secular growth are most meaningful for the longest periods over which some reasonable, stable trend fits the data well, and they must be calculated to avoid cyclical bias. For example, measuring the trend from a business cycle trough year to a peak year results in overestimation of the average growth rate; from a peak to a trough year, in underestimation. The selected initial and terminal years should therefore be in the same cyclical phase or have similar cyclical characteristics, for example, about the same unemployment or capacity utilization rates. This severely restricts the range of appropriate comparisons.[2]

Over long intervals measured in decades, trends dominate the business cycle, so here the cyclical bias, though often nonnegligible, matters less. Growth has been historically pervasive and persistent in the modern era, as illustrated by the following facts. Nearly every business expansion in the United States has carried total output and employment beyond the levels reached at the peak of the preceding cycle.[3] The recoveries in these variables have usually been faster after severe depressions than after mild declines (despite this, however, the recovery to the previous peak level has as a rule taken longer when the preceding contraction had been severe).[4]

2. See U.S. Bureau of the Census 1966. This publication (pt. V) presents real GNP growth rates for all possible combinations of initial and terminal years between 1890 and 1964 (the unemployment-rate estimates are not available before 1890). This amounts to 2,850 calculated growth rates for U.S. output. Out of these, only 360 (13%) refer to periods for which the unemployment rates (u) differ by less than 0.025 percentage points per year (i.e., $|u_t - u_T|/n < 0.025$, where the subscripts denote the initial and terminal years, and n is the number of years covered). For a more relaxed definition of "similar" u rates (difference of less than 0.1 point/year), the number of periods is 993 (34%). The number of all periods bounded by business cycle peak years between 1890 and 1964 is 190, out of which 36 (19%) would refer to similar unemployment rates on the first definition and 101 (53%) on the second.

3. The one conspicuous exception is the expansion of 1933–37, which followed the Great Contraction of 1929–33. Although among the longest and largest on record, it started from an unprecedentedly low level and was incomplete in the sense that even at its end unemployment was very high and per capita output lower than at the preceding peak.

4. For an interpretation of these findings and evidence, see Moore 1961, vol. 1, ch. 3, esp. pp. 86–109.

Over short intervals measured in years, the business cycle effects are typically preponderant. Therefore, serious errors are likely to result from the (unfortunately frequent) practice of evaluating and projecting growth rates on the basis of comparisons between arbitrary short unit periods that are relatively close to each other in time.[5]

The cyclical movements vary greatly in amplitude and duration. Severe depressions such as those of 1873–79, 1893–97 (interrupted only by a brief and incomplete recovery in 1894–95), 1907–8, 1920–21, 1929–33, and 1937–38 reduced growth strongly for some considerable time. Vigorous expansions such as those of 1879–82, 1897–99, 1908–10, 1921–23, 1938–45, 1949–53, and 1961–69 (the last three in wartime periods) raised the growth rates correspondingly. However, no less than 33 complete business cycles occurred in the United States between 1834 and 1975, and most of them have been mild. Short cycles make up a larger majority yet. Only 9 of the expansions have lasted longer than 3 years, and 5 of these were associated with major wars; about half (17) lasted 2 years or less. Contractions have been typically shorter than expansions: 25 (85%) did not exceed 2 years and 11 (33%) did not exceed 1 year. It is a historical fact that few peacetime cycles resulted in major disruptions of the secular growth trend of the U.S. economy.

This does not mean at all, however, that growth has been uniform or that no connection exists between cyclical variability and growth. In a century of U.S. progress, it is possible to identify several periods characterized by relatively high economic stability and several others during which stability was comparatively low. Table 7.1 shows that the average annual rates of growth in the economy's output (or real income) were generally higher in the former than in the latter segments.

The selection of the periods in both categories was guided by close inspection of charts for the available long time series on aggregate economic activity as well as by accounts in the literature on economic trends and fluctuations.[6] Each of the chosen segments comprises a number of complete business cycles measured from peak to peak (three contain 2 cycles each, four 3 cycles, and one 4 cycles). The four periods of "high" stability add up to 47 years, and so

---

5. The minimum distance should logically be at least one complete business cycle (measured from peak to peak, trough to trough, or between centered cycle averages). But business cycles vary greatly in duration and many are relatively short (see text below).

6. Friedman and Schwartz (1963a, p. 677) write: "We have characterized four segments of the 93 years of displaying a relatively high degree of economic stability: 1882–92, 1903–13, 1923–29, 1948–60. Each has also displayed a high degree of stability of the year-to-year change in the stock of money; the remaining periods have shown appreciably greater instability of the year-to-year change in both money and income." Table 7.1 uses the first three periods unchanged but extends the last one to 1948–69, to include the long expansion of the 1960s. My choice of the relatively unstable periods also agrees broadly with several characterizations by Friedman and Schwartz, who refer to "the disturbed years from 1891 to 1897" (p. 104) and "the years of economic turmoil" 1914–21 (p. 189). The 1930s, of course, witnessed the most severe contraction of modern times in 1929–33, then an "erratic and uneven" revival and another "unusually deep" contraction in 1937–38, which "proceeded at an extremely rapid rate" (p. 493). The large changes in the years of World War II and its immediate aftermath were due to the preparation for and conduct of wartime activities, inflation, and finally demobilization accompanied by a recession.

Table 7.1   **Growth Rates in Selected Periods of Relatively High and Low Economic Stability, GNP in Constant Dollars, 1882–1980**

| | | No. of Business Cycles (years) | Growth Rates in Real GNP (%) | |
| | | | | |
Line	Years[a] (1)	Covered[b] (2)	Average[c] (3)	S.D.[d] (4)
	A. Periods of Relatively High Economic Stability[e]			
1	1882–1892	3 (10)	5.3[f]	6.7[f]
2	1903–1913	3 (10)	3.4	6.1
3	1923–1929	2 (6)	3.5	3.8
4	1948–1969	4 (21)	3.9	2.6
	B. Periods of Relatively Low Economic Stability[e]			
5	1892–1899	2 (7)	3.1	6.8
6	1913–1923	3 (10)	2.4	8.6
7	1929–1948	3 (19)	2.5	9.4
8	1969–1980	2 (11)	2.7	3.1
	C. Summary[g]			
9	"High"- stability periods	12 (47)	4.0 (3.7)[h]	4.4 (3.7)[h]
10	"Low"- stability periods	10 (47)	2.6	7.4

Sources: Kendrick 1961 (GNP in 1929 dollars, 1879–1908); U.S. Department of Commerce, Bureau of Economic Analysis (GNP in 1958 dollars and in 1972 dollars, 1909–80); Nutter 1962 (combines U.S. estimates by Edwin Frickey, Solomon Fabricant, Warren Persons, and others). Most of the historical data and measures are taken from U.S. Bureau of the Census 1966.

[a]For each period listed in this column, the initial and terminal dates are business cycle peak years according to the NBER reference chronology for the United States.

[b]Number of complete peak-to-peak cycles from the initial to the terminal year. The number of years covered is shown in parentheses.

[c]Average annual growth rate between the initial and the terminal year, computed by the compound interest rate formula.

[d]Standard deviation, based on the annual growth rates for all years in the given period, as identified in cols. 1–2.

[e]See text.

[f]Industrial production (NBER, Nutter) estimates are used for the years 1882–88, real GNP (Kendrick) estimates for the years 1889–92 (the annual Kendrick figures begin in 1889). A comparison of the corresponding figures that are available for both series (decade averages for 1869–79 and 1979–88 and annual data for 1889–92) suggests enough similarity of relative change to permit the combined use of these estimates (e.g., the average annual growth rates based on the decade averages are 6.0% for industrial production, 6.3% for real GNP). If industrial production figures only were used for 1882–92, the entries in line 1, cols. 3 and 4, would have been 5.0% and 6.6%, respectively.

[g]Entries in line 9 refer to the periods in part A (lines 1–4); entries in line 10 refer to the periods in part B (lines 5–8). The entries in col. 2 are totals; those in cols. 3 and 4 are averages weighted by the number of years in each period.

[h]The first number covers all four periods in lines 1–4; the number in parentheses excludes the period 1882–92; that is, it covers the three periods in lines 2–4.

do the four periods of "low" stability (table 7.1, col. 2). Taken together, the comparisons refer to 94 years out of the total of 98 years covered (1882–1980). The data are most trustworthy for the 35 years after World War II and least trustworthy for the 32 years before World War I.

It is noteworthy that the effects of large business contractions outweigh those of major wartime expansions in two periods, 1913–23 and 1929–48. These segments belong to the low-stability, low-growth group B (lines 6 and 7). The 1948–69 period, which includes the Korean War and most of the Vietnam War, is classified in the high-stability, high-growth group A (line 4). The years 1969–80 witnessed the winding up of the Vietnam War and inherited little of its expansionary but most of its delayed inflationary effects. This period belongs in group B (line 8). Contemporaries have little doubt about the much discussed contrast between the turbulent 1970s, dominated by seemingly uncontrollable inflation, recessions, and energy problems, and the economically much more placid and prosperous decades of the 1950s and 1960s.

After the selection of the periods, standard deviations (s) of the annual growth rates within each of them were computed from historical statistics on real GNP (see table 7.1 for sources). These measures, shown in column 4, are consistent with the classification of the periods into the two categories: in terms of weighted averages, for example, s is 4.4 for group A and 7.4 for group B (lines 9 and 10). The average annual rates of growth in real GNP (g), calculated by the compound interest formula between the initial and terminal years of each period, are listed in column 3. They are throughout higher for the relatively more stable than for the less stable segments. On the average, g is 4.0% for group A, 2.6% for group B.

Table 7.1 is interesting and suggestive but far from conclusive. It is difficult to apply standard tests of statistical significance to results of this kind, since inevitably the data are uncertain, the sets of measures small, and the usual assumptions for inference from samples of independent, identically distributed observations appear to be of dubious validity. If all this is disregarded, test statistics are obtained which cannot reject the null hypothesis that the difference between the mean growth rates for groups A and B is due to chance.[7]

Moreover, I see no good general reason to expect any definite and uniform relationship between long-term growth and cyclical variability. It is possible for strong growth on the supply side to reduce the depth and duration of recessions (viewed primarily as declines in aggregate demand). But the opposite

---

7. The ratio of the (unbiased) variance estimates is 2.8, which according to the F-distribution with parameters (46, 46) is significant at both the 5% and the 1% levels; hence, the hypothesis of equal variances for the two groups would be rejected. However, an analysis of variance indicates that the within-group dispersion of the growth rates dwarfs the between-groups dispersion. This applies to both sets A and B as well as to the combination of the two. (The grand mean of the growth rates for all the individual years is 3.5%; the corresponding standard deviation is 6.2%.) On these tests, the "true" (population) means in the two sets A and B may not be different after all.

causal chain is no less plausible; that is, a more stable expansion of demand may generate more rapid growth. Strong recurrent spurts in demand (caused, e.g., by monetary accelerations) or in supply (caused, e.g., by uneven flows of technological innovation and business investment) can result in both more instability and more growth. Pronounced business cycles have certainly been a feature of many nations in the stage of rapid industrialization, while backward countries stagnated with relatively little economic instability but also little economic growth. In sum, one cannot help being agnostic here: different arguments and models can be made readily but there are few solid generalizations.

Still, one important proposition finds considerable support in experience as well as theory, namely, that both protracted high unemployment and protracted high inflation impede growth. Underutilization of productive capacities tends to reduce investment and tilt downward the potential (full employment) output curve. Uneven and largely unanticipated inflation (the usual type) impairs the signaling function of relative prices and acts as a bad tax, distorting resource allocation, hindering saving and productive investment, and fostering speculative activities.

7.3   Growth and Instability after World War II

In periods of substantial stability and satisfactory growth, the always attractive idea that the business cycle may have been conquered or rendered obsolete gains considerable publicity and acceptance. This often reflects a high confidence in government institutions and actions. In the 1920s, it was the Federal Reserve monetary policies that many hoped would maintain prosperity. In the 1960s, it was the tax cuts and fiscal fine-tuning generally. Unfortunately, the "return" of the business cycle has repeatedly proved such ideas to be pipe dreams or at least quite premature.

In the quarter century after World War II, however, business cycles have indeed been mild by historical standards. In Western Europe and Japan, sustained declines in the levels of output, employment, and real income and spending occurred only sporadically. Instead, alternations of above-average and below-average growth in these indicators of aggregate economic activity were observed recurrently, and the involved slowdowns soon came to be treated much as the mild recessions, partly because they had similar adverse effects on business and labor market conditions and partly because of heightened public sensitivity to any lapse from the high-growth path that lasted long enough to be widely recognized and decried.

The main reason for the apparent temporary suspension in these countries of the "classical" business cycle was clearly the extraordinary outburst of rapid growth from the nadir of the enormous destruction and deprivation of the mid-1940s. The economic legacy of World War II was here not only devastation of industry but also huge backlogs of unutilized, highly skilled resources and unsatisfied demand. Once reasonably sound currencies and free markets were restored, and international trade and capital flows revitalized, an era of great reconstruction, new investment, and technological progress set in to last a generation. As long as this favorable climate lasted, employment and output had steep upward trends, and cyclical setbacks assumed the form of retardations of growth rather than absolute declines. Thus it was not until 1966–67 that West Germany experienced its first postwar recession, with an actual decline (which was still quite moderate) in real GNP, industrial production, and related measures of overall economic activity.

In the United States and Canada, there was no wartime destruction, hence no stimulus of domestic reconstruction, but the backlog of demand after the war shortages was massive, and the incentives and resources for rapid growth were on hand, too. The widely expected postwar depression never materialized. The worldwide expansion of industry and trade obviously benefited the North American countries greatly. It is generally recognized that four business contractions as defined traditionally by the National Bureau (i.e., cumulative and widely diffused declines in activity) have occurred in the United States between 1948 and 1961, but all of them were mild. Then came the long economic expansion in the 1960s, which persisted beyond the expectations of most economists, although not without being modified by two mild slowdowns and presumably prolonged, first by a major tax reduction and later by the intensification of the war in Vietnam. At this point, the substantial moderation of the U.S. business cycle when compared with the pre–World War II patterns became quite apparent, and the important question was what accounts for that change and how lasting it would be.[8]

Of the domestic factors, one that is well documented and most probably important is the shift in the industrial composition of employment from cyclically highly sensitive sectors such as manufacturing, mining, and construction to relatively recession-proof sectors such as trade, services, and finance (Moore 1980, ch. 4; Zarnowitz and Moore 1977). Before the onset of the Great Inflation of the 1970s, most of the explanations of the relative shortness and mildness of recent recessions have also given much credit to institutional changes, notably the "built-in stabilizers" and bank deposit insurance. Discretionary fiscal and monetary policies had a mixed record but not without some relative successes (for further discussion and references, see Zarnowitz 1972a).

The loose term "stagflation" often used to describe the developments since about 1969 evokes the image of a slow-moving economy with sharply rising prices, but this is not exactly accurate. The cyclical fluctuations in this decade

---

8. To some, the events suggested that the business cycle in its traditional sense was, if not dead, too mild and sporadic to merit much interest. There was also rising interest in the "political cycle"—theories of how errors in macroeconomic stabilization policies or election-year politics can generate cyclical instability. But these interpretations did not turn out to have much long-term significance (see Lundberg 1968; Bronfenbrenner 1969; Zarnowitz 1972).

were relatively frequent and sharp, not only in real activity but also in the rate of inflation. The recessions became international in scope and more severe, but they were still short, even including the one in 1974–75, by historical comparisons. However, the average growth rates did decline considerably, and tendencies developed for both inflation and unemployment to drift upward (apart from their shorter cyclical movements). It was increasingly recognized that the expansion of the government's share and role in the economy has *de*-stabilizing and growth-inhibiting effects. Macroeconomic policies in this period oscillated between attempts to combat inflation and attempts to combat unemployment, with poor timing and for the most part indifferent or perverse results.

The decrease in the frequency, duration, and amplitude of business recessions has been accompanied by other changes, such as a reduction in the sensitivity of industrial prices to declines in final demand and an increase in the cyclical responsiveness of interest rates (Cagan 1966, 1975). That business cycles have changed significantly in various respects since the cataclysms of 1929–45 is hardly surprising when one considers the nature and scope of the concurrent changes in the economies, societies, and political systems involved. The changes in the cyclical behavior have been labeled "secular," but here caution is indicated if the term is meant to convey irreversible alterations or trends that can be projected. There is much evidence of, and good economic reasons for, the long-term shift in the composition of employment from goods-producing to service-producing industries, but it is not impossible to envisage technological change and organized efforts that would halt and even reverse that shift. Drastically different economic policies could alter the cyclical sensitivity of prices and interest rates.

In this respect, it is interesting to note that studies of business cycles in the pre–World War II era have not been able to document any strong *secular* or *discontinuous* changes in cyclical behavior.[9] Many industries undergo similar "life cycles"—phases of initially slow, then rapid, and finally again slow growth or possibly decay—as they introduce new products and techniques that flourish for some time but eventually encounter increasingly effective competition from newer and still better endowed industries. However, the economy comprises at any time all industries, at all their various life-cycle stages, so the industry growth patterns "wash out" in the aggregation, and the overall growth rates show no particular long-term evolution.[10]

9. See Burns and Mitchell 1946, ch. 10, where several tests are reported to have shown that the effects of secular changes on the following have been absent or slight: (1) the duration and amplitude of specific and business cycles; (2) business cycles and economic stages (Mills's hypothesis that the cycles tend to get shorter in the stage of rapid growth receives little support from the data); (3) business cycles before and after 1914.

10. Indeed, none of the once-popular theories of unidirectional trends in economic growth and instability such as Marx's projections of increasing pauperization and crises or Hansen's secular stagnation have been validated by tests of historical data.

With regard to *cyclical* changes in cyclical behavior, that is, the existence and nature of any patterns of long fluctuations, the results are mixed and in large part inconclusive. The Kondratieff swings of 50–60 years are hardly *general* as posited, for they show up mainly in prices, not production, and consist of too few episodes to be testable. Favorable evidence is cited for the notion that business cycle expansions have tended to be longer and contractions shorter during the upward phases of the long waves in prices than during the downward phases (Burns and Mitchell 1946, pp. 431–40; Moore 1980, pp. 31–32). However, history also shows that growth and deflation have not been incompatible; for example, over the decade 1869–79 as a whole, the price level declined strongly and almost continuously, while real income rose greatly (Friedman and Schwartz 1963a, pp. 29–44). There is much more evidence in support of the "Kuznets cycles," usually of some 15–25 years' duration, which have been traced back at least to the first half of the 19th century and are associated mainly with fluctuations in the growth of population, labor force, net immigration, building construction, and business formation (Burns 1934; Kuznets 1961; Abramovitz 1964; Easterlin 1968). But these movements, too, are much less general than the shorter business cycles, and much less is known about them.

In sum, the only types of movement that can be counted on to persist and matter for the economy as a whole are still only the two that are plainly visible in the comprehensive measures of economic activity and performance—the long-term growth and the business cycle. Both vary over time but retain their essential characteristics so that one can say about either that "plus ça change, plus c'est la même chose." Some of the changes in trends and cycles are significant and (at least partly and ex post) explainable but all elude any strict categorization and prediction. All of this applies to any of the developed economies with large private-enterprise sectors, despite the many differences among them.

7.4 Trend-Adjusted Fluctuations

The period of post–World War II reconstruction and international expansion of industry and trade may have been unique for the length of time during which growth in so many countries persisted at rates so high as to make business recessions rare and mild. Under more ordinary circumstances, such periods seem unlikely to last very long; and surely one lesson of recent history is that attempts to perpetuate them by inflationary policies are both ill-advised and ill-fated.

It was not accidental that the interest in growth cycles increased greatly on a worldwide scale as the good times with few recessions seemed to have no end. The many resulting studies, covering several countries, started appearing during the 1960s and continued into the next decade (Mintz 1969, 1974; Shinohara 1969, p. 76; Matthews 1969, p. 101; Waterman 1967; Sachverständigenrat zur Begutachtung der gesamtwirtschaftlichen Entwicklung 1968, pp. 100ff.; Tichy 1972, pp. 37ff.).

However, the idea of growth cycles, far from being new, has a rather long and interesting history. Methods of adjusting time series for seasonal variations and secular trends were applied early and frequently in statistical studies of business cycles. They resulted in several widely used indexes of general business conditions and trade for the United States, Germany, and Great Britain, all published between 1919 and 1926 in the form of seasonally adjusted series of percentage deviations from estimated trend (sometimes called "normal") curves.[11]

In his 1927 volume, Wesley Mitchell reviewed at length without basic disagreement the contemporary statistical techniques of time-series analysis and trend adjustment.[12] He did raise several "particularly insistent" questions about the existence and direction of any causal relation between the trends and the cyclical fluctuations, but only to note that they await answers which will require much further investigation (p. 233). In 1946, however, Burns and Mitchell argued against the sole reliance on trend-adjusted data in business cycle analysis on the ground that "cyclical fluctuations are so closely interwoven with . . . secular changes in economic life that important clues to the understanding of the former may be lost by mechanically eliminating the latter" (1946, p. 270). They favored conversion of the data into "cycle relatives," that is, percentages of the average value of the series during each completed cycle. This method eliminates in a stepwise manner the "intercycle" trends but retains the "intracycle" trends.

Full trend adjustment does suppress some part of the change that occurs during business cycles, which is a disadvantage insofar as the growth effects that are thus missed are of interest to the analyst.[13] On the other hand, working with deviations from trend should result in greater uniformities of the cyclical measures because the variance due to the secular change is eliminated or reduced. Isolating such uniformities can be instructive, and they turn out to be indeed much stronger after than before trend adjustments.[14] Thus a case

11. The U.S. indexes include those constructed by Warren Persons of Harvard University in 1919 and 1923; the statistical division of AT&T in 1922; Carl Snyder of the Federal Reserve Bank in New York in 1923 and 1924; and Edwin Frickey of Harvard in 1925. The work of Persons was particularly influential. Similar indexes were also prepared for Germany by E. W. Axe and H. M. Flinn in 1925, and for Great Britain by Dorothy Thomas in 1926.

12. Mitchell 1927, ch. 3, sec. 3, pp. 202–61; see also sec. 6, pp. 290–357, for a comprehensive discussion of the indexes identified in n. 11.

13. Consider, e.g., the industry life cycles noted earlier in the text. As Mitchell put it: "The inclusion of intracycle trends in cycle relatives helps to reveal and to explain what happens during business cycles. Rapidly growing industries affect business cycles otherwise than do industries barely holding their own or shrinking" (1951, p. 13).

14. For an early account of how cyclical measures tend to be more alike for trend-adjusted than for unadjusted data, both among and within series, see Burns and Mitchell 1946, ch. 7. On some confirming evidence from recent growth cycle studies, see text below.

can be made for a dual analysis addressed to both the classical business cycle and the growth cycle: useful lessons, which moreover should be largely complementary, can be drawn from cyclical measures based on both trend-unadjusted and trend-adjusted time series.[15]

An old and difficult practical problem in growth cycle analysis is that its results depend significantly on how and over what period the trend is fitted and whether and how it is extrapolated. Trends vary greatly and can be measured in many different ways, each of which has its particular strengths and limitations. Mathematical formulas (e.g., linear, quadratic, exponential, and logistic functions of time) often produce good approximations over limited historical periods only and lack the flexibility required to reflect the variations over time displayed by long-term movements in many economic time series. If moving averages are used to estimate such movements, they must be based on periods longer than the average duration of the cycles so as to yield smooth curves that cut through, and contain no significant elements of, the short-term fluctuations in the series. But when the moving-average period is too long, the advantage of greater flexibility is lost again; and even a reasonable choice of the period may not ensure that the trend is free of all traces of the cycle. Furthermore, the moving average must be centered, which implies the need for extrapolation at the beginning and end of the series over periods equal to half the number of months incorporated in the moving average.

In the NBER approach, which has been gradually improved over the past decade and is now widely applied in international studies, a flexible, smooth, nonlinear, and not necessarily monotonic trend is estimated by interpolation between segments of the series determined with the aid of long-term (75-month or 25-quarter) moving averages. Although no single ideal method of trend estimation exists, this procedure has been tested on many series and shown to have considerable merit for the purpose at hand. Its great advantage, moreover, is that it has been consistently applied to the main cyclical indicators for all large and many small industrialized, market-oriented economies. This work, a part of a large collaborative effort supported by several international and national organizations, was initiated in 1973 by Geoffrey Moore and Philip Klein (see Moore 1980, ch. 5).

The more technical detail on the adopted technique and a graphic illustration of how it works can be found in the literature (see Boschan and Ebanks 1978, pp. 332–35). It should be noted that the specific cycles in the resulting deviation-from-trend series are identified in the same way as those in the trend-unadjusted series.

The reference chronology of growth cycles is established by a close examination of the so-processed data for a country's main comprehensive indicators

---

15. Mitchell (1951, p. 14) recognizes that such double analyses would "add to our knowledge" but notes that they "would be so expensive as to reduce greatly the number of series we could cover." Present computational techniques remove this problem.

of economic activity (such as the series on total output, real income and sales, industrial production, employment). The criteria and procedures are practically the same as those employed in the NBER reference chronology of business cycles.[16] The difference is that growth cycle dates are derived from the observed consensus of the corresponding turning points in the *deviations from trend,* whereas business cycle dates are derived from the consensus of the turning points in the *levels* of the same indicators.

The schematic diagram for the United States in figure 7.1 (first panel) shows that a growth cycle downturn preceded each of the seven business cycle peaks of the 1948–80 period. In the last three cycles (since 1969), the low-growth phases lasted as long as 8–13 months before deteriorating into absolute declines. Thus, here retardations gave early and repeated (though admittedly still uncertain) signals of recession. On the four earlier occasions, in 1948–60, the leads of the decline in growth at peaks were much shorter, from 2 to 6 months. This shift may in part be attributable to the increased role of services: the rise in their output helped to offset the decline in output of goods and structures, and did so more efficiently in recent times. Also, the economy may have been propped up temporarily in the late stages of the recent expansions by buying and speculative activities associated with inflationary expectations and low real interest rates, which discouraged saving.

In sharp contrast to the early timing of the peaks, the troughs of the growth cycles coincided with those of the business cycles in each case except one (there was a short lag in 1954). On three occasions—in 1951–52, 1962–64, and 1966–67—low-growth phases interrupted business expansions but did not terminate them (i.e., here the slowdowns ended in a resumed high growth, not in a decline). Thus, as would be expected, growth cycles are more frequent than business cycles, for example, there were 10 growth cycle downturns in the 1948–80 period for the United States but 7 recessions.[17]

Growth cycles, then, tend to be relatively symmetrical: the U.S. record since 1948 yields average durations of 22 and 18 months for the high-growth and low-growth phases, respectively. In contrast, business cycles in the same period show a strong asymmetry: the expansions lasted on the average 49 months; the contractions, 10 months. The expansions have varied in duration much more than the high-growth phases have (the respective standard deviations are 27 and 11 months). Other important measures for growth cycles also show greater uniformity than their counterparts for business cycles. In particular, leading indicators, which are sensitive to all kinds of disturbances, tend to turn down in anticipation of business slowdowns as well as contractions.

16. On the identification of peaks and troughs of business cycles and growth cycles, see the brief statement and references in Moore 1980, ch. 1.
17. In figure 7.1, the latest U.S. recession was assumed to have ended in August 1980, which was also taken to mark the end of the latest low-growth phase. This date was tentative, based on the evidence available at the time of the writing, February 1981. Subsequent data revisions, however, identified July 1980. See Zarnowitz and Moore 1981.

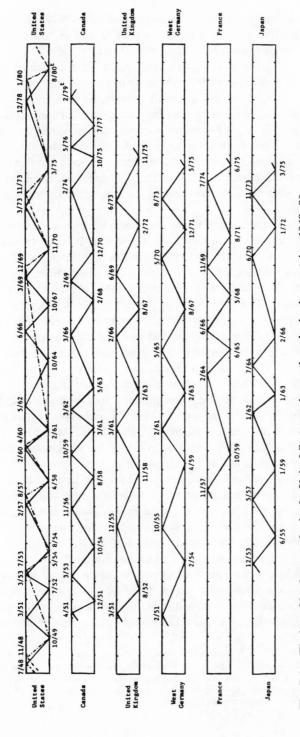

Fig. 7.1.   Timing of business cycles in the United States and growth cycles in six countries, 1948–80

Sources: For the U.S. business cycle and growth cycle chronologies, NBER; for the growth cycle chronologies of the other countries, Center for International Business Cycle Research.

Note: In each panel, the lines connect the dates of the consecutive peaks and troughs in growth cycles for the given country. The peak dates are listed above each panel, and the trough dates below. In the panel for the United States, the dashed lines connect the dates of the consecutive peaks and troughs in business cycles. The peak dates are listed above the panel, and the trough dates below, except where they coincide with the corresponding growth cycle dates. ' = tentative.

Hence, they have a better record of forecasting growth cycles than of forecasting business cycles (the slowdown predictions are treated as "extra turns" when attention is focused exclusively on the recessions).

The U.S. chronologies are more complete and better documented than those for most other countries, and the latter are in recent times predominantly limited to growth cycles. However, I have little doubt that many of the U.S. results (e.g., those concerning the greater frequency, symmetry, and relative predictability of growth cycles compared with business cycles) apply about equally to other developed market-oriented economies. Studies by Mintz and by Moore and his associates, as well as others abroad, indicate that "leading, coincident, and lagging indicators behave in much the same way in relation to growth cycles in other industrial countries as they do in the United States" (Moore 1980, p. 24).

Figure 7.1 suggests that most of the recent growth cycles have been international in scope, including those slowdowns that did not become recessions in the United States. That is, the low-growth phases of 1951–52, 1962–64, and 1966–67 had counterparts in Europe (indeed, as noted earlier, the first German recession after World War II occurred in 1966–67, overlapping the last of these episodes). The 1953–54 recession in the United States had but weak and spotty repercussions abroad (virtually limited to Canada and Japan). The recessions of 1957–58 and 1969–70 had more visible counterparts, although most of these took the form of growth retardations rather than absolute declines.[18] It is clear that the most serious recessions in the post–World War II period occurred in 1974–75 in all the countries covered and elsewhere in the trading world; most of these declines were preceded by slowdowns in 1973. The expansions that followed were soon, in 1976–77, interrupted by another cluster of low-growth phases, but not in the United States, where the next slowdown occurred only in 1979, followed by a brief but substantial decline in 1980. This last recession, too, spread internationally.

Figure 7.1 confirms what has long been observed and understood: business fluctuations tend to spread among countries linked by trade and financial transactions reflecting the international movements of goods, services, and capital. Expansions stimulate foreign trade and investments; slowdowns and recessions discourage them. The cyclical pattern of the U.S. economy impresses itself strongly upon a close partner of a relatively small economic size such as Canada. The diagrams for West Germany and the United Kingdom exemplify another close timing relationship. To be sure, there are also deviations, but the common rhythm is unmistakable for all the countries covered (and it extends to many others). It is often suspected that the chain of influence

18. In particular, in West Germany these were just mild slowdowns. France seems to have had more of a decline in 1958 only. The United Kingdom had lengthy retardations of a more pronounced variety and much less growth generally, but here too outright declines were rare and short. Japan, with the highest rates, also had the most frequent slowdowns outside of the United States and Canada, notably a sizable one in 1957–58.

runs mainly from the biggest country to the others (with the United States exporting its prosperity and its recessions), but this need not always be so: the proper model is one of multilateral interactions. In any event, the leads and lags disclosed by the chronologies vary greatly and cannot tell us much about the direction of the forces involved in the international transmission of cyclical movements.

7.5 Historical Dates and Durations of U.S. Business Cycles

According to the NBER chronology of U.S. business cycles, expansions have grown longer and contractions shorter. Table 7.2 demonstrates these tendencies by comparing the summary statistics on the durations of cycle phases for several periods, before and after such dividing years as 1855, 1919, and 1945. Wartime expansions have lasted longer than most of the others, but their exclusion does not alter the above finding (cf. table 7.2A, cols. 3 and 4). Before 1919, the peacetime expansions were on the average little longer than the contractions in business activity (the figures are 24 and 22 months, respectively). Afterward, they were more than twice as long (the corresponding averages are 32 and 15 months), and this despite the fact that the comparison includes the long depression of the 1930s and excludes three long wartime expansions. The vivid shift indicated by the average measures is somewhat further elaborated by the frequency distributions of short, intermediate, and long expansions and contractions (table 7.2B).

Of course, the data available to the NBER analysts for their work on identifying and dating the business cycles of history increased hugely in quantity and improved substantially in quality over time.[19] For the early decades, very few adequate time series exist, least of all in the most desirable form, which is comprehensive monthly or quarterly data on income, production, and employment. Here it was necessary to rely in the main on three sources, beginning with the descriptive evidence from "business annals" of contemporary opinion about the stage and spread of fluctuation in economic activity (Thorp 1926). The annals were next checked against indexes of business conditions and other series of broad coverage. Finally, arrays of cyclical turns in the more important monthly and quarterly series on individual processes were ascertained and closely examined so as to sharpen the choice of the reference dates.[20]

These studies of business cycle history replaced the concentration on financial crises, panics, and deep depressions, which was characteristic of the ear-

---

19. For example, U.S. industrial censuses are no more frequent than decennial from 1810 to 1899. They are quinquennial from 1888 to 1919, biennial to 1929, and irregular until the annual series of intercensal surveys begins in 1949. The data problems for the study of business cycles in other countries are on the whole greater yet. (The NBER chronologies extend over long stretches of time: for Great Britain, back to 1792; for France, to 1840; and for Germany, to 1866.)

20. For more on this procedure, see Burns and Mitchell 1946, pp. 76ff.

Table 7.2 The Duration of Business Cycles in the United States, 1834–1980

A. Average Measures, by Phase and Period

Line	Period (1)	No. of Cycles (2)	Mean Duration (S.D.), Months[a]				
			All Expansions (3)	Peacetime Expansions[b] (4)	All Contractions (5)	All Cycles (6)	Peacetime Cycles[c] (7)
1	1834–1855[d]	5	26 (20)	[e]	24 (15)	50 (23)	[e]
2	1854–1919	16	27 (10)	24 (7)	22 (14)	48 (19)	46 (19)
3	1919–1945	6	35 (26)	26 (15)	18 (13)	53 (22)	46 (16)
4	1945–1980	7	49 (27)	39 (12)	10 (3)	60 (27)	49 (11)
5	1834–1980	34	33 (20)	27 (13)	19 (13)	52 (21)	47 (17)

B. Frequency Distributions, by Phase and Period

Line	Period (1)	Expansions				Contractions			
		18 mos. and shorter (2)	19–36 mos. (3)	37 mos. and longer (4)	Total (5)	12 mos. and shorter (6)	13–24 mos. (7)	25 mos. and longer (8)	Total (9)
		Number							
6	1854–1919	3	12	1	16	3	10	3	16
7	1919–1980	1	5	7	13	7	5	1	13
8	1854–1980	4	17	8	29	10	15	4	29
		Percentage							
9	1854–1919	19	75	6	100	19	63	19	100
10	1919–1980	8	38	54	100	54	38	8	100
11	1854–1980	14	59	28	100	34	52	14	100

Source: National Bureau of Economic Research (for all reference dates used, except for August 1980, a tentative choice for the last trough; see fig. 7.1 and n. 17).

[a]Standard deviations of the duration estimates, in months, are given in parentheses.

[b]Excludes the Civil War and World War I expansions (line 2), the World War II expansion (line 3), and the Korean War and Vietnam War expansions (line 4). In line 5, all five of these wartime expansions are excluded.

[c]Excludes the cycles that contain the wartime expansions. See n. b.

[d]Measures in this line are based upon calendar year dates.

lier work in this area, with efforts to examine all business contractions, the mild ones as well as the severe ones. Mitchell noted that "the same developments which make it wise to substitute the concept of recession for the concept of crisis make it wise to recognize the shorter segments into which the long swings are frequently divisible. This change reduces the typical duration of American cycles to roughly one-half of the estimate commonest among theoretical writers" (1927, pp. 386–87). By the same token, the approach nearly doubles the number of basic observations (cycles) to be analyzed, acknowledging the great diversity of these fluctuations in length and size, but emphasizing their continuity. It presumes that the most severe and the mildest contractions are not of an entirely different species, even though they are certainly of a very different order of magnitude.

However, where consistent, comprehensive time series on the main aspects of aggregate economic activity are not available, the severity of business contractions and the vigor or expansions cannot be estimated with adequate confidence.[21] The evidence from business annals is deficient and susceptible of bias. Allowing for the lags of recognition, the consensus of contemporaries can determine rather well *that* business conditions have deteriorated or improved on a large scale and approximately *when* such shifts happened; it cannot tell us nearly as well just *how much* they deteriorated or improved. In a growing economy, downturns will attract more attention than upturns.[22] After a strong expansion, a mild decline (or even only a slowdown, if sufficiently long and diffused) may cause as much discomfort and alarm as a larger decline coming after a weaker expansion.[23] Hence it is possible that observers would tend to overstate the dimension of some of the movements in the former category, perhaps even mistaking at times a major retardation for a business contraction.

Time-series data permit some verification of the lessons from business annals. Moreover, they add valuable, though severely limited, quantitative information even for the earliest times covered. There are annual quantity series for individual but important items and monthly data for wholesale commodity prices, stock prices, bond prices, short-term interest rates, and (later) bank clearings. As noted before, indexes of business activity, which represent

21. This has been fully recognized by those who have done most to help remedy this situation. Thus Burns and Mitchell (1946, p. 402) state flatly, "Unfortunately, we lack at present reliable measures of the amplitude of successive business cycles." This conclusion still holds at least for the first half of the period covered by the NBER chronology.

22. Referring to the duration estimates derived from business annals, Mitchell (1927, pp. 421–22) states: "Our measurements are based solely upon the intervals between recessions. It would be desirable to check the results by a second set, based on the intervals between revivals. We have not attempted such a check, because business commentators have paid less attention to the upward than to the downward turning points of business cycles." (Note: In this discussion, business cycles are treated as having four phases—prosperity, recession, depression, and revival. The terms "recession" and "revival," then, refer to the turning zones.)

23. This is certainly consistent with the recent experience in fast-growing economies such as Japan.

weighted combinations of such series, have been popular in the early statistical studies of business cycles. It is unfortunate, however, that for the period before 1875 these indexes exist exclusively in trend-adjusted form. Clearly, it is difficult to distinguish business cycles from growth cycles in series that show deviations from trend only.

In this context, it is important to recall that the expansions and contractions of the early business cycles in the NBER chronology tend to be of nearly equal length—much like the phases of growth cycles and very unlike those of the later business cycles, in which the expansions are much longer than the contractions (compare lines 1–2 with lines 3–4 in table 7.2). Given this observation, and the limitations of the materials available for the identification of the early cycles, it is natural to ask whether some of these fluctuations may not be in the nature of growth cycles rather than business cycles. The reliance on business annals and trend-adjusted indexes, in particular, might well have produced a certain amount of bias in that direction.

The question, far from being purely academic or pedantic, is important in a basic sense, since it involves the reading of contemporary as well as historical trends. Thus it is well worth knowing whether business expansions have in fact grown longer and contractions shorter—or whether the evidence in table 7.2, which confirms that they have, is seriously flawed by a lack of consistency in the measurement of the fluctuations over time.

7.6   Amplitudes of Cyclical Movements: Contractions or Retardations?

Do all the "contractions" dated in the NBER reference chronology represent actual declines in economic activity or do some of them represent phases of below-average growth? It is much easier to raise this question than to answer it with sufficient confidence, for the already familiar reason that the data are so limited. A thorough review of the NBER chronology and the underlying materials is beyond the scope of this paper. Still, even a partial reexamination of the evidence could be of some help here, at least in determining the dimensions of the problem.

Table 7.3 reviews the period 1834–82, that is, that segment of the NBER reference cycle chronology for which there are no comprehensive measures or indexes of economic activity without trend adjustments. A comparison of columns 2 and 4, and of columns 3 and 5, shows that each of the NBER cycles corresponds to a cycle recognized in the U.S. business annals. It is this broad parallelism that interests us here, not the timing discrepancies, which seem considerable but are mainly due to the inevitable vagueness of the annals in this respect.

The measures in columns 6–11 are based on the only index of business activity in the United States available for these early decades, the Cleveland Trust Company index compiled in 1931 and intensively used by Ayres (1939). This is a weighted combination of trend-adjusted series on prices, physical

Table 7.3 Business Cycle Chronologies and Measures of Amplitude and Duration Based on Trend-Adjusted Time Series, United States, 1834–82

Line	NBER Reference Dates for Business Cycle			Business Annals[a]		Ayres's (Cleveland Trust Company) Index of Business Activity							
						Date and Value[b] of				Change[c]		No. of Months[d]	
	Peak (1)	Trough (2)	Peak (3)	Timing of Revival (4)	Timing of Recession (5)	Local	Low (6)	Local	High (7)	High to Low (8)	Low to High (9)	Below Trend (910)	Above Trend (11)
1	not avail.	1834	1836	L34–E35	Mid-37	10/34	− 7.4	2/37	+21.0	−13.5[e]	+28.4	16	23
2	1836	1838	1839	L38–E39	Fall 39	4/38	−11.8	3/39	+15.2	−32.8	+27.0	18	15
3	1839	1843	1845	L43–E44	May 45	2/43	−19.1	2/46	+ 4.5	−34.3	+23.6	68	9
4	1845	1846	1847	E47	L47	6/46	− 1.4	6/47	+14.3	− 5.9	+15.7	1[f]	24
5	1847	1848	1853	L48	L53–E54	12/48	− 5.4	3/54	+14.6	−19.7	+20.0	17	55[g]
6	1853	Dec. 1854	June 1857	L55	Mid-57	12/54	− 3.8	5/56	+10.1	−18.4	+13.9	6	27
7	June 1857	Dec. 1858	Oct. 1860	1859	L60	1/58	−13.0	9/60	+ 4.7	−23.1	+17.7	18	15[h]
8	Oct. 1860	June 1861	Apr. 1865	L61	L65	7/61	− 9.8	4/64	+ 9.8	−14.5	+19.6	23	27
9	Apr. 1865	Dec. 1867	June 1869	1868	E70	11/65	−14.0	6/69	+ 4.9	−23.8	+18.9	11	23[i]
10	June 1869	Dec. 1870	Oct. 1873	E71	Mid-73	10/70	− 4.8	1/73	+14.6	− 9.7	+19.4	5	33
11	Oct. 1873	Mar. 1879	Mar. 1882	L78–E79	L82	2/78	−12.7	1/81	+11.7	−27.3	+24.4	70	50

Sources: Cols. 1–3, Burns and Mitchell 1946, table 16, p. 78; cols. 4–5, Thorp 1926, ch. 1; cols. 6–11, Ayres 1939, app. A, table 9, col. 1.

[a]L denotes "late" (last half or quarter); E denotes "early" (first half or quarter). In referring to years, the first two digits are omitted.

[b]Refers to the lowest (col. 6) and highest (col. 7) value of the index in the given cycle, in percentage deviations from trend. The corresponding dates shown do not always coincide with the dates of business cycle troughs and peaks designated by Ayres.

[c]Amplitude of decline (−) in col. 8 and of rise (+) in col. 9, based on the corresponding entries in cols. 6 and 7.

[d]Months during which the index shows negative values (including the low in col. 6) are given in col. 10; months during which the index shows positive values (including the high in col. 7) are given in col. 11. Refers to consecutive months, except as noted below.

[e]From a high of +6.1 in 2/1832 to the low of −7.4 in 10/34 shown in col. 6.

[f]Except for the single low month of 6/1846, the index remained positive from 9/1845 through 6/1848, i.e., over intervals of 9 months and 24 months (as shown in col. 11).

[g]From 12/1849 through 9/1854, with two minor interruptions of 1 month each.

[h]From 3/1859 through 9/1859 and from 3/1860 through 10/1860 (small negative values in the 5 intervening months).

[i]From 7/1868 through 12/1869 and from 4/1870 through 8/1870 (small negative values in the 3 intervening months).

quantities, and pecuniary volumes of transactions or trade. As such, it contains considerable information but in a form that lends itself to much popular use and misuse; it ought to be handled with great care and caution. In particular, it is important to recognize that the annual movements in the index have a different meaning from the monthly movements, because the former reflect mainly changes in production and trade and the latter changes in commodity and security prices (the monthly series used as interpolators). Also, like other early indexes, this composite refers in large measure to durable goods, whose cyclical sensitivity tends to be high, which means that it may overstate the fluctuations of the economy at large.[24]

Contemporary testimonies and data broadly agree on the earliest developments covered, including a moderate decline in 1833–34, an expansion accompanied by much speculation in land through 1836, a financial panic followed by an incomplete recovery in 1837–38, and finally one of the longest and deepest depressions in U.S. history, marked by sharp deflation and repudiation of, or postponement of payments on, large amounts of private and state debts. In sharp contrast to that depression, which ended in 1843, the NBER-designated contraction of 1845–46 was a mild affair, which indeed is open to serious doubt: the episode may well have been one of a mere growth cycle retardation. Ayres speaks of "a minor dip in business in 1846"; his index stays positive, that is, above "normal," in all months but one from September 1845 through June 1848 (table 7.3, line 4).[25] The business annals describe a suspiciously short cycle in terms that are inconclusive but, compared to those used elsewhere, quite mild.[26] Moreover, several independent studies using mainly annual data on the volume of domestic and foreign trade fail to confirm the occurrence of a business contraction in these years. They suggest

24. In the period under review, the index comprised detrended series on commodity and security prices, imports and exports, ship construction, coal production, tons of registered shipping, and government finance (before 1855); later, pig iron consumption, railroad freight ton-miles, blast furnace activity, rail production, locomotive production, miles of new railroads, canal freight, and cotton consumption. For details, see Ayres 1939, app. C, pp. 204–5. Although the composition of the index is different for the years before and after 1855, tests for an overlap period are reported to indicate a very substantial similarity of the results from the two sets of series.

The Ayres index, now published by Ameri Trust Company (Cleveland) is reproduced in graphical form in many widely used economic textbooks, as a rule without any explanation. Although its historical use can be justified, its current use appears highly questionable (e.g., its entire course since 1961 is shown as somehow persisting well above its zero "long-term trend" line).

25. Ayres (1939, p. 11) stresses that in 1846 there was "no real depression. It may well be that conditions were then developing which may have initiated a real depression, but that renewed business activity was temporarily stimulated by the government expenditures of the Mexican War."

26. As summarized by Thorp (1926, p. 124), there was in 1845 a "slump ascribed to political difficulties. May; return to activity, October"; in 1846, there was a "slackening of activity to dullness" and, since May, war with Mexico and "severe pressure in money market." Mitchell notes in his introduction to Thorp's volume (pp. 42–43) that the annals imply for 1845–46 a cycle of about 1 year's duration when measured between successive recessions (i.e., downturns). This would have been a very short cycle indeed and one difficult to reconcile with the Burns-Mitchell 1946 definition, which has business cycles exceed 1 year in length.

a single business cycle between 1843 and 1848, with only a mild setback in 1845–46.[27]

The years 1853–54 saw rising interest rates and strongly declining security prices, and these financial developments dominate the accounts of the recession in Thorp's annals as well as in the statistical studies by Ayres and Cole. But the evidence of a contraction in real terms is weak, except with respect to business fixed investment. The construction of new railroad mileage dropped sharply, but Cole's index representing mainly the physical volume of domestic trade increased about 5% in 1854. Wholesale commodity prices show very little softness in this episode. Thus, here too, despite the general agreement in the literature, there is some room for doubt about the genuineness of the contraction (as distinct from undoubted financial trouble and a business slowdown).

Data are still scanty for the next 15 years, which include the Civil War, but they provide general support for the business contractions with the NBER-dated troughs in 1858, 1861, and 1867 (table 7.3, lines 7–9). It is fairly clear, however, that the last two of these were relatively mild, and the designation of 1865–67 as a contraction finds no support in annual production data, which show increases.[28] The latter observation applies a fortiori to the 1869–70 episode, which was much milder and shorter yet. Indeed, it is puzzling how to explain even a mild contraction at a time of the greatest acceleration in railroad investment. A careful study, which notes this fact, suggests that short-lived financial difficulties may have discouraged inventory accumulation, which played a relatively large role at the time (Fels 1959, pp. 96–97).

Again, it is possible that in terms of production, all that happened was a phase of below-average growth rather than an actual decline of cyclical proportions. In the absence of reliable, comprehensive data on intrayear output changes, no firm conclusion can be reached. But there is another important factor here, namely, the decidedly downward trend in prices, which prevailed for about 30 years after the Civil War. In such deflationary times, cyclical movements show up much more strongly in nominal (current dollar) aggregates of income and spending than in their real (constant dollar) aggregates.

27. Bullock and Micoleau (1931, p. 153) state that "the movement of foreign trade and that of commodity prices do not point to a depression or even a serious recession in business in 1846." Detrended indexes of the volume of domestic and foreign trade constructed by A. H. Cole from series on tonnage carried on canals and railroads, of vessels built, total merchandise shipped to and from abroad, etc., show declines in all NBER recession years during the period 1830–62, except in 1846 and 1854 (Cole 1930, p. 172; also Smith and Cole 1935, chs. 12 and 20). W. Gilbert (1933, p. 141) concludes that after 1843, "a level high enough to be characterized as prosperity was not achieved before 1846 and that the years 1844 and 1845 cannot be called prosperous years but rather years of broken and halting revival."

28. Frickey's index of industrial and commercial production (1899 = 100) has the following values: 13 in each of the 3 years 1860–62, 15 in 1863, 17 in both 1864 and 1865, 19 in both 1866 and 1867, and 20, 22, and 23 in 1868, 1869, and 1870, respectively. After adjustment for secular trend, the index fluctuates in broad conformity with the NBER chronology, declining in 1860–62, 1864–65, 1866–67, and 1869–70 (Frickey 1947, pp. 125–29).

(In inflationary times, the opposite is the case, as shown by recent experience.) Presumably, the high degree of price flexibility existing at the time has mitigated the output fluctuations. But a perceived deflationary trend generates expectations of further price declines, which are to some extent self-fulfilling (just as inflation generates partly self-validating expectations of further price rises). Such expectations are worrisome and can be seriously destabilizing, particularly since they are always clouded by uncertainty. The changes over time in the price level are generally quite uneven—for example, the deflation of 1865–96 was interrupted by several relatively short and weak upward price movements, mainly during business expansions. Thus price expectations are as a rule only roughly verified by the overall trend and often falsified by the shorter movements. Moreover, the dispersion of the changes in individual prices is high. The uneven declines in prices, values, and spending during the period under review were undoubtedly hurting many people. Business cycles are not, and cannot be, isolated from these developments. They cannot, therefore, be judged by their "real" elements alone.

The 1873–79 contraction was exceptionally long and by most accounts and measures very severe (see table 7.3, line 11, and table 7.4, line 1, which contains some additional information). However, the available evidence is heavily weighted with nominal series—prices, bank clearings, railroad revenues, imports—which fell sharply; the physical-volume series show shorter and smaller declines, mostly between 1873 and 1876.[29]

Beginning in the late 1870s, more comprehensive statistics are available monthly, and not only in trend-adjusted form. Table 7.4 lists the amplitudes of cyclical movements—percentage declines without trend adjustments, and an average of three indexes with such adjustments. This is useful information, but it must be interpreted with care, since each of these aggregates has considerable limitations and there is a considerable amount of duplication among them.[30]

29. Friedman and Schwartz (1963a, pp. 43–44) note that "the steady decline in prices from 1873 to 1879 probably led contemporary observers and certainly led later observers to overstate the severity of the contraction in terms of real output. . . . The contraction was severe. Yet an analyst who assessed the contraction on the basis of physical volume series alone would regard it as shorter in length and far less severe than it has generally been judged." Similarly, Fels (1959, p. 107) states that the "depression of the 1870s," though second only to that of 1929–33 in monetary statistics, was "nevertheless, in terms of output . . . singularly mild." This is strongly supported by Frickey's data.

30. Bank clearings outside New York City (the exclusion is designed to lessen the impact of financial transactions, largely in the stock and bond markets) have been widely used in the literature as a measure of aggregate economic activity. Since 1919, the better series of bank debits (also outside New York City and deflated) is used. See Macaulay 1938, table 30; Frickey 1942, pp. 338, 360–61; and Garvy 1959.

The Axe-Houghton index, which starts in 1879, is based on pig iron production, imports, bank clearings outside New York City, and revenue per mile of selected railroads. The Babson index is a base-year weighted aggregate of seasonally adjusted physical-volume or constant-dollar series, with coverage expanding from 11 to 33 components. It includes manufactures, minerals, agricultural marketings (but not farm production proper), construction, railway freight ton-miles, electric power, and foreign-trade volume. The weights are value-added data. See Moore 1961, 2:39–40,

The series used in table 7.4 show expansions and contractions corresponding to the NBER business cycle reference dates in all instances but two: the Babson index of physical volume of business activity did not decline in 1890–91 and the deflated bank debits paused but did not fall in 1926–27. However, a few of these movements have been questioned; for example, Ayres's index shows a mild decline in 1926–27, but he disregards it in his chronology, and the same applies in the case of Axe and Houghton.[31]

Despite the shortcomings of the underlying data, the amplitude measures in table 7.4 rank the cyclical episodes sensibly, that is, in broad agreement with the judgments expressed in the most informed and careful studies of American business cycles.[32] However, the rankings differ depending on whether trend-adjusted or unadjusted indexes are used. As would be expected, the declines are generally much larger and the rises much smaller in the former than in the latter series (cf. cols. 4 and 5 with the corresponding entries in cols. 6–13).

The fact that not only the trend-adjusted but also the unadjusted series match all but a few of the turning points in the NBER chronology can be said to confirm the latter in a broad and conditional sense. This means that it is primarily the occurrence of these cyclical movements approximately in the indicated periods that is supported by the data, rather than the precise dates of the peaks and troughs. It also means that the quality of the evidence depends on the degree to which the indexes used reflect the true cyclical movements in the economy at large. These movements cannot be observed well without more comprehensive, nonduplicative measures of aggregate economic activity. The available series, used as proxies for such measures, could either

---

for more detail. The AT&T index is described as "primarily a measure of manufacturing activity and the physical movement of commodities" (see Rorty 1923, pp. 159–60). In 1922, it comprised 12 items (identified with weights in Mitchell 1927, p. 295), but in earlier years its coverage was much slimmer. These three indexes (Axe-Houghton, Babson, and AT&T) are available without trend adjustments.

The trend-adjusted indexes used to compute the average cyclical amplitudes in cols. 4 and 5 of the table are those by Ayres and AT&T, plus the index presented and described in Persons 1931, pp. 8–9, 91, 111, 131, and 152–56.

31. See Ayres 1939, p. 45, and Axe and Houghton 1931. Ayres speaks of "a minor business downturn in 1927 which was not sufficiently important to be considered as marking the end of a cycle." But Burns and Mitchell (1946, p. 109) observe that "this decline [in the Ayres index] is a trifle longer and at least as large as the 1887–88 decline, and definitely larger though a little shorter than the 1869–70 decline, both of which Ayres considers as marking the end of a business cycle. A similar remark applies to Axe and Houghton." See also Burns and Mitchell 1946, table 27, p. 108 and text, for more on the comparison of NBER and other chronologies.

32. Burns and Mitchell (1946, table 156, p. 403) use the trend-adjusted indexes of Ayres, Persons, and AT&T to rank the amplitudes of U.S. expansions and contractions in 1879–1933. Moore (1961, table 3.6, pp. 104–5) extends these measures to cover the period 1854–1958. It should be noted that our review ends in 1929 and so excludes the Great Contraction of 1929–33 and the much shorter but deep contraction of 1937–38. The 1926–27 episode is believed to be the last one for which the data leave some uncertainty as to the nature of the cyclical developments involved. Hence, given my present objective, there was no point in going beyond the cycles of the 1920s.

Table 7.4   Measures of Amplitude of Cyclical Movement for Three Trend-Adjusted and Four Unadjusted Indexes of Business Activity, United States, 1873–1929

| Line | NBER Reference Dates for Business Cycles | | | Three Trend-Adjusted Indexes[a]: Average Change | | Deflated Bank Clearings[b] | | Axe-Houghton Index of Trade and Industrial Activity[c] | | Babson index of Physical Volume of Business Activity[d] | | AT&T Index of Industrial Activity[e] | |
	Peak (1)	Trough (2)	Peak (3)	High to Low (4)	Low to High (5)	Fall (%) (6)	Rise (%) (7)	Fall (%) (8)	Rise (%) (9)	Fall (%) (10)	Rise (%) (11)	Fall (%) (12)	Rise (%) (13)
1	Oct. 1873	Mar. 1879	Mar. 1882	−33.6[f]	+31.5	n.a.[g]	+89.7[h]	n.a.	+46.5[i]				
2	Mar. 1882	May 1885	Mar. 1887	−32.8	+26.0	−17.6	+62.2	−24.6	+37.1				
3	Mar. 1887	Apr. 1888	July 1890	−14.6	+21.3	−12.3	+36.4	− 8.2	+32.1				
4	July 1890	May 1891	Jan. 1893	−22.1	+21.1	−10.2	+23.0	−11.7	+16.8	n.m.[j]	+22.7[k]		
5	Jan. 1893	June 1894	Dec. 1895	−37.3	+27.8	−29.8	+39.6	−29.7	+37.3	−26.9	+35.9		
6	Dec. 1895	June 1897	June 1899	−25.2	+27.9	−16.0	+56.8	−20.8	+58.9	−15.3	+47.6		
7	June 1899	Dec. 1900	Sept. 1902	−15.5	+12.9	− 9.4	+30.9	− 8.8	+36.3	−12.2	+41.4	− 9.2	+38.5
8	Sept. 1902	Aug. 1904	May 1907	−16.2	+24.7	−10.5	+41.3	−17.1	+39.4	−14.2	+48.1	−17.6	+54.4
9	May 1907	June 1908	Jan. 1910	−29.2	+24.4	−25.4	+42.2	−31.0	+59.3	−22.7	+43.6	−29.1	+44.9
10	Jan. 1910	Jan. 1912	Jan. 1913	−14.7	+14.4	− 6.4	+16.1	−10.6	+25.6	− 9.0	−23.3	− 7.8	+30.8
11	Jan. 1913	Dec. 1914	Aug. 1918	−25.9	+35.7	−14.9	+59.2	−19.8	+49.2	−18.9	+56.8	−19.5	+52.3
12	Aug. 1918	Mar. 1919	Jan. 1920	−24.5	+19.5	−10.1	+37.4	−14.1	+23.2	−28.6	+34.2	−21.5	+28.9
13	Jan. 1920	July 1921	May 1923	−38.1	+36.7	−13.9	+24.2	−32.7	+68.5	−32.3	+65.0	−29.4	+60.1
14	May 1923	July 1924	Oct. 1926	−25.4	+21.7	− 7.5	n.m.	−22.7	+36.1	−17.2	+28.0	−20.5	+39.4
15	Oct. 1926	Nov. 1927	Aug. 1929	−12.2	+14.9	n.m.	+54.5[l]	−10.0	+21.6	− 9.5	+25.2	− 5.8	+24.9

Sources: See Table 7.3, for cols. 1–3 and on the Ayres index. Cols. 4–13: NBER files; Macaulay 1938, table 30, pp. A289–A296; Persons 1931; Rorty 1923, pp. 159–60 (AT&T index, trend adjusted). See also nn. *b, c, d,* and *e* below.

[a]Ayres's index of business activity compiled by the Cleveland Trust Company; index of industrial production and trade constructed by Warren M. Persons; and AT&T index of business activity. The Persons index begins in 1875; the AT&T index, in 1877. Each index is expressed in percentage deviations from its base (trend) line, and changes are computed between the extreme values of these deviations in each cycle; the entries below are averages of the corresponding changes in the three indexes.

[b]1875–1918, bank clearings; 1919–30, bank debits. NBER data (Macaulay), deflated by Carl Snyder's Index of General Price Level. Not adjusted for trend. Seasonally adjusted. Series begins in 1875.

[c]Furnished by E. W. Axe and Company, New York. Not adjusted for trend. Seasonal adjustment by compiler. Series begins in February 1879.

[d]Furnished by Babson's Reports, Inc. Not adjusted for trend. Seasonal adjustment by compiler. Series begins in January 1889.

[e]AT&T, Chief Statistician's Division (a confidential release, 6 Sept. 1944). Not adjusted for trend. Seasonal adjustment by compiler. Series begins in 1899.

[f]Based on the declines in the Ayres index, 1873–78, and in the Persons index, 1875–78.

[g]n.a. = data not available.

[h]Measured from the trough in 3/1878 to the peak in 6/1883; disregards a downward movement in the series from 7/1881 to 1/1882. See Burns and Mitchell 1946, chart 30, p. 255.

[i]Measured from the low of 2/1879 to the peak of 8/1882; disregards a downward movement in the series from 3/1880 to 1/1881.

[j]n.m. = no movement in the series corresponds to the NBER reference dates.

[k]Measured from the low in 9/1889 to the peak in 3/1892.

[l]Measured from the trough in 9/1923 to the peak in 11/1929.

underestimate or overestimate the true movements, but the greater risk would seem to be that of overestimation because the data appear to represent the cyclically sensitive sectors of the economy such as manufacturing better than they do the other sectors.

Of course, the serious nature of several contractions listed in table 7.4 is not in doubt. The decline in 1882–85 was among the longest and rather severe, although again more so in prices and money transactions than in production.[33] Generally poor business conditions and a protracted deflation characterized the 4½-year period from the beginning of 1893 to mid-1897, which saw two major contractions separated only by an abortive revival from the middle of 1894 through 1895. The debacles of 1907–8 and 1920–21 were both relatively short but very severe. There was also a serious decline in production and real income in the years 1913 and 1914, which was fully reversed only in 1915 by the inflow of orders from abroad as World War I intensified.[34]

The other contractions were definitely much milder, and some of them may well have been marked by retardations rather than absolute declines in total output. The one in 1887–88 is described as a brief "slight recession" in the business annals; it does not register as a decline in a number of important series but only as a retardation; and it is omitted from cyclical chronologies by some scholars.[35] The next contraction on the NBER list, attributed to monetary disturbances originating abroad in mid-1890, although shorter yet, is viewed as more pronounced, but not by much. After a brief but vigorous expansion following the depressed years 1893–97, another extremely mild contraction is identified by NBER in 1899–1900, which also does not show up in annual measures of output and real income.[36]

The first contraction of this century, in 1902–4, was rather lengthy but cer-

33. Frickey's (1947) annual index of industrial and commercial production (1899 = 100) has a peak of 48 in 1883 and a trough of 46 in 1885; in trend-adjusted form, the decline is from 109 (percentage of trend) in 1882 to 93 in 1885. See also Fels 1959, pp. 128–31.

34. For further evidence on the above episodes, see Fels 1959, chs. 10 and 11; Frickey 1947; Friedman and Schwartz 1963a, pp. 99–102, 108–13, 156–58, 196–97, and 231–32.

35. In particular by Kitchin (1923, pp. 10–16). Fels (1959, p. 142), agrees "that 1887–88 was about as mild as any contraction worthy of the name. The only difference of opinion to be found in the literature is whether it should be recognized as a cyclical contraction at all." He lists several monthly series for banking, imports, and railroad traffic and earnings that show no cyclical peaks in this period but also notes that investment in railroads and buildings did weaken. Frickey's index assumes the values 54, 60, and 61 in 1886, 1887, and 1888; in trend-adjusted form, the corresponding readings are 103, 107, and 104.

36. Beginning in 1889, annual figures on the value of net national product in 1929 dollars are available from Kendrick 1961. This series, due to Kuznets and Kendrick, shows increases of 4.3% and 2.7% in the "trough" years 1891 and 1900, respectively (in contrast to sizable declines in the depressed years 1893–94 and 1896). Similarly, Frickey's unadjusted index rises in both 1889–91 and 1899–1901 (but declines when trend adjusted in both 1891 and 1900). The monthly Babson index, which has a relatively good coverage of industrial output, moves along a low plateau but shows no decline from its beginning in 1889 through early 1891 (see n. 30 and table 7.4, line 4). For further information, see Friedman and Schwartz 1963a, pp. 94 (chart 8), 104, 136 (chart 13), and 139; also Fels 1959, pp. 166–71.

tainly not severe. Still, there is no reason to question that it was a true decline in aggregate economic activity as both real net national product and the index of industrial and commercial production had small losses (of about 1.8% and 1.5%, respectively) in 1904. Similarly, the contraction of 1910–12 was mild, although it too lasted about 2 years. Prices fell markedly in this period, while real net national product increased only slightly in 1910 (by 0.8%) and the index of industrial and commercial production fell 3.3% in 1911.[37]

The 1918–19 contraction as dated by the National Bureau was extremely brief (7 months) so it is not surprising that it is not registered in annual data. The amplitude measures of table 7.4, however, show it to have been more serious than most of the contractions discussed previously. It seems appropriate to regard it as a sui generis end-of-the-war recession along with the similarly short 1945 episode.

The last two cycles to be considered are those of 1923–29, a period of calmness before the storm, characterized by relatively stable economic growth and fairly stable prices. The contraction of 1923–24 was moderately brief and mild, but the Babson index suggests that it saw a decline in industrial production similar to those that occurred in 1895–97 and 1913–14 (cf. lines 6, 11, and 14 in table 7.4). The nature of the extremely mild 1926–27 phase is much more questionable, however. As already noted, some investigators excluded this movement from their cyclical chronologies (see n. 31). They may not have consistently followed their own criteria in doing so, but from the present point of view more doubt is justified. Even the sensitive industrial production indexes (Federal Reserve Bank, Babson) fell but relatively slightly—about 8% or 9%—in this period, and there is no good evidence that real income and total output declined, although money income probably did, a little, along with prices (R. A. Gordon 1951, p. 208, and references therein; also Friedman and Schwartz, 1963a, pp. 197 (chart 16) and 288).

In sum, this reappraisal suggests that generally the contractions in NBER chronology do represent cyclical declines in either real income and output or money income and spending or both the real and the nominal aggregates. In my view, it is necessary to consider both groups of variables: in the recent inflationary era, the cycles are mainly in the real aggregates, but in the past, when the price level fluctuated and long periods of deflation occurred, they were often more pronounced in the nominal aggregates.

Nevertheless, there are a few doubtful episodes. All of these go back to the 19th century, unless the recession of 1926–27 is questioned, which is a difficult, marginal case. The 1845–46 phase is most dubious, but 1869–70 is also of uncertain nature as are 1887–88 and 1899–1900. It seems impossible to refute the hypothesis that these were periods of below-average growth rather

37. The Nutter index of industrial production, based in large part on Frickey's data, shows a very similar decline in the same year (see ref. in table 7.1). See Friedman and Schwartz 1963a, pp. 173–74.

than actual declines. The same may apply to a few other minor contractions mentioned before, but it seems prudent not to press the matter. Although some factors point to retardations, others (such as the length of some of the phases or the behavior of prices and monetary and current-dollar series) point to the possibility of mild declines.

Suppose the four periods just listed are treated as growth cycle slowdowns, not business cycle contractions. This would make some business cycle expansions longer and larger. The effects on the averages are illustrated in table 7.5, which compares the figures from table 7.2, lines 1 and 2, with their counterparts, for fewer cycles obtained by including the slowdowns in expansions. Clearly, the differences between expansions and contractions are much increased. But the contrast with the business cycles of 1919–80 (based on the NBER chronology as in table 7.2, lines 3 and 4), though attenuated, is still in evidence.

7.7 Summing Up

This concluding section sums up a few points.

1. Severe depressions reduce economic growth strongly for some time; vigorous expansions, which often follow, have similar transitory effects in the opposite direction. Most of the cyclical movements, however, are short and mild. The last hundred years can be about evenly divided between a set of four periods of relatively high stability and a set of four periods of relatively low stability, each period being a sequence of two, three, or four complete peak-to-peak business cycles. In one set, the standard deviation of the annual growth rates in real GNP is 4.4%; in the other it is 7.4%. The corresponding average annual growth rates are 4.0% and 2.6%. These remarkably symmetric results suggest that growth was generally higher when stability was greater. Presumably, instability of aggregate demand and of the general price level impedes growth. However, long-term growth and cyclical variability depend partly on common and partly on different factors, and there seems to be no good general reason to expect any simple and stable relationship between them.

Table 7.5   Alternative Estimates of Duration of U.S. Business Cycles, 1834–1980

Period	No. of Cycles	Mean Duration (Standard Deviation), Months	
		Expansions	Contractions
1834–1855	5	26 (20)	24 (15)
1834–1855	4	36 (22)	27 (15)
1854–1919	16	27 (10)	22 (14)
1854–1919	13	37 (19)	23 (16)
1919–1980	13	43 (26)	14 (9)

2. Business cycles have changed in several important ways under the impact of the developments initiated during and after the cataclysms of the depression and war of 1929–45. Recessions are perceived as having decreased in frequency, duration, and amplitude; the apparent reasons for this lie in structural, institutional, and policy changes that have been much studied. But the process also introduced new destabilizing and growth-inhibiting elements. The recent changes in cyclical behavior are not necessarily irreversible alterations or trends that can be extrapolated.

3. The mildness of economic fluctuations after World War II led to a revival of the interest in growth cycles, that is, cyclical movements in trend-adjusted indicators. A great deal of valuable information for many countries has by now been assembled and evaluated on this basis. Growth cycles are relatively symmetrical in duration, in contrast to the recent business cycles, which consist of long expansions and short contractions. Measures of several important aspects of growth cycles show greater uniformity than their counterparts for business cycles. A comparison of the timing of recent growth cycles in the market-oriented economies linked by trade and financial transactions suggests a strong element of international diffusion of these movements.

4. The expansions and contractions of the early business cycles in the NBER chronology tend to be of nearly equal length, much like the phases of growth cycles and very unlike those of the more recent business cycles. But the early part of the chronology had to be constructed from very limited materials in the absence of the comprehensive monthly and quarterly indicators of economic activity that became available only in the past 40 years or so. Some of the early fluctuations could be in the nature of growth cycles rather than business cycles. Their identification relied to a considerable extent on business annals and trend-adjusted indexes of business conditions, which may be suspected of inducing some bias in this direction. A reexamination of the list of U.S. business cycles from 1834 through 1929 discloses some episodes regarding which there are good reasons to doubt that they involved general contractions in economic activity and not just phases of below-average growth. These instances are few, but they would be sufficient to cause a significant underestimation of expansions relative to contractions in the early (19th century) cycles. The doubts cannot be fully resolved with the limited information that is available.

8   The Regularity of Business Cycles

8.1   Introduction

Do business cycles have predictable periodicities? Do their phases die of old age? Or are the observed fluctuations merely random walks without past regularities of predictive value? These questions are central to modern macroeconomic dynamics and they have prompted a considerable amount of theoretical and empirical analysis. Yet the answers differ, with no apparent convergence to an agreement. There is much support for the notion that business fluctuations are just random deviations from growth trends, but also for theories that stress the essential regularity of features and even the uniformity of causes of expansions and contractions in macroeconomic activity.

This analytical situation is clearly both unsatisfactory and not uncommon. It could be due to any or all of the following: the controversial nature of the underlying issues and strong prior beliefs of the inquirers; neglect or selective use of the evidence; loose concepts and diversity of the business cycles of experience.

In this chapter, an attempt is made to comprehend the problems behind this apparent impasse by reviewing the literature and historical evidence. This approach lacks the terse elegance, but also the frequently spurious precision, of a single quantitative model or formula: the informed judgment it yields may well be more dependable.

This chapter was originally presented at the conference "Approaches to the Business Cycle" at McGill University, Montreal, Canada, on 25 March 1988. I thank the participants, and particularly the discussant, Anna J. Schwartz, for valuable comments. Any remaining errors are mine.

I would also like to thank Phillip Braun for valuable research assistance and Christine Verhaaren for efficient typing. Support from the Graduate School of Business of the University of Chicago, the National Bureau of Economic Research, and the Lynde and Harry Bradley Foundation is gratefully acknowledged. The research reported here is part of the NBER's research program in Economic Fluctuations. Any opinions expressed are those of the author and not those of the NBER.

Past studies, at the National Bureau of Economic Research (NBER) and elsewhere, have shown a persistence of sequential relationships and interactions among time series representing a wide range of economic, financial, or other variables. The common features of business cycles observed in the principal market-oriented economies consist mainly of the structure of lags and correlations connecting these "cyclical indicator" series. On the whole, this line of work suggests the existence of a recursive system that plays a central role in the generation and propagation of business cycles. It stresses the endogenous and deterministic, rather than the exogenous and random, elements of the process but stops short of expecting the longer-than-seasonal business fluctuations to have similar durations and amplitudes over time. This report is concerned only with the overall dimensions of business cycles, not with the characteristic interplay of the indicators, but the measures it presents are generally consistent with the view of the cycle just outlined.

The next section examines the implications of the NBER chronologies and other findings for the question, How regular in duration have business cycles been? There are brief discussions of the hypotheses and evidence concerning the incidence and coexistence of cycles with different periods—short, intermediate, and long. Some new pieces of evidence are introduced and assessments made. The analysis is extended to fluctuations in detrended series ("growth cycles") for the United States and other major countries since 1948.

The third section considers different theories for what they imply about the regularity of business cycles. The relevant concepts vary over a wide range: linear models with damping and white-noise shocks, models of the "political business cycle," and nonlinear models with limit cycles or irregularly oscillating growth. The problem of asymmetry in cyclical behavior deserves and receives particular attention, and some data and tests bearing on it are provided. I then approach the questions raised in the opening paragraph above in a different way, by considering the role of calendar versus historical time, and the predictability and costs of business cycles. The last section sums up the results.

8.2 Durations and Periodicities

8.2.1 Business Cycle Chronologies

The earliest dates of business cycle peaks (P) and troughs (T), compiled in annual terms from limited but well-explored information, suggest that between 1790 and 1860 both Great Britain and the United States experienced business cycles of the same overall frequency (14) and average duration (about 4.5 years). Table 8.1, however, also indicates that the individual phases and cycles varied greatly in length for both countries but particularly for the United States. Relative to the corresponding mean durations, the standard deviations tabulated for Britain have a range of 30%–63% and an average of

Table 8.1   Duration of Business Cycles in Great Britain and the United States, Annual, 1790–1858

Period	No. of Cycles	Expansion (T to P)		Contraction (P to T)		Cycle (T to T)		Cycle (P to P)	
		Mean (1)	S.D. (2)	Mean (3)	S.D. (4)	Mean (5)	S.D. (6)	Mean (7)	S.D. (8)
Great Britain									
1792–1826	7	3.6	1.5	1.1	0.4	4.7	1.5	4.7	1.4
1826–1858	7	3.0	1.5	1.6	1.0	4.6	1.6	4.6	2.3
1792–1858	14	3.3	1.5	1.3	0.7	4.6	1.5	4.6	1.8
United States									
1790–1826	7	2.8	1.6	2.4	1.9	5.1	3.0	4.6	1.5
1826–1855	7	2.4	1.5	1.7	1.1	4.1	1.7	4.2	1.7
1790–1855	14	2.6	1.5	2.0	1.5	4.6	2.4	4.4	1.6

Sources: Great Britain: Burns and Mitchell 1946, table 16, p. 79; United States: 1790–1833, Thorp 1926, pp. 113–26; 1834–55, Burns and Mitchell 1946, table 16, p. 78. See also Moore and Zarnowitz 1986, table A.2 and pp. 743–46.

Note: All entries are durations in years. P stands for peaks and T for troughs according to the annual chronologies. S.D. = standard deviation.

42%; for the United States the range is 33%–79% and the average is 54%. In Britain all but two of the expansions lasted 2–5 years and all but two of the contractions lasted 1 or 2 years. In the United States four expansions were shorter than 2 years and one was longer than 5 years; four contractions exceeded 2 years.

For periods between 1854 and 1938, monthly and quarterly as well as annual lists of reference dates are available for the two countries from the NBER study by Burns and Mitchell (1946); the chronologies for France and West Germany are somewhat shorter. The summary measures in table 8.2 indicate a substantial dispersion of the durations of business cycles and their phases as dated by the NBER. The S.D./mean ratios (coefficients of variation) average 40%–60% for expansions, close to 70% for contractions, and over 40% for full cycles, based on the longest periods listed (lines 4, 11, 14, and 17). The ranges of duration in months for the cycles before 1939 are as follows:

	United States	Great Britain	France	West Germany
Expansions	10–50	8–64	8–62	16–61
Contractions	7–65	6–81	8–68	12–61
Full cycles (T to T)	28–99	26–135	24–95	28–102

Thus conventional measures show large differences over time between the observed fluctuations in general economic activity, in terms of both overall length and division by upward and downward movements, for each of the four

Table 8.2   **Duration of Business Cycles in Four Countries, Monthly, 1854–1982 and Subperiods**

Period	No. of Cycles	Expansion (T to P) Mean (1)	S.D. (2)	Contraction (P to T) Mean (3)	S.D. (4)	Cycle (T to T) Mean (5)	S.D. (6)	Cycle (P to P) Mean (7)	S.D. (8)
		United States—All Cycles							
1. 1854–1919	16	27	10	22	14	48	19	49	18
2. 1919–1945	6	35	26	18	14	53	22	53	32
3. 1945–1982	8	45	28	11	4	56	27	55	30
4. 1854–1982	30	33	20	18	12	51	22	51	24
		United States—Peacetime Cycles[a]							
5. 1854–1919	14	24	7	22	14	46	19	47	19
6. 1919–1945	5	26	15	20	13	46	16	45	28
7. 1945–1982	6	34	15	11	4	46	13	44	19
8. 1854–1982	25	27	12	19	13	46	16	46	20
		Great Britain							
9. 1854–1919	11	42	13	30	22	70	29	73	30
10. 1919–1938	5	26	24	20	10	47	21	45	33
11. 1854–1938	16	37	18	26	19	63	29	64	33
		France							
12. 1865–1919	11	32	16	26	18	58	25	61	28
13. 1919–1938	6	24	11	15	8	39	14	38	10
14. 1865–1938	17	29	15	22	16	51	23	52	25
		West Germany							
15. 1879–1919	7	40	15	29	20	69	24	69	30
16. 1919–1932	3	29	12	23	15	40	18	53	22
17. 1879–1932	10	37	14	27	18	63	25	64	28

Sources: Burns and Mitchell, 1946, table 16 and chap. 4; Moore and Zarnowitz 1986, table A.3 and pp. 745–54.

Note: All entries are durations in months. For abbreviations see note to table 8.1.

[a]Exclude the wartime expansions (Civil War, World Wars I and II, Korean War, and Vietnam War), the immediate postwar contractions, and the full cycles that include wartime expansions and postwar contractions.

countries covered. But these statistics include outliers—some very long and very short expansions and contractions—which are relatively few and far between. It is important to allow for stochastic and exogenous elements in business cycle dynamics.

Here one might note first the tendency of wartime expansions to be protracted and of immediate postwar contractions to be brief. This is most apparent for the United States, mainly because peacetime expansions were on the whole longer in the other countries. When wartime cycles are excluded, substantially lower variability measures result, as shown in table 8.2 for the

United States (cf. lines 1–4 and 5–8). The coefficients of variation are reduced from 61% to 44% for expansions and from 43% to 35% for trough-to-trough cycles, 1854–1982.

The requirements for periodicity can be relaxed by treating the extreme-duration *classes* as "outliers." Ten of the 14 U.S. peacetime cycles of 1854–1919 had expansions in the range of 1.5–2.5 years, and 10 had contractions in the range of 1–2 years. All but 2 of these cycles (86%) lasted 2.5–4.5 years from trough to trough. This way of looking at the duration figures brings out better their central tendency, that is, the predominance in this era of American economic history of relatively short business cycle phases as defined by the NBER.

Note that even this truncation still leaves room for much variability (the 1-year ranges amount to a doubling of the lengths of the phases). Nevertheless, some contributors to the field are content to bestow the attribute of "periodicity" upon fluctuations so distributed.[1] This may be semantically legitimate, but the common practice seems to define periodicity more strictly. At any rate, judging from the NBER historical chronologies alone, business cycles are indeed best described as "recurrent but not periodic." This characterization is part of the much-quoted working definition of Mitchell 1927 and Burns and Mitchell 1946, which has survived well several decades of active research applications and testing.

In Europe business cycles were on the average longer and hence fewer than in the United States. Thus in the common period 1879–1938 trough-to-trough cycles numbered 17, 13, 14, and 10 in the United States, Great Britain, France, and Germany, respectively. The mean duration of the American cycles in that period was 4 years; the corresponding figures for the other economies are approximately 4.5–5.5 years. To account for most of the early cycles in the foreign countries, it is necessary to work with ranges of several years. Of the 11 British cycles of 1854–1919, for example, 7 lasted 4.5–8 years; 9 expansions were 2.5–4.5 years long, and 7 contractions were 2–3.5 years long. The results for France and West Germany are not very different.[2]

The average duration of phases during the interwar period (1919–38) is similar to that for the earlier decades in the case of the United States (table 8.2, lines 5 and 6). The phases are shorter than their pre-1919 counterparts elsewhere, except for the long contractions in Britain, where the economy was

1. A very clear example is Britton 1986; see pp. 1–4 for his general discussion of this issue with references to the literature. For an alternative treatment, see ch. 2 above.
2. Friedman and Schwartz raise the possibility that the greater number of turning points in the NBER reference chronology for the United States as compared with the United Kingdom may be due to the relatively greater abundance of statistics for the United States (1982, pp. 308–9). They note that the extra U.S. turns are concentrated primarily in the pre-1914 period, for which the U.K. chronology was based on scanty data; but also that the role of the British economy in the world was changed drastically by World War I, which may have also altered the pattern of the U.K. cyclical behavior. Their own chronologies differ little from those of the NBER: they omit two of NBER's U.K. dates (the 1901 trough and the 1903 peak) and add two U.S. dates (the 1966 peak and the 1967 trough) (1982, p. 74).

generally depressed much of that time (lines 9–10, 12–13, and 15–16). The dispersion measures are relatively high, reflecting the particularly diverse experiences of this turbulent era.

8.2.2   Multiple-Period and Long-Wave Hypotheses

The Burns-Mitchell definition imposes on business cycles certain minimum requirements of amplitude and scope as well as length, but only in very general and flexible terms. It thus allows for a great diversity of behavior, yet it treats the cycle as a single category. But some scholars prefer to use different concepts, which lead to hypotheses of several interacting cycles, each with its own characteristic frequency. It is then the combination of concurrent cycles with different intensities and durations that produces the seeming lack of periodicity. Different factors are responsible for major and minor cycles and perhaps still shorter subcycles. The existence of one or two types of a much longer wave comprising a number of the NBER-dated business cycles has also been asserted and investigated. It is clear that these approaches require more complex analyses and larger data bases than the common-cycle hypothesis.

Here it is important to recognize that business cycles involve numerous activities and are not adequately represented by specific cycles in any single variable; also, that no comprehensive time series exist to cover their long and varied history. For these reasons, it is more difficult to assess the relative amplitudes than the relative durations of business cycles, and indeed we know less about the former than the latter. But tests of models with multiple periodicities must rely on differences in the size as much as on those in the length of general economic fluctuations.

It is of course likely that durations and amplitudes of cyclical movements are positively correlated. The prevalence of short and mild recessions is consistent with this presumption. But the relationship is not easy to document and probably not strong, though it seems clearer for expansions than contractions (ch. 7, sec. 6; also Moore 1961, pp. 86–93). Certainly, the length of fluctuations is not a very reliable indicator of their size. Some of the U.S. contractions were long and severe (1839–43, 1873–79, 1929–33); some were long but moderate (1882–86, 1902–4); still others were short but severe (1907–8, 1937–38). Similar examples can be found for other countries.

Over nearly 150 years between the American Revolution and the low point of the Great Depression, U.S. wholesale prices followed long upward trends in three periods (1789–1814, 1843–64, and 1896–1920) and long downward trends in three intervening periods (1814–43, 1864–96, and 1920–32). In each of the intervals of secular inflation (deflation) expansions were long (short) relative to contractions. This relationship was also repeatedly observed and confirmed in the British, French, and West German data (Burns and Mitchell 1946, ch. 11; Moore 1983, ch. 15; Zarnowitz and Moore 1986, pp. 525–31). The dates of the uptrend-downtrend sequences in the price levels provide fair approximations to the "long waves" proposed by Kondratieff in

1926 and adopted with various modifications and interpretations by a number of economists over the years.[3] The long price movements are attributable largely to trends in money and credit creation and related influences of gold discoveries and wars. In the short run, prices generally tend to move procyclically around their longer trends, which presumably reflects a dominant role of fluctuations in aggregate demand.

A downswing phase of a long wave is supposed to be associated with average growth rates of technological innovation, capital formation, and industrial production that are lower than those in the preceding and following upswing phases. According to van Duijn 1983 (pt. 3), the results based on composite indexes aggregated across the main capitalist economies are broadly consistent with these hypotheses, whereas the tests for the individual countries tend to be negative, which is attributed to "national peculiarities" (p. 154). But there are so few of the long-wave phases that such results can hardly be conclusive. The evidence for the "1st Kondratieff" (before 1842–51) is shown to be defective. In the post–World War II period, the "4th Kondratieff" prosperity phase is dated 1948–66, followed by a "recession" in 1966–73 and a "depression" in 1973–. But this chronology is, to say the least, doubtful. The 1970s and 1980s have been much less depressed than the previous periods so classified, 1872–83 and 1929–37. Growth rates have declined but are positive most of the time in most places, and there is no general deflation and financial crisis.

More generally, the problem of identifying the long-wave turns with the available data is a truly formidable one (for early times, because of the paucity and defects of the information; for recent times, because of inevitable truncations and revisions). The smoothing out of the effects of other, much more pronounced movements (both the shorter cycles and the longest trend) presents no lesser difficulty. Several old and new tests of the long-wave and composite-cycle hypotheses produced largely negative results (Burns and Mitchell 1946, ch. 11; Adelman 1965; Howrey 1968). But here again the scarcity of relevant observations is a major problem, particularly for the tests based on spectral analysis. This recently favored method is well suited for the task of discovering hidden periodicities but only in relatively long, stationary, and homoscedastic time series, that is, under conditions that clearly do not obtain in the past context.

There is much disagreement about the very existence of some of the long waves even among the supporters of the concept, and more disagreement yet about the timing of the waves and their phases. This is in sharp contrast to business cycles, where chronologies from different sources are not very different and the NBER reference dates are widely accepted and used. There is

3. These include Schumpeter (1939); Dupriez (1947, 1978); Rostow (1978, 1980); Mandel (1980); and van Duijn (1983), who provides a useful critical survey of literature and evidence.

probably no better proof that the uncertainties surrounding the long waves are indeed unusually large.

Industrial production and early estimates of total output, when smoothed to reduce the influence of shorter business cycles, show 15- to 20-year fluctuations in the growth rates for the United States between 1840 and 1914. These movements, clearly associated with waves in the level of construction activity, are known as Kuznets cycles. Their explanation relies heavily on the role of population growth and notably the tides of immigration from Europe as sources of both additional labor supply and demand for new housing and other capital goods. The demographic forces are treated as interacting with economic developments, not as exogenous variables. Other important factors in these analyses include growth retardations in Europe, territorial and railway expansions in America, changes in the current balance and international capital flows, and constraints on the money supply under the prevailing specie standard.

Much has been learned from the literature dealing with these developments (e.g., Kuznets 1930; Burns 1934; Long 1940; Abramovitz 1964; Easterlin 1968). But some of the central elements in the Kuznets cycles as sketched above are now recognized as belonging to history. This type of fluctuation, therefore, is no longer evident in recent times, even though it is probably not entirely unrelated to long-term deviations from trends in the interwar and post–World War II periods (Abramovitz 1968; Rostow 1975).

8.2.3   Major and Minor Cycles

Unlike the deeply hidden long wave and the building cycle that apparently ceased to operate some time ago, major and minor cycles certainly exist as two very different categories, at least at the descriptive level. One can hardly object to this distinction as exemplified by the sequences of 1929–33–37 (the deepest contraction and a large but still incomplete recovery, both very long) and 1957–58–60 (a moderate and short interruption of growth). What is not so clear is how to define the major and minor cycles more precisely: whether they constitute a true, systematic dichotomy, and whether at least some major cycles consist of two or more minor ones.

Juglar (1862) was the first to observe that fluctuations in prices, interest rates, and other financial variables often lasted about 7–11 years. Kitchin (1923) stressed the primacy of 3- to 4-year cycles; the major cycles were to him "merely aggregates" of two or three minor ones (p. 10). In time it came to be widely believed that business investment in machinery and equipment plays a central part in the major, or Juglar, cycles, and inventory investment in the minor, or Kitchin, cycles. The former involve longer decision and implementation lags than the latter. Fixed capital lasts for years and cannot be adjusted to desired levels nearly as quickly as inventories that are normally disposed of in days, weeks, or at most months.

The NBER chronologies cannot be dichotomized into the Kitchin and the Juglar durations. Of the 14 cycles in Great Britain from 1792 to 1858, 6 lasted 3–4 years, 6 lasted 5–6 years, and 2 lasted 7 years each from trough to trough. The corresponding U.S. cycles include 3 of 2 years each, 4 of 3–4 years, 4 of 5–6 years, and 3 of 7–9 years. The monthly data used for 1854–1938 permit more detail. Let the classes of 30–54 months and 78 months or more serve as the Kitchin and Juglar durations, respectively: they would account for 31% and 25% of the observations for Britain, and 71% and 10% for the United States. The rest would fall in between, except for a few very short fluctuations. These measures, then, are definitely affirmative only on the historical prevalence of short cycles in the U.S. chronology.

Schumpeter (1935) held that "every Juglar so far observed . . . is readily . . . divisible into three cycles of a period of roughly forty months" (p. 8).[4] Nor surprisingly, no arrangement of the NBER consecutive business cycles into groups of three corresponds to the Juglar dates attributable to Schumpeter. Instead, his nine Juglar cycles marked off by troughs between 1848 and 1932 can be approximated by four groups of two cycles each, four of three cycles each, and one single cycle (Burns and Mitchell 1946, pp. 440–42).

But there is no good reason to insist on any particular fixed scheme of so many Kitchins per Juglar, and a more relaxed approach may be more instructive. When major cycles are marked off by troughs of severe depressions according to the U.S. monthly reference dates (in 1879, 1894, 1908, 1921, and 1933), their successive periods are roughly 15, 14, 13, and 12 years. The corresponding dates for Great Britain are not far off and they yield similar durations, namely, 16, 14, 13, and 11 years. These periods include 4, 4, 4, and 3 successive business cycles in the United States, and 2, 3, 3, and 3 business cycles in Great Britain. Burns and Mitchell admit that this result "suggests a fair degree of uniformity" and, upon further analysis, find some evidence of "a partial cumulation of successive cycles." Nonetheless, they conclude that "the [observed] relations are not sufficiently regular . . . to justify us in regarding the business cycles separated by severe depressions as subdivisions of long cycles" (1946, p. 460).

This is a tentative judgment conditioned by the deficient, available data, not a decisive rejection of all notions of periodicity. But whatever configurations of minor and major cycles may have prevailed in the half century here considered, they did not continue in the following era. The short but severe slump of 1937–38 occurred only 5 years after the end of the Great Contraction of 1929–33. After World War II, U.S. business expansions grew much longer and their durations more dispersed, in comparison with the pre-1945 and especially the pre-1919 cycles. This was due in large part, but by no means only, to the

---

4. Schumpeter also calculated that "the two complete Kondratieff units . . . contain each of them six cycles of from nine to ten years' duration." He attributed periodicities of 54–60 years, 9–10 years, and 40 months or "somewhat less" to the Kondratieff, Juglar, and Kitchin cycles, respectively. His full treatment admits some exceptions (1939, 1:161–74).

incidence of wars (cf. lines 1–8, cols. 1–2, in Table 8.2). On the other hand, contractions became much shorter and much less variable (cols. 3–4). Of the eight recessions since 1948, even the longest and largest (1973–75, 1981–82) were far less severe than earlier depressions, such as those of 1920–21 and 1937–38, let alone 1929–33 (see ch. 2, sec. 2.2, above; Moore and Zarnowitz 1986, pp. 767–71).

Thus if major cycles were to be defined as involving deep depressions, they could not be found at all in the economic history of the United States after the 1930s. What can clearly be identified is fluctuations in growth rates of total output that lasted longer than the average business cycle. Specifically, in 1948–55 and 1955–61, real GNP rose at compound annual rates of 4.4% and 2.2%, respectively. This period of 13 years included four recessions. In 1961–73 growth measured in the same terms was 4.0%; in 1973–86 it was 2.3%. This period of 25 years also included four recessions. But no indication of any definite periodicities emerges from this division.

To see this, note that the first of these two extended retardations was less than half the length of the second one, and the end of the latter is as yet undetermined. Note also the uneven incidence of business cycle phases within the two periods: 1948–55 and 1955–61 include two recessions each, 1961–73 only one, and 1973–86 three. Since 1973, growth rates fell well below the previous experience and expectations in all major capitalist economies. This may be due to a variety of sources of changes in labor and capital productivity distinguished in the studies of "growth accounting" (Maddison 1987). Oil price rises have attracted particular attention, but policy errors and disruptions first of high inflation and then disinflation are probably also among the major immediate causes of what happened.

To be sure, there is room for different interpretations of history, the more so the earlier and less reliable are the data. Long-wave proponents such as van Duijn perceive three Juglars in the postwar era, 1948–57, 1957–66, and 1966–73 (1983, ch. 9). But there was no business recession in the United States in 1966, only a short and mild slowdown; also, this breakdown does not produce any large differences between growth rates in output for the aggregate of the major countries (1983, p. 154).

Matthews (1959, pp. 208–10), using troughs in all contractions of manufacturing production except the shortest ones, counts seven major cycles for the United States between 1876 and 1938, with durations averaging 9 years (standard deviation, 3; range, 4–13). But he observes that "the periodicity is not really very good" and that "the circumstances surrounding the middling depressions were so diverse that it is difficult to regard them as the manifestation of a regular cyclical tendency" (1959, p. 211). Hence, he sees "distinct forces making for periodicity" at work only in the cycles of 3–4 and about 20 years, which were dominated by movements in inventory investment and house-building, respectively (1959, p. 214–15). For Great Britain, Matthews notes the early dominance of major cycles (of which four occurred in the relatively peaceful period 1825–65) ranging from 8 to 12 years and averaging 10 years (in addition to more numerous shorter and milder fluctuations). Between 1874 and 1907 four additional peak-to-peak cycles in national income occurred, lasting from 7 to 10 years and averaging 8 years, but these are attributed mainly to an alternation of two much longer, unsynchronized swings in domestic and foreign investment, a situation seen as unlikely to recur (1959, pp. 215–26).

In short, it is fair to say that direct inferences from time-series data in annual or shorter units, without resort to any elaborate smoothing or filtering procedures, lend little support to the concept of well-defined periodicities that apply to economic fluctuations across time and space. It is in the work of those authors who are sympathetic or committed to this concept that the problems encountered by the periodicity hypotheses are most visible.

8.2.4   Fluctuations in Detrended Series

The measures in Table 8.1 and 8.2 are based on the consensus of movements in time series that include long-term trends as well as cyclical fluctuations (only the seasonal variations are routinely removed). Alternative chronologies have been constructed from comovements of cyclical dimensions found in trend-adjusted data. In the upward (downward) phases of these "growth cycles," the economy grows at an average rate higher (lower) than its long-term trend rate. Hence not only absolute declines but also sufficiently large and long slowdowns can and do give rise to such detrended cycles.

Retardations often precede contractions, and then growth cycles have shorter upward phases, earlier peaks, and longer downward phases than the corresponding business cycles; that is, they are more nearly symmetrical. Sometimes a major slowdown occurs but no contraction follows, as in 1951–52, 1962–64, and 1966–67 in the United States (more recently, the period 1984–86 also turned out to fall into the same category). So growth cycles outnumber business cycles. However, it is also possible for a low-growth phase to include a short and incomplete business cycle recovery, though only one case of this sort has been documented so far: 1975–82 witnessed two business cycles but only one growth cycle.

When very strong upward trends prevail, growth cycles may replace business cycles; that is, phases of below-normal but still positive growth occur instead of contractions. In the long sweep of modern history, this appears to have happened on a large scale only in Europe and Japan during the great post–World War II reconstruction of the 1940s and 1950s. The condition may therefore be a temporary and uncommon one, except perhaps for small nations engaged in the process of rapid industrialization and buildup of exports. It is the observed postwar development that led to the contemporary definition of "growth cycles" and their dating for many countries (Mintz 1969; Klein and Moore 1985).

Since trends vary across the different indicator series for each country and generally also over time, their elimination might well reduce both the temporal variability and the spatial differentiation of the observed fluctuations. One would therefore wish to compare growth cycles with business cycles with respect to their regularities.

Table 8.3 suggests, first, considerable similarity between the durations of growth cycles in the principal economies with relatively unrestricted private enterprise and trade. The high-growth phases averaged 30–39 months for eight of the countries covered; 22 and 19 months for the United States and Canada. The low-growth phases averaged 17–22 months, except for United Kingdom and West Germany, with 28 and 30 months, respectively. Total growth cycles, whether marked off by troughs or peaks, lasted on the average a little over 4 years (about 5 years for Switzerland and 3 years for Canada, to take the range). Some of the discrepancies reflect differences in the time coverage. Inspection of the dates of successive growth cycles in the different countries reveals a good deal of correspondence between these chronologies. This confirms the old lesson that most of the larger fluctuations are transmitted or diffused internationally (see Moore and Zarnowitz 1986, sec. 8, for detail).

Second, the variability of growth cycle durations over time is less than that of business cycles but still large. For the United States, 1948–82, standard deviations are 50%, 52%, 45%, and 34% of the mean lengths of high-growth phases, low-growth phases, trough-to-trough growth cycles, and peak-to-peak growth cycles, respectively. The corresponding ratios for business expansions, contractions, and total cycle durations are 61%, 67%, 43%, and 47%. The range is 25–93 months for growth cycles; 28–117 months for business cycles. The results for other countries are similar; for example, the ranges of growth cycles in Japan, the United Kingdom, France, and West Germany are 40–99, 42–94, 41–70, and 41–98 months.

It is important to recognize that growth cycles are more difficult to identify than business cycles and are not as well defined and measured. In recent years, it was often taken for granted that trends and cycles have different causes and effects. They used to be treated as independent, for example, the long trend in real GNP as a deterministic function of time and the cycle as a stationary second-order autoregressive process around that time trend (Kydland and Prescott 1980; Blanchard 1981). This is now being strongly challenged by the view that the trends are themselves stochastic, and total output as well as other important macroeconomic series are stationary only after differencing (Nelson and Plosser 1982).

In an instructive article, Harvey (1985) argues in favor of a structured approach to modeling time series as containing unobserved stochastic trend and cycle components. He finds the properties of annual series on output, unemployment, consumer prices, and stock prices to be very different for periods ending in 1947 (with starting dates from 1860 to 1909) and the period 1948–70. For the earlier years "the cycle is an intrinsic part of the trend rather than

Table 8.3   **Duration of Growth Cycles in 10 Countries, 1948–1983**

Country	Period[a] (1)	No. of Cycles[b] (2)	High Growth (T to P) Mean (3)	S.D. (4)	Low Growth (P to T) Mean (5)	S.D. (6)	Cycle (T to T) Mean (7)	S.D. (8)	Cycle (P to P) Mean (9)	S.D. (10)
							Duration (months)			
1. United States	1948–82	9	22	11	21	11	44	20	41	14
2. Canada	1950–82	11	19	10	17	6	36	13	38	12
3. Japan	1953–83	6	35	17	18	3	48	13	53	19
4. Australia	1951–83	7	30	12	22	7	52	17	53	11
5. United Kingdom	1951–83	6	31	11	28	11	62	19	56	11
6. West Germany	1951–83	6	30	14	30	10	59	20	58	13
7. France	1957–79	5	33	19	20	6	47	16	52	19
8. Italy	1956–80	5	33	16	22	12	54	29	56	21
9. Netherlands	1950–79	7	30	14	19	5	51	16	49	18
10. Switzerland	1950–75	5	59	22	22	16	61	34	69	15

Source: For the United States, NBER. For other countries, Center for International Business Cycle Research.

Note: Growth cycle turning points mark the approximate dates when aggregate economic activity was farthest above its long-run trend level (P) or farthest below its long-run trend level (T). The selection of dates was based on visual inspection of computer-selected turns in coincident indicators for each country (such as GNP, personal income, employment, industrial production, and retail sales—in real terms, seasonally adjusted, and detrended). S.D. = standard deviation.

[a]From the first year with an identified growth cycle turn (P or T) to the last year with such a turn. The chronologies begin at different dates according to the availability of data. The absence of a recent date does not necessarily mean that a turn has not occurred.

[b]From P to P or from T to T, whichever number is larger.

a separate component that can just be added on afterwards." For 1948–70 "a faint cycle can be detected . . . [but a] stochastic trend model is sufficient," whereas "after 1970 . . . it could be argued that the reintroduction of a cyclical component is desirable" (p. 225). Not surprisingly, the short cycles of the early postwar period appear only faintly when annual units are used. The dispute continues but there is increasing evidence that the permanent components in business cycles are much larger than was previously assumed (Campbell and Mankiw 1987a, 1987b). All this may be interpreted as a revival of certain time-honored ideas: that trends are not very stable over long periods of time but subject to intermittent or sequential changes; that trends and cycles interact in various ways; and that, therefore, the separation of trends and cycles may be associated with serious errors (see ch. 7 for further discussion of this topic and references).

8.2.5 How Regular Are Investment Cycles?

What evidence is there that inventory investment is a source of minor cycles and fixed investment a source of major cycles? Studies of the historical record indicate that the relative importance of changes in business inventories is very large in short and weak fluctuations and much smaller in the long and strong ones, whereas the opposite is typically the case for investment in plant and equipment. Stocks of goods held for current production and sale are generally subject to prompter and less costly adjustments than stocks of structures and equipment on hand. Indeed, inventory investment is visibly more volatile than investment in plant and equipment. It is likely to drop in any recession, mild or severe, but will also at times show declines of some persistence during long business expansions. Fixed-capital investment has fewer "extra" movements of this kind. Yet comprehensive series on real investment of all types have a high degree of cyclical conformity; that is, they tend to move in broad swings whose duration and timing match well the business cycles as dated by NBER. If there are any systematic differences in periodicities here, they appear not to be sharp enough to be demonstrable by simple methods of comparing "specific cycles" in individual time series with "reference cycles" in aggregate economic activity.

The techniques of spectral analysis are well designed to serve the purposes of detecting and examining cyclical patterns or periodicities in large samples of data on stationary processes. They have been successfully used as such in the natural sciences and engineering. In econometric applications their usefulness is often limited by the small size of available samples of consistent data and the prevalence of nonstationary processes.

Most economic aggregates contain strong upward trends. Their short-period changes are highly autocorrelated and small relative to their contemporaneous levels. The power spectra estimated for such series show sharp peaks at the lowest, steep declines at rising, and flat declines at the highest frequencies.[5] Such convex curves relating power inversely to frequency (hence positively to the cycle period) were found to be relatively smooth, except for peaks at seasonal frequencies, and have been labeled "the typical spectral shape" (Granger 1966). In a spectrum so dominated by the long movement of the series, cyclical features turned out to be very diluted and difficult to identify. But this was soon recognized as a technical problem, not a proof of the unimportance of business cycles in general. For series that are trendless or detrended, more interesting spectra can be estimated. Differencing is often recommended and used. Howrey (1972) calculates spectra for real GNP and its major expenditure components in both first-difference and linear-detrended form. He finds using the change series preferable, but the results are generally consistent. His conclusion is that "these estimates indicate, from a descriptive point of view, the reality of three- to five-year business cycles, particularly in the investment series" (p. 617). The relative peaks that emerge lack statistical significance according to conventional tests, but this result is attributed to the shortness of the time series used.[6]

Another large problem in empirical applications of the analysis relates to the degree of smoothing used to produce the spectral density estimates. For very long consistent time series that may contain a large number of cycles, smoothing with weighted moving averages with many constants (a "truncation point" equal to one fourth or one third of the sample size, for example) can be appropriate. For the short series (small samples) usually available in economics, such smoothing may be too heavy. Hillinger (1986) contends that it results in attenuation of spectral peaks at business cycle frequency bands as in the "typical" spectral shapes. He presents unsmoothed spectra for quarterly series for 1960–84, which show pronounced peaks only at business cycle periods (roughly in the ranges of 3.5–8 and 3.5–10 years for West Germany and the United States, respectively). But the unsmoothed spectra, like the closely related periodograms, have unsatisfactory properties of their own and, in particular, lack consistency.[7]

Figures 8.1–8.4 and table 8.4 present the results of an exploratory application of spectral analysis to quarterly seasonally adjusted series on investment in inventories, equipment, nonresidential structures, and housing for the

5. This would be so whether the trends are deterministic or stochastic, and whether the underlying time-series models are of the ARIMA class or AR(1) with coefficients close to 1. For a discussion of the broad range of interpretations of spectra with this shape, see Granger and Newbold 1977, pp. 53–55, 63–65.

6. See Howrey, 1972, p. 624, where references to Adelman 1965 and Howrey 1968 are used to argue that studies of longer series "indicate more strikingly the relative importance of business-cycle variation."

7. That is, the variance of the estimate does not tend to zero as the sample size tends to infinity. Also, the covariance between estimates at different frequencies decreases steadily with the sample size, so that for long series the risk of finding spurious periodicities is high. But these are strong reasons to use high degrees of smoothing for large samples (increasing relative to the sample size); they are not good arguments for applying long moving averages to spectra of very short series that cover few business cycles.

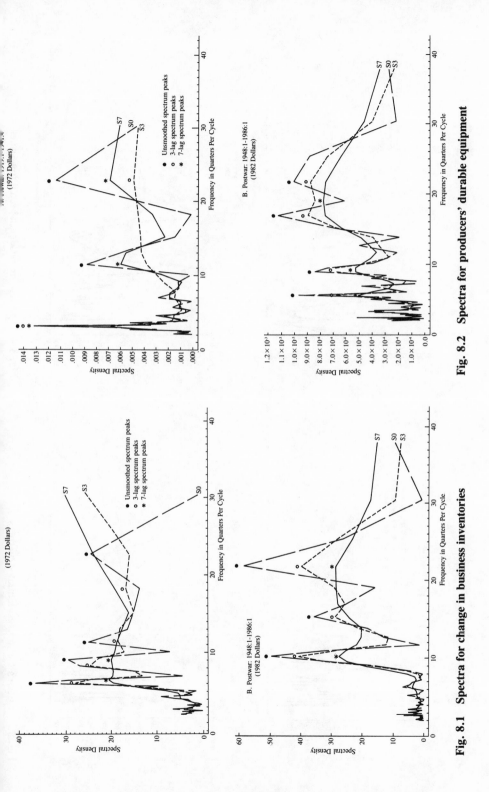

(1972 Dollars)

S7
S0
S3

● Unsmoothed spectrum peaks
○ 3-lag spectrum peaks
* 7-lag spectrum peaks

Frequency in Quarters Per Cycle

Spectral Density

.014
.013
.012
.011
.010
.009
.008
.007
.006
.005
.004
.003
.002
.001
.000

0 10 20 30 40

B. Postwar: 1948:1–1986:1
(1982 Dollars)

S7
S0
S3

*

Frequency in Quarters Per Cycle

Spectral Density

1.2 × 10⁻³
1.1 × 10⁻³
1.0 × 10⁻³
9.0 × 10⁻⁴
8.0 × 10⁻⁴
7.0 × 10⁻⁴
6.0 × 10⁻⁴
5.0 × 10⁻⁴
4.0 × 10⁻⁴
3.0 × 10⁻⁴
2.0 × 10⁻⁴
1.0 × 10⁻⁴
0.0

0 10 20 30 40

Fig. 8.2   Spectra for producers' durable equipment

(1972 Dollars)

S7
S3
S0

● Unsmoothed spectrum peaks
○ 3-lag spectrum peaks
* 7-lag spectrum peaks

Frequency in Quarters Per Cycle

Spectral Density

40
30
20
10
0

0 10 20 30 40

B. Postwar: 1948:1–1986:1
(1982 Dollars)

S7
S0
S3

*

Frequency in Quarters Per Cycle

Spectral Density

60
50
40
30
20
10
0

0 10 20 30 40

Fig. 8.1   Spectra for change in business inventories

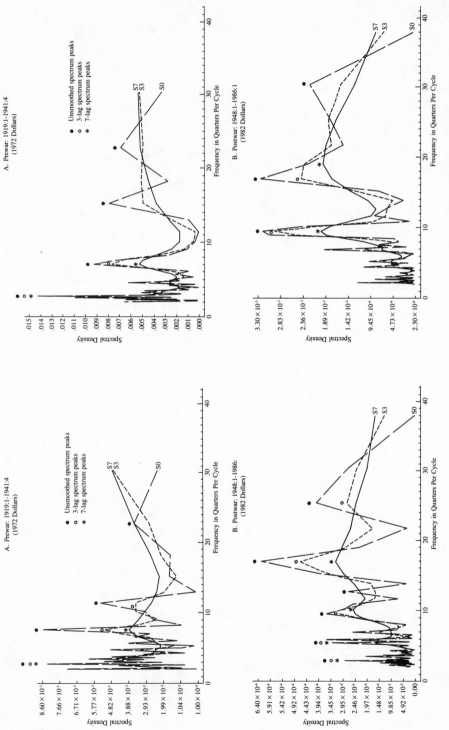

Fig. 8.3 Spectra for nonresidential structures

Fig. 8.4 Spectra for residential fixed investment

Table 8.4   **Peaks in Unsmoothed and Smoothed Spectra for Quarterly Series of Investment in Equipment, Nonresidential Structures, Inventories, and Housing, 1919–41 and 1948–86**

		Spectral Peaks (months)[b]							
		1919:1–1941:4[c]				1948:1–1986:1[d]			
Line	Type of Spectra[a] (degree of smoothness)	(1)	(2)	(3)	(4)	(5)	(6)	(7)	(8)
		Change in Business Inventories[a]							
1	Unsmoothed (S0)	18	27	34	68	(19)	30	46	65
2	Two lags (S3)	18	25	(34)	(55)	(19)	30	46	65
3	Four lags (S7)	19	(27)	. . .	. . .	(19)	30	. . .	(65)
		Producers' Durable Equipment[f]							
4	Unsmoothed (S0)	9	(21)	34	68	17	27	51	65
5	Two lags (S3)	9	(21)	34	68	17	28	(51)	(65)
6	Four lags (S7)	9	(21)	. . .	(68)	17	28	(57)	. . .
		Nonresidential Structures[f]							
7	Unsmoothed (S0)	8	21	46	68	9	28	51	76
8	Two lags (S3)	8	21	(55)	. . .	9	28	51	76
9	Four lags (S7)	8	21	. . .	. . .	(9)	30	51	. . .
		Residential Fixed Investment[f]							
10	Unsmoothed (S0)	8	23	34	68	(9)	28	51	91
11	Two lags (S3)	8	23	(34)	. . .	(9)	28	51	. . .
12	Four lags (S7)	8	23	. . .	. . .	(9)	28	57	. . .

Sources: 1919–41, Gordon and Veitch 1986 (updated version of data in Balke and Gordon 1986). 1948–86, Bureau of Economic Analysis, U.S. Department of Commerce, national income and product accounts.

[a]See figs. 8.1–8.4 for plots of these spectra and their peaks.

[b]Entries in parentheses refer to low or flat peaks.

[c]Estimates based on data in 1972 dollars.

[d]Estimates based on data in 1982 dollars.

[e]Inventory investment component of real GNP, used as reported.

[f]Change in the logarithms of the series (quarterly log differences).

United States, 1919–41 and 1948–86. Unsmoothed and lightly smoothed (3-lag and 7-lag) spectra are examined.[8] The post–World War II data come from the national income and product accounts compiled by the U.S. Department of Commerce, and the prewar data are new estimates by Gordon and Veitch (1986), all in constant dollars. The series on change in business inventories required no transformation; the other series, which show approximately log-linear trends, are cast in the form of relative rates of change (specifically, log differences).

The inventory series for 1948–86 show well-articulated peaks at periods of

8. The spectral windows were obtained with simple triangular weighting: 1 2 1 for the 3-lag and 1 2 3 4 3 2 1 for the 7-lag smoothed spectra. The SAS/ETS SPECTRA procedure was used in the calculations (see *SAS/ETS User's Guide,* 5th ed. [Cary, N.C.: SAS Institute, 1984], ch. 18).

30, 46, and 65 months in both the unsmoothed (S0) and 3-lag (S3) spectra. In the 7-lag (S7) spectrum, there is also a peak at 2.5 years and a gently rising plateau between 4 and 5.5 years. The prewar S0 has peaks at 18, 27, 34, and 68 months; S3 matches the first three of these well and the next one poorly; S7 is relatively high between 1.5–2 years only (cf. figs. 8.1A and 8.1B and table 8.4, lines 1–3). The strong procyclical movements of inventory investment in both the prewar and the postwar years is well documented (for a recent study of the 1929–83 period, see Blinder and Holtz-Eakin 1986). Measurement errors in the inventory investment data for the pre-1929 period may be responsible for the relative weakness of business cycle indications in the smoothed spectra for 1919–41.[9]

The 1948–86 spectra for producers' durable equipment show relative peaks at frequencies very similar to those located in the corresponding spectra for inventory investment, and these peaks show up in the smoothed curves as well, although much flattened. The 30- and 50-month peaks also appear, and more strongly, in the postwar spectra for both nonresidential and residential structures, but here there are some signs of much shorter and much longer cycles as well (cf. figs. 8.2–8.4 and table 8.4).

In the 1919–41 period, the 68-month cycle peaks appear in the S0 spectra for all three categories of fixed investment as well as for the change in business inventories but disappear or show up but weakly in the smoothed curves. The same is true of the 34-month peaks, except for nonresidential structures, where this cycle seems to be at least 1 year longer. The fixed-investment spectra also suggest some very short (9-month) and short (about 2-year) cycles.

In view of the unresolved problems and doubts noted earlier in this section, it seems best to treat these results simply as provisional without trying to test them in any formal way. Yet they are suggestive. The spectral peaks in table 8.4, col. 7, correspond to periods of 46, 51, and 57 months, all very close to the average durations of business cycles before and after World War II (53–56 months, see table 8.2, lines 2 and 3). The longest cycles, represented by relative peaks near 5.5–6.5 years (table 8.4, cols. 4 and 8), also fit in well with the observed durations of major macroeconomic fluctuations since 1919. This is not the case for those spectral peaks of inventory investment that correspond to periods of 1.5–2.5 years, which are shorter even than the average growth cycles of about 3.5 years (cf. table 8.4, lines 1–3, and table 8.3, line 1). But these results are at least in rough accord with the general notion that inventory investment generates short fluctuations, and indeed graphs of other

9. See Gordon and Veitch 1986, app. pp. 328–35, for a description of the data. Since their estimates of inventory investment were derived as residuals, they may have larger errors than the other series, especially for the early years covered. The Chow-Lin 1971 interpolation method was used to convert the annual series to quarterly observations. For producers' durable equipment, industrial production of producers' goods served as the basis for the interpolation; for plant and housing, industrial and residential building contracts and construction indexes were similarly employed.

spectrum estimates show similar local maxima (Howrey 1972; Hillinger 1986).

The observation that seems most difficult to explain is the apparent prominence of very short fluctuations in all divisions of fixed investment. More generally, the limitations of analyses and evidence of this type need to be stressed. Too many periodicities emerge in unsmoothed spectra; too few survive even relatively light smoothing. Aggregation across these and other components would be expected to produce much weaker and probably less periodic fluctuations in total output and employment.

8.3   Models and Problems

8.3.1   Limit Cycles and Random and Exogenous Shocks

Certain theories can produce strictly periodic fluctuations: a classic example is the nonlinear model of a limit cycle bounded between exogenously given "floor" and "ceiling" growth trajectories. [10] In the deterministic case, if the parameters of this model were to remain constant, the cycles would repeat themselves perfectly. This, of course, is not the observed or expected outcome, so random shocks must be added to nonlinear models too, but they play a relatively small role in systems with limit cycles. Major departures from periodicity may require changes over time in the basic parameters of models in this class. Such changes are indeed likely in a world with structural change and occasional large disturbances (e.g., wars). They are contemplated in discussions of some of these models but are not incorporated in the models or otherwise explained.

Random disturbances do have an essential part in the dynamically stable (i.e., damped) linear models, which, unless repeatedly shocked, cannot produce a continuing cycle. The output of such damped systems is represented

---

10. In Hicks 1950 the floor and ceiling lines have identical slopes equal to the long trend growth rate. The floor is set by the minimum rate of gross investment, which includes an autonomous part and maintenance of the current stock of capital; the ceiling is set by the limits on the resources available at full employment. Net investment is in large part induced by lagged changes in output, with a high value for the accelerator coefficient. Interacting with the lagged consumption-income (multiplier) relation, this accelerator would, in the unconstrained case, cause output to grow exponentially. But once set in motion by some initial impulse, an expansion will be slowed upon reaching the ceiling, and in the resulting downswing the accelerator is suspended until positive growth is again resumed when output falls to the floor and starts moving up along it.

It is important to note that the model could be relaxed in several ways to allow for differentiation of the endogenous and self-perpetuating cycles that it produces. (1) The accelerator could be such as to correspond to a cyclically explosive, rather than a monotonically explosive, solution. (2) Investment that is "autonomous"—that is, caused by factors other than the change in output—may fluctuate, say for technological or financial reasons. (3) Weak cycles may occur in which the ceiling is not reached. (4) Some variations may be admitted in the rate of growth of full-employment output and in the sizes and lag patterns of the accelerator and multiplier. See Hicks 1950, ch. 9.

by a second-order linear difference equation with a white-noise term u, that is, $y = ay_{-1} - by_{-2} + u$, with complex roots and $b < 1$ in absolute value (also, $a^2 < 4b$). When b is very close to unity, there is little damping and the periodicity is relatively high and easy to recognize; when b is lower (say, near 0.8), damping is strong and periodicity is weak and no longer visible. (For a demonstration of these relations by means of long-run stochastic computer simulations, see Britton 1986, pp. 7–9.)

It is only the small white-noise shocks densely distributed through time that serve as a possible source of periodicity in the damped linear models. Large specific shocks that are discontinuous and sporadic are likely to make business cycles and their phases less, rather than more, regular. Such disturbances can be caused by wars, large strikes and bankruptcies, price bubbles, foreign debt and financial crises, price cartel actions, and major shifts in fiscal and monetary policies. They will be particularly important when autocorrelated, which they probably often are. The conclusion of Blanchard and Watson (1986) that business cycles are affected by both small and large shocks but dominated by neither (and hence not "all alike") is plausible but as yet not well established.

As illustrated in chapter 9, simulations of large econometric models show them to possess weak cyclicality properties, to which relatively little is contributed by random noise. Serially correlated error terms in the model equations and exogenous variables have stronger effects, but generally the macroeconometric models are heavily damped and fail to account for much of the cyclical instability observed in past and recent data (Hickman 1972; Eckstein and Sinai 1986).

8.3.2 Government and the Business Cycle

The political business cycle (PBC) is a simple idea suggestive of periodicity: government policies aimed at winning elections for the party in power manage to manipulate inflation and unemployment so as to generate inverse cycles in the two variables, with turning points associated with the electoral campaigns and voting dates. Where the latter are fixed, as in the case of the 4-year presidential cycle in the United States, the so-induced fluctuations should have a strong tendency to be periodic. This hypothesis led to a considerable amount of interesting work on popularity functions relating electoral results to macroeconomic variables and reaction functions relating instruments to potential targets of economic policies. But the results vary and on the whole fail to be clearly supportive of the PBC models. This is not surprising, because it is doubtful that the contemplated policies can be sufficiently well timed and executed and, also, that the public will continually accept, or be fooled by, such policies if they succeed and tolerate them if they fail.

Business cycles go back a long time during the era of relatively small governments of limited economic functions and influence; but they have changed in various ways since, reflecting the evolution of the modern economy in both its private and public aspects (R. J. Gordon 1986). It is certainly important to study these changes and the role of government transactions, institutions, and policies in contemporary macroeconomic dynamics. But increasingly it is recognized that the most promising way to proceed in this direction is by treating the government as part of the endogenous process generating the economy's movement. Government policymakers as well as private agents react to actual and expected economic developments in pursuit of their objectives, despite the important (though partial) differences in the motivations, nature, and effects of their actions. There is both conflict and cooperation in the resulting process, with elements of complex games among the major partners, notably central banks and treasuries on one side and financial markets, business associations, and labor unions on the other.

Much hard work will have to be done to improve our understanding of these interactions, but some aspects of the story can be captured by extensions of current textbook models of the relations between output and interest rates (IS-LM) and output and prices (AD-AS). Fiscal and monetary policies affect IS and LM, respectively, and hence aggregate demand (AD); they also respond to shifts in IS, LM, AD, and aggregate supply (AS) that are caused by forces outside the government. What is needed is (1) to make the system dynamic by introducing lags and/or nonlinearities and (2) to make the policy variables endogenous by specifying how they react to changes in economic conditions. (However, this does not, in principle, preclude allowing for autonomous and stochastic elements in government actions, which are probably often substantial.)

The simplest approach is to use lags in the determination of prices (P) as well as output (Q), which may be due to slow and uncertain information, costs of rapid adjustments, desired implicit or explicit contract arrangements, or deviations from perfect competition. If then AD shifts up so that Q exceeds its full-employment level (Q^N) at the existing level of prices, there will occur a gradual upward adjustment in P and eventually also in expected prices (P^e). This will cause wages and other costs to rise and hence AS to move up, so that over time Q will fall back to Q^N. If AD shifts down and Q declines below Q^N, lagged downward adjustments of P and P^e will follow, so AS will move down and Q will slowly rise back to Q^N. The driving force here is the variation in demand; supply adjusts at prices and wages that are predetermined and slow to change, which explains the long lags involved.[11]

The fluctuations in AD could be the work solely of real forces in the private economy, as in the accelerator-multiplier interaction models, or solely of changes in money supply dominated by central-bank actions, as in a simple

11. In the presence of a long-term upward trend in P, this model would focus on the relation between Q/Q^N and the actual and expected inflation rates (p and p^e). When $Q/Q^N > 1$, inflation would accelerate (i.e., p and p^e would increase); when $Q/Q^N < 1$, p and p^e tend to decline. Another modification of the model is that some authors dispense with the concept of a short-run upward-sloping AS curve, keep the vertical AS curve at full employment, and work directly with shifts in the horizontal predetermined price levels. (Examples of these different treatments can be found today in most of the popular macroeconomic texts.)

exogenous monetarist model. An early formal model that combines real and monetary factors within a private economy is Hicks 1950 (chs. 11 and 12), where an IS-LM cobweb-type cycle is superimposed upon the nonlinear-accelerator core part of the system. This monetary cobweb results from the joint operation of long distributed lags in consumption and investment and shorter discrete lags in the demand for and supply of "bank money." This is an endogenous theory of a "monetary crisis" leading to a sharp rise in liquidity preference (a "credit crunch" in the more recent parlance).

Early students of business cycles saw no particular reason to give much attention to government activities. Keynesians have long treated the government as exogenous and having a large potential for reducing instability by countercyclical fiscal policies, income transfers and subsidies, or insurance schemes that keep up the volume of autonomous spending. The idea that government actions may be strongly destabilizing is still more recent, being due mainly to the rise of monetarism and its emphasis on the exogeneity and importance of monetary policy.

In the currently prevalent linear stochastic models, fiscal and monetary operations can produce either destabilizing shocks or stabilizing interventions, depending on how well they are timed, quantified, and executed. Some actions are taken to correct previous actions newly discovered to have been in error. So this approach permits a comprehensive treatment of policies and related variables, which can be revealing—if not pushed too hard.

Consider a monetary acceleration intended to revive a sluggish economy that has a cumulative lagged effect of fanning a business expansion into an inflationary boom, whereupon restrictive measures are taken that shift AD back and replace excess demand with excess supply. The concept of a cycle driven by such policy errors was popularized by the persistent monetarist criticism of the Federal Reserve, whose discretionary policies were time and again described as doing "too much too late." But it is hard to see how this argument can be generalized, and there is no sufficient evidence to support an attempt to do so. It would indeed be strange for such failures not to give rise to caution and learning but rather to be recurring with much the same negative results. Government miscalculations may well be common, but they do not offer a good basis for explaining the long existence and wide diffusion of business cycles.[12]

8.3.3   Nonlinearities

In linear models, time lags that cause overshooting in adjustments to equilibrium are essential to produce fluctuations in response to shocks. Nonlinear

---

12. In her (unpublished) comments on this chapter, Anna Schwartz has suggested that actions of monetary authorities may be endogenous in relation to minor cycles but not major cycles. Hence the absence of deep depressions in the post–World War II period could reflect caution and learning by the authorities. I agree that this may indeed be a partial reason for the postwar moderation of the business cycle (see ch. 2).

models can explain endogenously the existence and amplitude of a limit cycle without any shocks and explicit lags. (This is shown by a long line of work, from Kaldor 1940 and Goodwin 1951 on nonlinear investment-saving processes and cyclical profit shares to Schinasi 1982 on the integration of such functions and an IS-LM model with a government budget constraint.) But limit-cycle models need shocks to diversify the cycles and lags to determine their periods. And after all, it stands to reason that a successful explanation of how the "real world" economies move will have to include all these elements—random or exogenous disturbances and delayed reactions as well as nonlinearities.

Technical and scientific advances are facilitating work with reasonably comprehensive yet comprehensible models. Empirically, much is known about the role of leads and lags in business cycles. The part played by shocks is not so well understood and is more controversial despite (or perhaps because of) the current predominance of linear models that rely heavily on outside impulses of all sorts. The neglect of nonlinearities may well have led to an overstatement of the importance of random factors and perhaps also of policy changes treated as exogenous.

Nonlinear models now cover a wide range of business cycle theories: much of the work has Keynesian and some has Marxian flavor, but classical and neoclassical ideas are also represented (see the essays in Goodwin, Krüger, and Vercelli 1984 and in Semmler 1985). Grandmont (1985) shows that persistent deterministic fluctuations will emerge in an overlapping-generations (OLG) model in which markets clear and perfect foresight is obtained along the transition path through a sequence of periodic competitive equilibria. The basic condition is simply that the older agents have a greater preference for leisure. With the specified lag structure, cycles of different periods will typically coexist. The model has classical properties and generates some observed comovements, but it also suggests the possibility of an effective countercyclical monetary policy.[13]

Introduction of nonlinearities is necessary for modeling and analyses of a variety of theoretical ideas such as (1) time irreversibilities or ratchet effects employed in some early models of consumption and cyclical growth (Duesenberry 1949; Smithies 1957; Minsky 1959) and (2) discontinuities or jumps at certain parameter values that can differentiate the length of cycle phases or impose irregular fluctuations on long-term growth (from Goodwin 1951 to

---

13. Compare related results on other applications of the OLG approach that yield multiple rational-expectations solutions (ch. 2, sec. 4.6 gives a brief summary). Grandmont's system has the classical dichotomy: equilibrium prices are proportional to the stock of money, whereas real variables are determined in the goods market. Prices are positively correlated with output, and real interest rates are inversely correlated with output.

In contrast, a nonlinear model of capital accumulation in Foley 1986 shows how monetary and fiscal policies can fail to reduce cyclical instability and may even increase it. Here the accelerator amplifies the cycle, but liquidity effects eventually constrain it.

Day 1982, for example).[14] For these and other good reasons, this field of study is a promising and active one; but the work done so far is lopsidedly devoted to manipulations of highly aggregative and abstract models. What is badly needed is the development of tested knowledge of where the nonlinearities in the economy are located, how important they are, and what effects they have. This will require much careful examination of existing, and perhaps also collection of new, empirical data.

8.3.4 Asymmetries

An important point that did receive some attention recently is the possibility of basically asymmetrical cyclical behavior manifested in contractions that are on the average shorter and steeper than expansions. The view that such an asymmetry exists is far from new; as shown below, it found support in long historical evidence and was endorsed by some prominent economists several decades ago. But linear techniques are not capable of representing or explaining this type of behavior.

Mitchell (1927, pp. 330–34) noted that frequency distributions of month-to-month changes in trend-adjusted indexes of business activity for periods between 1875 and 1925 are slightly skewed to the left in each case. He wrote that "abrupt declines usually occur in crises; the greatest gains . . . come . . . as reactions after sudden drops"; also, "the number of declines is smaller than the number of advances, but the average magnitude of the declines is greater." He concluded that "business contraction seems to be a briefer and more violent process that business expansion."

Keynes appears to have narrowed the asymmetry from the total phases of rise and fall to the peak and trough zones. He wrote of "the phenomenon of the *crisis*—the fact that the substitution of a downward for an upward tendency often takes place suddenly and violently, whereas there is, as a rule, no such sharp turning-point when an upward is substituted for a downward tendency" (1936, p. 314).[15]

Table 8.5 shows average amplitude values (i.e., rates of change or slopes) for cyclical upswings and downswings in several long historical series with adjustments for secular trends. The measures are reproduced from Mitchell 1927 and Burns and Mitchell 1946 (or based on the data given therein; see notes to the table). For Mitchell's series in trend-adjusted form, the number of month-to-month increases tends to exceed that of declines only slightly (col. 2), whereas the absolute size of increases tends to be smaller than that of declines by varying differentials (cols. 3 and 4). The deposits series provides

14. The variety of slopes and shapes of the partly smooth, partly oscillating growth trajectories produced by recently developed purely deterministic models is remarkable (see Day 1982, fig. 1, p. 407), but it must be noted that these movements are much less persistent and more "chaotic" than those observed in economic aggregates during business cycles.

15. Hicks held a similar view of the asymmetry but less strongly. He related it to the "monetary deflation" that may accompany the real downturn and make it more severe (1950, pp. 115–18, 106–62). Keynes explained the "crisis" mainly by "a sudden collapse in the marginal efficiency of capital" (1936, p. 315).

Table 8.5   **Average Rates of Rise and Fall in Indexes of Business Activity, Unadjusted and Trend-Adjusted Monthly Data for the United States, 1875–1933**

	No. of Cycles[a]	Percentage Expanding[b]	Average Relative Amplitude per Month[c]			
			Rise	Fall	Rise	Fall
			Trend-Adjusted Data[d]		Unadjusted Data	
	(1)	(2)	(3)	(4)	(5)	(6)
Deflated clearings (Snyder)						
1875–1923 (M)	12	52	2.0	2.2	. . .	. . .
1884–1933 (B-M)	13	. . .	0.6	1.9	0.8	2.0
Clearings index (Frickey)						
1875–1914 (M)	10	51	4.0	4.2	. . .	. . .
1884–1914 (B-M)	9	. . .	0.7	1.6	1.0	1.8
AT&T index						
1877–1925 (M)	13	52	2.5	2.7	. . .	. . .
1900–1933 (B-M)	9	. . .	1.1	1.8	1.3	1.9
Deposits index (Snyder)						
1875–1923 (M)	13	47	3.0	2.8	. . .	. . .
Trade index (Persons)						
1903–1924 (M)	6	53	2.8	3.3	. . .	. . .
Pig iron production						
1897–1933 (B-M)	15	. . .	2.5	4.0	2.4	4.7
Railroad bond fields (Macaulay)						
1860–1931 (B-M)	16	. . .	0.62	0.65	0.56	0.94

Sources: (M) Mitchell 1927, tabulation on p. 333 and text, pp. 326–34. (B-M) Burns and Mitchell 1946, table 97, p. 291, and text, pp. 280–94.
[a]Number of complete specific cycles covered (trough-to-trough or peak-to-peak, whichever is larger). In (B-M) only corresponding cycles that show up in both unadjusted and trend-adjusted data are included (see n. *e*).
[b]Number of rises plus half the number of no change expressed as percentage of all month-to-month changes covered (calculated from data in Mitchell 1927, p. 333).
[c]Based on relative deviations from trend ordinates (M) or specific-cycle relatives (B-M).
[d]Trends calculated by original sources as smooth functions of time (oscillatory for bond yields, upward for the other series).
[e]Cycles in 1864–58, 1899–1905, and 1909–14 are omitted as noncorresponding.

the only exception here. The measures of Burns and Mitchell show the downswings as being on the average steeper (more rapid) than the upswings in every case. The differences are relatively large for both the unadjusted and the trend-adjusted series, except for railroad bond yields, where the trend is oscillatory (indeed downward most of the time; see Burns and Mitchell 1946, chart 36, p. 275).[16]

16. For electricity output in 1921–33, a strongly growing series, the rise and fall amplitudes are 1.0 and 0.8 in the unadjusted data and 0.5 and 0.7 in trend-adjusted data, respectively. This is an example of an asymmetry that is concealed by the trend in the original series, but it is based on two corresponding series only (Blatt 1983, p. 231).

Blatt finds the results reported by Burns and Mitchell for the detrended series to be very significant economically and statistically and infers that "a pronounced lack of symmetry is the rule" (1980; 1983, p. 232). He views this as a strong contradiction of the Frisch-type random shock theory of business cycles, which implies symmetrical fluctuations around trend.

De Long and Summers (1986) estimate coefficients of skewness in quarterly growth rates of real GNP and industrial production from post–World War II data for the six major OECD countries. The asymmetry hypothesis implies negative skewness. The estimates have negative signs in 9 out of 12 cases, but they are generally small relative to the calculated standard errors. For the United States, annual data show more evidence of negative skewness than quarterly data, particularly for GNP in the postwar period. Surprisingly, the skewness is positive (but not significant) for the U.S. quarterly real GNP series in 1891–1915 and 1923–40. The authors conclude (p. 176) that "it is reasonable in a first approximation to model business cycles as symmetric oscillations about a rising trend" since "GNP growth rates and industrial production growth rates do not provide significant evidence of asymmetry."

It would seem that this inference is too strong and probably premature, being based on uncertain assumptions and evidence. The standard errors of skewness are estimated from Monte Carlo simulations that assume the growth rates to be stationary third-order autoregression processes. The reasoning of Mitchell, Keynes, and Hicks attributes the asymmetry largely to the occurrence of sharp downturns in investment and/or monetary stringencies and financial crises. This is a plausible hypothesis, but it leads us to expect more asymmetry in the earlier era than after World War II; however, the De Long-Summers results unaccountably show the opposite. The GNP data inevitably are much less reliable for the former period. The Mitchell and Burns series used in table 8.5, though limited and partly overlapping in coverage, provide more observations and may well be on firmer ground. The evidence based on them is also less general and conclusive than it was interpreted to be, but it certainly should not be ignored or dismissed.

Neftçi (1984) rejects the null hypothesis of symmetry for unemployment in the United States in 1948–81 on the strength of tests applied only to data on the direction (not size) of changes in several series of jobless rates. De Long and Summers are critical of such tests for sacrificing power, but their own results confirm those of Neftçi even more strongly: quarterly U.S. data show positive skewness in unemployment and negative skewness in employment, both significant at the 5% level. However, they find no evidence of asymmetries in quarterly unemployment series for the five other OECD countries in 1950–79. This last result, though, relies heavily on difficult trend adjustments for large rises in European unemployment after 1973 assumed to be noncyclical; if not so detrended these series would appear strongly skewed. There is much that is unexplained and uncertain about these findings.[17]

---

17. When detrended and plotted to appropriate scales, the unemployment rate and (inverted) industrial production show closely similar fluctuations (see chart in De Long and Summers 1986,

It is true that the appearance of strong asymmetries in unadjusted time series is due to a large extent to the prevailing secular growth, and so is the fact that business expansions are much longer than contractions, as noted by De Long and Summers. But even series that contain no upward trends or from which such trends have been eliminated as well as possible often show visibly asymmetric behavior of the envisaged type. If no asymmetries occurred, the upswing and downswing phases of growth cycles should be about equal in length on the average over time. But table 8.3 shows that high-growth phases were typically longer than low-growth phases (cf. cols. 3 and 5).

Table 8.6 lists the differences between the average durations of high-growth and low-growth phases: they are all positive (col. 1). For the United States, Canada, and the United Kingdom, they are small (1–3 months); for West Germany, the difference is near zero. For the other six countries, they are much larger (9–17 months) and statistically significant at 2.5%–15% levels; the strongest evidence that high-growth phases tend to be longer comes from the measures for Japan, Australia, and the Netherlands (cols. 2–4).

Other indications that nonlinearities are neglected or concealed by currently popular methods of econometric and time-series analysis are scattered in recent literature (Blatt 1978; Britton 1986, pp. 50–52; Neftçi 1986). The conclusions range all the way from saying that these methods are very deficient (Blatt) to saying that they are the best available and unscathed by a search for asymmetries (De Long and Summers). Actually the search has so far been short and weak. The evidence is not very strong but on balance it suggests that business cycles do have potentially important nonlinear characteristics. Further research on this front is certainly needed.

8.3.5   Do Expansions Die of Old Age?

Late in 1985 many observers greeted the third anniversary of the continuing business expansion with a touch of worry. As measured by NBER, only 1 of the 6 peacetime expansions since 1945 lasted more than 39 months. Of the 14 comparable phases in 1854–1919, none survived more than 3 years, and of the 5 in 1919–45, only 1 did. Late in 1986 the same reasoning led to even stronger fears of a downturn. But by mid-1987 the expansion was nearing the peacetime record set recently in 1975–79 (58 months), and few forecasters expected a recession in the near future; and by early 1990 the new record exceeded the old one by more than 2 years. Far from being self-evident, the popular expectation that as an expansion grows older, the probability of its terminating increases should be viewed as a hypothesis open to much doubt and in need of full examination.

If business fluctuations were just random walks, then their past would have

---

p. 175). The timing differences between the two are partly systematic but small. Charts for other countries display much the same cyclical patterns in the corresponding series (Klein and Moore 1985, ch. 4 and app. 4A and 4B.) The test results may overstate the differences in skewness between output and employment.

Table 8.6   **Differences in Average Durations of High-Growth and Low-Growth Phases for 10 Countries, 1948–1983**

Country and Period Covered	Difference HG minus LG[a] (mo.) (1)	Degrees of Freedom[b] (2)	Standard Error $(s_\Delta)^c$ (3)	t-Statistic[d] (4)
1. United States, 1948–82	1.3	17	4.94	0.26
2. Canada, 1950–82	2.0	18	3.74	0.54
3. Japan, 1953–83	17.2	10	7.14	2.41[e]
4. Australia, 1951–83	8.7	13	4.86	1.79[f]
5. United Kingdom, 1951–83	2.9	11	6.19	0.47
6. West Germany, 1951–83	0.2	11	6.63	0.03
7. France, 1957–79	13.2	8	8.76	1.51[g]
8. Italy, 1956–80	11.2	8	8.97	1.25[h]
9. Netherlands, 1950–79	11.2	12	5.59	2.01[f]
10. Switzerland, 1950–75	16.8	8	11.96	1.40[g]

Source: Table 8.3.

[a]HG = average duration of high-growth phases; LG = average duration of low-growth phases.

[b]Equals $N_1 + N_2 - 2$, where N_1 = number of HG phases and N_2 = number of LG phases.

$${}^c s_\Delta = \left[\frac{(N_1 - 1)s_1^2 + (N_2 - 1)s_2^2}{N_1 + N_2 - 2}\right]^{1/2} \left(\frac{N_1 + N_2}{N_1 N_2}\right)^{1/2}$$, where s_1^2 and S_2^2 are variances of HG and LG phases, respectively.

[d]Entry in col. 1 divided by entry in col. 3.

[e]Significant at the 2.5% level.

[f]Significant at the 5% level.

[g]Significant at the 10% level.

[h]Significant at the 15% level.

no predictive value, and in particular the probability of a peak (trough) in any month of an ongoing expansion (contraction) would be a constant independent of the age of the phase. Indeed, McCulloch (1975) presents tests showing that the probability of termination is equal for "young" and "old" expansions, once the movement has exceeded some minimum duration, and that the same applies to contractions. This suggests to him that business fluctuations are merely like the "Monte Carlo cycles" the superstitious gamblers misperceive in their luck at casinos or racetracks, that is, pseudocycles with "no periodicity, rhythm, or pattern except perhaps a trend" (p. 303).

On the other hand, Neftçi (1982) offers a formula for an "optimal" prediction of cyclical downturns, one component of which is the probability of a peak this month based just on the length of the expansion to date. (The other is the probability of observing this month's value of the percentage change in the index of leading indicators when the trend in that index is upward.) Neftçi estimates the probabilities by smoothing the distributions of the observed phase durations and percentage changes in the leading index. Thus he expects the duration of an expansion in itself to be of some help in predicting the peak (mutatis mutandis, the same applies to contractions and troughs). A degree of success is claimed for this approach, and some modifications improve it further (Palash and Radecki 1985; de Leeuw, Missouri, and Robinson 1986; Niemira 1991).

McCulloch's tests present some technical problems: it seems that small changes in the underlying assumptions and data can lead to very different conclusions (de Leeuw 1987). But even if his results were entirely acceptable, his interpretation of them is not. Business cycles need not be strictly periodic to differ radically from purely random movements. The many important regularities well documented in studies of domestic, foreign, and international business fluctuations simply cannot be reconciled with the notion of "Monte Carlo cycles." Business cycles are far too persistent and pervasive for that, and they contain far too many common features with common explanations. In both relatively short and long, small and large expansions and contractions, some variables conform strongly, others weakly, some positively, others inversely. There are also systematic differences in cyclical amplitudes—and numerous recurring timing sequences as some variables tend to lead and others lag—at business cycle peaks and/or troughs.

Like the authors cited above, Hamilton (1989) models the business cycle as an outcome of a Markov process that switches between two discrete states, one representing expansions, the other contradictions. However, he assumes that the state transition probabilities are independent of the phase durations. This implies a constant hazard function $\lambda(\tau) = \lambda$ (where λ is the probability that a process will end after a duration, τ, given that it lasted until τ) and a memoryless exponential distribution of durations $f(\tau) = \lambda e^{-\lambda \tau}$ (Kiefer 1988). Diebold and Rudebusch (1990a), using NBER-designated business cycle phases, find that the null hypothesis of no duration dependence is not contradicted by the small sample of observations on postwar expansions. There is, however, some evidence of duration dependence in prewar expansions, postwar contractions, and, particularly, full cycles over the entire period covered (1854–1982). These results imply a weak stochastic form of periodicity, that is, a clustering tendency of intervals between successive peaks *or* troughs (and, at times, between successive peaks *and* troughs). They are entirely consistent with the historical analysis provided earlier in this chapter.

Neftçi's and related exercises suggest that the potential contribution of the phase duration measures and associated probabilities to the problem of forecasting business cycle turning points is likely to be modest, though probably not zero, as hypothesized by McCulloch. It would indeed be surprising to find otherwise. The probability of a peak during an expansion or of a trough during a contraction is clearly not just or even largely a function of the duration of the phase. Various combinations of internal stresses and imbalances with external disturbances, including major policy errors, can cut the life of an economic recovery short or bring on an unsustainable boom. Conversely, well-chosen policies and other favorable developments can prolong an expansion by helping to keep a slowdown in the economy from sliding into an absolute decline or a speedup from creating inflationary demand pressures. A recession may in itself create the conditions for the next upturn, or the recovery may be accelerated by stimulative policies.

What matters primarily, then, is not the passage of calendar time but what happens over time in and to the economy in motion. It is historical and psychological time, filled with events and processes, perceptions and actions. This is, of course, generally so in human affairs. There is a simple corollary: knowledge of the current phase of the business cycle and its age can help but must not be used in isolation. Its proper role is to assist in the interpretation of the contemporaneous movements of the economy by enabling us to compare systematically the present with the historical patterns of the indicators.

8.3.6   Predictability and Costs

Business cycle turning points, particularly peaks, tend to be associated with unusually large forecasting errors (see ch. 13 and 14 below). If the durations of expansions and contractions had been highly stable over extended periods, forecasters (and indeed economically active and observant people in general) should have long learned how to predict the timing of these phases with considerable accuracy. The fact that economic downturns and to a lesser extent upturns cause much surprise is therefore a strong prima facie argument against the hypothesis that business cycles are periodic. Since major slowdowns and recessions produce individual losses and social distress, there are surely major incentives to improve the related forecasts and decisions. Moreover, in the presence of continuing and recognizable periodicities, ways would presumably be found to reduce cyclical instability or to adjust to it so that it did relatively little harm to the economy at large.

Indeed, no grave and persistent economic and social problems are caused by seasonal fluctuations despite their broad diffusion and large quantitative importance. This is so because the seasonal cycles are generally close to being periodic and predictable. Business people, workers, and consumers possess much accumulated knowledge of how to cope with this type of anticipated instability, and there exist various institutional and market arrangements to help. True, seasonal variations have stochastic components that can be a source of significant forecasting and decision errors, but these are properly matters of private concern. In contrast, recurrent slumps that generate declines in sales, production, and incomes along with rises in unemployment clearly belong to the sphere of public interest, and so do recurrent inflationary or speculative booms.

It is certainly possible to conceive of causes of highly periodic, persistent, and costly cycles in total output and employment. They would have to be exogenous, inevitable, and themselves periodic. The classic case here is the weather cycle, whether due to variations in sunspot intensity or other factors (Jevons 1884; Moore 1914). But today such explanations lack all plausibility.

Moreover, such hypothetical externally imposed cycles would resemble seasonal fluctuations much more than business cycles.[18]

In short, the considerations of predictability and costs argue against the idea that business cycles are strongly and stably periodic. The existence of limited and variable periodicities, however, cannot be excluded.

8.4 Summary and Conclusions

The historical chronologies of business cycles provide evidence that is on the whole inconsistent with the hypothesis of strong overall periodicity, according to which these fluctuations tend to be of constant length. True, over long stretches of time similar average durations are obtained for the principal economies (about 4 years in the United States, 5 years in Great Britain), and most cycles fall within the ranges of ± 1 year around these means. But the dispersion measures for all cycle durations are large in absolute and relative terms everywhere. There is a sharp contrast in this respect between business cycles and the almost strictly periodic seasonal fluctuations.

Nevertheless, examples of approximate periodicity limited in time exist and deserve attention. Thus the 1958–82 turning-point comparisons, autocorrelations, spectral analysis, and autoregressions for the United Kingdom all support the statement that the "appearance of the trade cycle . . . is unusually, although not uniquely, periodic" (Britton 1986, p. 52). But a major (and fully recognized) difficulty with these results is that 25 years of data is a slender basis for determining cycles whose typical length may be 5 years. Yet over longer periods the structure of the economy is likely to change in ways that would alter the periodicity.[19]

Spectral analysis indicates a relative concentration of power around frequencies corresponding to the average duration of business cycles (near 4.5 years). Since these techniques are applied to trendless or detrended series, the average growth cycle duration (about 3.5 years) may be more relevant here, and spectral peaks that approximate it are found as well. These estimates, however, are of uncertain significance, and the approach also suggests other periodicities, including some that are clearly outside the range of observed nonseasonal fluctuations.

These observations suggest that business cycles defy simple characterizations, showing a strong tendency to recur and at times even near periodicity,

18. They would be longer and perhaps less regular than normal seasonal fluctuations, hence their social costs should be higher. But it could hardly be beyond the individual and collective ingenuity of people to find, in time, effective ways to reduce and allocate the burdens of such anticipated instability.

19. In fact, Britton's results for earlier periods in the modern history of Great Britain and for the United States since 1960 differ from his results for the United Kingdom in 1958–82, and the differences depend greatly on methods of estimation. Unlike for the United Kingdom, the evidence of periodicity for the United States (based on unemployment data) is found to be "relatively weak and doubtful" (1986, p. 44; for detail see ibid., chs. 1 and 4).

along with great diversity and evolution of phase durations. It is difficult but necessary to recognize such phenomena in the theoretical work on the subject.

Periodic business cycles are represented in the theoretical literature by a variety of models. The nonlinear accelerator-multiplier interactions can produce a limit cycle. Where elections are periodic, a political business cycle could conceivably have a parallel rhythm. These models have some rather evident and serious problems, and it does not redound to their advantage that they can generate periodicity that is more exact and general than consistent with likelihood and observation. But this does not mean that nonlinearities may safely be neglected; on the contrary, they are probably important and their empirical identification is much needed. In particular, there are some indications of asymmetrical cyclical behavior. One set of these is provided by historical trend-adjusted series whose downswings tend to be steeper than upswings. Another consists of estimated durations of growth cycle phases in the post–World War II period: for most countries surveyed, the periods of above-average growth tend to be longer than the periods of below-average growth.

The variability in length of business expansions and contractions is sufficiently large for the timing of cyclical turning points (particularly peaks) to be, demonstrably, very difficult to forecast. The age of a phase alone is not of much help in predicting the date of its end: what matters more is the dynamics of the evolving business situation. The regularity of business cycles manifests itself primarily in aspects of such dynamics—persistent comovements of specific indicators, the leads and lags involved, and so on. There is no evidence that close and lasting periodicities exist in the recurrence of socially costly recessions here or abroad, and there are good general reasons why they are not visible. Important hidden periodicities may well exist, although even they are not likely to be unique, well-defined, and stable.

9   Econometric Model Simulations and the Cyclical Characteristics of the Economy

9.1   Questions, Methods, and Data

This paper grows out of a comprehensive study which addresses some old but unsolved questions concerning several econometric models (Zarnowitz et al. 1972). The major substantive issue involved here was raised early in the literature: Do business cycles consist mainly of endogenous or exogenous movements? This is presumably an empirical problem, in the usual sense of being amenable to scientific treatment through formulation of suitable hypotheses that can be tested against the data. There is no dearth of either endogenous or exogenous or "mixed" theories, some of which can be and have been tested, though not always adequately or persuasively. Over the years, the subject of business cycles has attracted much systematic research and observation, which has added much to our factual knowledge. Nonetheless, the issue still resists a solution, and perhaps not surprisingly so, as it requires understanding the modern economy in motion to a degree not yet achieved.

It seems quite natural that a close connection should exist between the problem of how business cycles are generated and the method of studying the economy through building and analyzing econometric macromodels. Indeed, interest in testing various cyclical hypotheses first motivated Tinbergen to construct such models (1938–39). However, even now, more than five decades and several generations of aggregate econometric models later, disagreement abounds on how best to scale, specify, and estimate such models. The great gains in theory, information, and computational techniques and capacities have yet to be fully reflected in comprehensive systems of proved superi-

Reprinted from *The Business Cycle Today*, edited by Victor Zarnowitz, pp. 241–59 (New York: NBER, 1972).

The author is greatly indebted to Charlotte Boschan for helpful comments, to Josephine Su for valuable statistical assistance, to H. Irving Forman for the preparation of the figure, and to Gnomi Schrift Gouldin for editorial improvements.

ority. This presents a grave problem since what an econometric model suggests about the nature of business cycles may not be dependable if the model itself is not.

The study on which I report is, therefore, more properly described as a search for answers to these questions: Do the models under review generate cyclical behavior as defined and observed in the empirical business cycle studies, notably those of the National Bureau of Economic Research (NBER), which provide the main documentation on the subject? If so, to what extent are such fluctuations in the estimated series produced endogenously by the models, and to what extent are they attributable to external impulses? The aims of the study, then, will be recognized as very similar to those of the 1959 analysis of the annual Klein-Goldberger model by Irma and Frank Adelman (1959). Its scope, however, is substantially larger as the materials now available are much richer. Four different quarterly models are examined, to be labeled Wharton, OBE, FMP, and Brookings.[1] It is generally recognized that quarterly data are far more adequate in business cycle analysis than are annual data.

The methods employed also largely parallel the techniques used in the pioneering study by Adelman and Adelman (1959). Three types of complete-model simulations are analyzed, namely:

(a) Nonstochastic simulations over six-quarter periods beginning, alternatively, one, two, and three quarters before each of the business cycle turns that occurred during the model's sample period.[2] Each of these runs starts from new, correct initial conditions and uses ex post values for the exogenous variables.

(b) Nonstochastic simulations over the entire sample period covered by each model; also based on the initial conditions (actual value) at the beginning of that period and on the historical values of the exogenous variables.

(c) Stochastic simulations projecting the models for a period of 25 years starting at the end of the sample period. In these experiments, the exogenous variables are generally continued along smooth growth trends based on their compound interest rates of growth during the sample period.

One set of short and one of long nonstochastic simulations (a and b) was required for each model, but for the stochastic simulations (c) as many as 50 computer runs per model were made, so as to gain information on the variability of responses to different configurations of shocks and to avoid excessive reliance on any particular, and possibly idiosyncratic, shock distribution.

---

1. The abbreviations refer to the Wharton–Econometric Forecasting Unit model; the Office of Business Economics of the U.S. Department of Commerce model; the Federal Reserve Board-MIT-Penn. model; and the Brookings-SSRC model. The model variants on which this analysis is based are those developed by the summer of 1969 and explained in several papers prepared for the Harvard Conference on Econometric Models of Cyclical Behavior, November 1969.

2. The business cycle peaks and troughs are dated according to the NBER reference chronology (in quarterly terms) and are also referred to as reference turns.

Completed work covers nonstochastic simulations of type (a) for three models (Wharton, OBE, FMP), those of type (b) for all four models, and the stochastic runs for three (Wharton, OBE, and Brookings).

Regrettably, the results for the different models are not strictly comparable, for at least two reasons. First, the sample periods differ: the Wharton model covers 79 quarters, from 1948:3 through 1969:1; the OBE model covers 55 quarters from 1953:2 through 1966:4; the FMP model covers 44 quarters from 1956:1 through 1966:4; and the Brookings model covers 36 quarters from 1957:1 through 1965:4. Thus, the Wharton period includes four of the completed contractions or recessions in the postwar economic history of the United States (as well as such milder retardations as those of 1951–52, 1962–63, and 1966–67), the OBE period includes three, and the FMP period and the Brookings period each include two of these contractions. Such differences can strongly affect the relative performance of the models, and as a task for the future, it would be very desirable to recalculate the simulations with one common sample period for all included models. Second, models differ in coverage: in particular, what is endogenous in one of them may be exogenous in another. This must be accepted and only some partial remedies are available here depending on the cooperation of the model builders; but this study reduces the problem by concentrating upon a subset of selected variables that are basically common to, and endogenous in, all of the models covered.

The endogenous variables used in the simulations are listed in table 9.1, which classifies the series according to their typical timing at business cycle turns, as historically determined. The list includes eight series from the national income accounts, of which five are in constant and three in current dollars; five series relating to employment and unemployment, hours of work, and unit labor costs; four relating to commitments to produce durable goods and invest in equipment and housing; and three relating to interest rates and money. The main sources are the U.S. Department of Commerce, the Bureau of Labor Statistics (BLS), and the Federal Reserve Board (FRB). Most series are used after seasonal adjustment. In addition, three variables unclassified by cyclical timing and not included in table 9.1 were also represented in the simulations for all four models: the implicit price deflator for the GNP (P); private wage and salary compensation per labor-hour in dollars (W); and net exports in billions of 1958 dollars (NE). Some variables were selected because of their importance for macroeconomic theory in general and business cycle analysis in particular, some in view of their cyclical sensitivity and timing, and some for both reasons. With relatively few exceptions but frequent modifications, they appear in most of the recent econometric models of intermediate or large size.

Although simulation is a powerful tool of economic analysis, its inherent limitations are substantial. Inferences drawn from simulation results about the properties of the economic system are only as good as the model that is used as the analogue of that system. However, evidence from studies based on

Table 9.1   List of Variables and Data Definitions for Simulations of Four Models

Abbreviation	Variable by Timing Group	Available for Models:
	Leading Series	
1. *IH*	Investment in nonfarm residential structures[a]	Wharton, OBE, FMP, Brookings
2. *II*	Change in nonfarm business inventories[a]	Wharton, OBE, FMP, Brookings
3. *CPR*	Corporate profits before taxes and inventory valuation adjustment[b]	Wharton, OBE, FMP, Brookings
4. *AWW*	Average workweek, private employment, hours per week, BLS	Wharton, OBE, FMP, Brookings
5. *LH*	Total hours per person per annum in nonfarm private domestic sector, BLS	FMP
6. *OMD*	New orders, durable manufacturers' goods[a]	OBE
7. *UMD*	Unfilled orders, durable manufacturers' goods, end of quarter[a]	Wharton, OBE, Brookings
8. *OUME*	Unfilled orders, machinery and equipment industries, end of quarter[b]	FMP
9. *HS*	Private nonfarm housing starts, annual rate, thousands, Census	OBE
10. *M*	Demand deposits adjusted and currency outside banks[c]	OBE, FMP
	Roughly Coincident Series	
11. *GNP*	Gross national product[b]	Wharton, OBE, FMP, Brookings
12. *GNP58*	Gross national product in constant dollars[a]	Wharton, OBE, FMP, Brookings
13. *C*	Personal consumption expenditures[a]	Wharton, OBE, FMP, Brookings
14. *YP*	Personal income[b]	Wharton, OBE, FMP, Brookings
15. *LE*	Total civilian employment, millions of persons, BLS	Wharton, OBE, FMP, Brookings
16. *UN*	Unemployment rate, percentage (of labor force), BLS	Wharton, OBE, FMP, Brookings
	Lagging Series	
17. *ISE*	Investment in nonresidential structures and producers' durable equipment[a]	Wharton, OBE, FMP, Brookings
18. *RS*	Average yield, 4–6 months prime commercial paper, percentage per annum, FRB	Wharton, OBE, FMP, Brookings
	Government bill rate, percentage	Brookings
19. *RL*	Average yield, corporate bonds, Moody's, percentage per annum	Wharton, OBE, FMP, Brookings
	Government bond rate, percentage	Brookings
20. *L/CO*	Private employee compensation per unit of private GNP in constant dollars, OBE	OBE

[a]Annual rate, billions of 1958 dollars. National income accounts; OBE, Bureau of the Census, seasonally adjusted.

[b]Annual rate (except line 8), billions of current dollars. National income accounts; Bureau of the Census, seasonally adjusted.

[c]Daily average of quarter, billions of current dollars. Currency is exogenous; deposits are endogenous.

different models and applications to different periods may to some extent cumulate and reduce this weakness. This argues in favor of comprehensive and diversified coverage of econometric model simulations in business cycle analysis.

9.2 Six-Quarter Simulations around Business Cycle Turns

The determination of cyclical turning points in these nonstochastic simulations (described as type [a] above) presents considerable difficulties because the data refer to short, unconnected periods and it is sometimes uncertain whether the observed changes in direction are cyclically significant or merely reflect short random movements. This is particularly true when the suspected turns fall close to the beginning or end of the six-quarter period. Consideration of events outside this period—turns in the actual series that occurred shortly before or after—may be helpful, but it too is not always clearly legitimate. Alternative measures were, therefore, computed, one set including and the other excluding comparisons between outside actual and inferred simulated turns.[3] In some cases, doubts remained but were met by deciding in favor of recognizing turns in the simulations if this seemed at all reasonable.

Two models succeeded fairly well, and one (FMP) rather better, in reproducing the turns in the actual series at business cycle peaks and troughs. When the inferred turning points are included, the percentages of the turns matched are 60–67 for Wharton, 66–73 for OBE, and 76–90 for FMP (see table 9.2, lines 1–3, for the underlying numbers).[4] When they are excluded, the corresponding percentages are lower, averaging 58, 66, and 75 for the respective models.

The evidence does not indicate that the simulations beginning closer to the reference turn are systematically more successful than those beginning earlier. (The former, it may be noted, cover fewer specific-cycle turns in the actuals than do the latter.) Neither is the expectation that troughs are better reproduced than peaks definitely met, although troughs are often more sharply defined and more closely clustered. This may be due to the constancy of the lag structure used by the models. However, in the simulations that start one or two quarters prior to the reference dates, the percentages of troughs matched do tend to be somewhat higher than the corresponding figures for peaks.

Coincidences with the actual turns account for 21%, 39%, and 45% of the simulated turns in the six-quarter periods for the Wharton, OBE, and FMP

---

3. To illustrate such comparisons, if the actual series showed a peak shortly before the beginning of the simulation period and the simulated series continued downward locally, the latter was presumed to have produced a peak.

4. The higher attainment rate of the FMP model cannot be discounted simply on the presumption that fluctuations are more easily simulated for the period 1957–61; the better performance of the FMP model is retained also if the comparisons for all three models are limited to the turning points of this shorter period. Still, it is possible that the fits are better for 1957–61 and that this at least partly explains the superiority of the FMP model.

Table 9.2   Nonstochastic Six-Quarter Simulations around Reference Turns, Selected Statistics Relating to Cyclical Conformity, Timing, and Amplitudes of Simulated and Actual Series, Three Models

	Wharton Model (1949–61)		OBE Model (1954–61)		FMP Model (1957–61)	
	Actual (1)	Simulated (2)	Actual (3)	Simulated (4)	Actual (5)	Simulated (6)
Frequency of Turning Points (number)						
Simulations starting						
1. 3 quarters before reference turns	95	64	88	58	50	38
2. 2 quarters before reference turns	95	61	88	60	50	44
3. 1 quarter before reference turns	95	57	88	64	50	45
Relative Frequency of Leads and Lags (percentage of all turns)[a]						
Leading series						
4. Leads	46	80	55	70	45	33
5. Coincidences	44	2	36	10	31	30
6. Lags	10	17	9	20	24	37
Roughly coincident series						
7. Leads	39	88	38	55	32	47
8. Coincidences	48	2	50	21	53	19
9. Lags	13	10	12	24	15	34
Lagging series						
10. Leads	11	36	14	12	12	32
11. Coincidences	30	40	21	46	53	20
12. Lags	59	23	64	41	35	48
Average Percentage Amplitudes, by Cycle Phase[b]						
13. Expansions	7.8	6.4	7.4	3.5	7.6	3.7
14. Contractions	−7.0	−3.6	−6.6	−3.1	−6.5	−4.8

Note: Observations in lines 1–3 include, and those in lines 4–12 exclude, the inferred turning points in simulations corresponding to the known actual turns that occurred outside the simulation period. See text. For the classification of series by cyclical timing (lines 4–12), see table 9.1.

[a]The entries in cols. 2, 4, and 6 refer to all simulations regardless of starting date.

[b]The figures in cols. 2, 4, and 6 refer to simulations starting two quarters before reference turns (the results for the other simulations are similar). Expansions and contractions are phase movements in the actual and simulated series within the six-quarter periods.

models, respectively. The corresponding figures for leads of the simulated, relative to the actual, turns are 54%, 36%, and 19%, whereas for lags the percentages are 25%, 25%, and 36%. When the series are classified by historical timing groups and the comparisons are made relative to the business cycle peaks and troughs, leads are found to be much more frequent in the simulations than in the actuals for the Wharton simulations in all groups (table 9.2, lines 4–12, cols. 1–2). The same statement applies to the OBE model, though less strongly and not for the lagging series, but there is no comparable bias toward early turns in the FMP simulations (lines 4–12, cols. 3–6). On the whole, these simulations discriminate but weakly (and much less effectively than the actuals) between the historically leading, coincident, and lagging variables.

The simulated series show rises and falls that tend to be substantially smaller than their counterparts in the actual series within the selected turning-point segments (table 9.2, lines 13–14). Of course, nonstochastic simulations must be expected to vary less than the actuals on the average, because they do not include the component of random disturbances that is present in the actuals. However, this factor often seems to explain only a part of the observed underestimation of amplitudes. Good estimation and simulation of systematic, cyclical amplitude components is in any event desirable. The Wharton series approximate relatively well the average size of the actual rises; the FMP series give better results for the declines.

9.3   Sample-Period Simulations

In figure 9.1, each of the models shows the real GNP (taken to represent the aggregate economic activity) as declining during at least some portion of the first recession period covered. (For Wharton, this means the 1948–49 recession; for OBE, the one in 1953–54; and for FMP and Brookings, the one in 1957–58.) The Wharton and the FMP model also have *GNP58* contracting during the second recession, in 1953–54 and 1960–61, respectively. Neither Wharton nor OBE produces a fall in *GNP58* during either the 1957–58 or the 1960–61 recession. Although the FMP model does produce such declines in these two periods, it would be wrong to conclude that it is therefore better, because the initial conditions for this model, being as of 1956:1, are much closer to these episodes than the initial conditions for Wharton and OBE. Where the simulated series fail to match the declines in *GNP58,* they at least flatten off, however (e.g., Wharton and OBE in 1957–58, Brookings in 1960–61).

This leads to the important inference that there appears to be a progressive *dampening* of the fluctuations the further away a model's simulation proceeds from its initial-conditions period. This type of movement would be characteristic of a hypothetical economy representing a stable macrodynamic system insulated from external disturbances.[5] It is the response of such a system to the irregular but persistent outside shocks that is supposed to convert the damped fluctuations into a maintained movement of the type historically observed as the recurrent "business cycles."

---

5. The diminishing oscillations in this model originate in the divergencies from equilibrium that are likely to exist in any initial state of the system; they tend to disappear as the system approaches its equilibrium rate of growth. This hypothesis, completed by the notion that external disturbances or "erratic shocks" do in fact impinge upon the economy continually, gained influence following the important contribution by Frisch (1933).

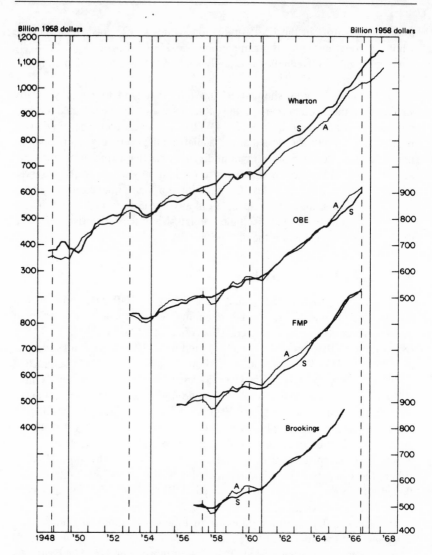

Fig. 9.1   Nonstochastic sample-period simulations of GNP in constant dollars, four models

Note: A = actual; S = simulated. Dashed vertical lines indicate business cycle peaks; solid lines, troughs. The last pair of such lines, however, refers to a business retardation in 1966–67, which did not develop into another recession.

Under this hypothesis, therefore, the failure of nonstochastic sample-period simulations to re-create the continuous cyclical developments that did actually occur need not constitute any adverse evidence about the structure of the underlying model. Instead, such results could be due to the suppression of the disturbance terms. It must be noted, however, that the simulations here reviewed use ex post values of exogenous variables. Changes in the latter include a large subset of "autonomous" shocks—variations in government expenditures, tax rates, monetary base, reserve requirements, population, exports, etc. Important effects of monetary and fiscal policy changes are thus incorporated. What these simulations suppress, then, is essentially the stochastic components of the endogenous variables. We cannot be certain that it is the disregard of this source of variability that is predominantly responsible for the errors of the nonstochastic sample-period simulations. There are undoubtedly misspecifications in the models, which could be just as important. The autocorrelations of the disturbance terms in some of the original structural equations are high enough to be disturbing. The failures of the simulations to track major cyclical movements can often be traced to the weakness of certain specific relations, for example, those for inventory investment or the price levels.

Nonstochastic simulations, which refer to the periods to which the models were fitted and use the correct ex post values of the exogenous variables, do not provide tests of the predictive powers of the models. They do, however, subject the models to rather demanding tests of a different kind, since in simultaneous estimation, errors are liable to cumulate across a model, and through the effects of lagged dependent variables, errors are also liable to cumulate over time. There is evidence that the calculated values do tend to drift away, though not necessarily continuously, in simulations that cover more than one or two business cycles. For trend-dominated variables such as *GNP, GNP58* or *C,* the drift appears sometimes as an increasing overestimation but more often as an increasing underestimation of the levels of the series. In fig. 9.1, the former is illustrated by the Wharton simulation for the 1960s and the latter by the OBE and FMP simulations in part of that decade.) Generally, the discrepancies between the levels of the simulated and actual (*S* and *A*) series are much greater than those between the corresponding quarterly changes. The reason lies in autocorrelated errors, which cumulate, thus throwing off base the long multiperiod predictions that are here involved.

Common to both short and long nonstochastic simulations is a strong tendency to underestimate the amplitudes of the observed cyclical movements. Contractions in the series, however, are often missed altogether by the simulations rather than merely underestimated. About one third of the recorded turning points are not matched by the sample-period simulations.

In table 9.3 are some measures of the kind that would be helpful to answer the question, how do the models compare with one another in terms of the relative accuracy of their simulations? (See lines 1–5.) However, because of

Table 9.3   Nonstochastic Sample-Period Simulations for Four Models, Average Error
Statistics and Relative Frequency Distributions of Leads and Lags at
Business Cycle Turns

	Wharton Model		OBE Model		FMP Model		Brookings Model	
	(1)	(2)	(3)	(4)	(5)	(6)	(7)	(8)
	MAERC % points	MAERC/ MAARC	MAERC % points	MAERC/ MAARC	MAERC % points	MAERC/ MAARC	MAERC % points	MAERC/ MAARC
Selected Variables[a]								
1. *GNP*	1.17	0.681	0.70	0.459	0.61	0.377	0.57	.363
2. *GNP58*	1.12	0.852	0.64	0.518	0.65	0.524	0.57	.428
3. *P*	0.27	0.453	0.24	0.488	0.22	0.429	0.22	.544
4. *ISE*	3.12	1.036	1.90	0.812	1.79	0.746	1.40	.557
5. *UN*	17.80	2.502	6.00	0.890	6.26	1.155	5.63	.895
	Relative Frequency of Leads and Lags (percentage of all turns)							
	Actual	Simulated	Actual	Simulated	Actual	Simulated	Actual	Simulated
Leading series[b]								
6. Leads	62	56	73	74	68	67	56	60
7. Coincidences	32	17	20	15	14	17	38	30
8. Lags	5	26	7	12	18	17	6	10
Roughly coincident series[b]								
9. Leads	35	44	38	42	31	30	27	33
10. Coincidences	51	9	50	17	50	30	60	33
11. Lags	14	48	12	42	19	40	13	33
Lagging series[b]								
12. Leads	8	32	8	11	17	30	18	60
13. Coincidences	42	23	21	28	42	20	45	20
14. Lags	50	46	71	61	42	50	37	20

[a]For meaning of the abbreviations, see table 9.1.
[b]For the classification of series by cyclical timing, see table 9.1.

the (already noted) differences in coverage among the models, this question
cannot be answered conclusively. The errors of the Wharton simulations are
on the average considerably larger than those of either the OBE or the FMP or
the Brookings simulations, except for the price level, *P,* where the differences
are small (compare cols. 1, 3, 5, and 7). But the Wharton simulations cover a
much longer period than the others, including the unsettled and difficult-to-fit
developments of the late 1940s and the Korean War.

Dividing the mean absolute errors of relative change (MAERC) by the
mean absolute values of actual relative change (MAARC) is a standardizing
procedure which probably tends to correct for the differences in the sample
periods but does not guarantee an unbiased comparison.[6] The resulting ratios

6. As elsewhere in the analysis of predictive accuracy, the comparisons with changes are on the
whole much more meaningful than those with levels. The smaller the ratio (MAERC)/(MAARC),
the better it speaks of the model; and a ratio that exceeds unity signifies that the errors are on the

(cols. 2, 4, 6, and 8) show smaller differences between the models than do the MAERC figures, but the models would be ranked rather similarly according to the two measures. (Brookings comes out somewhat better than FMP and OBE, and Wharton ranks fourth for most variables; for the price level, however, FMP and Wharton show the lowest ratios and Brookings the highest.)

The second part of table 9.3 (lines 6–14) shows that the simulations do discriminate broadly between the groups of leading and lagging indicators, but they do not carry this differentiation nearly as far as the actual timing distributions do. The OBE model yields good approximation for both leaders and laggers; the FMP and Brookings models for the leading series only. Brookings is particularly weak on the timing distribution for the laggers. The worst results are obtained for the six roughly coincident indicators, where exact coincidences make up 50%–60% of the timing observations for the actual series but only 9%, 17%, 30%, and 33% of the observations for the Wharton, OBE, FMP, and Brookings models, respectively.[7] It is for this category, too, that the simulations have the poorest record on cyclical conformity: the S series for *GNP* and other comprehensive aggregates of income, employment, and consumption show few turning points and frequently "skip" the peaks and troughs of business cycles.

9.4   Hundred-Quarter Ex Ante Simulations

These simulations (see type [c] above) have been computed only for the Wharton, OBE, and Brookings models, and their analysis is incomplete. Each of them covers a period of a hundred quarters, beginning past the space of sample experience (in 1968:3 for Wharton, in 1966:1 for OBE and Brookings). The "control solutions" (nonstochastic simulations) produce, over these long future periods, smooth series with uninterrupted growth trends for the comprehensive indicators of overall economic activity such as GNP, personal income, and employment. The trendlike control series contrast with the nonstochastic sample-period simulations that do show some recurrent, if damped, fluctuations. A probable reason for the contrast lies in the fact that in these control solutions, the exogenous variables are projected along smooth monotonic upward trends without any fluctuations. The historical series for the same variables, which were used in the nonstochastic sample-period simulations, often show considerable short-term fluctuations. However, this need not be the only or the main reason: another one may be provided by the specification errors on the models.[8]

---

average larger than the recorded changes; that is, the model does worse than a type of "naive" extrapolation.

7. Note that the large shares of leads and lags tend to approximately balance each other in this group (table 9.3, lines 9–11).

8. The control solutions suggest that at least in this context of long-term projections, all three models are confronted with difficult problems of internal consistency. They include some series

The lack of fluctuations in the control series for the comprehensive aggregates (GNP, etc.) indicates that none of these models generates cyclical movements endogenously. Evidently the models contain no mechanisms that would cause the simulated aggregates to fluctuate in the absence of shocks in either the exogenous quantities or in the relationships with endogenous variables.

The random shocks used in the stochastic simulations for the OBE and Wharton models were generated so that the expected value of the variance-covariance matrix of the shocks over the simulation period is equal to the variance-covariance matrix of the observed residuals over the sample period. In another set of experiments, serially correlated shocks were used, their lag correlations for a sufficiently large number of observations also being equal to the corresponding sample values obtained from the residual matrix.[9] For the OBE model, 25 simulations use serially uncorrelated random shocks and 25 use serially correlated shocks; for the Wharton model, the number is twice as large in each set. Only autocorrelated shocks were used in the 50 simulations for the Brookings model.

The stochastic simulations are strongly trend dominated for *GNP* in current and constant dollars and several other comprehensive aggregates (*YP, C, LE, P, W,* and *M*). There are systematic differences between the series with nonautocorrelated shocks (S_u) and those with autocorrelated shocks (S_c). The latter are far smoother than the former and hence tend to have larger average durations and smaller average percentage amplitudes of rises and declines.[10] The Wharton S_u series for *GNP* and *GNP58* show somewhat shorter and smaller declines than the sample-period actuals (*A*), while the S_c series show many fewer declines, all of them short and separated by overly long rises. In the corresponding OBE simulations of either type, declines are altogether rare, short, and small. The same can be said about the Brookings S_c series for *GNP* (in those for *GNP58,* declines are also small and short but more frequent). The simulated series that have weaker trends and stronger fluctuations (relating to investment processes, orders, unemployment, average workweek, and interest rates) tend to have shorter movements than the corresponding *A* series, in either direction. The S_c series often underestimate the length of the recorded movements of *A* less than the S_u series do.

---

that either are made to behave in a more or less arbitrarily predetermined fashion or are permitted to behave in ways that would seem difficult to rationalize. Such questionable simulations (as illustrated particularly by the control series for unemployment and interest rates) are perhaps best viewed as concomitants of the search for a broadly satisfactory control solution for the overall aggregates. In short, to get a plausible projection for GNP, the simulation of, say, the unemployment rate may have had to be compromised.

9. The method of generating the shocks is that of McCarthy (1972a).

10. A rise (decline) is used to denote any upward (downward) movement in a series, however short or small. In this analysis such changes are distinguished from cyclical movements that must be sufficiently long and pronounced to qualify as "specific-cycle" expansions and contractions (as defined by NBER).

These experiments suggest that the use of autocorrelated shocks is helpful in many but by no means all cases and that it works better for the more volatile series than for the comprehensive aggregates with dominant growth trends and subdued fluctuations. The declines in S_c tend to be longer but also smaller than those of S_u. The criterion of duration is presumably more important than that of amplitude.[11] When this is taken into account, the balance of the comparisons favors the S_c over the S_u simulations for most variables, but not without some important counterexamples (notably for *GNP* and *GNP58* in the Wharton model). In general, the cyclical aspects of the simulated series are much weaker than those observed in the historical series, in contrast to the long trends and short erratic variations that are often considerably stronger in the *S* than in the *A* series.

That the cyclical movements get blurred in the stochastic simulations could be due in large measure to the inadequate handling or scaling of the shocks, in particular to the neglect of disturbances in the exogenous variables. Hence we have also analyzed the relative deviations of shocked from control series, in the expectation that they would be more indicative of the cyclical effects of relatively weak impulses. This expectation was confirmed, but the ratios of the stochastic to the control series are also much more erratic than the shocked series proper, reflecting not only greater sensitivity to the effects of the shocks but presumably a telescoping of "measurement" errors as well. It is particularly the ratios of S_u to the control series that tend to be highly erratic; the ratios of S_c are much smoother and generally appear more plausible.

Ratios of the historical series to their exponential trends were computed to provide measures for the sample-period actuals that correspond to the measure for the simulated ratio series. As shown in table 9.4, lines 1 and 2, the trend-adjusted *GNP* series are better approximated by the S_c than by the S_u ratios, in terms of the durations (and therefore also the frequencies) of rises and declines. Comparisons of amplitudes alone would point to the reverse (lines 3 and 4), but, again giving more weight to the duration than to the amplitude criterion, the results for the ratio series generally favor the S_c over the S_u simulations, and do so rather more strongly than the findings based on the level comparisons. This conclusion also applies to the simulations for *GNP58* and other variables.

Using the ratio series, cumulated diffusion indexes (CDI) were constructed

---

11. The random shock hypothesis here considered asserts, in the formulation by Frisch (1933), that "the majority of the economic oscillations . . . seem to be explained most plausibly as free oscillations. . . . The most important feature of the free oscillations is that the length of the cycles and the tendency towards dampening are determined by the intrinsic structure of the swinging system, while the intensity (the amplitude) of the fluctuations is determined primarily by the exterior impulse." This suggests that the amplitudes of movements in the stochastic *S* series would depend mainly on the simulator's decision as to the magnitude of the shocks applied. They may be quite different from the amplitudes of the actuals, not because of any failure of the model to reproduce the basic structure of the economy, but because the impulses (shocks) have not been properly scaled.

Table 9.4 Stochastic 100-Quarter Simulations (Ratio Series) for Three Models, Selected Summary Measures of Duration and Amplitude and Relative Frequency Distributions of Leads and Lags at Turns in CDIs

	Wharton Model			OBE Model			Brookings Model	
	Sample-Period Actuals (A) (1)	Simulations with Nonautocorrelated Shocks (S_u) (2)	Simulations with Autocorrelated Shocks (S_c) (3)	Sample-Period Actuals (A) (4)	Simulations with Nonautocorrelated Shocks (S_u) (5)	Simulations with Autocorrelated Shocks (S_c) (6)	Sample-Period Actuals (A) (7)	Simulations with Autocorrelated Shocks (S_c) (8)
Quarterly movements in GNP (actual and simulated)[a]								
Durations (quarters)[b]								
1. Rises	3.4(2.1)	1.7(0.8)	2.2(1.4)	3.1(3.4)	1.9(1.1)	2.7(1.9)	3.3(1.7)	2.4(1.5)
2. Declines	2.6(1.6)	1.7(0.8)	2.3(1.9)	2.3(1.9)	1.9(1.1)	2.6(1.8)	2.5(1.3)	2.3(1.4)
Amplitude (percentage)[c]								
3. Rises	0.9	0.9(0.1)	0.4(.05)	0.6	0.4(.05)	0.3(.04)	0.8	0.34(0.06)
4. Declines	1.0	0.9(0.0)	0.4(.05)	0.6	0.4(.05)	0.3(.05)	0.9	0.33(0.06)

Relative Frequency of Leads and Lags (percentage of all turns)[d]

Group of variables[e]	Wharton Leads	Wharton Coincidences	Wharton Lags	OBE Leads	OBE Coincidences	OBE Lags	Brookings Leads	Brookings Coincidences	Brookings Lags
5. Leading	48	26	26	43	28	29	36	21	43
6. Roughly coincident	23	43	34	22	47	30	33	44	23
7. Lagging	28	21	51	24	25	51	31	24	45

Note: See text for the explanation of simulations with nonautocorrelated and autocorrelated shocks (S_u and S_c), of the form in which they are used here (as ratios to the corresponding control series), and of the timing comparisons underlying the entries in line 5–7 (observations at reference—CDI—peaks and troughs).

[a]Actual (A): relative deviation of GNP from its exponential trend. Simulated (S_u and S_c): relative deviation of shocked from control series for GNP. On the meaning of "rises" and "declines," see n. 10. The entries in lines 1–4, cols. 2, 3, 5, and 6 are based on all available simulation runs.

[b]For A: mean duration, with standard deviation in parentheses. For S: mean duration per run, with mean standard deviation of the durations "within the run" in parentheses.

[c]For A: mean amplitude. For S: mean amplitude per run, with standard deviation of means per run in parentheses (in percentages, at quarterly rate).

[d]Based on comparisons of the turning points in the simulated ratio series with the corresponding reference dates—peaks and troughs in the CDIs.

[e]Classified according to the timing of the historical series. See table 9.1.

for three randomly chosen runs of the Wharton model and three of the OBE model. For either model, the selection includes one set of series based on S_u and two based on S_c simulations. For the Brookings model, the CDI indexes were computed for two sets of the S_c series. The indexes are of the "historical" type: after the cyclical turning points have been identified in each of the simulated ratio series in a given set, the percentage of the series undergoing specific-cycle expansion is calculated for each quarter and then the deviations of these percentage figures from 50 are cumulated. Each of the CDIs shows reasonably well defined cyclical movements, whose turning-point dates can be used as a reference chronology with which to compare the timing of the simulated series in the given set. The average durations of the specific cycles in the CDIs (about 13, 15, and 18 quarters for Brookings, OBE, and Wharton, respectively) are smaller than those of the postwar (1948–68) cycles in trend-adjusted *GNP* and *GNP58* (18–20 quarters). This reflects mainly short expansions in the indexes, but the overall differences for some of the runs are not large.

In general, the series resulting from simulations with autocorrelated shocks conform better to the reference indexes (CDIs) than the series resulting from simulations with nonautocorrelated shocks, because the former have fewer "extra" turns than the latter. The comprehensive indicators of national product, income, and expenditures, which historically rank high on conformity, also score relatively well according to these comparisons.

There is considerable correspondence between the relative timing of the ex ante stochastic simulations and of the historical data for the same variables, as indicated by the average leads and lags of the ratio series at the major turns in the CDIs. Indeed, the distributions of the timing observations for the ratio series (table 9.4, lines 5–7) appear to be appreciably better than those for the sample-period simulations in identifying the coinciders. However, they are not so sharp in differentiating between the groups of typical leaders and laggers (see table 9.3, lines 6–14), particularly because of discrepancies relating to several of the leading series. Also, the total picture is less favorable than the distributions alone would imply, for many turns in the more volatile ratio series (particularly from the S_u runs) cannot be matched with the reference turns, and some that can be are difficult to date, so that the timing comparisons are rather uncertain.

9.5 Concluding Remarks

To produce any cyclical movements, the models included in this study seem to require perturbations in either the exogenous variables or the relationships with endogenous variables or both. Even the best stochastic simulations here obtained—those with serially correlated shocks to the equations—show only residual cyclical elements, much weaker than those observed in the historical series used in the estimation of the models. This is a disappointing result, assuming that it is reasonable to expect the stochastic simulations to reproduce the recent pattern of the economy's movement at least over several years beyond the sample period. Errors in either the estimates of the disturbances or in the structure of the models could account for this finding.

The absence of shocks or fluctuations in the projected exogenous variables is an unrealistic feature that is likely to be partly responsible for the weakness of the cyclical elements in the stochastic ex ante simulations. Further experiments should test whether this weakness can be remedied by imposing more or less sporadic disturbances on the exogenous factors—or, better, to what extent it can be reduced. There are some indications that the role of such exogenous movements may be large, but the evidence is still very fragmentary (Green, Liebenberg, and Hirsch 1972). Moreover, it is possible that the general picture conveyed by the simulations is seriously distorted by specification errors in the models; certainly, important errors of this sort would tend to obscure the meaning of the evidence that the simulations can provide.[12] Future simulation studies, therefore, should be combined with a comparative analysis of misspecifications in the models covered.

A more limited task that could be readily accomplished with the materials already collected is to examine larger samples of the stochastic simulations. Also, to compare the models with regard to their ability to approximate the main characteristics of major short-term fluctuations of the economy, there is need for more standardized simulations—at least for a suitable common sample period for the different systems. Finally, the simulation studies should be extended to other recent models and to revised versions of the included models. The more varied the assortment of the represented systems, the more we are likely to learn from this research.

---

12. This point was repeatedly made in discussions at the 1969 Harvard conference. See Bert G. Hickman's (1972) introduction to *Econometric Models of Cyclical Behavior.*

III   Indicators

10   Cyclical Indicators: Structure, Significance, and Uses

10.1   Roughly Coincident Indicators and the Dating of Business Cycles

Economic indicators, as a general category, are descriptive and anticipatory data used as tools for business conditions analysis and forecasting.[1] There are potentially as many subsets of indicators in this sense as there are different targets at which they can be directed. For example, some indicators may relate to employment; others to inflation.

This brings to mind the uses of such time series as lagged explanatory variables in econometric models and regression equations. But there is a different, established meaning to what is often called the "indicator approach." This is a system of data and procedures designed to monitor, signal, and confirm cyclical changes, especially turning points, in the economy at large. The series that serve this purpose are selected for being comprehensive and systematically related to business cycles and are known as *cyclical indicators*.

Business cycles are recurrent sequences of alternating phases of expansion and contraction that involve a great number of diverse economic processes and show up as distinct fluctuations in comprehensive series on production, employment, income, and trade—aspects of aggregate economic activity. The end of each expansion is marked by a cluster of peaks in such series; the end of each contraction, by a cluster of troughs. Analysts at the National Bureau of Economic Research (NBER) base the dating of business cycle peaks and troughs on the identification and analysis of such clusters, that is, the consensus of the corresponding turning points in the principal *coincident indicators*. This is done because (1) the comovement of the indicators is itself an essential characteristic of the business cycle; (2) no single adequate measure of aggregate economic activity is available in a consistent form for a long historical

---

1. This section draws in part on Zarnowitz and Moore 1977, p. 476–507. It is also based in part on Zarnowitz 1987, as are some other sections of this chapter.

period; and (3) economic statistics generally are subject to error, so that the evidence from a number of independently compiled indicators tends to be more reliable than the evidence from any individual series. The NBER reference chronologies of business cycle peaks and troughs (Burns and Mitchell 1946, ch. 4; Moore 1961, chs. 5 and 6; Zarnowitz and Moore 1977, 1981; Moore and Zarnowitz 1986) are widely used in academic as well as current business research.

Figure 10.1 illustrates the process of dating business cycles with the aid of 12 indicators in real terms for 1972–76. This period was one of a slowing expansion, a mild downturn followed by an accelerating contraction, an abrupt upturn, and more gradual recovery. It was complicated by an unanticipated rise in inflation following highly stimulative monetary and fiscal policies of 1971–72; exogenous increases in prices of raw materials and agricultural products during 1973; and the oil embargo and huge hikes in energy costs in 1973:4 and 1974:1. Real retail sales peaked as early as March 1973, industrial production in June 1974, employee-hours in nonagricultural establishments as late as October 1974. Despite this considerable scatter of dates, there was a definite concentration of peaks in the series on output, real income and sales, and inverted unemployment around November 1973 and 1973:4 (the x's denote the specific-cycle turns on the chart).

The troughs in the specific cycles for the twelve series show less of a scatter, but here too retail sales in constant dollars turned up early (November 1974) and employment late (June 1975). The other ten series all reached their local minima in March 1975 or 1975:1.

Aspects of general economic activity admit of different measurements, and their alternative statistical representations contain largely unknown data errors. For these reasons, evidence from two or more closely related or partly overlapping series is considered in deciding on when recessions began and ended.

No aggregates in current dollars are shown in the figures presented here but the original work on dating the contraction of 1973–75 included an examination of seven such series (GNP, final sales, value of goods output, personal income, retail sales, manufacturing and trade sales, and wages and salaries in manufacturing, mining, and construction; see Zarnowitz and Moore 1977). The nominal totals represent the original form in which many economic transactions take place and are motivated and recorded. In times of stable prices or cyclical alternation of inflation and deflation, such series would show distinct rises and declines in levels and be given much weight in the process of dating business cycles. However, in times of continuing strong inflation the current-dollar aggregates often do not decline at all in recessions.[2] The deflated series

2. For example, of the seven series listed at the beginning of this paragraph, only the last two had specific-cycle contractions at any time in the period covered (and brief and shallow at that, corresponding to the last and worst part of the contraction in late 1974 and early 1975). See Zarnowitz and Moore 1977, p. 479 and 482 for charts of the levels and deviations from trend for the nominal indicators in 1972–76.

and indexes of physical volume are then given decisive weight as representing more closely what is commonly understood by "recession" and "recovery." When trend adjusted, however, the nominal indicators commonly show significant declines that indicate their participation in growth cycles.

The choice of November 1973 for the business cycle peak and March 1975 for the business cycle trough was ultimately based on judgmentally weighted evidence from the series displayed in figure 10.1. It is confirmed by the composite index shown on figure 10.2, which covers eleven real indicators.[3]

A diffusion index based on the same series shows in cumulated form the excess of the percentage of indicators expanding over the percentage contracting, using cyclical peaks and troughs to define these phases. As plotted on figure 10.2, this index reached a high plateau in November 1973 and drifted neither upward nor downward for about a year thereafter (meaning that about half of its components were expanding and half contracting). This series, which summarizes the underlying data in a complementary but less informative way, is only in a very broad sense consistent with the choice of the November 1973 peak but supports strongly the March 1975 trough date.

How prompt and confident the determination of a business cycle peak or trough can be depends on how close the consensus of the corresponding specific-cycle turn is. When the latter are widely dispersed, as in the case of the 1973–74 peaks, the dating is difficult and must not be rushed; when they are not, as in the case of the 1975 troughs, the recognition that a new phase of the cycle has begun is relatively easy and quick. Gradual downturns and sharp upturns characterized several postwar business cycles, whereas the opposite was true of the major interwar cycle, where the declines took much less time to start than to end.

In sum, this example demonstrates one important use of the cyclical indicators, namely, the identification and dating of business contractions and slowdowns. The construction of the historical reference cycle chronologies at NBER was always based on a similar detailed inspection of the available data, mainly for those indicators considered to have "roughly coincident" timing. (Of course, the statistical information for the more distant past has been much more limited.) The January 1980 business cycle peak was the first determined by a formally constituted NBER Committee on Business Cycle Dating convened on June 3, 1980 (for a report, see Zarnowitz and Moore 1981).

10.2   Growth Cycles and Business Cycles

Figure 10.3 presents the turning points in the corresponding trend-adjusted series used to date growth cycles. The specific-cycle peaks in these data fall

---

3. These are the same series as in figure 10.1, except that the rate of unemployment is omitted (the number of unemployed is retained). Composite indexes are computed by standardizing the monthly percentage changes in the component series so as to prevent the more volatile series from dominating the index; averaging the standardized changes for each successive month; and cumulating the results into a monthly index.

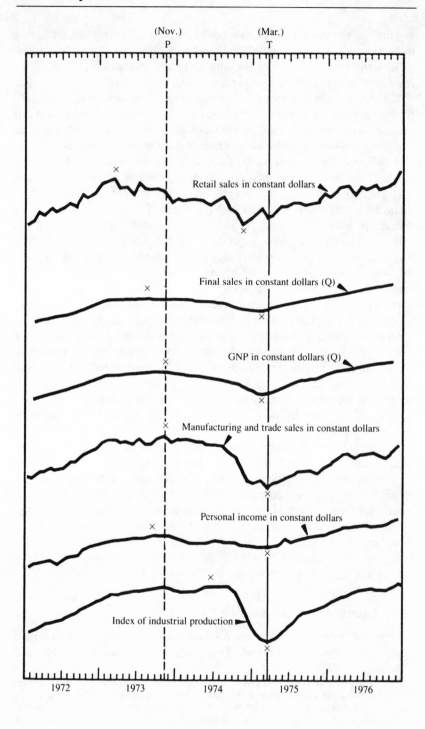

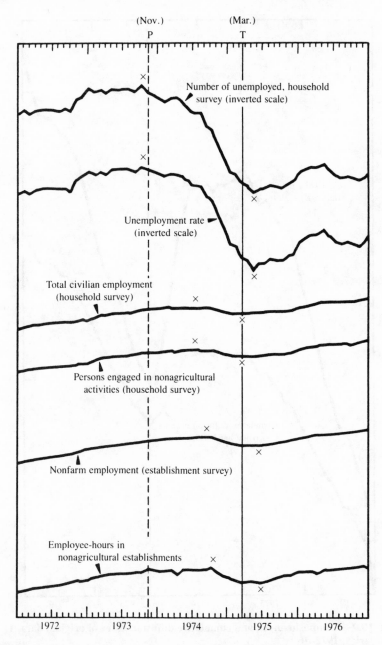

Fig. 10.1   Selected measures of aggregate economic activity, levels, 1972–76
Note: The *x*'s denote specific-cycle turns.

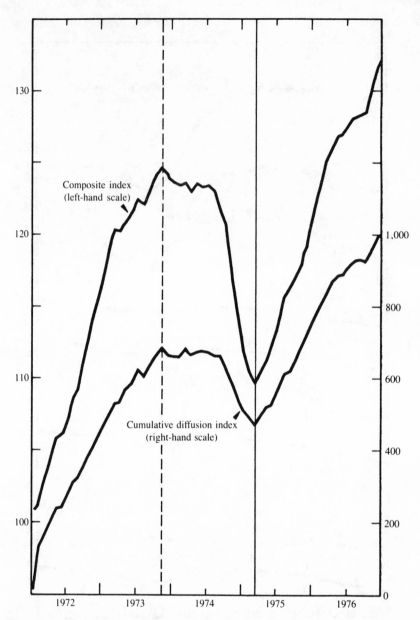

Fig. 10.2   Composite index and cumulative diffusion index of original data, 11 real series, 1972–76

into two groups: 1973:1 or March for GNP, sales, and personal income in constant dollars; and September–November 1973 for industrial production and the employment and unemployment series. As the slowdown preceded the recession, most of the peaks in the detrended indicators occurred earlier than their counterparts in the original series. In contrast, the trough dates were generally unaffected by the trend adjustments, which is typically the case when the upturn is well articulated. When the recovery starts slowly, the troughs in the detrended series tend to lag behind the corresponding troughs in the unadjusted series.

Figure 10.4 shows that the composite index based on the deviations from trend of the eleven real indicators reached a peak in March 1973 and varied only a little during the next nine months. This marks the peak of the growth cycle, that is, the beginning of the 1973 slowdown that turned into a recession near the end of the year. The index clearly stopped falling and started rising in March 1975, the date of the trough in both the business cycle and the growth cycle. The corresponding cumulative diffusion index in the lower part of figure 10.4 provides roughly consistent evidence.

Each of the seven recessions of 1948–80 was preceded by a phase of positive but below-average growth, but these slowdowns lengthened from 2–6 months for the first four of the peaks to 8–13 months for the last three. The long slowdowns marked the ends of the expansions of 1961–69, 1970–73, and 1975–80, and were related to intensified inflation and price shocks, government interventions, reduced rates of private investment and productivity, and the increasing role of service employment. Only the short and weak expansion of 1980–81 ended without any significant slowdown.

If long slowdowns always ended in recessions, they would be very helpful to those engaged in predicting (as distinct from dating) business cycle peaks. But some growth cycle declines interrupt rather than disrupt business cycle expansion (as discussed in chapters 6 and 7). It turns out to be particularly hard to distinguish between these two types of slowdown on a current or timely basis.

10.3   Timing of Specific Cycles: Leading and Lagging Indicators

Differences among business cycles are naturally reflected in the behavior of cyclical indicators. In a growing economy expansions must be on average larger than contractions in terms of output, employment, etc., and they are also likely to be longer. The individual cycles and their phases, however, vary greatly in duration and amplitude. These differences are systematically related to the scope or diffusion of cyclical movements among different units of observation (e.g., activities, regions, industries). Vigorous expansions are generally more widespread than weak expansions; severe contractions are more widespread than mild contractions. Consider diffusion indexes, that is, time series showing the percentage of components in a given aggregate that are

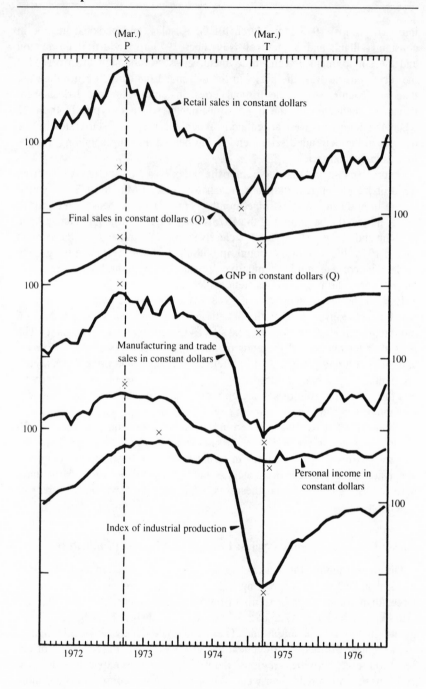

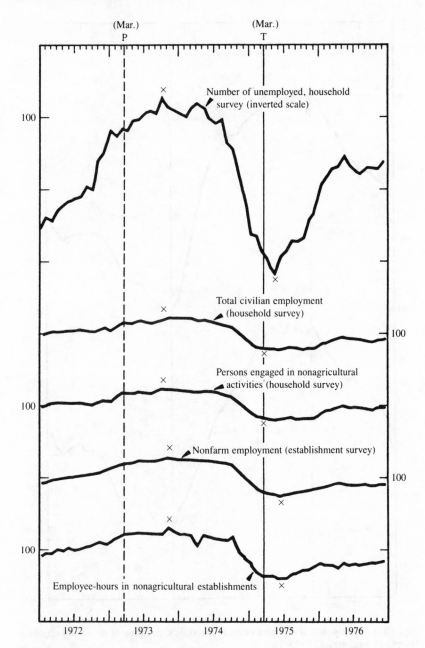

Fig. 10.3   Selected measures of aggregate economic activity, deviations from trend, 1972–76

Note: The *x*'s denote specific-cycle turns.

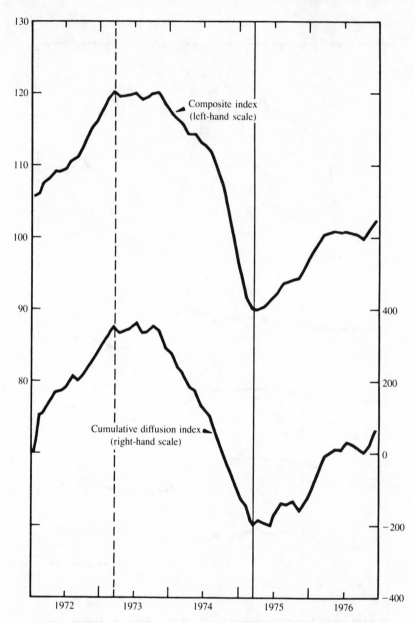

Fig. 10.4   Composite index and cumulative diffusion index of deviations from trend, 11 real series, 1972–76

rising in each successive unit period. Such indexes are correlated with the rates of change in, and tend to lead the levels of, the corresponding aggregates. Information about the direction of the change, hence surveys designed to produce timely diffusion measures on actual or expected sales, prices, profits, etc., are popular in many countries.

As observed across a wide spectrum of variables, the specific cycles differ greatly and in part systematically. What matters particularly in the present context is the characteristic variation of cyclical indicators with respect to their relative *timing*. Thus many economic time series, called *leading indicators*, tend to reach their turning points *before* the corresponding business cycle turns. There are also many series that tend to reach their turning points *after* the peaks and troughs in the business cycle, and they are the *lagging indicators*.

The leading series represent largely flow and price variables that are highly sensitive to the overall cyclical influences but also to shorter random disturbances; hence they show large cyclical rises and declines but also high volatility. Coincident series such as those shown in figure 10.1 have cyclical movements that generally come closer to one-to-one correspondence with business expansions and contractions, and are much smoother. At the same time, the fluctuations in the approximately coincident indicators tend to be smaller than those in the more responsive leaders. Lagging indicators include some massive stock variables which move cyclically much less yet and are extremely smooth.

The tripartition according to timing is not exhaustive and not always so simple. Apart from series that do not conform to business cycles at all or have irregular timing, there are some that have mixed timing (e.g., lead at peaks and lag at troughs, or vice versa).

Gradual changes in timing also appear in some variables, reflecting the effects of structural or institutional changes. For example, the index of industrial production lagged at most of the business cycle peaks in 1920–37 but led at most of the peaks in 1948–81. Although short intervals prevailed among these observations in both periods, the timing of production was more nearly coincident in the interwar than in the postwar cycles. This may be due to the decline of the share in employment of the sectors covered by this index (manufacturing, mining, and electric and gas utilities). Against the backdrop of the rising size and weight of broadly defined services, it is now possible for the index of industrial production to turn down without pulling the rest of the economy promptly into a recession. Employment in goods-producing industries actually declined in 1967 and 1985–86, years of continued expansion. Total nonfarm employment now tends to have more short lags and fewer short leads and coincidences compared with its historical timing at business cycle turns. This is likely to be attributable to the rising trend and weight of overhead labor and service jobs.

10.4   Alternative Interpretations and Uses of Lagging Indicators

A large majority of indicators show positive conformity to business cycles, that is, they tend to increase in expansions and decrease in contractions subject to leads or lags that are small in comparison to the durations of their cyclical movements. Some indicators, such as the rates of unemployment, delinquent loans, and business failures, show inverse conformity by typically increasing in contractions and decreasing in expansions. Their timing is measured on an inverted basis by matching their specific-cycle peaks (troughs) with business cycle troughs (peaks).

Some series, such as those on the monetary growth rates, have very long leads when treated on the positive basis and shorter lags when treated on the inverted basis. The influence from money to business would argue for the former interpretation (downturns in monetary growth cause recessions; upturns cause recoveries); the influence from business to money may favor the latter interpretation (e.g., recessions cause increases, and recoveries cause decreases, in the currency and reserve ratios). Theory does not make the choice very easy, since it is agreed that the influences run both ways. The finding that the dispersion of the timing comparisons is less when computed on the positive plan supports the matching of like turns used in the early monetarist studies (see Friedman 1964, pp. 14–15).

Alternative interpretations also apply to another set of important cyclical relations. When treated on an inverted basis, the principal lagging indicators become long leaders. Interest rates usually rise early in business contractions but decline later as pressures of the demand for credit ease and banks acquire more reserves. But these declines signal reductions in the cost of credit, which stimulate borrowing for more real investment and future production; in this sense, they can be linked, with leads, to the next business revival, which they are helping to bring about. The interest rates tend to decline through the early recovery stages of expansion, and the later they turn up as a result of tighter credit supply, the longer the expansion is likely to last (Cagan 1969). Long records support the inference that bond yields lag and bond prices (approximately, inverted yields) lead at both peaks and troughs in aggregate economic activity.

Other lagging series, like interest rates, also measure or reflect the costs of doing business: unit labor cost, inventories carried in manufacturing and trade, and business loans outstanding. The costs of inputs of labor, materials, and capital will rise eventually during expansions as more and more industries get to operate close to full-capacity utilization and higher. A large increase in such costs relative to the levels of actual and expected prices would have strong deterrent effects on new orders and contracts, credit extensions, etc. This mechanism can produce a deteriorating "profit squeeze," depress business confidence and new investment, and be instrumental in bringing on a slowdown or even a recession. Conversely, declines in the overall level of financial, production, and inventory costs during contractions improve the actual and expected profit margins and pave the way for an upturn in the leading and, later, the coincident indicators of general economic activity.

In fact, turning points in the lagging series occur before the opposite turning points in the leading series on average and with great regularity. The median troughs of a group of 30 lagging series led the median peaks of a group of 75 leading series in anticipation of each of the fifteen business cycle downturns between 1887 and 1937. The median peaks of the laggers led the median troughs of the leaders thirteen times (and coincided twice) ahead of each of the fifteen business cycle upturns between 1888 and 1938. The average leads were 12 months at peaks of the leaders and 7 months at troughs. Analogous comparisons based on twelve leading and six lagging indicators for 1949–82 produce seven leads in as many observations at peaks and seven leads out of eight observations at troughs (one coincidence). Here the means are − 16 and − 4 months respectively. The dispersions of the individual timing comparisons around these averages are large mainly because of a few outliers.[4]

Table 10.1 presents for the same groups of indicators a summary of timing at business cycle turns (rather than relative to each other). The entries in columns 1, 3, and 5 make clear that the inverted laggers provide the earliest signals of both peaks and troughs, followed by the leaders, and eventually confirmed by the laggers (the coincident series are not included). The leads tend to be longer at peaks than at troughs, particularly so for the first group and in the postwar period, when expansions increased and contractions decreased greatly in duration. The lags tend to be longer at troughs than at peaks in the same period.

10.5   Differences and Shifts in Timing at Peaks and Troughs

According to a count based on 103 series with long records, leads and lags were equally frequent at peaks of the pre-1919 business cycles, whereas at troughs leads were twice as frequent as lags. In 1919–38, the ratio of leads to lags was approximately 5 to 4 at both peaks and troughs. In a very comprehensive sample of 188 series for 1948–70, leads outnumbered lags by more than 7 to 2, but the two categories were almost in balance at troughs (see table 10.2, lines 1–3).

Differences between the pre-1939 sample and the post-1947 sample cannot explain the observed shifts in timing. Thus a set of 40 long series that extend through 1970 gives very similar results (lines 4–5). Moreover, a subset of 28 series that cover five business cycles in 1920–38 and five in 1948–70 provides

4. Omitting one very long lead associated with the business downturn of 1937 reduces the mean for the early observations at peaks from − 12 to − 10 and the standard deviation from 11 to 4. Omitting another unusually long lead associated with the revival of 1933 reduces the mean lead for the early observations at troughs from − 7 to − 5 and the standard deviation from 9 to 4. The postwar comparisons include smaller outliers associated with the peaks of 1953 and 1980.

Table 10.1   Leads and Lags of Groups of Cyclical Indicators, Means and Standard Deviations, 1885–1982 and Subperiods

	1885–1919[a]		1948–82[b]		1885–1982[c]	
	Mean	S.D.	Mean	S.D.	Mean	S.D.
Type of Turn and Group	(1)	(2)	(3)	(4)	(5)	(6)
	Leads (−) or Lags (+) at Peaks					
Median trough, lagging[d]	− 17	11	− 26	12	− 20	12
Median peak, leading	− 5	4	− 10	6	− 7	5
Median peak, lagging	+ 6	4	+ 5	3	+ 5	4
	Leads (−) or Lags (+) at Troughs					
Median peak, lagging[e]	− 13	9	− 7	3	− 11	8
Median trough, leading	− 6	3	− 3	2	− 5	3
Median trough, lagging	+ 7	5	+ 10	5	+ 7	5

Sources: 1885–1938: Moore 1950, table 11, based on 75 leading and 30 lagging series. 1948–82: BCD, October 1977, app. F and subsequent issues, based on 12 leading and 6 lagging series. For a list of all observations used (leads and lags at the individual business cycle turns), see Zarnowitz and Moore 1986, tables 9.15 and 9.16.

Note: S.D. = standard deviation.

[a]Covers 14 business cycle peaks in 1887–1913 and 1920–37 (August 1918 omitted) and 14 business cycle troughs in 1885–1914 and 1919–38 (April 1919 omitted).

[b]Covers 8 business cycle peak in 1948–81 and 8 business cycle troughs in 1949–82.

[c]Covers 22 business cycle peaks and 22 business cycle troughs.

[d]Data for the November 1948 peak not available.

[e]Data for the May 1885 trough not available.

confirming evidence (lines 6–7). The latter sample also shows that leads at peaks grew much longer in the postwar as compared with the interwar cycles, and lags at peaks grew shorter. The differences are much smaller for the comparisons at troughs, where both the leads and the lags became moderately smaller (see the last two lines in table 10.2).

The NBER reference cycle chronology has been subjected to several reviews, most recently in Moore and Zarnowitz 1986 (see also chapter 7). It is unlikely to contain errors sufficiently large and systematic to be responsible for the above-noted asymmetries and shifts in the distributions of the cyclical timing comparisons.[5]

What then can explain these observations? It is possible for strong upward trends to skew the timing of many indicators toward lags at peaks and leads at troughs. The differences between the measures for the pre-1919 and 1919–38 cycles are consistent with this simple hypothesis, because the interwar period as a whole was marked by reduced upward trends (less real growth and more deflation). But the distributions shifted even further toward leads at peaks and lags at troughs in 1948–70, despite the higher growth and inflation trends then

5. For early discussions of this point, see Moore 1961, ch. 7, esp. pp. 222–25; and Mitchell 1951, pp. 73–75.

Table 10.2   Distributions of Leads and Lags at Business Cycle Peaks and Troughs in Prewar, Interwar, and Postwar Periods

	Time Series (no.) (1)	Timing Observations (no.) (2)	Business Cycle Peaks			Business Cycle Troughs		
Period			Leads (%) (3)	Coincidences (%) (4)	Lags (%) (5)	Leads (%) (6)	Coincidences (%) (7)	Lags (%) (8)
			A. Nonmatching Samples					
Before 1919	103	1,263	46	9	46	62	8	30
1919–38	103	919	50	12	38	46	19	36
1948–70	188	1,442	75	7	20	36	21	43
			B. Matching Samples					
Before 1939	40	562	48	11	40	55	12	32
1948–70	40	343	72	8	20	43	19	38
1920–38	28	259	55	11	34	45	17	38
1948–70	28	236	73	8	19	43	16	41

Addendum: Mean Lead (−) or Lag (+), in Months

	All Observations		Leads at Peaks	Lags at Peaks	Leads at Troughs	Lags at Troughs
	Peaks	Troughs				
1920–38	−2.0	+1.1	−6.8	+5.0	−6.0	+9.7
1948–70	−7.5	+1.0	−11.0	+3.1	−4.4	+7.2

Note: In some lines, the entries for leads, coincidences, and lags in cols. 3–5 or 6–8 fail to add up exactly to 100 due to rounding. Each of the 103 series used in lines 1 and 2 has a record beginning before 1919 and extending through 1938 and has been accepted for cyclical conformity and timing in either the full period covered or 1919–38. This sample was examined in Moore 1950 (reprinted in Moore 1961, pp. 222–25). The sample of 188 series (line 3) includes all indicators evaluated in the 1972–75 Bureau of Economic Analysis (BEA) review. The sample of 40 series (lines 4 and 5) is a subset of the longest series from the same BEA collection (10 start in 1857–89, 24 in 1907–21, and 6 in 1926–29). The sample of 28 series (lines 7–9) is a subset of the previous one that covers 5 peaks and 5 troughs of business cycles in 1920–38 and an equal number of turns of either type in 1948–70.

prevailing (cf. lines 1–3 in the table). This is contrary to the hypothesized trend effects.

The most likely explanation of the contrast between the interwar and the postwar distributions of the measures of timing at peaks and troughs derives from the reasons for the moderation of business cycles (chapter 3). Structural, institutional, and policy changes tended to support the forces of expansion and counteract those of contraction. The economy grew more responsive to the former and more resistant to the latter. Hence recessions, once recognized as such, were not permitted to endure and deepen but ended in relatively concentrated and symmetrical upturns. Expansions survived weaknesses in the cyclically sensitive sectors more easily than before; and when such slowdowns did worsen and spread so as to bring about a decline in aggregate activity, the process was now often much more protracted than it used to be. The slowdowns that preceded the business cycle peaks were accompanied by many leads in sensitive indicators and generally much dispersion of the specific-cycle peaks.[6]

Expansions were much longer and contractions much shorter in 1948–70 than in 1920–38, and this probably helps explain the differences in the average size of leads and lags between the two periods, as shown in the last section of table 10.2. The hypothesis is that the lags at initial troughs and the leads at terminal peaks tend to increase with the length of expansions, whereas the lags at initial peaks and the leads at terminal troughs increase with the length of contractions. This implies that cyclical timing relations are more stable in terms of business cycle time than in terms of calendar time (see chapter 6, sec. 6.3).

The evidence from the data used in table 10.1 and from the phase durations in peacetime business cycles of 1887–1982 is on the whole consistent with the above hypothesis. The correlations between the durations of business expansions on the one hand and the leads and lags internal to the corresponding expansions on the other are all positive, and half of them are quite high (table 10.3, lines 1–4). The analogous correlations with business contractions are also positive (except one that is effectively zero), but most are smaller (lines 5–8). This presumably reflects the fact that many contractions were similar in being short, particularly in the postwar period, and the same applies to the recent average leads at troughs. With more observations of greater variety, it seems plausible that the hypothesis would receive stronger support.[7]

There is also related evidence that the lengths of the leads or lags at successive turning points are positively correlated (Zarnowitz and Moore 1986, pp. 565, 568–71). These correlations refer directly to the intervals between the turns in the indicator series and make no use of the business cycle chronology. They too apply as well to comparisons between opposite turns as to those between like turns. All of this is certainly consistent with the idea that cyclical influences run from lagging to leading indicators as well as in the opposite direction. As detailed in the next two sections, these dynamic interactions form an integral part of business cycles, helping to shape and being themselves shaped by the movement of aggregate economic activity (coincident indicators).

6. It is well to observe that this prevalence of flat downturns and sharp upturns is the direct opposite of the asymmetry noted for the pre-1939 sample of indicators, which was attributed by Mitchell (1951, p. 75) "mainly to a difference between peaks and troughs in the average character of the arrays of specific-cycle timing dates. . . . At the peaks these arrays are on the average relatively compact and symmetrical; at the troughs the arrays are more dispersed and skewed toward leads."

7. Consider a diversified collection of indicators, all extending over the same stretch of time, which includes an equal number of business expansions and contractions. The number of specific-cycle turns that match business cycle turns (peaks and troughs combined) is about equally divided between business expansions and contractions. If contractions are short and expansions long, for example, the density of the turns in the series and their proximity to the business cycle turns should on the average be greater in contractions than in expansions.

Table 10.3   Correlations between Leads and Lags of Groups of Indicators and
                  Durations of Business Cycle Phases, 1885–1982 and Subperiods

		Correlation Coefficients (r)		
Line	Statistic[a]	1885–1938 (1)	1948–82 (2)	1885–1982 (3)
	A. With Durations of Business Expansions[b]			
1	Leads at peaks of MdT-Lg	+.87	+.97	+.89
2	Leads of MdT-Lg relative to MdP-L	+.78	+.95	+.51
3	Leads at peaks of MdP-L	+.50	+.51	+.57
4	Lags at initial troughs of MdT-Lg	+.12	+.82	+.41
	B. With Durations of Business Contractions[c]			
5	Leads at troughs of MdP-Lg	+.90	+.43	+.88
6	Leads of MdP-Lg relative to MdT-L	+.82	+.60	+.75
7	Leads at troughs of MdT-L	+.21	−.01	+.37
8	Lags at initial peaks of MdT-Lg	+.19	+.64	+.26

Sources: See table 10.1

[a]Abbreviations: Md, median; T, trough; P, peak; Lg, lagging group; L, leading group. For example, line 1 refers to "median trough, lagging group."

[b]Number of observations per entry in cols. 1, 2, and 3 is 14, 5, and 19, respectively.

[c]Number of observations per entry in cols. 1, 2, and 3 is 14, 6, and 20, respectively.

10.6   Economic Process and Cyclical Timing

Business cycle indicators have been selected, analyzed, and reviewed in a long series of comprehensive and detailed studies (Mitchell and Burns 1938; Moore 1950, 1961; Shiskin 1961a; Moore and Shiskin 1967; Zarnowitz and Boschan 1975a, 1975b). The results include a cross-classification of all individual indicators by types of economic process and characteristic timing in recessions and recoveries.

Table 10.4 summarizes this material for the 112 series included in the section on "Cyclical Indicators" in *Business Conditions Digest (BCD)*, a monthly report of the Bureau of Economic Analysis (BEA) in the U.S. Department of Commerce.[8] The indicators are divided into seven groups representing major economic processes and into more than thirty smaller subgroups. For each of the latter, part A (B) of the table lists the median leads or lags at business cycle peaks (troughs) of 1948–80.

The proportions of leaders, coinciders, and laggers are 57%, 22%, and 21% at peaks and 44%, 20%, and 36% at troughs, respectively. More series anticipated recessions than recoveries in this representative collection of post-

---

8. *BCD* (called *Business Cycle Developments* before 1968) began publication in 1961 and was discontinued in March 1990. From April 1990 on, data and charts on business cycle indicators are published in a new section of *Survey of Current Business*, another monthly report by the BEA.

Table 10.4   Cross-classification of Indicators by Economic Process and Cyclical Timing

Economic Process	Leading (L) (no. of series)	Median Lead (−) or Lag (+) (mo.)	Roughly Coincident (RC) (no. of series)	Median Lead (−) or Lag (+) (mo.)	Lagging (Lg) (no. of series)	Median Lead (−) or Lag (+) (mo.)
			A. At Seven Business Cycle Peaks, 1948–80[a]			
I. Employment & unemployment (15 series)	Marginal employment adjustments (3)	−11 to −13	Comprehensive employment (5)	0 to −3	Unemployment, long-term & average duration (2)	0, +1
	Job vacancies (2)	−7, −9				
	Comprehensive unemployment (3)	−3 to −5				
II. Production & income (10 series)	Capacity utilization (2)	−6 to −11	Comprehensive output & income (4)	0 to −3		
			Industrial production (4)	0 to −3		
III. Consumption, trade, orders, & deliveries (13 series)	New & unfilled orders (4)	−5.5 to −12	Consumption & trade (4)	0 to −3		
	Change in unfilled orders, vendor performance (2)	−6, −11				
	Consumer sentiment, car buying, real retail sales (3)	−5.5 to −12				
IV. Fixed capital investment (18 series)	Formation of business enterprises (2)	−10, −13	Business investment expenditures (6)	−2.5 to +1		
	Residential construction (3)	−10 to −13				
	Business investment commitments (7)	−2 to −9				
V. Inventories & inventory investment (9 series)	Change in inventories (4)	−4 to −11			Manufacturing & trade inventories (4)	+3 to +8
	Materials & supplies on hand & on order (1)	−2				
VI. Prices, costs, & profits (19 series)	Stock prices (1)	−9.5			Unit labor costs (4)	+5 to +10
	Sensitive commodity prices (3)	−5 to −10			Labor share (1)	+10
	Profits & profit margins (8)	−6 to −24.5				
	Cash flows (2)	−6, −6				

B. At Seven Business Cycle Troughs, 1949–80[b]

Economic process	Indicator group (no. of series)	At peaks	Indicator group (no. of series)	At troughs
VII. Money and credit (28 series)	Changes in money & liquid assets (3)	−7 to −20	Interest rates: On market securities (6)	0, +0.5
	Real money balances (2)	−11, −16	Charged by banks (2)	
	Credit flows (5)	−9 to −11	Private debt outstanding (4)	
	Credit difficulties (2)	−9, −14		
	Bank reserves (2)	−3, −4.5		
	Velocity of money (2)			
	64 series		*25 series*		*23 series*
Total: 112 series				
I. Employment & unemployment (15 series)	Marginal employment adjustments (3)	0 to −1	Comprehensive employment (4)	
			Insured unemployment rate (1)	0
			Job vacancies (2)	0 to 0
			Employment population ratio (1)	0
			Comprehensive unemployment (2)	0 to 0
			Unemployment: long-term & average duration (2)	0 to +1
II. Production & income (10 series)	Industrial production (nondurable manufactures) (1)	−1	Comprehensive output & income (4)	
			Industrial production (3)	
			Capacity utilization (2)	
III. Consumption, trade, orders, & deliveries (13 series)	New orders, change in unfilled orders (4)	−1 to −3	Manufacturing & trade sales (2)	−1 to −3
	Vendor performance (1)	−4	Car buying (1)	−1 to −3
	Production of consumer goods, retail sales (3)	−2	Unfilled orders (1)	0
	Consumer sentiment index (1)			0, −1
IV. Fixed capital investment (18 series)	Formation of business enterprises (2)	−1, −1.5	Nonresidential fixed investment, total, equipment (2)	−1, −1.5
	Contracts & orders, plant and equipment (4)	−1 to −2	Output of business equipment (1)	0, 0
	Residential construction (3)	−2 to −3	Construction contracts, BIC (1)	
			Nonresidential fixed investment, structures (1)	
			Capital appropriations, BIC (2)	
			Business investment expenditures (2)	

Far-right timing values: +1 to +2; +3.5, +4; +1 to +4; +1, +2; +3; +3, +3; +5, +8; +2; +1; +2; +3; +1, +5; +4, +4

(continued)

Table 10.4   Continued

Economic Process	Leading (L) (no. of series)	Median Lead (−) or Lag (+) (mo.)	Roughly Coincident (RC) (no. of series)	Median Lead (−) or Lag (+) (mo.)	Lagging (Lg) (no. of series)	Median Lead (−) or Lag (+) (mo.)
V. Inventories & inventory investment (9 series)	Change in inventories (4)	−1 to −5.5			Inventories on hand & on order (5)	+3 to +13
VI. Prices, costs, & profits (19 series)	Stock prices (1)	−4	Profits with inventory valuation & capital consumption adjustments (3)	0 to 0	Unit labor costs (4)	+9 to +13
	Sensitive commodity prices (3)	−1 to −7			Labor share (1)	+13
	Profits & profit margins (5)	−2 to −4				
	Cash flows (2)	−2, −2				
VII. Money and Credit (28 series)	Changes in money & liquid assets (3)	−3 to −9	Velocity of money (GNP/M1) (1)	−1.5	Velocity of money, PI/M2 (1)	+12.5
	Real money balances (2)	−3, −4			Bank reserves (2)	+2.5, +5
	Credit flows (5)	−1 to −3			Outstanding debt (4)	+2.5 to +7
	Credit difficulties (2)	0, −2			Interest rates (8)	+2 to +16
Total: 112 series	49 series		23 series		40 series	

Source: U.S. Department of Commerce, Bureau of Economic Analysis, *Handbook of Cyclical Indicators: A Supplement to the Business Conditions Digest* (1984), table 8, pp. 172–73.
[a]November 1948, July 1953, August 1957, April 1960, December 1969, November 1973, January 1980.
[b]October 1949, May 1954, April 1958, February 1961, November 1970, March 1975, July 1980.

war indicators. Moreover, the average leads were in general markedly longer at downturns than at upturns. The opposite applies to the lags, which tended to be both fewer and shorter at peaks.

The general conspectus of timing relationships that are typical of business cycles was introduced in chapter 2 (see table 2.4 and text); table 10.4 extends and quantifies that schematic representation. Read horizontally, the table shows the within-process sequences: for example, marginal employment adjustments (average workweek, overtime hours, claims for unemployment insurance) led at business cycle peaks by long intervals, job vacancies by intermediate intervals, and unemployment by short intervals; comprehensive employment had roughly coincident timing; and long-term unemployment and average duration of unemployment lagged. At troughs, the sequence was somewhat different in that job vacancies and most unemployment series lagged. Read vertically, the table shows which variables in different economic-process groups had similar timing. To illustrate, marginal employment adjustments, new orders for consumer goods, business investment commitments (new appropriations, orders and contracts for capital goods), change in inventories, stock prices, corporate profits, and money change and credit flows, all led at both peaks and troughs.

Series on job vacancies and unemployment (inverted) illustrate the mixed category of leads at peaks and lags at troughs. This is because employment typically rises slowly in both the initial and the late stages of a business expansion, whereas the labor force grows at a fairly steady pace.[9] Capacity utilization rates exemplify series that lead at peaks and coincide at troughs, presumably again reflecting the recent patterns of flat downturns and sharp upturns.

Most indicators, however, tend to either lead at both types of turn or be roughly coincident or lag at both. The identities of the leaders, coinciders, and laggers remain unchanged over long stretches of time, as documented by repeated reviews of their performance. That is, the medians in table 10.4 are generally quite representative in the sense that leads prevail heavily for the series listed on the left, rough coincidences (including leads and lags of 3 months or less) for the series listed in the middle, and lags for the series listed on the right. But it should be noted that this qualitative continuity coexists with a good deal of variation in the *magnitudes* of the *individual* leads (lags) recorded over time for a particular leading (lagging) indicator.

Table 10.5 lists the medians and ranges of the leads and lags for the same groups of indicators at the 1981 peak and the 1982 trough of the severe recession that issued in the long expansion of the past decade. Comparisons of the corresponding entries in this table and table 10.4 confirm that the timing classifications established some time ago in the *BCD* generally held up well. As

---

9. The reasons why employment recovers relatively slowly lie in the initial uncertainties about the prospects for an enduring expansion and the concurrent rises in the average workweek and labor productivity. The reasons why employment grows less in late than in midexpansion stages lie in demand slowdowns or supply constraints or both.

Table 10.5   Timing of Groups of Indicators in the Recession and Recovery of 1981–83

		Median Lead (−) or Lag (+) (mo.)	
Line (1)	Group (no. of series) (2)	Business Cycle Peak: July 1981 (3)	Business Cycle Trough: November 1982 (4)
	I. Employment and Unemployment (15 series)		
1	Marginal employment adjustments (3)	−6 (−3 to −7)	−2 (+1 to −2)
2	Job vacancies (2)	−8 (same)	−2 (same)
3	Comprehensive employment (5)	0 (0 to −7)	+2 (0 to +4)
4	Comprehensive unemployment (3)	0 (0 to +1)	+1 (0 to +1)
5	Average duration & long-term unemployment (2)	+3 (+1, +5)	+5 (+1, +9)
	II. Production and Income (10)		
6	Capacity utilization (2)	−3.5 (−2, −5)	0 (same)
7	Comprehensive output & income (4)	+1 (−1 to +2)	−0.5 (0 to −3)
8	Industrial production (4)	+ 0.5 (0 to +1)	0 (0 to −6)
	III. Consumption, Trade, Orders, and Deliveries (13)		
9	Change in unfilled orders; vendor performance; retail sales (4)	−3.5 (+1 to −7)	−7.5 (−3 to −10)
10	New orders (3)	−2 (same)	−1 (same)
11	Unfilled orders; production of consumer goods (2)	0 (same)	0 (same)
12	Manufacturing & trade sales (2)	0 (−1, +1)	−1 (same)
13	Index of consumer sentiment; car buying (2)	+1 (same)	−10 (−8, −12)
	IV. Fixed Capital Investment (18)		
14	Formation of business enterprises (2)	−2 (−1, −3)	−3 (−2, −4)
15	Business investment commitments (5)	−3 (−3 to −8)	−3 (+1 to −3)
16	Capital appropriations (2)	0 (−2, +2)	+ 0.5 (−3, +4)
17	Business investment expenditures (6)	−2.5 (0 to −4)	+3 (0 to +6)
18	Residential construction (3)	−10 (−8 to −10)	−12 (−9 to −13)
	V. Inventories and Inventory Investment (9)		
19	Inventory investment (4)	−0.5 (+1 to −2)	0 (0 to −5)
20	Inventories on hand & on order (5)	+4 (0 to +6)	+7 (+1 to +8)
	VI. Prices, Costs, and Profits (19)		
21	Sensitive commodity prices & stock prices (4)	−9.5 (−8 to −12)	−9 (+1 to −14)
22	Corporate profits & margins after taxes (4)	−5 (−2 to −8)	+3 (0 to +3)
23	Same with inventory valuation and capital consumption adjustments; price/unit labor costs ratio (4)	+4 (+1 to +4)	−9 (0 to −9)
24	Corporate cash flows (2)	−0.5 (+4, −5)	−9 (same)
25	Unit labor costs & labor share (5)	+16 (+10 to +19)	+12 (+9 to +20)
	VII. Money and Credit (28)		
26	Changes in money supply & liquid assets (3)	−11 (−6 to −13)	−9 (0 to −14)

Table 10.5   Continued

| | | Median Lead (−) or Lag (+) (mo.) | |
| | | Business Cycle Peak: July 1981 | Business Cycle Trough: November 1982 |
Line (1)	Group (no. of series) (2)	(3)	(4)
27	Real money supply (2)	n.t.	− 17.5 (− 13, − 22)
28	Velocity of money (2)	+ 1 (same)	+ 8.5 (+ 8, + 9)
29	Credit flows—change in debts (5)	− 2 (+ 6 to − 9)	− 1 (+ 1 to − 9)
30	Credit difficulties (2)	n.t.	n.t.
31	Bank reserves (2)	n.t.	n.t.
32	Interest rates (8)	+ 1.5 (− 2 to + 2)	+ 5 (+ 2 to + 8)
33	Outstanding debt (4)	+ 14 (same)	+ 8.5 (+ 8, + 11)

Note: The entries in cols. 3 and 4 are medians of leads and lags for the groups of indicators listed in col. 2 and (in parentheses) the ranges of the corresponding observations for the individual series in each group. Where the group consists of two series only, both observations are listed. Where all observations for the group are identical, the designation is "(same)." Where no timing comparisons can be made for any series in the group, the entry reads "n.t." (no specific turning points matching the 1981 business cycle peak or the 1982 business cycle trough). For the identification of the source and the series covered, see table 10.4.

would be expected, however, there were individual abberations. The downturn in July 1981 occurred abruptly, cutting short a recovery that began only a year earlier. Because there was no slowdown, some series that typically lead at peaks were tardy this time: the index of consumer sentiment, consumer expenditures on automobiles, and change in business inventories. At the November 1982 trough, job vacancies had a short lead instead of the usual lag, and business investment and profits turned upward late instead of close to the reference date.

10.7   How the Indicators Performed before and after World War II

The first list of indicators of both revivals and recoveries, based on data available through 1938, appeared in Moore 1950. Later Moore (1979) compared the historical timing record of these series in periods of varying lengths between 1860 and 1938 (mostly interwar years) with the record of the same series or their current equivalents in 1948–75. This is a rather demanding test of the postsample performance for the indicators, considering the many profound differences between the U.S. economy before 1938 and after 1948.

Table 10.6 is a summary of the main findings from Moore 1979. Of the 21 indicators originally selected in 1950, 15 continued to be carried in the *BCD* through 1979. The other six were replaced by related series available from the same source. For three leading indicators and one lagging, the substitutes are very close; for the two coincident indicators, much less so (see the notes to

Table 10.6   Prior and Subsequent Performance of Three Groups of Indicators
              Selected and Classified in 1950

	At Business Cycle Peaks			At Business Cycle Troughs		
	Leading[a]	Roughly Coincident[b]	Lagging[c]	Leading[a]	Roughly Coincident[b]	Lagging[c]
	Average Lead (−) or Lag (+), in Months					
Through 1938	− 6	0	+ 5	− 5	− 2	+ 3
1948–75	− 12	− 2	+ 3	− 2	+ 1	+ 4
	Percentage of Timing Comparisons in Appropriate Class					
Through 1938	80	72	88	81	67	72
1948–75	89	60	68.	71	84	73

Source: Moore 1979, pp. 408–9 (reprinted in Moore 1983, ch. 24, pp. 376–77).

[a]The leading group includes eight series: liabilities of business failures; Dow-Jones index of industrial common stock prices (S&P 500 index in 1948–75); new orders, durable goods, value; residential building contracts, floorspace (new building permits, private housing units, number in 1948–75); commercial and industrial building contracts, floorspace; average workweek, manufacturing; new incorporations, number; wholesale price index, 28 basic commodities (industrial materials price index, 13 commodities in 1948–75).

[b]The roughly coincident group includes eight series: employment in nonagricultural establishments; persons unemployed, number; corporate profits after taxes; bank debits outside New York (manufacturing and trade sales, value, in 1948–75); freight car loadings (value of goods output, 1972 dollars, in 1948–75); industrial production index; gross national product, value; wholesale price index, industrial commodities.

[c]The lagging group includes five series: personal income, value; retail sales, value; consumer installment debt, value; bank rates on business loans; manufacturers' inventories, book value (manufacturing and trade inventories, book value, in 1948–75).

the table for details). To simplify and save space, only the overall group averages are shown here, but the underlying observations at individual turns are on the whole consistent with the conclusion that the postwar data tend to support the choices and classifications made 30 years earlier on the strength of the pre-1938 information.

In particular, it is clear that the leaders as a group continued to lead, though by longer intervals at peaks and shorter ones at troughs. The laggers continued to lag. Among the 1948–75 timing comparisons for the series designated as leading indicators in 1950, the relative frequency of leads increased moderately at peaks and decreased at troughs. The lagging indicators performed worse at peaks but equally well at troughs in the postwar as compared with the pre-1938 sample period.

10.8   How to Explain the Cyclical Sequences

There are good reasons to expect the observed cyclical timing sequences to persist, as they indeed do. To a large extent, established procedures and technologies determine which series move early and which late relative to each other. For example, before funds for new capital projects are disbursed, they must be appropriated; before plants are built, construction contracts are placed; before equipment is paid for and installed, it must be ordered; before expenditures on residential investment are recorded, building permits are taken out and housing starts are counted.

Moreover, new investment commitments come close to representing investment planning on the demand side, and payments for capital goods and their production, delivery, or installation represent more nearly investment realizations on the supply side. Where substantial gestation lags intervene, the distinction is important. Thus, according to the theory of desired stock-flow adjustments, planned investment should lead total output, including consumption as well as (realized) investment. The flexible accelerator theory also applies to inventories, where it suggests that inventory investment tends to lead sales and that the ratio of manufacturing and trade inventories to the corresponding sales lags.

Additional explanations derive from monetary and financial arrangements. The rate of change in business and consumer credit outstanding leads because new loans serve to finance investment in processes that are themselves leading (in inventories, housing, and consumer durables; also in plant and equipment, where the loans are taken out early in the process). Here too, there are timing sequences that reflect stock-flow relationships: net increments lead; totals lag. Credit flows have large early movements, but debt aggregates are smooth and sluggish. Money growth rates are very volatile but tend to lead by variable, though mostly long, intervals. Monetary aggregates themselves are dominated by upward trends and show persistent declines only in cycles with severe contractions. However, real money balances, such as the broadly defined money supply M2 deflated by a consumer price index, declined well ahead of several recent peaks in total output and employment and rose well ahead of troughs. That is, in late stages of expansion (contraction) money increased less (more) than prices. Here both endogenous and exogenous elements are important; notably, changes in the nominal money stock depend on the policy-controlled changes in the monetary base.

Interest rates (much influenced by the actual and expected changes in money, credit, and prices) tend to lag. This does not mean that they are to be viewed as only a result, not a cause, of the economy's cyclical course and future: they are both. Changes in the level and structure of interest rates are important codeterminants, along with risk premiums, of discount factors and stock returns, cost of finance, and investment opportunities. Expectations of changes in the price level vary across the economy and over time, and interest rates adjust to these changes, in ways that are not directly or reliably observable, let alone predictable. Nominal rates play an important role in the interactions of money demand and supply. Therefore, nominal rates matter at least as much as real rates in business cycle developments.

Cost-price-productivity-profit linkages give rise to other cyclical sequences. Changes in prices of sensitive materials precede changes in producer and consumer prices. Changes in labor productivity (output per hour) lead; changes in unit labor cost lag. As a result of these tendencies connected with cyclical movements in sales and the rates of utilization of labor and capital, profit margins and totals show early and large fluctuations. (For further discussion of the subjects of this and the preceding paragraph, see chapters 2, 3, and 4.)

Stock prices track and anticipate the broad movements of corporate earnings (leading) and interest rates (lagging) and relate positively to the former, inversely to the latter. This helps explain the cyclicality and early timing of broadly based indexes of common stock prices. Long records of such indexes, in the United States and abroad, document that bear markets tend to begin well before business contractions and bull markets well before expansions. But the indexes also show additional, sizable movements because stock prices are apparently quite sensitive to noncyclical short-term influences or shocks as well.

Some timing relations reflect directly the changing state of the economy. Thus delivery periods get progressively longer just before and during recoveries and especially in booms, when orders back up and strain the capacity to produce; and they get progressively shorter when an expansion slows down and a contraction develops. This explains the leads of vendor performance (percentage of companies receiving slower deliveries). The early timing of the change in unfilled orders can be explained similarly. The ratio of unfilled orders to sales measures roughly the number of months it would take for the backlog of work to be eliminated at the current levels of activity. When expansions slow gradually, as they did on several recent occasions, these indicators peak early along with the capacity utilization rates. This helps account for the long leads at the corresponding business downturns of other series, too, notably indexes of consumer expectations, new orders for consumer goods and materials, and contracts and orders for plant and equipment.

Last but not least, there is a simple rationale for the sequences among the labor market series. Changes in hours are less binding than changes in the number employed, so the average workweek in manufacturing leads because it is altered early in response to uncertain signs of shifts in the demand for output. Initial claims for unemployment insurance change slightly ahead of the overall unemployment rate, whereas long-term unemployment and the jobless rate among persons unemployed 15 weeks and over lag behind. People with the least qualifications and weakest attachments to the labor force lose jobs early and gain jobs late whenever the economy slows and declines.

10.9   Significance in Macro and Micro Theories

The existence of regular timing sequences among economic time series is necessary but not sufficient to demonstrate that some indicators are likely to lead, others to have approximately coincident timing, and still others to lag at *business cycle turns*. What is needed in addition is (1) that the movements involved have cyclical dimensions with respect to duration and amplitudes and (2) that the coincident indicators, which include the aggregates of input and output as implied by the definition of business cycles, occupy central positions in many of the sequences. Both requirements are amply satisfied, as already demonstrated by our measures.

The indicators in current use play important roles in many areas viewed as critical in business cycle theories. This is illustrated in table 10.7, which is based on a long series of studies (for references, see chapters 2 and 5 and Moore 1983, pp. 347–51).

The literature on business cycles, though rich in ingenious hypotheses of varying plausibility and compatibility, produced no unified theory (chapter 2).

Table 10.7   **Business Cycle Theories and Indicator Sequences: A Conspectus**

Theories or Models	Some Main Factors	Evidence from Time Series
Accelerator-multiplier models; hypotheses on autonomous investment, innovations, and gestation lags	Interaction between investment, final demand, and savings	Large cyclical movements in business investment commitments (orders, contracts) lead total output and employment; smaller movements in investment realizations (shipments, outlays) coincide or lag
Inventory investment models	Stock adjustments in response to sales changes and their effects on production	Inventory investment tends to lead; its declines during mild recessions are large relative to those in final sales
Old monetary overinvestment and current monetarist theories	Changes in the supply of money, bank credit, interest rates, and the burden of private debt	Money and credit flows (rates of change) are highly sensitive, early leaders; velocity, market rates of interest, and credit outstanding coincide or lag
Hypotheses of cost-price imbalances, volatility of prospective rates of return, and expectational errors	Changes in costs and prices, in the diffusion, margins, and totals of profits, and in business expectations	Profit variables and stock price indexes are sensitive early leaders; unit labor costs lag

Source: See references in text.

There is evidence in support of a number of different models that focus on period-specific or sector-specific aspects of the economy's motion. Monocausal theories may help explain some episodes but are invalidated by long experience.

Some more or less formal models have been developed recently to explain why some of the leading indicators lead. Popkin (1984, 1990) stresses the importance of intermediate transactions between producing units rather than with final purchasers, and of the production of goods rather than services. He argues that the latter are only weakly cyclical; it is the goods-producing industries, mainly manufacturing, that are most sensitive to business cycles. Therefore, manufacturing is and should be strongly represented on the list of principal leading indicators used in composite indexes. The series concerned include new orders for consumer goods and materials, contracts and orders for plant and equipment, the average workweek of production workers in manufacturing, vendor performance, change in manufacturing inventories on hand and on order, and the percentage change in sensitive materials prices. All of these, except the last one, are in real terms. Popkin builds, estimates, and simulates a quarterly log-linear model linking final demand (sales) with intermediate manufactures. Retailers place orders for finished goods, whose producers react by changing unfilled orders and/or inventories and/or output. These adjustments determine the profit margins over costs of labor and materials and, hence, output prices, given the wages and material prices paid. The results show that the amplitudes of cyclical fluctuations transmitted from final sales are systematically greater for the manufacturers of materials than for the manufacturers of finished products, and greater for the latter than for the retailers. The magnification appears in ratios of cyclical to control solutions of the model for outputs, inventories, new orders, and prices. The analysis recalls earlier studies of vertical (interstage) transmission of demand movements through changes in new and unfilled orders and inventories (Zarnowitz 1962, 1973; Mack 1967; Childs 1967).

A model of the short-run behavior of a firm that attempts to minimize the costs of meeting expected demand is shown by de Leeuw (1991) to be consistent with the relative timing and amplitudes of new orders, output, shipments, employment, average hours, and changes in unfilled orders and inventories—under many but not all conditions. The outcomes of model simulations depend on whether production is to order or to stock; on whether the initiating disturbances occur in actual or expected demand or productivity; and on whether the expectations are formed adaptively or on the assumption of perfect foresight. Tests based on regressions of alternative measures of output growth on lagged values of employment growth, changes in inventories and unfilled orders, and alternative proxies for expected demand are found to be on the whole encouraging.

According to de Leeuw (1989), it is possible that business cycles reflect to a large extent movements in certain fundamental forces ("prime movers") such as "monetary and fiscal policies, regulatory decisions, foreign economic developments, demographic shifts, new technologies, droughts or bumper crops, and a few others" (p. 23). Yet few prime movers are included in the lists of principal leading indicators for the United States and other countries.[10] After considering several possible reasons and remedies for this, de Leeuw develops a "prime-mover–based" leading index by means of a regression of output on M2, cyclically adjusted federal expenditures, exports, relative import prices, inflation, and the GNP gap (where the first two of the variables listed are taken as first differences in logs, and the next three as second differences to proxy for unexpected changes). An index obtained by transformation of the values produced by the above regression declined only slightly and irregularly in 1955–57 and 1968–69, leading by long intervals but not distinctly at the 1957 and 1970 peaks in the coincident index; its movement was essentially trendless and random in the 1950s and dominated by a rising trend in the 1960s. In 1970–88 this index of prime movers acquired more cyclicality and definitely declined in 1973–74 and 1978–81, with long leads at the peaks of 1973 and 1980. It skipped the recessions of 1953–54 and 1960 and failed to signal the 1981 peak (see de Leeuw 1989, chart 2).

The performance of this construct as a leading indicator is relatively weak, in my view. Moreover, de Leeuw's results are not surprising. As noted in chapter 3, the effects of fiscal policy on aggregate economic activity have not been particularly consistent. Also, our vector autoregressive model estimates in chapter 12 confirm that fiscal variables contribute little to the determination of changes in real GNP in the presence of several much more powerful variables, notably an index of selected leading indicators. Monetary policy had stronger effects but also lacked consistency and contained important endogenous components. In the 1980s the volatility of growth rates increased for all monetary aggregates, and their performance as cyclical indicators deteriorated (see Cagan 1990). Deflation helps and M2 is still a relatively good choice among the monetary series (as is the monetary base, according to Cagan). But other areas produce better leading indicators (e.g., in real investment, credit, sensitive prices).

---

10. The U.S. composite index of leading indicators contains one series classified by de Leeuw as a prime mover, namely, the deflated money supply. The Organization for Economic Cooperation and Development (OECD) has identified leading indicators in 21 countries, and out of 180 such series 36, or 20%, are designated prime movers in de Leeuw 1989, table 1. (These include 18 money supply series, 8 export series, 8 terms-of-trade series, and 2 leading indicators for neighboring countries.) Of the leading indicators for 10 countries as selected at Columbia University's Center for International Business Cycle Research (CIBCR), only 3% are so designated. The CIBCR indicators are by design generally similar to those chosen for the United States in the NBER and BEA studies (P. A. Klein and Moore 1985); the OECD indicators deviate more from the U.S. selections. It should be noted that both the OECD and the CIBCR international indicators refer directly to growth cycles rather than business cycles.

Enough has been said on the reasons for the observed behavior of the indicators and their links to micro and business cycle theories to weaken if not disprove the charge of "measurement without theory." If the reasons are simple, so much the better.

10.10   Modeling with Cyclical Indicators

The development of modern macroeconomic models was closely related to the idea of interdependence among the major components of aggregate income and output. Correspondingly, the econometric implementation of these models was closely related to the development and structure of national income and product accounts (NIPA). The builders of macroeconometric models drew heavily on the NIPA data, first in annual and later in quarterly form. Also, the models soon acquired a Keynesian orientation, which meant a shift from the direct interest in business cycles (which dominated at the beginning: Tinbergen 1938–39) to a preoccupation with the determinants of levels of aggregate output and employment in the short run.

In contrast, the development of the indicators was from the beginning motivated by the need for timely detection or prediction of business cycle turning points (the first one was the revival from the slump of 1937–38; see Mitchell and Burns 1938). The objective being the analysis of current business conditions and the forecasting, recognition, measurement, and appraisal of recessions and recoveries, the approach uses mainly monthly, and to a lesser extent quarterly, times series. The indicators are generally endogenous variables (not exogenous "prime movers"); that is, they influence the economy and are influenced by it. The traditional NBER approach, with its emphasis on the dichotomies of contraction and expansion, peak and trough, seems to lend more support to endogenous and nonlinear theories than to exogenous and linear theories of the business cycle. On the other hand, most macromodels are not fundamentally nonlinear and rely heavily on outside forces and shocks to account for the very existence of business cycles (chapters 6 and 9).

The evolution of macroeconomics led to progressively less dependence of both the theoretical and the econometric models on the early Keynesian ideas and progressively more dependence on principles of optimization and market clearing. The theory underlying the system of cyclical indicators is largely of a different type, namely, the dynamics of plans and expectations under uncertainty and of institutional and physical constraints in processes of production and investment.

All these differences of objective, concept, data, and method make it difficult to combine cyclical indicators and econometric models in some comprehensive and systematic way. Yet the two approaches are complementary in important respects. The indicators are indispensable for the analysis of the current course and near future of the economy. As such the required data need to be systematically collected, monitored, and processed into appropriate composite indexes (the latter will be discussed in chapter 11). For years now this task has been performed by the Commerce Department (BEA), which amounts to a de facto endorsement of the indicator methodology by the federal government.[11] The active macroeconometric models, which have meanwhile grown greatly in size and complexity, are not well equipped to track the current developments and forecast or at least recognize promptly the key business cycle events. But they are designed to make quantitative quarterly and/or annual forecasts from sets of estimated economic relationships, and indeed this is increasingly their main function. In actual practice, there are probably few professional forecasters with macromodels, and few experienced users of quantitative forecasts who would ignore the signals from indicators.[12]

Some leading indicators are regularly included in large econometric models. For example, vendor performance acts as an important determinant of industrial prices and inventory investment in the Data Resources, Inc. (DRI), model (Eckstein 1983). Housing starts are related to the variables governing the demand for housing services, the stock of housing, and cost and availability of mortgage financing; then residential construction is estimated as a moving average of starts. Contracts and orders for plant and equipment could be treated similarly but are not (more attention is paid to survey data on investment intentions). The labor input in the production function is represented by the product of employment and the average hours worked. The distinction between the fast short-run adjustment of weekly hours and the slower adjustment of the number of workers is made in one version of the Wharton model (L. R. Klein 1990). The demand functions for money and other financial assets generally follow the modern portfolio theory, but with many elaborations in the large-scale models, and the monetary base or unborrowed reserves are treated as an exogenous variable subject to control by the Federal Reserve. Price indexes for raw and intermediate industrial materials play an important role but as early indicators of inflation rather than changes in real activity.

It is clear that these uses of the leaders, though important, are quite different from those made of the same variables in the indicator approach. They are more indirect, partial, and limited. The interdependence of timing, stressed in the indicator system, receives no special consideration in the models. There is aggregation by time, because it is still difficult to construct monthly models, and the lag specifications are often crude.

Yet some model builders report making intensive use of monthly indicator data. As discussed by L. R. Klein (1990, pp. 104–5), the recent "Pennsylvania approach" is as follows. Selected monthly series, including many cyclical indicators, leading and others, are estimated and extrapolated by means of formal time-series models (e.g., ARIMA, VAR). Averaged into quarterly val-

11. Many state governments and foreign countries have followed the United States in compiling their own leading indicators and indexes.
12. Incidentally, the same applies to the makers and users of "judgmental" forecasts. For more on these matters, see chapters 13, 14 and 18.

ues, they are then used to project many GNP components for the current quarter and one quarter ahead. Constant-term adjustments, or "add-factors," are applied to the results obtained from the model equations to make them agree reasonably well with the indicator-based estimates. Longer solutions are produced by simulation techniques with the add-factors retained in the model. This method permits a combination of high- and lower-frequency magnitudes calculated, respectively, from the monthly indicators and the quarterly model.

Small forecasting models that incorporate selected leading indicators along with third-order autoregressions and that use pooled international data have been found to generate relatively accurate and efficient predictions of annual and quarterly growth rates of real output for eight European countries and the United States (Garcia-Ferrer et al. 1987). Such forecasts, while much more limited in scope than those produced by elaborate international efforts using large econometric models, are also much less costly yet quite competitive in quality. The leading indicators used include real stock returns and growth rates in money supply for each country and all countries combined. [13]

10.11   Conclusion and Brief Preview of Part III

This chapter has been concerned mainly with the systematic aspects of cyclical indicators and their analytical characteristics and functions. But the principal uses of the indicators are in forecasting. Here it becomes essential to construct the composite indexes of leading, coincident, and lagging indicators from preselected series. Such indexes, and particularly those designed to lead, can be built, applied, and assessed in various ways. They are the subject of chapter 11.

It remains to offer some concluding and forward-looking remarks. When used collectively, the indicators provide over the course of business cycles a revolving flow of signals. Shallow and spotty declines in the leading series provide only weak and uncertain warnings; a run of several large declines increases the risk of a general and serious slowdown or recession. The latter may suggest some stabilizing policy actions that, if effective, could falsify the warning. The coincident indicators confirm or invalidate the expectations based on the behavior of the leaders and any related policy decisions. The lagging indicators provide further checks on the previously derived inferences, in particular on any early designation of the timing of a business cycle term. Moreover, for reasons stated earlier (sec. 10.4), they also act as predictors when used in inverted form.

Macroeconomic forecasting, which the indicator system is designed to aid, must be essentially consistent with the ascertained regularities of business fluctuations. Some of these "stylized facts" may be difficult to reconcile with

---

13. It is interesting to note that to my knowledge, the large models generally do not include indexes of stock prices or returns.

the preconceptions of the general-equilibrium theory, but this does not diminish the value of the indicator analysis. The real problems with the indicators are mainly practical. Large amounts of random noise, large revisions of originally published figures, and short lead times (which occur mostly at troughs of short recessions) detract from the usefulness of some leading series. Those irregular variations and data errors in its components that are independent tend to cancel out in the leading index, which is therefore relatively smooth. As a result, the problem of extra turns or false warnings is reduced, but it is not eliminated.

Chapter 11 will discuss why and how the composite indexes are constructed and used and with what results, as assessed by repeated tests. Chapter 12 examines the role of a combination of leading indicators in the framework of a simple VAR model that also includes total output, monetary and fiscal variables, and interest and inflation rates.

11 Composite Indexes of Leading, Coincident, and Lagging Indicators

11.1 Objectives, Standards, and Assessments

11.1.1 Reasons for Combining Indicators into Indexes

In concurrence with much of the literature, this book argues that there is no *single* proven and accepted cause of *all* observed business cycles.[1] Instead, there are a number of plausible and not mutually exclusive hypotheses about what can cause downturns and contractions, upturns and expansions. Similarly, no *single* chain of symptoms exists that would invariably presage these developments. Instead, there are a number of frequently observed regularities that seem likely to persist and play important roles in business cycles but are certainly not immutable. The study of modern economic history reveals a mixture of unique and common characteristics in each recorded business cycle. It also suggests that certain systematic changes in short-term macro-dynamics can be linked to long-term changes in the economy's structure and institutions and the government's role and policies.

All this combines to explain why it has proved so difficult to make progress toward a unified theory of business cycles, despite the great ingenuity of the theorists and considerable gains in tested knowledge achieved in the empirical work on the subject. Now, for the same reasons, the performance of individual indicators in any given period is apt to vary depending on which causal elements are dominant and how their working manifests itself. In particular, some leading indicators turn out to be most operative and useful in one set of conditions, and others in a different set. To increase the chances of getting true signals and reduce those of getting false ones, it is therefore advisable to rely on a reasonably diversified group of leading series with demonstrated

---

1. This section is based in part on Zarnowitz and Boschan 1975a, as are some other paragraphs of this chapter.

predictive potential. This suggests combining selected leaders into an appropriately constructed index and monitoring changes in that index as well as in its components on a regular basis. The argument can be readily generalized to composite indexes of roughly coincident indicators and of lagging indicators as well.

Second, the measurement errors in individual indicators are often large, especially in the most recent observations based on preliminary data. To the extent that the data errors in the different indicators are independent, the risk of being misled can be reduced by evaluating the signals, not from any one series viewed in isolation, but from a number of related series. The latter, however, must be sufficiently differentiated and not just provide different measurements for essentially the same variables. This is because multiple counting should be avoided inasmuch as it results in unintended overweighting of some elements in an index.

The third reason is an enhancement of predictive ability that can be achieved by the reduction of pure "noise." In general, indicators tend to react not only to sustained cyclical fluctuations but also to frequent disturbances of all kinds, for example, major strikes and foreign wars. This is particularly true of the sensitive leading indicators. Hence, the month-to-month changes in these series (after elimination of any seasonal elements) usually reflect the short erratic movements much more than the longer cyclical ones. By combining the series into an index, some of that noise is eliminated; that is, a well-constructed composite index can be much smoother than any of its components.

The corollary of these arguments for constructing indexes from selected series with common timing patterns is that a failure of an individual indicator does not refute the method. Rather, such a failure merely impairs and, if repeated, ultimately invalidates the particular series concerned. Unless the underlying economic process is significantly altered, the problem reduces to getting a better representation for it by improving the series or replacing it with one that would perform satisfactorily. On the other hand, even a failure on a single occasion would have strong negative implications for the indicator approach if it extended to a whole set of principal series combined in an index.

11.1.2   Criteria for the Evaluation of Indicator Performance

Historically, six criteria were applied in assessing and selecting the NBER cyclical indicators. They refer to the following questions:

1. How well understood and how important is the role in business cycles of the variables represented by the data? (The judgment on this is quantified in the score for *economic significance.*)

2. How well does the given series measure the economic variable or process in question (*statistical adequacy*)?

3. How consistently has the series led (or coincided or lagged) at business cycle peaks and troughs (*timing at recessions and revivals*)?

4. How regularly have the movements in the specific indicator reflected the expansions and contractions in the economy at large (*conformity* to historical business cycles)?

5. How promptly can a cyclical turn in the series be distinguished from directional change associated with shorter, irregular movements (*smoothness,* which is inversely related to the degree of statistical noise)?

6. How promptly available are the statistics and how frequently are they reported (*currency* or timeliness)?

A formal, detailed weighting scheme according to the above criteria was first developed and applied in Moore and Shiskin 1967. In the Zarnowitz and Boschan studies (1975a, 1975b, 1975c), a revised version of the same approach was used. The scores for each of the six major characteristics and their many relevant components were computed on the 0-to-100 scale and then combined into a total score by means of the weights.[2]

The evaluation of economic significance is difficult and inevitably subjective; hence much of it was handled by preselection, with the minimum acceptable score set at 70%. The scores for all other criteria were based on essentially objective statistical measures. Thus, the quality of the reporting system is assessed according to whether it is set up directly for statistical purposes, is a by-product of an administrative system, or is nonexistent (as for series estimated indirectly from related variables). Other aspects of statistical adequacy include the coverage of process (full enumeration, probability sample, other) and of time period (full month, or 1 week, or 1 day per month, etc.); the availability of estimates of sampling and reporting errors; the length of the series and comparability over time (breaks are penalized); and the frequency of revisions (none, once a reporting period, or more often). More recently, the revisions were given a more elaborate treatment and a separate score reflecting their relative size as well as frequency.[3]

The cyclical timing performance of an indicator is appraised mainly according to the probability that the observed number of timing comparisons of a given type will be equaled or exceeded by chance. The dispersion of the leads and lags about their means is also taken into account but with a smaller weight (of about 20% of the total timing score). The leads and lags of the series are

2. In 1967, the first four criteria received weights of 20% each; the last two received weights of 10% each. The results referred to the period before 1966 (as far back as the data were available but with a heavy preponderance of the evidence from the post–World War II years). The timing of the indicators at peaks and troughs was handled symmetrically.

In 1975, criteria 1, 2, and 4 received weights of 1/6 each, timing 2/15, smoothness 2/15, and currency 1/10. The results referred to the period 1947–70. An asymmetrical distribution of the cyclical timing comparisons at peaks and troughs of the postwar period was applied. Cf. Moore and Shiskin 1967, pp. 22–27, and Zarnowitz and Boschan 1975a, pp. 2–4.

3. For more detailed information on scoring for statistical adequacy, errors and revisions, smoothness and currency, see chapter 13 below. Also, on these and the other scores for the components of the 1966 and 1975 indexes, see Moore and Shiskin 1967 and Zarnowitz and Boschan 1975a and 1975b.

measured at the NBER-established references dates for business cycle peaks and troughs separately.

Conformity is evaluated by relating the number of business cycle phases that are matched by the specific-cycle movements (expansions and contractions) in the given series to the total number of phases covered and then computing the probabilities for the observed records. Other elements of the conformity score are the frequencies of "extra" movements in the indicators that do not match the phases of general business fluctuations and can result in misleading "false signals." The amplitudes of cyclical changes in the series are also accounted for here (the larger and more distinct movements score higher).[4]

Smoothness depends on the relationship between the irregular and the trend-cycle components of the series adjusted for seasonal variation. Large erratic variations are common among many leading indicators and constitute the main defect in some. Smoothing the data with short, trailing moving averages can be advantageous for some erratic series that have long leads and high currency scores (i.e., are compiled frequently and released promptly). To put it differently, trade-off relationships exist between the smoothness, currency, and timing characteristics (e.g., moving averages increase smoothness but reduce currency and possibly the lead times).

11.1.3   The Indicator Scores and Selection of Index Components

Table 11.1 presents means and standard deviations of each of the principal component scores and of the total scores for 108 cyclical indicators that were regularly presented in *BCD*. These statistics refer to data for 1947–80. The series are classified by cyclical timing (pt. A) and by economic process (pt. B). Listed in part A are also the scores of the composite indexes of leading, coincident, and lagging indicators as well as of the groups of series included in each of these indexes.

The major purpose of the original scoring efforts in the mid-1960s and again in the early 1970s was to help select the most consistently cyclical series for the indicators section of *BCD*. This explains in large part why the overall average scores in the table (col. 8) are all relatively high and clustered. They do not differ greatly across either the economic process or the cyclical timing groups.

It is also to be noted that the differences between the component scores are generally large and often significant but that they offset each other to a large extent. For example, the leaders as a group rank well below the coinciders with respect to smoothness, but the reverse obtains for revisions (see lines 1–2 and 5–6). Production and income series (lines 20–21) score high on timing

---

4. Within the total score for conformity, probability gets a maximum of 50, extra turns 30, and amplitude 20 points.

Table 11.1   **Means and Standard Deviations of Scores of Cyclical Indicators, 1947–80**

Line	Timing (1)	Conformity (2)	Smoothness (3)	Currency (4)	Statistical Adequacy (5)	Revisions (6)	Economic Significance (7)	Total (8)
A. CLASSIFIED BY CYCLICAL TIMING (108)								
All Leading Series (47)								
1	76	68	57	57	78	72	74	71
2	11	18	27	29	12	22	7	6
Components of the Leading Index (12)								
3	79	72	68	80	75	65	74	74
4	10	16	20	10	8	30	9	5
All Roughly Coincident Series (18)								
5	86	77	87	57	80	52	82	78
6	18	7	15	28	8	18	11	8
Components of the Coincident Index (4)								
7	95	82	95	74	77	40	88	82
8	5	4	10	13	5	16	5	6
All Lagging Series (26)								
9	81	72	85	62	75	82	78	77
10	16	15	17	32	13	20	5	6
Components of the Lagging Index (6)								
11	86	71	87	75	73	70	80	78
12	6	18	16	18	15	24	6	8
Unclassified (17)								
13	75	77	78	72	74	75	76	75
14	18	16	22	26	14	18	8	8
Composite Indexes (3)								
15L	86	72	100	80	77	0	90	75
16C	100	86	100	80	77	20	90	83
17Lg	92	86	100	80	73	0	90	78
B. CLASSIFIED BY ECONOMIC PROCESS (108)								
I. Employment and Unemployment (15)								
18	84	85	81	80	71	83	81	81
19	9	9	16	0	13	18	10	5
II. Production and Income (10)								
20	93	80	92	56	74	46	84	79
21	9	6	10	31	11	16	8	7
III. Consumption, Trade, Orders, and Deliveries (13)								
22	75	72	71	71	81	63	70	73
23	22	15	21	18	7	18	10	9
IV. Fixed Capital Investment (18)								
24	80	73	68	52	79	67	74	73
25	15	12	23	30	9	22	5	4
V. Inventories and Inventory Investment (9)								
26	77	64	71	50	77	64	77	70
27	15	17	38	11	9	17	5	6

Table 11.1   **Continued**

Line	Timing (1)	Conformity (2)	Smoothness (3)	Currency (4)	Statistical Adequacy (5)	Revisions (6)	Economic Significance (7)	Total (8)
			VI. Prices, Costs, and Profits (17)					
28	76	61	72	40	73	75	75	69
29	17	15	14	32	9	22	5	6
			VII. Money and Credit (26)					
30	77	68	65	70	82	82	78	75
31	14	19	33	30	17	19	5	7

Source: U.S. Department of Commerce, Bureau of Economic Analysis 1984, table 7, pp. 169–71.
Note: In each section, except Composite Indexes (lines 15–17), entries in the first line are means of the scores of the individual series, and entries in the second line are the corresponding standard deviations. Entries in lines 15–17 are the mean scores of the leading (L), coincident (C), and lagging (Lg) composite indexes. Series are seasonally adjusted except for those that appear to contain no seasonal movement. The number of series in each group is shown in parentheses.

(which is here typically coincident) but low on currency and revisions (the data from GNP accounts are quarterly and subject to several and often large alterations). The series relating to consumption and trade do worse on timing, conformity, and smoothness but better on currency, statistical adequacy, and revisions (lines 22–23). In sum, the dispersion across the different groups of indicators is much greater for the average scores of the individual attributes than for the average total scores. The standard deviations within the groups, too, tend to be much larger for the component than for the overall scores.

The indicators included in the leading, coincident, and lagging indexes were chosen from the best-scoring series in the respective timing categories. Obviously, high consistency of procyclical or countercyclical behavior, that is, high conformity or coherence (correlation with business cycles, allowing for any systematic leads or lags), is a desirable characteristic of any index component. Timing consistency is particularly important. In addition, prompt availability of reasonably accurate data is an essential requirement for an index that is to be used in current business analysis and forecasting. This means that the component series should be released frequently with short publication lags. Thus, beginning with the 1975 list, the composite indexes of the U.S. Department of Commerce include monthly series only.[5]

As implied by these observations, the components of the leading index per-

5. Dropping GNP from the coincident index and corporate profits from the leading index involved very difficult decisions in view of the importance of the represented variables. Real GNP is, of course, the central measure of total output, but the data are quarterly and much revised. Important studies of business cycles (notably Mitchell 1913, 1927) ascribe a major role to profits; also, there is evidence of a strong tendency for total corporate profits to lead. But few concepts are more difficult to measure than profits in the true economic sense. Data on corporate profits are compiled only on a quarterly basis and are available only with long delays and sequences of revisions.

form better than the average leading series on timing, conformity, and, particularly, smoothness and currency. However, this is partly paid for by lower scores on revisions and (to a lesser extent) statistical adequacy. Due to these offsets, the overall advantage of the index component series is modest (cf. lines 1 and 3). Similar statements can be made about the coincident and lagging series (cf. lines 5 and 7, and 9 and 11). Note that larger differences would be shown had the index components been excluded from the "all series" groups.

The indexes themselves score as well or better than the averages of the corresponding component series in all categories except revisions. The gains from combining the indicators are considerable for timing, conformity, and currency but much larger yet for smoothness, especially in the case of the leading indicators. However, until very recently, the indexes earned zero or very low scores for revisions, mainly because each of them contained some series that were not available in time to be included in the first release. No estimates of the contributions of the missing components were made, so that a month later, when the lagging data first appeared, the indexes typically showed large revisions. Hence, the advantages elsewhere were again largely dissipated here (cf. lines 3 and 15, 7 and 16, and 11 and 17). The two tardy components were eliminated from the Department of Commerce leading index in 1989 with the intention of radically reducing the size of the revisions in that index (Hertzberg and Beckman 1989; for detail, see table 11.3 and text below).

Clearly, more is required of a good index than of a good single indicator. For reasons already stated, the indexes should be reasonably diversified in their economic coverage in order to have the potential to function well in the longer run or under widely varying conditions. Also, each different variable of interest should be given the best and broadest representation possible. Consequently, the selection of index components favored comprehensive series drawn from all major economic process groups that fit into the given timing pattern. At times, the implementation of this principle involved some costs in terms of lower scores than would be available otherwise (i.e., from collections of series less diversified and/or less aggregative).

The existing indexes are designed to lead (or coincide or lag) at both peaks and troughs of business cycles. This is restrictive since it excludes series with mixed timing patterns, which prevail in some areas for reasons that are well understood (see chapter 10, sec. 6). Such series (i.e., those that lead at peaks and lag at troughs or vice versa) are included in the "unclassified" group in table 11.1 (lines 13–14). Note that these indicators score on average about as well as the other groups.

Recall also that in recent business cycles leads have been much more common, but also much more variable, at peaks than at troughs. As shown in table 11.2, the timing scores averaged considerably less at peaks than at troughs for most indicators. Of the timing groups, only the laggers score slightly higher

Table 11.2   **Mean Scores of Groups of Cyclical Indicators and Composite Indexes, Timing at Peaks and Troughs, 1947–80**

Classified by Timing[a] (no. of series) (1)	Mean Timing Score Peaks (2)	Mean Timing Score Troughs (3)	Classified by Economic Process[b] (no. of series) (4)	Mean Timing Score Peaks (5)	Mean Timing Score Troughs (6)
All L series (47)	48	78	I (15)	58	85
L I components (12)	62	79	II (10)	73	87
Leading index (1)	76	94	III (13)	41	76
All C series (18)	57	81	IV (18)	49	82
C I components (4)	53	91	V (9)	57	69
Coincident index (1)	96	97	VI (17)	44	74
All Lg series (26)	76	71	VII (26)	66	65
Lg I components (6)	88	83			
Lagging index (1)	94	82	All series (108)	55	76
Unclassified (17)	46	76	All index components	67	82

Source: See table 11.1.
[a]Abbreviations: L = leading; I = index; C = roughly coincident; Lg = lagging.
[b]Groups are identified by roman numerals as in table 11.1. See table 11.1 for the titles of these economic process groups.

at peaks than at troughs, and of the economic process groups only the money and credit series (VII) do so. However, the timing performance is much better and more balanced between peaks and troughs for the composite indexes than for the corresponding "all series" groups.

11.1.4   Measurement Errors

Macroeconomic indicators are obtained by processing and aggregating primary data that as a rule contain a variety of errors, both random and systematic.[6] The errors in the components may either offset or reinforce each other in the aggregate. The procedures for the derivation of economic macromeasures can themselves contribute to the inaccuracy of the resulting time series. The more complex the process and the more numerous the estimations and approximations that are involved, the greater are the chances of substantial defects, with conceptual, procedural, and statistical ingredients that are difficult to isolate and assess.

As shown by the pervasiveness and persistence of revisions in economic statistics, some of the errors are of the kind that can be reduced only partially

6. Systematic errors may arise from nonprobability sampling or inadequate sampling or faulty enumeration. Respondents and/or collectors of the data may be poorly informed or poorly motivated or both. Concealment and falsification are possible. In short, the data vary greatly in coverage and quality, depending on the knowledge and cooperation of the people who make them. For further discussion of these and other matters covered in this section of the text and the next one, see Zarnowitz 1982c.

and gradually. To be prompt and frequent, as demanded for current business analysis and forecasting, information on important indicators must often take the form of preliminary figures subject to repeated and possibly large alterations. The discrepancies between the successive releases of a time series represent for the most part errors resulting from large lags in the availability of primary data. Although other errors created by conceptual and procedural problems may well be more serious, they tend to be less identifiable. Their detection and correction occurs only sporadically, as a result of benchmark revisions and definitional changes that cause "breaks," that is, discontinuities in several of the major indicator series.

Some of the cyclical indicators included in the BEA indexes have only occasional and mostly minor revisions (average workweek, layoff rate, unemployment duration) or no revisions at all (stock prices, vendor performance, the prime rate). However, for most of the index components the first preliminary figure A_1 (issued in the current month for the previous one) is revised 1–4 times in as many successive months (A_i, $i = 2, 3, 4$). The first two changes generally account for a very high proportion of the total revision.[7]

Let the error term in successive revisions be defined as $E_{it} = A_{it} - A_{1t}$. For most indicators, both the averages taken without regard to sign and the standard deviations of E_{it} tend to increase with i, the index of the time distance between the revisions. The mean errors are predominantly negative, suggesting underestimation of levels in the early data, but they are mostly small and independent of i. Tests that $a_i = 0$ and $b_i = 1$ in the regression equations $A_{it} = a_i + b_i A_{1t} + e_{it}$ produce mixed results. Although for most indicators the F- and t-ratios are not clearly significant, they are so for some series that are based on indirect estimation and, in their early version, seriously incomplete data. The measurement errors revealed by the revisions are not systematically larger in the leading than in the coincident or lagging indicators. The revisions are typically fewer and less diffused over time in the monthly indicators than in quarterly aggregates from the national income and product accounts.[8] However, very large and frequent revisions are found in both sets of time series for such important variables as inflation, monetary changes, inventory investment, and profits.[9] Adjustments for price changes and other procedures that are inevitably intricate and approximate in nature tend to add to the probable error.

For the composite indexes of cyclical indicators, incomplete coverage in

7. For quantitative evidence, see Zarnowitz 1982c, pp. 93–103. This and the following paragraph present in brief the main qualitative findings from this study.

8. The GNP revisions extend from those in each of the three months following the quarter to which the data refer, through those in July of each of the three successive years, to the large but infrequent benchmark overhauls that are important in the historical sense rather than for any practical current purposes. See Zellner 1958; R. Cole 1969b.

9. In recent times, series for various monetary aggregates have been published at monthly and weekly intervals and revised almost as frequently (see, e.g., Pierce et al. 1981). On the importance of revisions in the GNP implicit price deflator, see Keane and Runkle 1990, pp. 722–24. On measures of inventory investment and corporate profits, see Zarnowitz 1982c, pp. 95–96.

the early releases has long presented a major practical problem. In the absence of good and timely estimates for the missing components, this problem is a particularly serious one for series to be used in forecasting such as the leading indexes. Further difficulties in the application and testing of these series arise from occasional discontinuities due to changes in the composition, weights, or other technical aspects of the indexes. (About all of this more will be said later in this chapter.)

Measurement errors are very common in economic data and they affect economic behavior, analysis, and forecasting; yet their role is not well understood. For example, consider tests of the predictive value of the leading index (l) based on forecasts of real GNP (q) obtained from lagged values of q and l. Should l be represented by preliminary values because these alone are available to an authentic ex ante forecaster? And should q be represented by final values because these alone represent the "truth" to be predicted? To answer yes to both questions implies that the forecasts are expected to eliminate correctly the cumulative future errors in the series on real GNP growth (as revealed by the whole string of statistical and conceptual revisions). But these errors may be both highly significant and to a large extent unforecastable. Moreover, the lagged values of q in their final form are unknown to the real-time forecaster. In sum, tests of this type could be severely biased against finding l a good predictor of q because the measures used leave large errors in l but not in q.[10]

Testing forecasts against revised instead of initial values of the target series *may* result in a spurious rejection of the hypothesis that the forecasts are rational or unbiased (cf. Keane and Runkle 1990). However, the errors in the predicted variable can have different consequences, depending entirely on their nature. If the errors are small and random, they will matter little or not at all. If they are significant and systematic but largely predictable, they should optimally be taken into account by the forecaster (see chapter 13).

On the assumption that the revisions, as intended, cumulatively improve the data,[11] they provide important information: the larger, the less stable, and the more stretched out in time they are, the less dependable are the most recent statistics relating to the current economic situation. For series that are not revised, this information is simply lacking: they may or may not have significant measurement errors. The absence of revisions, or the cessation of further revisions, does not prove the absence of errors.

Measures of statistical adequacy help assess the quality of a time series but offer no substitute for the quantitative estimates of error available from the revisions. For 110 *BCD* indicators as of 1975–80, scores for these character-

---

10. Diebold and Rudebusch 1990b follow a method analogous to that described in the text paragraph above, but their target variable is industrial production, which is not as strongly affected by errors that can be inferred from data revisions as real GNP is. See section 11.3.4 below.

11. This is not always true: it is not unusual to find some revisions, in a chain of several, which increase, rather than reduce, the discrepancy between the prior and the final estimate.

istics averaged 70 (out of 100), fell heavily in the 60–79 range, and were not systematically differentiated by broad categories of economic process and cyclical timing.[12]

11.1.5 Information Lags

Fourteen of our cyclical indicators are weekly or daily series that can be smoothed with a minimum loss of timeliness and provide monthly estimates the same month or early in the next month; 67 are monthly series available with lags of 1 month (48), 2 months (15), and 3 month (4); and 29 are quarterly series available some time during the next quarter. The currency scores are 100 for a series that is collected at least weekly, 20 for a quarterly series, and intermediate for monthly series—the lower the score, the longer the lag of release.

Even if a series is available promptly, its month-to-month movement may be so obscured by either seasonal change or irregular variation (noise) as to shed little light on the longer, cyclical movements and trends that are of primary interest for current business analysis and forecasting. To the extent that the seasonal fluctuations are distinct, independent, and stable, they can be reasonably well measured and eliminated (most indicators are presently reported in seasonally adjusted form). The noise element varies greatly across the indicators, as shown by measures computed for each of them in the Bureau of the Census X-11 program of decomposition and seasonal adjustment. The ratio $\bar{I}_i/\bar{C}_i$ compares the irregular to the trend-cycle component of the given series, the average changes in the two being measured over i unit periods. As the span i is increased, $\bar{C}_i$ builds up while $\bar{I}_i$ shows little (and no systematic) change, so the ratio generally declines. The shortest span i, in months, for which $\bar{I}/\bar{C} < 1$ is called MCD (months for cyclical dominance). The smoother a series, the smaller are its $\bar{I}/\bar{C}$ and MCD values. In a set of 81 weekly and monthly indicators, 30 series had MCD = 1, 21 series had MCD = 2, and 30 series had MCD≥3 (37%, 26%, and 37%, respectively). For 29 quarterly indicators, the corresponding frequencies were 4 (14%), 13 (45%), and 12 (41%).

A cross-classification of the series by scores for currency and smoothness shows no tendency for the two ordinal scales to either agree or disagree with each other systematically (see Zarnowitz 1982c, table 4 and pp. 108–10). The coefficient of rank association is here $G = .07$, and the probability of the true value of G being different from 0 seems extremely low (Goodman and Kruskal 1954, 1963). Across the series, then, our measures of the data-release lag (currency) and the signal-detection lag (smoothness) are uncorrelated. By adding these lags for each series, one can obtain a rough estimate of the total lag involved in extracting information from the data.

---

12. See Zarnowitz 1982c, text and table 3, pp. 103 and 106–8. The series show more dispersion within than across such categories.

Table 11.3   **Estimated Information Lags for 110 Cyclical Indicator Series**

Information Lag (months) (1)	Weekly or Monthly (no.) (2)	Quarterly (no.) (3)	All (no.) (4)	All (%) (5)
2	22	0	22	20.0
3	25	0	25	22.7
4	18	4	22	20.0
5	6	13	19	17.3
6	3	11	14	12.7
7	4	1	5	4.6
8	1	0	1	0.9
9	2	0	2	1.8
Total	81	29	110	100.0
Average lag (months)	3.6	5.3	4.1	. . .

Source: Zarnowitz 1982c, text and table 4.

Note: The information lag is the sum of the data-release lag (1–3 months) and the signal-detection lag (1–6 months). The information lags of 2–4 months consist of data-release lags of 1–2 months and signal-detection lags of 1–3 months; the longer information lags include data-release lags of 3 months and signal-detection lags of 4–6 months.

Table 11.3 shows that the lags so calculated vary from 2 to 9 months for the weekly and monthly indicators and from 4 to 7 months for the quarterly indicators. The 41 series (37% of the sample) that have lags of 5 or more months account for about half of the sensitive indicators of fixed and inventory investment, prices, costs, profits, money, and credit. The estimates are conservative in the sense that they ignore whatever could be done to shorten the information lags by skillful data analysis (e.g., use of weekly and monthly data to correct deficit or anticipate tardy monthly and quarterly information) and forecasting (e.g., projections of lead-lag relationships). On the other hand, they are understated because the signal-detection lags are derived from revised observations rather than current figures, which are frequently preliminary and contain more statistical noise. On average, the underestimation is probably 1 or 1.5 months for all the series covered but higher, perhaps 1–3 months, for those series with significant revisions.[13]

Incomplete or defective information can contribute to expectation and decision errors. Furthermore, the longer and more staggered the information lags, the longer will such errors persist and the costlier will be their effects, detection, and correction. The actual lags and errors are unlikely to be a major source of business cycles but can surely play a significant role in their propagation (see chapter 2, secs. 2.4.3 and 2.4.5).

13. These are rough estimates, based on simple methods applicable to large volumes of data at relatively low costs, but they yield generally plausible results. They are, to my knowledge, not contradicted by other studies that use different techniques posing higher data requirements (for further detail and references, see Zarnowitz 1982c, pp. 111–12).

Informational lags and errors impede learning and prediction, yet to counteract them, longer and better forecasts are required. An effective reduction of the time needed to assess the state of the economy in the present and near future is itself a modest but significant forecasting achievement. The leading and confirming indexes can help the forecaster advance further along this way.

11.2   The Composition, Timing Records, and Construction of Composite Indexes

11.2.1   The Present Indexes

The currently published indexes of leading, coincident, and lagging indicators incorporate revisions that the Commerce Department (BEA) introduced in February 1989. Table 11.4 presents a summary of the timing records of these indexes and their components. The measures refer to the seven peaks and seven troughs of business cycles in 1953–82.

The leading index consists now of 11 series drawn from five economic process groups (it includes no series on production or income and none related to inventories). Three cyclically sensitive and important variables that were represented in the past are no longer: corporate profit, the flow of credit, and inventory investment. This is regrettable and presumably due to the deficiencies of the data, which one greatly wishes were remedied. The inclusion of quarterly or tardy monthly series would necessitate either releasing the index with long delays, using some monthly proxies first, or adding the data for these variables only after the initial estimate of the index had been published (at the cost of large index revisions). None of the alternatives are appealing. As a result, the index is somewhat less broadly based than some of its predecessors (see table 11.5 and text below). On the other hand, the new index has the advantage that all of its components are promptly available and subject to smaller revisions than the excluded series. This should make the successive estimates of the index for any month less variable and therefore easier to interpret with some confidence.

Two of the leading series on the 1989 list (*BCD* code numbers 1 and 5) are early indicators of labor market developments; three (8, 20, 92) are built wholly or partly from data on new and unfilled orders received by manufacturers; two (19, 99) are indexes of cyclically sensitive prices of assets (common stocks) and inputs (industrial materials); and 1 each represent residential investment commitments (29), the speed of deliveries (32), consumer expectations (83), and the deflated money stock (106). Except for the newly added index of consumer expectations, all these indicators stand for variables that in one form or another were given some attention in earlier vintages of the leading index as well. The coverage still relies heavily on manufacturing, construction, and selected market and trade data. Efforts to find and add leading indicators of services and international activity have so far met with little success (the change in the consumer price index for services is included in the new composite index of lagging indicators). The available time series in these areas are generally dominated by longer trends and not very cyclical.

Only the future can reveal the predictive potential and usefulness in application of the new indexes and their components, but it is somewhat reassuring to know that at least in the past the cyclical timing of the selected series has been fairly consistent. For the 11 leading indicators, the mean (median) leads at peaks had a range of 7–16 (8–15) months. The standard deviations varied from about 3 to 13 and were smaller than the corresponding means in each case except one (index of consumer expectations). At troughs, the leads were much shorter, averaging 1 month or less for four of the series and 2–5 months for the others. Here the dispersion (S.D.) measures show the same order of magnitude as the means. In other words, the leaders at peaks often had only very short leads or a more nearly coincident timing at troughs (compare cols. 1–3 and 4–6 in the first section of table 11.4). The means (S.D.) of the leads of the composite index itself were approximately 10 (6) and 5 (4) months at business cycle peaks and troughs, respectively (the median lead at troughs was only 2 months).

It will be recalled that the peak-trough differences in timing extend to a great many cyclical indicators (chapter 10). Whereas the leads tend to be much longer at peaks than at troughs of the postwar business cycles, the lags tend to be longer at troughs than at peaks. Indeed, the latter shows up as a clear contrast for the present lagging index of the Commerce Department (BEA) and for each of its seven components (see the last section in table 11.4). In short, the observations for the principal indicators and indexes reflect a more broadly observed phenomenon.

The timing differences are very likely related to the asymmetries of postwar business cycles. We are already familiar with the relevant facts: expansions have typically been much longer and more gradual than contractions. Long-term growth accounts for a part but not all of the apparently strong asymmetries (see chapter 8, sec. 8.3.4). The results of the indicator analysis suggest that separate leading indexes for peaks and troughs could have some significant advantages. In 1975, experimental indexes of this type were constructed with partially positive results (see Zarnowitz and Boschan 1975a, n. 23). They met with the criticism of being too complicated and costly to maintain and use, but recently a very different analysis gave independent support to the same idea (Diebold and Rudebusch 1989).[14]

None of the three composite indexes failed to match any of the recorded 14 business cycle turns of 1953–82, and the same is true of 17 of their component series (table 11.4, col. 7). The series real M2 missed 6 turns, 1 lagging series missed 4, and 3 series (one in each timing category) missed 2 turns, or

---

14. "[T]he use of two indexes, an 'expansion index' and a 'contraction index,' constructed with different components and component weights, could enhance predictive performance" (Diebold and Rudebusch 1989, pp. 386–87).

Table 11.4 Leading, Coincident, and Lagging Indexes and Their Components, Summary Measures of Timing at Business Cycle Peaks and Troughs, 1953–82

	Leads (−) or Lags (+), in Months						B.C. Turns Missed (7)	Extra S.C. Turns (8)
	B.C. Peaks			B.C. Troughs				
	Median (1)	Mean (2)	S.D. (3)	Median (4)	Mean (5)	S.D. (6)		
Leading indicators								
1. Average weekly hours, manufacturing	−10	−9.7	6.6	−1	−1.0	1.0	0	4
5. Average weekly initial claims (inverted)	−11	−10.1	7.0	0	−0.1	2.0	0	4
8. Manufacturers' new orders, consumer goods and materials[a]	−13	−12.1	6.8	−1	−1.4	2.5	0	4
32. Vendor performance, slow deliveries	−9	−10.0	9.4	−4	−4.4	4.2	0	4
20. Contracts & orders, plant & equipment[a]	−8	−7.0	4.2	−1	0.1	4.1	0	2
29. Building permits, new private housing units	−11	−15.0	7.8	−3	−5.4	4.9	0	4
92. Change in manufacturers' unfilled orders[a]	−12	−12.9	7.4	−2	−3.0	3.2	0	6
99. Change in sensitive materials prices[b]	−8	−9.3	8.9	−2	−2.7	2.3	0	6
19. Index of stock prices, 500 common stocks	−9	−9.7	2.6	−4	−4.7	1.8	0	10
106. Money supply, M2[a]	−15	−16.0	6.7	−2.5	−3.5	2.4	2	2
83. Index of consumer expectations	−9	−11.6	12.6	−4	−3.9	3.1	6	4
910. Composite index of 11 leading indicators	−8	−9.7	6.1	−2	−4.6	4.1	0	4
940. Ratio, coincident index to lagging index	−12	−14.6	6.8	−1	−2.6	3.7	0	4

Coincident indicators

41. Employees on nonagricultural payrolls	+2	+1.4	4.9	+1	+0.9	1.1	0	0
51. Personal income less transfer payments	+0.5	+1.0	1.3	−1	−1.0	0.9	2	0
47. Index of industrial production	0	−1.3	2.6	0		0.6	0	2
57. Manufacturing & trade sales[a]	−3	−4.3	3.3	−1	−1.1	1.8	0	0
920. Composite index of 4 roughly coincident indicators	0	−1.6	2.3	−0	−0.6	1.1	0	0

Lagging indicators

91. Average duration of unemployment (inverted)	+1	0	3.6	+8	+9.4	4.9	0	0
77. Ratio of manufacturing and trade inventories to sales	+9	+9.9	4.4	+14	+18.4	13.0	0	4
62. Change in index of unit labor cost, manufacturing	+6	+7.3	4.7	+9	+9.4	2.2	0	10
109. Average prime rate charged by banks	+3	+4.3	3.2	+14	+17.9	19.0	0	4
101. Commercial and industrial loans[a]	+5	+5.7	5.9	+9.5	+9.8	6.0	2	2
95. Ratio of consumer installment credit to personal income	+5	+5.6	3.1	+7	+6.8	3.8	4	4
120. Change in consumer price index for services[b]	+3	+1.8	6.4	+5	+8.3	9.4	0	6
930. Composite index of 7 lagging indicators	+3	+4.7	3.8	+7	+8.4	4.9	0	2

Source: U.S. Department of Commerce, Bureau of Economic Analysis, *Business Conditions Digest (BCD)*, December 1989, p. 104.

Note: The numbers preceding the titles of the series are the *BCD* series numbers. The list of indicators used in this table is the one introduced by the Bureau of Economic Analysis in February 1989 and used presently (see Hertzberg and Beckman 1989). The table is based on leads or lags of specific peak or trough dates that mark the cyclical turning points in the individual indicator series at the corresponding reference peak or trough dates that mark the cyclical turning points in the overall business activity. Seven business cycles are covered, with the following NBER reference dates: peaks, 7/53, 8/57, 4/60, 12/69, 11/73, 1/80, and 7/81; troughs, 5/54, 4/58, 2/61, 11/70, 3/75, 7/80, 11/82.

Abbreviations: B.C. = business cycle; S.C. = specific cycle; S.D. = standard deviation.

[a]1982 dollars.

[b]Smoothed by an autoregressive moving-average filter developed by Statistics Canada.

1 phase, each. Earlier indexes had similarly good records in the sense of having missed very few business cycle turns. Of course, it helps that this is a retrospective analysis using currently available, revised data; spotting the turns ex ante in preliminary data is at times much more difficult. Even so, missing the turning points of business cycles is definitely not the most important type of error for these indicators; giving false signals is.

This is readily seen from the contrast between the rare instances of business cycle turns missed and the high frequencies of extra specific-cycle turns missed (cf. cols. 7 and 8). Each of the leading series had some cyclical movements of its own that were not correlated with the general economic fluctuations. The modal number of extra turns was 4, some series had 2 and 6, but one (the stock price index) had 10. Interestingly, a very similar statement can be made about the lagging indicators, except that one of these had no extra turns (one, the index of unit labor cost, had 10).

As would be expected, the four comprehensive coincident indicators show a record of almost one-to-one correspondence with business cycle peaks and troughs, that is, a minimal number of errors of either type. About one third of the individual comparisons at peaks and half of those at troughs were exact coincidences (0), with the rest divided between mostly short leads and lags. Employment was slightly lagging.

The coincident index itself led at three peaks, lagged at two troughs, and had the timing 0 at each of the other nine business cycle turns. The ratio of this index to the lagging index (which reflects inversely the role of costs of labor, inventory, and finance; see chapter 10) tended to lead, by long intervals at peaks and short ones at troughs.

11.2.2   Five Successive Lists of Leading Indicators, 1950–89

The first list of NBER business cycle indicators was based on a study of nearly 500 series that varied in length but ended in 1933 (Mitchell and Burns 1938). It included 71 series "tolerably consistent in their timing in relation to business cycle revivals" and a subset of 21 "most trustworthy" of these indicators. The next review used about 800 series through 1938, classified them by timing, and selected indicators of recession as well as revival (Moore 1950). After another decade, it was possible to analyze still more series and extend the measures through 1958 (Moore 1961). Revised short and supplementary lists of indicators were shown, along with the first composite index of leading indicators. In 1966 another study introduced an explicit scoring plan and used it to evaluate more than a hundred series (Moore and Shiskin 1967). The results included new long and short lists of U.S. indicators classified by cyclical timing and economic process, and corresponding composite indexes.

In 1972–75, the BEA conducted a comprehensive appraisal of cyclical indicators and indexes with the cooperation of members of the NBER staff (Zarnowitz and Boschan 1975a and 1975b). Between 1967 and 1975 inflation intensified and two recessions occurred (1970 and 1973–75). Some of the old nominal indicators needed to be deflated to perform well under the new conditions; other revisions became advisable for other reasons, including as usual changes in the available data. The last, rather limited review of the indicators was completed by the BEA staff in 1989.

Table 11.5 presents the complete record of all the revisions in the short lists of the leading indicators for both revivals and recessions from 1950 through 1989. These are also the lists of the components of the successive composite leading indexes since 1960. The numerous footnotes cite the reasons for each of the changes made, as given at the time. They also cover any interim revisions made between the five dates when the new lists were published. Because the table provides detailed references and documentation, the text to follow is limited to a few general explanations.

A quick glance at table 11.5 seems likely to give the impression of great variability, as if almost all selections were transitory and the composition of the lists or indexes was quite unstable over time. But this would be very misleading. A closer look shows that each list retained several series from the previous one and that most of the changes were substitutions or additions within the same economic process groups (see Summary at the end of the table). In other words, most of the revisions replaced some series with other representations of similar variables. Often the reason was the availability of new data deemed conceptually or statistically superior or the discontinuation of old data. Some changes, as noted earlier, were dictated by considerations of timeliness; others, by unpredictable events in government or business (see, e.g., nn. *d* and *k;* the latter had partly to do with the lack of good current data on new business telephones after the breakup of AT&T in 1982). To be sure, at times errors were made and reversed when recognized (see nn. *e* and *cc*).

To the extent that revisions take time but improve the data, there is inevitably a conflict between the promptness and accuracy of estimates and forecasts. But the presumption that the more recent indexes are better does not mean that the earlier ones have failed. On the contrary, as shown in chapter 10, sec. 10.7, the 1950 indexes, though based on pre-1938 data, would have performed reasonably well in terms of timing at the business cycle turns of 1948–75.

11.2.3   Index Construction Methods and Revisions

There are six basic steps in the calculation of a composite index in the traditional NBER-BEA style. (1) Month-to-month percentage changes are computed for each component series expressed originally as levels.[15] Series expressed as changes are differenced. (2) For each series, the changes obtained in step 1 are divided by their long-run average without regard to sign.

---

15. Formulas ensuring symmetrical treatment of positive and negative changes are used. For a more detailed narrative and algebraic explanation of the methodology, see U.S. Department of Commerce, Bureau of Economic Analysis 1984, pp. 65–69.

Table 11.5   **Five Successive Lists of Leading Indicators, 1950–89**

Group & Number of Economic Process[a]; Title, Source, & No. of Series[b]	Indicator Lists of				
	1950 (1)	1960 (2)	1966 (3)	1975 (4)	1989 (5)
Marginal Employment Adjustments (I)					
Average workweek, production workers, manufacturing (3; 1)	x	x	x	x	x
Gross accession rate, manufacturing[c]		x			
Nonagricultural placements, all industries[d]			x		
Layoff rate, manufacturing[e]		x		x	
Average weekly initial claims, state unemployment insurance inverted (2; 5)					x
Orders & Deliveries—Consumption & Trade (III)					
New orders, durable goods, industries, current dollars (2; 6)[f]	x	x	x		
New orders, consumer goods & materials, constant dollars (1, 2; 7)				x	x
Change in manufacturers' unfilled orders, durable goods, constant dollars, smoothed (2; 26)[g]					x
Vendor performance—slower deliveries diffusion index (32)[h]				x	x
Index of consumer expectations (83)[i]					x
Formation of Business Enterprises (IV)					
New incorporations, number (13)	x				
Net change in business population, Q[j]		x			
Index of net business formation (1; 12)[k]			x	x	
Business Investment Commitments (IV)					
Commercial & industrial building contracts, floorspace (9)[l]	x	x			
Contracts & orders for plant & equipment, current dollars[m]				x	
Contracts and orders for plant and equipment, constant dollars (1, 2; 20)[n]				x	x
Residential Construction Commitments (IV)					
Residential building contracts, floorspace[o]	x				
Housing starts, new private units (2; 28)		x			
Building permits, new private housing units (2; 29)[p]				x	x
Inventory Investment (V)					
Change in business inventories, current dollars, Q (1; 245)[q]		x			
Change in book value, manufacturing & trade inventories (1, 2; 31)[r]			x		
Net change in inventory on hand & on order, constant dollars smoothed (1, 2; 31)[s]				x	

Table 11.5   Continued

Group & Number of Economic Process[a]; Title, Source, & No. of Series[b]	Indicator Lists of				
	1950 (1)	1960 (2)	1966 (3)	1975 (4)	1989 (5)
Sensitive Commodity Prices (VI)					
Wholesale price index, 28 basic commodities[f]	X				
Industrial materials price index[u]		X	X		
Percentage change, WPI of crude materials, excluding foods & feeds, smoothed (1, 3; 99)[v]				X	
Percentage change in a revised index of sensitive materials prices (1, 3; 99)					X
Stock Prices (VI)					
Dow-Jones index, industrial stock prices[w]	X				
S&P stock price index, 500 common stocks (19)[x]		X	X	X	X
Profits and Profit Margins (VI)					
Corporate profits after taxes, current dollars, Q (1; 16)[y]	X	X			
Ratio, price to unit labor cost, manufacturing (1, 3; 26)[z]			X		
Credit Difficulties (VII)					
Current liabilities of business failures (14)[aa]	X	X			
Credit Flows (III)					
Net change in consumer installment credit (4; 113)[bb]		X			
Money (VII)					
Money supply, M1, in constant dollars (1, 4; 105)[cc]				X	
Money supply, M2, in constant dollars (1, 4; 106)[cc]					X
Percentage change in total liquid assets, smoothed (1, 4; 104)[dd]				X	
Summary Number of:					
Component series in each list	8	12	12	12	11
Series unchanged from previous list	n.a.[ee]	4	5	4	7
Substitutions within same group	n.a.	4	4	5	2
Additions within same group	n.a.	2	2	1	2
Additions in new group	n.a.	2	1	2	0
Deletions from previous list		4	3	3	2

Sources: Moore 1950, 1961; Moore and Shiskin 1967; Zarnowitz and Boschan 1975a; Hertzberg and Beckman 1989. See text for more detail.

[a]Roman numerals denote economic processes. See table 11.1 for the titles.

[b]The first number in parentheses following the title of the series denotes the source as follows: 1. U.S. Department of Commerce, Bureau of Economic Analysis; 2. U.S. Department of Commerce, Bureau of the Census; 3. U.S. Department of Labor, Bureau of Labor Statistics; 4. Board of Governors of the

(*continued*)

Table 11.5   Continued

Federal Reserve System. The second number in parentheses identifies the series in the *BCD* and the *Survey of Current Business* (*SCB*). The numbers are given only for the series carried most recently in the *BCD* or currently in the *SCB*. For the corresponding information on the other series, see footnotes below.

[c]Source 3; old *BCD* series no. 2. Replaced in 1966 by nonagricultural placements (source 3; old *BCD* series no. 4), which "provide broader coverage and prompter availability" (Moore and Shiskin 1967, p. 69; henceforth M-S). Discontinued in February 1982.

[d]Replaced in September 1969 by average weekly initial claims for state unemployment insurance (see note *e* below). Stated reason: Shift in emphasis of the public offices of the U.S. Department of Labor from total placements to services for disadvantaged workers. These services take more staff time than is required for qualified workers. The effect of this policy change has been to slow down the number of placements. Data not updated since June 1970, discontinued July 1971 (see *BCD*, September 1969 and July 1971, p. III).

[e]Source 3; old *BCD* series no. 3. Omitted in 1966 because "workweek and placements enough for short list" (M-S). Reinstated to replace average weekly initial claims in 1975 because "layoff rate leads more consistently at troughs" (Zarnowitz and Boschan 1975a, p. 6; henceforth Z-B). Discontinued in February 1982 and replaced again with average weekly initial claims.

[f]Replaced in 1975 by a series of real new orders received by manufacturing industries producing primarily consumer goods and materials. This allows separation of these orders from orders for equipment, which are aggregated with contracts for plant (see note below). Deflation needed for better cyclical performance since the late 1960s because of persistent rise in the general price level (Z-B).

[g]Includes the on-order portion of the series net change in inventories on hand and on order in constant dollars, which was dropped from the leading index in 1989 because the current data for the on-hand portion are not available in time to be included in the initial estimate of the index. Covers all durable goods, including also capital goods and defense products. (See Hertzberg and Beckman 1989, pp. 97–98; henceforth H-B).

[h]Based on surveys by Purchasing Management of Chicago and, since 1989, by the National Association of Purchasing Management. "Best available indicator of changes in delivery lags" (Z-B).

[i]Compiled by the University of Michigan's Survey Research Center. "Added to provide a new dimension to the leading index" (H-B).

[j]Source: Office of Business Economics, U.S. Department of Commerce. Quarterly. Replaced the monthly Dun and Bradstreet, Inc., series on new incorporations in 1960 because the latter "is occasionally affected strongly by changes in legislation, especially in the tax laws, . . . and partly because the net changes take account of discontinuances" (Moore 1961, p. 66; henceforth M61). Discontinued after 1959:4 and replaced by the monthly index of net business formation. For references and comparisons, see M61, ch. 14).

[k]Original sources: Dun and Bradstreet, Inc., and Bureau of the Census. Suspended from the index in March 1987. This series "deteriorated as a measure of change in business population, primarily because of the poor quality of one component of the series and the unavailability of data of another component in the time for inclusion in the initial release" (see *BCD*, February 1987, p. III).

[l]Source: McGraw-Hill Information Systems Company. Replaced in 1966 by contracts and orders for plant and equipment (see note *m* below) because of "poor timing and conformity record since 1950. The equivalent value series, plus privately owned public utilities, is included in the series on contracts and orders" (M-S).

[m]"Most comprehensive series on new investment commitments by business enterprises"; new since 1960 list (M-S).

[n]"Deflation is needed for better cyclical performance since the late 1960's" (Z-B).

[o]Source: F. W. Dodge Corp. Replaced by housing starts in 1960 because starts are "less erratic . . . and currently published more promptly" (M61, p. 65).

[p]Compared with housing starts, "permits series is smoother" (M-S).

[q]Volatile but persistently leading, especially at peaks, since 1939 (M61, pp. 68–69).

[r]Replaced the quarterly inventory investment in 1966 because "monthly series more current" (M-S).

[s]"Concept of including stocks on order is better. Deflation is needed for better cyclical performance" (Z-B).

Table 11.5   **Continued**

ʳSource: BLS. Unweighted geometric mean of relatives for 28 products.

ᵘSource: BLS. Includes daily prices of 13 raw or simply processed materials. Conformed more closely to business cycles than the broader index, which includes prices of foodstuffs "subject to vagaries of weather conditions and government farm price policies" (M61, p. 69).

ᵗ"Percent change is better than level. Leads are more consistent, especially since the late 1960's (Z-B). Revised in 1989 to improve the methodology and date consistency (H-B).

ʷSource: Dow-Jones & Co., Inc. Unweighted mean of prices of 30 industrial stocks.

ˣSource: Standard & Poor's Corp. New monthly index of prices of 500 common stocks introduced in 1957; before then coverage smaller but increasing (from 198 stocks in 1918 to 480 in 1957). The S&P index has the advantage of greater coverage and diversification compared with the Dow-Jones index.

ʸDropped from the index in 1975 because of being "quarterly and tardy (low score for currency)" (Z-B).

ᶻOld *BCD* series no. 17. Ratio of price to unit cost, manufacturing, dropped from the index in 1975 because it "failed to lead at the last three business cycle troughs (1958–70)" (Z-B).

ᵃᵃSource: Dun & Bradstreet, Inc. Dropped from the index in 1966 because of "poor timing and conformity record since 1948" (M-S).

ᵇᵇIncluded in the index in 1966 because of "wide cyclical movements and consistent leads" (M-S). Dropped from the index in 1975 with the comment that it "lacks timeliness. In recent period, very erratic and more nearly coincident than leading at troughs" (Z-B).

ᶜᶜDeflated by the consumer price index. Included in the index in 1975 as an "important measure of the quantity of money in real terms. Good scores for indicator performance" (Z-B). Replaced in March 1979 by M2 money supply deflated by the CPI. The more comprehensive monetary aggregate was favored by changes due to deregulation of banking, new interest-earning and highly liquid types of deposits, and greater incentives to economize on the use of money.

ᵈᵈIncluded in the index in 1975 as a "comprehensive measure of changes in wealth held in liquid form by private nonfinancial investors" (Z-B). Replaced in February 1983 by change in business and consumer credit outstanding (1, 4; 111), which had a better record of cyclical conformity and timing in recent years. The credit change series was dropped from the index in January 1989.

ᵉᵉn.a. = not applicable.

This standardization makes the mean absolute value for each so-transformed series equal to 1, and it prevents the more volatile series from dominating the index. (3) For each month, the values of all available component series obtained in step 2 are averaged.[16] (4) The resulting changes are then adjusted for the leading (L) and lagging (Lg) indexes so that their long-run absolute averages are equal to that of the coincident index (C). This index standardization procedure (division by the ratio of long-run averages L/C and Lg/C, respectively) has the purpose of facilitating the use of the three indexes as a consistent system. (5) The so-modified average changes are cumulated into a "raw" index for each of the three sets of indicators. (6) A common trend is established for the three indexes, which can be viewed as a linear approximation to the secular movement in aggregate economic activity.[17] The trend adjustment

16. Before the last BEA revision (i.e., through January 1989) the average was a weighted one, with the total scores of the series serving as weights. Since then, in the computation of the revised indexes, the components of each index are assigned equal weights. The change had relatively little effect because the weights based on the scores of the series were not very different from 1 (see Hertzberg and Beckman 1989, p. 99).

17. Before 1989 the target trend was the average of the long trends in the four components of the coincident index (0.268% per month). For the latest revised indexes, the trend is that of real GNP (0.261% per month). Clearly, the two trends are almost the same, so the effect of this change was minimal (Hertzberg and Beckman 1989, p. 100).

enhances the usefulness of the indexes by making them differ only with respect to short-term, mainly cyclical movements.

In three decades of development, the composite indexes of leading, coincident, and lagging indicators spread to many countries, aided by and promot-
ing the growth of information about national and international economic fluctuations (Klein and Moore 1985; Moore and Moore 1985). Following Mintz
1969, methods of combining series in terms of deviations from trend or rates
of growth were devised to track growth cycles, which have become more common than business cycles. These methods share the several basic elements of
index construction listed above, but they adapt them depending on the treatment of trends and weighting and differ in many technical details. Interesting
work on composite index construction has been done in Australia (Haywood
1973) and by the British Central Statistical Office (CSO 1976), Statistics Canada (Rhoades 1982), the Organization of Economic Cooperation and Development (OECD 1987), and Japan's Economic Planning Agency (EPA, since
the early 1970s). A useful comparison of these methods is provided in Boschan and Banerji 1990, where a procedure is suggested that uses the standard
deviation of smoothed, detrended series as the standardization factor. The amplitude standardization is at the core of the construction of these indexes. It is
itself a form of weighting that equalizes the volatility of the index components. Scoring is useful in choosing the component series but weighting based
on the scores may or may not be helpful (it could be redundant). Transformations of the individual series are needed to induce stationarity as appropriate
in each particular case.

The U.S. composite indexes are updated near the end of each month by
computing the preliminary figures for the previous month and recomputing a
number of preceding values.[18] From time to time, recomputations are made to
incorporate longer term, benchmark and seasonal revisions. In addition, the
standardization factors for the components and the indexes, and the trend adjustment factors, are updated at longer intervals.[19]

These statistical revisions, as well as the definitional revisions (compositional and weight changes), make it necessary to differentiate clearly between
the uses of preliminary estimates and the revised index data. Evaluations of
the latter have their role in historical and analytical contexts, but authentic ex
ante or real-time forecasting always involves preliminary values. Diebold and
Rudebusch (1987) examined the stochastic properties of the first-released data
and subsequent revisions for the Department of Commerce index of leading
indicators. They report that in 1983–87 the revisions (particularly the earliest
ones, which contained the most information) behaved approximately as if
they were errors of efficient forecasts. This was not the case in 1979–81, when
measurement errors due to the missing index components were much more
severe.

18. For 11 months before 1987 and for 5 months in the latest revised indexes.
19. Eight times between August 1970 and January 1989.

11.3   Forecasting with Leading Indicators

11.3.1   Some General Observations

By their own testimony, practicing forecasters use leading indicators widely, along with other methods and information. In predicting the course of the economy in the near future, business economists generally rely on "a complicated combination of quantitative and qualitative elements—with a heavy emphasis placed upon the exercise of judgment" (Butler, Kavesh, and Platt 1974, p. 207). The major expenditure components of GNP are forecast with the aid of theory, statistical procedures such as regression, and assumptions about policy and other external changes. The GNP accounting framework and checks and adjustments for consistency and plausibility are then used to derive the overall forecasts. As documented in chapter 13 (sec. 13.8), evidence from surveys shows that most professional analysts of the short-term economic outlook favor this flexible and eclectic approach, labeled the "informal GNP model." When asked to rank items on a short list of general forecasting techniques according to their own usage, most respondents chose the informal GNP model as first. But very few replies referred only to this or any other single method; combinations prevail heavily. Many of the surveyed forecasters reported using leading indicators and outside macroeconometric models, which were given predominantly second or third ranks. (Of course, some forecasters work primarily with their own full-scale econometric models, but their number is relatively small.) Anticipations surveys and "other methods" (such as time-series analysis) received fewer references and were cast mostly in subsidiary roles.

The methods are broadly defined and jointly applied so that it is hardly possible to isolate and assess the contribution of each (more on this in chapter 13). The surveys provide no measures of just how well the leading and confirming indicators and indexes serve their users, although they affirm credibly that these time series are in fact regularly and extensively employed as tools for the analysis of current and forecasting of future business conditions.

To test the predictive value of the leading indicators, it is necessary to specify the data (usually a leading index and/or its components); the target (all changes in some representation of aggregate economic activity; turning points in business cycles or the selected aggregate); and the procedure or rule to be applied (regressions of coincident on leading variables; filtering of the leading series to forecast peaks and troughs). A double dichotomy has emerged in the literature. (1) Some writers concentrate on the prediction of turning points, arguing that this is the most appropriate or the most important function of leading indicators, and that the economy behaves differently in the vicinity of peaks and troughs or differently in expansions than in contractions. Others use the leaders simply as linear predictors of all successive values of some measure of economic activity. (2) Most tests of either sort have been based on revised data as of the time of the study, but some have tried to re-create the actual, real-time forecasting situation by employing preliminary data available at the time of the forecast.

11.3.2   Tests of Turning-Point Predictions

Several studies attempted to evaluate leading indicators and indexes as predictors of cyclical turns, that is, sustained changes of direction in aggregate economic activity. Such appraisals require that a set of filtering rules be considered. Not each monthly wiggle in the leading index need be significant, and excessive concern with a single month's movement must be severely discouraged.

Vaccara and Zarnowitz (1978a, 1978b) considered two very simple rules. (1) Let three consecutive monthly declines in the leading index (1975 version) signal a downturn, and three consecutive rises, an upturn. This yielded mean leads of 8.8 and 3.2 months at business cycle peaks and troughs in 1948–76, no missed turns, and five "extra cycles."[20] Because 3 months must elapse before a turning point is identified, a minimum lead of 4 months is required for a sufficiently early warning. Leads at least this long did occur at all five peaks covered but only at three of the six troughs. (2) As an alternative, treat each directional change in the trailing 6-month moving average of the index as a turning-point signal. This rule reduces the requisite effective lead time to 2 months. The mean leads are here 5.6 and 1.0 months at peaks and troughs, respectively. Again, there are no missed turns and five false signals each of peaks and troughs.

Earlier, Hymans (1973) applied the rule of two consecutive monthly declines (rises) in expansion (contraction) to the leading index constructed in 1966. As might have been expected, this resulted in an unacceptably large number of false predictions, particularly of peaks. The assumption that the forecaster has timely knowledge of the current phase of the business cycle is hardly justified in the critical periods around peaks and troughs. Hymans constructed an alternative index of leading indicators based on spectral analysis, using the same components as the 1966 NBER index. This method combines indicator components corresponding to four cyclical periodicities (of 60, 40, 30, and 24 months) and so filters out false signals much more effectively, but at the cost of strongly reducing the size and frequency of the leads.

Filtering rules typically involve trade-offs of currency for accuracy: the more smoothing, the fewer the extra turns but also the shorter the effective lead time at true turns. This is so whether one requires longer runs (more months of maintained direction of movement) or longer spans (more months over which to measure the change). To get better signals, the magnitude of changes in the indicators should be taken into account as well as their direction.

---

20. Three extra cycles were associated with the growth cycle slowdowns in 1950–51, 1962, and 1966. The other two involved declines that lasted only 3 months each.

Combining selected leading series into indexes can greatly reduce the frequency of false predictions of turning points but cannot eliminate the problem. The leading indexes issue warnings not only of recessions but also of cyclical retardations, that is, phases when the overall real growth rates fall below their long-term average but remain positive (except possibly for an occasional brief slippage below 0). In sum, these indexes predict best the "growth cycles" in trend-adjusted aggregates of output and employment. This was found to be true as well for Japan, Canada, and Western Europe (Moore 1983, chs. 5 and 6). What is needed, therefore, is a method that would allow us to discriminate in a timely fashion between recessions and major slowdowns and thereby safeguard against the main type of "extra turns" that occur in practical forecasting.

To this purpose, a sequential signaling system has been devised and tested with some promising results in Zarnowitz and Moore 1982. The long-term trends built into both the leading and the coincident indexes are 3.3% per annum, and the standard deviations of their random components are approximately 1.0%. Now consider smoothed 6-month percentage changes in these indexes, calculated at compound annual rates from preliminary data available at the time of forecast.[21] This yields two trendless series to be labeled the "leading index rate" (L) and the "coincident index rate" (C). The procedure is to monitor their movements on a current basis, paying special attention to two percentage bands: 3.3 ± 1.0 and 0 ± 1.0. The first signal of a business cycle peak (P1) occurs when the leading index rate falls below the upper band, while the coincident index rate, which will typically be higher, remains nonnegative. In short, P1: $L < 2.3$, $C \geq 0$. The second signal of a peak is observed when the leading rate falls below the lower band and the coincident rate falls below the upper band; that is, P2: $L < -1.0$, $C < 2.3$. The third and last signal (P3) is defined by $L < 0$, $C < -1.0$; that is, the coincident rate falls below the lower band, and the leading rate remains negative. A signal is invalidated when either index rate, after declining across a band, rises again above it; it is not invalidated when L or C merely backs up into the band and stays there.

Table 11.6 presents the record of these signals based on historical data for the period through September 1976 and on preliminary data thereafter. The four slowdowns not followed by recessions (in 1951, 1962, 1966, and 1984) were all associated with prompt P1 signals. In 1951, P2 followed P1 by 4 months, adding to uncertainty, but in the other instances there were no further warnings. The absence of P2 should have ruled out a false prediction, and the absence of P3 a false identification, of a business cycle peak. That the signals would have been reasonably timely on most occasions is suggested by the following overall timing means (standard deviations): P1 led P2 by 5 (2)

---

21. This is done by dividing the current month's index by the average of the 12 preceding months and raising the ratio to the 12/6.5 power (the center of the average is located 6.5 months before the current month).

Table 11.6 Sequential Signals of Slowdown and Recession, 1951–90

Dates of Signals[a]				Leads (−) or Lags (+), in Months, at Business Cycle Peaks				Leads (−) or Lags (+) in Months, at Growth Cycle Peaks		
P1 (L < 2.3, C ≥ 0) (1)	P2 (L < −1.0, C < 2.3) (2)	P3 (L < 0, C < −1.0) (3)	Business Cycle Peak[b] (4)	P1 (5)	P2 (6)	P3 (7)	Growth Cycle Peak[b] (8)	P1 (9)	P2 (10)	P3 (11)
3/51	7/51	...	none	...	...	...	3/51	0	+4	...
6/53	8/53	9/53	7/53	−1	+1	+2	3/53	+3	+5	+6
1/56	7/56	9/57	8/57	−19	−13	+1	2/57	−13	−7	+7
9/59	6/60	9/60	4/60	−7	+2	+5	2/60	−5	+4	+7
5/62	...	...	none	...	...	...	5/62	0	...	...
6/66	...	...	none	...	...	...	6/66	0	...	...
6/69	11/69	4/70	12/69	−6	−1	+4	3/69	+3	+8	+13
8/73	1/74	3/74	11/73	−3	+2	+4	3/73	+5	+10	+12
11/78	5/79	3/80	1/80	−14	−8	+2	12/78	−1	+5	+15
6/81	8/81	10/81	7/81	−1	+1	+3	none	...	...	...
7/84	...	...	none	...	...	...	6/84	+1	...	...
11/87	8/90[c]	10/90	7/90	[d]	+1	+3	2/89	−15	+18	+20
Averages: sample period (before 10/1976)										
Mean lead (−) or lag (+)				−7	−2	+3		−1	+4	+9
Standard deviation				7	6	2		6	6	3
Averages: postsample period (since 10/1976)										
Mean lead (−) or lag (+)				−8	−2	+3		−5	+12	+18
Standard deviation				9	5	1		9	9	4

Source: Zarnowitz and Moore 1982; reprinted in slightly updated form in Moore 1983, table 4-7.

[a]For full definition of the signals, see text. Revised data for the indexes (taken from U.S. Department of Commerce, Bureau of Economic Analysis 1977) are used prior to October 1976; preliminary data (taken from various issues of *BCD* through March 1990 and the Survey of Current Business for April 1990 to July 1990) are used for the period October 1976 to June 1990.

[b]Dated according to the NBER reference chronologies.

[c]An earlier P2 signal (2/90) was canceled in 5/90 when L > 1.0.

[d]The early 11/87 signal cannot be meaningfully related to the business cycle peak of July 1990.

months, P2 led P3 by 5 (5) months, and growth cycle peaks led business cycle peaks by 7 (4) months.

Sequences of all three signals occurred before each of the seven recessions covered, and only at these times.[22] They were short and concentrated when there was little or no warning from a prior slowdown, as in 1953 and 1981; they were long and spread out when protracted slack phases preceded the downturns. If very early signals are "premature" in the sense of lacking credibility, P1 and P2 in 1956 and P1 in 1978 would qualify as such because each of these events anticipated the corresponding business cycle peaks by more than a year.

The "band approach" to sequential signaling produced no false alarms at all during the turbulent years 1976–83 (the first half of our postsample period).[23] This success is probably attributable in part to the fact that no slowdown-without-recession occurred in that period. But the P1 signals also announced and accompanied the 1984–86 retardation in its first 1.5 years; then T2 and T3 signals predicted the end of this phase in its last year (table 11.7).[24] Another P1 signal appeared first in November 1987, after the stock market crash, but it was neither canceled nor confirmed by P2 before the new slowdown, which is now known to have started in or about February 1989. A P2 warning flashed in February 1990 but was canceled in May and reinstated in August; and a P3 signal confirmed the downturn in October.

At business cycle troughs, the first signal (T1) occurs when the L rate rises across the lower band (0 ± 1%) while the C rate remains less than 1.0%. The second signal (T2) is given when L rises across the upper band (3.3 ± 1%) and C rises above 1.0%. The third signal (T3) requires that both L and C cross the upper band from below, that is, rise above 4.3%. False signals of troughs are defined, analogously to those of peaks, as reverse crossing through the bands. They are infrequent and therefore relatively unimportant. As demonstrated in table 11.7, the signals of business cycle troughs are less dispersed but much tardier than those of peaks. Full recognition of peaks (P3) required 1–5 months after the event, not long considering the irreducible lags of measurement and detection in noisy data. In contrast, full recognition of troughs (T3) required 5–13 months (cf. col. 7 in tables 11.6 and 11.7). The longer lags at troughs simply reflect the lack of earlier signals from the indicators.

22. Sufficient data are not available to make the calculations for the 1948 peak, but P3 arrived no later than January 1949 and possibly earlier.

23. The reverse crossings through the bands, which constitute the false signals in this approach, are very infrequent for both index rates, L and C, whether preliminary or first revised data are used. Also, the percentages of the observations falling into the two bands have been relatively small for L and C in 1948–81 (but larger in the 1980s). In contrast, spurious turning-point predictions abound in the alternative "level approach" when currently available preliminary data are used. In this system, critical levels of 3.3% and 0% perform the functions of the bands 2.3%–4.3% and − 1.0%– + 1.0%, respectively. When the first revised data are used, which implies a delay of 1 month, the frequency of false signals is greatly reduced. See Zarnowitz and Moore 1982.

24. In growth cycles where no P3 signal is reached, T1 is usually skipped (but see table 11.7, n. *c*). T2 then may cancel a previous P1 or P2 signal; T3 marks renewed above-average growth.

Table 11.7   Sequential Signals of Recovery, 1949–86

Dates of Signals[a]			Business Cycle Trough[b]	Leads (−) or Lags (+), in Months, at Business Cycle Troughs			Growth Cycle Trough[b]	Leads (−) or Lags (+), in Months, at Growth Cycle Troughs		
T1 (L > 1.0, C < 1.0) (1)	T2 (L > 4.3, C > 1.0) (2)	T3 (L > 4.3, C > 4.3) (3)	(4)	T1 (5)	T2 (6)	T3 (7)	(8)	T1 (9)	T2 (10)	T3 (11)
8/49	1/50	3/50	10/49	−2	+3	+5	10/49	−2	+3	+5
1/52[c]	3/52[d]	8/52	none	...	...	...	7/52	−6	−4	+1
5/54	11/54	12/54	5/54	0	+6	+7	8/54	−3	+3	+4
6/58	10/58	11/58	4/58	+2	+6	+7	4/58	+2	+6	+7
3/61	6/61	8/61	2/61	+1	+4	+6	2/61	+1	+4	+6
...	2/63	5/63	none	...	...	...	10/64	...	−20	−17
...	5/67	11/67	none	...	...	...	10/67	...	−5	+1
11/70	5/71	12/71	11/70	0	+6	+13	11/70	0	+6	+13
6/75	9/75	11/75	3/75	+3	+6	+8	3/75	+3	+6	+8
9/80	12/80	4/81	7/80	+2	+5	+9	7/80	+2	+5	+9
7/82	4/83	6/83	11/82	−4	+5	+7	12/82	−5	+4	+6
...	12/85	4/86	none	...	...	...	1/87	...	−13	−9

Averages: sample period (before 10/1976)

Mean Lead (−) or Lag (+)				+1	+5	+8		−1	0	+3
Standard Deviation				2	1	3		3	9	8

Averages: postsample period (since 10/1976)

Mean Lead (−) or Lag (+)				−1	+5	+8		−2	−1	+2
Standard Deviation				4	0	1		5	10	10

Source: Zarnowitz and Moore 1982, reprinted in slightly updated form in Moore 1983, table 4-8.

[a] See n. *a* in table 11.6.

[b] See n. *b* in table 11.6.

[c] Note that the C rate fell below 1% but not below 0 in the slowdown of 1951–52; that is, no P3 occurred before this T1 signal.

[d] The C rate fell below 0 for a single month in July 1952, probably in connection with the major steel strike, but both L and C rates rose sharply beginning in August.

As for the *average* timing at business cycle peaks, P1 led by 7–8 months in both the sample and the postsample periods, P2 led by 2–4 months, and P3 lagged by 2–3 months. Shorter leads and longer lags characterized the timing of the same events at growth cycle peaks. T1 tended to signal business cycle troughs at approximately the time of their occurrence, T2 5 months later, and T3 8 months later. At growth cycle troughs, the leads and lags of the T signals were on average shorter but much more dispersed.

In terms of the latest revised data first published by the Department of Commerce in March 1989, the means (standard deviations) of the leads or lags of the signals, in months, are as follows:

	P1	P2	P3	T1	T2	T3
At business cycle turns	−7 (6)	−3 (5)	+2 (1)	0 (2)	+5 (1)	+8 (3)
At growth cycle turns	−2 (6)	+4 (5)	+9 (3)	−1 (2)	−1 (9)	+4 (8)

These statistics are closely similar to those computed from earlier and preliminary data in tables 11.6 and 11.7 (all discrepancies fall in the range of −1 to +1 months). To be sure, comparisons of individual observations disclose some larger effects of the revisions, but even so, few of the differences would matter greatly.

11.3.3   Probabilities of Recession and Recovery

Several recent papers discuss the implications of the assumption that macroeconomic variables are subject to two different probability distribution functions, one of which applies in business expansions and the other in contractions. The switches from the former to the latter or vice versa are supposed to occur suddenly at random time points and be unobserved; they can only be inferred from the data according to some model and prediction rules. Thus Neftçi (1982) splits the data on the composite index of leading indicators for 1948–70 into "downturn regimes" and "upturn regimes," apparently relying in the main on judgment. He then smoothes the historical frequency distributions of the monthly changes in the index with a 3-month centered moving average to estimate the probability distributions separately for the two regimes. His formula for assessing the probability of recession is recursive and dynamic in that it includes the previous month's outcome and cumulates the probabilities from 0 at the start of each expansion to 100% at the end. It also involves a prior probability distribution based on the assumption that the likelihood of a downturn increases slightly in each month as the expansion ages.[25]

25. Let p_t be the probability of an imminent peak this month (p_{t-1}, last month); let p_t^e be the probability that the latest observation came from the distribution for expansions, and p_t^c that it came from the distribution for contractions; and let Π_t be the prior probability of a peak based solely on the length of expansion to date. Then

$$p' = \frac{[p_{t-1} + \Pi_t (1 - p_{t-1})p_t^c}{[p_{t-1} + \Pi_t(1 - p_{t-1})p_t^c] + [(1 - p_{t-1})p_t^e(1 - \Pi_t)]} .$$

A signal of a nearby recession is issued when the probability computed by the formula exceeds a preset level of confidence. Neftçi, in two illustrations using the 90% level, shows that the leading index would have given warnings of recession in August 1973 and April 1979 (1982, pp. 238–40).[26]

The assumption that the life expectancy of an expansion is a steadily declining function of its duration is questionable (see chapter 8, sec. 8.3.5) and so is Neftçi's judgmental dating, which deviates considerably from the NBER chronologies. The distinction between business cycles and growth cycles needs to be made explicit in this context. The target dates are never clearly defined, which makes it difficult to assess the proposed method and verify its results (the definition of a recession as two consecutive declines in GNP [see 1982, p. 232] is simply inadequate). But these defects of implementation do not detract from the importance of Neftçi's basic idea that prediction of turning points can be treated as an optimal stopping-time problem (Shiryayev 1978). The concept stimulated much interesting work on how the statistical technique of sequential analysis can best be used to determine when the cumulative information justifies announcing a turning point, given the cost of a false signal and a preset margin of error.

Applying this analysis to the performance of the leading index at post-1948 business cycle peaks, Palash and Radecki (1985) report the following estimates, in months: 7/53, − 1; 8/57, − 14; 4/60, − 5; 12/69, − 1; 11/73, − 3; 1/80, − 6. These lead times do not differ much from those of the P1 signals in table 11.6, column 5, but the absence here of any prior warning of the 1981 downturn is troubling. Also, the probability approach produces signals of slowdowns as well as recessions but, unlike the band approach, does not attempt to distinguish between the two by means of additional information.[27]

Diebold and Rudebusch 1989 is a comprehensive evaluation of cyclical turning-point forecasts from historical data on the BEA composite index of leading indicators for December 1949 to December 1986. The method is a Bayesian sequential probability recursion (SPR), which retains some aspects of Neftçi's approach and modifies others.[28] Here all probabilities are used directly as forecasts, and the stopping rule is not applied. A measure of *accuracy* for a set of n such forecasts is the quadratic probability score

26. Note the closeness of these dates to their counterparts in table 11.6, cols. 1 and 2 (a P1 signal in 8/73 and a P2 signal in 5/79).

27. Thus the results of Palash and Radecki include continuous predictions of recession from 4/51 to 5/52 (the slow-growth phase of the Korean War cycle; cf. table 11.6, line 1). They also show a 6-month lead at a misnamed "business cycle peak" of 12/66, which corresponds to the P1 signal of 0 at the growth cycle peak of 6/6 in table 11.6.

28. Among the retained elements is the assumption that the composite leading index (CLI) has the following simple probability structure: $\Delta CLI = \alpha^u + \varepsilon_t^u$ in expansions; $\Delta CLI = \alpha^d + \varepsilon_t^d$ in contractions (where the α's are constants and the ε's are independently and identically distributed random variables with means of 0). The densities corresponding to the two regimes, f^u and f^d, are estimated by fitting normal distribution functions to the CLI data partitioned according to the specific-cycle peaks and troughs in the index that match the NBER business cycle turns. The probability of a turning point is taken to be independent of the duration of the phase; hence the transition priors are constant.

$$QPS = \frac{1}{n} \sum_{t=1}^{n} 2(p_t - r_t)^2,$$

where r_t is the realization corresponding to the predicted probability, p_t (it equals 1 when a turning point has occurred and 0 otherwise). QPS has a range from 0 (best) to 2 (worst). A measure of *calibration* (i.e., closeness of predicted probabilities to observed relative frequencies) is the global squared bias, GSB = $2(\bar{p} - \bar{r})^2$, where $\bar{p}$ and $\bar{r}$ are means of p_t and r_t, respectively. GSB, too, ranges from 0 to 2. Forecasts are also scored on other criteria, notably their local discriminating power, or *resolution,* which reflects the extent to which different probability values are followed by different realizations. All scores are for several forecast horizons (1, 3, 5, 7, 9, and 13 months). Only symmetric loss functions are considered.[29] However, the performance of the leading indicators tends to be asymmetric and such that the index would presumably score better if missing a true turn mattered more than calling a false turn.

The SPR forecast scores on accuracy (QPS) at peaks increase from .29 for the shortest to .49 for the longest horizon. Surprisingly, these results are worse than those obtained from the simple rule that yields probabilities of 1 when the leading index shows three consecutive declines (3CD) and of 0 otherwise (the scores for these 3CD forecasts increase from .19 to .34 in the 1–9 months range). Even the naive forecast of zero probability of a downturn throughout earns lower (i.e., better) scores than SPR. The optimal constant-probability forecast, where the constant is chosen to minimize QPS for expansions, performs much better than any of these methods. However, constant priors can be found that optimize the posterior probability predictions via SPR, and this method (SPR*) produces about equally good results (scores of .04–.39). Also, both SPR and SPR* show higher relative accuracy when the LPS measures are substituted for QPS (see n. 29), whereas 3CD performs poorly here.

At troughs, SPR* generally scores best; the naive forecast worst. The optimal constant-probability forecast for contractions comes in a close second; SPR third. The scores generally increase with the horizon in the range of 1–7 months (e.g., from .27 to .48 for SPR under QPS).[30]

The SPR predictions tend to overpredict the probabilities of turning points; the naive no-change predictions obviously underpredict them. All other examined types of forecast, from the simple 3CD rule to the sophisticated SPR*, are well-calibrated or unbiased (i.e., have GSB $\approx$ 0 for all horizons). The resolution scores show SPR and SPR* to be moderately and about equally informative, whereas the naive and constant-probability forecasts are, of course, by their very nature of no value in this respect.

29. They are implied by both QPS and an alternative, the log probability score (LPS). The LPS penalizes large errors more heavily than QPS does, and so the absolute level of the scores tends to be higher for LPS than for QPS (cf. tables 1 and 2 in Diebold and Rudebusch 1989, p. 382).

30. The longer predictions show improvements that are correctly recognized as artificial. Because the postwar recessions were short (all but one less than a year), it was easy to predict that they would end after 9 or 11 months.

In absolute terms, all predictive techniques performed worse in contractions (at troughs) than in expansions (at peaks). In relative terms, the SPR method performed best in contractions. The longer their horizon (time span to target), the less accurate would the probabilistic turning-point predictions typically be. This is a general property of optimal forecasts and a widely observed regularity, as documented in part IV of this book.

The Diebold and Rudebusch 1989 analysis is ex post in the sense that their probability densities are estimated over the entire sample and their data on the leading index represent the latest "final" revisions. An ex ante evaluation based on rolling probability densities, preliminary and partially revised data, and the SPR method (Diebold and Rudebusch 1991) yields closer approximations to real-time out-of-sample forecasts. Not surprisingly, the so-constructed ex ante forecasts are less accurate than their ex post counterparts. The main reason is probably data errors rather than pure forecast errors. As we have seen, not only are the component series of the leading index subject to frequent short-term statistical revisions but they have not all been available in time for inclusion in the first preliminary values of the index; moreover, the composition of the index itself was altered on several occasions. The probability forecasts based on preliminary data reflect all these measurement errors and could be very sensitive to the compositional changes in particular. But the NBER business cycle turning-point dates (the target of these forecasts) are established retrospectively, in light of historical, revised information. Many important macroeconomic series (e.g., real GNP) undergo repeated and often relatively large revisions, and forecasters on the whole predict the future values of these variables better in preliminary than in revised form.[31]

Hamilton (1989) applies a nonlinear iterative filter to quarterly growth rates in real GNP for 1952–84 and reports the maximum likelihood estimates of the parameters of the underlying process. He notes that one possible outcome of this use of Markov switching regression to infer regime changes might have been an identification of above-trend ("fast") and below-trend ("slow") growth phases. However, this was not the case; instead, the best fit to the data separated periods of positive growth from periods of negative growth (recession). Indeed, the dates of the switches determined by this method agree quite well with the NBER business cycle chronology.[32]

Hamilton's statistical analysis extends that of Neftçi. That its results agree so well with the results of the historical NBER studies is remarkable. But here again it is well to remember that the focus of all of this work is on the U.S.

31. For evidence, see Zarnowitz 1967 and R. Cole 1969a; for more on the general properties of macroeconomic forecasts, see part IV below. True ex ante predictions must use preliminary data for the most recent periods, and the effective weight of this information will often be large. Thus the forecasts are apt to have more in common with the early than with the later revised values of the target variables.

32. The only large discrepancies are associated with Hamilton's peak dates of 1957:1 and 1979:2, which coincide with oil price increases (the NBER dates are 1957:3 and 1980:1). Elsewhere the differences are mostly zero; in a few cases, ±1 quarter.

business cycle chronology derived from ex post information. Slowdowns are more frequent than recessions, the two are not so easily distinguishable on a current basis, and leading indicators are sensitive to both. Growth cycles attract much popular and official attention, particularly abroad, and the concept receives support from some contemporary theories. The leading and confirming indicators in Europe and Japan are mostly geared to fluctuations in deviations from trend.

Niemira 1991, using the Neftçi method, finds the timing of the probability signals from the Department of Commerce index of leading indicators to have been on average coincident with U.S. growth cycle turning points in 1951–86.[33] The individual signals show considerable dispersion, however, particularly at peaks. The 1962–64 growth cycle was missed. On the whole, the slowdowns and speedups might often have been recognized with relatively little delay but seldom detected early. Much the same can be said about the applications of the method to Japan and West Germany (where short lags prevail) and the United Kingdom (where the lags are longer).

In short, the probability approach has a broad appeal a priori on general statistical grounds and helps extend the range of uses of the leading indexes. Still, its results can only be as good as the predictive potential of these indexes allows. This is true as well for the method of sequential signaling by leading and coincident index growth rates, which retains its usefulness.[34]

11.3.4 Regression-Based Approaches

Leading indexes and their components can be used to predict not only turning points but also future values of macroeconomic aggregates with coincident timing tendencies. For example, consider the ordinary regression of dq_t on $d\ell_{t-1}$, where d denotes first differences in logs ($\Delta\ln$) and q refers to real GNP and ℓ refers to the index of leading indicators. Let the parameter estimates based on quarterly data for 1948–69 be used to compute one-quarter-ahead forecasts of real growth in 1970–76, and then reestimate for 1948–70 and 1971–76 and so on. As shown in Vaccara and Zarnowitz 1978, this very simple procedure yields root mean square errors of about .01 (close to the standard errors of regression) and mean errors near 0. The correlations between the out-of-sample predictions and realizations range from .68 to .74. Adding dq_{t-1}, $d\ell_{t-2}$, and $d\ell_{t-3}$ does not improve the results significantly, but adding lagged changes in the inverted lagging index, dv, does. A chain of predictions can extend the span of forecasts of real growth: dq_{t+2} is obtained from $d\ell_{t+1}$, which is itself obtained from dv_t. Measures of relative accuracy

33. Whether the confidence levels of 90% or 95% are used apparently makes little difference, and Niemira opts for the latter. The growth cycle chronology is that used in studies of the NBER and the Center for International Business Cycle Research (CIBCR). Comparisons with other chronologies such as Beveridge and Nelson 1981 are shown to yield much worse results.

34. See section 11.3.2 above on the application of this method to U.S. business and growth cycles. Reports by Moore on the continuing work at the CIBCR indicate that applications to other countries also provide useful information on their growth cycle developments.

suggest that the forecasts with composite indexes are definitely "in the ball park," that is, not at all far behind the much more complex and expensive GNP forecasts of econometricians and business economists.[35]

Auerbach (1982) estimates jointly (1) the regression of a cyclical variable dy on its own lagged values and on those of the leading index, $d\ell$, and (2) the regression of $d\ell$ on its component series. Monthly rates of change in either the unemployment rate or the industrial production index serve as dy, monthly rates of change in the BEA index of 1975 vintage serve as $d\ell$, and the lags range from 1 to 10 months. The weights estimated from Auerbach's equation (2) for the sample period 1949–77 vary considerably across the index components and differ depending on which of the two cyclical variables is used. The regression weights help to obtain a better within-sample fit for the unemployment rate, but the BEA index with approximately equal weights performs better in out-of-sample predictions for both variables. These results prove robust to different choices of sample period (1949–73, 1968–73) and forecast period (1973–77 and subdivisions). The stability of equations is rejected when using the estimated index with "optimal" regression weights but accepted when using the BEA index. Exclusion of those component series that did not individually help explain dy worsens the out-of-sample prediction performance of the BEA index.

Leading indicators contribute to the determination of national output and some other major economic aggregates in vector autoregressive (VAR) models, as shown in chapter 12. Continuing work in this area, conducted by me jointly with Phillip Braun, is now producing updated regression estimates and out-of-sample predictions with selected indexes. The latter include combinations of new-investment commitments for plant and equipment and housing (ℓ_2) and of most of the other components of the BEA leading index used in the late 1970s and 1980s (ℓ_8). Table 11.8 compares forecasts from four VAR models. The first model (A) includes real growth, inflation, money growth, and the interest rate; another (B) adds ℓ_2; the third (C) adds ℓ_8 instead; and the fourth (D) includes all six variables. The sample period is 1949–82; the forecast period is 1983–89.

The ratios of model B to model A root mean square errors (RMSE) show that when ℓ_2 is included, forecasts of real growth (q) improve for the first three quarters but deteriorate for longer spans. Interestingly, ℓ_2 helps to raise the accuracy of forecasts of inflation (p) and the level of interest rates (I) at all horizons (cols. 1–3). The RMSE ratios for C/A tell us that ℓ_8 contributes to the forecasts of q over quarters 1–4, to those of p over some intermediate and longer spans, and to those of I over most spans. However, most of the C/A

---

35. Leading indicator predictions of changes in the coincident index (dc) were on the whole more accurate than the predictions of dq, according to the results by Vaccara and Zarnowitz. One possible reason is that the coincident index has smaller measurement errors than real GNP; another, that it has more of a tendency to lag slightly. (Errors in component series often average out in an index, and employment lags slightly behind output much of the time.)

Table 11.8   **Measures of Net Predictive Value of VAR Models with and without Selected Leading Indexes: Forecasts for 1–12 Quarters Ahead, 1983–89**

	Ratios of Root Mean Square Errors (%)								
	Model B/Model A			Model C/Model A			Model D/Model A		
Span in Quarters	q (1)	p (2)	l (3)	q (4)	p (5)	l (6)	q (7)	p (8)	l (9)
One	81	83	93	93	100	92	83	80	91
Two	86	82	96	96	103	100	96	81	102
Three	76	89	96	95	99	97	82	89	101
Four	101	90	92	98	98	94	99	90	92
Five	114	92	92	110	100	81	117	90	89
Six	125	94	94	110	99	94	122	91	93
Nine	102	94	95	123	97	94	117	92	91
Twelve	102	96	97	107	99	95	101	96	92

Note: Model A includes four variables: q, m, I, and p. Model B includes the same variables plus l_2. Model C replaces l_2 with l_8. Model D includes all six variables: q, m, I, p, l_2, and l_8. The variables are defined as follows ($\Delta \ln$ = first difference in natural logarithm): q = $\Delta \ln$ real GNP; m = $\Delta \ln$ money supply M1; I = commercial paper rate; p = $\Delta \ln$ GNP implicit price deflator; l_2 = $\Delta \ln$ index of new-investment commitments (contracts and orders for plant and equipment; building permits for private housing); l_8 = $\Delta \ln$ index of eight leading indicators (average workweek, manufacturing; average initial claims for state unemployment insurance; vendor performance—percentage of companies receiving slower deliveries; change in sensitive materials prices; new orders for consumer goods and materials, constant dollars, manufacturing industries; index of net business formation; change in inventories on hand and on order, constant dollars, manufacturing and trade; index of 500 common stock prices). Cols. 1, 4, 7 refer to forecasts of real GNP growth; cols. 2, 5, and 8, to forecasts of inflation; cols. 3, 6, and 9, to forecasts of the interest rate.

ratios are higher than the corresponding B/A ratios, which suggests that the net predictive value of ℓ_8 is less than that of ℓ_2 (cf. cols. 1–3 and 4–6). When both ℓ_2 and ℓ_8 are included, some gains are achieved, particularly in forecasting p, as indicated by the D/A ratios (cols. 7–9). It might appear that the contributions of ℓ_2 and ℓ_8 are small (most of the ratios, in percentages, are in the 90s), but one should remember that the benchmark VAR model A is not an easy one to beat (consisting as it does of four principal macroeconomic variables, each quarterly series being taken with four lags, plus constant terms and time trends).[36]

Finally, Diebold and Rudebusch in their most recent evaluation (1990b) look at the contribution of the Department of Commerce leading index (LI) to monthly forecasts of industrial production (IP) that also use the lagged values of IP. They report that LI has a considerable net predictive value when both series (used in logarithms of the levels) are taken in the "final" revised form, but not when LI is the preliminary series and IP is the revised one. In the latter

36. The autoregressive elements are particularly strong for p, m, and I but relatively weak for q, l_2, and l_8, as indicated by F-statistics. The most significant influences on q are those of the interest rate and the leading indexes. Compare the similar results of the F- and t-tests reported in chapter 12.

case, of course, the past LI values would be available to the "real-time" forecaster but the past IP values would not. Here again, my interpretation of their results is that they primarily reflect the measurement errors in the preliminary LI series (as in Diebold and Rudebusch 1989; see sec. 11.3.3 above).

11.4 Recent and Expected Innovations

11.4.1 New Methods and Experimental Indexes

An experimental index of coincident indicators by Stock and Watson (1989, 1991a) is built on the assumption that all comovements of the included time series are attributable to a single unobserved factor (the "aggregate economic activity" or "state of the economy").[37] The underlying linear stochastic model is specified in log differences, so the common dynamic factor is $\Delta \ln C_t$; in addition, the relative change in each of the coincident variables covered is supposed to include a random component u_t that collects the variable-specific movements and measurement errors. The u's are thought of as uncorrelated with $\Delta \ln C_t$, with each other across the component series, and over time, at all leads and lags.

The Stock-Watson (S-W) coincident index includes four series, three of which it shares with the BEA index. One series is slightly different (employee-hours are used by S-W and number of employees by BEA, both for the nonfarm sector). The two indexes are very similar but the cyclical movements are somewhat smaller in the S-W composite and the upward trend is weaker (Stock and Watson 1989, p. 366).

The S-W formalization of the coincident index is methodologically interesting but rather restrictive. It certainly does not imply that business cycles have a single common cause, or that they can be reliably dated according to the movements of a single coincident index, BEA or S-W (cf. Stock and Watson 1989, pp. 352–55; Zarnowitz and Braun 1989, p. 399). A broader range of variables, nominal as well as real, would require more than one factor.

The new S-W leading index is both conceptually and structurally very different from the older NBER and BEA indexes. Calculated from a modified VAR model with seven selected leading variables, it is a forecast of the 6-month-ahead growth rate of the S-W coincident index ($\ln C_{t+6|t} - \ln C_{t|t}$). The selection involved an extensive search through a large array of series limited to the sample period 1960–88, using models with up to nine lags in each of the leading series and four lags in $\Delta \ln C$. Stock and Watson recognize that the danger of overfitting is particularly large here (1989, p. 367). A good in-sample fit would be expected and is largely confirmed (Zarnowitz and Braun

---

37. See Sargent and Sims 1977 for an early study of an unobserved one-index model of multivariate time series.

1989). But in the absence of out-of-sample tests, doubts arise about just how well this index would have performed over past periods with very different characteristics or how well it will do in the future.

The S-W leading index includes no series on money and credit, inventory investment, consumption, delivery lags, sensitive commodity prices, and stock prices. Three of its seven components relate to interest rates: change in the 10-year Treasury bond yield (I_{10}); the 6-month risk spread, commercial paper rate minus Treasury bill rate (CP − TB); and the yield curve, 10-year to 1-year Treasury bond spread ($G10 − G1$). The other components are the building permits for private housing units (BP); manufacturers' unfilled orders for durable goods, in constant dollars (DUO); the trade-weighted nominal exchange rate (EXN); and part-time work in nonagricultural industries due to slack (PTW). BP is a level series; the others are smoothed growth rates.

Only two of the seven S-W leaders are also included in the BEA index (BP and DUO, but the latter in the form of absolute change, not rate of growth). A series such as EXN, with a short and poor record of cyclical conformity and timing, would not have qualified under the selection criteria used in the indexes constructed in the past (Moore and Shiskin 1967; Zarnowitz and Boschan 1975a, 1975b). Although theoretical considerations support inclusion of this important variable, they do so equally for other variables that have been omitted, particularly those relating to real investment, profits, credit, and money.

The level of interest rates tends to move procyclically with lags (the prime rate is a component of the BEA index of lagging indicators), but as shown earlier, such laggers when inverted become long leaders. The I_{10} component contributes only mildly to the S-W index.[38] The yield curve ($G10 − G1$) is more effective, and the public-private spread (CP − TB) is by far the most effective, according to the tests reported by S-W and Zarnowitz and Braun 1989 (but see sec. 11.4.3 below for some qualifications).

The S-W leading index would probably gain from broader and more diversified coverage, including at least some of the more effective components of the BEA index. Its reliance on interest rates and spreads seems too heavy: the predictive power of these variables in the past was not always as strong as in recent times, and it may not always prove as strong in the future (Sims 1989, pp. 396–97). Indeed, the S-W index failed to predict the July 1990 business cycle peak. However, most leading indicators performed rather poorly on this occasion. (Stock and Watson 1991b), perhaps because the 1991 downturn was aggravated and accelerated (though not necessarily caused) by the Iraqi invasion of Kuwait on August 2. The BEA leading index declined in July, synchronously with the general economic activity.

---

38. See, e.g., fig. 5(F) in Stock and Watson 1989, p. 371. Also, note that "interestingly, including a measure of ex ante real rates (with various measures of expected inflation) does not improve the performance of the LEI [i.e., S-W] index" (p. 385).

11.4.2   Do Stock Prices Belong in the Leading Index?

Probably no major leading indicator met with more criticism in recent times than the stock price index (particularly after the crash of October 1987). Stock prices reflect profit expectations and presumably help determine consumption (wealth effect) and cost of capital, hence business investment decisions (q-ratio). Some studies offer strong support for the power of market changes to predict output (Fama 1981; Fischer and Merton 1984); others provide mixed evidence on the theoretical consequences of stock price movements (see references in chapter 2 and Cagan 1990). The verdict of most recent tests is essentially negative.[39]

I find the long-term cyclical record of stock prices as leading indicators in the United States and other developed economies (Canada, Japan, and Western Europe) to be good in the relevant relative terms. The market indexes have performed worse than the composite indexes, but this is true of other individual indicators as well. Their recent record leaves much to be desired, but it would seem premature to eliminate the S&P 500 index from the U.S. leading index. As summed up in table 11.9, all but three of the U.S. business contractions since 1873 were preceded and accompanied by substantial declines in the market.[40] So stock prices signaled well the actual recessions and recoveries. However, they performed poorly with respect to the other type of error by giving many false signals (i.e., containing many extra turns). Of the 12 significant declines in the S&P index in 1946–82, 5 (42%) were not associated with recessions. Interestingly, the conformity of stock prices to business cycles, as measured by both types of error, was excellent in 1873–1919 and much worse in the later era of the Federal Reserve and rising government size and interventions (cf. table 11.9, cols. 4 and 5). Yet one should also consider that the tendency of the market to lead actually strengthened in the postwar period (cols. 6–7). Also, the market declines associated with recessions and major slowdowns were typically larger and longer than the other declines.[41]

11.4.3   New Proposals and Need for Further Work

The study by Stock and Watson suggests that the BEA index could be significantly improved by the inclusion of some functions of interest rates, par-

39. Stock and Watson (1989, p. 388) conclude that the marginal predictive value of S&P 500 in helping to predict their coincident index is "modest." Fredman and Niemira (1990), working with the components of the latest BEA composite index of leading indicators, consider the same stock price series the main candidate for replacement. For a rather more optimistic appraisal, however, see Niemira 1990a.

40. The exceptions consist of the mild, indeed marginal, recession of 1926–27, the short one in the first half of 1980, and the 1945 episode related to the end of World War II.

41. The bear markets in 1962 and 1966 are related to business slowdowns; those in 1946, 1977, and 1983–84 are not. The outliers are the short but steep decline in 1962 and the long but gradual decline in 1976–78. The average amplitudes per month of cyclical contractions in common stock prices are close to 2% for each of the three subperiods distinguished in table 11.9. For more detail on timing and amplitudes of stock price indexes in the United States, see Moore 1983, ch. 9, and Zarnowitz 1987–88. On the timing of market indexes at postwar growth cycle turns in eight countries, see Klein and Moore 1985.

Table 11.9   **Selected Measures of Cyclical Conformity and Timing, Common Stock Prices, 1873–1986**

Period	No. of Turning Points Covered in Business Cycles (B.C.)[a] (1)	No. of Turning Points Covered in Stock Price Cycles (S.C.)[b] (2)	No. of B.C. and S.C. Turning Points Matched[c] (3)	% of B.C. Turns Skipped[d] (4)	% of Extra S.C. Turns[e] (5)	% of Leads[f] At B.C. Peaks (6)	% of Leads[f] At B.C. Troughs (7)
1873–1919	24	24	24	0	0	83	75
1920–1945	12	10	8	33	20	75	75
1946–1986	16	24	14	13	42	100	100
1873–1986	52	58	46	12	21	87	83

Sources: Morgenstern 1959, ch. 10; Moore 1983, ch. 9; *BCD,* April 1987, p. 105; Zarnowitz 1987–88, p. 14.

[a]As dated by the NBER. Every entry includes an equal number of B.C. peaks and B.C. troughs.

[b]Refers to specific-cycle peaks and troughs (in equal numbers for every entry) in the S&P monthly index of common stock prices. For 1873–1919: index compiled by Cowles Commission and S&P, includes virtually all industrial public utility, and railroad stocks traded on the New York Stock Exchange. For 1918–56: monthly average of S&P weekly index, coverage increasing from 198 to 480 stocks. 1957–86: S&P index of 500 common stocks.

[c]B.C. turns matched by like turns in the monthly S&P 500 index.

[d]Equals in terms of the column numbers $[(1) - (2)/(1)]100$.

[e]Equals in terms of the column numbers $[(2) - (3)/(2)]100$.

[f]Based on all timing observations at matched B.C. and S.C. turns (see cols. 3 for the numbers and nn. a–c).

ticularly the risk spread. Some measure of the slope of the yield curve is another candidate that receives support from both historical analyses (Kessel 1965; Cagan 1966) and recent tests (Keen 1989; Fredman and Niemira 1990).

Corporate bond prices led at each peak and each trough of the eight complete business cycles of 1948–82, but they have a much longer record of consistent cyclical behavior (Mitchell and Burns 1938). The Dow-Jones index, a simple average of daily closing bond prices for each month, had very long and highly variable leads at peaks (with a mean and a range of 27 and 10–58 months, respectively). Its leads at troughs were more moderate but also long relative to the observed distributions of such leads and the durations of business contractions (they ranged from 3 to 13 months and averaged 7 months). Bond prices, of course, move inversely to bond yields. Their long downward trend in the postwar period reflects the rise in the price level and the gradual diffusion of inflationary expectations.[42]

The Dow-Jones bond price average is included in the new long-leading index of the CIBCR along with the money supply (M2) in constant dollars, new housing permits, and the ratio of the price to unit labor cost in manufactur-

42. For detail on corporate bond prices as a leading indicator, see Zarnowitz 1990.

ing.[43] The long-leading index is designed to help remedy the old problem of very short leads at business cycle troughs of the existing composites. It is also intended to provide a forecasting tool with a somewhat longer forward reach and to be tested against the movements in the short-leading index (and vice versa). Its peaks (troughs) lead the corresponding turns in the BEA index on average by 4 (5) months (see Moore and Cullity 1990).

Seven of the 11 components of the new short-leading CIBCR index are the same as or nearly equivalent to the indicators included in the BEA leading index in its present form. The remaining components include a new index of net business formation, a new layoff rate series, growth rate in real domestic nonfinancial debt, and the diffusion index of inventory change from the monthly survey of the National Association of Purchasing Management. Each of these series represents an important cyclical variable with a tendency to lead well known from the results of closely related data used in the past.[44]

With larger samples of better data and a careful choice of evaluation methods, we should be able to draw important distinctions between types of fluctuations and turning points. As noted earlier, some indicators lead only at peaks, others only at troughs, and neither of these groups should be ignored. Also, some indicators may rank high as predictors of business cycle turns but low as predictors of growth cycle turns, or vice versa.[45]

Much more work needs to be done to extend and improve the set of useful indicators of major changes in general economic activity. This applies not only to the leading series but also to the roughly coincident and lagging series.

43. The first two of these series are also components of the BEA leading index (with the minor difference that BEA uses an index of permits, and CIBCR uses the number of permits). The ratio series is a new monthly indicator of profit margins (see Boschan and Moore 1990).

44. For analyses of these indicators, see Moore 1990, ch. 2; Moore and Cullity 1990; Klein and Moore 1990; and Zarnowitz and Moore 1990. For criticism of the two series included in the BEA index but not in the CIBCR indexes (change in constant-dollar unfilled orders for durable goods and the index of consumer expectations), see Moore 1990, pp. 12–14.

45. Fredman and Niemira 1990 evaluate 17 leading indicators separately at the two sets of turns in 1948–82, using a Neftçi-type technique. In signaling business cycle turns, the ratio of the coincident to the lagging index ranks first, the yield curve second, I_{10} fourth, the BEA leading index fifth, and the "credit risk" (CP − TB) last. In signaling growth cycle turns, the BEA leading index ranks first, credit risk fifth, the yield curve eleventh, I_{10} fifteenth, and the C/Lg ratio last!

12   Major Macroeconomic Variables and Leading Indexes

12.1 Background and Objectives

How the economy moves over time depends on its structure, institutions, and policies, all of which are subject to large historical changes. It would be surprising if the character of the business cycle did *not* change in response to such far-reaching developments as the Great Contraction of the 1930s and the post-Depression reforms, the expansion of government and private service industries, the development of fiscal and other built-in stabilizers, and the increased use and role of discretionary macroeconomic policies. It is consistent with our priors that the data for the United States and other developed market-oriented countries generally support the hypothesis that business contractions were less frequent, shorter, and milder after World War II than before (R. J. Gordon 1986; see chapter 3).

Although business cycles have moderated, they retain a high degree of continuity, which shows up most clearly in the comovements and timing sequences among the main cyclical processes.[1] An important aspect of this continuity is the role of the variables that tend to move ahead of aggregate output and employment in the course of the business cycle. The composite index of leading indicators combines the main series representing these variables. Several studies point to the existence of a relatively close and stable relationship between prior changes in this index and changes in macroeconomic activity (Vaccara and Zarnowitz 1977; Auerbach 1982; Zarnowitz and Moore 1982; Diebold and Rudebusch 1989). Yet, the currently popular, small reduced-form

---

This chapter is co-authored with Phillip Braun and is reprinted from *Analyzing Modern Business Cycles: Essays Honoring Geoffrey H. Moore*, ed. P. A. Klein, chap. 11 (Armonk, NY: M. E. Sharpe, 1990).

1. For assessments and references concerning the U.S. record, see Moore 1983, chs. 10 and 24; and Zarnowitz and Moore 1986.

macro models make little or no use of the leading indicators.[2] We suspect that the reason is lack of familiarity. The role of the indicators is probably often misperceived as being purely symptomatic. Heterogeneous combinations of such series resist easy theoretical applications. On a deeper level, the notion that the private market economy is inherently stable led to an emphasis on the role of the monetary and fiscal disturbances. Interest in the potential of stabilization policies had a similar effect in that it stimulated work on models dominated by factors considered to be amenable to government control.

This orientation is understandably appealing but can easily become one-sided and error-prone, both theoretically and statistically. For example, a simple vector autoregressive (VAR) model in log differences of real GNP, money, and government expenditures suggests the presence of strong lagged monetary and fiscal effects on output.[3] However, it is easy to show that these relationships are definitely misspecified. One way to demonstrate this is by adding changes in a leading index that excludes monetary and financial components so as not to overlap any of the other variables. In this expanded model, the dominant effects on output come from the past movements of the leading index, while the roles of the other variables (including the lagged values of output growth itself) are greatly reduced (see sec. 12.4). In general, omitting relevant variables in a VAR will cause the standard exogeneity tests, impulse responses, and variance decompositions to be biased, as shown in Lütkepohl 1982 and Braun and Mittnik 1985.

The first objective of this chapter is to examine the lead-lag interactions within larger sets of important macroeconomic variables, including interest and inflation rates along with output, monetary, and fiscal variables, and a nonduplicative leading index. The rationale for including this index is twofold: (1) The changes in the leading index can be interpreted broadly as representing the early collective outcomes of investment and production (also, less directly, consumption) decisions. As such, they presumably reflect the dynamic forces that shape the basic processes within the private economy and account for the continuity of business cycles. Both aggregate demand and aggregate supply shifts are involved, but the demand effects may be stronger in the short run. (2) The addition of the leading index helps us overcome the bias due to the omitted variables. The index stands for a number of important factors that would otherwise be omitted. It would not be practical to include the several individual series to represent these variables.

We work with equations that include up to six variables plus constant terms and time trends. They are estimated on quarterly series, each taken with four lags, which means using up large numbers of degrees of freedom. Given the size of the available data samples, it is not possible for such models to accommodate more variables and still retain a chance to produce estimates of param-

---

2. Large econometric models incorporate some individual indicators but probably suboptimally and not in a comprehensive and systematic way.
3. This recalls the old St. Louis Fed model with its reliance on "policy variables" only.

eters in which one could have some confidence. It is, of course, easy to think of additional, possibly important variables whose omission might cause some serious misspecifications. All VAR models face this dilemma, but the only way to avoid it is by assuming a full structural model, which could be still more deficient. We seek some partial remedies in alternative specifications guided by economic theory and history as well as comparisons with related results in the literature.

Although the format adopted is that of a VAR model, the implied system-wide dynamics (i.e., impulse response functions and variance decompositions) are beyond the scope of this study. These statistics seek to describe behavior in reaction to innovations, require longer series of consistent data than are actually available,[4] and are probably often very imprecise even for smaller systems (see Zellner 1985 and Runkle 1987 with discussion). In contrast, there is sufficient information to estimate the individual equations well, even with more lagged terms. We find that much can be learned from attention to the quality and implications of these estimates, which are logically prior to inferences on overall dynamics but carry no commitment to the particular interpretations of a VAR model.

The second and related objective is to extend the analysis to the periods between the two world wars and earlier in another effort to study the continuity and change in U.S. business cycles. To evaluate any persistent shifts or the secular evolution in the patterns of macroeconomic fluctuation, it is of course necessary to cover long stretches of varied historical experience. Estimates of the interrelations among the selected variables are calculated from quarterly seasonally adjusted data for three periods: 1886–1914, 1919–40, and 1949–82. Generally, we look for the similarities and differences within the three periods that are suggested by this exercise.

Historical data are scanty and deficient, which inevitably creates some difficult choices and problems. The next part of this chapter discusses this and lists the variables and series used. The following section discusses the applied methods and presents tests that determine what transformations must be used on any of the series to validate our statistical procedures. Then the results are examined, focusing on simple exogeneity and neutrality tests for a succession of models as well as on interperiod comparisons. The final section sums up our conclusions and views on the need for further work.

12.2 Data

12.2.1 The Selected Variables and Their Representations

Table 12.1 serves as a summary of the information on the data used in this study. It defines the variables and identifies the time series by title, period,

---

4. With $m = 6$ variables and $k = 4$ lags, $km^2 = 144$. For the sample period 1949:2–1982:4 covered by our postwar series, the number of degrees of freedom is 109.

Table 12.1   List of Variables, Symbols, and Sources of Data

Number (1)	Variable[a] (2)	Periods[b] (3)	Form[c] (4)	Symbol[d] (5)	Source[e] (6)	Notes on Derivation[f] (7)
1	Real GNP (1972 dollars)	1,2,3	$\Delta\ln$	q	B&G	Annual data from F&S 1982 and Kuznets 1961 and Commerce NIPA (1981ff. since 1889), interpolated quarterly by Chow-Lin (1971) method using the Persons (1931) index of industrial production and trade
2	Implicit price deflator	1,2,3	$\Delta\ln$	p	B&G	(nominal GNP/real GNP) × 100
3	Monetary base	1,2,3	$\Delta\ln$	b	B&G	Based on data in F&S 1970 and 1963a through 1914 and R. J. Gordon and Veitch 1986 for 1949–82
4	Money supply, M1	2,3	$\Delta\ln$	m_1	B&G	1919–46: R. J. Gordon and Veitch 1986; 1947–58: old M1, *FRB*: 1958–82: new M1, *FRB*
5	Money supply, M2	1,2,3	$\Delta\ln$	m_2	B&G	1886–1907: F&S 1970; 1907–14 and 1919–80; R. J. Gordon 1982a; 1980–82: *FRB*
6	Commercial paper rate	1,3	In level	I	B&G	1886–89: in New York City, from Macaulay 1938; 1890–1914, 1919–80: 4–6 month prime, from R. J. Gordon 1982a; 1981–82: 6 month, from *FRB*
7	Commercial paper rate	2	Δ	i	B&G	do.

No.	Series	Period[b]	Transformation[c]	Symbol[d]	Source[e]	Notes[f]
8	Federal expenditures	1	ln level	GX	Firestone	Based on *Daily Treasury Statements of the United States* (see Firestone 1960, app. pp. 76–86, and data, seasonally adjusted, pp. 97–111)
9	Federal expenditures	2	Δln	gx	Firestone	do.
10	Fiscal index	3	ln level	G	Blanchard	From Blanchard 1985 and Blanchard and Watson 1986, app. 2.2; based on data for government spending, debt, and taxes
11	Diffusion index, 75 leading series	1	Δln	ℓdc	Moore	Analyzed in Moore 1961, vol. 1, ch. 7; based on specific-cycle phases; data from Moore 1961, vol. 2, p. 172
12	Amplitude-adjusted (composite) index, six leading series	2	Δln	ℓd	Shiskin	Analyzed in Shiskin 1961a, pp. 43–55; Data from NBER files
13	Composite index of leading indicators	3	Δln	ℓ	Commerce	The composite index of 12 leading indicators minus three components: M2 in constant dollars, change in business and consumer credit outstanding, and the index of stock prices, from *BCD*

[a] All variables are used as quarterly series.

[b] Period 1: 1886–1914; period 2: 1919–40; period 3: 1949–82.

[c] Δln: first difference in natural logarithm; Δ: first difference.

[d] Small letters are used for rates of change or absolute changes; capital letters are used for levels of the series.

[e] B&G: Balke and Gordon 1986, app. B. Firestone: Firestone, 1960, app. tables, Blanchard: Blanchard and Watson 1986, app. 2.2. Moore: Moore 1961. Shiskin: Shiskin 1961a. Commerce: U.S. Department of Commerce, Bureau of Economic Analysis.

[f] F&S: M. Friedman and Schwartz. NIPA: national income and product accounts. *FRB: Federal Reserve Bulletin.* NBER: National Bureau of Economic Research. *BCD: Business Conditions Digest* (U.S. Department of Commerce).

symbol, and source. Some notes on the derivation of the underlying data are included as well.

The table includes 11 different variables and 23 segments of the corresponding series, counting one per time period (cols. 2 and 3). No equation contains more than six variables. Some variables have different representations across the three periods covered because consistent data are not available for them. Further, unit root tests indicate that in some cases, levels of a series ought to be used in one period and differences in another. (These tests and the required transformations are discussed in sec. 12.3, which covers the statistical framework.) As shown in column 4, natural logarithms are taken of all series except the commercial paper rate. Federal expenditures in 1886–1914, the fiscal index in 1949–82, and the interest rate in both of these periods are level series; in all other cases first difference series are used.

Lowercase letters serve as symbols for variables cast in the form of first differences; capital letters for those cast in levels (table 12.1, col. 5). The series relating to output (q), prices (p), the alternative monetary aggregates (b, m_1, m_2), and interest (I or i) are staple ingredients of small reduced-form, or VAR, models. They appear in the table on lines 1–7. Of the additional series, three represent fiscal variables (8–10). For the postwar period, there is an index combining federal spending, debt, and taxes (G). For the interwar and prewar periods, there are two segments of the federal expenditures series (gx and GX, respectively).

Finally, there are three different indexes of leading indicators (11–13). The only such series presently available for 1886–1914 is a diffusion index based on specific cycles in individual indicators (ldc). The composite indexes for 1919–40 and, particularly, for 1949–82 (ld and l, respectively) are much more satisfactory.

12.2.2 Data Sources and Problems

The "standard" historical estimates of GNP before World War II, based mainly on the work of Kuznets, Kendrick, and Gallman, are annual at most. We use the new quarterly series for real GNP and the implicit price deflator from Balke and Gordon (1986b).[5] These data are constructed from the standard series by means of quarterly interpolators which include the Persons 1931 index of industrial production and trade before 1930, the Federal Reserve Board (FRB) industrial production index for 1930–40, constant terms, and linear time trends. The use of interpolations based on series with narrower coverage than GNP is a source of unavoidable error if the unit period is to be shorter than a year.[6]

---

5. New annual estimates of nominal GNP, the implicit price deflator (1982 = 100), and real GNP for 1869–1929 are presented in Balke and Gordon (1989). This study develops some additional sources for direct measurement of nonmanufacturing output and the deflator. It concludes that real GNP was on the average about as volatile as the traditional Kuznets-Kendrick series indicate, but that the GNP deflator was significantly less volatile.

6. The Persons index consists of a varying assortment of weighted and spliced series on bank clearings outside New York City, production of pig iron and electric power, construction contracts,

The historical annual estimates of U.S. income and output leave much to be desired, but it is difficult to improve on them because the required information simply does not exist. The series have been recently reevaluated, leading to new estimates by Romer (1986 and 1987) and Balke and Gordon (1988). Romer's method imposes certain structural characteristics of the U.S. economy in the post–World War II period on the pre–World War I data. This produces results that contradict the evidence of postwar moderation of the business cycle by prejudging the issue (Lebergott 1986; Weir 1986; Balke and Gordon 1988). It is mainly for this reason that we do not use Romer's data. The basic source of historical monetary statistics (monthly since May 1907, biennial earlier) is Friedman and Schwartz 1970. Here, too, interpolations based on related series are applied in early years. The data for money (like those for income, output, and prices) improve over time but are never without serious problems. The interwar and postwar series are produced by the FRB.

Market interest rates are more easily and much better measured than the macroeconomic aggregates and indexes on our list. The commercial paper rate series (Macaulay 1938 and FRB) is of good quality, at least in a comparative sense.

The Blanchard fiscal index is designed to measure "the effect of fiscal policy on aggregate demand at given interest rates" (Blanchard and Watson 1986, p. 149). This series moves countercyclically most of the time, hence presumably retains in large measure elements of built-in tax-and-transfer stabilizers. For the earlier periods, no comparable comprehensive index is available, and we use the series on federal expenditures from Firestone (1960).

From the Commerce Department's leading index for 1949–82, we exclude real money balances (M2 deflated by the consumer price index) and change in business and consumer credit outstanding. This is done to avoid overlaps or conflicts with the monetary variables covered in our equations. The stock price component (Standard & Poor's index of 500 common stocks) may be strongly affected by monetary and fiscal developments, and adopting a conservative bias, we remove it as well. This newly adjusted composite index consists of nine series representing primarily the early stages of fixed capital investment, inventory investment, and marginal adjustments of employment and production.[7]

The only composite index of leading indicators available in the literature for the interwar period covers six series: average workweek, new orders for

---

railroad car loadings and net ton-miles of freight, indexes of volume of manufacturing and mining, etc. The compilation is spotty and uneven, particularly before 1903. A few other historical indexes of business activity are available but they have similar limitations (see chapter 7).

7. These indicators are average workweek, manufacturing; average weekly initial claims for unemployment insurance; vendor performance (percentage of companies receiving slower deliveries); change in sensitive materials prices; manufacturers' orders in constant dollars, consumer goods and materials industries; contracts and orders for plant and equipment in constant dollars; index of net business formation; building permits for new private housing units; change in manufacturing and trade inventories on hand and on order in constant dollars.

durable-goods manufacturers, nonfarm housing starts, commercial and industrial construction contracts, new business incorporations, and Standard & Poor's index of stock prices. The index is presented and discussed in Shiskin 1961a. Its method of construction is very similar to that presently used for the Commerce index.[8] The coverage of the Shiskin index, though narrower, also resembles that of the postwar index, particularly when the money and credit components are deleted from the latter. The one major difference is that the interwar index is based on changes in the component series over 5-month spans, whereas the postwar index is based on month-to-month changes.[9]

Unfortunately, no composite index of leading indicators exists for the pre–World War I period. To compute such an index from historical data would certainly be worthwhile but also laborious; the project must be reserved for the future. In the meantime, we report on some experimental work with the only available series that summarizes the early cyclical behavior of a set of individual leading indicators. The set consists of 75 individual indicators whose turning points have usually led at business cycle peaks and troughs. It covers such diverse areas as business profits and failures, financial market transactions and asset prices, bank clearings, loans and deposits, sensitive materials prices, inventory investment, new orders for capital goods, construction contracts, and the average workweek. Moore (1961) presents a diffusion index showing the percentage of these series expanding in each month from 1885 to 1940. The index is based on cyclical turns in each of its components: a series is simply counted as rising during each month of a specific-cycle expansion (and declining otherwise). Clearly, the type of smoothing implicit in this index construction is ill-suited for our purposes as it was designed for a very different task of historical timing analysis. Nevertheless, for lack of any other measure, we use this diffusion index by cumulating its deviations from 50 and taking log differences of the results.

12.3   The Statistical Framework

12.3.1   Method of Estimation

Conflicting macromodels draw support not only from different theoretical rationalizations of economic behavior but also, when implemented econo-

---

8. Percentage changes in each component series (computed so as to ensure symmetrical treatment of rises and declines) are standardized, that is, expressed as ratios to their own long-run mean, without regard to sign. The resulting changes are averaged across the series for each month and then cumulated into an index. Simple averages are used by Shiskin, and weighted averages by Commerce, but this makes little difference since the Commerce weights, based on performance scores of the selected indicators, are nearly equal. Also, the Commerce index has a trend adjusted to equal the trend in the index of coincident indicators (which is close to the trend in real GNP), whereas the Shiskin index has no such adjustment (Shiskin 1961a, pp. 43–47 and 123–25; U.S. Department of Commerce 1984, pp. 65–70).

9. Except for the inventory and price components, which are weighted 4-month moving averages, trailing.

metrically, from different empirical priors imposed on the data. Dissatisfaction with the "incredible identification" of existing large-scale simultaneous equation systems led to the recent popularity of vector autoregressions, which treat all variables as endogenous and shun unfounded *a priori* restrictions. The method has been used in attempts to discriminate among alternative explanations of money-income causality (Sims 1980a).

This chapter examines the interactions within a larger set of macroeconomic variables than that considered in the money-income causality studies. The particular statistics that interest us in this context are exogeneity and neutrality tests for the selected macrovariables within the different time periods.

Define $x_{s,t}^i$ as a generic variable with s denoting the time series $(q, p, b, \ldots)$ and i denoting the time frame (prewar, interwar, postwar). For each series and time frame, we estimate ordinary least squares regressions of the form (the superscript i is henceforth omitted for simplicity)

$$(1) \qquad x_{s,t} = \alpha_s + \beta_s t + \sum_{r=1}^{R} \sum_{j=1}^{J} \gamma_{r,j} x_{r,t-j} + e_t,$$

where $R = 3, \ldots$ up to 6 series and $J = 4$ quarterly lags. The neutrality test is a t-statistic which tests the null hypothesis

$$(2) \qquad H_0: \sum_{j=1}^{J} \gamma_{s,j} = 0$$

against the alternative that the sum is not equal to 0. The exogeneity test is an F-statistic which tests

$$(3) \qquad H_0: \gamma_{s,1} = \ldots = \gamma_{s,k} = 0$$

against the alternative that not all γ are equal to 0.

12.3.2 Unit Roots and Transformations

Since the work of Nelson and Plosser (1982), much interest has been paid to the existence of unit roots in macroeconomic time series. The magnitudes of the secular and cyclical components of these series receive primary attention in the work of Cochrane (1988) and Campbell and Mankiw (1987). Sims, Stock, and Watson (1986) also consider the role unit roots play in hypothesis testing with VARs. They show that to interpret correctly exogeneity and neutrality tests using standard asymptotic theory, it is necessary to transform the data to zero-mean stationary series. Moreover, Stock and Watson (1987) shed new light on the long-debated problem of money-income causality by taking nonstationarities into account. Therefore, because of both an explicit interest in the results and also the necessity of having stationary series to employ standard asymptotic theory, we calculate a set of unit root tests.

We test the null hypothesis

(4)
$$x_{s,t} = \sum_{j=1}^{J} p_{s,j} x_{s,t} + e_t$$

against the general alternative

(5)
$$x_{s,t} = \mu_s + \psi_s t \sum_{j=1}^{J} p_{s,j} x_{s,t} + e_t$$

with $\Sigma\, p_{s,i} < 1$ and, depending on the test, with and without ψ_s restricted to be 0. Rejection of the null hypothesis implies that the series does not contain a unit root and is stationary either around its mean, when ψ_s is restricted to be 0, or around a time trend, when ψ_s is not so restricted.

The unit root tests are presented in Tables 12.2, 12.3, and 12.4 for the postwar, interwar, and prewar sample periods, respectively. Part A of each table includes the tests for a single unit root for each series, calculated using levels. Part B contains tests for a second unit root calculated using first differences.

Because there is no uniformly most powerful test for unit roots, we use two different sets of test statistics. To test the hypothesis that a series is stationary around its mean, we estimate the Dickey-Fuller $\hat{\tau}_\mu$ statistic and the Stock-Watson q_f^μ statistic. These statistics restrict ψ_s in the alternative hypothesis (eq. [5]) to be 0. To test the hypothesis that a series is stationary around a linear time trend, we estimate the Dickey-Fuller $\hat{\tau}_\tau$ statistic and the Stock-Watson $q\tau_f$ statistic.

The Dickey-Fuller statistics are calculated by estimating via ordinary least squares (OLS) the following transformation of equation (5):

(6)
$$x_{s,t} = \mu_s + \psi_s t + \phi_{s,1} x_{s,t} + \sum_{j=2}^{J} \phi_{s,j}(x_{s,j+1} - x_{s,t-j});$$

and calculating the adjusted t-statistic for $\phi_{s,t}$ as

(7)
$$\hat{\tau}_\mu = \frac{\phi_{s,1} - 1.00}{\text{SE}(\phi_{s,1})}$$

with and without ψ_s restricted to be 0. $\text{SE}(\phi_{s,1})$ is the typically reported standard error of ϕ_s. The critical values for these statistics are tabulated in Fuller 1976.

The Stock-Watson test statistics we use are based on the more general Stock-Watson $q_f(k, m)$ test for common trends in a vector of time-series variables. The statistic is simply

(8)
$$q_f(k, m) = T[\text{Re}(\hat{\lambda}) - 1],$$

where $\hat{\lambda}$ is the largest real (Re) root of the sample autocorrelation matrix and T is the number of observations. The $q_f(k, m)$ statistic tests the hypothesis of k versus m unit roots for an n-vector time series ($m < k \leq n$). For the univar-

Table 12.2   **Univariate Tests for Unit Roots and Time Trends for the Postwar Sample: Quarterly Data, 1949:1–1982:4**

Series[a]	Unit Root Test Statistics[b]				t-Statistics[c]	
	$\hat{\tau}_\mu$	q_f^μ	$\hat{\tau}_\tau$	q_f^τ	Time	Constant
	A. Tests on Levels[d]					
Q	− 1.92	− 0.61	− 1.90	− 7.82	2.17	2.04$^+$
M_1	4.21	1.39	0.53	0.44	0.71	− 3.23*
M_2	2.22	0.41	− 1.56	− 2.92	2.09$^+$	− 1.74°
B	3.12	0.58	− 1.45	− 0.74	2.81*	− 2.64*
G	− 2.90$^+$	− 15.56$^+$	− 4.76*	− 36.21**	− 3.34**	− 2.81*
L	− 1.54	− 1.48	− 3.38°	− 17.83°	4.51**	1.72
I	− 1.78	− 7.00	− 3.73$^+$	− 24.96$^+$	3.17*	1.89°
P	3.16	− 0.13	0.68	− 0.08	0.89	− 1.89°
	B. Tests on Differences[d]					
q	− 5.09*	− 85.86**	− 5.41*	− 88.41**	− 1.72°	4.52**
m_1	− 2.67°	− 54.56**	− 4.21*	− 89.71**	4.20**	3.51**
m_2	− 2.84°	− 24.10**	− 4.07*	− 48.73**	3.21*	3.24*
b	− 3.29$^+$	− 37.60**	− 4.73*	− 65.18**	4.37**	3.08*
g	− 6.28*	− 114.65**	− 6.24*	− 114.63**	0.50	− 0.33
ℓ	− 7.26*	− 87.91**	− 7.39*	− 88.68**	− 1.19	3.79**
i	− 3.42$^+$	− 115.49**	− 3.30°	− 115.48**	− 0.06	0.64
p	− 3.30$^+$	− 39.14**	− 4.20*	− 67.00**	2.94*	3.05*

[a]On the definitions of the variables, see table 12.1. Capital letters denote levels (in logs, except for I) Lowercase letters denote first differences (in logs, except for i).

[b]$\hat{\tau}_\mu$ denotes the Dickey-Fuller (1979) statistic computed using a regression with four lags. q_f^μ is the Stock-Watson (1986) statistic, also from a regression with four lags. $\hat{\tau}_\tau$ and q_f^τ are again, respectively, the Dickey-Fuller and Stock-Watson statistics calculated using a time trend.

[c]t-statistics for the time and constant coefficient estimated from a regression of the variable on four own lags with time trend and without.

[d]Significance level at the 1/10 of 1% level is denoted by ** (except for the Dickey-Fuller tests, for which 0.001 significance levels are not tabulated); at the 1% level by *; 5% level by $^+$; and 10% level by °.

iate tests used here, the null hypothesis (eq. [4]) is one unit root, $k = 1$, against the alternative (eq. [5]) of no unit root, $m = 0$. The critical values for the q_f^μ and q_f^τ statistics are tabulated in Stock and Watson 1986.

We also test for the order of any deterministic components in these series. We regressed the level and first difference of each series against a constant, time, and four of its own lags. Likewise we tested for significant drift terms by replicating this estimation without a time trend. The last column reports the t-ratio on the constant term.

Looking at the results for the postwar sample (table 12.2), only the fiscal index is stationary in levels around its mean as well as around a time trend. The leading index and the commercial paper rate are stationary in levels around a time trend only. All postwar series are stationary in first differences, with significant time trends occurring for all three money series and prices.

Table 12.3   Univariate Tests for Unit Roots and Time Trends for the Interwar Sample: Quarterly Data, 1919:1–1940:1

Series[a]	$\hat{\tau}_\mu$	q_f^μ	$\hat{\tau}_\tau$	q_f^τ	Time	Constant
			Unit Root Test Statistics[b]		*t*-Statistics[c]	
			A. Tests on Levels[d]			
Q	−1.21	−8.74	−1.90	−11.33	1.71°	1.60
M_1	0.29	1.05	−0.87	−3.15	2.17+	0.05
M_2	−0.94	−2.55	−1.63	−5.71	1.78°	1.18
B	3.06	3.14	0.48	−1.49	2.17+	−2.28+
GX	0.06	−1.36	−3.07*	−13.65	3.33*	0.04
LD	−1.53	−4.99	−1.78	−7.04	−1.23	2.33+
I	−1.42	−4.26	−3.38*	−16.68	−2.93*	0.66
P	−3.38*	−8.74	−3.11	−11.33	−1.26	3.28**
			B. Tests on Differences[d]			
q	−3.33*	−35.18**	−3.22+	−35.64	0.59	0.96
m_1	−2.67°	−21.32**	−3.05	−23.96**	1.80°	1.08
m_2	−3.33*	−21.02**	−2.58	−20.41**	0.89	0.89
b	−2.25	−58.90**	−4.30*	−76.41**	3.76**	1.79°
gx	−5.85*	−90.52**	−6.72*	−99.09**	2.20+	0.90
ℓd	−4.80*	−57.41**	−4.77*	−54.29**	0.16	0.00
i	−5.43*	−49.00**	−5.38*	−48.95**	0.33	−1.21
p	−5.64*	−35.18**	−6.10*	−35.65**	−2.07	−1.26

[a]On the definitions of the variables, see table 12.1. Capital letters denote levels (in logs, except for *I*) Lowercase letters denote first differences (in logs, except for *i*).

[b]$\hat{\tau}_\mu$ denotes the Dickey-Fuller (1979) statistic computed using a regression with four lags. q_f^μ is the Stock-Watson (1986) statistic, also from a regression with four lags. $\hat{\tau}_\tau$ and Q_f^τ are again, respectively, the Dickey-Fuller and Stock-Watson statistics calculated using a time trend.

[c]*t*-statistics for the time and constant coefficient estimated from a regression of the variable on four own lags with time trend and without.

[d]Significance level at the 1/10 of 1% level is denoted by ** (except for the Dickey-Fuller tests, for which 0.001 significance levels are not tabulated); at the 1% level by *; 5% level by + ; and 10% level by °.

We infer from this that it is necessary to take first differences of real GNP, money, and prices.

Although the tests indicate the leading index is stationary in levels around a time trend, we decided to perform our subsequent analysis using first differences. This is because the leading index has a built-in nonstationary component constructed from the trend of the coincident index (see U.S. Department of Commerce 1984, pp. 65–69). Because this nonstationary component is implicitly related to the trend rate of growth of GNP and we take first differences of GNP, we also take first differences of the leading index. According to Sims, Stock, and Watson (1986), the presence of significant trends in the series of money and price changes makes it necessary to include a time trend in our equations to permit us to use standard asymptotic theory to interpret the exogeneity and neutrality tests.

For the interwar period (table 12.3), the unit root tests are more difficult to

Table 12.4   **Univariate Tests for Unit Roots and Time Trends for the Prewar Sample: Quarterly Data, 1886:1–1914:4**

Series[a]	Unit Root Test Statistics[b]				t-Statistics[c]	
	$\hat{\tau}_\mu$	q_f^μ	$\hat{\tau}_\tau$	q_f^τ	Time	Constant
			A. Tests on Levels[d]			
Q	−0.93	−0.93	−2.24	−15.22	3.11*	1.20
M_2	0.00	−0.45	−2.04	−6.50	1.85°	1.31
B	0.17	−0.10	−1.94	−19.77	2.11⁺	2.28⁺
GX	−1.17	−2.23	−3.64*	−43.42**	4.04**	1.52
LDC	−2.84°	−5.66	−4.24*	−21.90⁺	2.66*	2.15⁺
I	−5.10*	−49.94*	−6.30*	−56.93**	−2.68*	4.59**
P	0.45	0.91	−1.35	−2.74	2.35⁺	−0.15
			B. Tests on Differences[d]			
q	−5.18*	−70.48**	−5.18*	−70.77**	−0.68	3.19*
m_2	−4.09*	−161.64**	−8.04*	−39.39**	0.38	3.17*
b	−5.88*	−161.65**	−5.88*	−161.86**	0.60	3.87**
gx	−6.60*	−150.58**	−6.58*	−150.58**	−0.40	−1.80°
ℓdc	−7.45*	−68.23**	−7.71*	−63.13**	−1.40	2.02⁺
i	−6.98*	−123.60**	−6.95*	−123.59**	−0.18	0.09
p	−5.72*	−113.51**	−6.15*	−117.50**	2.11⁺	1.30

[a]On the definitions of the variables, see table 12.1. Capital letters denote levels (in logs, except for I). Lowercase letters denote first differences (in logs, except for i).

[b]$\hat{\tau}_\mu$ denotes the Dickey-Fuller (1979) statistic computed using a regression with four lags. q_f^μ is the Stock-Watson (1986) statistic, also from a regression with four lags. $\hat{\tau}_\tau$ and Q_f^τ are again, respectively, the Dickey-Fuller and Stock-Watson statistics calculated using a time trend.

[c]t-statistics for the time and constant coefficient estimated from a regression of the variable on four own lags with time trend and without.

[d]Significance level at the 1/10 of 1% level is denoted by ** (except for the Dickey-Fuller tests, for which 0.001 significance levels are not tabulated); at the 1% level by *; 5% level by ⁺; and 10% level by °.

interpret because of the small sample size (87 observations). For levels (pt. A), the Dickey-Fuller tests indicate that the interest rate is stationary around a time trend and the price level is stationary around its mean. The Stock-Watson tests contradict these particular results, however, bringing into question the power of these tests (see Dickey and Fuller 1979 for power calculations of $\hat{\tau}_\mu$). Looking at the tests on differences (pt. B), the tests indicate that all of the interwar series are stationary, except for the Dickey-Fuller tests for m_1 and m_2 around a trend and the monetary base around its mean. However, these particular tests again contradict the Stock-Watson tests. Because of these results, we act conservatively and use first differences of all of the interwar series. Moreover, following the arguments for the postwar sample, a time trend is also necessitated by the significant t-ratios for m_1, b, and g on the trend coefficients.

Finally, for the prewar sample (table 12.4) it is sufficient to take first differences only of real GNP, the monetary base, M_2, and the implicit price deflator, whereas the series on government expenditures and the interest rate can be left in levels. Again, although the tests indicate the leading diffusion index is stationary in levels around a trend, we instead use first differences of this series in our subsequent analysis. This is because the trend is artificially induced via the accumulation of the original series. A time trend is also included because of the significant trend coefficient for inflation.

12.4 The Results

12.4.1 Factors Influencing Changes in Real GNP: A Stepwise Approach

1949–1982

Table 12.5 is based on regressions of real GNP growth on its own lagged values (q_{t-i}, i = 1, . . . ,4) and the lagged values of from two to five other selected series, plus a constant term and time. Each variable has the form shown in table 12.1, col. 4, as indicated by the tests discussed previously. The calculations proceed by successively expanding the set of explanatory variables, in four steps. First, only the lagged terms of q are used along with the corresponding values of a fiscal and a monetary variable. The inflation group is added next, and then the interest-rate group. The last step includes the leading-index terms as well.

This table and those that follow are standardized to show the F-statistics for conventional tests of exogeneity and, underneath these entries, the t-statistics for the neutrality tests, that is, for the *sums* of the regression coefficients of the same groups of lagged terms for each variable. The estimated individual coefficients are too numerous to report and their behavior is difficult to describe in the frequent cases where their successive values oscillate with mixed signs. It seems advisable, however, to show at least the summary t-ratios in each equation. When sufficiently large, these statistics suggest that the individual terms in each group are not all weak or not all transitory, that is, that they do not offset each other across the different lags.

In the 1949–82 equations with three variables only, the lagged q terms are always significant at least at the 5% level; each of the monetary alternatives makes a contribution (m_2 is particularly strong); and the fiscal index G is relatively weak, except when used along with the monetary base b (table 12.5, pt. A, eqs. [1]–[3]). Adding inflation (p) is of little help in explaining q, but on balance the coefficients of p are negative and some may matter (eqs. [4]–[6]). When the commercial paper rate (I) is entered, it acquires a dominant role at the expense of the other (especially the monetary) variables (eqs. [7]–[9]).[10] Finally, equations (10)–(12) show that of all the variables considered,

10. The addition of I reduces further the statistics for p. The simple correlation between I and p in 1949–82 is about 0.7. During the latter part of the postwar era, inflation spread and accelerated and financial markets became increasingly sensitive to it. Since I depends on the real interest rate (R) and expected inflation (i.e., forecasts of p, probably based in part on p_{t-i}), our results suggest an independent role for R in codetermining q.

Table 12.5 Rate of Change in Real GNP (q) Regressed on Its Own Lagged Values and Those of Other Selected Variables: Tests of Exogeneity and Significance, Quarterly Data for Three Periods between 1886 and 1982

Equation No.	df[a]	Lagged Explanatory Variables[b]	Test Statistics[c] for q (1)	b, m_1, m_2 (2)	G (3)	p (4)	I, i (5)	$\ell, \ell d, \ell dc$ (6)	t (7)	$\bar{R}_2$ (8)
			A. Sample Period 1949:2–1982:4							
1	121	q, b, G	4.2*	3.4*	3.1+					0.26
			1.6	-0.7	2.7*				1.3	
2	121	q, m_1, G	2.9+	3.1+	1.6					0.26
			1.1	1.1	1.6°				-0.3	
3	121	q, m_2, G	3.1+	5.3**	1.3					0.30
			0.8	2.7*	0.9				-1.5	
4	117	q, b, G, p	3.5*	3.2+	2.1°	0.8				0.26
			1.2	0.1	2.2+	-1.6			1.4	
5	117	g, m_1, G, p	2.1°	3.5+	1.1	1.3				0.27
			0.6	1.7°	0.9	-1.8°			-0.3	
6	117	q, m_2, G, p	2.3°	5.2**	1.0	0.9				0.30
			0.8	2.4+	0.8	-0.8			-1.0	
7	113	q, b, G, p, I	2.0°	2.4+	0.9	0.3	4.7**			0.34
			0.4	-1.2	0.7	0.4	-3.2*		3.0*	
8	113	q, m_1, G, p, I	2.3°	2.0°	0.7	0.4	4.0*			0.34
			-0.7	2.3+	-0.8	-0.6	-3.2**		0.5	
9	113	q, m_2, G, p, I	2.0	2.3°	1.0	0.8	2.8+			0.34
			0.2	1.0	0.7	0.1	-2.4+		0.5	
10	109	q, b, G, p, I, ℓ	1.3	1.3	1.7	0.7	3.7*	4.4*		0.41
			-1.9	-0.1	-0.6	1.3	-3.3**	3.7**	1.1	
11	109	q, m_1, G, p, I, ℓ	2.7+	2.4°	2.5+	0.4	4.6**	6.0**		0.44
			-3.1*	2.2*	-1.8°	0.9	-3.8**	4.7**	-0.5	

(continued)

Table 12.5   Continued

Equation No.	df[a]	Lagged Explanatory Variables[b]	q (1)	b, m_1, m_2 (2)	G (3)	p (4)	I, i (5)	$\ell, \ell d, \ell dc$ (6)	t (7)	$\bar{R}_2$ (8)
12	109	q, m_2, G, p, I, ℓ	1.7	2.1°	2.4+	0.9	3.2+	5.3**		0.43
			-2.3	0.6	-1.0	1.5	-3.1*	4.4**	0.2	
		B. 1920:4–1940:4								
13	67	q, b, gx	7.0**	5.2**	6.7**					0.44
			3.0*	1.4	-1.4				-0.7	
14	67	q, m_1, gx	2.6	3.9*	5.3***					0.40
			0.7+	2.0+	-1.3				-0.5	
15	67	q, m_2, gx	4.6*	4.0*	5.2*					0.41
			1.7°	0.9	-1.5				0.4	
16	63	q, b, gx, p	5.2**	5.3**	5.6**	0.9				0.43
			3.0*	1.4	-1.5	-0.8			-0.4	
17	63	q, m_1, gx, p	1.1	5.0*	3.9*	1.7				0.43
			0.8	2.7*	-0.8	-2.0+			-0.4	
18	63	q, m_2, gx, p	2.4°	4.6*	3.6*	1.2				0.42
			1.6	1.6	-1.0	-1.7°			0.8	
19	59	q, b, gx, p, i	4.8*	4.4*	5.3**	0.8	0.2			0.41
			2.9*	1.5	-1.4	-0.6	-0.5		-0.5	
20	59	q, m_1, gx, p, i	0.8	4.2*	3.6*	1.8	0.3			0.40
			0.6	2.7*	-0.8	-2.1+	0.5		-0.5	
21	59	q, m_2, gx, p, i	2.1°	3.9*	3.6*	1.4	0.3			0.39
			1.2	1.7°	-1.0	-1.7°	0.3		0.8	
22	55	$q, b, gx, p, i, \ell d$	1.4	4.1*	3.0+	1.3	0.2	3.9*		0.50
			-0.6	1.3	-1.0	-0.1	-0.2	2.6*	-0.7	

Eq.	df[a]	Variables[b]	(1)	(2)	(3)	(4)	(5)	(6)	(7)	(8)
23	55	*q, m₁, gx, p, i, ℓd*	2.0	3.5*	1.9	1.9	0.2	3.5*		0.49
			−1.4	2.4+	−0.7	−1.4	0.7	2.3+	−0.7	
24	55	*q, m₂, gx, p, i, ℓd*	1.9	3.7*	1.7	1.2	0.6	4.0*		0.49
			−0.8	1.5	−0.5	−1.2	0.4	2.2+	0.4	

C. 1886:2–1914:4

Eq.	df[a]	Variables[b]	(1)	(2)	(3)	(4)	(5)	(6)	(7)	(8)
25	101	*q, b, G, x*	8.9**	0.2	0.7					0.21
			0.9	0.3	1.1				−1.2	
26	101	*q, m₂, GX*	3.0+	5.3**	0.2					0.34
			−0.5	2.2+	0.3				−0.6	
27	97	*q, b, GX, p*	7.2**	0.2	0.8	1.7				0.23
			1.3	0.4	1.4	−1.7*			−1.4	
28	97	*q, m₂, GX, p*	3.0*	5.0**	0.2	1.6				0.36
			−0.6	2.6*	0.3	−1.8°			−0.4	
29	93	*q, b, GX, p, I*	4.0*	0.3	0.3	1.7	3.3*			0.30
			0.0	0.7	0.6	−1.7°	−2.4+		−1.0	
30	93	*q, m₂, GX, p, I*	2.4+	3.0+	0.2	1.6	1.6			0.37
			−0.8	2.2+	0.1	−1.7°	−1.4		−0.4	
31	89	*q, b, GX, p, I, ℓdc*	4.0*	0.3	0.1	1.5	3.7*	0.7		0.29
			−0.3	0.7	0.5	−1.4	−2.4+	−0.7	−1.1	
32	89	*q, m₂, GX, p, I, ℓdc*	2.6+	3.5*	0.1	1.6	2.3°	1.2		0.38
			−1.1	2.2°	−0.4	−1.5	−1.8°	−1.2	−0.4	

[a]Degrees of freedom.

[b]See table 12.1 for definitions of the variables and sources of the data.

[c]The first line for each equation lists the F-statistics for groups of lagged values of each variable covered (cols. 1–6) and squared correlation coefficients for the sums of regression coefficients (col. 8). The second line lists the t-statistics for the sums of regression coefficients of the same groups (cols. 1–6) and for the time trend (col. 7). Significance at the $\frac{1}{10}$ of 1% level is denoted by **; at the 1% level by *; at the 5% level by +; and at the 10% level by °.

the rate of change in the leading index exerts the statistically most significant influence on q. Five of the test statistics for l are significant at the 0.1% level; one at the 1% level. The level of interest rates represented by l retains its strong net inverse effect on q. The direct contributions of m_1, m_2, and G to the determination of real GNP growth are much fewer and weaker; those of b and p are altogether difficult to detect.[11]

Alternative calculations show that when l is added to the equations with the monetary and fiscal variables only, the effects of these variables on q are again drastically reduced. Had we retained the money, credit, and stock price components in the leading index, the role of the index in these equations would have been even stronger and that of the other regressors generally weaker.[12] In any event, the evidence indicates that the quarterly movements of the economy's output in 1949–82 depended much more on recent changes in leading indicators and interest rates than on recent changes in output itself, money, the fiscal factor, or inflation.

Conceivably, longer lags could produce different results, so we checked to see what happens when eight instead of four lags are used. These tests suggest some gains in power for the lagged q and G terms, but the leading index and the interest rate still have consistently strong effects. However, we do not report these statistics because the restriction to lags of one–four quarters is dictated by the limitations of the available data. With eight lags, for example, the number of degrees of freedom is reduced from 109 to 81 for the six-variable equations.

1919–1940

In the equations for the interwar period, all variables appear in the form of first differences. In the first subset (table 12.5, pt. B, eqs. [13]–[15]), q depends positively on its own lagged values and those of the monetary variables and inversely on the recent values of federal expenditures gx. All the F-statistics are significant, most highly so. On the other hand, inflation contributes but little to these regressions, as shown by the results for equations (16)–(18) (only two t-tests indicate significance and none of the F-tests). Further, no gains at all result from the inclusion of the change in the commercial paper rate (eqs. [19]–[21]).

11. These results are not inconsistent with b influencing q with longer lags via changes in m_1 or m_2 or l, or with a negative effect of inflation uncertainty on output, which is found in some studies that work with higher moments or forecasts of inflation (see Makin 1982; Litterman and Weiss 1985; chapter 17).

12. It should be noted that the index is robust in the sense of not being critically dependent on any of its individual components or their weights. Thus, any large subset of these indicators can produce a fair approximation to the total index under the adopted construction and standardization procedures. Some of the components are known to have good predictive records of their own (e.g., stock prices, as shown in Fischer and Merton 1984), but the leading index outperforms any of them on the average over time. The reductions in coverage and diversity detract from the forecasting potential of the index but, up to a point, only moderately. And, as in the present case, they may often be advisable for analytical purposes.

In contrast, there is strong evidence in our estimates for 1919–40 that the lagged rates of change in the index of six leading indicators (ld) had a large net positive influence on q. Four of the corresponding test statistics are significant at the 1% level and two at the 5% level (pt. B, col. 6). In equations (22)–(24), ld shows the strongest effects, followed by the monetary variables; gx is significant only in one case; and the tests for lagged q, p, and i terms are all negative.

On the whole, the monetary series appear to play a somewhat stronger role in the interwar than in the postwar equations; whereas the leading series appear to play a somewhat weaker role. It should be recalled, however, that l is a more comprehensive index than ld and is based on better data. Even for the series that are more comparable across the two periods, the quality of the postwar data is probably significantly higher. Further, the reliability of the results for 1919–40 suffers from the small-sample problem: the number of observations per parameter to be estimated here is little more than half the number available for 1949–82.

In light of these considerations, it seems important to note that the interwar results resemble broadly the postwar results in most respects and look rather reasonable, at least in the overall qualitative sense. The leading indexes are highly effective in the regressions for both periods. The main difference between the two sets of estimates is that the commercial paper rate contributes strongly to the statistical explanation of q in 1949–82, but the change in that rate does not help in the 1919–40 regressions (cf. col. 5 in pts. A and B of table 12.5). We checked whether interest levels (I) would have performed significantly better than interest changes (i) in the interwar equations, and the answer is no.

1886–1914

For the pre–World War I period, the equations with three variables indicate strong effects on q of its own lagged values and those of m_2, but no significant contributions of either the monetary base or government expenditures (table 12.5, pt. C, eqs. [25]–[26]). The inflation terms add only a weak negative influence, as shown in the summary t-statistics for equations (27)–(28).

The recent values of the commercial paper rate have substantial inverse effects on the current rate of change in real GNP, particularly in the equations with the base and after the change in the diffusion index of leading indicators (ldc) is added (eqs. [29]–[32]). The ldc index itself appears to be ineffective. In light of the major importance of the leading indexes in the postwar and interwar equations, this negative result is probably attributable mainly to the way ldc is constructed. (Recall from a previous discussion that this index uses only the historical information on specific-cycle turning points in a set of 75 individual indicators.)

12.4.2   Test Statistics for Six-Variable Equations

1949–1982

Each of the monetary variables (b, m_1, m_2) depends strongly on its own lagged values and those of the interest rate (I), as shown by the corresponding F-values in table 12.6, equations (1)–(3). The I terms have coefficients whose signs vary, and their t-statistics are on balance small, though mostly negative. The fiscal index (G) appears to have a strong positive effect on m_1, and the time trends in column 7 are important. The effects of the other variables are sporadic and weak.

G is more strongly autoregressive yet. It also depends positively on b and m_2 and inversely on I, the change in the leading index l, and time (eqs. [4]–[6]).

Inflation (p) also depends mainly on its own lagged values, according to equations (7)–(9). A few relatively weak signs of influence appear for b, I, and G. The time trends are significant. These results are consistent with a view of the price level as a predetermined variable adjusting slowly with considerable inertia. Monetary influences on p involve much longer lags than are allowed here.

The interest rate depends most heavily on its own recent levels, as is immediately evident from equations (10)–(12). Still, some significant inputs into the determination of I (which yields R^2 as high as 0.95) are also made by other factors, notably m_1 and l.

As for l, it is not strongly influenced by either its own recent past or that of the other variables. The largest F-values here are associated with the interest rate in equations (13) and (14) and with inflation in equation (15).

The corresponding tests for real GNP (q) equations have already been discussed in the previous section (relating to the estimates in the last six lines of table 12.5, pt. A). It is interesting to note that very few significant F- or t-statistics are associated with the lagged q terms according to our tests (table 12.6, col. 1).

1919–1940

Tests based on the interwar monetary regressions indicate high serial dependence for m_1 and m_2 but not b (table 12.7, eqs. [1]–[3]). The base is influenced strongly by recent changes in output (q), moderately by those in the leading index (ld). There are signs of some effects on m_2 of ld and p, but no measurable outside influences on m_1.

Equations (4)–(6) for the rate of change in government expenditures (gx) produce F-statistics that are generally low and significant only for the lagged values of the dependent variable. The same applies to equations (10)–(12) for the change in the interest rate (i).

The rate of inflation (p) depends heavily on its own lagged values, too (eqs.

Table 12.6   **Tests of Exogeneity and Significance, Six-Variable Equations: Quarterly, 1949–82**

Equation No.[a]	Dependent Variable[b]	q (1)	b, m_1, m_2 (2)	G (3)	p (4)	I (5)	ℓ (6)	t (7)	$\bar{R}_2$ (8)
					Test Statistics[c] for				
1	b	1.7	10.5**	1.2	1.5	3.4*	2.9+		0.71
		1.8°	3.2**	−0.2	0.1	−0.9	1.7°	2.6*	
2	m_1	1.1	3.3*	3.3*	1.3	8.0**	0.4		0.54
		0.6	1.5	2.0+	0.7	−0.4	1.2	3.3*	
3	m_2	0.7	7.3**	0.8	0.4	10.6**	0.4		0.76
		0.4	3.7**	0.3	−0.2	−1.6°	0.3	2.9*	
4	G	1.1	2.4+	36.0**	0.7	3.5*	0.1		0.87
		−0.8	2.4+	9.7**	−0.7	−0.1	−0.2	−2.9*	
5	G	0.7	1.3	28.3**	1.0	3.6*	0.1		0.86
		−0.6	1.6	8.6**	−1.7°	−0.9	0.1	−2.3+	
6	G	0.7	2.4+	34.8**	1.1	2.6+	0.4		0.87
		−0.4	1.8°	9.6**	−1.9°	0.1	1.2	−2.7*	
7	p	1.1	2.5+	2.3°	0.5	2.8+	9.1**		0.63
		0.7	−1.8°	2.6*	−1.1	0.7	4.6**	3.0*	
8	p	1.0	0.8	1.1	0.3	1.7	8.7**		0.61
		−0.4	0.9	1.5	−0.3	1.0	4.0**	1.2	
9	p	1.0	1.6	2.1°	0.2	1.6	8.4**		0.62
		0.5	−1.9+	2.5*	−0.8	0.2	4.1**	3.0*	
10	I	1.8	1.3	0.2	4.1*	81.0**	3.0+		0.94
		1.1	−0.4	−0.5	0.5	13.1**	1.7°	0.9	
11	I	2.8+	6.6**	0.2	1.6	98.1**	1.9		0.95
		0.7	0.2	−0.1	0.5	14.8**	1.6	0.9	
12	I	1.8	2.1°	0.2	3.4*	68.0**	2.4+		0.95
		1.5	−0.8	−0.0	0.3	12.5**	1.2	1.5	
13	ℓ	1.2	1.1	1.9	1.8	3.8*	1.3		0.45
		0.1	−1.8°	2.2+	0.2	−1.4	−1.3	3.6**	
14	ℓ	1.2	1.6	1.6	2.2°	4.0*	2.5+		0.46
		−1.0	0.6	1.6°	1.0	−1.1	−2.4+	2.3+	
15	ℓ	1.0	1.2	1.7	2.1°	1.2	2.5+		0.45
		−0.4	−0.5	2.1+	0.9	−1.1	−2.5*	2.3+	

[a]Sample period: 1949:2–1982:4. Degrees of freedom: 109.
[b]See table 12.1 for definitions of the variables and sources of the data.
[c]F-statistics on the first line and t-statistics on the second line for each equation. Significance at the $\frac{1}{10}$ of 1% level is denoted by **; at the 1% level by *; at the 5% level by + ; and at the 10% level by °.

[7]–[9]). Some of the test statistics suggest that m_1, ld, and perhaps i may influence p slightly over the course of a year.

Interestingly, according to equations (13)–(15), ld is affected much more strongly by the recent monetary changes than by its own lagged values. There are also some signs of influence of gx on ld. This raises the possibility that monetary and fiscal changes, including those due to policy actions, may affect real GNP with long lags through the mediating role of the leading indicators

Table 12.7   Tests of Exogeneity and Significance, Six-Variable Equations: Quarterly,
                  1919–40

Equation No.[a]	Dependent Variable[b]	q (1)	b, m_1, m_2 (2)	g (3)	l (4)	i (5)	p (6)	t (7)	$\bar{R}_2$ (8)
					Test Statistics[c] for				
1	b	3.5	0.1	1.4	2.6[+]	0.7	0.7		0.40
		2.8**	−0.3	1.3	−1.7°	−1.4	−0.7	3.7**	
2	m_1	0.3	8.2**	1.4	0.9	0.1	1.3		0.55
		−0.1	3.3*	−1.7°	−0.3	−0.2	0.7	1.5	
3	m_2	0.6	4.6*	1.7	2.1°	0.7	2.2°		0.60
		0.3	2.8*	−2.4[+]	0.7	−0.3	1.6	1.1	
4	gx	1.9	1.1	2.7[+]	1.4	1.5	0.8		0.36
		−1.8	−1.2	−2.0[+]	1.4	0.4	1.5	2.1[+]	
5	gx	1.6	1.2	2.2[+]	1.5	1.0	0.7		0.36
		−1.9	−0.4	−1.8°	1.7	0.4	1.5	1.5	
6	gx	1.3	1.2	3.3[+]	1.2	0.9	0.9		0.36
		−1.5	−1.4	−2.3[+]	1.5	0.3	1.9°	1.7	
7	p	0.7	0.2	1.0	1.7	1.7	5.1*		0.54
		0.5	−0.2	1.4	1.4	−2.1[+]	1.9°	1.1	
8	p	1.2	2.2°	1.5	2.1°	1.4	6.2**		0.60
		0.2	−0.5	1.2	2.0[+]	−1.4	2.0[+]	1.4	
9	p	1.4	1.4	1.2	2.3[+]	2.0	5.7**		0.58
		0.7	−1.3	0.7	1.6	−1.6	2.2[+]	1.6	
10	i	0.6	0.7	0.5	1.3	2.7[+]	0.3		0.14
		−0.6	0.9	0.9	1.1	0.9	0.8	−0.7	
11	i	0.5	0.1	0.4	1.0	2.7[+]	0.3		0.10
		−0.1	0.1	1.0	0.7	0.7	0.6	−0.0	
12	i	0.6	0.9	0.7	1.3	2.6[+]	0.3		0.15
		−0.4	0.8	1.5	0.9	0.7	0.2	−0.1	
13	ld	1.1	4.7*	2.2°	3.0[+]	0.8	1.4		0.39
		−1.1	2.4[+]	−1.4	2.2[+]	−0.6	−0.1	−1.4	
14	ld	1.3	4.6*	1.5	2.0°	0.5	1.8[+]		0.39
		−1.8°	3.0*	−1.1	1.7°	0.6	−1.7	−0.7	
15	ld	1.3	7.4**	2.0°	2.7[+]	1.5	1.5		0.47
		−1.2	2.1[+]	−1.0	1.9°	0.5	1.6°	0.7	

[a]Sample period: 1920:4–1940:4. Degrees of freedom: 55.
[b]See table 12.1 for definitions of the variables and sources of the data.
[c]F-statistics on the first line and t-statistics on the second line for each equation. Significance at the $\frac{1}{10}$ of 1% level is denoted by **; at the 1% level by *; at the 5% level by [+]; and at the 10% level by °.

(ld). But note that this is suggested only by the estimates for the interwar period, not by those for the postwar era.[13]

Comparing Tables 12.6 and 12.7 and drawing also on Table 12.5 (pts. A and B, eqs. [10]–[12] and [22]–[24]), we observe that q depends strongly on

13. The difference could be related to the fact that the interwar index includes, while the postwar index excludes, the stock price series. Financial asset prices and returns are probably subject to stronger monetary and fiscal influences than other leading indicators are.

the leading indexes (l, ld) in both periods and on the monetary factors in the interwar period. The autoregressive elements are weak in q, l, and ld and strong (as a rule dominant) in the other variables according to the interwar as well as the postwar estimates. The effects of q on the other factors are generally weak or nonexistent.

1886–1914

The F-statistics for the own-lag terms are significant in all the pre–World War I equations, highly so (at the 0.1% level) for the monetary, fiscal, leading, and interest series, less so for q and p (see table 12.8 and table 12.5, pt. C, eqs. [30]–[32]). The leading index ldc for 1886–1914 is very strongly autocorrelated, in contrast to the indexes ld for 1919–40 and l for 1949–82. This reflects the construction of the prewar index, which assumes smooth cyclical movements in the index components (see section on data sources and problems).

Prewar changes in the monetary base are poorly "explained," mainly by own lags and those of government expenditures (GX) and the commercial paper rate (I). The corresponding changes in the stock of money (m_2) are fitted much better by lagged values of m_2 itself, I, and p. And as much as 94% of the variance of GX is explained statistically, mainly by lagged GX terms and the time trend. (See table 12.8, eqs. [1]–[4]).

The estimates for inflation (p) are problematic. They suggest that p was influenced positively by lagged money changes but also inversely by its own lagged values and those of I and ldc. The R^2 coefficients are of the order of 0.2–0.3 (eqs. [5]–[6]).

The equations for the interest rate (eqs. [7]–[8]), besides being dominated by autoregressive elements, indicate some short-term effects of q (with plus signs) and m_2 (minus). These results seem generally reasonable.

The leading diffusion index ldc (eqs. [9]–[10]) depends primarily on own lags, with traces of positive effects of q and p and negative effects of I. In view of the probable measurement errors involved (mainly in the ldc series), the serviceability of these estimates is uncertain.

12.5   Conclusions and Further Steps

The following list of our principal findings begins with a point of particular importance, which receives clear support from the better quality of the data available for the postwar and interwar periods.

1. Output depends strongly on leading indexes in equations which also include the monetary, fiscal, inflation, and interest variables (all taken in stationary form, with four quarterly lags in each variable). Hence, models that omit the principal leading indicators are probably seriously misspecified.

2. Short-term nominal interest rates had a strong inverse influence on output (specifically, the rate of change in real GNP) during the 1949–82 period.

Table 12.8   Tests of Exogeneity and Significance, Six-Variable Equations: Quarterly, 1886–1914

Equation No.[a]	Dependent Variable[b]	Test Statistics[c] for							
		q (1)	b, m_2 (2)	GX (3)	p (4)	I (5)	ℓdc (6)	t (7)	$\bar{R}_2$ (8)
1	b	0.7	7.3**	2.0°	0.3	2.8⁺	0.9		0.14
		1.4	−3.7**	1.7°	0.1	2.8*	0.6	−1.1	
2	m_2	1.1	20.8**	0.5	1.7	2.8⁺	4.2*		0.59
		−1.8	5.2**	−0.2	−1.4	−2.0⁺	0.6	−0.2	
3	GX	0.9	0.4	10.8**	0.2	0.9	0.3		0.94
		−0.4	0.9	5.1**	−0.4	−1.4	0.5	3.7**	
4	GX	1.6	0.9	9.2**	0.3	0.4	0.1		0.94
		−1.0	1.1	4.6**	0.2	−0.9	0.4	3.7**	
5	p	1.4	1.2°	1.5	3.3*	3.7*	1.8		0.23
		−0.3	2.0⁺	−0.3	−2.7*	−2.6⁺	−1.6°	0.1	
6	p	2.3°	2.8⁺	2.1°	3.3*	2.7⁺	2.5⁺		0.28
		−1.8°	3.2*	−1.0	−3.1*	1.4	−2.3*	1.1	
7	I	2.6⁺	1.9	0.7	2.3°	11.4**	1.5⁺		0.49
		2.8*	−2.5*	0.1	1.2	4.6**	2.3⁺	−0.4	
8	I	1.9	2.3°	0.7	1.7	8.1**	0.8		0.51
		2.3⁺	−1.2	−0.5	1.2	3.5**	1.3	0.1	
9	ℓdc	1.8	0.3	1.9	55.6**	2.2°	2.0°		0.72
		2.3⁺	0.4	−0.5	6.6**	−1.7°	0.4	−0.2	
10	ℓdc	1.3	0.3	1.9	56.3**	2.2°	2.1°		0.72
		−1.8°	0.3	−0.5	6.7**	−1.5	0.1	−0.1	

[a]Sample period: 1886:2–1914:4. Degrees of freedom: 89.

[b]See table 12.1 for definitions of the variables and sources of the data.

[c]F-statistics on the first line and t-statistics on the second line for each equation. Significance at the ¹⁄₁₀ of 1% level is denoted by **; at the 1% level by *; at the 5% level by ⁺; and at the 10% level by °.

When interest is included, the effects of the monetary and fiscal series are reduced (this resembles the results of some earlier studies; cf. Sims 1980a). When the leading index is also included, most of the monetary effects are further diminished.

3. In the interwar period, the role of money appears greater, and the fiscal and interest effects tend to wane. In the prewar (1886–1914) equations, output is influenced mainly by its own lagged values and those of the money stock and the interest rate. The other factors, including a diffusion index based on specific cycles in a large set of individual leading series, have no significant effects. However, this probably reflects errors in the data, especially the weakness of the available leading index.

4. The monetary, fiscal, and interest variables depend more on their own lagged values than on any of the other factors, and the same is true of inflation, except in 1886–1914. The opposite applies to the rates of change in output and (again, except in 1886–1914) the leading indexes. None of the variables in question can be considered exogenous.

5. The reported unit root tests are consistent with earlier findings that most macroeconomic time series are difference-stationary (see Nelson and Plosser 1982 on annual interwar and postwar data, and Stock and Watson 1987 on monthly postwar data). The major exceptions to this are the prewar and postwar fiscal and interest series.

Our work offers some suggestions for further research. The following steps at least should be considered:

(*a*) Construct a satisfactory composite index of leading indicators for the periods before World War II from the best available historical data.

(*b*) Compute variance decompositions and impulse response functions for alternative subsets of up to four variables represented by the quarterly series used in this paper.

(*c*) Do the same computations for larger sets of six variables by using monthly data. This would complement the results obtained here for individual equations in the same sets; further, it would permit comparisons with some recent smaller VAR models estimated on monthly data. The main problem with this approach is that no suitable monthly proxies for GNP may be found.

(*d*) Update the postwar series and check on predictions beyond the sample period, for example, for 1983–88.

(*e*) Try to find out where the explanatory or predictive power of the leading index is coming from by testing important subindexes relating to investment commitments, profitability, etc.

(*f*) Compare the implications of this paper with those of the most recent and ongoing studies of leading indicators (de Leeuw 1988, 1989; Stock and Watson 1988a, 1988b).

IV Forecasting

13   On Short-Term Predictions of General Economic Conditions

Part IV (chapters 13–18) is about forecasting the course of the economy in the near future, that is, up to 2 years, or eight quarters, ahead. Only the true ex ante predictions that are nontrivial and verifiable are considered, and only for a relatively small number of principal U.S. macroeconomic variables, real and nominal. The period covered is limited to the last three or four decades by the availability of the forecasts, but the spectrum of sources and methods covered is broad. Empirical studies of how macroeconomic forecasts and expectations are formed and what their properties and accuracy are have useful lessons despite their relatively short history. This chapter will serve as an introduction and guide to the subject; the chapters that follow deal much more thoroughly with several of its dimensions. [1]

13.1   Functions and Contents

Economic forecasts refer to economic aspects of unknown events, whether in the past, present, or future. It is of course the future that attracts most attention, since the practical purpose of the forecasts is to help formulate and improve public and private plans and decisions, which are necessarily forward looking. Formal forecasts of economists attempt to take into account the collective effects of these decisions, but they also influence in various ways and degrees the informal expectations of consumers, investors, business managers, and government officials.

The "unknown events" come in many different types and forms. The most common and regular targets of macroeconomic forecasting are the rates of growth in real GNP and its major expenditure components, the unemployment

---

1. Some of sections below draw in part on material in my earlier publications (Zarnowitz 1972b, 1974) and update it.

rate, and inflation and interest rates. Many professional forecasts are more detailed and extend to such cyclically sensitive series as corporate profits, industrial production, and housing starts. Large econometric model services help predict hundreds of variables that are of interest to subscribers. Financial forecasters concentrate on stock and bond prices and yields and on exchange rates, all of which are highly volatile, responsive to a continuous flow of news and rumors that affect traders' expectations, and notoriously difficult to predict.

Indeed, it is often argued that financial and other major economic series behave largely as random walks and hence cannot be predicted at all. But the overall stock market movements over intermediate and longer horizons, for example, have clearly strong trend-cycle components. They are both persistent and pervasive (large majorities of individual stock prices participate), anticipatory of business cycle and growth cycle turns, and related to other highly cyclical variables, notably corporate profits and (inversely) interest rates.[2]

Predicting routine events in economics and business generally takes the form of periodic forecasts of time-series values. In addition, there are events of special concern such as the turning points of business and growth cycles, financial panics and major bankruptcies, strikes, international crises and wars, and so on. Forecasters may or may not try to anticipate cyclical turns with the aid of leading indicators, but in any event their time-series predictions have implications for the timing of these events that need to be monitored and checked. Exogenous shocks, such as a sharp rise in oil prices due to a foreign cartel action or a threat of war, are not amenable to economic forecasting but their consequences for general business activity are.

Real aggregates and price indexes typically have upward trends reflecting economic growth and inflation, respectively; nominal aggregates expand for both reasons. Growth trends are long-term movements that dominate comprehensive output, employment, and related income and expenditure series in real terms across decades. In the period covered by our forecasts, inflation too has been persistent as well as pervasive. Cyclical fluctuations prevail over intermediate horizons of several quarters and years. In the shortest run, measured in weeks and months, changes in most economic time series are heavily influenced by irregular variations from random causes and by intrayear, approximately periodic, seasonal movements. But the forecasts are generally in quarterly and annual units, and they aim at seasonally adjusted values wherever seasonal movements exist; furthermore, the random noise in the series is unforecastable. In practice, then, the systematic part of the time series covered by the short-term macroeconomic forecasts (as defined above) consists of elements of trend and, to a larger extent, cyclical movements.

It follows that a forecast should be judged successful if it approximates well that systematic part of its target (which includes the effects of past shocks and

2. See chapter 11, sec. 11.4.2, for more detail and references.

seasonal innovations to the extent they are knowable). But this task is generally much more difficult than it sounds. Movements that are "systematic" are persistent or recurrent, but they are by no means predetermined, periodic, or repetitious. As noted earlier, trends and cycles interact with each other and contain stochastic elements. The economy in motion is a complex of dynamic processes, subject not only to a variety of disturbances but also to gradual and discrete changes in structure, institutions, and policy regimes. No wonder that there are few (if any) constant quantitative rules (e.g., time-invariant linear econometric equations) to help the macroeconomic forecaster effectively and consistently over more than a few years or from one business cycle to another.

13.2   Sources and Uses

Business and economic forecasting in the United States today is a highly diversified "industry" of significant size. A large majority of its members are business economists whose main function is to provide information to improve managerial decisions. The membership of the National Association of Business Economists grew rapidly from 322 in 1959 (the year NABE was founded) to 1,682 in 1969 and 2,749 in 1979; it peaked at 3,491 in 1983, declined to 3,098 in 1987, and rose to more than 3,300 in 1989 and 1990. By far most of these people are professionals working for private companies in manufacturing, finance, trade, services, consulting, etc.; some are in government at all levels and in academic institutions. They use macroeconomic forecasts in their work as inputs to assessments of prospects for their own activities or concerns (firms, industries, regions), but only a minority are regular producers of such forecasts. Thus the "macro panel" of NABE (which quarterly updates predictions of annual changes in real GNP and components, inflation and interest rates, and other aggregative variables) now has 125 participants, and the actual number of regular macroeconomic forecasters is probably of the order of 200–250.[3]

The forecasting units vary in size from individuals and small teams to sizable economic divisions of some large corporations and multibranch specialized consulting and forecasting firms. Some of the last operate large-scale econometric models and provide customer services internationally.[4] The demand for macroeconomic forecasts is to a substantial degree met by subscriptions to such services and also to publications that frequently survey groups of professional forecasters and list their individual and average predictions.[5]

---

3. I am very grateful to David L. Williams, secretary-treasurer of NABE, for help in collecting the factual information used in the text paragraph above. The membership figures exclude student and institutional members.
4. Among the largest and best known are Wharton Econometric Forecasting Associates, Inc. (WEFA), and Data Resources, Inc. (DRI). See Adams 1986 and Eckstein 1983.
5. Monthly surveys of forecasters available by subscription are the *Blue Chip Economic Indicators* (since 1978) and *Economic Forecasts: A Worldwide Survey* (since 1984). A quarterly survey in the public domain was conducted by NBER and the American Statistical Association from

Since the supply comes from a small number of relatively large producers and many small ones, the forecasting industry can be described as a mixture of oligopolistic and competitive elements. But it is also arguable that the market for forecasts is one of monopolistic competition as the overall number of sellers is large, the products are differentiated in several respects, and the barriers to entry seem low. In other countries, macroeconomic forecasting is generally much more concentrated, either in a few private sources or in government agencies and publicly supported economic research organizations.[6]

U.S. government forecasts that are designed to serve as inputs into the economic policy-making originate in several agencies: the Council of Economic Advisers (CEA), the Office of Management and Budget (OMB), the Treasury, Federal Reserve Board (FRB), and the Bureau of Economic Analysis (BEA) in the Department of Commerce. Many of these forecasts are for internal uses only and based on economists' models and judgments (FRB and BEA have their own macroeconometric models). The official forecasts that are published, such as those of the CEA in the *Economic Report of the President* (January or February of each year), are end products of interaction among top policymakers as well as their economic advisers.

Those who must forecast regularly and frequently are likely to be absorbed by technical requirements of their profession: monitoring and processing information, analyzing current economic and political developments, preparing reports, and interpreting results. Most are pragmatic and use all data and approaches that they deem helpful to improve their predictions; few spend much time on working with and testing specific theoretical models. The principal scientific and academic use of the forecasts is to test the various hypotheses, models, and methods employed by the forecaster, but this task is largely left to the outside observer. The same applies to another, quite different but also important aspect of predictions of economic change, namely, that they may be useful in providing data to study how expectations are formed, transmitted, and revised.

All these are definitely bona fide uses of forecasts. But some forecasts are at least occasionally and secondarily used as means of communicating intentions and influencing opinion, which may bias them or make them otherwise questionable.

In short, economic and business forecasters serve many different masters.

1968:4 to 1990:1. It is being continued, in essentially unchanged form, by the Federal Reserve Bank of Philadelphia.

6. The former case is well represented by Canada: see the instructive analysis in Daub 1987, ch. 6. The latter situation prevails in several European countries. For example, in Germany six economic research institutes dominate the field; elsewhere the most influential forecasts originate in ministries of finance and economic affairs, central banks, universities, and research institutes. There are probably many private business forecasts as well but few are collected and publicized. For a comprehensive index of organizations engaged in macroeconomic forecasting worldwide, see Cyriax 1981.

Much of their output is communication to the business or government administrators who employ their services; some is being done for the outside world: peers, professionals, the interested public. And it is not unusual for their products to have both internal and external uses. For example, an econometric model developed at a university may serve as a basis for scientific work and also as a source of forecasts circulated to business subscribers; aggregate forecasts by the economic staff of a corporation are a basic input to micropredictions of sales, etc., but are also used in the company's publications and speeches by its executives; and so on.

Forecasters face all sorts of conflicts of evidence and opinion, which they often resolve by various internal compromises; since their work is essentially conjectural, much of this seems inevitable. The multipurpose nature of some forecasts may complicate the situation considerably by bringing forth some conflicts of interest as well.

13.3 Quality and Accuracy

The decision maker who knows the cost of acquiring and using the forecast and the returns attributable to it should in principle be able to evaluate the quality of the forecast exactly, at least in retrospect. This is an ideal condition but good approximations to it may exist in massive routine applications of simple methods to replicable problems. Thus a manufacturing company with thousands of products must use low-cost time-series models for purposes of inventory control and production scheduling; it can experiment with alternative models and choose the most cost-effective ones with considerable confidence. However, economic forecasting generally cannot be reduced to such situations. In macroforecasting especially, there is a wide choice of sophisticated models and techniques, a major role for judgment, but little opportunity for any controlled experimentation. Microlevel information required for a comparative analysis of costs and returns is usually confidential and not available to an outside observer; on a macrolevel, such information may not exist at all or be very underdeveloped and costly.

However, with reasonably reliable and prompt information, it is possible to assess short-term aggregate forecasts in a meaningful way by ex post comparisons with actual outcomes. Verifiability so defined is a necessary condition for the forecasts to be potentially useful. Hence it seems natural to view the overall *accuracy* of a given set of predictions as the principal single aspect of their *quality*, that is, goodness in use. But accuracy is relative and it depends on other characteristics that differentiate forecasts such as scope, span, and timeliness. These too codetermine quality and are in principle amenable to objective measurement.

Comparisons of accuracy are often impeded because the differences among forecasts with respect to their other attributes are difficult to allow for by standardization or classification. The lack of information about the costs of forecasts may seem to be a principal obstacle. But cost levels and differentials have been greatly reduced by computer technology and competition among forecast makers and collectors. Although surely relevant, they are probably no longer of major importance for ranking macroeconomic predictions produced by different sources and methods.

Information about the models or the reasoning behind the forecasts is clearly desirable in general and critical for some purposes of research and knowledge. Many business forecasts come with general explanations of the underlying assumptions and arguments, and econometric model services sell large amounts of numerical detail on the equations and adjustments used in their control solutions, alternative simulations, etc. But it is much easier to assess the accuracy of forecasts than the quality of economic analysis and judgment, and the information necessary for the latter task is often neither provided to nor demanded by commercial and lay users.

It is true that a prediction can be "correct for the wrong reasons"—although based on assumptions contrary to fact, it may fortuitously produce only a small error. The converse is also possible, as when a model supported by theory and past experience fails because of some unanticipated shock. This suggests that a quantitative analysis of forecast errors is not sufficient; a qualitative analysis of how each prediction was derived is needed to evaluate the forecasts. However, this argument can be carried too far. Individual predictions may indeed suffer from excusable assumptions about "exogenous," perhaps noneconomic, events, but if a forecaster's performance is below par on the average over time, it is hard to accept wrong assumptions as a justification.[7]

More generally, a few sporadic successes or failures do not prove that a given source or method of forecasts is or is not accurate. To reduce the role of chance, measures of average accuracy are needed, and they are the more informative the longer and more varied the periods covered. Unfortunately, the available samples of forecasts are mostly small, since few forecasters have produced long, consistent time series of verifiable predictions.[8]

In the end, knowing the size of prediction errors is necessary for any appraisal of the consequences of these errors, although it is usually not sufficient. In choosing the products of different forecasters, users act rationally when they prefer those with comparative advantages in past accuracy or at least attach to them greater weights.[9]

7. It is generally prudent for the forecaster to state carefully his or her basic assumptions, and the information may help the forecast users and judges. However, surrounding predictions with hedges against all kinds of unforeseeable events detracts from their usefulness, particularly for business purposes.
8. The samples are numerous and diverse in terms of sources, methods, variables, and predictive horizons, but this "cross-sectional" richness is not a good substitute for the paucity of long time series of forecasts.
9. Whether superior forecasters exist is a related but separate matter, about which more later in sections 13.8 and 13.9 and chapter 15.

13.4   Summary Measures of Absolute Accuracy

The choice between different measures of accuracy depends upon the forecaster's or user's conception of how errors of different types and sizes reduce the usefulness of the forecast. For example, if the loss depends simply on the size of the difference between the predicted and actual value, the appropriate summary measure is the mean absolute error (MAE). If large errors in either direction are considered much more serious than the small ones, squares of the differences should be used, and the proper average is the root mean square error (RMSE). [10]

In still different situations, the sign as well as the size of the error may matter so that the loss function is asymmetric, with underestimates preferred to overestimates, or vice versa. For example, if management would rather err on the side of too low than too high inventory holdings, it may prefer underestimates of sales, that is, penalize them less than overestimates in weighting. However, it does not follow that such a user should favor forecasts with a built-in corresponding "bias": it seems best for the forecaster to produce best unbiased predictions and for the user to apply to the results whatever his or her loss function is, by appropriately weighting the errors. One can conceive of an indefinite number of diverse individual loss functions; for example, turning-point errors may be treated as particularly serious, errors smaller than some present threshold values may be ignored as implying a zero loss, and so on. But little is known about the distribution of user performance, and for practical reasons of general acceptability and comparability, only a few simple types of error measures are commonly in use (mostly MAE and RMSE).

Table 13.1 covers a large number of predominantly judgmental forecasts by business economists and some others, summed up in two sets; the principal government forecast; and the longest series of forecasts made by econometricians working with a family of macroeconomic models. The group averages from surveys of forecasters conceal the dispersion of errors in the predictions of individual participants, which is often large, and they are always more accurate over time than most of their components (see chapters 15 and 16). For the end-of-year predictions of nominal GNP growth in the year ahead, the MAEs show these broad "consensus" forecasts to be about as accurate as the government and econometric forecasts (cf. cols. 2 and 6 with 4 and 8, lines 2–4). These measures refer to periods between 1963 and 1989, range from 0.8 to 1.3 percentage points, average 1.0, and have a standard deviation of 0.2. The earliest available collection of forecasts, for 1956–63, shows a larger MAE of 1.6 percentage points (line 1).

Similarly, the comparisons across the different sets of annual forecasts of

---

10. The RMSE is a particularly convenient measure mathematically and statistically because it is optimal under a quadratic loss criterion, corresponds to the ordinary least squares estimation procedure, and lends itself to decomposition into systematic (bias, inefficiency) and residual variance components. The MAE corresponds to an alternative V-shaped loss function, where the cost of (loss due to) error depends linearly on the absolute size of the error.

Table 13.1 Annual Forecasts of Percentage Changes in Nominal and Real GNP and IPD: Mean Absolute Errors and Mean Errors, 1956–89

Line	Period Covered (1)	Private Judgmental Forecasts, Mean[a] MAE (2)	ME (3)	CEA MAE (4)	ME (5)	ASA-NBER, Median MAE (6)	ME (7)	Michigan Model (RSQE)[b] MAE (8)	ME (9)	Preliminary Data[c] MAE (10)	ME (11)	Mean Absolute % Change[d] (12)
						Gross National Product (GNP)						
1	1956–63	1.6	−0.4							0.5	−0.3	5.0
2	1963–76	1.0	−0.7	0.9	−0.2			1.3	−0.5	0.3	−0.3	7.9
3	1969–76	0.8	−0.4	0.8	0.2	1.0	−0.3	1.0	−0.1	0.3	−0.3	8.4
4	1969–89			1.0	0.2	1.2	−0.1			0.5	−0.5	8.4
						GNP in Constant Dollars (RGNP)						
5	1959–67	1.3	−0.9					1.0	−0.5	0.5	−0.2	4.3
6	1962–76			1.1	0.6			1.4	0.2	0.4	−0.1	4.1
7	1969–76			1.2	0.8	1.0	0.7	1.6	0.8	0.3	0.1	3.6
8	1969–89			1.0	−0.3	1.1	−0.1			0.6	0.0	3.2
						GNP Implicit Price Deflator (IPD)						
9	1959–67	0.6	0.2					0.7	0	0.3	−0.3	1.9
10	1962–76			1.0	−0.5			1.0	−0.5	0.4	−0.3	4.2
11	1969–76			1.4	−0.6	1.3	−0.9	1.4	−0.9	0.4	−0.4	5.9
12	1969–89			1.0	0.03	1.2	−0.2			0.6	−0.4	5.6

Sources: Lines 1–3, 5–7, and 9–11: based on tables 14.1, 14.2, and 14.3 (see chapter 14 for detail). Lines 4, 8, and 12: based on author's files and calculations; see also Moore 1983, tables 26.3 and 26.4; *Economic Report of the President;* and *Budget of the U.S. Government.*

Note: MAE (mean absolute error) = $1/n \Sigma |E_t|$, where $E_t = P_t - A_t$; P_t is the predicted value and A_t is the actual value (first estimate); and Σ denotes summation over all n years covered. ME (mean error) = $1/n \Sigma E_t$. All measures refer to annual percentage changes and are in percentage points.

[a]Line 1: forecasts from (1) *Fortune* magazine; (2) Harris Bank; (3) IBM; (4) National Securities and Research Corporation, (5) NICB Economic Forum; (6) School of Business Administration, University of Missouri; (7) Prudential Insurance Company of America; (8) University of California in Los Angeles (UCLA) Business Forecasting Project; (9) Livingston Survey; mean; and (10) N.Y. Forecasters Club, mean. Lines 5 and 9: sources 2, 4, 5, and 8.

[b]Research Seminar in Quantitative Economics of the University of Michigan.

[c]Based on the first official estimates following the year for which the forecast was made as compared with the revised data from U.S. Department of Commerce, BEA, 1977; SCB, 1991.

[d]Computed from preliminary data (first estimates for year t published in year $t + 1$).

real GNP growth (RGNP) show fairly small and unsystematic differences in overall accuracy for each of the four periods covered between 1959 and 1989. Here the MAEs have a range of 1.0–1.6 percentage points, mean of 1.2, and standard deviation of 0.2 (lines 5–8).

For the corresponding forecasts of inflation in terms of the implicit price deflator (IPD), the MAEs have a wider range of 0.6–1.4 percentage points, a mean of 1.1, and standard deviation of 0.3. However, the interforecast differences in each line are particularly small here (lines 9–12).

The errors in table 13.1 are measured from preliminary data first published after the end of the forecast target year. This allows us to compare the arithmetic and absolute means of these forecasting errors with the corresponding averages for the measurement errors defined as differences between the percentage changes in the preliminary and revised data. The MAEs of the preliminary data, so computed, have a range of 0.3–0.6 and average 0.4 (col. 10); they are quite sizable compared with the MAEs of the forecasts proper, which have a range of 0.6–1.6 and average 1.1. (Compare these measures also with the mean absolute percentage changes in preliminary data, which interestingly increased over the successive periods for IPD and GNP but decreased for RGNP; see col. 12.) The early data tended to underestimate the revised data by about −0.3 (col. 11).

Predictions of the rates of change in GNP and RGNP made *quarterly* for the year ahead show similar MAEs of 1.1–1.4 even for most subperiods of the difficult decade of the 1970s, but they show much higher MAEs of 1.8–3.2 percentage points for some recent intervals (1978–85 for nominal, 1974–78 and 1981–85 for real growth; see table 18.2 below). The corresponding measures for IPD inflation fall in the 1.1–1.6 range. The worst errors coincide with major cyclical changes such as the recessions of the mid-1970s and early 1980s and the disinflation of 1981–85.

The absolute or squared errors increase systematically with the span of forecast in quarters. For example, the MAEs of the GNP growth predictions in 1970–75 fall in the ranges of 0.4–0.5, 0.8–1.0, 1.7–1.9, and 2.8–3.5 for one, two, four, and eight quarters ahead, respectively (see table 14.5).

13.5 When and Why Growth and Inflation Were Underpredicted or Overpredicted

In the 1950s and 1960s forecasters generally underpredicted the nominal GNP growth in years of cyclical expansion—that is, most of the time. This implies negative averages of errors measured as differences, predicted minus actual values. Thus, the errors of eight sets of GNP forecasts for 1953–70, in billions of dollars, had means of −2.5 for the base (current-year) levels, −4.0 for the base-to-target changes, and −6.5 for the target (next-year) levels.[11] Positive errors (i.e., overestimates of GNP changes or levels) occurred

---

11. The level errors are equal to the algebraic sums of the corresponding base and change errors. For the sources of the eight forecasts, see table 13.1, n. *a*.

in this period in only six years, each of which was associated with a recession or a major slowdown (1954, 1958, 1960, 1962, 1967, and 1970). The largest underestimation errors occurred in times of booming economic activity, later accompanied also by rising inflation (1955, 1965–66, and 1968–69) (for details see Zarnowitz 1974, table 5 and pp. 578–80).

Thus the underestimation of GNP changes probably reflected in the main an underestimation of real growth. The few year-to-year decreases were more often missed (i.e., increases were predicted instead) than either under- or overstated. RGNP forecasts are not available for the early postwar period, but predictions of the index of industrial production (IP) are and they provide some confirming evidence. Of the seven sets of IP forecasts between 1951 and 1963, all but one have negative mean errors of changes and all but two have negative mean errors of levels (Zarnowitz 1967, table 4, p. 34).[12]

Scattered annual forecasts of the consumer and wholesale price indexes in 1949–67, assembled and examined in Zarnowitz 1969b, show no evidence of an overall bias for CPI and a prevalence of overestimates for WPI. Forecasters tended to underestimate the large changes and to overestimate the small changes in the indexes, and most of the price changes in this period were relatively small. There is much extrapolative inertia in these forecasts, although most of them were more accurate than naive model projections and produced definite positive correlations between the predicted and actual index changes. This evidence too is consistent with the hypothesis that it was mainly real growth that was underpredicted in the GNP forecasts summarized here.

The overall timidity of these predictions can be understood only in their historical context. Forecasters used the available data, which referred mainly to the interwar period, while dealing with the very different economic environment of the postwar era. Many expected a replay of what happened after World War I, repeatedly using analogies that turned out to be basically false. The recession of 1948–49 occurred later and was less severe than they had projected. Before the proper lessons from the errors were drawn, the shocks of the Korean War created new uncertainties. The recessions that followed in 1953–60 were relatively mild but discouragingly frequent (three in 8 years).

However, forecasters gradually learned to expect higher rates of economic growth. RGNP increases were strongly underestimated in 1959–67 but *overestimated* in 1962–76. That the nominal GNP forecasts were on average too low in the latter period must be attributed entirely to the underprediction of the rate of increase in IPD (cf. lines 5, 6, and 10, odd columns, table 13.1).

In fact, inflation accelerated greatly in the late 1960s and, especially, in the middle and late 1970s, due to the monetary overstimulation during the Viet-

12. Weighted mean errors, in index points 1947–49 = 100, are approximately 0.8 for base levels, −1.0 for changes, and −0.1 for target levels. Note that IP is less affected by the underestimation of growth than GNP is. This is related to the fact that IP is in real units and has a smaller trend and larger cyclical component (its forecasts suffer more from turning-point errors; see Zarnowitz 1972b, pp. 194–95).

nam War and then the unusual supply and price shocks and the public and policy reactions to them. Bouts of inflation alternated with poorly managed efforts to disinflate. Real activity declined mildly in 1970, more seriously in 1974–75. The turning points in both inflation and output were generally missed; so the rises in IPD were increasingly underpredicted at the same time that the rises in RGNP were increasingly overpredicted between 1962 and 1978. These errors offset each other to produce GNP forecasts with mostly negative but on average small errors (cf. lines 2–3, 6–7, and 10–11, odd columns).

Finally, inflation peaked in 1980–81 and decreased gradually to much lower levels in the following five years. Predicted rates moved down with a lag, thus tending to overestimate actual rates. Later, inflation increased again, but slowly, which was on the whole well anticipated. RGNP growth was underestimated in 1980, when the recession turned out to be milder than expected, and in the years of strong recovery and expansion (1983–84, 1988); it was greatly overestimated in 1982, after a severe downturn cut short an unusually weak and brief rise in activity. However, more than half the time, in both the 1970s and the 1980s, the errors of the annual forecasts for all three variables were moderate (less than one percentage point), and on the whole the under- and overestimates balanced each other well, as can be seen from the results for 1969–89 (lines 4, 8, and 12).

13.6   Bias or Cyclical Errors?

Persistent under- or overprediction of actual values suggests a failure to avoid bias by learning from past errors. Thus it is desirable that the mean error of a set of forecasts not differ statistically from zero. Also, forecasts should be efficient, that is, uncorrelated with their own errors, else again the presence of a systematic error is inferred.

These requirements are certainly logical and indeed are often treated as almost obvious and minimal in the literature. Yet they are based on assumptions that are only too frequently shown to be false in practice, namely, that the behavioral patterns of and relations among the variables concerned are essentially time invariant and known. In reality, the processes underlying the time series to be predicted are not necessarily stable, because they reflect the changing structure and institutions of the economy and perhaps shifts in economic policies and behavior. Correspondingly, forecasting models and techniques also do not remain unchanged for long. The available samples of consistent and comparable predictions are in many cases too small to establish the existence and evaluate the importance of systematic errors. Finally, measurement errors may distort and fragment both the time-series data and the related forecasts.

For any or all of these reasons, ex post tests can and do find evidences of bias and/or inefficiency even in forecasts which would be judged very good ex ante (those that come from respected professional sources or enjoy wide support when made or are based on state-of-the-art models). It seems unlikely that these forecasts are in fact systematically deficient in the sense of having persistent yet avoidable errors. More plausibly, such errors are themselves period specific and of the kind that could not be readily detected and corrected at the time when the forecasts were made.

Forecasts of inflation by individual respondents to the quarterly ASA-NBER surveys in 1968–79 provide an instructive example in this context. Tests presented in chapter 16 show a high proportion of these forecasts to be biased and inefficient, in contrast to the corresponding predictions for five other aggregative variables, where the incidence of such errors is low. In addition, there is evidence that the average forecasts of inflation from the same surveys are inconsistent with the hypothesis of unbiasedness for the period 1970–74 but not for 1975–79 and 1980–84 (Hafer and Hein 1985, esp. pp. 390–92). It makes good sense to argue that changes in inflation were particularly difficult to predict in the first half of the 1970s because of novel exogenous developments and shocks. There was the breakdown of the Bretton Woods arrangements and transition to the floating exchange regime; the imposition and elimination of wage and price controls; international food shortages and huge price increases; and the oil embargo and quadrupling of oil prices. The resulting elements of inescapable surprise must be taken into account in assessments of the generally poor forecasts of inflation rates in this period, which lagged behind the actual rates and underestimated them greatly most of the time (see chapter 14, sec. 14.5 for an analysis by subperiods).

In chapter 16, the forecasts are compared with the last data available prior to the benchmark revisions of 1976 and 1980. Keane and Runkle (1990) show that when instead the preliminary (first release) data are used, the proportions of bias and inefficiency in the one-step-ahead inflation forecasts are much smaller, so that the rationality hypothesis can no longer be rejected. Their estimation and replication work is very careful and proficient but their explanation relies too heavily on measurement errors to be really persuasive. Systematic yet unpredictable errors in inflation *data* may well have been concentrated in the first half of the 1970s like the similar large errors in inflation *forecasts*, and for much the same reasons. Early estimates have much in common with extrapolations. Otherwise, it is not clear why data errors should have been so critical for the forecasts of inflation but not for the other variables that tend to be subject to larger revisions.[13] In general, the issue of whether or

---

13. This is certainly true for GNP and such of its components as the change in business inventories, a series notorious for grave measurement problems and errors. Most of the data used to deflate GNP come from the components of the CPI and the producer price index (PPI), and these microdata usually do not have large revisions, except for changes in weights and seasonal factors. The revisions in the IPD series to which the ASA-NBER inflation forecasts refer are thus presum-

not forecasts are unbiased or "rational" must surely hinge on much more than the choice between preliminary and revised data.[14]

Early studies found that forecasters often underestimated changes in micro- and macroeconomic variables, and they discussed the meaning and possible sources of this phenomenon (Theil [1958] 1965, ch. 5; Zarnowitz 1967, ch. 4). But longer time series of forecasts that are now available show greater frequencies of overestimates in the recent years and little evidence of any overall bias. This is illustrated in table 13.2 for the government and private predictions of annual rates of change in nominal and real GNP and IPD, 1969–89. The mean errors of both the CEA and the ASA-NBER survey forecasts are all fractional, small relative to the corresponding standard deviations, and statistically not different from zero by conventional tests (lines 5, 11, and 16).[15] On the whole, overestimates were just slightly more numerous in the CEA set, and underestimates were slightly more numerous in the ASA-NBER set; and neither type of error was systematically larger in size (cf. lines 1–2, 6–7, and 12–13).

By far the largest errors are found in the third category, where the predicted changes differ from the actual changes in sign. Such directional or turning-point errors occurred in the annual forecasts of table 13.2 only for RGNP (line 8). They relate to some of the years of business cycle contraction and troughs, namely, 1970, 1974, and 1982, and are all positive.[16]

This suggests that it is the failure to predict business downturns that is the major shortcoming of these forecasts. More general evidence comes from comparisons of the accuracy of forecasts classified ex post by the cyclical nature of their target periods. In each case, as shown by the absolute values of their mean errors and by their standard deviations and MAEs, the forecasts for contraction and trough years have been much worse than the forecasts for expansion and peak years (cf. lines 3–4, 9–10, and 14–15). The results for quarterly predictions confirm and amplify this conclusion (chapter 18, sec. 18.2.2).

---

ably due in large measure to shifts in the GNP expenditure weights. It is easy in retrospect to relate large shifts in spending patterns to the disturbances of the 1970s. Finally, figure 1 in Keane and Runkle 1990, p. 723, suggests that the discrepancies between the initial and final estimates of IPD were greater in the first than in the second half of their sample period (1968–86), certainly in levels.

14. It cannot be taken for granted that forecasters aim to predict initial values rather than try to come closer to the true values. To the extent that revisions are systematically related to some past information, rational forecasters should be able to take them into account.

15. The ratios of the means to their standard errors are all very small (less than 0.3), but there is no good reason here to make the assumptions of independence, etc., that underlie the simple significance (t) tests.

16. For more evidence on the importance of turning-point errors, based on a larger sample of earlier annual forecasts, see chapter 14, sec. 14.3. Such errors play an even greater role in quarterly forecasts, as discussed in Zarnowitz 1967, pp. 72–80, 114–20, and Zarnowitz 1974, pp. 584–90.

Table 13.2   Types of Error in Two Sets of Annual Forecasts of Nominal and Real GNP Growth and IPD, 1969–89

		CEA				ASA-NBER, Median			
Line	Type of Error[a]	No. (1)	ME[b] (2)	S.D.[c] (3)	MAE[d] (4)	No. (5)	ME[b] (6)	S.D.[c] (7)	MAE[d] (8)
		Gross National Product (GNP)							
1	Underestimates	9	−0.8	0.4		13	−1.0	0.8	
2	Overestimates	12	1.0	1.1		7	1.5	1.0	
3	B.C. expansions	16	−0.0	1.1	0.9	16	−0.4	1.2	0.9
4	B.C. contractions	5	1.0	1.7	1.2	5	0.9	2.4	1.8
5	Total	21	0.2	1.3	1.0	21	−0.1	1.6	1.2
		GNP in Constant Dollars (RGNP)							
6	Underestimates	8	−0.9	0.6		9	−1.2	0.9	
7	Overestimates	9	0.8	0.6		8	0.5	0.3	
8	Directional errors	3	2.3	0.8		3	2.8	1.7	
9	B.C. expansions	16	0.1	1.0	0.8	16	−0.5	1.1	0.8
10	B.C. contractions	5	1.1	1.7	1.7	5	1.7	2.1	2.1
11	Total	21	0.3	1.3	1.0	21	0.1	1.6	1.1
		GNP Implicit Price Deflator (IPD)							
12	Underestimates	9	−1.2	1.0		10	−1.4	1.7	
13	Overestimates	11	0.9	0.7		11	1.0	0.7	
14	B.C. expansions	16	−0.0	1.0	0.8	16	0.1	1.2	1.0
15	B.C. contractions	5	−0.0	2.2	1.7	5	0.8	2.9	1.8
16	Total	21	0.0	1.4	1.0	21	−0.2	1.7	1.2

[a]Underestimates: sign P = sign A and $P < A$. Overestimates: sign P = sign A and $P > A$. Directional errors: sign $P \neq$ sign A. B.C. expansions: errors of forecasts relating to years of business cycle expansion and peaks. B.C. contractions: errors of forecasts relating to years of contraction and troughs.

[b]ME = mean error.

[c]S.D. = standard deviation.

[d]MAE = mean absolute error. Not shown where equal to the corresponding ME value without regard to sign.

13.7   Relative Accuracy

Measures of absolute accuracy, by comparing predicted and actual values, show how much the former deviate from the unattainable state of perfection (no errors). More realistic criteria are found in comparisons of the accuracy of forecasts of different types and from different sources. Some common benchmarks of predictive performance are provided by models that mechanically extrapolate information contained in the past record of the series to be predicted. The appropriate models vary with the characteristics of the variables and periods concerned. In short, forecasts are best evaluated in relative terms and by more than one yardstick.

Consider four examples of "naive models": N1, which projects forward the last observed level of the predicted variable; N2, which adds to that level the last known change; N2*, which similarly projects the average of past changes;

and N3, based on an autoregressive equation with five terms. All of eight sets in an early collection of annual forecasts of GNP and IP for periods ending in 1963 proved to be superior to N1 and N2, and all but one also to N2* and N3 (Zarnowitz 1967, table 16 and pp. 86–90; N2* in this case averages changes since 1947). A partial extension of this study through 1969 shows forecasts continuing to outperform N1 and N2*, as summed up in table 13.3, lines 1–4. However, the forecasts grew much worse relative to N2 in the middle and late 1960s. This is because extrapolations of last change in GNP are at their very best in times when no major fluctuations occur in either output or inflation. Of course, this was a transitory advantage as nominal growth is seldom so well sustained.

The relative accuracy measures in table 13.3 are ratios of RMSEs of the forecasts to the corresponding RMSEs of the selected extrapolative models. The annual CEA and ASA-NBER predictions of nominal GNP growth easily outperform the last-change projections (N2), with ratios in the range of 0.46 to 0.54 for 1962–89 and subperiods (line 5). The forecasts of real GNP growth compare still more favorably with N2 (line 8), but those of IPD inflation do worse, with ratios of 0.72 for CEA and as high as 0.98 for ASA-NBER in 1969–79 (line 11).

The ratios to N4, the projections of the moving average of changes in the last four years, are somewhat higher than the N2 ratios, but they too show the forecasts of GNP and RGNP in a strong comparative position (lines 6 and 9). For IPD, however, N4 is less demanding than N2 (line 12).

Finally, N5 is hypothetical and forward looking in that it projects the mean of actual changes in the forecast period, a statistic knowable only ex post; but it is also extremely naive in the sense that it assumes a constant prediction in each successive unit period. The RMSE of these "random-walk-with-trend" projections equals the standard deviation of the future actuals. Interestingly, N5 performs much like N4 here, being just a little weaker for GNP and RGNP and slightly stronger for IPD (cf. lines 6–7, 9–10, and 12–13).

The upshot is that the annual forecasts under study are generally much more accurate than an array of simple mechanical extrapolations. The only exception is the inflation forecasts from surveys when compared with N2 since 1964 and also with N4 and N5 in 1969–79 (lines 2 and 11–13, cols. 2 and 7). The conclusion is supported by other recent studies, notably McNees 1988b (see also table 18.1 and text below for additional results and references).

However, it can be argued that the naive models represent minimal standards. The economic models and reasoning, technical skills, professional experience, and informed judgment when combined should enable the modern forecaster to do much better. Indeed, he or she is now expected to satisfy the demand for frequent predictions of developments over sequences of several quarters into the future; the old practice of year-end forecasting for the year ahead is no longer sufficient. So quarterly multiperiod forecasts are now prepared routinely by econometric service bureaus in great detail and by many

Table 13.3 Annual Forecasts of Nominal and Real GNP and IPD: Comparisons with Selected Naive Models, 1953–89

Line	Ratio of RMSEs Forecast to Naive Model[a]	Average of Four Sets of Private Judgmental Forecasts (predictions of levels and changes in current dollars)			CEA (predictions of percentage change)			ASA-NBER, Median (predictions of percentage change)		
		1953–63 (1)	1964–69 (2)	1953–69 (3)	1962–74 (4)	1975–89 (5)	1962–89 (6)	1969–79 (7)	1980–89 (8)	1969–89 (9)
		Gross National Product (GNP)								
1	N1	0.41	0.28	0.33						
2	N2	0.56	1.05	0.64						
3	N2*	0.66	0.43	0.50						
4	N3	0.72								
5	N2				0.53	0.46	0.48	0.54	0.53	0.53
6	N4				0.61	0.55	0.58	0.58	0.67	0.63
7	N5				0.69	0.54	0.59	0.54	0.78	0.63
		GNP in Constant Dollars (RGNP)								
8	N2				0.47	0.34	0.41	0.46	0.42	0.45
9	N4				0.54	0.35	0.44	0.52	0.44	0.49
10	N5				0.59	0.43	0.51	0.59	0.54	0.58
		GNP Implicit Price Deflator (IPD)								
11	N2				0.72	0.72	0.72	0.98	0.74	0.92
12	N4				0.61	0.49	0.54	0.93	0.39	0.73
13	N5				0.50	0.46	0.46	0.98	0.37	0.72

Sources: Cols. 1–3: based on Zarnowitz 1967, table 16, p. 87, and Zarnowitz 1974, table 3, p. 574. Cols. 4–6; based on Moore 1983, tables 26-3 and 26-4, pp. 442–45 and 448–49; *Economic Report of the President; Budget of the U.S. Government.* Cols. 7–9: based on author's files and calculations.

[a] RMSE (root mean square error) $= \sqrt{1/n \, \Sigma \, (E_t)}$, where $E_t = P_t - A_t$; P_t is the predicted value and A_t is the actual value (preliminary estimate which appears in February of year $t + 1$). N1 refers to the projection of the last observed level (for year $t - 1$); N2 to that of the last observed change; N2* to that of the average change from 1947 to year $t - 1$. N3 projects the average return between the present value of the series and its past values (based on regressions of A_t on A_{t-i}, $i = 1, 2, \ldots, 5$). N4 projects the moving average of the last four observed changes (for A_{t-i}, $i = 1, \ldots, 4$). N5 assumes that the mean of the actual values in the forecast period is known and projects it each year.

"The forecasts come from (1) *Fortune* magazine ("Business Roundup"); (2) Harris Trust and Savings Bank; (3) Prudential Insurance Company of America; and (4) University of Missouri School of Business Administration.

business economists for an array of important macroeconomic variables. These forecasts can be tested against extrapolations from state-of-the-art times-series models, which include the univariate ARIMA (autoregressive integrated moving-average) models and the multivariate VAR (vector autoregressive) models. Chapter 18 shows that the record of such tests for three macroeconometric models and group forecasts from a business outlook survey is mixed. For some variables and periods the forecasts are less accurate than either ARIMA, VAR, or BVAR (Bayesian vector autoregressions) but the opposite is true in about two thirds of the comparisons (see table 18.3, pt. B).

Sophisticated time-series models have important lessons for forecasters on how to decompose, detrend, deseasonalize, and use the stochastic properties of the series for predictive purposes. They can help avoid bias in forecasting for processes that are reasonably stable over the periods covered. Economists' forecasts include extrapolative along with other, analytical and judgmental elements; thus comparing the errors of forecasts with the errors of corresponding projections from time-series models can yield estimates of the net predictive value of the combined nonextrapolative components of the forecast (which can be positive, zero, or negative). [17] Tests of relative accuracy based on such comparisons pose standards that may be difficult to exceed but that may not be sufficient to establish the usefulness of those forecasts that meet them. This is because the strength of the time-series models generally lies in good projections of recent trends that, however, tend to lag behind actual developments and fail to give timely signals of broad changes in the economy (turning points in growth rates and levels of income, output, prices, etc.). But it is precisely such signals that are most needed by users of short-term forecasts of general economic conditions.

13.8   Forecasting Methods and Results

During the period 1968–81, the quarterly ASA-NBER surveys regularly collected information on some methodological characteristics of the forecasts. The questionnaire asked the participants which of several listed tools they used and what the relative importance of these items was in their own work. Large majorities reported using the "informal GNP model," an eclectic and flexible approach with large elements of judgment (Butler and Kavesh 1974). This "model" actually covers a variety of procedures whereby the major expenditure components of GNP are predicted and combined into an overall forecast, in nominal and real terms. The last step usually involves various adjustments that may be iterative and are designed to make the forecast internally consistent and reasonable in light of the currently available information and beliefs. Table 13.4 tells us that over 70% of the respondents used this

---

17. For an early discussion and examples, see Mincer and Zarnowitz 1969 and other essays in Mincer 1969a.

Table 13.4   Forecasting Methods Used in the ASA-NBER Quarterly Economic Outlook Surveys, 1968–70, 1974–75, and 1980–81

	Informal GNP Model (1)	Leading Indicators (2)	Anticipations Surveys (3)	Econometric Model—Outside (4)	Econometric Model—Own (5)	Other Methods (6)
	Seven Surveys 1968:4–1970:2 (496 replies)[b]					
% using	77	72	65	42	23	17
% ranking first[c]	57	14	2	7	7	8
% ranking second	13	32	24	10	7	4
% ranking lower[d]	7	24	40	26	10	5
	Six Surveys 1974:1–1975:2 (308 replies)[e]					
% using	71	49	53	56	25	14
% ranking first[c]	50	5	1	9	16	7
% ranking second	13	30	18	24	7	4
% ranking lower[d]	7	25	33	22	3	3
	Six Surveys 1980:1–1981:2 (198 replies)[f]					
% using	74	49	42	53	27	19
% ranking first[c]	56	12	1	13	13	9
% ranking second	13	21	16	14	6	5
% ranking lower[d]	4	14	25	25	7	5

Sources: American Statistical Association and National Bureau of Economic Research, *Quarterly Survey of Economic Outlook,* various issues; author's files and calculations.

[a]Write-in but often not specified.

[b]The August 1969 survey was held in connection with the ASA annual meeting and attracted a very large number of respondents (128, including 46 regular panelists). Participation in the other surveys varied from 49 to 83 and averaged 61.

[c]Most important.

[d]Ranks 3 to 6 (least important).

[e]Participation varied from 46 to 62 and averaged 51.

[f]Participation varied from 24 to 46 and averaged 31.

general approach and 50% or more ranked it as first (col. 1). These proportions remained remarkably steady while the survey participation rates declined over time (many casual forecasters who participated in the early years dropped out, leaving a much smaller core of regular forecasters only).

Leading indicators were also employed by about 70% of the survey membership in 1968–70 but later that share declined to about 50%. They were ranked second by most respondents (col. 2). Anticipations surveys received references from 65% of members in 1968–70, 42% in 1980–81, and generally lower ranks (col. 3).

Users of outside econometric models accounted for more than 40% of the early survey members and more than half of those in the 1970s and early 1980s. These forecasters preferred other methods and ranked the outside models second or lower (col. 4). About one fourth of the respondents had their own econometric models, and most of them (but perhaps surprisingly not all and not in the early years) ranked these models first (col. 5). Finally, "other methods" (e.g., time-series models) were specified by fewer than 20% of the participants and preferred by about half of them (col. 6).

The different methods tend to complement each other, for example, new readings on monthly cyclical indicators and the latest results from an investment or consumer anticipations survey may be used to modify forecasts from econometric models or the informal approach. It is therefore understandable that the predominant forecasting practice is to use various combinations of these methods or techniques in a more or less judicious fashion. Indeed, this is the single most important lesson to be drawn from the replies to the question on methods as elicited in the ASA-NBER surveys. The reported rankings differ widely, reflecting the backgrounds, interests, and preferences of the individuals; but no one method is widely treated as if it were self-sufficient and always superior to each of the others.

In an effort to establish whether the forecasters' methodological choices were associated with significant differences in predictive accuracy, I first examined regressions of the individual errors of GNP forecasts on dummy variables representing different methods, one equation for each survey and for each predictive horizon (Zarnowitz 1971, pp. 65–68). The estimates related to the early surveys with high participation rates and used alternatively the classification by first ranks only and by lower ranks as well. Few of the coefficients were found to be significant (less than one in six at the 5% level, for example). The results suggested in general an absence of systematic differences between the contributions to the forecast errors of the main listed methods.[18]

A 1975 study by Su and Su, based on the 1968:4–1973:2 ASA-NBER forecasts of absolute and percentage changes and levels of GNP, RGNP, IPD, and the unemployment rate, compared the accuracy of the respondents who ranked first the informal GNP model with those who preferred econometric models (own or outside), leading indicators, and other methods. The four groups varied in their relative performance by variable, span, and type of forecast (changes vs. levels) but none surpassed the others *consistently.*[19]

Table 13.5, based on a large number of time series of individual forecasts of rates of change in GNP, RGNP, and IPD between 1968 and 1980, presents measures of average accuracy by method that omit occasional forecasters and aggregate across predictions for the current quarter and three quarters ahead. (Providing more detail and evidence for other variables would not alter the conclusions; see Zarnowitz 1983, pp. 84–85). The differences between the average RMSEs listed in the table are, line by line, very small and of uncertain significance; indeed, when rounded off to one decimal point, all but a few of them would disappear. However, it may be worth noting that when first ranks

18. Most of the significant coefficients referred to the thinly populated and apparently inferior groups such as "other methods" and, for the first ranks, anticipations surveys.

19. See Su and Su 1975, pp. 603–5. All four subsamples generated larger errors than the consensus forecasts because of larger variances.

Table 13.5   Average RMSEs of ASA-NBER Survey Forecasts, by Methods Ranked First and Lower, 1968–80

Variable	Informal GNP Model (1)	Leading Indicators (2)	Anticipations Surveys (3)	Econometric Model—Outside (4)	Econometric Model—Own (5)	Other Methods (6)
	According to First-Ranked Method					
GNP, % change	0.96	1.00	0.99	0.89	1.09	1.15
RGNP, % change	1.14	1.24	1.22	1.05	1.25	1.27
IPD, % change	0.71	0.79	0.85	0.72	0.76	0.83
	According to Lower-Ranked Method					
GNP, % change	1.03	0.97	0.95	0.98	0.76	0.97
RGNP, % change	1.19	1.12	1.10	1.13	1.12	1.18
IPD, % change	0.76	0.72	0.71	0.71	0.72	0.87

Sources: ASA-NBER, *Quarterly Survey of Economic Outlook,* various issues; for more detail, see Zarnowitz 1983.

Note: This table covers 79 individuals in at least 12 of the 46 quarterly surveys in the period from 1968:4 through 1980:1. The entries represent averages of RMSEs of forecasts for the current survey quarter and three quarters ahead. The errors are measured as differences, percentage predicted change minus percentage actual change, for each successive nonoverlapping target quarter. Measures in lines 1–3 refer to responses of those forecasters who reported using the given method as primary (ties for the first rank are not included). Measures in lines 4–6 refer to the responses of those forecasters who reported using the given method but ranking it second through sixth.

only are considered (lines 1–3), outside econometric models tend to have the smallest errors, with the informal approach a close second. When lower ranks are used (lines 4–6), own econometric models, leading indicators, and anticipations surveys have more favorable relative positions.

This is consistent with the view that combining the different procedures helps, particularly when done by experienced forecasters. Thus our sample measures indicate that subscribers perform somewhat better than model proprietors on average over time, and the probable reason is this: the former group is dominated by large companies using well-known econometric service bureaus and their own professional staffs, whereas the latter group includes some individuals who are exclusive users of their own models and some teams of experts selling their large-model forecasts and advice.

Some broadly corroborative evidence is also available from other sources. According to the annual surveys of the National Association of Business Economists (NABE) in 1975–79, 52%–60% of members preferred "eclectic judgmental" methods, and 22%–28% preferred "eclectic econometric" methods (Conlan and Wickersham 1982). A special mail survey sent to the Blue Chip forecasters in 1987 showed the following mix of average contributions to predictions of real growth, inflation, and interest rates: judgment, 48%; econometric model, 28%; time-series analysis, 24% (based on more detailed figures in Batchelor and Dua 1990, p. 5). Even the organizations with their own large-scale econometric models assigned sizable weights to judgment (20%–50%, on average about 30%) and other elements such as time-series methods, current data analysis, and interaction with others (10%–20%). Thus, these forecasters estimated the contributions of their models as such at 45%–80% (on average 60%).[20]

Some of the lists mix techniques and theories. For example, the NABE members' classification in 1980 and 1981 includes, in addition to the large judgmental and econometric groups (averaging 49% and 26%), "rational expectations" (12%), "monetarists" (6%), and other or nonrespondents. Batchelor and Dua (1990) report on an attempt to cross-classify the Blue Chip forecasters by "ideology" (Keynesian, monetarist, supply-sider, RE, Austrian, other) and "technique" (three categories, as noted above). They find some support for the inference that the Keynesian-econometric combination had an advantage over others, but note that individuals in their sample generally relied on more than one technique and used elements of more than one theory. Also, Keynesian models and econometric methods were developed earlier than the modern versions of the other theories and methods, so they may have gained adherents with more practical and diverse experience.[21]

13.9   Search for the Best and the Complementarity of Suboptimal Forecasts

The classical research strategy of economists looking into the future is to form conditional expectations based on an "optimal" model. This involves the use of the preferred theory of the behavior of economic agents as constrained by the available resources and the institutional framework; identification of the endogenous variables and the relationships among them; specific assumptions about economic policies and exogenous events or developments; approximations with existing data, statistical estimation of the model parameters, and derivation of predictions. This line of attack led to the macroeconometric models and forecasts.

But macroeconomic theories differ and no one is demonstrably superior and generally accepted. The complexity and changing dynamics and structure of the economy make it costly and difficult to collect the required information and learn from it on a current basis. Testing of the theories is impeded and ideological differences persist. Even substantial agreement on fundamentals

20. See McNees 1981, p. 7. The weights come from 11 sources of macroeconomic forecasts: BEA, Chase, DRI, General Electric Co., Georgia State University, Kent Economic Institute, Manufacturers Hanover Trust, RSQE (Michigan), Townsend-Greenspan & Co., UCLA, and Wharton.

21. The weights placed on the listed theories by the average responses to the May 1987 Blue Chip survey were as follows: Keynesian, 43%; monetarist, 20%; supply side, 12%; rational expectations, 8%; Austrian 4%; other, 13%. Batchelor and Dua examined annual forecasts of real growth, inflation, and the Treasury bill rate made by 44 respondents on selected dates in 1976–86 (1990, pp. 4–10).

of rational behavior is not sufficient to resolve conflicts of views on what constitutes credible restrictions in the econometric models of the economy. The selections of endogenous versus exogenous variables are particularly controversial.

Moreover, some of the best-known macroeconometric models are so very large that they are unwieldy and difficult to comprehend, often posing excessive data requirements and resorting to ad hoc theories and arbitrary assumptions in dealing with detailed relations about which little is known. Many features of the existing models viewed as "Keynesian" are not acceptable to critics of diverse persuasion: monetarist, rational expectations, public choice, supply side. This applies notably to the treatment of economic policies as exogenous, basically benevolent, and effective not only in principle but also often in practice. But the critics have yet to produce their own, and evidently better, econometric models of the economy.

The interest of academic economists in practical econometric forecasting, never strong to begin with, was much reduced by the recent controversies, which partly explains the rise in popularity within the profession of new statistical methods of univariate and multivariate time-series prediction. Econometric forecasts were compared successively with simple autoregressive (AR), ARIMA, VAR, and BVAR forecasts. The challengers claimed that the time-series models have the advantage of low costs and replicability but yet are competitive with the best-known complex and expensive econometric models with respect to many, though not all, variables, horizons, and periods; or that the econometric forecasts are inefficient in that lower errors can be obtained by combining them with some time-series models (Nelson 1972; Cooper 1972; Cooper and Nelson 1975; Lupoletti and Webb 1986; Litterman 1986).

In their countercriticism, econometricians noted correctly that only their forecasts have the potential advantages of being based on models with identifiable structures and specific assumptions about exogenous variables and the possibility to explain and simulate as well as predict. However, they also argued that their models require the use of prior knowledge in structural specification and inspection of the equation residuals before each forecast is made. The charge against the time-series models is that they fail to take proper advantage of economic theory, may be restricted to too few variables and too many lags, and are unlikely to predict well over longer horizons (Howrey, Klein, and McCarthy 1976; Runkle 1987). A lively debate about the methods of evaluation, the linkages between, and the relative performance of time-series and econometric models has continued for years and shows no signs of exhaustion.[22]

22. The following papers are cited for their innovative nature or because they review the subject (some are accompanied by several comments): Zellner and Palm 1974; Wallis 1977, 1989; Armstrong 1978; Zellner 1979; Fildes 1985; Longbottom and Holly 1985; McNees 1986; Dhrymes and Peristiani 1986; Clemen and Guerard 1989.

At the same time that the econometricians and time-series analysts engaged in a competition guided by the principle of constructing optimal predictive models, considerable work was being done on combining multiple individual forecasts of various types. This research demonstrates that such combinations generally improve forecast accuracy, often substantially and by very accessible and inexpensive methods, including simple averaging (see Clemen 1989 for a survey with annotated bibliography). I first presented and discussed the evidence on gains from aggregating individual GNP forecasts in 1967 (pp. 5 and 123–26); a more recent and more comprehensive analysis is given in chapter 15 of this volume. Much has been learned from two decades of effort to develop a theory of optimal forecast combinations, which however does not promise a single best rule but rather suggests different procedures depending on the underlying assumptions and purposes (Winkler 1989).[23]

The idea of combining forecasts is to some critics inconsistent with the principle of optimal information-processing and modeling: an econometric structure that does not "emcompass" what can be predicted by a time-series extrapolation, for example, is simply misspecified (Chong and Hendry 1986). Further, combining (like time-series models) can result only in unconditional forecasts and may generate internal inconsistencies, for example, predictions of GNP components that do not add up to predictions of total GNP.

In a world in which economic processes and relations tended to be stable and identifiable from good data promptly available at low cost, pooling of information would always be preferred to pooling forecasts (which in this case should not vary much anyway). But ours is a very different world where "economic change is a law of life" (Burns 1968, p. 226); new surprises and uncertainties continually arise, and valuable information is costly and at no time exclusively possessed by any single expert or embodied in any single model. Timely short-term forecasts for the economy under such conditions can hardly afford the costs of collecting all the relevant data and knowledge. Thus combining forecasts may be justified here as a practical way to aggregate the pieces of information that are available to forecasters, and the procedure can be formalized along Bayesian lines (Winkler 1989).

In particular, combining bona fide outside forecasts with different characteristics is an expedient method for a decision maker to reduce the large-error risk associated with relying on one particular model or one individual's judgment.[24] Here then is an appropriate role for *users* (and collectors and analysts) of the forecasts. However, the essential function of *makers* of forecasts is very different, namely, to *add* some predictive value to the sum of diverse infor-

23. The literature advanced from combinations of unbiased one-step forecasts with weights constrained to sum to 1 (Bates and Granger 1969) through unconstrained least squares (Granger and Ramanathan 1984) to Bayesian prior-information and shrinkage techniques (Clemen and Winkler 1986; Diebold and Pauly 1990). For a study of particular interest to macroeconomists, see Bischoff 1989.

24. A close and often noted analogy is with an investor's strategy to reduce risk through portfolio diversification.

mational inputs acquired from outside (data, tools, interactions with others). Unless a forecaster produces some such "value-added," his or her product will not be sufficiently differentiated to make a contribution to the combined forecast and to be of continuing interest to informed users.

13.10   Model and Judgment

At the most basic level, two ingredients can be distinguished that are blended in the making of almost any macroeconomic forecast: (1) some more or less systematic technique or model and (2) judgment in choosing and modifying ingredient (1) and adjusting its results. Some forecasters wish to reduce judgment to the choice of the procedure and rely mainly on the model in the interest of objectivity, replicability, and avoidance of biases of perception and assessment. Uses of time-series models that require little or no individual fine-tuning, such as unrestricted univariate or vector autoregressions, provide good examples. Others exercise their judgment much more extensively so as to apply prior knowledge and experience in diagnosing the changing conditions and flexibly adapting the current forecast to them. This is illustrated by the practices not only of many business economists who have no formal models of their own but also of those econometricians who often judgmentally adjust many predictions generated by their models in attempts to improve their accuracy.

The major role of such constant-term adjustments in macroeconometric forecasting of the 1960s is amply demonstrated in studies by Evans, Haitovsky, and Treyz (1972) and Haitovsky and Treyz (1972) (for an interpretation, see also Zarnowitz 1972b). First, the ex ante predictions by teams equipped with the then-representative large models, Wharton and Office of Business Economics (OBE) (Department of Commerce), are much more accurate with than without judgmental adjustments (i.e., in their final form as issued, XA*, rather than in the intermediate, unpublished stage as generated mechanically from the models, XA). This is summed up in table 13.6, which also indicates that the reductions in the MAEs produced by the adjustments are particularly large for the shortest predictive spans (lines 1–4, cols. 1–3).[25]

Second, the errors of ex ante forecasts are on average smaller in absolute size than the errors of the corresponding ex post forecasts that incorporate the same adjustments: the MAE ratios XA*/XP* tend to fall in the 0.6–0.8 range (lines 5–8, cols. 1–3). This is surprising, since XP* use the reported realized values of the exogenous variables and should on this account be more accurate than XA*, which use the projected values of these variables. Although the forecasters' adjustments are themselves a source of errors that may either reinforce or offset the errors in the models and external extrapolations, their net

25. The results for some other variables are similar. See, e.g., Zarnowitz 1972b, table 6 and pp. 218–22.

Table 13.6   **The Effects of Judgmental Adjustments on the Accuracy of Forecasts with Several Macroeconometric Models**

Line	Variable[a]	Two Models, 1967:2–1969:3[b]			Four Models, 1980s			
		1Q (1)	4Q (2)	All (3)	1Q (4)	4Q (5)	8Q (6)	All[c] (7)
		MAE Ratios: XA*/XA[d]			*% of Predictions Improved by Judgment[e]*			
1	GNP	0.2	0.6	0.4	66*	47	65	59
2	RGNP	0.2	0.9	0.6	55	50	50	52
3	UR	0.3	0.6	0.5	60	48	50	53
4	Total	0.2	0.7	0.5	62*	57	58	59
		MAE Ratios: XA*/XP*[f]			*% of RMSEs Reduced by Judgment[g]*			
5	GNP	0.6	1.1	0.8	100	50	50	67
6	RGNP	0.7	0.7	0.8	75	25	25	42
7	UR	0.8	0.8	0.7	75	50	50	58
8	Total	0.7	0.9	0.8	76	68	63	69

Source: Cols. 1–3; based on Haitovsky and Treyz 1972, table 1 and p. 319. Cols. 4–7: based on McNees 1990, table 4 and pp. 46–48.

[a]GNP = nominal GNP; RGNP = real GNP; UR = civilian unemployment rate. Total refers to averages for the same 3 variables (cols. 1–3) and for 21 variables covered (cols. 4–7).

[b]Averages for the Wharton model and the OBE model forecasts. 1Q and 4Q denote one quarter ahead and four quarters ahead, respectively. "All" refers to averages for 1Q, 2Q, 3Q, 4Q, and 1-year-ahead forecasts.

[c]Refers to averages for 1Q, 4Q, and 8Q (eight quarters ahead) forecasts.

[d]MAE = mean absolute error. XA* = judgmentally adjusted ex ante forecasts, XA = unadjusted ex ante forecasts.

[e]Percentage of times that adjusted predictions were more accurate than those generated mechanically. Total number of observations for 1Q forecasts in line 4 is 841. An asterisk after a number indicates that it is significantly different from 50 at the 90% confidence level.

[f]XP* = judgmentally adjusted ex post forecasts. XA* and XP* incorporate the same adjustments.

[g]RMSE = root mean square error. The number of the RMSEs in each of cols. 4–6 is 4 (lines 5–7) and 71 (line 8).

effect was apparently to partially compensate for the other inaccuracies. Both outside information and judgment can help correct for errors that an unaided model would commit, but uncontrolled interactions between the different categories of errors may present a serious problem.[26]

Comparisons of Wharton and OBE forecasts of GNP and RGNP in 1966–69 with largely judgmental forecasts by business economists yield mixed re-

---

26. On cases where the ex post forecast errors exceed the ex ante ones without adjustments, which suggests that model misspecifications are more than offset by errors in the exogenous inputs, see Zarnowitz 1972b, pp. 27–28 (also, cf. comments by Okun and Eckstein in Zarnowitz 1972b, pp. 319–22).

sults (Zarnowitz 1972b, tables 7 and 8, pp. 222–27). The adjusted ex ante forecasts of Wharton and OBE hold an edge over two sets of the other forecasts but not two others (including ASA-NBER group median predictions). The ex post forecasts are somewhat less accurate.

These comparisons are of limited value because the available samples of forecasts that can be matched are small, and they refer to old models that have been much revised since. Some new results are presented in McNees 1990 for "four prominent macroeconometric forecasters . . . who . . . have provided data on both their publicized (adjusted) and mechanical (unadjusted) forecasts (pp. 46–47). Table 13.6 gives a summary (cols. 4–7). Judgment improved 55%–66% of the individual predictions for one quarter ahead and reduced 75%–100% of their RMSEs. Here the adjustments tend to receive much help from data on weekly and monthly indicators. For longer spans, the proportions are considerably lower but in general still 50% or higher overall.[27]

Counts of how often judgmental adjustments improved accuracy do not tell us how large the reductions in the averages of absolute or squared errors were. Even so, the new measures seem to leave judgment a smaller role than the old ones do. This could be due to the more recent models being better specified or including more efficient predetermined rules for adjusting residuals or some other reasons. An analysis of the relation between errors of published (adjusted) forecasts and errors of mechanical forecasts suggests that the judgmental adjustments, although mostly helpful, are more often than not too large; the forecasters would do better if they relied on them somewhat less and on their own models somewhat more (McNees 1990, pp. 49–51). But additional evidence is needed to clarify this important aspect of the actual use of macroeconometric models in forecasting.

In my view, it is still largely valid to conclude, as past research did, that the contributions of professional judgment and experience to the accuracy of macroeconomic predictions tend to be both important and positive. After all, an economist's knowledge and analysis of current developments, which a model cannot have, should be able to improve on the mechanical forecasts from that model. This need not at all be inconsistent with psychologists' findings that cast doubt on the value of untrained and unmotivated "common sense" in experimental predictive environments.

13.11   New Comprehensive Comparisons

A detailed study of the forecasting performance of the NBER-ASA Quarterly Economic Outlook Survey 1968:4–1990:1 has been completed very recently (Zarnowitz and Braun 1991). The results confirm that the dispersion across the individual participants' forecasts is typically large and rising with

27. Compare col. 4 with cols. 5–7 in the table. A conspicuous exception is the RMSEs for RGNP in line 6, cols. 5–7. For more detail on more variables, see McNees 1990, table 4.

the length of the predictive horizon. Errors of the average change forecasts cumulate over longer spans with great regularity for a variety of time series. Errors of marginal change and level forecasts, too, often increase with the distance to the target quarter, although by smaller margins and less regularly.

The more autocorrelated variables such as real GNP and consumption are much easier to forecast, and are much better predicted, than variables with high random variability such as residential investment and change in business inventories (all forecasts of series with trends refer to percentage changes). Inflation was underestimated and poorly predicted by most forecasters most of the time.

Simple averaging across the corresponding responses to each successive survey results in group mean forecasts that are generally much more accurate than the majority of individual forecasts. However, for some variables and periods the combinations work much better than for others. The more differentiated and the more complementary the information embodied in their components, the better are the group mean (consensus) forecasts.

Table 13.7, which covers rates of change in GNP, RGNP, and IPD from 1968:4 to 1990:1, compares the mean individual and the consensus forecasts from the NBER-ASA surveys with some representative econometric and time-series forecasts. The econometric predictions are those based on the model of the University of Michigan Research Seminar in Quantitative Economics (RSQE), the longest available series of consistent forecasts of this type. The BVAR forecasts use the five-variable, six-lag quarterly model introduced in chapter 12 (with M2). The Sims probabilistic model is also of the BVAR type

Table 13.7   **Nine Sets of Forecasts Ranked according to Their Average RMSEs, Three Variables, 1968:4–1990:1**

Line	Forecast	Gross National Product (GNP) ARMSE (1)	Rank (2)	GNP in Constant Dollars (RGNP) ARMSE (3)	Rank (4)	Implicit Price Deflator (IPD) ARMSE (5)	Rank (6)
1	NBER-ASA median	1.90	4	1.94	7	1.53	7
2	NBER-ASA consensus	1.586	1	1.58	3	1.21	5
3	Michigan (RSQE)	1.98	5	1.87	5	1.42	6
4	BVAR(A)	2.69	8	1.90	6	1.62	8
5	BVAR(B)	1.89	3	1.40	1	1.03	3
6	Sims(A)	2.30	7	2.08	8	.97	2
7	Sims(B)	1.594	2	1.47	2	.66	1
8	Sims-Todd ARIMA(A)	3.05	9	2.26	9	1.69	9
9	Sims-Todd ARIMA(B)	2.03	6	1.60	4	1.09	4

Source: Zarnowitz and Braun 1991, table 29.

Note: ARMSE (average root-mean-square error) is computed by taking the mean of the RMSEs across the five spans 0–1, . . . , 0–5. The smallest ARMSE is ranked 1, and the largest ARMSE is ranked 9, for each of the three variables.

but allows time variation in coefficients and forecast error variance; it is a nonlinear, nine-variable, five-lag model (Sims 1989; for an earlier version, see Litterman 1986). The univariate ARIMAs are as specified in Sims and Todd 1991. All these time-series models are estimated with the presently available data that incorporate all revisions; hence the forecasts based on them are in this sense ex post. But the forecasts are generated sequentially, using only the information preceding the date of the forecast.

Two alternative assumptions, A and B, are employed for the comparisons in table 13.7. Variant A is that the last-known values of the variables concerned refer to the previous quarter, $t-1$; variant B is that they refer to the current quarter, t. A is preferred because the quarterly data for t are not known to the real-time forecasters, but B is to some extent justified because the forecasters do know and use some monthly and weekly data released in quarter t (and the latest economic news generally). The truth falls somewhere in between but probably more often closer to A than B, for two reasons: (1) the forecasters' information about the most recent developments is limited and deficient; (2) the forecasters use preliminary data, and the time-series models use revised data.

For variant A comparisons, the average RMSEs of the consensus (group mean) survey forecasts are the lowest for GNP and RGNP and the second lowest for IPD, following the Sims (A) model (lines 1–4, 6, and 8). The variant B comparisons are rather strongly biased in favor of the ex post forecasts with time-series models. The ARMSEs are all much lower for the variant B predictions than for their variant A counterparts (cf. lines 4, 6, and 8 with lines 5, 7, and 9). When all nine sets of forecasts listed in table 13.7 are considered, the Sims (B) model ranks 2, 2, and 1 for GNP, RGNP, and IPD, respectively. The corresponding ranks of BVAR (B) are also high: 3, 1, and 3. The ARIMA forecasts tend to be less accurate.[28]

13.12   A Preview

The last part of this book develops several themes already introduced and some additional ones. Chapter 14 argues that the accuracy and properties of forecasts depend heavily on the economic characteristics of the periods covered but only weakly and not systematically on the differences among the forecasters. Offsets between errors in the corresponding predictions of real growth and inflation are demonstrated and analyzed. Multiperiod quarterly forecasting is shown to pose much greater difficulties than annual forecasting.

Chapter 15 discusses the variety of predictions covered by quarterly business outlook surveys. Combining individual forecasts from different professional sources—business analysts, academic economists, corporate execu-

28. Note that these results conceal the differences between the forecast horizons, which are sometimes important, and that the rankings for some other variables differ considerably. Thus, the Michigan forecasts rank higher for the longer spans and are best for the rate of unemployment.

tives—can result in significant gains. Thus the group mean forecasts are on the average over time more accurate than most of the component sets. But there is also a moderate degree of consistency in the relative performance of a large number of the survey members.

Chapter 16 presents extensive results from testing for bias and serially correlated errors in a collection of time series of quarterly forecasts with several horizons and for several variables. It argues against the presumption of rationality in the sense that one should not expect the macroeconomic forecasts to be typically either uniform, unbiased, or self-fulfilling. The tests are more favorable to composite group forecasts than to most of the individual forecast sets, and less favorable to predictions of inflation than to those of other variables, including RGNP growth and unemployment.

Chapter 17 uses unique survey data on matched point and probabilistic forecasts of inflation and GNP growth to study how the degree of consensus among forecasters is related to the degree of uncertainty as revealed by the diffuseness of the appropriate probability forecasts. This means that the disagreement among forecasters tends to understate uncertainty but that rising disagreement often indicates rising uncertainty. Also, there is evidence that expectations of higher inflation generate greater uncertainty about inflation, and that the latter has adverse effects on real growth.

Finally, chapter 18 finds no evidence that U.S. macroeconomic forecasts have grown systematically worse, that is, less accurate, more biased, or both (as some critics have charged). True, large errors in predictions of both real growth and inflation occurred in some recent years (the mid- and late 1970s and early 1980s) but these were times of high concentration of unanticipated shocks and setbacks. The major failures of forecasting are shown to be related mainly to the incidence of slowdowns and contractions in general economic activity. Accordingly, progress in forecasting will require better handling of the difficult problem of turning-point prediction. There is need to combine econometric and time-series models with uses of leading indicators to reduce the length and variability of the lags in recognizing recessions (see also Zarnowitz and Moore 1991).

14   An Analysis of Annual and Multiperiod Quarterly Aggregate Forecasts

14.1   On Some Uses and Limitations of Forecast Data

How and how well economists forecast, and how much their predictions help or hurt public and private decision making, are matters that ought to receive much attention from the profession. This is so not only because of their direct interest to the authors, users, and critics of the forecasts, but also because of their intrinsic but less evident academic interest. What is the practical applicability of economic analysis in this critical area? What is the quality of foresight and counsel that can be expected of responsible economists? These are broad questions which are not easy to answer, but they are basic and surely deserve to be tackled. This requires that we systematically confront forecasts as indications of how economists ex ante thought events were likely to unfold with ex post knowledge of what actually did happen and how. The aims, from the least to the most ambitious, are (1) to measure forecast errors, (2) to explain them, and (3) to learn how to reduce them in the future.

Success in forecasting may be occasional and fortuitous or intuitive, but progress in forecasting, to the extent it is possible, can only come from advances of science, not art or chance. It presupposes that sufficiently important and persistent regularities in economic processes and relationships exist and

Reprinted from the *Journal of Business* 52 (January 1979): 1–33. © 1979 The University of Chicago. All rights reserved.

The author is grateful to Dennis Bushe, Thomas Kutzen, and Robert Osterlund for assistance with research and preparation of this paper; to Stephen K. McNees and Linda G. Martin for comments and aid with the data; and to Otto Eckstein, Geoffrey H. Moore, and Arthur M. Okun for criticisms and suggestions based on an earlier draft. This report was supported by grants from the National Science Foundation and the Earhart Foundation to the National Bureau of Economic Research and by a grant from the Center for the Management of Public and Nonprofit Enterprise, Graduate School of Business, University of Chicago.

are properly identified and used. Learning processes are involved, which can be time-consuming and discontinuous, reflecting in part the shifts and discontinuities in the economic change itself, in part the inadequacies of measurement and analysis.

Data on economic forecasts generally cover short time periods. Long time series of consistent predictions simply do not exist. Few if any forecast sets are fully identified according to the many aspects and dimensions that matter (source, target, timing, assumptions, data, models, and methods used), so that it is often difficult to determine what constitutes a suitable "sample" of forecasts of a given type. Moreover, few forecasters leave their models and techniques unchanged for long as they seek improvements and try to adapt to new developments in the economy. Hence, a particular forecaster's past record is often a highly uncertain basis for inferences about future performance.

Even more hazardous, if not irresponsible, are attempts to grade forecasters on the evidence of how well they predicted change in a particular short period, say, a year or a few years. Clearly, on any single occasion some forecasters will be ahead of others by sheer chance or for some idiosyncratic reasons. Strong evidence of significant and stable differences over time is required to rank the forecasting individuals, groups, or models with a modicum of confidence, and such evidence is essentially lacking (Zarnowitz 1967, 1971; Christ 1975; McNees 1975).

The proliferation in recent years of multiperiod quarterly macroforecasts offers no substitute for long historical series. These are rich data containing much interesting material that certainly deserves to be carefully recorded and analyzed. However, such forecasts, and their errors, tend to be internally correlated in at least two ways: (1) serially, within each sequence made from a given base period, and (2) across the successive sequences, which overlap and thus refer partially to the same target period. Each multiperiod forecast is a joint product of the common information, technique, and judgment used, and each depends on previous forecasts of which it is to some extent a revision. Thus, errors in the data, models, procedures, and judgments, autocorrelated disturbances, and certain types of distributed lags are all likely to induce interdependencies within and between the multiperiod forecasts. The resulting complex correlation structures resist estimation, given the small samples of comparable predictions from any given source. Consequently, measures of average accuracy, bias, etc., calculated from such samples are difficult to interpret from the viewpoint of statistical inference (Spivey and Wrobleski 1978).

Two conclusions are surely valid. First, small-sample studies of forecasts are still needed and can be instructive, but their limitations must be recognized. Second, it is necessary to compile and examine forecast records extending as far back in time as possible, so as to gain information, take a longer view of forecasting behavior and performance, and place the short records of recent predictions in a proper perspective. Historical data on post–World War

II forecasts assembled in the 1960s by the National Bureau of Economic Research (NBER) provide a good base here, which I was able to partially extend and update. Some preliminary results for annual forecasts of three variables are reported below.

14.2   The Record of Annual GNP Forecasts since 1947

In the early post–World War II period, most forecasts were made near the end of the calendar year for the next year and most referred to GNP in current dollars. The evidence we have on such forecasts goes back to 1947 but is quite fragmentary for the late 1940s and early 1950s.

The period of transition from the war economy witnessed the largest errors on record in the GNP forecasts. Even after the 1945–46 predictions were shown to have greatly underestimated the then-prevailing levels of economic activity (L. R. Klein 1946), expectations of a business slump stubbornly persisted. One small, reputable group of private forecasters came up with an average prediction for 1947 of a 6% decline in GNP, whereas the actual change turned out to be a rise of about 11%. For 1948 the group predicted a fractional decline, but GNP instead advanced again at much the same surprisingly high rate. The failure of forecasts during these years was widespread, with but a few partial exceptions; the developments of the time could not have been predicted well with estimates based on data and relationships for the 1930s and false analogies with the early post–World War I period, and were not. When a recession finally came late in 1948, it proved shorter than many had expected. A "consensus forecast" by more than 30 respondents polled in December 1948 anticipated well the decline of nearly 2% in GNP during 1949, but a year later the same group was wide of the mark in predicting a drop of 3:5%, whereas GNP actually staged a strong comeback in 1950 with a rise exceeding 10% (though it should be noted that the latter resulted in part from the onset of the Korean War in June 1950).

The evidence for the period 1953–76 is summarized in table 14.1 in terms of comparisons between the predicted and the actual annual percentage changes. It is generally instructive to analyze forecast errors in terms of levels, absolute changes, and percentage changes, but if a choice must be made for succinctness, there are several good reasons for using percentage changes where technically appropriate, particularly for variables with strong trends. (1) What is predicted in the first place is change from the last known or estimated level, and percentage changes often depend less on the levels and are more stable and comparable over time than dollar changes. (2) Percentage change forecasts are apt to be less affected by data revisions. (3) Some important measures of predictive performance, such as correlations with actual values, are much more meaningful for change forecasts than for level forecasts. (4) It is the rates of growth in economic aggregates (income, output, prices) that are of main interest to analysts and policymakers.

The forecasts are made late in the year $t - 1$ or, in a few cases, very early in the target year t; typically, the forecasters know the official estimates for the first three quarters but not for the last quarter of the year $t - 1$. The actual changes used to compute the errors are based on the first official estimates for the year t published early in the following year $(t + 1)$. These are provisional values which are themselves partly near-term predictions, and subsequent revisions indicate that the errors in the early data are by no means negligible (cols. 10–11).[1] On the average, without regard to sign, these revisions are about one-third the size of the forecast errors (lines 5–8). The errors are computed by subtracting the actual from the predicted (or estimated) changes, and they are predominantly negative, which shows that both forecasts and the provisional figures strongly tend to understate the changes in GNP (lines 9–12). By far most of these underestimated changes are increases (for a review of similar findings of earlier studies, see Zarnowitz 1972b).

Table 14.1 discloses a substantial correspondence between the forecasts and the realizations. The predicted changes approximate the actual ones well in each period covered, the averages of the former being generally less than 1 percentage point smaller than the averages of the latter (lines 1–4). Where the mean actual changes increased (as from 5% per year in 1956–63 to 8% per year in 1963–76), so did the mean predicted changes; moreover, the discrepancies between the two diminished in the latter years. The forecasts are in all cases considerably more accurate than the naive model which assumes that next year's percentage change will be the same as that of the previous year and more accurate than the—somewhat less naive—trend extrapolation model, which projects the average percentage change of the 4 previous years. Collectively, the mean absolute error (MAE) of forecasts is less than half that of the first naive model (lines 5–8, col. 8), and the ratio of the two declines from 0.47 in 1956–63 to 0.43 in 1963–76 and 0.34 in 1969–76. The corresponding ratios for comparisons of the forecasts with the 4-year moving average ("trend") extrapolations (col. 9) are 0.84, 0.56, and 0.44.

The average error measures are important, but they fall far short of telling the whole story. Measures of correlation (which unfortunately are often omitted from forecast evaluations) are needed to show how well the predicted changes have tracked the actual changes over time. The r^2 coefficients for the forecasts covered in table 14.1 are all positive and significant, generally exceeding .5 and, for the more recent periods, averaging .7 or higher (lines 13–

1. In some evaluations, forecasts are adjusted for the differences between the forecaster's own estimates of the base (current actual value) and the revised base figures (see McNees 1975, pp. 7–9, and Eckstein 1978, p. 320, for arguments in favor of that practice). My own view is that it is more instructive to study the base revisions separately as one of the sources contributing to the total error, that is, to compute and compare both the level errors unadjusted and the absolute change errors adjusted for base revisions. For percentage change errors, which to save space are alone used here, I agree with McNees (1975, p. 9) that "it is not clear what adjustments for data revisions would be appropriate or even possible." Preliminary calculations indicate that the effects of revisions on errors computed in this form are small and not systematic.

Table 14.1 Summary of Measures of Error for Annual Predictions of Percentage Change in GNP, 1953–76

Line	Period and No. of Years Covered	Livingston Survey, Mean Forecast[a] (1)	Selected Private Forecasts, Mean[b] (2)	N.Y. Forecasters Club, Mean Forecast[c] (3)	ASA-NBER Survey, Median Forecast[d] (4)	Economic Report of the President[e] (5)	Michigan Model[f] (6)	Wharton Model[g] (7)	Extrapolations Last Change[h] (8)	Extrapolations Average Change[i] (9)	Actual Preliminary[j] (10)	Actual Revised[k] (11)
			Mean Absolute Percentage Change, Predicted and Actual									
1	1953–76 (24)	5.7	6.0	...	...	...	...	...	...	...	6.6	6.9
2	1956–63 (8)	4.3	4.7	4.0	...	...	...	...	...	...	5.0	5.3
3	1963–76 (14)	7.1	7.2	...	...	7.6	7.2	7.6	...	...	7.9	8.2
4	1969–76 (8)	8.1	8.0	...	8.1	8.6	8.3	8.2	...	...	8.4	8.8
			Mean Absolute Error, in Percentage Points									
5	1953–76 (24)	1.6	1.2	...	...	...	...	...	3.1	2.3	.5	...
6	1956–63 (8)	1.7	1.4	1.7	...	...	...	...	3.4	1.9	.5	...
7	1963–76 (14)	1.1	.9	...	...	.9	1.3	.8	2.3	1.8	.3	...
8	1969–76 (8)	1.0	.6	...	1.0	.8	1.0	.9	2.6	2.0	.3	...
			Mean Error, in Percentage Points									
9	1953–76 (24)	−1.0	−.7	...	...	...	...	...	−.3	−.1	−.5	...
10	1956–63 (8)	−.4	−.1	−.8	...	...	...	...	−.2	−.4	−.3	...
11	1963–76 (14)	−.8	−.6	...	...	−.2	−.5	−.3	−.3	−.6	−.3	...
12	1969–76 (8)	−.3	−.4	...	−.3	.2	−.1	−.2	−.3	−.5	−.3	...
			Squared Correlation (r²); between Predicted and Actual Change									
13	1953–76 (24)	.739	.792	...	...	...	...	...	.012	.054	...	...
14	1956–63 (8)	.634	.497	.563	...	...	...	...	.155[l]	.038	...	...
15	1963–76 (14)	.717	.791	...	...	.752	.603	.689	.006	.079	...	...
16	1969–76 (8)	.780	.875	...	.768	.834	.746	.669	.002	.000	...	...

[a]Based on surveys conducted by Joseph A. Livingston, syndicated columnist with the *Philadelphia Inquirer,* and published in the *Philadelphia Bulletin* and *American Banker.* Of the semiannual surveys, only the end-of-year ones are used here; they typically cover answers to a questionnaire mailed in November and appear in a "Business Outlook" column late in December. The participants in these surveys, listed at the end of the *Bulletin* columns, varied in number between 44 and 62.

[b]Average of end-of-year annual GNP forecasts from the following sources: (1) *Fortune* magazine ("Business Roundup"); (2) Harris Trust and Savings Bank; (3) IBM Economic Research Department; (4) National Securities and Research Corporation; (5) NICB (now Conference Board) Economic Forum; (6) Robert W. Paterson, University of Missouri; (7) Prudential Insurance Company of America; (8) UCLA Business Forecasting Project. The earliest of these predictions were made in October; the latest in January. Most but not all of the forecasts in each of these eight sets are available in published form; those for the period ending in 1969 were analyzed in NBER studies of economic forecasting (Zarnowitz 1967, 1972b, 1974).

[c]Of the semiannual forecasts of this group, only the end-of-year ones are included. The group mean forecasts used here cover individual predictions varying in number between 31 and 39. These data, too, were analyzed in NBER studies (see ref. in n. *b*), but no forecasts were collected for the period after 1963. The predictions for 1956–58 were made in October; those for 1959–63 in December.

[d]Source: Quarterly releases by the American Statistical Association and the National Bureau of Economic Research, published in the ASA *AmStat News* and the NBER *Explorations in Economic Research.* Median forecasts from the November surveys only are used. The membership in these surveys varied between 45 and 84. See Zarnowitz (1969a) and Su and Su 1975.

[e]Forecasts by the Council of Economic Advisers (CEA) as stated in the *Economic Report* (usually as the midpoint in a relatively narrow range). As a rule, the *Economic Report* appears in January. For some earlier studies of these forecasts, see Moore 1969a, 1977d; Zarnowitz 1972b; Fellner 1976, pp. 118–24; McNees 1977.

[f]Published ex ante forecasts from the Research Seminar in Quantitative Economics (RSQE) of the University of Michigan. Based on several working models (see Suits 1962; Hymans and Shapiro 1970, 1974). The forecasts are those released in connection with the University of Michigan annual "Conference on the Economic Outlook," occurring usually in November (in 1974 and 1975, December).

[g]Source: *Wharton Economic Newsletter,* Econometric Forecasting Unit, Wharton School of Finance and Commerce, University of Pennsylvania. Forecasts based on a series of versions of Wharton models (see Evans and Klein 1967; Evans, Klein, and Saito 1972b; McCarthy 1972; Duggal et al. 1974). The forecasts here covered are dated in November or (as in 1971 and 1973–75) in December.

[h]Assumes that next year's percentage change will be the same as that of the previous year. The actual changes used are those based on the preliminary estimates explained in n. *j* below.

[i]Assumes that next year's percentage change will be the same as the average percentage change in the 4 previous years. On the actual changes used, see n. *j*.

[j]Based on the first official estimates following the year for which the forecast was made.

[k]Based on current data taken from U.S. Department of Commerce, Bureau of Economic Analysis, *Handbook of Cyclical Indicators, A Supplement to the Business Conditions Digest* (May 1977).

[r]*r* is negative.

16, cols. 1–7). In contrast, the corresponding coefficients for the extrapolations (cols. 8 and 9) are zero or near zero (where larger, r is negative). These results mean that the extrapolations can account for little or none of the variation in year-to-year changes in GNP, while the forecasts have captured most of this variation.

Because sufficiently long and consistent annual time-series data for GNP are not available, no attempt was made here to test the forecasts against higher standards provided by more effective extrapolation methods such as the autoregressive integrated moving-average (ARIMA) models. However, recent comparisons of quarterly forecasts with such models show the forecasts to be on the average more accurate (Hirsch, Grimm, and Narasimham 1974; Christ 1975; Spivey and Wrobleski 1978), and I would expect this to be a fortiori true for the annual forecasts and particularly with respect to the correlations with the actual values.

The evidence supports the conclusion that the end-of-year forecasts of current-dollar GNP next year had a reasonably satisfactory record of accuracy since 1953. Indeed, in comparisons with earlier forecasts (Sapir 1949; Okun 1959; Zarnowitz 1967), that record improved considerably in the 1960s and even in the 1970s, a turbulent period presumed to have been particularly difficult to forecast.

It must be noted that our collection is certainly no random sample, including as it does the official administration forecasts and several of the most reputable and influential sets of private predictions by business and academic economists (see notes to table 14.1). It is also true that our data and measures have some shortcomings that must not be overlooked. In particular, the estimates of the current position (ECP) which the forecaster actually used as the starting point or base are not always reported. In some cases, therefore, the base values had to be imputed, which was done using data as of the (precise or approximated) date of the forecast plus such information as was available on how the forecaster derived his ECPs on other occasions. The imputations, even though carefully made, undoubtedly contain some errors. However, these errors are definitely not such as to invalidate the broad conclusions of this paper.[2]

It is difficult to draw more detailed inferences concerning the relative accuracy of the different forecast sets covered from these results. One reason is that the forecasts differ appreciably with regard to their precise dates, and it is known from previous research that later predictions have a significant advantage over earlier ones (Zarnowitz 1967; McNees 1975). It is apparent, however, that the average error and correlation measures do not show large, consistent differences among these forecast sets. This is in agreement with earlier

2. Other possible errors, also not critical, might arise from the fact that some of our forecasts, lacking directly reported annual predictions, are averages of forecasts for shorter periods within the coming year. This could cause some deviations from the span or target period intended by the forecasters (Carlson 1977).

findings which together strongly suggest that the search for a consistently superior forecaster is about as promising as the search for the philosophers' stone (Zarnowitz 1971; McNees 1973, 1975, 1976; Christ 1975).

A few further observations seem warranted. Although the forecasters included differ in many respects, even a detailed inspection reveals few sharp contrasts between their predictions for the same years. Of course, competent forecasters use common data and techniques, regularly interact, and are often similarly influenced by recent events and current attitudes and ways of thinking. The genuine ex ante forecasts here considered are all to a large extent "judgmental." Large doses of judgment enter, mostly helpfully, the forecasts derived with the aid of econometric models (see, e.g., Haitovsky, Treyz, and Su 1974). This could well tend to reduce the dispersion among the corresponding predictions of this type; there is indeed some evidence that errors of ex ante forecasts with econometric models vary less than errors of ex post forecasts made without judgmental adjustments (Christ 1975). At the same time, many so-called judgmental forecasters also use some more or less explicit econometric equations or models, "outside" or "own" (Zarnowitz 1971; Su and Su 1975). While published forecasts by ranking practitioners are often developed with particular skill and care, group average forecasts greatly benefit over time from cancellations of individual errors of opposite sign (Zarnowitz 1967, 1972b). At any given time, the deviations between corresponding forecasts from different sources are likely to be reduced by the working of these balancing factors. Thus, it is not surprising that forecasts for the same variable and target period tend to be similar. Indeed, the correlations between pairs of the forecast sets included in table 14.1, computed for the four periods distinguished therein, are significantly higher than the correlations between predictions and realizations recorded on lines 13–16. The r^2 coefficients for eight pairs of the predicted percentage change series all exceed .8, and some are considerably higher.

Of the 110 observations in our seven forecast sets, about 64% are underestimates of change and 34% are overestimates. By far most of the latter refer to years marked by economic recessions (1954, 1960, 1970, 1974) or slowdowns (1962, 1967). The provisional GNP values show but two year-to-year declines in the period covered in table 14.1: in 1954, which the forecasts overstated, and in 1958, which the forecasts missed (accounting for the only turning-point errors in this sample). Thus underestimation was limited to the increases in GNP; moreover, it was most pronounced when the increases were particularly large, as in 1953, 1955–56, 1965–66, 1968–69, and 1973.

These results suggest the presence of "systematic" errors, but not in the sense of a bias that could have been readily escaped or corrected in advance. It seems difficult to discount them as merely another manifestation of the familiar tendency of forecasts to underestimate the observed changes (which, for series with random elements, is a property of even unbiased and efficient forecasts [Mincer and Zarnowitz 1969; Hatanaka 1975]). What is underestimated here is the average annual rate of growth in a series which, as properly recognized by the forecasters, is trend dominated and seldom declines from year to year. This outcome can be traced to the forecasters' tardy recognition of high-growth phases ("booms") and, increasingly, of inflation speedups, but it was also mitigated by their even tardier recognition of business recessions and slowdowns. Such movements are recurrent and not purely random; they have important, detectable regularities as shown by historical studies of business cycles; but they are also nonperiodic and indeed vary a great deal over time, so their predictability remains very limited. In any event, simple "learning from past errors" would not have been of much use here as the errors of these forecasts generally have zero or very low autocorrelations.

14.3   Annual Forecasts of Real GNP and the Price Level

It is difficult to obtain and verify consistent forecasts of GNP in constant dollars and the implicit price deflator (IPD) that would cover more than just the most recent period. Few business forecasters in the 1950s and 1960s made systematic efforts to decompose their predictions of current-dollar GNP into quantity and price elements. Of the forecasters with econometric models, who paid more attention to real GNP, only two (the University of Michigan and Wharton Econometric Forecasting Associates) have longer records.[3]

Table 14.2 shows that the predicted changes in real GNP, taken without regard to sign, differed from the actual changes by less than 1 percentage point on the average (lines 1–3). The predicted changes tend to be smaller than the actual ones, except for the Council of Economic Advisers (CEA) forecasts (col. 3), where the reverse obtains. The MAEs of the forecasts average a little over four tenths of those of the simple last-change extrapolations in 1959–67 and 1962–76, about one third in 1969–76 (lines 4–6, col. 6). Comparisons with extrapolations of the average percentage change of the 4 previous years give very similar results, except for 1959–67, where the forecast errors average about two thirds of the extrapolation errors (lines 4–6, col. 7).

Correlations between the predicted and actual changes are all significantly positive, and they too suggest some improvement in recent years: the r^2 coefficients for 1969–76 are higher than those for the earlier and longer periods (lines 10–12). It is interesting to observe that all but one of them exceed the corresponding coefficients for current-dollar GNP forecasts, particularly so for the predictions with the Wharton models and the ASA-NBER group medians (from quarterly surveys regularly conducted by the American Statistical Association and evaluated by the National Bureau of Economic Research)

3. Some of the econometric forecasts were released at more than one date near the end of the year, and in more than one version depending on the data used or policy assumptions made. In all but a few doubtful instances where somewhat arbitrary decisions had to be made, the forecasts chosen are those preferred by the forecaster or, lacking stated preferences, those which embodied assumptions most common to the forecasts made at the time.

Table 14.2   Summary Measures of Error for Annual Predictions of Percentage Changes in Real GNP, 1959–76

Line	Period and No. of Years Covered	Selected Private Forecasts, Mean[a] (1)	ASA-NBER Survey, Median Forecast (2)	Economic Report of the President[b] (3)	Michigan Model (4)	Wharton Model (5)	Extrapolations		Actual	
							Last Change (6)	Average Change (7)	Preliminary (8)	Revised (9)
				Mean Absolute Percentage Change, Predicted and Actual						
1	1959–67 (9)	4.1	…	…	3.7	…	…	…	4.3(5.0)[c]	4.5
2	1967–76 (15)	…	…	4.4	3.8	…	…	…	4.1	4.05
3	1969–76 (8)	…	3.3	4.0	3.5	3.2	…	…	3.6	3.3
				Mean Absolute Error, at Percentage Points						
4	1959–67 (9)	1.3	…	…	1.0	…	2.7	1.7	.5	…
5	1962–76 (15)	…	…	1.1	1.4	…	2.8	2.6	.4	…
6	1969–76 (8)	…	1.0	1.2	1.6	.9	3.7	3.6	.3	…
				Mean Error, in Percentage Points						
7	1959–67 (9)	−.9	…	…	−.5	…	−.6	−1.1	−.2	…
8	1962–76 (15)	…	…	.6	.2	…	−.3	.1	−.1	…
9	1969–76 (8)	…	.7	.8	.8	.5	−.15	.7	.06	…
				Squared Correlation (r²) between Predicted and Actual Change						
10	1959–67 (9)	.445	…	…	.531	…	.306[d]	.000	…	…
11	1962–76 (15)	…	…	.775	.617	…	.012	.049[d]	…	…
12	1969–76 (8)	…	.936	.857	.709	.941	.001	.320[d]	…	…

Note: For sources and explanations of the data used in cols. 2–9, see nn. *d–k*, respectively, in table 14.1.

[a] Average of end-of-year annual forecasts of real GNP inferred from the forecasts of current-dollar GNP, the consumer price index (CPI), and the wholesale price index (WPI) from the following sources: (1) Harris Trust and Savings Bank; (2) National Securities and Research Corporation; (3) NICB (Conference Board) Economic Forum; (4) Robert W. Paterson, University of Missouri; (5) UCLA Business Forecasting Project. These forecasts were obtained by dividing the forecasts of GNP, as reported in current dollars, by the composite price-level forecasts. The latter are weighted sums of the reported forecasts of CPI and WPI, the weights being .647 and .353, respectively (the first of these proportions represents the average ratio of consumption expenditures to GNP in the period 1953–64). For further detail and analysis of the individual forecasts in this set, see Zarnowitz 1969b; see also table 14.1, n. *b*.

[b] The forecasts for 1962, 1963, 1965, and 1968 must be inferred from statements in the *Report*; they are confirmed by the CEA as approximately correct, though not in all cases precisely correct (Moore 1977d). The other forecasts are all based on figures given in the *Report* and so are fully verified.

[c] The figure in parentheses is based on preliminary GNP figures deflated by weighted averages of the corresponding data for CPI and WPI (with weights as given in n. a. above). This series of "actual" values is comparable to the forecasts used in col. 1 only.

[d] *r* is negative.

(compare table 14.2, line 12, and table 14.1, line 16). In contrast to the reasonably high correlations for the forecasts proper, those for the extrapolations (cols. 6–7) are here again extremely low or negative.

These summary measures, then, present the annual forecasts of real GNP in a generally favorable light. However, the accuracy of these forecasts varied greatly in different years, which at times seriously impaired their usefulness, and this does not show up in the summary. As suggested by the averages with regard to sign (lines 7–9), the usual tendency of forecasts to underestimate changes prevailed in the first half of the period 1959–76 but not in the second half. Actually, the errors varied considerably in each subperiod, primarily reflecting cyclical change and in particular the disturbing effects of missed downturns. Real GNP turned down in 1954, 1958, 1970, and 1974, but of the 10 predictions for these years which are available, 8 specified continued rises and only 2 succeeded in signaling declines. Again, and not surprisingly, nearly all of the significantly large overestimation errors refer to the years during which national output grew at relatively low or decreasing rates, and most of the larger underestimation errors refer to the years of high real-growth rates.

It is of considerable interest to note that the turning-point errors are much larger than other errors (on the average about 2½–3 times larger, for all forecasts in this collection). Thus, even though relatively few, these directional errors had a strong adverse impact on the overall accuracy of the real GNP forecasts, as indicated by the following tabulation:

	No.	MAE, % Points	% of Total Absolute Error
Underestimation errors	33	1.12	46.8
Overestimation errors	21	.92	24.4
Turning-point errors	8	2.85	28.8

This evidence contradicts the argument that turning-point errors matter little because they are few and far between (see, e.g., Samuelson 1976). But the argument goes further to say that such few large errors are the necessary (and small) price to pay for the avoidance of many large errors "between turning points" by means of optimal estimation procedures such as least squares. However, it is not clear that these procedures imply more than that the variance of the predicted changes must be less than that of the actual changes (and progressively declining as the forecast span is lengthened). It has never been demonstrated that a trade-off between errors at major turning points and other errors exists, and it would seem a counsel of despair for the forecasters to accept it as inevitable. Prediction of cyclical turns in such series as real GNP, though certainly difficult, is not necessarily impossible, particularly on an annual basis (note the good record in forecasting troughs). In sum, there are indeed strong reasons for makers and users of economic forecasts to give a great deal of attention to turning-point errors. Actually, most of them realize this, as is shown by the acknowledged need for and practice of analyzing such errors (Hickman 1972; Adams and Duggal 1974; Fromm and Klein 1976). However, there is certainly much need for improvement here, and room for some new initiatives (e.g., on how to use current signals from leading indicators, see Vaccara and Zarnowitz 1978).[4]

The worst single year for the predictions covered in table 14.2 was 1974, on the eve of which forecasters across the field missed the onset of a serious recession. This and the smaller turning-point errors for 1970 are the main reasons for the rise in the average errors of these forecasts in 1969–76 compared with the earlier years. But the rise in the absolute errors was not large, and it is well to recall that at the same time there was some improvement in accuracy as measured by the criteria of comparisons with extrapolations and correlations of predicted with actual changes (compare lines 4–6 and 7–12, cols. 3–4 and 6–7, in table 14.2). Limited evidence from one longer series of forecasts suggests that real GNP was predicted with similar average errors in the two 8-year periods, 1953–60 and 1969–76, with much smaller errors in the relatively quiet years 1961–68.

Although the forecasts of real GNP are about as good relative to our simple extrapolative benchmark models as are the forecasts of GNP in current dollars, they are less accurate in terms of comparisons of the errors with the actual percentage changes to be predicted. The point is that the extrapolations perform substantially better for nominal GNP than for real GNP. This can be shown by dividing the error of extrapolation into the size of the actual change, without regard to sign, which gives the following overall ratios for the $X1$ (last change) and $X2$ (average change) models:

GNP—$X1$, 0.44; $X2$, 0.30.   Real GNP—$X1$, 0.78; $X2$, 0.68.

These results accord with expectations, since the growth rates in constant-dollar GNP varied considerably more than those in current-dollar GNP. The ratios of forecast error to extrapolation error average about 0.4 when $X1$ is the standard, 0.5–0.6 when $X2$ is, and the results are much the same for either variable.

Table 14.3 surveys the performance of forecasts of percentage changes in the price level (IPD) that match the real GNP predictions covered in table 14.2. On the average, the predicted inflation rates fall short of the actual ones by fractions of 1 percentage point (lines 1–3). The 1959–67 forecast sets are less accurate than simple last-change extrapolations (line 4), and the other sets

---

4. Eckstein (1978, p. 321) expresses doubt on this score, saying that "for example, leading indicators began to fall in August 1974. . . ." But this applies only to the indicators in current dollars; the present leading index based largely on series in constant dollars or physical units turned down in June 1973, 5 months before the date of the NBER reference peak, and kept falling. Similarly, nominal GNP declined only slightly for a single quarter in 1975, quarter 1 (hereafter indicated as 1975:1), while real GNP declined for six quarters between 1973:4 and 1975:1.

Table 14.3   Summary Measures of Error for Annual Predictions of Percentage Changes in the Price Level, 1959–76

Line	Period and No. of Years Covered	Selected Private Forecasts, Mean[a] (1)	ASA-NBER Survey, Median Forecast (2)	Economic Report of the President[b] (3)	Michigan Model (4)	Wharton Model (5)	Extrapolations — Last Change (6)	Extrapolations — Average Change (7)	Actual — Preliminary (8)	Actual — Revised (9)
				Mean Absolute Percentage Change: Predicted and Actual						
1	1959–67 (9)	1.5	...	...	1.9	...	...	...	1.9(1.4)[c]	2.0
2	1962–76 (15)	...	...	3.7	3.8	...	...	...	4.2	4.5
3	1969–76 (8)	...	4.9	5.3	5.0	5.3	...	...	5.9	6.2
				Mean Absolute Error, in Percentage Points						
4	1959–67 (9)	.6	...	...	.7	...	.3	.7	.3	...
5	1962–76 (15)	...	...	1.0	1.0	...	1.3	1.4	.4	...
6	1969–76 (8)	...	1.3	1.4	1.4	1.4	2.0	2.1	.4	...
				Mean Error, in Percentage Points						
7	1959–67 (9)	.2	...	...	0	...	−.1	.04	−.3	...
8	1962–76 (15)	...	...	−.5	−.5	...	−.2	−1.0	−.3	...
9	1969–76 (8)	...	−.9	−.6	−.9	−.6	−.2	−1.2	−.4	...
				Squared Correlation (r^2) between Predicted and Actual Change						
10	1959–67 (9)	.389	...	...	.424	...	.365	.068[d]	...	...
11	1962–76 (15)	...	...	.768	.682	...	.536	.508	...	...
12	1969–76 (8)	...	.526	.581	.454	.604	.166	.059	...	...

Note: For sources and explanations of the data used in cols. 2–9, see nn. *d–k*, respectively, in table 14.1.

[a] Average of end-of-year annual forecasts of the composite price level (a weighted sum of forecasts of CPI and WPI).

[b] See table 14.2, n. *b*.

[c] The figure in parentheses is based on weighted averages of data for CPI and WPI. This series of actuals for the composite price level is comparable to the forecasts used in col. 1 only (cf. table 14.2, n. *c*).

[d] *r* is negative.

outperform the naive models by relatively small margins, much less than those observed for the GNP series. The naive models work comparatively well here, with errors averaging about three tenths of the actual changes in IPD. Projections of the last change are in this case better than those of the average change (cols. 6–7), which is the reverse of the situation for GNP in both current and constant dollars. The forecasts underestimated strongly (much more than the last-change extrapolations) the average inflation since 1961 (lines 7–9). The predicted and actual percentage changes in the price level are all positively correlated, but the correlations for 1969–76 are generally lower than their counterparts for GNP and, still more so, for real GNP (lines 10–12).

Forecasts of inflation often have much in common with projections of the last observed rate of inflation. To illustrate, correlations between the errors of these forecasts and the errors of the corresponding extrapolations produce the following r^2 coefficients: Michigan (1959–76), .51; CEA (1962–76), .78; ASA-NBER (1969–76), .95; Wharton (1969–76), .80. For growth rates in real GNP, the correlations between forecast errors and extrapolation errors are also positive but throughout lower, in most cases much lower. These results are not surprising, and they have a positive aspect inasmuch as forecasts should be closer to extrapolations of a given type in those cases where such extrapolations are more effective (for an elaboration, see Mincer and Zarnowitz 1969). However, our comparisons are constrained to naive models which presumably do not represent high standards for economic forecasting. In particular, price-level forecasts that are highly correlated with last-change extrapolations must share the property of the latter to lag a year behind the actual rates of inflation. Indeed, the correlations between the predicted changes and the previous year's actual changes are all positive and high: the r^2 coefficients for the four sets of IPD forecasts listed earlier in this paragraph are .76, .87, .81, and .72, respectively. These are far higher than the r^2 between successive actual changes, which range from .17 to .54 depending on the period (col. 6).

The annual percentage changes in real GNP (RGNP) are inversely related to those in IPD and positively related to those in current-dollar GNP, while the last two variables do not show a strong or stable association. The relationships between the predicted changes generally parallel the actual ones. This is illustrated by the r^2 coefficients tabulated below.

	1962–76			1969–76		
	Actual	Michigan	CEA	Actual	Michigan	CEA
RGNP-IPD	.567(−)	.328(−)	.528(−)	.646(−)	.472(−)	.651(−)
RGNP-GNP	.297	.210	.222	.644	.464	.491
IPD-GNP	.020	.217	.068	.085(−)	.004	.022(−)

The errors of the forecasts are similarly interrelated. Table 14.4 demonstrates a pervasive pattern of negative correlation between errors in forecast-

Table 14.4   Correlations between Errors of Forecasts of Percentage Changes in Nominal GNP, Real GNP, and IPD, 1962–76

		Squared Correlation (r^2) between Forecasts Errors		
		For RGNP and IPD	For RGNP and GNP	For IPD and GNP
Line	Source of Forecast	(1)	(2)	(3)
1962–76 (15 years):				
1	Economic Report (CEA)	.297(−)	.359	.114
2	Michigan model	.494(−)	.429	.006
1969–76 (8 years):				
3	Economic Report (CEA)	.677(−)	.004	.259
4	Michigan model	.684(−)	.209	.014
5	Wharton model	.340(−)	.036	.466
6	ASA-NBER survey, median	.525(−)	.013	.351

Note: The sign (−) following the r^2 coefficient indicates that r is negative.

ing real growth and inflation (col. 1). The tendency for these errors to be offsetting, which benefits the forecasts of GNP in current dollars, is most strongly in evidence for the more recent years. When forecasters overestimated real growth, or missed a downturn and projected continued growth instead, they typically also underestimated inflation, as in 1969–71 and 1973–74. Underprediction of real growth occurred in 1972 and 1975–76 in combination with overprediction of inflation.

These observations, which have some precedents (Moore 1969a, 1977a, Zarnowitz 1969b), are consistent with a view of the world in which nominal GNP changes are predicted directly and relatively well, but their division into real and price changes continues to pose great problems. Many forecasters may agree with that view in general terms, and some subscribe to models consistent with it (a specific example might be the St. Louis model, in which the dollar change in total GNP expenditure is determined mainly by the dollar change in a measure of money stock). However, most macroeconometric models, including the two sets covered here, have separate aggregate-real-demand, output, and price-level equations, and it is not at all clear why they should predict GNP better in current than in constant dollars. In fact, some studies of the recent performance of quarterly models arrive at the opposite conclusion, namely, that the results for real GNP are better than those for nominal GNP because of deficient price forecasts (Duggal et al. 1974; Eckstein, Green, and Sinai 1974). The available evidence seems too limited and too mixed to permit any conclusive generalizations on this point. But it is interesting to observe that the importance of output errors versus price errors may vary with changes in the relative roles of real versus nominal factors and disturbances: in the 1970s the errors of the GNP forecasts were for the most

part better correlated with the IPD errors than with the RGNP errors, whereas
in the 1960s the contrary situation obtained (table 14.4, cols. 2–3).

14.4 Quarterly Multiperiod Forecasts, 1970–75: An Overall Appraisal

Here the forecasts and actual data refer to overlapping sequences of quarters, not simply to a series of successive years. Our materials cover 22 quarters from 1970:3 through 1975:4, a period for which forecasts from several
new sources are available. First estimates for the preceding year, taken from
the data prior to the 1976 benchmark revision of the national income accounts,
serve as comparable realizations. Comparisons with the revised data will require a fully integrated treatment of forecast errors and measurement errors.
In short, we now deal with much more complex forecasts but basically treat
the predictions and actual data in the same straightforward fashion as before.

Four of the sources use formal macroeconometric models combined with
judgmental adjustments and (often several alternative) assumptions about exogenous factors. These include, in alphabetical order: Bureau of Economic
Analysis of the U.S. Department of Commerce (BEA); Chase Econometric
Associates, Inc. (Chase); Data Resources, Inc. (DRI); and Wharton Econometric Forecasting Associates, Inc. (Wharton). Each of these forecasters predicts more than 100 variables each quarter, for sequences of up to 8 quarters
ahead, so each can be said to produce regular and relatively detailed forecasts
of the short-term course of the U.S. economy. However, the models used differ in several important respects, such as size and selection of the exogenous
variables. Thus, the BEA model is currently viewed as of "medium" scale (it
has 98 equations, of which 58 are stochastic); Chase is "large" (it has 150
equations, of which 125 are stochastic); so is Wharton (which has 201 equations, of which 67 are stochastic); and DRI is "very large" indeed (with 718
equations, 379 of which are behavioral).[5]

Forecasts by a group associated with the General Electric Company (GE)
use individual econometric relationships in an iterative process involving a
large amount of judgmental prediction; they are not based on a formal model
of simultaneous equations. This system also is large enough to produce forecasts of over 100 variables. In addition, the ASA-NBER median forecasts are
included as a benchmark set of composite predictions. The surveys attract a
representative cross section of professional forecasters, mainly business but
also academic and government economists. The number of participants varies, averaging about 50 per survey. Their methods and techniques differ, but
informal use of models and judgment prevails. The averages of the individual

5. See Intriligator 1978, table 12.12, pp. 454–56, for the numbers of equations and other
summary characteristics of the models. Fromm and Klein (1976, table 1, p. 2) define the scale of
a model, based on the number of equations, as follows: very small = 9 or less, small = 10–49,
medium = 50–119, large = 120–99, very large = 200 or more.

predictions from the surveys trace well the trends in what is sometimes called the "standard" or "consensus" forecast.

As shown in table 14.5, lines 1–6, the MAEs of GNP forecasts are close to 1 percentage point (like the annual forecasts, see table 14.1) for 2 quarters ahead and about half of that or less for 1 quarter ahead. Over longer spans, the MAEs rise more or less steadily by increments varying generally from 0.2 to 0.5 of 1 percentage point for each additional quarter. The MAEs approach 2 percentage points for 4-quarter spans and exceed it for 5-quarter spans; similarly, they approach 3 percentage points for 7-quarter spans and exceed it for 8-quarter spans. Consistent with earlier findings and interpretations for various types of multiperiod forecasts (see, e.g., Zarnowitz 1967, pp. 60–72), the MAEs increase somewhat less than in proportion to the extension of the span. The errors in forecasts of percentage changes expressed on a per-unit-of-time basis (roughly, MAE divided by the length of the effective span) are substantially stable, neither rising nor declining systematically as the forecast reaches further into the future. The same applies to the errors of the implicit predictions of changes during the successive single quarters covered; it is the cumulation of these intraforecast ("marginal") change errors that technically accounts for the tendency of errors in the total predicted changes to grow with the span.[6]

Where both forecasts and realizations refer to increases (as they do most of the time by far in the case of GNP), errors of positive sign denote overestimation and errors of negative sign denote underestimation of actual change. For the short spans of 1–4 quarters, the mean errors (ME) are in all but one instance positive for BEA, Chase, and DRI, while they are, on the contrary, negative throughout for ASA-NBER, GE, and Wharton (table 14.5, lines 7–12). In absolute terms, these averages are predominantly small, however (less than $|0.2|$ except for the ASA-NBER errors, which are larger). For the longer spans of 5–8 quarters, the MEs are generally negative, much larger absolutely, and rising with the span. As will be shown below, the overall MEs conceal large errors of opposite sign in the forecasts for some of the different economic phases of the period 1970–75.

The r^2 coefficients for the correlations between the predicted and actual changes in GNP exceed .6 or .7 for 1-quarter ahead (like the annual forecasts) and exceed .4 or .5 for 2 quarters ahead (lines 13–18). They are generally much smaller for the longer spans, mostly in the .1–.3 range, in a few cases (interestingly, for the middle, rather than the longest, spans) near zero.

Theil's inequality coefficients are remarkably similar for the different forecast sources and horizons, falling mostly between 0.2 and 0.3 (lines 19–24). This indicates that these forecasts are all much better than a naive model ex-

---

6. Note that fewer observations are available for the longer spans (table 14.5, n. *b*). This reduces the comparability of the measures reported for the different spans but does not eliminate it entirely.

Table 14.5   **Summary Measures of Error for Quarterly Multiperiod Predictions of Percentage Change in GNP, 1970–75**

		Span of Forecast in Quarters[b]							
Line	Forecast Set[a]	One (1)	Two (2)	Three (3)	Four (4)	Five (5)	Six (6)	Seven (7)	Eight (8)
		Mean Absolute Error, in Percentage Points							
1	ASA-NBER	.51	1.03	1.44	1.67	2.10	. . .	. . .	. . .
2	BEA	.46	.84	1.36	1.67	2.27	. . .	. . .	. . .
3	Chase	.42	1.03	1.32	1.68	2.22	2.73	3.19	3.49
4	DRI	.53	1.04	1.43	1.94	2.43	2.69	2.95	2.80
5	GE	.42	.95	1.34	1.71	2.19	2.59	2.88	3.25
6	Wharton	.40	.98	1.60	1.68	1.92	2.35	2.83	3.07
		Mean Error, in Percentage Points[d]							
7	ASA-NBER	.06	−.27	−.38	−.39	−.91	. . .	. . .	. . .
8	BEA	.05	.11	.10	.11	−.22	. . .	. . .	. . .
9	Chase	.01	.04	.02	.08	−.14	−.66	−1.48	−2.34
10	DRI	−.01	.11	.05	.11	.01	−.42	−1.12	−1.69
11	GE	−.14	−.15	−.30	−.15	−.15	−.44	−.95	−1.68
12	Wharton	−.12	−.10	−.19	−.12	−.15	−.69	−1.32	−2.17
		Squared correlation (r^2) between Predicted and Actual Changes							
13	ASA-NBER	.612	.615	.262	.168	.384	. . .	. . .	. . .
14	BEA	.704	.597	.201	.032	.007	. . .	. . .	. . .
15	Chase	.752	.451	.107	.058	.127	.134	.179	.293
16	DRI	.632	.469	.069	.000[e]	.008	.102	.249	.600
17	GE	.753	.577	.284	.159	.132	.180	.227	.225
18	Wharton	.773	.453	.099	.148	.252	.349	.310	.440
		Theil's Inequality Coefficient (U)							
19	ASA-NBER	287	.270	.266	.242	.210	. . .	. . .	. . .
20	BEA	.250	.256	.271	.266	.251	. . .	. . .	. . .
21	Chase	.241	.287	.294	.268	.236	.218	.198	.189
22	DRI	.284	.292	.299	.295	.272	.218	.182	.148
23	GE	.245	.260	.260	.243	.233	.204	.181	.172
24	Wharton	.223	.291	.306	.249	.215	.186	.183	.171

[a]See text on the sources and abbreviations used.

[b]Number of forecasts covered per set: ASA-NBER, BEA; 22, 21, 20, 19, and 17 for spans 1–5, respectively; Chase, DRI, GE, Wharton; 22, 21, 20, 19, 18, 17, and 16 for spans 1–7, respectively; 15 (Chase, Wharton), 14 (DRI), and 12 (GE) for span 8.

[c]MAE $= 1/n\Sigma|e_t|$, where $e_t = P_t - A_t$, $P_t =$ predicted percentage change, $A_t =$ actual percentage change, and $n =$ number of forecasts covered (for the given set, variable, period, and span).

[d]ME $= 1/n\Sigma e_t$ (see n. c).

[e]r is negative.

[f]$U = \sqrt{\Sigma e_t^2/\Sigma A_t^2}$ (see n. c).

trapolating the last-recorded percentage change (for which $U = 1$). That model, it should be noted, is but a minimal standard for economic forecasts. It is worth noting that the U coefficients do not increase with the forecast span; in fact, they decline slightly below .2 for the longest spans.

The next two tables have the same format as table 14.5, which facilitates presentation and comparisons of these measures. Real GNP have MAEs (in percentage points) rising from .5–.6 for 1 quarter ahead to 5–6 for 8 quarters ahead, that is, somewhat more than in proportion to the measured span (table 14.6, lines 1–6). The errors for the two shortest spans are not much larger than those for GNP in current dollars, but the errors for the longest spans are 50%–100% larger. The unusually rapid buildup of the MAEs can be traced in large part to turning-point errors. In quarterly multiperiod forecasting, turning points are more frequent and more difficult to predict than in annual forecasting, but the errors associated with them matter much more yet. Here, missing a turn often means that a whole chain of predictions for the subsequent observations is badly off.

The MEs of these forecasts are all positive, which is largely due to the effects of missing or underestimating the declines in real GNP during the recession (table 14.6, lines 7–12). The MEs also cumulate continuously and rapidly here, quite unlike those for the nominal GNP forecasts.

Relative to the size of the actual percentage changes, the real GNP errors are on the average much larger than the current-dollar GNP errors. Note that the inequality coefficients in table 14.6, lines 19–24, rise from .4 or more for the shortest to .7 or more for the longest forecasts. (In contrast, let us recall, the corresponding statistics in table 14.5 vary in the vicinity of .2 for all spans.)

In terms of correlations with the actual changes, on the other hand, the real GNP forecasts look favorable. The r^2 coefficients are throughout rather surprisingly high in table 14.6, averaging over .8 for 1 quarter ahead, over .7 for 2, 5, and 6 quarters ahead, and over .6 for the other spans (lines 13–18). They are much higher than the r^2 coefficients for GNP in table 14.5, particularly for the longer forecasts.

The MAEs of forecasts of inflation in terms of the GNP IPD are once more of the order of .5 or less 1 quarter ahead, approximately 1 percentage point 2 quarters ahead (table 14.7, lines 1–6). However, they cumulate very rapidly, especially in the range of the longer forecasts. The figures for the 4-quarter-ahead predictions are here on the average about 5 times as large and the figures for 8 quarters ahead are more than 13 times as large as those for the 1-quarter span.

This exceptionally strong, much more than proportional buildup of errors reflects a progression of underestimates of inflation rates. The MEs in table 14.7 are all negative (lines 7–12) and average about $-.2$, -1.5, and -5.5 percentage points for the spans of 1, 4, and 8 quarters, respectively.

The r^2 coefficients for the IPD inflation forecasts are generally higher than

Table 14.6   **Summary Measures of Error for Quarterly Multiperiod Predictions of Percentage Change in Real GNP, 1970–75**

Line	Forecast Set[a]	One (1)	Two (2)	Three (3)	Four (4)	Five (5)	Six (6)	Seven (7)	Eight (8)
				Span of Forecast in Quarters[b]					
		Mean Absolute Error, in Percentage Points[c]							
1	ASA-NBER	.56	1.24	1.89	2.43	3.09	...	...	...
2	BEA	.56	1.37	2.14	2.80	3.17	...	...	...
3	Chase	.51	1.11	1.81	2.46	3.29	4.19	4.95	5.31
4	DRI	.61	1.37	2.08	2.75	3.52	4.15	4.78	5.58
5	GE	.50	1.20	1.75	2.15	2.80	3.80	4.76	5.15
6	Wharton	.45	1.18	1.73	2.00	2.48	3.18	4.24	4.92
		Mean Error, in Percentage Points[d]							
7	ASA-NBER	.10	.32	.76	1.30	1.71	...	...	...
8	BEA	.32	.68	1.12	1.71	1.83	...	...	...
9	Chase	.17	.51	.92	1.46	1.98	2.38	2.63	2.82
10	DRI	.26	.77	1.20	1.82	2.59	3.16	3.66	4.72
11	GE	.00	.22	.36	.95	1.53	2.09	2.46	2.58
12	Wharton	.02	.35	.72	1.22	1.71	2.17	2.69	2.90
		Squared Correlation (r^2) between Predicted and Actual Change							
13	ASA-NBER	.846	.789	.698	.684	.746	...	...	...
14	BEA	.829	.754	.642	.512	.508	...	...	...
15	Chase	.839	.817	.727	.703	.733	.710	.604	.596
16	DRI	.793	.745	.598	.584	.785	.827	.741	.638
17	GE	.808	.741	.677	.661	.772	.764	.661	.662
18	Wharton	.820	.672	.651	.745	.816	.781	.730	.580
		Theil's Inequality Coefficient (U)[e]							
19	ASA-NBER	.461	.532	.618	.663	.660	...	...	...
20	BEA	.476	.585	.675	.756	.701	...	...	...
21	Chase	.433	.502	.607	.673	.711	.741	.758	.741
22	DRI	.504	.622	.721	.769	.781	.774	.774	.836
23	GE	.427	.498	.548	.606	.627	.676	.714	.694
24	Wharton	.398	.543	.582	.563	.555	.584	.632	.662

[a]See text on the sources and abbreviations used.

[b]Number of forecasts covered per set: ASA-NBER, BEA: 22, 21, 20, 19, and 17 for span 1–5, respectively; Chase, DRI, GE, Wharton: 22, 21, 20, 19, 18, 17 and 16 for spans 1–7, respectively; 15 (Chase, Wharton), 14 (DRI), and 12 (GE) for span 8.

[c]$MAE = 1/n\Sigma|e_t|$, where $e_t = P_t - A_t$, P_t = predicted percentage change. A_t = actual percentage change, and n = number of forecasts covered (for the given set, variable, period, and span).

[d]$ME = 1/n\Sigma e_t$, (see n. c).

[e]$U = \sqrt{\Sigma e_t^2/\Sigma A_t^2}$ (see n. c).

those for the forecasts of percentage change in nominal GNP (except for a few short predictions) but throughout lower than the corresponding statistics for the real-growth forecasts. They range from .23 to .71 and tend to decrease as the spans lengthen (table 14.7, lines 13–18).

The inequality coefficients U average .31 for the shortest and .48 for the

Table 14.7   **Summary Measures of Error for Quarterly Multiperiod Predictions of Percentage Change in the Price Level, 1970–75**

Line	Forecast Set[a]	Span of Forecast, in Quarters[b]							
		One (1)	Two (2)	Three (3)	Four (4)	Five (5)	Six (6)	Seven (7)	Eight (8)
		Mean Absolute Error, in Percentage Points[c]							
1	ASA-NBER	.45	1.02	1.64	2.26	3.14	...	...	...
2	BEA	.44	1.10	1.86	2.55	2.96	...	...	...
3	Chase	.39	1.02	1.64	2.29	2.98	3.87	4.88	5.69
4	DRI	.54	1.11	1.69	2.37	3.05	4.04	5.17	6.78
5	GE	.39	.90	1.49	1.96	2.37	3.06	4.08	4.79
6	Wharton	.35	.79	1.38	1.95	2.76	3.57	4.54	5.53
		Mean Error, in Percentage Points[d]							
7	ASA-NBER	− .26	− .64	− 1.20	− 1.82	− 2.77	...	...	...
8	BEA	− .24	− .57	− 1.07	− 1.70	− 2.18	...	...	...
9	Chase	− .15	− .49	− .96	− 1.50	− 2.33	− 3.31	− 4.42	− 5.48
10	DRI	− .27	− .70	− 1.22	− 1.85	− 2.82	− 3.88	− 5.12	− 6.78
11	GE	− .12	− .36	− .70	− 1.20	− 1.85	− 2.78	− 3.76	− 4.57
12	Wharton	− .14	− .46	− .96	− 1.44	− 2.02	− 3.08	− 4.29	− 5.34
		Squared Correlation (r^2) between Predicted and Actual Change							
13	ASA-NBER	.651	.587	.474	.410	.385	...	...	...
14	BEA	.574	.388	.309	.217	.210	...	...	...
15	Chase	.600	.440	.394	.287	.246	.233	.320	.381
16	DRI	.478	.426	.412	.346	.401	.398	.384	.371
17	GE	.657	.633	.508	.440	.438	.457	.524	.676
18	Wharton	.714	.711	.652	.566	.502	.495	.494	.396
		Theil's Inequality Coefficient U[e]							
19	ASA-NBER	.325	.341	.382	.408	.458	...	...	...
20	BEA	.338	.382	.410	.445	.446	...	...	...
21	Chase	.311	.358	.377	.410	.438	.462	.480	.496
22	DRI	.375	.388	.397	.422	.444	.475	.508	.540
23	GE	.284	.286	.326	.354	.369	.395	.416	.410
24	Wharton	.265	.270	.307	.339	.365	.399	.436	.465

[a]See text on the sources and abbreviations used.

[b]Number of forecasts covered per set: ASA-NBER, BEA: 22, 21, 20, 19, and 17 for spans 1–5, respectively; Chase, DRI, GE, Wharton: 22, 21, 20, 19, 18, 17, and 16 for spans 1–7, respectively; 15 (Chase, Wharton), 14 (DRI), and 12 (GE) for span 8.

[c]MAE $= 1/n\Sigma|e_t|$, where $e_t = P_t - A_t$, P_t = predicted percentage change, A_t = actual percentage change, and n = number of forecasts covered (for the given set, variable, period, and span).

[d]ME $= 1/n\Sigma e_t$ (see n. c).

[e]U $= \sqrt{\Sigma e_t^2 / \Sigma A_t^2}$ (see n. c).

longest inflation forecasts, displaying a systematic but gradual increase with the span (lines 19–24). They are higher than their counterparts for the current-dollar GNP forecasts but lower than those for the real GNP forecasts.

A critical point revealed by the comparison of our tabulations is that the quantity and price ingredients of the GNP forecasts show a pattern of offsetting errors in the quarterly as well as annual data. The MEs of real-growth predictions are all positive; those of inflation predictions, all negative. Matched by source and span, these statistics have similar absolute values for most of the shorter forecasts. As a result, the MEs of the current-dollar GNP forecasts for spans 1–4 vary in sign but are generally small. For the longer spans 5–8, however, the negative MEs of the inflation forecasts outweigh the positive MEs of the real-growth forecasts, often by large margins. Consequently, the MEs of the longer forecasts of percentage changes in GNP are almost without exception negative (denoting underestimation) and for the most part relatively large.

Forecasts from the different sources are comparable only in a limited and qualified sense. Not only do the models vary in scale and choice of exogenous variables (and practically nothing can be done to allow for these differences), but there are also some systematic discrepancies in the timing of the predictions. The GE forecasts are typically made early in the quarter.[7] Late forecasts are often somewhat more accurate than those released earlier, since they enjoy advantages of additional and more current information.[8] Some of the sources produce forecasts 2 or even 3 times a quarter, but so far we have been able to obtain only one set of predictions for each of them; with more information, it will be possible to increase the number of sets which are more nearly comparable in terms of the release dates.[9]

Despite the many difficulties that beset them, comparisons between forecasts are needed and will inevitably be made. Some summary statements on the apparent relative accuracy of the forecasts are therefore in order here, but they must be interpreted with great caution and cannot support any strong conclusions. According to the MAEs, Wharton and GE forecasts of both real growth and inflation rank high (i.e., they have relatively low MAEs), but as already noted, these sets, particularly GE, have the advantage of late timing. Among the four "early-quarter" forecasters, Chase and ASA have better records than BEA and DRI for most of the 1–5-quarter forecasts of percentage changes in real GNP and IPD, but BEA ranks overall higher than the others for the corresponding nominal GNP predictions. Of the four, only Chase and DRI predict over longer (6–8-quarter) spans, and here DRI has somewhat lower errors for the growth rates in nominal and real GNP, and Chase has somewhat lower errors for inflation.

The differences between the MAEs across sources are mostly small; their precise significance is unknown but probably in many cases low. Other mea-

---

7. For the release dates, see McNees 1975, p. 39; 1976, p. 41.

8. For evidence, see Zarnowitz 1967, pp. 126–30 and McNees 1975, pp. 22–30; 1976, pp. 31 ff.

9. Three of the sources predict more than once each quarter, and the calendar of the releases suggests the following classification for them (EQ, MQ, and LQ denote early-quarter, mid-quarter, and late-quarter forecasts, respectively):

      Chase: EQ, LQ   DRI: EQ, MQ, LQ   Wharton: EQ, MQ

sures of forecasting performance such as the correlations between predicted and actual changes often yield different rankings of the forecast sets. I conclude that the surveyed measures do not show any of the forecasters to be consistently and generally superior to others. This result is consistent with other evaluations which find that the rankings of forecasters vary depending on the variables, periods, and spans covered as well as on the criteria and measurements applied. [10]

14.5   Quarterly Multiperiod Forecasts: An Analysis by Subperiods

The period 1970:3–1975:4, although short, was unusually varied and marked by major disturbances and drastic changes in the economy's course. It is useful to divide it into the following parts, as suggested by the contemporary business cycle and inflationary developments: (1) *1970:3–1973:1:* End of the mild 1970 recession followed by an expansion that accelerated in 1972, with relatively stable inflation. (2) *1973:1–1973:4:* Slower real growth and a sharp inflation speedup (materials shortages, runups in commodity prices, oil embargo). (3) *1973:4–1975:1:* Recession, severe in its last 2 quarters, accompanied first by a further rise and then by a downturn in the rate of inflation. (4) *1975:1–1975:4:* Sharp upturn and the initial recovery phase, with a further decline in inflation.

One question is whether forecasts that originated in these four subperiods show significantly different characteristics and performance. The other is whether forecasts for these subperiods (i.e., those that aimed at the corresponding groups of target quarters) are so differentiated. It turns out that the answers to both questions are definitely yes.

To illustrate the first point, the expansion phase 1 produced forecasts that underestimated growth in dollar GNP mainly because they underestimated inflation. The percentage changes in real GNP were partly underpredicted, partly (in some longer forecasts) overpredicted, but whether negative or positive the MEs of these forecasts were small. In general, the record of the forecasts that were made during period 1 was good in terms of both the ME and the MAE figures, even for the long spans. In contrast, the slowdown phase 2 produced real-growth predictions with very large positive MEs and inflation forecasts with very large negative MEs (underestimation errors). These errors balanced each other so that the MEs for the nominal GNP predictions were moderate (and mostly negative, except for the longest forecasts). The reces-

10. The findings of this study should and will be carefully compared with those of other appraisals of the same forecasts, but the task is still to be completed. Differences between the error measures used are difficult to allow for and they becloud the results of such comparisons. Nonetheless, it is interesting to observe that the 1975 and 1976 studies by McNees report rankings of forecasting performance for GNP, real GNP, and IPD that resemble rather well the results of the present evaluation. (McNees also shows that the forecasters often score quite differently for other variables.)

sion phase 3 gave rise to even larger positive MEs in the real-growth forecasts as the declines were repeatedly missed and, when finally recognized, underestimated. These errors were larger absolutely than the negative errors on the price side, which reflected a continuing underestimation of inflation, so that the predictions of the growth rates in nominal GNP had consistently positive MEs in subperiod 3.

The above summary is based on charts (not reproduced here) which show the average errors (MAE and ME) by span and by subperiod in which the forecasts originated.[11] These charts look very similar for the different models. They show in each case the same striking differences between the forecasts made in subperiods 1, 2, and 3. The suggested inference is that concurrent predictions from different sources and models have common patterns such that their errors depend strongly and similarly on the characteristics of the time of their origin.

In a second exercise, the forecasts were assigned to the four subperiods according to their target quarters, not their base quarters, as illustrated in figures 14.1–14.3. Here the samples are partitioned differently; hence the resulting patterns diverge from those obtained on the first plan, but the conclusion is analogous. The type and size of forecast errors depend critically on the economic properties of the target periods vis-à-vis those of the periods of origin. Forecasters perform best when the two periods are alike, belonging to the same already recognized phase—for example, a continuing expansion as in 1971–72 (most of subperiod 1). They perform worst when the target falls into a new phase, particularly when the latter departs sharply from the currently established pattern (forecasts made in subperiods 2 and 3 and those for subperiods 3 and 4 provide many examples, particularly in the long-span categories). Such period characteristics are much more important determinants of forecast errors than are any differences among the forecasters.

Figure 14.1 shows that all six forecasters persistently underestimated the percentage changes in GNP for subperiods 1 and, much more strongly, 2. All of them overestimated GNP changes in their short forecasts for subperiod 3 (from 1 to 3 or 4 quarters ahead) and underestimated changes in the longer forecasts for the same phase. Overestimates prevailed in all sets for the last phase covered, subperiod 4. As would be expected, MAEs typically increase with the span in any phase, and so do MEs when taken without regard to sign. In subperiod 4, however, the average errors behave in an unusual fashion, first increasing and then decreasing with the lengthening span (the rises refer to spans 1–5; the declines to spans 6–8). This is due to offsets between the real-growth forecasts with positive MEs and the inflation forecasts with negative MEs (see figs. 14.2 and 14.3).

Overall, figure 14.1 demonstrates for the GNP forecasts that the average

---

11. No averages for phase 4 are used on this basis, since they contain too few observations in the truncated sample.

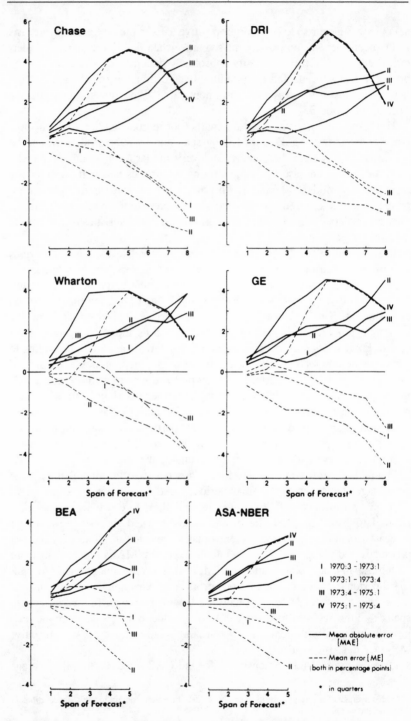

Fig. 14.1   Quarterly multiperiod forecasts of percentage changes in GNP, average errors by subperiod and span, two models, 1970–75

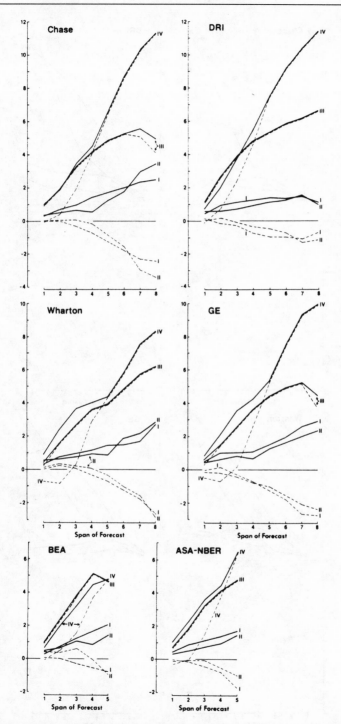

Fig. 14.2   Quarterly multiperiod forecasts of percentage changes in real GNP, average errors by subperiod and span, two models, 1970–75

Note: For key, see fig. 14.1.

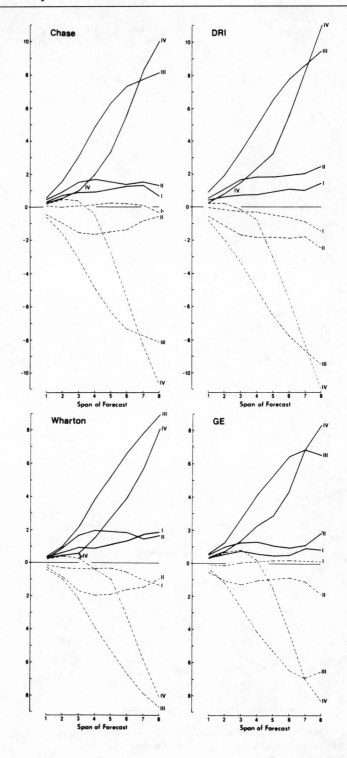

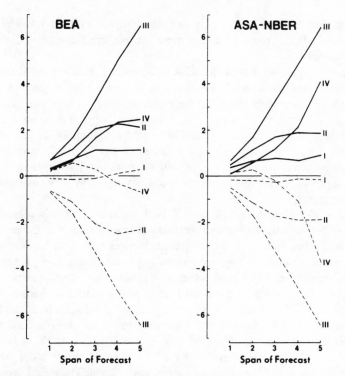

Fig. 14.3   Quarterly multiperiod forecasts of percentage changes in the IPD, average errors by subperiod and span, two models, 1970–75
Note: For key, see fig. 14.1.

error patterns by subperiod and span are substantially similar across the different sources covered. As will be seen below, much the same statement applies to the MAE and ME patterns for the real GNP and IPD forecasts.

Figure 14.2, which covers the real-growth forecasts, shows underestimates dominating the relatively moderate errors for the expansion and slowdown phases 1 and 2. The errors for the recession phase 3 and, particularly, for the 1975 recovery phase 4 are much larger, and they cumulate far more rapidly over the longer spans. The MEs for the two latter subperiods are positive and, for the long forecasts, as large as the MAEs or nearly so. Here the huge errors derive mainly from the forecasters' failure to predict the declines in real GNP and, to a lesser extent, from underestimation of the declines that were predicted.[12] The buildup of errors tapers off at the long end of the forecast range

12. The change errors, $P_t - A_t$ (see table 14.5 for the definitions), are positive where $P_t > 0$ and $A_t > 0$ and also where $P_t < 0$ and $A_t < 0$ but $|P_t| < |A_t|$. These cases dominate in fig. 14.2 the results for both the recession phase 3 and the recovery phase 4. Although real GNP reached a trough in 1975:1 and increased thereafter, the actual changes over longer spans ending in 1975 are negative: that is, real GNP was lower during period 4 than in 1973 (period 2) and during most of 1974 (period 3).

in subperiod 3, but it is strikingly fast throughout in subperiod 4, where the MAEs and MEs increase tenfold or more between the 1-quarter span and the 8-quarter span.

Figure 14.3 shows that the inflation forecasts had relatively small errors in subperiod 1 and considerably larger and on the average all negative errors in subperiod 2; in neither phase did the errors increase strongly with the span. In contrast, the recession period 3 witnessed very large inflation errors, dominated throughout by underestimates and cumulating rapidly. The short forecasts for the initial recovery phase 4 had small errors, mostly with positive means, indicating overestimation of inflation rates that just began to decline. The long forecasts for this last subperiod, however, show very large underestimation errors.

A close examination of figures 14.1–14.3 discloses certain appreciable differences between the forecasters' performances with respect to the particular variables, subperiods, and spans covered. For example, DRI has smaller errors than Chase in predicting real growth 5–8 quarters ahead for phases 1 and 2, but larger errors than Chase in the corresponding forecasts for phases 3 and 4; in predicting growth over the short range of 1–4 quarters, Chase is on balance ahead of DRI. The average accuracy record of inflation forecasts favors GE over Wharton for phase 1 and Wharton over GE for phase 4; for 2 and 3, the picture is mixed, with Wharton scoring as well as GE, or a little better, in the short range but worse than GE in the long range. However, all of these are matters of detail, and the differences are typically small. The main lesson from the comparisons of the MAE and ME patterns is that the similarities greatly outweigh the differences between the forecasters' performance records.

14.6   Concluding Observations

The end-of-year forecasts of annual percentage changes in GNP earn good marks for overall accuracy when judged according to realistic, rather than ideal, standards. Moreover, they are found to have improved in the period since the early 1960s compared with the previous years after World War II.

The corresponding forecasts for GNP in constant dollars (real growth) and IPD (inflation) are weaker. The former suffer from large turning-point errors; the latter from large underestimation errors. But the errors in forecasts of real growth are negatively correlated with the errors in forecasts of inflation, which helped to make the nominal GNP predictions more accurate. In recent times, these correlations were connected with the unexpected concurrence of accelerating inflation and slowing, then declining output rates. Optimistically, and probably also from a lingering faith in a simple Phillips trade-off, forecasters kept anticipating less inflation and more growth. But in the late 1950s and early 1960s, it was the relative stability of the price level that caused widespread surprises, and offsetting errors resulted from the opposite combination of overestimates of inflation and underestimates of real growth.

Forecasts of inflation are not much better than projections of the most recently observed inflation rates, and they lag behind the actual rates much like such projections. The deficiency of price-level forecasts, documented in this and other studies, surely impairs the general ability of economists to analyze the prospects for the economy. Improvements will require major advances in our knowledge, presumably through research based on carefully worked out data (abstract speculation abounds, but good information and observation are rare in this area).

The favorable record of annual GNP predictions does not imply that forecasters can perform well the more difficult task of predicting quarterly changes in GNP within the year ahead or even beyond it. Forecasts for the year as a whole can be satisfactory when based on a good record for the first 2 quarters; they tend to be more accurate than forecasts with longer spans.[13] An examination of the recent multiperiod predictions shows that the errors for real GNP and IPD cumulated rapidly beyond the spans of 2–4 quarters. Previous studies have shown the cumulation to be as a rule less than proportional to the increase in the span, but in this period the buildup of errors was much greater than usual. No doubt in less turbulent times the longer forecasts can be considerably more accurate, but this fair-weather argument is not very persuasive or helpful. At the present time, the predictive value of detailed forecasts reaching out further than a few quarters ahead must be rather heavily discounted. Again, what is critical here is theoretical analysis and empirical research that would lead to improvements in our ability to predict broad movements in the price level and business cycle turning points. Despite setbacks, there is still no reason to give up moderate hopes for an ultimate advance on these fronts.

13. Also, errors of predictions for the individual parts of the year at times offset each other to some degree (Zarnowitz 1967; McNees 1973, 1974). These gains from aggregation over time resemble those from aggregation over sectors (GNP is predicted with smaller average errors of relative change than are most of its components; see Zarnowitz 1967, 1972b; Fromm and Klein 1976).

15 The Accuracy of Individual and Group Forecasts

Empirical studies of forecasts and expectations based on survey data have generally concentrated on the performance of time series of *averages* of the participants' responses. As a rule, these represent means or medians for groups whose size and composition vary over time. This raised the possibility of serious aggregation errors due to the neglect of the cross-sectional and distributional aspects of the data: differences among the individual and subgroups, sampling variation, consistency and representativeness of the employed averages. That such matters can be important is not in doubt, but they seem to have attracted relatively little attention in the literature. [1]

This chapter examines the accuracy of a large number of individual forecast series and of the corresponding average forecast series from a quarterly survey conducted by the author for the National Bureau of Economic Research in collaboration with the American Statistical Association. The survey questionnaire is mailed by the ASA in the middle month of each quarter to a list of persons who are professionally engaged in forecasting the course of the econ-

Reprinted from the *Journal of Forecasting* 3 (Jan.–March 1984): 11–26. © 1984 John Wiley & Sons, Ltd. Reprinted by permission of John Wiley & Sons, Ltd.

Financial support from the U.S. National Science Foundation and aid of the Graduate School of Business of the University of Chicago and NBER are gratefully acknowledged. The author is greatly indebted to Louis Lambros for helpful suggestions and efficient research assistance. Earlier versions of this paper were presented in workshops at the University of Chicago and Stanford University, at the annual meeting of the American Association for the Advancement of Science in Washington, D.C., on 8 January 1982, and at the Third International Symposium on Forecasting in Philadelphia on 6 June 1983. The paper has benefited from comments of the participants, of many colleagues, and anonymous referees.

1. An early study which dealt with certain characteristics of the relation between aggregate and individual forecasts is Zarnowitz 1967, pp. 123–26. A more recent analysis of disaggregated data from surveys of inflation forecasts is Figlewski and Wachtel 1981.

omy, and regular reports on the results are released in the third month.[2] The respondents are economists, mainly from corporate business and finance but also from independent consulting firms, government agencies, and academic and research organizations. This study covers 79 individuals (persons or firms) who participated in at least 12 of the 42 surveys in the period from 1968:4 to 1979:1.[3]

The forecasts relate to rates of change in four variables: gross national product in current and constant dollars (labeled GNP and RGNP), the GNP implicit price deflator (IPD), and consumer expenditures for durable goods (CEDG). The errors of percentage change forecasts are

$$(1)\ e_{t+j} = \begin{cases} \left(\dfrac{P_t - A_{t-1}^*}{A_{t-1}^*} - \dfrac{A_t - A_{t-1}}{A_{t-1}} \right) \times 100, & \text{if } j = 0; \\[2em] \left(\dfrac{P_{t+j} - P_{t+j-1}}{P_{t+j-1}} - \dfrac{A_{t+j} - A_{t+j-1}}{A_{t+j-1}} \right) \times 100, & \text{if } j = 1, \ldots, 4. \end{cases}$$

Here P is the predicted level and A is the actual level according to the last national income and product accounts data released prior to the major benchmark revisions of January 1976 and December 1980. A_{t-1}^* is a preliminary estimate which is the most recent "actual" value available at the time of the forecast (since A_t is unknown, P_t is a true prediction with a horizon of about one quarter). The subscripts refer to the survey quarter t, which is the date when the forecast was made, and to the target quarter, $t + j$, which is the date to which the forecast refers (since all this applies to any of the forecasters and to any of the variables covered, other subscripts are omitted).

It will be noted that equation (1) contains differences between the successive levels predicted in a multiperiod forecast made at time t, namely, $P_t - A_{t-1}^*$ for the current quarter ($j = 0$) and $P_{t+j} - P_{t+j-1}$ for any of the next four future quarters ($j = 1, \ldots, 4$). Accordingly, these are errors of the implicit marginal or "intraforecast" change predictions whose targets are successive quarterly intervals (0–1, 1–2, . . .), which do not overlap.[4]

For two variables, change in business inventories (CBI) and the unemployment rate (UR), the forecast errors are defined as

$$(2)\qquad E_{t+j} = P_{t+j} - A_{t+j}, \qquad j = 0, 1, \ldots, 4,$$

2. The reports, prepared by the NBER, are now published in the *NBER Reporter* and in *AmStat News*. They discuss mainly the median predictions of current interest. For some of the broader historical evaluations, see Moore 1969a, 1977c; Zarnowitz 1972b, 1979; Fair 1974; Christ 1975; McNees 1975, 1976; Su and Su 1975.

3. For further discussion and analysis of the ASA-NBER forecast data, and references to the literature, see Zarnowitz 1983.

4. In contrast, forecasts of average changes over increasing spans (0–1, 1–2, . . .) have overlapping target periods, and they are therefore necessarily intercorrelated. On the definitions, measures, and merits of level and change errors, see Zarnowitz 1967, pp. 32–35, and 1979, p. 6, and McNees 1973, pp. 7–10.

that is, as differences, predicted level minus actual level. These series, unlike the others, which have strong upward trends, can be treated as stationary. Here it is the levels that are of primary interest, not the rates of change as in the cases of RGNP (real growth) and IPD (inflation).

The questions addressed are the following: How accurate are the individual forecasts relative to the corresponding group averages? How representative are the latter of the former? What are the distributions across the individuals of the summary measures of error for the period covered? How do the results compare across the different variables and predictive horizons? The paper is a progress report on a comprehensive study of a large and diversified collection of U.S. macroeconomic predictions. [5]

15.1 Measures of Relative Accuracy and Consistency

The root mean square error (RMSE) of the ith individual's set of predictions can be written as

$$(3) \qquad M_i = \left(\frac{1}{n_i} \sum_{t \in N_i} \varepsilon_{it}^2 \right)^{1/2}$$

for any variable and forecast horizon. [6] Here $\{N_i\}$ is the set of the target periods of the ith forecasts, and n_i is the number of predictions in that set. The numbers and dates of the surveys covered differ across the individuals, and the error series ε_{it} in equation (3) have gaps at times when any of the forecasters missed any of the surveys, which happened frequently. [7]

Next we construct series of group means predictions that match the series for each individual precisely in terms of the variable, horizon, and periods covered. Thus for each series of predictions by a particular forecaster (denoted by the subscript i) there is now a corresponding series of group averages (g_i) of predictions by all those forecasters in our sample who responded to the same surveys. In our simplified notation, the RMSE for the group mean series is

$$(4) \qquad M_{gi} = \left(\frac{1}{n_i} \sum_{t \in N_i} \varepsilon_{gt}^2 \right)^{1/2}.$$

Ratios of RMSEs, M_i/M_{gi} provide convenient measures of the relative accuracy of individual forecasts. They are comparable in a way in which absolute errors for sets of predictions that differ in target dates are not. For any

---

5. For a report on tests of bias or rationality, see Zarnowitz 1983.

6. For level forecasts (UR and CBI) $\varepsilon_{it} = E_{it}$; for percentage change forecasts (the other variables) $\varepsilon_{it} = e_{it}$. Again there is no need here to complicate the formula by adding subscripts for the variable and target period.

7. Recall that, to be included, a forecaster must have participated in at least 12 surveys, but the surveys need not be consecutive. The mean number of surveys covered is 23, with a standard deviation of 8; the minimum is 12; the maximum 37 (out of a total of 42).

target category, the most accurate individuals will have $M_i < M_{gi}$, and the proportion of such forecasts can vary over a wide range. However, if all forecasters participated in every survey (no gaps), then the average of the corresponding RMSEs across the individuals could not exceed the group RMSE. That is,

$$\frac{1}{m} \sum_{i=1}^{m} M_i \geq M_g$$

for a group g consisting of m regular participants, provided that

$$\varepsilon_{gt} = \frac{1}{m} \sum_{i=1}^{m} \varepsilon_{it}$$

(which is easily demonstrated for simple level forecasts).[8]

It follows that a group average forecast has a built-in advantage vis-à-vis individual forecasts: a strategy of random selection among the latter will involve a greater risk of error than that of using the average. However, this by no means precludes that some individuals may be superior forecasters whose performance has been above-average over time due to better skills or methods. It is indeed of particular interest to compare the individuals with survey averages which represent reasonably accessible and efficient forecasting benchmarks. Data on the median forecasts from the ASA-NBER surveys (which resemble the overall group means used later in this study) are summarized after each survey and published regularly, after having been first communicated to the survey members. They reflect the views of many respected professional forecasters and are among the best known and most widely used predictions for the U.S. economy.

Contemporaneous expectations for a given target may be distributed more or less symmetrically about their mean, but over time the individual's positions within these distributions are likely to fluctuate. For most people, most of the time, the predictive record may be spotty, with but transitory spells of relatively high accuracy. A series of group averages is helped by offsetting errors, in particular by the cancellation of individual errors of opposite sign.[9] But the gains from combining generally good professional forecasts into a set of composite predictions (e.g., the group means) depend on the existence of

---

8. This is a special case of Minkowski's inequality. See Hardy, Littlewood, and Pólya 1964, theorem 24, pp. 30–31. I am indebted to Michael Rothschild and Edward George for a clarification of this point.

M_i is here defined as $\left(\frac{1}{n}\sum_{t=1}^{n}\varepsilon_{it}^2\right)^{1/2}$ and M_g as $\left[\frac{1}{n}\sum_{t=1}^{n}\left(\frac{1}{m}\sum_{t=1}^{m}\varepsilon_{it}\right)^2\right]^{1/2}$.

Average M_i will be equal to M_g only when the forecasts and hence their errors ε_i, are proportional.

9. See Zarnowitz 1967, p. 125, for a related discussion. Stekler and Thomas (1980) use "penalized MSE" measures involving sums $\Sigma_i(e_{it})^2$ rather than $(\Sigma_i e_{it})^2$ to determine the importance of offsetting errors in component forecasts (e) for the evaluation of aggregate forecasts.

independent elements in the individual forecasts. It is these facts that will be found of primary importance in our comparative analysis.

15.1.1   The M_i/M_{gi} Ratios: Individuals versus Group Averages

Inspection of graphs for 30 distributions of ratios of RMSEs, M_i/M_{gi} (one for each of the six variables and five target quarters) shows that every one of them is skewed to the right. This is illustrated in figure 15.1, which includes the graphs for the shortest horizon ($j = 0$) and the same-quarter-year-ahead target ($j = 3$), those periods being labeled Q0 and Q3, respectively. If the forecasts ε_{it} were independent normal variables, then ε_{it}^2 and their sums would have chi-square distributions. This may help explain the skewness of the distributions of the RMSE ratios shown in figure 15.1.

It is clear that only minorities of the individuals had ratios of less than 1, that is, outperformed the group averages over time. Summing up the evidence from all such graphs (for Q0, . . . , Q4), the best (lowest) ratios fall between 0.7 and 0.9, the worst (highest) between 1.4 and 2.2. The means of the ratios (marked $\hat{M}$) are all located to the right of the unity (broken vertical) lines, as they would have to be if the inequality referred to before (see text and n. 8) applied strictly. The histograms tend to get tighter and also, often, less skewed for the more distant quarters.[10]

Table 15.1 shows that the mean ratios are remarkably close: when rounded, all but 9 of the 30 statistics are 1.1. The higher mean ratios, ranging from 1.2 to 1.4, refer to the shortest predictions, for Q0 and, less so, for Q1. The standard deviations of the M_i/M_{gi} ratios tend to decrease strongly with the distance to the target quarter, from Q0 to Q3.[11] An exception is CBI, where the horizon of the expectations apparently does not matter much (all the means are approximately 1.1 and the decline in the dispersion of the ratios is very small).

The proportions of the better-than-average forecasters ($M_i/M_{gi} < 1$) vary strongly with the target quarter for some variables, much less so for others. Thus for UR the range is 8%–42%; for CBI it is only 29%–38%. Averaged across Q0–Q4, the figures fall between 20% for GNP and 33% for CBI (see the last section of table 15.1).

It is known from past studies (and shown again below) that the average accuracy of forecasts varies considerably across the individuals, variables, and target periods. Highly volatile series such as CEDG and CBI are much

---

10. See Zarnowitz 1982b, pp. 16–18, for a chart showing all the graphs discussed in the text above.

11. The series for Q0, Q1, Q2, and Q3 start in 1968:4, 1969:1, 1969:2, and 1969:3, respectively, and extend to 1979:1. The series for Q4 start in 1969:4 and end in 1979:1 but miss the first three quarters in 1970, 1971:1, and 1975:3 (because a few surveys did not ask for the Q4 predictions). For these reasons, the number of the surveys covered is 42 for Q0, 41 for Q1, 40 for Q2, 39 for Q3, and 33 for Q4. Our comparisons are somewhat impaired by these disparities; in particular, the relatively large figures for Q4 compared with those for Q3 probably reflect the drop in survey coverage.

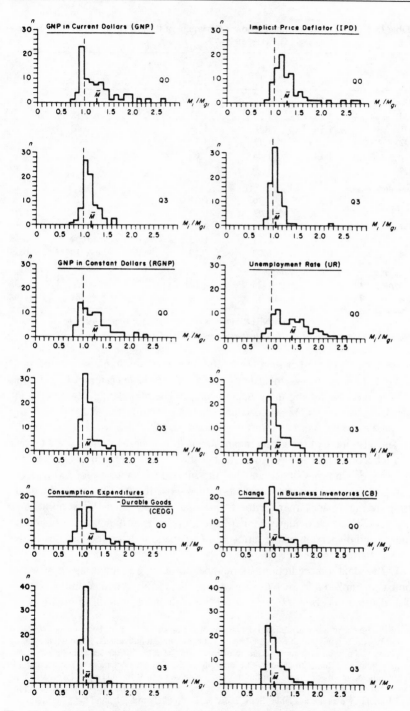

Fig. 15.1 Seventy-nine individual forecasts of multiperiod changes in six aggregate variables, comparison with group mean forecasts, 1968–79

Table 15.1   Means and Standard Deviations of the M_i/M_{gi} Ratios, by Variable and Target Quarter, 1968–79

	GNP (1)	IPD (2)	RGNP (3)	UR (4)	CEDG (5)	CBI (6)
Means						
Q0	1.25	1.29	1.25	1.43	1.18	1.10
Q1	1.16	1.16	1.14	1.19	1.10	1.11
Q2	1.13	1.11	1.11	1.11	1.07	1.09
Q3	1.14	1.08	1.09	1.08	1.06	1.10
Q4	1.17	1.10	1.12	1.08	1.08	1.10
Standard deviations						
Q0	0.38	0.36	0.31	0.36	0.28	0.20
Q1	0.21	0.23	0.18	0.24	0.18	0.21
Q2	0.18	0.16	0.15	0.19	0.11	0.19
Q3	0.17	0.18	0.15	0.18	0.09	0.18
Q4	0.24	0.20	0.19	0.19	0.10	0.19
Percentage of cases where $M_i/M_{gi} < 1$						
Average	20	26	22	29	24	33
Range	13–35	11–37	18–27	8–42	19–31	29–38

Source: Based on quarterly ASA-NBER business outlook surveys, 1968:4–1979:1.
Note: On coverage and symbols used, see text and figure 15.1.

more difficult to predict than relatively smooth, trend-dominated series such as GNP. In general, the uncertainty and difficulty (hence errors) of prediction tend to increase for the more distant future. The remarkable degree of standardization in the M_i/M_{gi} ratios stands in sharp contrast to the diversity of the average accuracy measures for the individuals, M_i.

The advantage of the group means M_{gi} is the greatest for the nearest targets and it becomes less and less important as the predictions reach out further into the future. One may speculate that the individual forecasts for Q0 and Q1 contain more independent information than those for Q2–Q4, hence the gains from averaging are larger for the former than for the latter.[12] The abilities to predict CBI are particularly limited, even for the nearest quarters, so here the means and dispersion of the ratios M_i/M_{gi} depend little on the distance to the target quarter $j = 0, 1, \ldots, 4$).

Earlier data, on predictions by members of a large group of business economists organized into the New York Forecasters Club, produce similar results. The distributions of M_i/M_{gi} ratios for 6-month and 12-month forecasts of in-

12. The large means and standard deviations of the ratios for Q0 may be associated with the disparities in the quality of the current data available to different individuals. Although the survey questionnaire provides the most recent information on the values of the series to be predicted, some respondents choose to use different jump-off levels, which may be more or less accurate. It is not quite clear why the figures for the shortest predictions of UR should be particularly high, as table 15.1, col. 4, shows them to be, but it is suggestive that this is the only variable covered for which monthly data are available. Some individuals are likely to lag behind the majority in absorbing these monthly data (and related weekly information on unemployment claims).

dustrial production in 1947–63 show strong positive skewness, with most of the values falling between 1.0 and 1.3, the classes below 0.8 almost empty, and the average values all concentrated in the narrow range 1.1–1.2.[13]

15.1.2 Rank Tests of Predictive Consistency

Success in one class of predictions (say, for GNP in Q1) may or may not coincide with success in another class (say, GNP in Q4, or for IPD). If the degree of coincidence were very low (e.g., if very few people managed to "beat" the group mean in more than one class), then the success, being rather isolated, might be attributable more to chance than to better techniques or skills.

The NBER-ASA survey participants have been ranked according to the M_i/M_{gi} ratios for each of the variables and target quarters covered. The correlations among the resulting ranks could be either close to zero (indicating very little consistency in the relative performance of the forecasters across different variables or predictive spans) or significantly negative (those who succeed in one category tend to fail in another) or significantly positive (those who succeed in one category also tend to succeed in others).

The rank correlations are presented in table 15.2, both across the variables for each target quarter and across target quarters for each variable. All the correlations are positive and in general they appear to be significantly so (see note to table 15.2). Thus, there is some degree of consistency in the predictive performance of the individuals as revealed by their M_i/M_{gi} ranks.

People who predict relatively well the rates of change in nominal GNP also tend to do so for the rates of change in real GNP: the average rank correlation coefficient $\bar{\rho}$ is 0.74 in this case. For variables that are not so closely related, the correlations are much lower (e.g., $\bar{\rho} = 0.23$ for CEDG and IPD, and also for CEDG and UR). However, only 15 of the 75 coefficients ($\rho \neq 1$) in part A of the table are less than 0.2. The overall mean of the ρ statistics is 0.36.

For any of the variables, people who rank high (low) in predicting one quarter also tend to rank high (low) in predicting the next quarter. The ρs for Q0–Q1 average 0.61, those for Q1–Q2, Q2–Q3, and Q3–Q4 average 0.52–0.55 (see pt. B of table 15.2). For nonadjoining target periods, the rank correlations are lower, $\bar{\rho}$ being 0.40 where the distance is two quarters (Q0–Q2, Q1–Q3, and Q2–Q4) and 0.31 where it is three quarters (Q0–Q3 and Q1–Q4). The further apart the target periods, the less correlated are the values to be predicted, and the above results suggest that the ranking consistency declines correspondingly. But the reductions in the rank correlations vary considerably in size and regularity, being most pronounced for CEDG, least for GNP. When averaged over the quarters Q1–Q4, the $\bar{\rho}$ coefficients are relatively low for

---

13. See Zarnowitz 1982b, p. 22, for a chart showing these results in detail. GNP forecasts made by members of the same group in the period 1956–63 (Zarnowitz 1967, pp. 123–26) tell much the same story.

Table 15.2   Rank Correlations among Participants in ASA-NBER Surveys according to Ratios of Individual to Group RMSEs. Multiperiod Predictions for Six Aggregate Variables, 1968–79

A. Across Variables, for Each Target Quarter[a]

Target quarter Q0

	GNP	IPD	RGNP	UR	CEDG	CBI
GNP	1.00					
IPD	0.57	1.00				
RGNP	0.83	0.65	1.00			
UR	0.42	0.43	0.39	1.00		
CEDG	0.69	0.56	0.69	0.50	1.00	
CBI	0.40	0.41	0.36	0.21	0.42	1.00

Target quarter Q1

	GNP	IPD	RGNP	UR	CEDG	CBI
GNP	1.00					
IPD	0.23	1.00				
RNGP	0.77	0.48	1.00			
UR	0.20	0.39	0.40	1.00		
CEDG	0.43	0.20	0.50	0.30	1.00	
CBI	0.39	0.31	0.38	0.22	0.38	1.00

Target quarter Q2

	GNP	IPD	RGNP	UR	CEDG	CBI
GNP	1.00					
IPD	0.35	1.00				
RGNP	0.66	0.48	1.00			
UR	0.23	0.48	0.27	1.00		
CEDG	0.27	0.15	0.21	0.12	1.00	
CBI	0.41	0.43	0.32	0.36	0.31	1.00

Target quarter Q3

	GNP	IPD	RGNP	UR	CEDG	CBI
GNP	1.00					
IPD	0.27	1.00				
RGNP	0.69	0.33	1.00			
UR	0.41	0.44	0.49	1.00		
CEDG	0.21	0.05	0.14	0.19	1.00	
CBI	0.28	0.42	0.15	0.37	0.03	1.00

Target quarter Q4

	GNP	IPD	RGNP	UR	CEDG	CBI
GNP	1.00					
IPD	0.44	1.00				
RGNP	0.76	0.51	1.00			
UR	0.39	0.49	0.31	1.00		
CEDG	0.18	0.17	0.17	0.06	1.00	
CBI	0.49	0.36	0.38	0.19	0.21	1.00

Average Q0–Q4

	GNP	IPD	RGNP	UR	CEDG	CBI
GNP	1.00					
IPD	0.37	1.00				
RGNP	0.74	0.49	1.00			
UR	0.33	0.45	0.35	1.00		
CEDG	0.36	0.23	0.34	0.23	1.00	
CBI	0.32	0.39	0.32	0.27	0.27	1.00

B. Across Target Quarters, for Each Variable[b]

	Q0	Q1	Q2	Q3	Q4
GNP in current dollars (GNP)					
Q0	1.00				
Q1	0.51	1.00			
Q2	0.18	0.19	1.00		
Q3	0.14	0.18	0.40	1.00	
Q4	0.50	0.32	0.40	0.47	1.00
GNP in constant dollars (RGNP)					
Q0	1.00				
Q1	0.57	1.00			
Q2	0.33	0.47	1.00		
Q3	0.05	0.19	0.48	1.00	
Q4	0.38	0.19	0.33	0.33	1.00
Consumer expenditures for durable goods (CEDG)					
Q0	1.00				
Q1	0.66	1.00			
Q2	0.53	0.43	1.00		
Q3	0.12	0.07	0.14	1.00	
Q4	0.14	0.00	0.04	0.08	1.00

	Q0	Q1	Q2	Q3	Q4
Implicit price deflator (IPD)					
Q0	1.00				
Q1	0.55	1.00			
Q2	0.45	0.68	1.00		
Q3	0.41	0.54	0.60	1.00	
Q4	0.39	0.52	0.51	0.62	1.00
Unemployment rate (UR)					
Q0	1.00				
Q1	0.64	1.00			
Q2	0.38	0.78	1.00		
Q3	0.32	0.62	0.85	1.00	
Q4	0.27	0.53	0.75	0.92	1.00
Change in business inventories (CBI)					
Q0	1.00				
Q1	0.70	1.00			
Q2	0.63	0.76	1.00		
Q3	0.51	0.56	0.81	1.00	
Q4	0.57	0.62	0.63	0.76	1.00

Note: For rankings without ties, the variance of ρ equals $n/(n-1)$ (Kendall 1948, p. 46). For $n = 75$, therefore, the standard error $s_\rho = 1/\sqrt{(0.74)} = 0.1162$ (for $n = 79$, $s_\rho = 0.1124$; for $n = 80$, $s_\rho = 0.1132$). Hence, all entries $\rho \geq 0.23$ in the table are significant at the 5% level, and all $\rho \geq 0.20$ at the 10% level.

[a] These measures refer to 75 individuals who participated in at least 12 quarterly ASA-NBER business outlook surveys 1968:4–1979:1 and predicted all six variables covered. The acronyms for the variables are identified in part B of the table. Q0–Q4 refer to the current and the four successive future quarters. The rank correlation coefficients shown are Spearman's $\rho = 1 - [6\Sigma d^2/(n^3 - n)]$, where d is the rank difference and n is the number in each ranking.

[b] These measures refer to the sample covered in fig. 15.1:79 individuals for each of the variables except CEDG (80). The rank correlation coefficients are Spearman's ρ.

CEDG, GNP, and RGNP (0.27–0.33) and high for IPD, UR, and CBI (0.55–0.66).

15.2 Distributions of Summary Measures of Error

It is instructive to examine the distributions of the statistics that sum up the records of the individual forecasters. The discrepancies in time coverage reduce the comparability of absolute accuracy measures across the respondents to the surveys. However, in the ASA-NBER data there appears to be no significant bias due to missed observations. No pattern has been found to suggest that the participants covered selected the times of their responses in any systematic manner; rather it is random factors (absences, work pressure, negligence) that account for the allocation of the missed surveys among the individuals. Interest in the overall picture provided by the summary measures of each forecaster's performance is also enhanced by the fact that the number of surveys (42) is relatively large and the coverage of each is adequate (on the average, 43 participants with a standard deviation of 9).[14]

The distributions of the summary measures of error for the individual forecasts are further compared with the corresponding measures for the overall group forecasts. The latter refer to the series of mean predictions, of which there are 30, one for each of the targets covered (6 variables $\times$ 5 horizons). These averages comprise all forecasters who predicted the given target at any time during the period under study, so that the series are continuous, each including predictions from all surveys covered. Thus the RMSE for any of these group mean g) series is simply

$$(5) \qquad M_g = \left(\frac{1}{n} \sum_t \varepsilon_{gt}^2\right)^{1/2}, \qquad t = 1, 2, \ldots, n,$$

where n is the total number of consecutive surveys (42 $-j$ for Q0–Q3, 33 for Q4; see n. 11).

15.2.1 Overall Accuracy

For each of the six variables, the means of the individual RMSEs taken across the target quarters Q0, . . . , Q4 exceed the corresponding RMSEs for the overall group mean forecasts. The ratios of the summary statistics of error (entries in col. 2 of table 15.3 divided by those in col. 5) vary from 1.04 to 1.16 and average 1.11.

The performance of the series of group mean forecasts is also superior to the average performance of the series of individual forecasts in terms of correlations with the actual values. The averages of the $\bar{r}^2$ coefficients for the individuals vary between 0.14 and 0.28, except for the unemployment rate, a

---

14. See Zarnowitz 1983 for more numerical detail on the forecast samples from the ASA-NBER surveys.

Table 15.3   **Selected Overall Accuracy Statistics for Individual and Group Mean Forecasts, Six Variables, 1968–79**

	Individual Forecasts[a]			Group Mean Forecasts[b]			Actual Values[c]		
Variable	ME (1)	RMSE (2)	$\bar{r}^2$ (2)	ME (4)	RMSE (5)	$\bar{r}^2$ (6)	Mean (7)	S.D. (8)	RMSV (9)
GNP	−0.11	1.00	0.22	−0.13	0.88	0.29	2.18	1.09	2.93
IPD	−0.39	0.78	0.21	−0.38	0.67	0.27	1.50	0.67	1.64
RGNP	0.28	1.21	0.28	0.25	1.05	0.35	0.68	1.24	1.41
UR	−0.14	0.67	0.66	−0.10	0.62	0.69	5.78	1.68	6.02
CEDG	−0.28	4.04	0.14	−0.36	3.68	0.18	2.25	3.97	4.57
CBI	−1.72	10.00	0.27	−1.77	9.57	0.44	9.19	10.87	14.23

[a]These measures refer to the sample covered in fig. 15.1 (75 individuals forecast CEDG; 79 individuals forecast each of the other variables). They are means of the corresponding statistics for the five target quarters. Q0, . . . , Q4. ME = mean error; RMSE = root mean square error; $\bar{r}^2$ = squared coefficient of correlation, corrected for the degrees of freedom.
[b]These measures refer to the overall group mean forecasts m_g (see eq. [5] and text) and are means of the corresponding statistics for the target quarters Q0, . . . , Q4.
[c]For the definition of actual values, see text. For the nominal and real gross national product (GNP and RGNP), IPD, and CEDG, the measures refer to percentage changes; for UP and CBI, they refer to levels. S.D. = standard deviation (corresponding to the means in col. 7): RMSV = root mean square value computed as $\sqrt{[(\text{mean})^2 + (\text{S.D.})^2]}$.

relatively smooth level series, where the $\bar{r}^2$ is 0.66 (col. 3). They are 60%–80% lower than their counterparts for the overall group means (col. 6), except again for UR, where the margin in favor of the aggregate is much smaller.

The mean errors have negative signs for all the variables, with the important exception of RGNP. This reflects the familiar tendency toward underestimation of changes in most forecasts. The average overestimation of real growth observed in our data is largely explained by the fact that after a decade of relative stability and an extraordinarily long business expansion, the 1970s gave rise to a novel phenomenon commonly called stagflation and an unexpectedly serious recession. As would be expected, since the individual predictions are randomly distributed over the same period as that covered by the overall group mean series, the two sets of forecasts have much the same mean errors (cf. cols. 1 and 4).

As a rule, it is some simple average rather than the underlying individual forecasts from economic outlook that are regularly published and used, and it is certainly worth knowing that the predictive value of the former tends to be measurably greater than that of the latter; but how accurate have the mean predictions been, considering the accessible data and techniques? One approach to answering this broad question would be through comparisons with benchmark predictions from time-series models appropriately selected to fit the characteristics of the variables in question and estimated with data available at the time the ex ante forecasts to be assessed were actually made. This task is beyond the scope of the present paper. To gain some insight into the orders of magnitude involved, however, it is useful to compare the average forecast errors with the average values of the outcomes for each of the target series, and some summary statistics are provided for this purpose in the last section of table 15.3.

Plainly, the absolute values of the mean errors are at least smaller than the mean actual values in every case, and they are indeed for most of the variables quite small in these terms (cf. cols. 1 and 4 with col. 7). More telling, the RMSEs are less than the corresponding root mean square values of the target series, again in most cases by large margins (cf. cols. 2 and 5 with col. 9). The RMSEs for the group mean forecasts are also generally less than the standard deviations of the actual values (cols. 5 and 8). The predictions of UR and GNP rank as the first and second best in all of these comparisons; IPD and RGNP rank lowest when the ME figures are used; RGNP and CEDG when the RMSE figures are.

15.2.2 Characteristics of the Distributions

The medians of the RMSEs for the individual forecasts are with few exceptions lower than the means, but by relatively small margins (see table 15.4, cols. 1 and 4). This indicates a weak tendency for these distributions to be skewed to the right, that is, toward the large RMSEs.

In virtually all instances, the averages of the individual RMSEs exceed the RMSEs for the corresponding group mean forecasts (compare the entries in cols. 1 and 4 with their counterparts in col. 6). The measures for the group mean tend to be closer to the lower quartile than to the median of the distribution of the individual RMSEs (cf. cols. 3, 4, and 6). This is roughly consistent with the earlier finding, based on more strictly comparable measures, that the overall proportion of cases in which $M_i < M_{gi}$ is about 26% (table 15.1).

The more distant the target quarter, the larger tend to be the prediction errors, as demonstrated by the increases from Q0 to Q4 of the entries in columns 1 and 3–6 of table 15.4. However, the increases taper off: the forecasters on the average predict Q0 substantially better than Q1, and Q1 still noticeably better than Q2, but their ability to anticipate Q3 is not much less limited than their ability to anticipate Q2, and the same applies even more to Q4 versus Q3. In short, these measures suggest that the RMSEs tend to approach asymptotically a high plateau at the more distant target quarters.

Note that these results apply to the marginal prediction errors for each successive quarter (in a shorthand notation used earlier, to changes 0–1, 1–2, . . .). To the extent that such errors are positively correlated, their cumulation can produce much greater increases in the average prediction errors for changes over increasing, overlapping spans (0–1, 0–2, . . .).[15]

---

15. The buildup of *average* prediction errors with increasing spans is a general phenomenon to be expected and is well documented in forecast evaluations. However, some evidence for earlier periods has shown *marginal* errors varying narrowly and irregularly over the range of several

The absolute dispersion measures (standard deviations in col. 2 and inter-quartile ranges implied by cols. 3 and 5) increase from Q0 to Q4 for UR, decrease for CEDG, and behave rather irregularly for other variables, such as GNP and RGNP. In contrast, relative dispersion measures, namely, the coefficients of variation S.D./M (ratios of entries in col. 2 to those in col. 1) show strong tendencies to decrease for the more distant target quarters. They are also on the average similar for most of the variables (ranging from 0.23 to 0.26, except for CEDG and CBI, where they are 0.19 and 0.31, respectively).

The group mean forecasts have tracked the actual changes better than the average individual forecasts: the correlation measures in column 9 of table 15.4 are, with but a few exceptions, higher than those in column 7. The listed $\bar{r}^2$ coefficients decline strongly with the lengthening horizon between Q0 and Q2, much less so for Q3 and Q4, for both the individual and group mean forecasts. Only for UR, where the correlations are high for reasons already noted, do these declines extend clearly through the entire target range (Q0–Q4). The dispersion of the $\bar{r}^2$ coefficients across the individuals declines as the distance to the target quarter increases, except for UR, where the opposite happens (col. 8).

15.3   Summary and Interpretations of Findings

The results of the study support the following statements:

1. The group mean forecasts from a series of surveys are on the average over time more accurate than most of the corresponding sets of individual predictions. This is a strong conclusion, which applies to all variables and predictive horizons covered and is consistent with evidence for different periods and from other studies. It is based on an intensive analysis of a large collection of authentic macroeconomic forecasts, in two forms: (1) individual-to-group RMSE ratios M_i/M_{gi}, which turn out to be predominantly larger than 1.0; and (2) distributions of summary measures of accuracy, in which the series of the overall mean predictions M_g place better than half or more of the individuals.

2. The minorities that did succeed in outperforming the group averages vary in size across the variables (from 20% for GNP to 33% for CBI) and, particularly, across the horizons Q0–Q4 (e.g., 11%–37% for IPD, 8%–42% for UR). In each of the 30 categories combining specific variables and target quarters, most of the forecasters show RMSEs exceeding those of the strictly comparable group mean forecasts, and in most of the categories these majorities are large. The M_i/M_{gi} ratios average 1.1 and cluster between 0.9 and 1.4.

---

quarters ahead, without any systematic upward drift (Zarnowitz 1967, pp. 64–72, 1979, pp. 18–19; McNees 1973, pp. 24–25). The present results may differ because of the nature of the period covered (and Zarnowitz 1979 provides some support for this hypothesis), but they also inspire more confidence than those of other studies, being based on much larger samples of better controlled data.

Table 15.4   RMSEs and Correlations between Predicted and Actual Values, Selected Distributional Statistics by Variable and Target Quarter, Individual and Group Mean Forecasts, 1968–79

| Quarter Predicted | RMSEs | | | | | | Squared Correlations ($\bar{r}^2$) | | |
| | Individual Forecasts | | | | | Group Mean M_g | Individual Forecasts | | Group Mean M_g |
	M (1)	S.D. (2)	LQ (3)	Me (4)	UQ (5)	(6)	M (7)	S.D. (8)	(9)
GNP in current dollars (GNP)									
Q0	0.77	0.27	0.58	0.68	0.92	0.66	0.49	0.22	0.63
Q1	0.95	0.26	0.78	0.92	1.05	0.86	0.24	0.16	0.31
Q2	1.06	0.19	0.96	1.07	1.15	0.96	0.13	0.12	0.18
Q3	1.10	0.26	0.92	1.10	1.23	0.98	0.12	0.13	0.16
Q4	1.12	0.28	0.94	1.08	1.22	0.94	0.12	0.15	0.18
Implicit price deflator (IPD)									
Q0	0.55	0.16	0.45	0.49	0.60	0.42	0.45	0.20	0.64
Q1	0.69	0.16	0.58	0.66	0.77	0.59	0.28	0.18	0.35
Q2	0.79	0.16	0.69	0.78	0.87	0.70	0.14	0.12	0.17
Q3	0.88	0.19	0.78	0.86	0.95	0.77	0.10	0.10	0.12
Q4	0.98	0.21	0.86	0.94	1.09	0.88	0.10	0.10	0.08
GNP in constant dollars (RGNP)									
Q0	0.85	0.28	0.67	0.78	0.96	0.70	0.60	0.18	0.75
Q1	1.09	0.28	0.91	1.03	1.26	0.95	0.38	0.17	0.48

Q2	0.22	1.24	1.13	1.25	1.37	1.12	0.18	0.13	0.25
Q3	0.25	1.39	1.22	1.36	1.53	1.23	0.10	0.11	0.10
Q4	0.31	1.46	1.25	1.39	1.69	1.23	0.12	0.15	0.16
Unemployment rate (UR)									
Q0	0.06	0.22	0.17	0.21	0.26	0.16	0.97	0.02	0.99
Q1	0.11	0.46	0.38	0.44	0.51	0.41	0.86	0.06	0.91
Q2	0.17	0.71	0.60	0.67	0.81	0.65	0.68	0.12	0.75
Q3	0.23	0.94	0.78	0.91	1.09	0.88	0.48	0.17	0.53
Q4	0.24	1.04	0.88	1.00	1.19	0.98	0.32	0.19	0.27
Consumer expenditures for durable goods (CEDG)									
Q0	0.96	3.37	2.64	3.10	3.85	2.87	0.40	0.25	0.63
Q1	0.78	4.16	3.79	4.13	4.60	3.77	0.11	0.15	0.13
Q2	0.71	4.24	3.82	4.22	4.68	4.04	0.05	0.07	0.01
Q3	0.65	4.44	4.12	4.41	4.78	4.09	0.05	0.07	0.01
Q4	0.69	3.98	3.47	3.99	4.47	3.64	0.08	0.08	0.13
Change in business inventories (CBI)									
Q0	2.65	8.21	6.70	8.10	9.61	8.07	0.36	0.21	0.55
Q1	3.06	9.17	7.06	8.89	11.86	9.11	0.31	0.22	0.51
Q2	3.36	10.42	8.22	10.08	12.87	9.79	0.25	0.19	0.41
Q3	3.32	10.99	9.16	11.12	13.10	10.08	0.20	0.18	0.40
Q4	3.00	11.22	9.13	11.14	13.12	10.80	0.21	0.17	0.35

Note: The measures refer to those individuals who participated in at least 12 of the quarterly ASA-NBER business outlook surveys in 1968:4–1979:1 (75 for CEDG; 79 for each of the other variables). Q0 denotes the current (survey) quarter, Q1–Q4 the following four quarters (for details on coverage by target quarter, see n. 11). M = mean; S.D. = standard deviation; Me = median; LQ = lower quartile; UQ = upper quartile; and M_g = overall group mean (see eq. [5] and text). The $\bar{r}^2$ are corrected for the degrees of freedom.

3. Rank correlations among the respondents according to the same ratios are positive for all variables and target quarters, and they are statistically significant in most cases by the conventional tests. For this result to obtain, a moderate degree of consistency must have existed in the relative performance of a sufficient number of the survey members. It is still true, as earlier reports also indicate, that no single forecaster has been observed to earn a long record of superior overall accuracy,[16] and indeed nothing in the present study would encourage us to expect any individual to reach this elusive goal. But a small number of the more regular participants in the ASA-NBER surveys did perform better in most respects than the composite forecasts from the same surveys.

4. To go beyond the observations in point 3, a further study of the characteristics, methods, and results of the forecasters with the best records will be needed. To mention just one question of interest, it remains to be seen whether weighted combinations of selected forecasts from this subgroup would yield significantly large and persistent gains in accuracy, but our results do not rule out this possibility.[17] It seems more doubtful that weighting could be applied with much benefit directly to large numbers of forecasts from the surveys.[18]

5. Absolute measures of error depend strongly on the characteristics of the predicted variables and vary accordingly, in contrast to the standardized M_i/M_{gi} ratios. For example, relatively smooth series such as the unemployment rate and growth in nominal GNP are easier to predict and are in fact much better predicted than the more volatile series such as growth in real GNP and the IPD inflation, as indicated by comparisons of average size and variability of forecast errors and realizations.

6. The overall composite forecasts M_g have RMSEs that are for almost all categories smaller than the medians, and indeed often close to the lower quartiles, of the distributions of the RMSEs for the corresponding individual forecasts. Also, the correlations of predicted with actual values ($\bar{r}^2$) are typically higher for M_g than for most of the individuals, frequently by substantial margins. These results are apparently unrelated to the differential characteristics of the variables covered.

7. The location and dispersion statistics for the distributions of the RMSE and $\bar{r}^2$ measures display much diversity but also some apparent regularities. The medians tend to be smaller than the means, suggesting some positive skewness in the RMSE distributions. Although the standard deviations of the individual RMSEs and $\bar{r}^2$ coefficients vary greatly across the different variables, the coefficients of variation do not.

16. See, for instance, Zarnowitz 1967, pp. 123–32 and McNees 1979, pp. 4–17.

17. On weighted combinations of forecasts, see Bates and Granger 1969 and Granger and Newbold 1977, pp. 269–78.

18. Under circumstances that are not infrequently encountered in practice, equal weighting schemes have been found to yield more accurate composite forecasts than differential weighting schemes derived by least squares; see Einhorn and Hogarth 1975.

8. There is a general tendency for the errors to increase in absolute size with the time distance to the target quarter, but by decreasing margins. Also, correlations between predictions and realizations typically decline as the target period recedes into the future, but again more so for the nearest than for the more distant quarters. The relative dispersion measures tend to decrease with the predictive horizon for the RMSEs and rise for the correlation statistics, whereas the absolute dispersion measures show no common patterns of change.

Forecast makers and users may draw the following conclusions from these findings and some related results in the literature:

1. It is advantageous for the experts to consider various methods and sources of prediction, including the recent evolution of the "consensus" of expectations. Good practitioners absorb a great deal of common information, which tends to both improve their forecasts and make them similar. At any point in time, luck may count as much as skill in ranking the forecasters, but on the average over time those who use better models, techniques, and judgments are likely to score significantly above average. It is these individuals or teams, working in large measure independently, that contribute to any successful forecasting which deserves attention, whereas mere opinions of the "follow-the-leader" or similar types do not.[19]

2. Just as there are gains to the forecast makers from combining different, relevant, and complementary approaches, so there are gains to the forecast users from combining predictions from different sources, provided that the latter are sufficiently independent. This suggests that decision and policy makers do well to consult the leading surveys of economic and business forecasters as well as any of their favored individual sources. Where available, measures of dispersion of the forecasts are worth monitoring along the averages.

3. The survey averages include some econometric and many judgmental forecasts. They are neither better nor worse than the predictions from the well-known econometric service bureaus in any systematic sense; the detailed comparisons differ by variable, span, and target period. Forecasts from the major econometric model services generally benefit from judgmental adjustments. Although very influential, they are themselves also influenced by other predictions originating in large industrial corporations, financial institutions, and government agencies. Such cross-effects blur somewhat the distinctions between the forecasts involved, but they stop far short of eliminating them. The interactions persist because they are deemed useful.

---

19. Thus I do not believe that the results of this study or other evidence "support the wisdom of changing forecasts to go along with the crowd" (Silk 1983). First, the "crowd" itself is a select one here and, second, a sizable minority of individuals was shown to have produced forecasts superior to the overall averages.

16   Rational Expectations and Macroeconomic Forecasts

16.1 Questions and Data

16.1.1 On Economics of Expectations and Surveys of Forecasts

Recent theorizing about expectations has concentrated on market rewards that motivate people to use all of the information that can be acquired cost-effectively. The rational expectations hypothesis (REH) assumes that a sufficiently large number of agents know "how the world works"; that is, they properly identify the structure of their environment and succeed in exploiting the existing profit opportunities. Their expectations are decisive for what transpires in the marketplace and are reflected in the equilibrating behavior of prices and other endogenous variables (Muth 1961; Poole 1976). Prices in a market may incorporate all of the information that matters, even though price expectations of many, perhaps even most, traders do not meet the rationality criterion. The competitive game of economic prediction cannot be comprehended by treating expectations as if they were single valued and universally shared; it is important to distinguish between *individual* and *market* expecta-

Reprinted from the *Journal of Business and Economic Statistics* 3 (October 1985): 293–311. © 1985 American Statistical Association.

This study is part of the National Bureau of Economic Research Program on Economic Fluctuations. Parts of an earlier version were presented at the annual meeting of the American Association for the Advancement of Science in Washington, D.C., on January 8, 1982, and before the Econometric and Statistical Colloquium at the University of Chicago. The author thanks the participants for useful comments. He is grateful to Craig Ansley, Edward George, John Huizinga, Robert Kohn, and Arnold Zellner for helpful discussions, and to the anonymous referees for criticisms that resulted in much improvement of the first submission. He is particularly indebted to Louis Lambros and Hanan Jacoby for valuable suggestions and research assistance and to Paul Flignor and Scott Katzer for help with computations. Financial support from the National Science Foundation and aid of the Graduate School of Business of the University of Chicago and NBER are gratefully acknowledged. The usual disclaimer applies.

tions. (For an early argument that rational market reactions may coexist with much individual "irrationality," see Becker 1962; a more recent discussion is in Mishkin 1981a.)

A model consisting of isolated competitive auction markets in which only price signals count is easy to conceive and manipulate, but of limited interest. In a modern economy, not all markets are of this type; uncertainty and a high degree of interdependence exist. Hence important signals are being transmitted by quantities as well as prices, and by global variables as well as local variables. Aggregate measures such as real GNP growth, inflation, unemployment, sensitive cyclical indicators, changes in money and credit, interest rates, and exchange rates are widely monitored and selectively used. For most of the macrovariables, *market* expectations are nonexistent or unobservable, but it is evident that numerous predictions are being regularly made and used throughout the economy. Macropredictions serve as important inputs to micropredictions.

Not surprisingly, professional business analysts and economists produce the bulk of the macroeconomic predictions, for both public and internal uses, and many of them participate in periodic business outlook surveys. It might be argued that these are the *forecasts* of people who study the economy (experts), which are quite unlike the *expectations* of those who act in the economy (agents). On the one hand, the experts are usually credited with more knowledge of the economy at large than the agents have. On the other hand, the experts are often charged with being less strongly motivated to predict optimally than the agents, who are seen as having more at stake.

In practice, the distinction between agents and experts is at this point very blurred. Macroeconomic forecasters, who sell their services to governmental and corporate decision makers and often compete as well in the market for public attention, are treated as "experts," but they are certainly also "agents" in their own right. Indeed many of them are influential agents who have passed critical market tests, as certified by their positions and the rewards their forecasts and advice have earned them in the business world. It can be presumed that, in general, they do have incentives to perform well and strive to do so.

Consistent with this view, it is appropriate that the results of business outlook surveys have received alternative interpretations in the literature. They are treated either as agents' expectations (e.g., in tests of whether they conform to the hypotheses of rational or adaptive expectations) or as experts' forecasts (e.g., in comparisons with predictions from particular econometric models). (For examples and further references, see Theil 1965; Mincer 1969b; Mincer and Zarnowitz 1969; Zarnowitz 1974, 1979; McNees 1978; Nelson 1975; Carlson 1977; Wachtel 1977; Pearce 1979; Figlewski and Wachtel 1981; and Gramlich 1983.) This article will adopt the first of these perspectives.

An ideal survey would use a large, properly constructed random sample to ensure that the respondents represent well the universe of those whose expectations count and a system of rewards and penalties to ensure that the respondents have a stake in their responses. Of course, the ideal surveys do not exist, and the actual ones may be far from ideal. If a survey yields inferior or biased predictions, it is possible that carelessness, poor information, or other failings of particular respondents are to blame, which should not be generalized. The evidence may be distorted and the results misinterpreted because of reporting errors, outliers, undue reliance on averages from small samples, spotty participation, or limited time coverage. But detailed knowledge of and attention to the data can go far toward safeguarding against such pitfalls. This article benefits from the author's direct involvement with the management of the surveys to be discussed.

16.1.2   Tests of Rationality

The strictest interpretation of rational expectations is that a forecast $P_{ijt} = P_{i,t+j}$ equals the mathematical expectation of the corresponding target variable $A_{jt} = A_{t+j}$ conditioned on the relevant subset of the available information I (data and models). Here i refers to the source, t to the date, and j to the span or horizon of the forecast. Formally,

$$(1) \qquad \forall i, t, j \exists I_{t-1}: P_{ijt} = E(A_{jt} \mid I_{t-1}), \qquad i = 1, \ldots, N;$$
$$t = 1, \ldots, T; j = 0, \ldots, S,$$

where E is the expected-value operator. There is no restriction on the span of the forecast (S may equal T), but the dating assumes for simplicity a one-period information lag. Thus the shortest forecasts ($j = 0$) are made in and for the period t, the next longer ones ($j = 1$) are made in t for $t + 1$, and so on, and all of these simultaneous multiperiod forecasts are based on I_{t-1}.

In (1) the information set I_{t-1} is taken to be common to all individuals. But if all were able and willing to use exactly the same data and the same models in the same way, then their simultaneous forecasts for any given target would be identical, that is, $\forall i, t, j: P_{ijt} = P_{jt}$. Presumably, I_{t-1} would then indeed contain all of the pertinent information generated in the economy. The forecasts would be unbiased, indeed tending to be self-fulfilling whenever A_{jt} depends on actions of economic agents based on P_{jt}. The forecast errors $\varepsilon_{jt} = P_{jt} - A_{jt}$ would reflect solely the irreducible variation of the actual values; that is, P_{jt} would be optimal in the sense of having minimum error variances (the analog of perfect foresight in a stochastic world).

Both general reasoning and specific evidence indicate that this case is far from reality. Valuable information is limited and unevenly diffused, and its costs and returns to individuals with different skills and interests vary. There is uncertainty and disagreement as to the data and models to be used for the same predictive purpose. Some data are preliminary and subject to unpredictable revisions; some models contradict others, so not all can be true. Those forecasters who use better data and models will be less frequently misled, and their expectations will be on the average more accurate. Furthermore, depending on the forecasting objective and the appropriate model, the criterion of unbiasedness may apply to some variables but not to others. Thus rationality does not mean the use of unbiased predictors in all cases (as shown in Grossman 1975).

Finally, even if forecasters use the same information for the same purposes, they may have different loss functions, in which case their forecasts would differ. For those whose loss functions are asymmetrical, the use of biased predictors may be optimal.

For all of these reasons, one would not expect individual forecasts to be generally uniform, unbiased, or self-fulfilling. Studies of survey data confirm the existence of substantial differences among concurrent and corresponding forecasts from different sources (Figlewski and Wachtel 1981; Jonung 1981; Zarnowitz 1984a).

If the reported forecasts are based on individual-specific, not general, information, then (1) is replaced by

$$(2) \qquad \forall t, j \qquad P_{ijt} = E(A_{jt}|I_{ijt-1}).$$

Here, for any given variable, the data and models used are those selected by the source, and the information may also vary for different predictive horizons.

Under (2), unlike under (1), the forecasts or expectations P_{ijt} cannot, of course, be all optimal; moreover, there is no longer any strong presumption that they will tend to be unbiased, with identically and independently distributed errors. People interact in making predictions and attempt to learn from their own errors and those of others. This process may be thought of as one of striving to reduce the gap between the individual and the general information sets, I_i and I, at any point in time. This means that each agent or forecaster tries to predict the average or prevailing forecast or what others are likely to predict that forecast will be. But this is a difficult, in principle open-ended, task. Individual rationality does not necessarily imply convergence of individual expectations and consistency of individual plans, at least not in the short-run reference frame of the forecasts under consideration (cf. Frydman and Phelps 1983).

It remains true that an individual forecaster's errors $\varepsilon_{ijt} = P_{ijt} - A_{jt}$ can satisfy any or all of the following criteria, each of which is desirable:

$$(3) \qquad \forall t, j \qquad E(\varepsilon_{ijt}) = 0,$$

$$(4) \qquad \forall t, j \qquad E(P_{ijt}\varepsilon_{ijt}) = 0$$

and,

$$(5) \qquad \forall t, j, k \neq 0 \qquad E(\varepsilon_{ijt}\varepsilon_{ijt-k}) = 0.$$

Forecast sets that meet all of the preceding criteria are accurate on the average or in the long run; they are uncorrelated with their own errors; and their errors are independent in the sense of being serially uncorrelated. They may differ across sources in that some display larger, and others smaller, random errors, but all are free of systematic errors defined as failures to conform to (3)–(5).

One way to check on the extent to which genuine forecasts from surveys satisfy these criteria of rationality is by estimating the regression equations

$$(6) \qquad A_{jt} = \alpha_{ij} + \beta_{ij} P_{ijt} + u_{ijt}$$

and then testing the joint null hypothesis H_0: $(\alpha_{ij}, \beta_{ij})$ = (0, 1) for each target variable covered. If H_0 is accepted, $A_{jt} = P_{ijt} + u_{ijt}$ and $E(u_{ijt}) = 0$; that is, the forecasts are unbiased.

Some tests of H_0 assume that $E(u_{ijt}) = 0$, $E(u_{ijt}^2)$ = σ_{ijt}^2, and $E(u_{ijt} u_{ijt-k}) =$ 0 for $k \neq$ 0. But it is possible for a forecast set to satisfy (3) or (4) or both but not (5), or vice versa. We must therefore examine separately the serial correlation and other properties of the forecast errors.

The advantage of this approach is that no specification is needed of what data and models the forecasters could and should have used; the only information required for the tests is matching time-series data on forecasts and realizations. As a rule, the outside observer has no way of knowing what the information set of a particular forecaster contains; indeed, even the producer of the forecast would probably often find it difficult to define the contents of that set clearly and exhaustively. (This statement is presumably more valid for judgmental than for econometric or time-series forecasts; but true ex ante predictions of all kinds virtually always include important judgmental elements.) On the other hand, the criteria used here are still weak, since rational expectations imply the efficient use of pertinent information, not just unbiasedness and serially uncorrelated errors. The forecaster's own past errors are only a part of his or her information set.

16.1.3   Sources of Evidence, Definitions of Measures, and Scope of Study

Owing to the efforts of the National Bureau of Economic Research (NBER), in collaboration with the American Statistical Association (ASA), a large amount of information has been assembled on the record of forecasting changes in the U.S. economy. The data are believed to represent well the contemporary state of the art in this area.

Each quarter, the NBER examines the results of a questionnaire mailed by the ASA. (For the quarterly reports on each survey, see *NBER Explorations in Economic Research* through 1977 and *NBER Reporter* since 1978. The corresponding ASA reports have appeared in the *American Statistician* and since 1974 in *AmStat News*. The forecasts have also been published and discussed in *Economic Outlook USA,* a report by the Survey Research Center at the University of Michigan. On the origin of the survey and the design of the questionnaire, see Zarnowitz 1969c.) The survey reaches a broadly based and diversified group of persons who are regularly engaged in the analysis of current and prospective business conditions. Most of the respondents are from the world of corporate business and finance, but academic institutions, government, consulting firms, trade associations, and labor unions are also represented. The format of the survey remained unchanged from its inception in 1968:4 through 1981:2, with forecasts covering on each occasion the current and the next four quarters, for 11 time series representing the principal measures of national output, income, consumption, investment, the price level, and unemployment. (Since 1981:2 the coverage has been substantially extended. The surveys also have regularly collected unique data on the methods and assumptions used by the participants and on the probabilities they attach to alternative prospects concerning changes in output and prices. For references to some evaluations of the overall results from the ASA-NBER surveys, see Zarnowitz 1984a.)

Past work on the survey data has concentrated on summary measures, group medians, or means, whereas this article is part of a comprehensive study of forecasts by individual respondents in the ASA-NBER group. Furthermore, unlike the many recent studies that consider only expectations of inflation, this report covers other important aggregate variables as well.

The body of the data consists of 42 consecutive surveys covering the period from 1968:4 through 1979:1. Altogether, the list of those who replied to any of the questionnaires includes 172 names (which are treated confidentially). Many individuals responded only once or a few times, however, and some decision had to be made on the minimum number of survey responses that would qualify a participant for inclusion. It was set at 12, which left 79 individuals in the sample. (There are a few exceptions where a series contains less than 12 observations. These refer to the longer horizons and arise because some forecasters occasionally predicted fewer than four quarters ahead. For example, of the 395 $\dot{P}_{ij}$ series for GNP, 16 [4%] have 10 or 11 observations each, all but four of them for Q4.)

Four of the variables covered have strong upward trends, and it is not their levels that are of major interest, but rather their rates of change that reflect the real growth or inflation or both. These are gross national product (GNP) and consumer expenditures for durable goods (CEDG), both in current dollars; GNP in constant dollars (RGNP); and the GNP implicit price deflator (IPD). For these series, forecast errors are measured as differences, predicted minus actual percentage change $(\dot{P}_{ijt} - \dot{A}_{ij})$. The definitions employed are

$$\text{(7)} \qquad \dot{A}_{jt} = \left(\frac{A_{t+j} - A_{t+j-1}}{A_{t+j-1}} \right) 100, \qquad j = 0, \ldots, 4,$$

and

$$\text{(8)} \qquad \dot{P}_{ijt} = \left(\frac{P_t - A^*_{t-1}}{A^*_{t-1}} \right) 100, \qquad \text{if} \quad j = 0$$

$$= \left(\frac{P_{t+j} - P_{t+j-1}}{P_{t+j-1}} \right) 100, \qquad \text{if} \quad j = 1, \ldots, 4.$$

The change in business inventories (CBI), a current-dollar series, is in first-difference form and does not appear to have a trend. The unemployment rate (UR) represents the percentage of the civilian labor force that is unemployed and is dominated by short-term, mainly cyclical movements, not a long-term trend. For these two variables, therefore, forecast errors are measured as differences, that is, predicted level minus actual level ($P_{ijt} - A_{jt}$). (For further references to the treatment of level and change errors, see Zarnowitz 1984a.)

The ASA-NBER surveys are taken in the first half of each quarter, at a time when the most recent data available would be the preliminary estimates for the preceding quarter, which are marked A^*_{t-1} in (8). (An exception is the UR series, which is available monthly.) Consequently, the P figures for the current quarter ($j = 0$) are authentic ex ante forecasts whose span is approximately one quarter.

The "actual" values are not well defined for many economic variables, such as GNP and components, that are subject to several, often sizable, revisions. Here they are represented by the last data available prior to the benchmark revisions of January 1976 and December 1980. These are presumably the "best" of those estimates that are conceptually comparable to the corresponding survey predictions. It should be noted that this procedure imposes on the forecasters the burden of predicting future revisions that are assumed to remove observational errors. An alternative is to compare the forecasts with provisional data that are closer to the most recent figures that were available to the forecaster. The most informative approach is one that integrates the analysis of data errors and of predictive errors, which would be a good task for another article. (On the role of preliminary data and revisions in economic measurement and prediction, see Cole 1969b; Howrey 1978; and Zarnowitz 1979, 1982c.)

The differences between the successive levels predicted in a multiperiod forecast made at time t, $P_{t+j} - P_{t+j-1}$, are implicit predictions of changes over the successive subperiods covered. Note that each of these marginal ("intraforecast") predictions covers a single quarterly interval, so the target periods do not overlap.

In all, about 400 quarterly time series of forecasts are available for each of the six variables (five series for as many target quarters per each of the 79 individuals and the group averages). The volume and quality of the data are such as to permit an intensive study of several aspects of the economic predictions. Neglect of data problems explains why some survey evaluations yielded mixed and partly contradictory results of limited applicability. (A case in point is the series of surveys of economic forecasters conducted semiannually since 1947 by Joseph A. Livingston, a syndicated financial columnist: Carlson 1977; Pearce 1979; and Figlewski and Wachtel 1981.) The problems relate to the timing of the survey, its consistency, and the effective forecasting spans involved; changes in composition over time; the role of outliers; and reporting errors. A careful proofreading of the data is needed to detect simple mistakes of calculation, copying, and typing that chance or neglect will always occasion in some replies. The voluminous ASA-NBER materials were submitted to such an audit with the aid of a computer and, where needed, inspection of the original submissions. Although the number of mistakes identified by this means turned out to be very small in relative terms, failure to eliminate them would have adversely affected the evaluation of several individual records.

Section 16.2 presents the evidence on the question of bias in multiperiod predictions by individuals and groups. Section 16.3 addresses the problem of serially dependent residual errors and discusses tests for autocorrelation in the "knowable" forecast errors. Finally, section 16.4 sums up the results and places them in the context of earlier related work.

16.2 Testing for Bias in Multiperiod Predictions

16.2.1 Distributions of the Regression and Test Statistics

Regressions of the actual on the predicted values have been computed for each of the 79 individuals who participated in at least 12 surveys and also for the series of means of the corresponding predictions. For nominal and real GNP, the price index, and consumer durables (GNP, RGNP, IPD, and CEDG), percentage changes were used as in

$$(9) \qquad \dot{A}_{jt} = \alpha_{ij} + \beta_{ij}\dot{P}_{ijt} + u_{ijt}, \qquad j = 0, \ldots, 4; t = 1, \ldots, T.$$

For the unemployment rate (UR) and inventory investment (CBI), levels A_{jt} and P_{ijt} were used instead. Estimation of the regressions requires certain assumptions about the probability distribution of the disturbances u_{ijt}. The simplest and most common approach is to assume that $E(u_{ijt}) = 0$, $\text{var}(u_{ijt}) = \sigma_{ij}^2$, and the u_{ijt}'s are uncorrelated for each forecaster and target variable covered. The technique of ordinary least squares (OLS) applies in this case. The sample least squares estimates $\hat{\alpha}$ and $\hat{\beta}$ (the subscripts may now be dropped for simplicity) lend themselves to statistical tests of the joint null hypothesis that the true (population) parameters of the relation between A and P are $\alpha = 0$ and $\beta = 1$. A sufficiently high F-ratio refutes that hypothesis, suggesting that the forecasts contain some systematic errors.

Table 16.1 represents the evidence from the full collection of 790 P_{ij} and 1,560 $\dot{P}_{ij}$ forecast series. To provide a background of descriptive statistics, the OLS estimates of the intercepts and slope coefficients are summarized in columns 1–4.

The means of $\hat{\alpha}_{ij}$ ($\bar{\alpha}$) tend to increase with j, the distance to the target quarter, at least from Q0 through Q3, for most variables (col. 1). In contrast, the means of $\hat{\beta}_{ij}$ ($\bar{\beta}$) typically decrease (col. 3). The standard deviations of $\hat{\alpha}_{ij}$ and $\hat{\beta}_{ij}$ both tend to rise as the predictive horizon lengthens, with only a few exceptions (cols. 2 and 4). These measures indicate a great deal of dispersion, reflecting partly differences in the ability of the individuals to produce un-

Table 16.1   Sets of Multiperiod Forecasts for Six Aggregate Variables, 79 Participants in ASA-NBER Surveys, 1968–79: Distributions of Regression Statistics and Tests of Bias

| Quarter Predicted | Mean Values of Individual Statistics[a] | | | | | | | Percentage of Forecasters with Significant Tests[b] | | | |
	$\bar{\alpha}$ (1)	S.D.$_\alpha$ (2)	$\bar{\beta}$ (3)	S.D.$_\beta$ (4)	F (5)	t_α (6)	t_β (7)	$F(s)$ (8)	$F(l)$ (9)
GNP in current dollars (GNP)									
Q0	.38	.76	.87	.32	12.7	15.2	12.7	0	21.7
Q1	.81	.75	.65	.34	10.1	17.7	19.0	3.0	15.2
Q2	1.17	.88	52	.41	11.4	26.6	17.7	3.0	17.4
Q3	1.27	1.06	.46	.51	16.5	26.6	24.1	3.0	26.1
Q4	1.12	1.24	.50	.59	11.4	20.2	16.5	0	19.6
Implicit price deflator (IPD)									
Q0	.42	.42	.81	.33	26.6	19.0	17.7	11.8	37.8
Q1	.72	.51	.69	.42	46.8	36.7	17.7	20.6	66.7
Q2	1.03	.48	.48	.42	57.0	48.1	20.3	23.5	82.2
Q3	1.20	.46	.36	.41	64.6	43.0	17.7	20.6	97.8
Q4	1.27	.66	.42	.65	58.2	38.0	16.5	8.8	95.6
GNP in constant dollars (RGNP)									
Q0	−.12	.36	1.06	.31	10.1	19.0	12.7	2.9	15.6
Q1	−.29	.48	1.04	.43	8.9	7.6	8.9	0	15.6
Q2	−.11	.65	.80	.59	8.9	7.6	8.9	0	15.6
Q3	.01	.72	.62	.64	12.7	2.5	7.6	0	22.2
Q4	−.27	1.19	.72	1.04	15.2	0	12.7	0	26.7
Unemployment rate (UR)									
Q0	−.01	.26	1.00	.05	2.5	3.8	3.8	0	4.3
Q1	−.01	.76	1.01	.14	2.5	2.5	3.8	0	4.3
Q2	.29	1.17	.98	.22	3.8	3.8	3.8	0	6.5
Q3	1.01	1.38	.88	.26	12.7	7.6	8.9	3.0	19.6
Q4	1.80	2.12	.75	.39	10.1	16.5	11.4	0	17.4
Consumer expenditures for durable goods (CEDG)									
Q0	.99	.87	.93	.45	20.0	12.0	13.3	6.5	29.5
Q1	1.26	1.16	.43	.55	6.7	8.0	16.0	0	11.4
Q2	1.55	1.16	.27	.67	8.0	8.0	10.7	3.2	11.4
Q3	1.41	1.70	.26	.82	2.7	2.7	13.3	3.2	2.3
Q4	.57	1.88	.59	.92	4.0	5.3	4.0	0	6.8
Change in business inventories (CBI)									
Q0	2.76	3.54	.88	.52	16.2	20.3	8.9	11.8	19.6
Q1	1.81	4.54	.93	.61	10.0	13.9	13.9	2.9	15.2
Q2	2.18	5.61	.82	.80	6.3	10.1	5.1	5.9	6.5
Q3	2.22	5.72	.78	.74	3.8	6.3	3.8	0	6.5
Q4	2.97	4.84	.78	.59	3.8	6.3	2.5	2.9	4.3

[a]The entries in cols. 1 and 2 are the means ($\bar{\alpha}$) and standard deviations (S.D.$_\beta$) of the $\hat{\alpha}_{ij}$ estimates from the regressions of actual values on the individual forecasts. The entries in cols. 3 and 4 are the means ($\bar{\beta}$) and standard deviations (S.D.$_\beta$) of the $\hat{\beta}_{ij}$ estimates from the same regressions. See text and eq. (9). The regressions are estimated by OLS. All figures refer to those individuals who participated in at least 12 surveys: 75 for CEDG, 79 for each of the other variables.

Table 16.1   Continued

ᵇThe significance level is 5% for all tests. The percentages in cols. 5–7 refer to all participants in at least 12 surveys (same coverage as in cols. 1–4); col. 8, to those who responded to 12–19 surveys (31–34); and col. 10, to those who responded to 20 or more surveys (44–46). The F-tests are for the joint null hypothesis that $\alpha = 0$ and $\beta = 1$; the t_α tests, for the hypothesis that $\alpha = 0$; and the t_β tests, for the hypothesis that $\beta = 1$. If the null hypothesis is true, the statistic for the joint test should have an F-distribution with 2 degrees of freedom in the numerator and $n - 2$ df in the denominator (where n, the number of observations, varies across the individuals). The appropriate t-tests are two-tailed, using the t-distribution with $n - 2$ df.

biased forecasts, partly differences in coverage (the samples are smaller for Q4 than for the other horizons), and partly differences between the variables (forecasts differ sharply across the individuals for volatile series that are especially difficult to predict, such as CBI).

A sharp contrast between the predictions of inflation and those of the other variables is shown by the relative frequencies of the individual forecast series that failed to pass the joint test for unbiasedness at the 5% significance level (col. 5). For IPD, about half of the computed F-ratios exceed the critical $F_{.05}$ values, whereas for GNP and RGNP the corresponding frequencies are 12% and 11%, respectively; for UR, CEDG, and CBI, they were 6%–8%.

According to the separate t-tests for regression intercepts and slopes, the incidence of $\alpha \neq 0$ is much higher for IPD than for GNP, whereas the incidence of $\beta \neq 1$ is similar for the two variables (cols. 6 and 7). These tests suggest that the high F-ratios observed for the inflation forecasts are associated to a larger extent with the deviations of α from 0 than with the deviations of β from unity. The t_α-tests are also relatively unfavorable to the inventory investment (CBI) forecasts, but for the real growth and consumer durables (RGNP and CEDG) forecasts, it is the results of the t_β-tests that appear to be more damaging.

The test results do not show a common pattern of systematic dependence on the time horizon j. Thus for IPD the frequencies of significant F- and t_α-ratios increase sharply between Q0 and Q2 or Q3, but those of the t_β-ratios do not (cols. 5–7). The frequencies for UR generally tend to rise, whereas those for CEDG and, particularly, CBI tend to decline as the target quarter recedes into the future. The figures for the other variables show on the whole smaller or more irregular fluctuations.

16.2.2   The Effects of Sample Size

Although rich in comparison with the few small samples used in most studies of economic forecasts, our data also have some important limitations that need to be recognized. The forecast series are numerous but much shorter than would be desirable (inevitably so, since our surveys began only in 1968). The minimum requirement of participation in at least 12 surveys improves the data by eliminating the occasional respondents. But the average number of observations per series is still no more than 23, with a standard deviation of 8.

The conventional 1% and 5% significance levels imply low probabilities of wrongly rejecting the null hypothesis H_0 when it is true but also high probabilities of wrongly accepting H_0 when it is false. For small sample sizes, therefore, these tests have very low power against the alternative composite hypothesis that is merely a negation of H_0 (i.e., H_1: $\alpha \neq 0$, $\beta \neq 1$). As shown in Zellner 1984, several issues arise at this point: the asymmetric treatment of H_0 and H_1 in classical tests, the associated uncertainty about the choice of significance levels that are appropriate for different sample sizes, and the "sharpness" of null hypotheses. Although the problems are well known in principle, they are almost habitually disregarded in applied economic and econometric literature.

A simple experiment strikingly illustrates the importance of the sample size in this context. The frequencies of the F-ratios that are significant at the 5% level are throughout very much lower for the forecasters who participated in 12–19 surveys than for those who participated in 20 or more surveys (table 16.1, cols. 8 and 9). Indeed, the proportions for the first subset, $F(s)$, are typically 0 or less than 5% and average 1.9%, except for IPD, where they range between 9% and 24% and average 17.1%. In contrast, the proportions for the second subset, $F(l)$, are concentrated between 10% and 25% and average 14.4%, except again for IPD, where they range between 38% and 98% and average 76.0%! Clearly, had only the shorter series been at our disposal, they would have led us to an overly favorable appraisal of the forecasts, though not without a correct warning about the relatively high incidence of bias in the predictions of inflation.

It should be noted that the predictions of both groups of forecasters—those with the shorter (s) and those with the longer (l) series—are spread about equally across the 1968–79 period, so the large discrepancies between the reported results for $F(s)$ and $F(l)$ cannot be attributed to differences in the periods covered. For the 42 surveys of 1968:4–1979:1, the mean (standard deviation) of the participation numbers is 43 (9); for the two subsets of 21 surveys each, 1968:4–1973:4 and 1974:1–1979:1, the corresponding figures are 48 (8) and 38 (8), respectively. Thus some attrition occurred in the number of forecasters per survey. Its effect was about the same, however, for the two groups of forecasters; for set s, the proportion of observations in the earlier period is 0.61; for set l, it is 0.64.

To increase power, higher significance levels may be employed. Table 16.2 shows that the $F(s)$ frequencies at the 10% level exceed their counterparts at the 5% level by factors ranging from 3 to 14. In contrast, the $F(s)$ frequencies at the 1% level are all 0, misleadingly suggesting that no bias at all exists in this group of relatively short forecast series (cf. cols. 2, 5, and 8). For the longer series, however, the decision to use 10% instead of 5% as the significance level would have made little difference in these conclusions, and even at the 1% level the negative results on the inflation forecasts are very evident in the $F(l)$ entries (cols. 3, 6, and 9).

Table 16.2   **Summary of Results for Tests of H_o: $\alpha = 0$, $\beta = 1$; Two Groups of Forecasters, Six Variables, 1968–79**

	Percentage of Forecasts with F-Ratios That Are Significant at the								
	1% Level			5% Level			10% Level		
Variable	F (1)	$F(s)$ (2)	$F(l)$ (3)	F (4)	$F(s)$ (5)	$F(l)$ (6)	F (7)	$F(s)$ (8)	$F(l)$ (9)
GNP	3.0	0	5.2	12.4	1.8	20.0	21.0	11.5	27.8
IPD	19.2	0	33.8	50.6	17.1	76.0	69.1	46.5	86.2
RGNP	2.3	0	4.0	11.1	.6	19.1	20.5	8.2	29.8
UR	0.5	0	0.9	6.3	.6	10.4	15.4	8.5	20.4
CEDG	2.3	0	4.1	8.3	2.6	12.3	14.7	9.0	18.6
CBI	.8	0	1.3	8.0	4.7	10.4	17.2	14.7	19.1

Note: The abbreviations for the variables are identified in table 16.1. The entries in cols. 1, 4, and 7 refer to all individuals who participated in at least 12 of the quarterly ASA-NBER surveys in the 1968:4–1979:1 period (75 for CEDG, 79 for each of the other variables). The entries in cols. 2, 5, and 8 refer to those who responded to at least 12 but fewer than 20 of the surveys (31 for CEDG, 34 for IPD and RGNP, and 33 for each of the other variables). The entries in cols. 3, 6, and 9 refer to those who responded to 20 or more of the surveys (44 for CEDG, 45 for IPD and RGNP, and 46 for each of the other variables).

16.2.3   Confidence Regions

Consider the ratio

$$(10) \quad F = [1/2(c_{11}c_{22} - c_{12}^2)s_u^2][c_{11}(\hat{\beta} - \beta)^2 + c_{22}(\hat{\alpha} - \alpha)^2 - 2c_{12}(\hat{\alpha} - \alpha)(\hat{\beta} - \beta)],$$

where s_u^2 is the variance of the calculated regression residuals and c_{ij} is the (i, j)th element in the variance-covariance matrix of the estimated coefficients, divided by s_u^2. The confidence region for $\hat{\alpha}$ and $\hat{\beta}$ is given for any selected confidence coefficient g by $F \leq F_g$, where the probability $\Pr(F < F_g) = g$. It is an ellipse centered at $(\hat{\alpha}, \hat{\beta})$, and the higher g, the larger the ellipse ($g = .99, .95, .90$ correspond to the significance levels of 1%, 5%, and 10%, respectively, in the tests of H_0). In the present context, it is of interest to compare the confidence regions for selected short and long series of forecasts.

For purposes of illustration, two forecasters were chosen: one coded "8" who participated in 13 consecutive surveys, 1972:1–1975:1; the other "48," whose record includes 33 consecutive surveys, 1968:4–1976:4. Using their Q0 forecasts of inflation and real growth, figure 16.1 shows the concentric ellipses associated with the confidence levels of .99, .95, and .90. The ellipses for the shorter series are much larger and spaced much more widely apart than those for the longer series (about twice as long and twice as wide, measured by the major and minor axes). As the figure demonstrates (and other such comparisons would generally confirm), the conventional use of high g

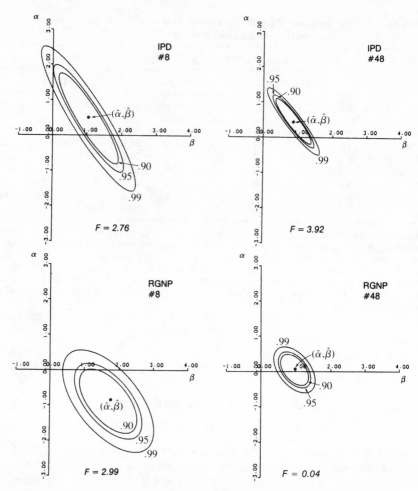

Fig. 16.1   Confidence regions for selected forecasts of inflation (IPD) and real growth (RGNP).

Note: The critical values $F_{.99}$, $F_{.95}$, and $F_{.90}$ are 2.86, 3.98, and 7.24, respectively, for the smaller sample; the corresponding values for the larger sample are 2.48, 3.31, and 5.36. The calculated values are listed in the figure.

values in analyzing small sets of predictions can be quite costly in terms of the precision sacrificed to reduce the probability of type I errors.

The high incidence of bias in the inflation forecasts is on the whole reaffirmed by this analysis (note the F values in fig. 16.1 and the location of the [0, 1] points relative to the boundaries of the confidence regions). That the ellipses have downward-sloping major axes indicates that $\hat{\alpha}$ and $\hat{\beta}$ are negatively correlated, which simply reflects the fact that the mean values of the forecasts are positive. (An elementary property of the two-variable regression model is that $\text{cov}(\hat{\alpha}, \hat{\beta}) = -\bar{x} \text{ var } \hat{\beta}$, where $\bar{x}$ is the mean of the explanatory variable. In the preceding regressions the forecasts play the role of x.)

16.2.4 Mean Errors

The tests summarized in tables 16.1 and 16.2 suggest the presence of certain systematic errors in some of the forecasts. An analysis of the distributions of the mean errors of the forecasts helps to identify the probable nature of such errors.

A tendency toward underestimation of change, which has long been observed in a great variety of forecasts, can arise in unbiased as well as biased predictions (Mincer and Zarnowitz 1969, pp. 15–20). Table 16.3 shows that almost all forecasters underestimated inflation and did so increasingly for the more distant future. In contrast, real growth as measured by the rates of change in RGNP was predominantly overestimated in this period of an unexpected deterioration in both inflation and the cyclical business performance. On the average, these overestimates rise steadily with the predictive horizon. The underestimates of the price component and the overestimates of the quan-

Table 16.3   **Selected Statistics on the Distribution of Mean Errors in Individual Forecasts, 1968–79**

	Variables Predicted					
Quarter Predicted	GNP (1)	IPD (2)	RGNP (3)	UR (4)	CEDG (5)	CBI (6)
Means (standard deviations) of the mean errors[a]						
Q0	−.12 (.21)	−.16 (.14)	.04 (.24)	.04 (.05)	−.92 (.67)	−2.40 (1.95)
Q1	−.07 (.20)	−.30 (.17)	.23 (.22)	−.01 (.11)	−.36 (.70)	−1.88 (2.28)
Q2	−.13 (.19)	−.39 (.18)	.26 (.23)	−.12 (.17)	−.27 (.77)	−1.39 (2.82)
Q3	−.13 (.21)	−.49 (.17)	.35 (.24)	−.29 (.23)	.03 (.76)	−1.10 (3.10)
Q4	−.08 (.29)	−.61 (.21)	.53 (.31)	−.32 (.27)	.15 (.80)	−1.85 (2.80)
Percentage of under (over) estimates[b]						
Q0	71 (29)	89 (11)	34 (66)	14 (86)	91 (9)	95 (5)
Q1	63 (37)	96 (4)	11 (89)	47 (53)	64 (36)	85 (15)
Q2	76 (24)	98 (2)	14 (86)	80 (20)	65 (35)	71 (29)
Q3	73 (27)	99 (1)	10 (90)	92 (8)	52 (48)	69 (31)
Q4	62 (38)	99 (1)	2 (98)	86 (14)	41 (59)	73 (27)

[a]The errors are defined as the predicted minus the actual value, so minus (plus) signs are associated with under (over) estimates. For GNP, IPD, and CEDG, the mean error is computed in percentage change terms as $\bar{P}_{ij} - \bar{A}_{ij}$; for UR and CBI, it is computed in terms of levels as $\bar{P}_{ij} - \bar{A}_{ij}$, for any ith individual and jth target quarter. (See text and eqs. (7) and (8) for definitions of P_{ij}, A_{jt}, $\bar{P}_{ij}$, and $\bar{A}_{ij}$; the overbars indicate averaging over time t.) The means of the mean errors across the individuals are without, the corresponding standard deviations are within, the parentheses.

[b]The percentage of individual forecasters with mean errors that are negative (positive) is shown without (within) the parentheses. The number of individuals covered is 75 for CEDG, 79 for each of the other variables (all forecasters who participated in at least 12 quarterly ASA-NBER surveys in the period 1968:4–1979:1).

tity component tend to cancel each other in the predictions of rates of change in the current-dollar GNP, where the mean errors are negative for most individuals but on the average very small throughout (cf. table 16.3, cols. 1–3). Underpredictions prevail for the unemployment rate in Q2–Q4 (consistent with the overprediction of real growth) and for business inventory investment, whereas the record for the rates of change in consumer durables is more mixed (cols. 4–6).

16.2.5   Estimates and Tests for Group Mean Forecasts

Consider now the regressions of the actual values on the series of means of the corresponding predictions by all individuals included in this study. Table 16.4 shows that the results vary greatly across our 30 different categories. The absolute values of the regression intercepts $|\hat{\alpha}|$ often increase with the predictive horizon, whereas the signs of these estimates are about equally mixed (col. 1). All of the slope coefficients ($\hat{\beta}$) are positive, but they otherwise display no common regularities (col. 2).

For GNP, the values of α do not deviate significantly from 0 nor the values of β from unity, according to the F- and t-ratios (cols. 3–5). In contrast, the F-tests strongly reject H_0 for the inflation forecasts, particularly in the more distant quarters, and the t-statistics suggest that this is attributable mainly to $\alpha > 0$. The estimates for UR show a striking dependence on the horizon, but bias is here strongly indicated in the longest forecasts only. Elsewhere it is the short predictions that are apparently biased, which could be due to measurement errors in estimating the base of the forecast. Here the t-ratios often suggest inefficiency in the sense of $\beta > 1$.

The incidence of bias does not appear to be systematically related to either the relative accuracy of the forecasts or the relative smoothness of the target series. Thus the percentage changes in GNP are far more volatile than the levels of UR, which helps to explain why the $\bar{r}^2$ coefficients are so much higher for the latter, but the F- and t-tests are much more favorable to GNP than to UR. There are strong indications of bias in the forecasts of IPD inflation and none in those of the far more variable rates of change in CEDG beyond Q0. In general, bias does not imply particularly large errors, and some of the forecasts that appear to be highly biased are indeed relatively accurate (notably for UR, but also for the short predictions of IPD, RGNP, and CBI).

The Durbin-Watson (DW) statistics listed in table 16.4, column 7, suggest that the residual disturbances from the regressions of actual on predicted values for GNP, RGNP, and CEDG are essentially free of first-order serial correlations when 5% significance points are used. On the other hand, the DW tests for IPD and UR strongly indicate the presence of positively autocorrelated residuals, and most of the results for CBI point with less force in the same direction.

The well-known property of positively autocorrelated residuals is to bias downward the standard errors and upward the $\bar{r}^2$ values (while leaving the

OLS regression estimators unbiased and consistent). The loss of efficiency—underestimation of sampling variances of the regression coefficients—may in some cases invalidate the results of these tests, which motivates some subsequent analysis (sec. 16.3.2).

16.2.6 Pooling the Forecasts

Let all individual series of forecasts for a given variable and span be stacked into one $NT \times 1$ vector $\mathbf{P}$. Let $\mathbf{A}$ denote the $NT \times 1$ vector for the corresponding actual values, which includes N terms A_t in each of the T unit periods to match an equal number of predictions P_{it}, $i = 1, \ldots, N$. Then the simplest model that combines time-series and cross-sectional data from business outlook surveys such as that of ASA-NBER can be written as

$$(11) \qquad\qquad \mathbf{A} = (\iota\ \mathbf{P})\boldsymbol{\gamma} + \mathbf{u},$$

where $\boldsymbol{\gamma}' = (\alpha\ \beta)$, ι is an $NT \times 1$ vector of 1's, and $\mathbf{u}$ is an $NT \times 1$ vector of residual errors. In (11) the parameters α and β are assumed to be fixed and common to all forecasters. With the data used in this article, each of such regressions would include some 1,600–1,800 observations. Such pooling might seem to offer a way to obtain more powerful and precise tests of the REH.

Figlewski and Wachtel (1981) used a regression like (11) to relate actual inflation to pooled individual forecasts of inflation from the semiannual Livingston survey (1,864 observations). They first estimated the equation by OLS and then reestimated by weighted least squares to allow for large differences in the residual variance over time. (In the weighted regression each observation is divided by the standard error of the residuals for the given time period as calculated by OLS.) They reported both regressions but not the test statistics, noting merely that "the F-test clearly indicates forecast bias" (p. 3) for the results.

The model under consideration is seriously misspecified, however. In each unit period, the dependent variable A_t takes on a single value, whereas the independent variable P_{it} takes on N values. Thus for any two forecasters k and l,

$$(12) \qquad\qquad u_{kt} - u_{lt} = \beta(P_{lt} - P_{kt})$$

in each of the T periods. Assuming that $\beta \neq 0$ and $P_{kt} \neq P_{lt}$ (to exclude entirely implausible and uninteresting cases), the differences among the errors mirror the differences among the predictions. For any given target in any single period, say A_1 for $t = 1$, P_{i1} and u_{i1} ($i = 1, \ldots, N$) have equal variances and a correlation of -1. This cross-sectional dependence of contemporaneous predictions and errors will cause $\text{cov}(P_{it}, u_{it})$ to be nonzero in the pooled model (11), even if for the individual forecast series the condition that the P's and u's are independent holds. In other words, the estimate of β in (11) is biased away from unity.

Table 16.4   Regressions of Actual on Predicted Values and Tests of Bias, 30 Series of Group Mean Forecasts, OLS Estimates, 1968–79

Quarter Predicted	Regression Estimates[a]		F-Ratio[b] for α = 0, β = 1	t-Tests[c] for		Squared Correlation[d] ($\bar{r}^2$)	Durbin-Watson[e]	Additional Statistics[f]		
	α	β̂		α = 0	β = 1			Standard Error	Dependent Variable	
									Mean	S.D.
	(1)	(2)	(3)	(4)	(5)	(6)	(7)	(8)	(9)	(10)
Gross national product (GNP)										
Q0	-.42	1.26	2.17	-1.28	1.72§	.63	2.36°	.64	2.23	1.06
Q1	-.03	1.06	.28	-.05	.24	.32	2.00°	.87	2.23	1.06
Q2	.31	.91	.39	.49	-.30	.18	1.92°	.96	2.25	1.06
Q3	.23	.95	.36	.29	-.13	.16	1.95°	.99	2.27	1.06
Q4	.02	1.03	.16	.22	.07	.12	1.61°	.95	2.27	1.01
Implicit price deflator (IPD)										
Q0	-.08	1.17	4.37#	-.39	1.26	.64	1.35+	.39	1.53	.64
Q1	.37	.93	5.95*	1.37	-.35	.33	1.06+	.53	1.56	.65
Q2	.75	.67	8.02*	2.41#	-1.35	.14	.79+	.60	1.58	.65
Q3	.94	.56	10.23*	2.81*	-1.66	.08	.69+	.63	1.60	.65
Q4	1.08	.50	11.54*	2.65*	-1.47	.03	.62+	.67	1.67	.68
Real gross national product (RGNP)										
Q0	-.36	1.44	6.02*	-2.70#	3.45*	.75	2.47×	.63	.69	1.26
Q1	-.64	1.54	3.30#	-2.56#	2.22#	.49	2.09°	.91	.66	1.28
Q2	-.70	1.54	1.82	-1.82§	1.38	.26	1.80°	1.10	.66	1.28
Q3	-.58	1.33	1.27	-1.08	.61	.11	1.63°	1.20	.66	1.28
Q4	-1.21	1.80	3.22§	-1.83§	1.26	.16	1.26+	1.13	.59	1.24

Unemployment rate (UR)										
Q0	−.05	1.00	2.89§	−.48	.22	.99	1.42+	.15	5.92	1.45
Q1	.05	.99	.01	.17	−.16	.91	.86+	.42	5.97	1.40
Q2	.51	.93	.74	1.04	−.90	.76	.60+	.42	5.97	1.40
Q3	1.35	.81	3.06§	2.13§	1.84§	.59	.42+	.82	6.09	1.27
Q4	1.98	.71	3.57#	2.45#	−2.22#	.43	.30+	.87	6.22	1.15
Consumer expenditures for durable goods (CEDG)										
Q0	.08	1.62	8.19*	.17	3.22*	.63	2.18+	2.47	2.30	4.05
Q1	.02	1.25	.47	.02	.56	.14	2.52×	3.81	2.22	4.11
Q2	.62	.84	.16	.47	−.26	.02	2.42°	4.07	2.19	4.11
Q3	.58	.83	.10	.38	−.24	.01	2.45°	4.09	2.20	4.10
Q4	−2.00	2.05	.79	−1.17	1.26	.12	2.30°	3.53	1.96	3.77
Change in business inventories (CBI)										
Q0	−.50	1.39	4.05#	−.27	1.99§	.55	1.88°	7.54	9.78	11.23
Q1	−3.15	1.65	4.41#	−1.25	2.47#	.48	1.34+	8.48	10.38	11.80
Q2	−3.98	1.69	3.13§	−1.25	2.09§	.38	1.40+	9.30	10.56	11.81
Q3	−5.94	1.84	3.17§	−1.65	2.27#	.37	1.22+	9.41	10.50	11.82
Q4	−6.21	1.83	2.41	−1.39	1.92§	.32	1.13+	10.07	11.35	12.20

[a]The series of levels are used for UR and CBI; series of percentage changes, for the other variables. All measures refer to the means of predictions by those respondents to the quarterly ASA-NBER surveys, 1968:4–1979:1, who participated in at least 12 surveys. The series used in each of the regressions for Q0–Q3 contain 42 observations for as many surveys; the series for Q4 contain 37 observations each. See text for further explanations.

[b]The critical values of $F(2, 40)$ at the indicated significance levels are: 6.04 (.5%), 5.18 (1%), 4.06 (2.5%), 3.23 (5%), and 2.41 (10%). The critical values of $F(2, 35)$ are slightly higher. *means significant at the 1% level; #, at the 5% level; and §, at the 10% level.

[c]For the meaning of symbols *, #, and §, see n. b.

[d]Corrected for df.

[e]Corrected for the gaps in the data for Q4. °means null hypothesis of no first-order serial correlation in the u's is accepted at the 5% significance level; ×, result indeterminate; and +, positive serial correlation present. The 5% significance points of d_l and d_u for $n = 40$ and $k = 1$ are 1.44 and 1.54, respectively.

[f]Standard error of the regression: $\Sigma u^2/n - 2$. S.D.: standard deviation of the dependent variable (actual values).

The misspecified error structure of (11) makes this a basically inappropriate model. The least squares estimates of α and β are biased even in large samples when $\text{cov}(P, u) \neq 0$. This is clear from an evaluation of their probability limits: plim $\hat{\beta} = \beta + [\text{cov}(P, u)/\text{var}(P)]$. If $\text{cov}(P, u) < 0$, as seems likely in view of (12), then the slope estimates from (11) will be biased downward, and the intercept estimates upward. Table 16.5 provides a few illustrations. A comparison of the corresponding entries in columns 1 and 2 of tables 16.5 and 16.4 shows that the estimates of α are much higher and those of β much lower in the pooled regressions than in the group mean regressions. (The same is true of the estimates reported by Figlewski and Wachtel: compare their eq. [3] for the average forecasts with their OLS pooled regression in footnote 6.) The standard errors are extremely low (the t-ratios high) in table 16.5, and the calculated F-values are significant even at the .1% level. For the short forecasts of UR, a is very close to 0 (.4) and b to 1 (.99), yet F is still as high as 34. The results in table 16.4 are far more favorable. The examples are typical and will suffice.

Suppose that the roles of actuals and forecasts are reversed as in

$$(13) \qquad \mathbf{P} = (\mathbf{\iota}\, \mathbf{A})\boldsymbol{\delta} + \mathbf{v},$$

where $\boldsymbol{\delta}' = (\alpha'\ \beta')$. Here for any given target value such as A_1, there is a distribution of the individual predictions P_{i1} with $E(P_{i1}) = \alpha' + \beta'A_1$ and $\text{var}(P_{i1}|A_1,) = \text{var}(v_{i1})$. If $(\alpha', \beta') = (0, 1)$, the *mean* forecasts are unbiased. Indeed, the group mean forecasts from a series of surveys are on the average

Table 16.5   Pooling the Survey Forecasts: Some Examples

Quarter Predicted	$A = (\iota\, P)\,\gamma + u$ (Eq. [11])[a]					$P = (\iota\, A)\delta + v$ (Eq. [13])[b]	
	a (1)	b (2)	$\bar{r}^2$ (3)	F (4)	n (5)	a' (6)	b' (7)
Gross national product (GNP)[c]							
Q0	.58 (.05)	.77 (.02)	.39	66.6	1,819	.99 (.04)	.50 (.01)
Q3	1.49 (.08)	.35 (.03)	.06	181.0	1,694	1.74 (.04)	.16 (.02)
Implicit price deflator (IPD)[c]							
Q0	.62 (.03)	.67 (.02)	.37	228.1	1,808	.49 (.03)	.56 (.02)
Q3	1.34 (0.4)	.25 (.03)	.04	786.7	1,685	.85 (.04)	.17 (.02)
Unemployment rate (UR)[d]							
Q0	.04 (.02)	.99 (.004)	.97	34.0	1,796	.12 (.02)	.99 (.004)
Q3	1.39 (.11)	.80 (.02)	.49	127.9	1,673	2.06 (.09)	.60 (.02)

[a]Cols. 1 and 2: OLS estimates of $\gamma = (\alpha, \beta)$ and their standard errors (in parentheses). Col. 3: squared correlation coefficient corrected for df. Col. 4: F-ratio for $(\alpha, \beta) = (0, 1)$ with 2 and $n - 2$ df. Col. 5: number of observations.
[b]OLS estimates of $\delta' = (\alpha', \beta')$ and their standard errors (in parentheses).
[c]Percentage changes.
[d]Levels.

over time more accurate than most of the sets of component individual predictions, though they are not always unbiased (see chapter 15 and preceding text). Model (13) yields answers to some interesting questions; for example, do forecasters perform better for some values of A than for others? This model, too, however, seems essentially unsuited for our present purpose. First, one of the proper criteria of our tests, namely, the independence of predictions and errors, is directly contradicted here, since P is a function of v. Second, it is natural to think of forecasts as being available before the unknown stochastic realizations, which suggests choosing P as the independent and A as the dependent variable, not the other way round. (Implicitly, if the possibility of *both* [11] and [13] is admitted, P, as well as A, is being considered a random variable. On the debate about the alternative interpretations and applicability of "classical" vs. "bivariate" regression, see Maddala 1977, pp. 97–101.)

The estimates of α' and β' are no more informative than those of α and β as far as the tests of our basic hypothesis are concerned. (See table 16.5, cols. 6 and 7 and compare the corresponding entries in cols. 1 and 2.) Note that $\bar{r}^2$ and N are the same for equations (11) and (13). Furthermore, $(\alpha, \beta) = (0, 1)$ for (11) implies that

$$(\alpha', \beta') = \left[\bar{P} \left(1 - \frac{\text{var}(P)}{\text{var}(A)} \right), \frac{\text{var}(P)}{\text{var}(A)} \right]$$

for (13), and the F-tests calculated either way on this basis lead to the same conclusions. The quite different null hypothesis that $(\alpha', \beta') = (0, 1)$ is also strongly rejected by the data.

In short, pooling macroeconomic survey forecasts of this type cannot be properly done within the general regression framework discussed earlier. Allowing the parameters of such models to vary across individuals and time, though in principle desirable, would not resolve this problem. Rather it should be instructive to work directly with forecast errors, using variance decomposition methods to isolate and study time as well as individual effects; but this is a task best left for another article.

16.3 Testing for Dependencies in Errors

16.3.1 Autocorrelated Disturbances and Bias

Tests for serial correlations among the regression residuals u_{ijt} (eq. [9]) have been made for all series that are sufficiently long and complete. These data refer to the forecasts by 18–20 individuals (depending on the target) who participated in more than 12 *consecutive* surveys. The nonconsecutive predictions by the same forecasters are omitted. The series number 452, vary in length from 13 to 33, and average 19 quarters. There is adequate coverage here for spans Q0–Q3; the samples for Q4, which are smaller, are not included.

The serial correlation coefficients are defined, on the assumption of homoscedasticity, as

(14) $\hat{\rho}_k = \widehat{\text{cov}}(u_t, u_{t-k})/\widehat{\text{var}}(u_t)$, $k = 1, \ldots, 6$.

The Ljung-Box-Pierce statistic Q serves as a convenient test for the presence of autocorrelation in such sets of the $\bar{\rho}$'s. In the present context, it is calculated by

(15) $$Q = n(n+2) \sum_k^6 (n-k)^{-1}\hat{\rho}_k^2,$$

which is approximately distributed as chi-square with six degrees of freedom (df). (If the errors formed random uncorrelated sequences, the $\{\hat{\rho}_k\}$ would themselves be uncorrelated, with variances equal to $(n - k)/n(n + 2)$. For large values of n and relatively small m, the variances approximate $1/n$ and $Q = \Sigma_k^m \hat{\rho}_k^2 \sim \chi_m^2$. In view of the small size of the available samples, it seemed advisable to avoid these common approximations. See Box and Pierce 1970.)

Most of the Q-statistics computed for the inflation and unemployment forecast series are found to be statistically significant at the 5% and 10% levels, and the frequencies are particularly high for IPD (see table 16.6, cols. 2–4). In contrast, the other variables suggest a relatively moderate incidence of autocorrelated residual errors. The frequencies of significant Q's increase from Q0 to Q3 for IPD, UR, and CBI, but appear to be unrelated to the predictive horizon for the other variables.

We next match up for each individual the results of the Q-tests with those of the previously discussed F-tests and show the percentage distribution of the forecasts according to the significance, at the 10% level, of both statistics (table 16.6, cols. 5–8). Although gaps in the data impair the comparability of the measures underlying this cross-tabulation, the broad indications obtained are of sufficient interest. Serial correlation in the error terms may produce large values of the F-statistics, wrongly causing them to reject the null hypothesis. For two thirds of the inflation (IPD) forecast series, both Q and F are significant, but elsewhere such cases are infrequent (col. 5), and those in which neither statistic is significant abound (col. 8). Except for the IPD and UR sets, the F's are likely to be more significant when the Q's are not (cf. cols. 5 and 7). Autocorrelation of error terms without bias is also often found, most prominently so for UR (col. 6).

16.3.2 Generalized Least Squares Estimates

Models with autoregressive errors of the form

(16) $A_t = \alpha + \beta P_{gt} + u_t$ and $u_t = e_t - \sum_{i=1}^{j} \rho_i u_{t-i}$

Table 16.6   Frequencies of Significant Q- and F-Statistics for Selected Forecast Sets, Six Variables, 1968–79

Variable	No. of Forecast Series[a] (1)	Significance Level of Q-Statistics[b]			Significance at the 10% Level[c]			
		1% (2)	5% (3)	10% (4)	Q and F (5)	Q only (6)	F only (7)	Neither (8)
GNP	75	12.0	21.3	35.3	6.6	25.0	22.4	46.0
IPD	80	47.5	68.8	73.8	66.2	7.5	17.5	8.8
RGNP	75	5.3	16.0	17.3	4.0	13.3	21.3	61.3
UR	71	33.8	53.5	62.0	14.1	47.9	0	38.0
CEDG	71	2.8	11.3	22.5	5.0	37.5	7.5	50.0
CBI	80	17.5	32.5	43.8	8.5	14.1	18.3	59.2

Note: Cols. 2–8 are percentages based on entries in col. 1.
[a]Each series includes consecutive observations only, by participants in more than 12 surveys.
[b]Refers to the Box-Pierce statistics as defined in eq. (15) with 5 df. See text.
[c]Refers to the set of Q- and F-statistics matched by individuals, as explained in the text. Except for rounding, the sum of the corresponding entries in cols. 5–8 is 100.0.

were estimated for the mean forecast series P_{gt}. Here e_t is a normally and independently distributed error term and j equals 1, 2, and 3 for Q1, Q2, and Q3, respectively. (The procedure used is AUTOREG [*SAS/ETS User's Guide,* 1980 edition, pp. 8.1–8.7]. It is not applicable to data with missing values, hence the exclusion of Q4 from table 16.7.] Table 16.7 shows that for GNP none of the estimates of the autoregressive parameters ρ_i are significant, confirming the absence of serial correlation among the residuals from the OLS regressions. The generalized least squares (GLS) and OLS estimates also show no significant differences for the forecasts of RGNP in Q2 and Q3 and those of CEDG. If $\alpha = 0$ and $\beta = 1$, the forecast errors would optimally follow moving-average (MA) processes of the order $j - 1$ (Granger and Newbold 1977, pp. 121–22). The results reported in table 16.7, columns 6–8, for Q3 and perhaps Q2 are suggestive of the presence of such processes.

There is no doubt about the presence of first-order autocorrelations in the error terms of the OLS regressions for inflation and inventory investment, and here the GLS estimation results in large reductions of the test statistics. Still, at least two of the F-ratios for IPD in table 16.7 are significant at the 10% level.

Finally, there is no visible improvement in the cases of RGNP—Q1 and UR—Q3, where the F- and t-ratios in table 16.7 are indeed larger than the corresponding entries in table 16.4. The $\hat{\rho}_i$ estimates indicate the presence of a second-order autoregressive process in the error terms of the OLS regressions for UR.

16.3.3   Ex Ante Errors in Individual Forecasts

The actual values employed in the previous sections include all of the nonconceptual (prebenchmark) revisions in the data. These revisions presumably

Table 16.7   Regressions of Actual on Predicted Values and Tests of Bias, 18 Series of Group Mean Forecasts, GLS Estimates, 1968–79

Quarter Predicted	Regression Estimates a (1)	b (2)	F-ratio for $\alpha=0$, $\beta=1$ (3)	t-Test for $\alpha=0$ (4)	$\beta=1$ (5)	Estimated Autoregression Coefficients $\hat{\rho}_1$ (6)	$\hat{\rho}_2$ (7)	$\hat{\rho}_3$ (8)	Squared Correlation $(\bar{r}^2)$ (9)	Durbin-Watson (10)
Gross national product (GNP)										
Q1	−.02	1.06	−.04	.24	.01				.31	1.99°
Q2	.27	.93	.45	.47	−.27	−.02	.17		.19	1.97°
Q3	.15	.99	.44	.21	.03	−.02	.18	.01	.12	1.95°
Implicit price deflator (IPD)										
Q1	.60	.75	2.56§	1.49	−.84	−.47*			.10	2.06°
Q2	1.15	.36	2.95§	2.14*	−1.58	−.48*	−.07		.06	2.13°
Q3	1.03	.49	2.27	1.64	−1.04	−.59	−.12	.03	.08	2.12°
Real gross national product (RGNP)										
Q1	−.64	1.54	3.58#	−2.67#	2.32#	.06			.50	2.02°
Q2	−.74	1.59	1.98	−1.91§	1.48	−.08	.11		.24	1.92°
Q3	−.28	1.01	.65	−.44	.01	−.18	.03	−.07	.04	1.99°
Unemployment rate (UR)										
Q1	.41	.93	.46	.88	−.94	−.54*			.78	1.40+
Q2	.85	.87	1.14	1.46	−1.36	−1.03*	.55*		.66	.91+
Q3	2.65	.58	4.99#	3.15#	3.00*	−1.31*	.80*	−.18	.25	.74+
Consumer expenditures for durable goods (CEDG)										
Q1	−.06	1.30	.87	−.08	.80	.29§			.20	2.14°
Q2	−.17	1.25	.43	−.17	.55	.27§	.19		.10	2.09°
Q3	−.68	1.47	.77	−.66	.99	.30§	.21	.19	.12	2.11°
Change in business inventories (CBI)										
Q1	−2.56	1.59	2.31	−.77	1.74	−.31#			.33	1.70°
Q2	−3.25	1.60	1.85	−.88	1.56	−.35#	.18		.26	1.87°
Q3	−6.10	1.86	2.57§	−1.50	2.05§	−.44#	.16	.13	.28	1.81°

Note: See sec. 16.3.2 on the model and computer procedure used. On the meaning of the measures and symbols, see notes to table 16.4.

bring the data closer to the "true" values that one would like to have predicted. (Indeed, some forecasters state for the record that they should be tested for their ability to predict revised, not preliminary, values.) But it is important to recognize that such data, and hence the estimates derived from them, are all ex post in nature. The residual errors from our regressions could not have been *known* to the forecasters on a current basis. The requirement that such errors be free of serial correlation is therefore not a straightforward test of rationality in the sense of efficient use of contemporaneous information.

The following tests allow for this problem by using series of past errors defined as in section 16.1.2 and based exclusively on data that were available to participants in the successive surveys. The underlying argument is that the forecasters could and should have used this information so as to exploit and thereby eliminate all systematic elements in it. It must be noted, however, that keeping track of the many successive revisions in complex data, particularly the quarterly national income and product accounts, is not a small or low-cost operation in which forecasters can be expected to engage routinely. The analysis that follows required the creation of a comprehensive computer file of successive vintages of the data covered.

Drawing upon that record, the ex ante forecast error series for each individual and target variable are compiled. The autocorrelation functions for these errors are estimated as

(17)
$$\hat{\rho}_k = \sum_{t=1}^{T-k} \varepsilon_{t+j}\varepsilon_{t+j-k} \bigg/ \sum_{t=1}^{T} \varepsilon_{t+j}^2, \qquad j = 0, \ldots, 3;$$
$$k = j+1, \ldots, j+6.$$

Here ε_{t+j} represents the error of forecast made at time t for the jth target quarter, and $\hat{\rho}_k$ is the sample autocorrelation coefficient for the lag k. The omission of $\hat{\rho}_k$ for $k \leq j$ reflects the fact that the information available at time t includes the errors of past predictions through the previous quarter $(t - 1)$ but does not include the errors of the current predictions for $t + j$. For example, the errors of the Q0 forecasts will not be known until a quarter later, hence they are not yet available to the forecasts for Q1, Q2, and Q3, which are all made at the same time as those for Q0. The lack of current knowledge, then, impedes the elimination of significant autocorrelations for $\hat{\rho}_k$ where $k \leq j$. This argument applies here specifically to $\hat{\rho}_1$ for Q1, Q2, and Q3; to $\hat{\rho}_2$ for Q2 and Q3; and to $\hat{\rho}_3$ for Q3.

The autocorrelation coefficients $\hat{\rho}_k$ are computed for the errors in forecasts of those individuals who participated in more than 12 consecutive surveys, the same sample as that used before in the context of table 16.6. The test statistics Q_j are then calculated by (15) with $6-j$ df. The results are summarized in table 16.8.

The critical 10% significance level is widely used in practice as a cutoff for the Q-test, and on this criterion the joint hypothesis that all of the examined autocorrelation coefficients are 0 cannot be rejected for more than half of the

Table 16.8 **Chi-Squared Tests of Autocorrelations of Errors in Selected Forecast Sets, Six Variables, 1968–79**

Quarter Predicted	No. of Forecast Series[a] (1)	% of Forecasts with Q-Statistics[b] Significant at the Level of			% of Forecasts with $\hat{\rho}_k > 2/\sqrt{n}$ (5)
		1% (2)	5% (3)	10% (4)	
Gross national product (GNP)					
Q0	19	21.0	31.6	47.4	52.6
Q1	19	15.8	36.8	57.9	36.8
Q2	19	0	5.3	26.3	0
Q3	18	11.1	11.1	16.7	11.1
Implicit price deflator (IPD)					
Q0	20	45.0	60.0	60.0	60.0
Q1	20	20.0	45.0	80.0	60.0
Q2	20	30.0	50.0	50.0	50.0
Q3	20	45.0	60.0	75.0	85.0
GNP in constant dollars (RGNP)					
Q0	19	10.5	31.6	31.6	15.8
Q1	19	0	15.8	15.8	10.5
Q2	19	0	5.3	10.5	5.3
Q3	18	0	33.3	50.0	5.6
Unemployment rate (UR)					
Q0	18	22.2	27.8	27.8	22.2
Q1	18	22.2	33.3	38.9	33.3
Q2	18	33.3	44.4	44.4	55.6
Q3	17	23.5	52.9	58.8	47.1
Consumer expenditures for durable goods (CEDG)					
Q1	18	0	16.7	33.3	11.1
Q2	18	0	11.1	16.7	0
Q3	17	0	0	5.9	0
Change in business inventories (CBI)					
Q0	20	15.0	35.0	45.0	60.0
Q1	20	10.0	45.0	45.0	35.0
Q2	20	25.0	60.0	65.0	80.0
Q3	20	15.0	40.0	45.0	20.0
Summary Variable:					
GNP	75	12.0	21.3	37.3	25.3
IPD	80	35.0	53.8	66.2	63.8
RGNP	75	2.7	21.3	26.7	9.3
UR	71	25.4	39.4	42.3	39.4
CEDG	71	5.6	16.9	23.9	9.9
CBI	80	16.2	45.0	50.0	48.8

Source: Quarterly ASA-NBER surveys, 1968:4–1979:1.

[a]Includes forecasts of those individuals who participated in more than 12 consecutive surveys. The few observations available for Q4 are excluded.

[b]Refers to the Box-Pierce statistics as defined in eq. (15), with $6-j$ df. See text.

[c]Covers all forecasts used in this table, summarized across the four target quarters, Q0–Q3.

error series covered. The best results are obtained for the RGNP and CEDG forecasts (see cols. 2–4 and the summary in table 16.8). In contrast, two thirds of the series for IPD, half or more of those for CBI, and the long forecasts of UR have Q-statistics that are significant. Thus in many cases forecasters appear to have failed to treat their own past errors efficiently as data to learn from. (One can think of various possible reasons for this: inconsistent or deficient information, models, and judgments, surprisingly large and frequent disturbances.)

It should be noted that these chi-squared tests are neither strong nor direct. (For example, a value of Q below the 10% level indicates a probability of less than 90% that the hypothesis that the errors are not white noise is true. For more detail and examples, see Pindyck and Rubinfeld 1981, pp. 549–50.) An additional test is performed by inspecting all individual $\hat{\rho}_k$ coefficients to see how many of them fall outside the range of 2 standard deviations from 0. The results, listed in the last column of table 16.8, generally agree well with our earlier conclusions.

16.3.4   Ex Ante Errors in Group Mean Forecasts

Table 16.9 presents sample estimates of the autocorrelation functions (eq. [17]) for the errors in the ASA-NBER group mean forecasts. If the error series, each of which contains 42 observations, were white noise, the standard deviation of $\hat{\rho}_k$ would be approximately .154. Of the 108 entries in columns 1–6 of the table, 82 are smaller than .154 in absolute value; 22 fall between .154 and .301; and only four exceed .301, that is, are outside the range of ± 2 standard deviations from the mean 0. Inflation forecasts account for eight of the observations in the second and all four observations in the third group.

Not surprisingly, the Q-statistics are definitely significant for the IPD errors, but the same does not apply to the other series, where they are actually rather small, with only a few exceptions (col. 7). In several cases, the calculated Q's decline between Q0 and Q3, notably so for GNP and CEDG.

There is no indication that the absolute values $|\hat{\rho}_k|$ are systematically related to the lag k. In particular, they do not tend to decline as k rises (for IPD the $\hat{\rho}_6$ values, all negative, are particularly large). It is not clear that the autocorrelations of higher order deserve much attention, but it certainly cannot be assumed that all of them are 0. (In an earlier study based on ex post errors in the group mean forecasts and using as many as 12 autocorrelation lags, some of the $\hat{\rho}_k$ coefficients for $k > 6$ were found to be large and significant [see Zarnowitz 1982a, table 9 and text]. However, one would expect the autocorrelations to be on the whole lower for the errors that are knowable ex ante than for the ex post errors.)

Table 16.9   Tests of Autocorrelation of Errors in 24 Series of Group Mean Forecasts, 1968–79

Quarter Predicted	Estimated Autocorrelation Coefficients[a]						Box-Pierce Statistic[b]
	$\hat{\rho}_1$ (1)	$\hat{\rho}_2$ (2)	$\hat{\rho}_3$ (3)	$\hat{\rho}_4$ (4)	$\hat{\rho}_5$ (5)	$\hat{\rho}_6$ (6)	(Q_j) (7)
GNP in current dollars (GNP)							
Q0	−.18	−.15	−.04	−.06	−.17	.14	5.11
Q1		−.16	−.11	−.08	−.07	.11	2.84
Q2			−.05	−.02	.05	.08	.92
Q3				.09	.03	.10	.92
Implicit price deflator (IPD)							
Q0	.35	.20	.23	.01	−.13	−.34	16.54#
Q1		.21	.22	.12	−.14	−.26	9.66§
Q2			.24	.11	−.17	−.32	10.14#
Q3				.12	−.20	−.41	11.09#
GNP in constant dollars (RGNP)							
Q0	.01	−.04	.01	−.10	−.18	.07	2.57
Q1		−.09	−.02	−.11	−.17	−.00	2.37
Q2			.01	−.02	−.09	−.05	53
Q3				.03	−.06	−.09	.72
Unemployment rate (UR)							
Q0	.04	−.18	−.05	−.12	−.15	.16	4.77
Q1		−.11	−.24	−.17	−.11	.04	5.53
Q2			−.22	−.20	−.09	.03	4.78
Q3				−.14	−.08	−.00	1.25
Consumer expenditures for durable goods (CEDG)							
Q0	−.29	−.09	−.22	.19	.07	.12	9.07
Q1		−.15	−.14	.13	−.03	.12	3.52
Q2			−.12	.10	.04	.02	1.31
Q3				.13	−.00	.06	1.00
Change in business inventories (CBI)							
Q0	.11	−.02	−.09	.07	−.09	.05	1.70
Q1		−.02	−.12	.01	−.11	−.03	1.37
Q2			−.07	.02	−.11	−.04	1.01
Q3				.02	−.01	−.04	.12

Source: Quarterly ASA-NBER surveys, 1968:4–1979:1.

[a]For level errors in UR and CBI and for percentage change errors in the other variables. All measures refer to the means of predictions by those individuals who participated in at least 12 surveys. See eq. (17) and text.

[b]See eq. (15) and text. # means significant at the 5% level, §, at the 10% level.

16.5 Summary and Conclusions

16.5.1 Main Results

1. The hypothesis of unbiasedness is rejected at the 5% significance level for 362 of the 2,350 forecast series examined. Nearly half of these rejections refer to the inflation forecasts, where they account for 44.3% of the tests. For the other five variables, the percentage of rejections is 9.6. It is evident that the forecasts of inflation show much more bias than the others.

2. The contrast extends to each target quarter but is particularly sharp for the longer horizons, as illustrated by the following percentages rejected:

	Q0	*Q1*	*Q2*	*Q3*	*Q4*
IPD forecasts	25	44	53	59	54
Other forecasts	12	7	8	9	9

3. About 4 out of 10 of the respondents participated in fewer than 20 of the surveys covered, producing relatively short forecast series for which the power of the tests is low. Higher significance levels and confidence region analysis are used to cope with this small-sample problem. The previously derived broad conclusions on the incidence of bias are not altered.

4. Inflation has been underestimated most of the time during the 1970s in both the short and, particularly, longer forecasts. Mainly for this reason, the mean errors are predominantly negative for all nominal variables covered. They tend to be positive for the predictions of rates of change in real GNP.

5. Because in each unit period there is only one actual value but many individual predictions for any target variable, pooled regressions yield biased estimates of the parameters. They result in unreliable tests that greatly overstate the extent of bias in the forecasts.

6. For inflation and unemployment, most of the regressions of actual on predicted values have serially correlated residual error terms, and the frequencies of this result increase with the predictive horizon (distance from the target quarter). For the other variables, only minorities of the tests indicate the presence of such dependencies. The latter increase the risk of falsely rejecting the null hypothesis of unbiasedness. However, cases in which separate tests indicate both bias and autocorrelated residuals appear to be relatively infrequent, except for inflation.

7. For the series of group mean forecasts, the tests do not reject H_0: (α, β) = (0, 1) for GNP (Q0–Q4), RGNP (Q2, Q3), UR (Q1, Q2), and CEDG (Q1–Q4). Elsewhere there are evidences of bias, weak in some cases and strong in others, such as the shortest forecasts for RGNP and CEDG, intermediate forecasts for CBI, and all forecasts (but particularly the longer ones) for IPD. These results are from tests based on OLS regression estimates; tests that use GLS estimates produced fewer and weaker rejections of the unbiasedness hypothesis.

8. Rationality in the sense of efficient use of relevant information implies

the absence of systematic elements in series of errors from the forecaster's own predictions, where such errors are measured strictly in the form in which they could have been known at the time of the forecast. Tests of autocorrelation among errors so measured are again unfavorable for most individual forecasts of IPD and many forecasts of CBI and UR and considerably more favorable for the other variables. There is no evidence of a common dependence of these results on the forecasting span.

9. The corresponding tests for the group mean forecasts confirm the negative verdict on the inflation expectations, but they find little evidence of serial correlation among the ex ante errors of the other forecasts for lags of up to six quarters.

16.5.2   Related Findings

Recent work using survey data has been preoccupied with tests for the rationality of inflation expectations. The most frequently used series consists of one-step-ahead group forecasts from the semiannual Livingston surveys. The balance of the evidence is that these data reject the hypothesis that (α, β) = $(0, 1)$. This conclusion is consistent with the results of Pesando (1975), Carlson (1977), Wachtel (1977), Moore (1977c), Pearce (1979), Figlewski and Wachtel (1981), and Gramlich (1983). Tests that do not reject the hypothesis were reported by Mullineaux (1978, 1980a).

Another set of data much examined in this context comes from the surveys of consumer attitudes of the University of Michigan Institute for Social Research (ISR; Juster 1979; Huizinga 1980; Curtin 1982). The questions on "prices of things you buy," once concerned solely with the *direction* of the expected changes, now also seek to classify the rates of change into a few broad *size* categories. The creation of a group forecast series from such data requires a rather elaborate ex post procedure of quantifying qualitative responses. Some of the studies find that the unbiasedness hypothesis cannot be rejected for the ISR data; others merely find that it is "not so decisively rejected" as the inflation forecasts by other groups (Gramlich 1983, p. 163). In all, there is not much convincing evidence here in favor of the REH. Claims that households predict inflation "more rationally" than economic and business forecasters receive some support, but they are based on comparisons that seem strained and inconclusive.

The plant and equipment surveys of the Commerce Department's Bureau of Economic Analysis yield forecasts by businessmen of price changes for goods and services and capital goods purchased; these data fail to pass the test for unbiasedness decisively (de Leeuw and McKelvey 1981; Gramlich 1983).

Data from the European and Japanese surveys, mainly of consumers, require quantification of categorical responses. The results of the tests are here mixed but in large measure negative (Aiginger 1981; Papadia 1982; Visco 1984).

The regressions of actual on predicted inflation have also been found to produce serially correlated residuals, which some of the studies interpret as another departure from rationality. But the correctness of this view depends on the (generally unexamined) extent to which the calculated regression error terms constitute information knowable at the time of the forecast.

McNees (1978) applied tests of unbiasedness to forecasts from three well-known econometric service bureaus, Chase, Data Resources, Inc., and Wharton. The periods covered are short—5.5 or 6 years beginning in 1970:2—so the power of these tests is low, and the results are in part difficult to rationalize. For the multiperiod forecasts of inflation, the F-statistics are generally significant but much higher for the GLS than the OLS estimates. For real growth, the situation is reversed and the null hypothesis is consistently accepted for predictions over more than one quarter when GLS is used. The results for UR are mixed, with indications of bias in the longer but not the short forecasts.

According to a study by Hafer and Hein (1985), the average ASA-NBER forecasts of inflation were more accurate in 1975–79 and 1980–84 than in 1970–74. In the last two subperiods and in the full period 1970–84, they outperformed the inflation forecasts from a time-series (ARIMA) model and an interest-rate model (similar to Fama and Gibbons 1982). The first half of the 1970s was clearly among the most trying times for the forecasters generally (Zarnowitz 1979). But this is not to say that the forecast period somehow explains or excuses the observed failures of the forecasts to avoid bias and inefficiency. After all, it is precisely in times of highly variable inflation and real growth rates that the incentives to use data and predict efficiently are especially high. Moreover, as suggested by the present study, much of the variation among the forecasts is attributable to differences between the sources, models, variables, and horizons involved; it simply cannot be explained by differences in the periods covered.

17   Consensus and Uncertainty in Economic Prediction

17.1 Concepts and Problems

Although all forecasts are by their very nature probabilistic statements, most economic predictions quote but a single value to be assumed by a certain variable, without specifying the attached probabilities. Often many such point forecasts are available for a given target variable from a business outlook survey. If they show a high degree of agreement, does this indicate that the forecasters confidently expect the outcome they commonly predict to come true? More generally, does the dispersion of the point forecasts reflect their authors' uncertainty (i.e., their relative *lack* of confidence)? This paper deals with these and other related questions, drawing on a set of data that is very rare in economics in that it includes related point and probabilistic forecasts from the same sources.

17.1.1 Consensus

Averages from economic outlook surveys are frequently called "consensus" forecasts or treated as such. The term has entered the popular discourse without having been defined in a generally accepted way. But it is clear that the degree to which a survey average is representative of the collected individual predictions can vary greatly depending on the nature of the underlying distribution. There may be no meaningful consensus if the distribution of the point

This chapter is co-authored with Louis A. Lambros and is reprinted from the *Journal of Political Economy* 95 (June 1987): 591–621. © 1987 The University of Chicago. All rights reserved.

The authors are much indebted for helpful comments on an earlier draft of this paper to James Heckman and two anonymous referees. They also thank Walter Baehrend, Douglas Scott Katzer, Walter R. Teets, and Christine Verhaaren for efficient help with research and typing. Financial support from the National Science Foundation to the National Bureau of Economic Research (NSF grant SES-7920361) and aid from the Graduate School of Business of the University of Chicago are gratefully acknowledged. Any remaining errors are those of the authors.

forecasts in question is highly diffuse or multimodal because of large differences among the underlying models. On the other hand, a consensus would be strongly in evidence for any unimodal, symmetrical, and sufficiently tight distribution (see Schnader and Stekler 1979). The inverse aspect of the consensus is the dispersion of a sample of point forecasts, which can be measured simply by their standard deviation.

In predicting the value an aggregate variable is to assume in a given period, individuals and groups use in part the same public information and the same established techniques and relationships. The common elements induce some positive correlation across the resulting forecasts. Insofar as the makers and users of the forecasts interact and influence each other, directly or indirectly, the correlation of corresponding expectations would be reinforced. That such interdependencies may be substantial is suggested by the existence of informal exchanges and organized polls of opinion, market arrangements for the sale of expert advice, and media dissemination of public forecasts. A frequently encountered surmise is that many forecasters are risk averters who do not wish to deviate much at any time from the views of the future that appear to be prevalent. If so, the distribution of the approximately contemporaneous point forecasts for a given target would be further tightened around an influential "consensus" value.

But there are also important limitations and countertendencies to this process. Only the hypothetical expectations containing all the pertinent information generated in the economy are necessarily self-fulfilling; actual forecasts, even if widely shared, are not since they are inevitably based on partial and imperfect knowledge. No mechanism has been discovered to ensure the convergence of the forecasts to a unique and stable equilibrium path. Attempts to predict average opinion or what others are likely to predict that average to be and so forth run into the frustrating "infinite regress" problem. Certainly, genuine predictions intended to guide the decision making or affect views in the marketplace do not merely mimic one another. Thus simple averages of forecasts from successive business outlook surveys have proved to be more accurate over time, and also less biased, than most of the corresponding forecast sets of the individual participants. Evidently there is a good deal of independent information in the individual forecast series so that their collinearity is limited, and combining them yields net gains in predictive power (Zarnowitz 1967, pp. 123–26; 1984a; 1985a).[1]

17.1.2 Uncertainty

In a number of recent studies, which are cited below, high (low) dispersion of predicted price changes across survey respondents is interpreted as being

---

1. On methods to choose a diversified "portfolio" of forecasts and weights that reduce the variance of the resulting composite, see Bates and Granger 1969 and Newbold and Granger 1974. On the conditions under which unweighted aggregate predictions are optimal or nearly optimal, see Einhorn and Hogarth 1975 and Hogarth 1978.

indicative of high (low) "inflation uncertainty." Thus uncertainty is here simply identified with the inverse of what was labeled "consensus" in the preceding subsection.

It is important to recognize that this approach does not involve any direct measurement of uncertainty in the usual sense of that term. The latter is a function of the distribution of the probabilities that a forecaster attaches to the different possible outcomes (values) of the predicted event (variable). The tighter this distribution, the lower is the associated uncertainty.

For an informed outside assessment of uncertainty so defined, therefore, some sufficient knowledge of the probabilities involved would seem necessary. Inferences from point forecasts do not produce such knowledge; they may or may not provide helpful clues in its absence. When the standard deviation of a set of corresponding predictions by different individuals is taken to indicate uncertainty, the underlying assumption is that this interpersonal dispersion measure is an acceptable proxy for the dispersion of intrapersonal predictive probabilities or beliefs held by the same individuals. The validity of this assumption can by no means be taken for granted; it is an empirical question that is best answered by direct measurement and testing.

Some events do have stable and known distributions of outcomes; others do not. It is generally easier to predict stationary than nonstationary variables, transitory than permanent changes, smooth trends than abrupt turning points. The stabler and more knowable the underlying "objective" probability distributions are, the greater presumably is the accuracy of the forecasts and the confidence with which the subjective probabilities of the predicted outcomes are held. The concept of uncertainty adopted here applies in principle to any probabilistic forecast, whether held with a high or a low degree of confidence.[2]

Simple schematic diagrams suffice to show the important distinction between consensus and uncertainty and how the two may be related. In figure 17.1 the point forecasts reported by the individuals A, B, and C are viewed as the expected values of their respective probability distributions. The degree of *consensus* among the three (or any number of) survey respondents is said to be "high" when their point forecasts are clustered, "low" when they are widely dispersed. The degree of *uncertainty* is said to be high when the predictive distributions of A, B, C, . . . are diffuse, low when they are tight. As illustrated in panels *a* and *b* of the figure, high consensus may be associated with either low or high uncertainty. Similarly, low consensus may be associated with either low or high uncertainty (panels *c* and *d*).

Suppose, however, that both uncertainty and consensus depend on the accuracy record of the recent point forecasts. The better that record, the tighter

---

2. Thus no use is made in this paper of the distinction between "risk" and "uncertainty" (Knight 1921; Keynes 1936), which has important implications in other contexts (chapter 2; Meltzer 1982).

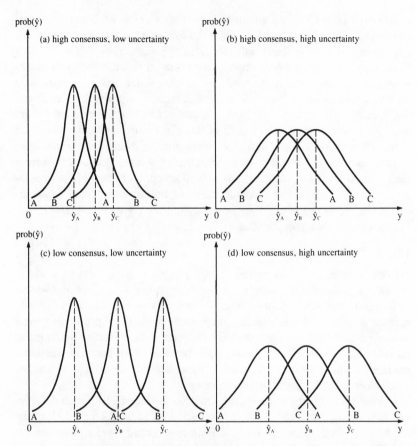

Fig. 17.1   Examples of contrasting combinations of consensus and uncertainty
Note: Curves A, B, and C represent the probability distributions of alternative forecasts from
sources A, B, and C, respectively. The probabilities prob(y) are measured vertically; the
different values of the predicted variable (y) are measured horizontally. The point forecasts are
y_i, (i = A, B, C, . . .).

will be the individuals' predictive probability distributions and the smaller
will be the differences among their new point forecasts. In other words, forecasting successes should be associated with high consensus and low uncertainty; forecasting failures, with low consensus and high uncertainty. If so,
then the combinations *a* and *d* in figure 17.1 would have higher probabilities
of occurrence than the opposite combinations *b* and *c*.

Bomberger and Frazer (1981) tested the relationship between the dispersion
of the individual forecasts of inflation (σ_t) and a weighted average of past
errors in these forecasts ($\sqrt{S_t}$), using data from a semiannual survey of economic forecasters conducted by Joseph A. Livingston, a syndicated financial

columnist.[3] They found a high positive correlation ($r^2 = .77$) between the two measures, which they argued supports the use of σ_t as a proxy for inflation uncertainty. However, this result, though suggestive, is inconclusive. Past forecast errors represent only one of the presumptive determinants of uncertainty; others, more future-oriented, are at least as important. They include the latest readings on the various influential indicators, the recent trends and prospective shifts in economic policies, and changes in the external factors affecting business and finance. Each of these is a source of signals that often diverge and are subject to different interpretations, and hence of uncertainty.

There is also a statistical problem here: the serial correlation of errors from the Livingston survey predictions could well account for much of the association between σ_t and $\sqrt{S_t}$. The predominant finding from a number of studies of inflation forecasts is that they generally fail the conventional tests of unbiasedness, efficiency, or consistency.[4]

17.1.3 Hypotheses and Tests

For any time series, increased volatility tends to be associated with decreased predictability. Thus the more variable inflation is, the less of it will be anticipated. But when inflation rises to unusually high levels, it is likely to become more volatile. Repeated policy attempts (a) to keep unemployment low by stimulating spending and (b) to counter the resulting intermittent bursts of inflation inevitably produce monetary instability. People increasingly realize how this process works, and so anticipated inflation will rise and become more variable, augmenting uncertainty.

Extensions of this hypothesis attribute adverse real effects to such developments. High and volatile inflation raises frictions in the markets and lowers productivity. Prior contracts delay adjustments toward shorter commitments and more indexation. The effectiveness of relative prices in guiding and coordinating economic actions is impaired as distinguishing signals from noise in the observed absolute prices becomes increasingly difficult. These arguments have been used in attempts to explain positive comovements of inflation and

3. Livingston's June and December columns, published in the *Philadelphia Bulletin* and the *Philadelphia Inquirer*, refer to the levels of the predicted variables 6 and 12 months hence. The initially published average forecasts contain frequent adjustments intended to allow for large changes in the data between collection and publication. Carlson (1977) concluded that these adjustments cannot be justified, and he eliminated them by reworking the averages from the original individual forecasts. The effective spans of the forecasts were now assumed to be 8 and 14 months. Subsequent research work generally relied on the means and standard deviations of the Livingston forecasts in the form published by Carlson. Bomberger and Frazer used these data for the 8-month forecasts in 1952–77. Their S_t measure is an average of squared past errors of the individual forecasts with a geometrically weighted lag distribution.

4. On the evidence for the Livingston data, see Pesando 1975, Carlson 1977, Wachtel 1977, Pearce 1979 and Figlewski and Wachtel 1981 (more favorable results are reported in Mullineaux 1978, 1980a). On the evidence from other surveys of economists, consumers, and business executives, see also de Leeuw and McKelvey 1981, Gramlich 1983, and Zarnowitz 1985a.

unemployment rates as in the "stagflation" of the 1970s (M. Friedman 1977), as well as the role of monetary shocks and price misperceptions in business cycles (Lucas 1975, 1977).

Evidence from actual price index data on the whole supports the idea that a positive relationship exists between the rate of inflation and its variability over time (R. J. Gordon 1971; Okun 1971; B. Klein 1975). Additional support comes from international cross-section studies that suggest that countries with higher average rates of inflation tend to have higher standard deviations or mean absolute changes of inflation (Logue and Willett 1976; Jaffee and Kleiman 1977; Foster 1978).

Wachtel (1977) shows that the inflation expectations of economists and consumers (collected by Livingston and the Survey Research Center of the University of Michigan, respectively) have had large errors, mostly of underestimation. Nevertheless, these data contribute to equations for consumption, prices, wages, and interest rates when used along with other determinants (for some qualifications, see de Menil 1977). Cukierman and Wachtel (1979) find that for both of these surveys, the variance of inflation predictions across the respondents increases with the variance of measured inflation.

According to Mullineaux (1980b), the unemployment rate U_t falls with the unexpected part of the current inflation rate, $\pi_t^u = \pi_t - \pi_t^e$, and rises with σ_{t-i} and U_{t-j}, where π_t^e and σ_t are Carlson estimates of means and standard deviations of the Livingston survey forecasts, and the lags $i = 0, \ldots, 11$ and $j = 0, \ldots, 4$ years. However, the interpretation of these equations is difficult because of the use of long distributed lags in the presence of highly autocorrelated variables, notably U and σ. The cumulative effects on U of σ and, especially, π^u are weak in the sense that they require long lags to get significantly large with the expected signs.

In Levi and Makin 1980, the percentage change in employment dN_t depends positively on π_t^u and inversely on σ_t. The equations yield significantly positive correlations only when σ_t is included.[5] Makin (1982) relates dN_t, or its counterpart for output, to "anticipated" and "unanticipated" money growth rates, current and lagged, and to σ_{t-i}, $i = 0, 1$. Again, inflation uncertainty represented by σ is found to act as a significant depressant (the other conclusion is that anticipated money has substantial initial effects in stimulating real economic activity). These studies do not rely critically on distributed lags and are therefore more convincing.

Expectational data from the same surveys have also been used in several recent studies of the determinants of nominal yields (i_t) on bonds free of default risk. Here typically a reduced-form "Fisher equation" is estimated, where i depends on π^e, σ, and some factors affecting aggregate demand and

---

5. For 1948–75, however, the $\bar{R}^2$ coefficients are low, about .1–.2. For 1965–75, a period of rising and more variable inflation, they are much higher: near or above .6.

supply such as exogenous expenditures and money growth rates (or surprises).[6] Levi and Makin (1979), Bomberger and Frazer (1981), and Makin (1983) present regression estimates that show that the interest rates are negatively influenced by the current values of σ_t or distributed lags in this variable. However, Barnea, Dotan, and Lakonishok (1979) and Brenner and Landskroner (1983) report positive coefficients of σ or related proxies, while Melvin (1982) has a positive but not significant coefficient, which he suggests may be due to defects of the survey measure and the consequent errors-in-variables bias toward zero.

These apparently contradictory results may merely indicate that the sign of the effect of σ on i is not clear. The argument is that inflation uncertainty depresses both real investment and savings as borrowers and lenders are discouraged by expected volatility of relative and absolute prices. If the impact on investment dominates, the net effect of σ on the after-tax real rate and hence on i will be negative; if the impact on savings dominates, that effect will be positive (Makin 1983).

The models under review are products of the 1970s, a period of rising inflation; it is not clear that they pass the test of the disinflation in the 1980s. The sharp decline in actual inflation was accompanied by less volatility of price change. There can be little doubt that it induced lagging but substantial reductions in expected inflation and presumably also in the associated uncertainty. Yet, even when real growth was positive, the rates of productivity, investment, and saving remained on the whole low in these years (puzzlingly so to many observers), except for the strong but brief recovery in 1983–84. Interest rates declined generally but much less than inflation.[7] Recent attempts to explain these developments rely on various special factors.

17.1.4 Further Steps

Evidently, economics of uncertainty is an important and active field of study, with interest centering on inflation.[8] Just as clearly, there is as yet little well-tested knowledge about it.

The approach to be followed here is to elicit information on uncertainty from time series of probabilistic forecasts. Section 17.2 presents the data and measures we have developed.

6. Some of these studies also consider the roles of taxes, real rates, and lags, whereas others are limited to the gross effects on i_t of π^e_t and σ_t or related measures. For comprehensive surveys of the literature, see Tanzi 1984.
7. Note that the downward movement of the rates occurred entirely during the recessions of 1980 and 1981–82 as well as the slowdown after mid-1984; it was interrupted and partially reversed in the intervening recoveries.
8. Uncertainty about real growth prospects has received little attention in recent literature. The effects of changes in the "confidence" of consumers, investors, and business people are often emphasized, but these changes themselves and their determinants are extremely difficult to measure and analyze. What is needed here is probabilistic forecasts for real economic activity. Our surveys provide such materials but only since mid-1981 (see sec. 17.2).

Section 17.3 discusses the results based on these materials and compares them with the results obtained by means of the point forecast proxies for uncertainty. This is presumably the best way to answer the empirical question of just how well the indirect measures have worked. The use of matched probabilistic and point forecast sets allows us to examine directly how consensus and uncertainty are related and also whether expectations of higher inflation breed more inflation uncertainty (secs. 17.3.1–17.3.4). Next we explore ways to bring together the measures derived from our series of probabilistic forecast distributions and the measures derived from the Livingston point forecast data. This cross-section analysis is then extended to reexamine the hypotheses discussed above on how inflation uncertainty affects real economic activity and inflation rates (secs. 17.3.5–17.3.7).

Section 17.4 sums up our conclusions.

17.2   Data and Measures

17.2.1   Properties of Surveys and Samples

The survey conducted quarterly since 1968 by the American Statistical Association (ASA) and the National Bureau of Economic Research (NBER) is, to our knowledge, unique in regularly yielding numerical replies on predictive uncertainty. A questionnaire, mailed to a broadly based and diversified list of persons who are professionally engaged in the analysis of current and prospective business conditions, asks for forecasts on a number of important macroeconomic variables including the gross national product in current dollars (GNP) and in constant dollars (RGNP) and the GNP implicit price deflator (IPD). These predictions refer to the current and the next four quarters and to the current and next year.

In addition to these point forecasts, the ASA-NBER survey provides probabilistic forecasts for IPD and GNP (through mid-1981) and for IPD and RGNP (thereafter). For each of the paired variables, a list of percentage intervals (e.g., 10.0–10.9, 9.0–9.9, etc.) is included, with blank spaces to write the numbers in. The replies represent the chances in 100 that the forecaster associates with the changes falling in the selected intervals.

Although the numbers refer to *annual* changes, they come from *quarterly* surveys so that the effective horizons of the predictions vary substantially. Of principal interest are the probabilistic forecasts for the change from year $t - 1$ to year t that were issued in the four consecutive surveys from the last quarter of $t - 1$ through the third quarter of t. The distances between the dates of these surveys and the end of the target year are approximately 4½, 3½, 2½, and 1½ quarters. We shall refer to these categories simply as horizons (H) 4, . . . , 1. They account for the bulk of the more than 4,600 reported probabilistic forecast distributions for 1969–81 and can be regularly matched with the point forecasts made by the same persons for the same targets.

The total number of persons who responded to any of the 51 ASA-NBER surveys taken during the period 1968:4–1981:2 is 192; the number of those who participated in at least 12 surveys is 80. The latter subset of "regular" respondents is the main source of evidence in this paper, but we analyzed the total set as well to make sure that the selection does not bias our results in any particular way.

Data from the completed questionnaire forms available in the NBER files were screened so as to (1) strictly match the probabilistic and point forecasts made by the same persons for the same targets and (2) eliminate unusable replies and obvious reporting errors. The last step improved the quality of microdata in our sample but had minimal effects on the aggregate measures obtained since the proportion of the forecasts excluded was very small.

The final collection for the group of regular forecasters includes 1,673 and 1,705 individual probability distributions for GNP and IPD, respectively. The shortest forecasts (H1) account for about 19% of these data, H2 for 27%, H3 for 28%, and H4 for 26%.[9]

17.2.2   Aggregate Probabilistic and Point Forecast Series

Summary statistics such as the mean, standard deviation, skewness, and kurtosis were calculated for each of the individual probability distributions.[10] Uniform distribution within each of the selected intervals was assumed. Thus the kth-order moment about zero of the distribution is computed by numerical integration as

$$(1) \qquad \mu_k^o = \sum_i p_i \left(\frac{u_i^{k+1}}{k+1} - \frac{l_i^{k+1}}{k+1} \right),$$

where p_i is the probability assigned to the ith interval ($\Sigma_i p_i = 1$), and l_i and u_i are the lower and upper limits of the ith interval, respectively. Since unit intervals are used, the mean ($k = 1$) reduces to $\Sigma_i p_i[(l_i + u_i)/2]$. The mean forecast implicit in the jth respondent's probability distribution for horizon h and year t will be denoted as ϕ_{jht}.

For each ϕ_{jht} there is a matching point forecast f_{jht}. The latter numbers are computed from corresponding estimates and predictions of *quarterly levels* of GNP and IPD. For example, in the fourth quarter of year t_{04}, a respondent would use data on the "actual" values of GNP in the preceding quarters

---

9. The probabilistic predictions issued in the second and third quarters of year $t - 1$ (H6 and H5) and in the fourth quarter of year t (H0) are excluded. Such replies are available only for the years 1974, 1980, and 1981. Also, only 136 (about half) of them have point counterparts. The probabilistic distributions with the horizons of 6 and 5 quarters cannot be matched with point forecasts at all, and those with the zero horizon lack interest since by the fourth quarter of t most of the target year is already over. In addition, 210 faulty or unusable replies were eliminated by editing the questionnaires for degenerate distributions with single "100" entries (116), cases in which the probabilities do not add up to 1.00 (47), and mistaken applications to real rather than nominal GNP (47).

10. The results reported below are not affected by skewness and kurtosis, and no use will be made of these measures in this paper.

($\ldots A_{02}$, A_{03}) and make predictions through the end of the year $t + 1$ (P_{04}, P_{11}, $\ldots$, P_{14}). Accordingly, the annual percentage change forecast for any j and t and for $h = 4$ is

$$(2) \qquad f_4 = \left(\frac{P_{11} + P_{12} + P_{13} + P_{14}}{A_{01} + A_{02} + A_{03} + P_{04}} \right) 100.$$

Similarly, f_3 made in the first quarter of the year $t + 1$ would equal the ratio $100(\Sigma_{j=1}^{4} P_{ij} / \Sigma_{j=1}^{4} A_{0j})$, where the P's and A's are the new quarterly level predictions and estimated realizations, respectively (note that P_{04} is now replaced by A_{04}). Still more recent predictions and estimates would be available for f_2 (including A_{11} instead of P_{11}) and f_1 (including also A_{12} instead of P_{12}).

The individual ϕ and f predictions are used next to construct annual time series of group averages. Thus the means of the individual probability distributions are averaged across all members of the sample for the given survey as in

$$(3) \qquad \sum_{j} \phi_{jht} = \Phi_{ht}.$$

The matching point forecasts are similarly averaged over the same individuals according to

$$(4) \qquad \sum_{j} f_{jht} = F_{ht}.$$

These steps produce 2×4 aggregate probabilistic forecast series and again 2×4 aggregate point forecast series (for GNP and IPD, and $h = 1, \ldots, 4$, in each case).

17.2.3   Regular and Occasional Forecasters

Whether or not the sporadic respondents are included makes hardly any difference in terms of the aggregate results. For both GNP and IPD, the corresponding average measures in the total set and the regular set are extremely close. This applies to mean forecasts, mean errors, and the overall dispersion statistics for point forecasts and probabilistic forecasts alike, as demonstrated in table 17.1, lines 5–6, 11–12, and 17–18. Correlations between the two sets are so uniformly near unity, even after squaring and adjusting for the degrees of freedom, that there is no need to list them. Suffice it to note that the $\bar{r}^2$ between the matched "all" and "12 +" mean forecasts exceed .99 for either variable at each horizon and that they are not much lower for the other statistics. For example, the average $\bar{r}^2$ is .96 for the series of standard deviations of the corresponding probabilistic forecasts.

The evidence from the ASA-NBER surveys presented below is based on the forecasts by the "regular" respondents only, that is, those who participated in 12 or more surveys. There are several good reasons for working with this group. Earlier studies of the samples of individual forecasts from these sur-

Table 17.1   Summary Statistics for Point Forecasts and Mean Probability
Forecasts of Annual Percentage Changes in GNP and IPD, 1969–81

		Gross National Product		Implicit Price Deflator	
Line	Horizon (quarters)[a] (1)	Point Forecasts (2)	Mean Probability Forecasts (3)	Point Forecasts (4)	Mean Probability Forecasts (5)
		Mean Forecasts			
1	1	8.8 (2.8)	8.4 (2.6)	6.6 (1.9)	6.6 (2.1)
2	2	8.9 (2.6)	8.8 (2.4)	6.2 (2.2)	6.4 (2.2)
3	3	9.0 (2.2)	9.0 (2.1)	6.2 (2.4)	6.4 (2.4)
4	4	8.7 (2.1)	8.6 (2.0)	5.2 (1.8)	5.5 (1.8)
5	1–4	8.9 (2.4)	8.7 (2.3)	6.1 (2.1)	6.2 (2.1)
6	1–4 (all)	8.8 (2.4)	8.7 (2.3)	6.1 (2.1)	6.2 (2.0)
		Mean Errors[b]			
7	1	− .44 (1.32)	− .79 (1.14)	− .19 (.47)	− .22 (.54)
8	2	− .62 (1.13)	− .73 (1.01)	− .50 (.73)	− .38 (.80)
9	3	− .64 (.97)	− .70 (1.01)	− .72 (1.13)	− .52 (1.16)
10	4	− .88 (.85)	−1.01 (.88)	−1.20 (1.42)	− .92 (1.47)
11	1–4	− .65 (.18)	− .81 (.14)	− .65 (.42)	− .51 (.30)
12	1–4(all)	− .67 (.21)	− .84 (.19)	− .66 (.43)	− .50 (.31)
		Standard Deviation[c]			
13	1	.39 (.11)	.81 (.06)	.34 (.21)	.76 (.06)
14	2	.63 (.23)	.91 (.07)	.46 (.20)	.83 (.08)
15	3	.90 (.31)	.98 (.10)	.68 (.34)	.90 (.11)
16	4	1.14 (.22)	.98 (.08)	.70 (.19)	.86 (.07)
17	1–4	.76 (.32)	.92 (.08)	.54 (.23)	.84 (.08)
18	1–4 (all)	.83 (.43)	.94 (.08)	.59 (.20)	.84 (.08)

Note: All entries refer to the samples of regular forecasters except those in lines 6, 12, and 18, which refer to the samples of all forecasters. Entries are means; entries within parentheses are the corresponding standard deviations. All measures are in percentage points, referring to percentage changes at annual rates.

[a]Horizons 1, 2, 3, and 4 refer to forecasts of change from year $t - 1$ to year t made in the third, second, and first quarters of year t and the fourth quarter of year $t - 1$, respectively; 1–4 refers to forecasts for all four horizons combined. See n.14 and the text for more detail.

[b]Entries in lines 7–10 are averages of the series shown in fig. 17.1.

[c]Entries in lines 13–16 are averages of the series shown in fig. 17.2.

veys (see chapters 15 and 16) had to impose some minimum-response restrictions since the sporadic respondents could not be individually evaluated because of a paucity of data. The "12 or more" rule was used there to good advantage, and the approach is followed here in the interest of consistency and comparability. The elimination of occasional forecasts also has the advantage of reducing the variation of the coverage over time.[11]

11. Many individuals responded only once or a few times, mainly to the early surveys. Each of the 80 "regulars" had an adequate exposure: the range is 12–34 surveys, with a mean of 23 and a standard deviation of 8. The numbers of participants per survey in this sample average 41, with a standard deviation of 10 and a range of 21–60.

17.3 Results

17.3.1 Mean Forecasts and Errors

Figure 17.2 shows a remarkably close agreement between paired series of group mean errors of probabilistic and point forecasts and, by implication, also between the corresponding mean forecast series.[12] Indeed, Φ_{ht} and F_{ht} are highly correlated in each of the eight cases, with $\bar{r}^2$ ranging from .881 to .992 for GNP and from .981 to .995 for IPD. The matched series have very similar average levels, as can be seen in table 17.1, lines 1–12.

This is a strong finding of considerable significance. Evidently, the respondents on the whole equated their preferred (point) forecasts to the expected values (weighted means) of their predictive probability distributions. To be sure, not all did so at all times, but a large majority did most of the time. Thus large $\phi - f$ discrepancies being well defined as exceeding 1 percentage point, only about one in four of the regular respondents had 20% or more of such deviations on the record, and only one in twenty had 40% or more.

For unbiased forecasts, these results seem mildly suggestive of symmetrical loss functions, but they are not inconsistent with bias or asymmetrical loss functions for many of the individuals involved. Indeed, figure 17.2 indicates that the surveyed forecasts are not free of bias. Of the 46 mean errors of probabilistic predictions for GNP, H1–H4, 35 (76%) are negative; the parallel count for IPD is 31/46 (67%). The proportions of underestimates among the mean errors of point predictions are 76% for GNP and 74% for IPD. Not only are the underestimates more numerous than the overestimates, but they also are visibly larger overall. On the average, the errors of both the probabilistic and the point forecasts are negative for either variable at each horizon (table 17.1, lines 7–12). The absolute values of these mean errors tend to increase with the horizon, especially for IPD, where the corresponding variability measures do so as well (see entries in parentheses).[13]

17.3.2 Series of Dispersion Measures

Figure 17.3 compares the series of the means of the standard deviations calculated from the individual probability forecast distributions ($\bar{s}_\phi$) with the series of standard deviations for the corresponding sets of point forecasts (s_f). For the GNP growth rates, $\bar{s}_\phi > s_f$ in each year at H1 and in all but two years at H2, but the differences between $\bar{s}_\phi$ and s_f are much smaller and less systematic at H3 and H4. For the IPD inflation rates, $\bar{s}_\phi$ exceeds s_f as a general rule

---

12. Note that $(\Phi_{ht} - A_t) - (F_{ht} - A_t) = \Phi_{ht} - F_{ht}$. Also, for any group of respondents indexes $j = 1, \ldots, n$, $\Sigma_j^n(\phi_j - A) = \Phi - A$ and $\Sigma_j^n(f_j - A) = F - A$ (this applies to any h and t, so these subscripts are omitted for simplicity).

13. Unlike inflation, which was heavily underestimated in this period, real GNP growth rates were on the average overestimated, so that the *quarterly* point forecasts of changes in nominal GNP show little bias (see chapters 14 and 16). However, the mean errors of GNP forecasts for the successive quarters, while small, are generally negative, and they cumulate. This produces much larger underestimation errors in the *annual* forecasts.

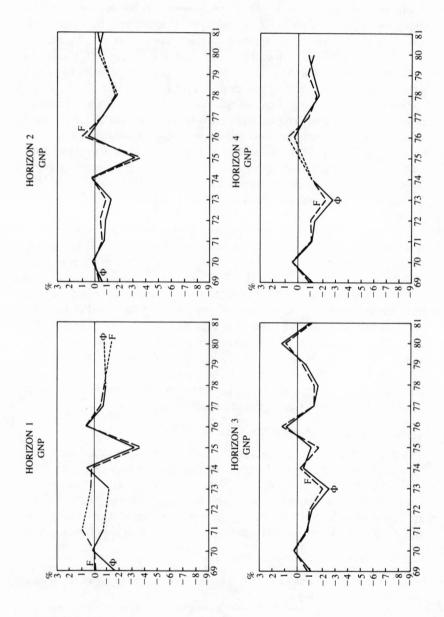

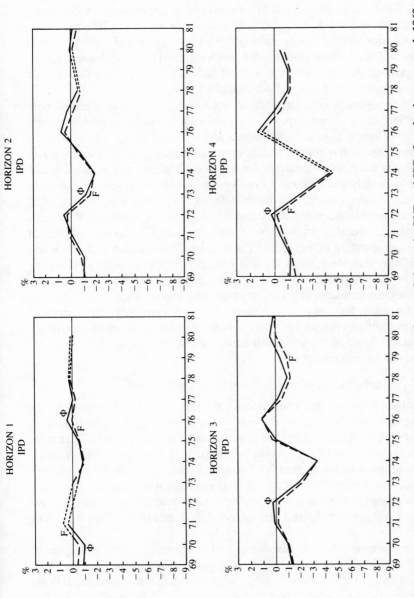

Fig. 17.2 Mean errors in point and probabilistic forecasts of rates of change in GNP and IPD, four horizons, annual, 1969–81

Note: Long-dashed lines refer to mean errors of group forecasts (F_m); solid lines refer to mean errors of group probabilistic forecasts (Φ_m); short-dashed lines indicate missing observations. The actual values used to compute the forecast errors are the last estimates available prior to the benchmark revisions of January 1976 and December 1980.

(with exceptions of one year each at H1 and H2 and two years each at H3 and H4). The $\bar{s}_\phi$ series fluctuate much less over time than their s_f counterparts.

Table 17.1 quantifies some of the inferences from these graphs (lines 13–16). The $\bar{s}_\phi$ series (cols. 3 and 5) are relatively stable, as shown by the figures in parentheses, and they increase only mildly between H1 and H3. In contrast, the s_f series (cols. 2 and 4) are volatile and increase strongly and monotonically with the horizon from much lower levels at H1. The differences $\bar{s}_\phi - s_f$ are positive and relatively large in six of the eight categories (for GNP H3 the difference is small; for GNP H4 it is negative).

Disturbances to aggregate demand and the price level come largely without warning and are unanticipated; most are then followed by gradual adjustments. There is a great deal of inertia and resilience in the economy, whose normal condition is growth, and the agents-observers know it. It seems, prima facie, unlikely that uncertainties about demand growth and inflation would vary as widely and erratically from year to year as the s_f series do, even in turbulent times, and that they would differ so much across the horizons. What can reasonably be expected is that increases in the volatility of change, whether in spending or prices, will in time generate irregular upward drifts in the corresponding uncertainties. The $\bar{s}_\phi$ series show in each case much less variability than the s_f series but also generally higher and more gently rising levels. We find the behavior of $\bar{s}_\phi$ easier to rationalize with respect to the presumptive measures of uncertainty than the behavior of s_f.

Our results thus suggest that consensus statistics probably often understate the levels of uncertainty. They may also overstate the variations in uncertainty. Measures based on the probabilistic forecast distributions should be more dependable on both counts.

17.3.3   Is Predictive Dissent a Symptom of Uncertainty?

Table 17.2 shows that a unit increase in s_f may add only a fraction to $\bar{s}_\phi$: the regression coefficients are of the order of .1–.2, where they appear significant at all (col. 4). The intercepts are all very similar, somewhat above .7 for inflation, higher for the rates of change in GNP (col. 3). The Durbin-Watson statistics are not very low, generally close to 1.5 (col. 5). Of the 12 correlations listed, five are significant at the 1% level or better, which includes the results from pooling the data across the horizons, and two others are significant at the 10% level; none of the rest presumably differs statistically from 0 (in four cases $\bar{r}^2 = 0$).

The evidence, then, is mixed, much of it suggesting that s_f and $\bar{s}_\phi$ are at most weakly related. But this needs to be qualified by two observations. First, all but two of the correlations listed (both for the shortest forecasts, H1) are positive. Second, when larger samples are obtained by pooling and when there are no missing observations (H3), the results rather clearly indicate a positive association between s_f and $\bar{s}_\phi$. Thus there is some direct empirical support here for what is often taken for granted, namely, that greater interpersonal differentiation of expectations is a symptom of greater uncertainty.

The reasons why this support is not stronger may lie in certain offsetting effects. Thus one can argue that it is precisely when uncertainty is high that people will have strong incentives to reduce the risk of making eccentric errors and will invest more resources in interactive prediction (see sec. 17.1.1). To the extent that this is true, it would tend to make the individual expectations (point forecasts) more closely bunched at such times; that is, it would produce elements of inverse correlation between s_f and $\bar{s}_\phi$.

A warning is in order at this point. Our findings are based on small samples of observations. Pooling the data can help but is no substitute for longer series of matching point and probabilistic forecasts. Collection and processing of more information of this type should in time produce more conclusive results.

17.3.4   Inflation Expectations and Uncertainty

Our data permit direct tests of the hypothesis that changes in anticipated inflation tend to cause parallel changes in uncertainty about inflation. This idea plays an important role in theories that view rising (and high and volatile) inflation as a major source of adverse real effects (see sec. 17.1.3).

Table 17.3 shows that the regressions of inflation uncertainty measured by $\bar{s}_\phi$ on inflation expectations measured by Φ give results that are generally consistent with the hypothesis. The effects of Φ on $\bar{s}_\phi$ are all positive, and they are strong for all except the shortest (H1) forecasts, as shown by the t-ratios on b, the Durbin-Watson statistics, and the correlations (lines 1–4, cols. 3–6). Pooling yields good results, too, especially when dummy variables are used to capture the horizon effects (lines 5–6).

In contrast to this direct supportive evidence from the probabilistic forecast distributions, the consensus measures from the point forecasts contribute little here. The effects of F on s_f are weak generally and apparently trifling for H1 and H2, although the correlations between the two variables are all positive (lines 7–10). Pooling does not help, except for the significant horizon effects (lines 11–12).

That higher Φ is associated with higher $\bar{s}_\phi$ for inflation does not mean that a similar relationship should be expected to exist for GNP, which reflects changes in total output as well as in the price level. There is no presumptive reason why increased rates of real growth ought to induce greater uncertainty about growth prospects, for example. Indeed, the correlations between $\bar{s}_\phi$ and Φ for GNP are extremely low, with $\bar{R}^2 = 0$ for each horizon. The pooled regressions show no significant effects of Φ on $\bar{s}_\phi$ either.[14] Much the same applies to the F and s_f series derived from the GNP point forecasts, where one

---

14. When dummy variables for the horizons are used, they alone contribute to the regression, as shown by the following estimates:

$$\bar{s}_\phi = \quad .798 + \quad .0014\phi + \quad .099d_2 + \quad .171d_3 + \quad .174d_4,$$
$$\qquad (14.9) \qquad (.25) \qquad (2.8) \qquad (5.0\ ) \qquad (4.9)$$
$$R = .664, \bar{R}^2 = .386.$$

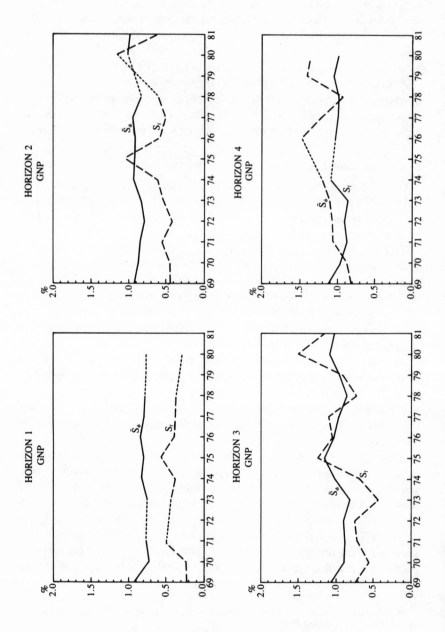

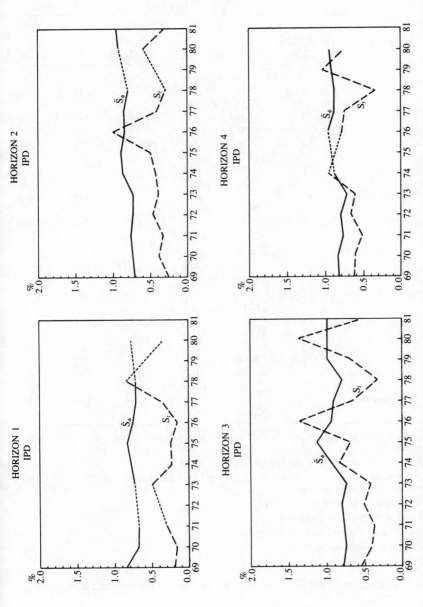

Fig. 17.3 Standard deviations and probabilistic forecasts of rates of change in GNP and IPD, four horizons, annual, 1969–81

Note: Long-dashed lines refer to standard deviations of point forecasts (s_f); solid lines refer to standard deviations of probabilistic forecasts (s_ϕ); short-dashed lines indicate missing observations.

Table 17.2   **Relating Time Series of Standard Deviations of Point and Probabilistic Forecasts, Annual Percentage Changes in GNP and IPD, 1969–81**

			Regression Estimates[a]			Correlations[b]	
Line	Horizon (quarters) (1)	No. of Observations (2)	a (3)	b (4)	Durbin-Watson (5)	r (6)	$\bar{r}^2$ (7)
			Gross National Product				
1	1	10	.885 (12.5)	−.118 (−.7)	2.08	−.237	0
2	2	12	.810 (15.8)	.157 (2.0)**	1.64	.545**	.226
3	3	13	.753 (12.1)	.255 (3.9)*	1.03	.758*	.536
4	4	11	.934 (6.3)	.044 (.3)	1.48	.114	0
5	H1–H4, pooled	46	.764 (28.8)	.209 (6.7)*	1.48[†]	.710*	.493
6	With dummies[c]	46	.744 (25.6)	.168 (3.6)*	1.59[†]	.756*	.530
			Implicit Price Deflator				
7	1	10	.785 (21.2)	−.078 (−.8)	1.63	−.280	0
8	2	12	.774 (12.6)	.120 (1.0)	.79	.295	0
9	3	13	.772 (11.9)	.181 (2.1)**	1.97	.534**	.221
10	4	11	.736 (9.0)	.179 (1.6)	1.27	.467	.131
11	H1–H4, pooled	46	.740 (27.0)	.182 (4.1)*	1.59[†]	.525*	.259
12	With dummies[d]	46	.714 (23.1)	.131 (2.6)*	1.56[†]	.606*	.306

[a]The regression equations are $\bar{s}_\phi = a + bs_f$ (with the time subscripts omitted; there are no lags); t-ratios are in parentheses.

[b]Multiple correlation coefficients R and $\bar{R}^2$ appear in lines 6 and 12.

[c]The coefficients of the dummy variables H2, H3, and H4 (and their t-ratios) are .059 (1.8)**, .086 (2.2)***, and .049 (1.0), respectively.

*Significant at the 1% level for two-tail tests.

**Significant at the 10% level for two-tail tests.

***Significant at the 5% level for two-tail tests.

[†]Exceeds the upper bound of the 1% point.

of the correlations is negative and only one (for H4) is positive and significant at the 10% level.

17.3.5   Cross-Survey Analysis

The literature discussed in section 17.1.3 makes extensive use of measures based on the point forecasts of inflation from the Livingston surveys. How are

Table 17.3   **Relating Standard Deviations to Means of Probabilistic and Point Forecasts of Inflation, 1969–81**

Line	Horizon (quarters)[a] (1)	Regression Estimates[b]		Durbin-Watson (4)	Correlations[c]	
		a (2)	b (3)		r (5)	$\bar{r}^2$ (6)
	Probabilistic Forecasts					
1	1	.686 (11.3)	.011 (1.2)	1.56	.404	.058
2	2	.600 (25.4)	.036 (10.1)*	1.78	.954*	.902
3	3	.620 (13.6)	.043 (6.4)*	1.66	.887*	.767
4	4	.660 (16.5)	.037 (5.3)*	1.91	.869*	.728
5	H1–H4, pooled	.653 (18.6)	.030 (5.6)*	.70	.647*	.406
6	With dummies[d]	.540 (18.6)	.033 (9.0)	1.72[†]	.868*	.730
	Point Forecasts					
7	1	.218 (.8)	.018 (.5)	1.87	.167	0
8	2	.383 (2.0)	.011 (.4)	2.00	.130	0
9	3	.299 (1.2)	.061 (1.6)	2.50	.432	.114
10	4	.446 (2.5)	.049 (1.5)	2.72	.455	.119
11	H1–H4, pooled	.415 (3.2)	.022 (1.1)	1.46[†]	.167	.006
12	With dummies[e]	.089 (.6)	.376 (2.2)	2.30[†]	.599*	.296

[a]For the corresponding numbers of observations, see table 17.2.
[b]The regression equations are $\bar{s}_\phi = a + b\Phi$ for the probabilistic forecasts (lines 1–6) and $s_f = a + bF$ for the point forecasts (lines 7–12) with the time subscripts omitted (there are no lags); t-ratios are in parentheses.
[c]Multiple correlation coefficients R and $\bar{R}^2$ appear in lines 6 and 12.
[d]The coefficients of the dummy variables H2, H3, and H4 (and their t-ratios) are $-.077$ (3.5)*, .143 (6.7)*, and .139 (6.2)*, respectively.
[e]The coefficients of the dummy variables H2, H3, and H4 (and their t-ratios) are .132 (1.3), .353 (3.6)*, and .417 (3.9)*, respectively.
*Significant at the 1% level for two-tail tests.
[†]Exceeds the upper bound of the 1% point.

these data related to our series of probabilistic forecast measures? This question clearly needs to be addressed, but the differences between the Livingston and the ASA-NBER survey formats impede obtaining the answer.

One approach is to combine the Livingston forecasts made late in the year $t-1$ for the first half of year t with those made in the middle of year t for the second half. The resulting annual averages, called LIV6, are paired with the means of the ASA-NBER forecasts with horizons H4 and H2 for year t, labeled ANB6. The component predictions of LIV6 and ANB6 have similar dates,[15] but the targets of the former are semiannual and those of the latter are annual. This complication is avoided by an alternative procedure, which is to match the projections for t from the late $t - 1$ surveys of Livingston and ASA-NBER H4 (we refer to these series as LIV12 and ANB12).

For all these differences, plus the fact that the Livingston surveys aim at the rate of change in consumer prices (CPI) while the ASA-NBER surveys aim at inflation in terms of the IPD, the mean forecasts for LIV6 and ANB6 and for LIV12 and ANB12 are highly correlated, as demonstrated in table 17.4, lines 1–2. Of course, these associations are not quite as close as those between the F and Φ series within the ASA-NBER set.

More remarkable yet, the correlations between the s_f series for LIV and the $\bar{s}_\phi$ series for ANB are rather high and significant at the level of 1% or less (lines 3 and 4). There is more evidence here that low (high) consensus indicates high (low) uncertainty than in the relationships between the s_f and $\bar{s}_\phi$ series within the ASA-NBER set as examined in table 17.2 and section 17.2.3.

It is true that the significance of these results is difficult to assess, given the smallness of the available data samples. Pooling cannot be used here to alleviate the problem. The Durbin-Watson statistics are not very low, but the residuals from some of the regressions appear to be positively autocorrelated.

In the ANB series used in table 17.4, H3 figures are interpolated in the instances in which H2 or H4 figures are not available. However, to guard against a possible bias from this procedure, alternative regressions were calculated discarding all observations for which the H2 or H4 forecasts are missing.[16] The main results of this procedure for the equations $s_f = a + b\bar{s}_\phi$ are the following: for LIV6–ANB6, $b = 5.600$ (3.6); D-W $= 2.31$, $r = .784$; for LIV12–ANB12, $b = 3.988$ (3.8); D-W $= 2.34$, $r = .788$ (t-ratios and r significant at the 1% level in a two-tail test). Compared with their counterparts in table 17.4, the values of the t-ratios and r are lower here and the Durbin-Watson statistics much higher. The finding that the LIV s_f series are positively related to the ANB $\bar{s}_\phi$ series remains intact, so the interpolations seem to have little to do with it.[17]

15. The Livingston midyear and end-of-year surveys are taken about a month after the corresponding ASA-NBER surveys (see table 17.4, n. a).

16. This "classical least squares" method of dealing with the problem of missing observations is used throughout elsewhere in this study.

17. There is also no evidence that the interpolations cause any serious distortions in the other equations estimated in table 17.4. Without interpolations, the t-ratios of b and r values are somewhat higher in lines 1 and 2, somewhat lower in lines 5–8, but all are still significant at the level of 1% or less. The Durbin-Watson statistics are generally higher, exceeding 2.3 in all but three cases, which suggests that the interpolations might have induced some autocorrelation in the residuals from the regressions of table 17.4.

Table 17.4   Relating the Uncertainty and Consensus Measures for the ASA-NBER and Livingston Inflation Forecasts, 1969–81

Line	Survey Data[a] (1)	Regression Estimates[b]			Correlations	
		a (2)	b (3)	Durbin-Watson (4)	r (5)	$\bar{r}^2$ (6)
	Mean Forecasts (F, φ)					
1	LIV6, ANB6	−.811	1.040	1.48	.937*	.868
		(−1.0)	(8.9)*			
2	LIV12, ANB12	−.553	1.024	1.56	.956*	.906
		(−.9)	(10.8)*			
	Standard Deviations (s_f, $\bar{s}_\phi$)					
3	LIV6, ANB6	−3.058	5.470	1.29	.849*	.696
		(−3.4)	(5.3)*			
4	LIV12, ANB12	−1.854	3.480	1.50	.811*	.625
		(−2.7)	(4.6)*			
	Standard Deviations on Mean Forecasts					
5	LIV6 (s_f, F)	.426	.217	1.73	.898*	.789
		(2.1)	(6.8)*			
6	LIV12 (s_f, F)	.280	.169	1.78	.906*	.804
		(1.9)	(7.1)*			
7	ANB6 ($\bar{s}_\phi$, φ)	.615	.040	1.63	.954*	.902
		(24.5)	(10.6)*			
8	ANB12 ($\bar{s}_\phi$, φ)	.637	.041	1.17	.891*	.774
		(15.3)	(6.5)*			

[a]LIV6 are annual F and s_f series for inflation (CPI) based on forecasts from surveys taken in December of year $t - 1$ for the first half of year t and in June of t for the second half of t. LIV12 are corresponding series based on December ($t - 1$) forecasts for year t. ANB6 are annual φ and $\bar{s}_\phi$ series for inflation (IPD) based on forecasts taken in November of $t - 1$ and May of t for the year t. ANB12 are corresponding series based on November ($t - 1$) forecasts for year t.

[b]The regression equations are of the form $F = a + b\phi$ for lines 1–2, $S_f = a + b\bar{s}_\phi$ for lines 3–4, $s_f = a + bF$ for lines 5–6, and $\bar{s}_\phi = a + b\Phi$ for lines 7–8. The F and s_f series refer to LIV6 and LIV12; the Φ and $\bar{s}_\phi$ series to ANB6 and ANB12. t-ratios are in parentheses. The number of observations is 13 in each regression (for one missing observation in the H2 series and two in the H4 series, the corresponding values of H3 are interpolated).

*Significant at the 1% level for two-tail tests.

What probably does help explain these results is that they are based on 6-month and, to a larger extent, 12-month forecasts, omitting the shortest horizon for which the association between s_f and $\bar{s}_\phi$ may be much weaker, as table 17.2 would suggest. In any event, table 17.4 provides direct support for the uses of the Livingston σ series as a proxy measure of uncertainty. This seems to be the first evidence of this kind, and as such it is both noteworthy and favorable.

The last section of table 17.4 confirms that $\bar{s}_\phi$ rises with Φ (cf. lines 7–8 and table 17.3, lines 1–6), but it also shows that s_f rises with F for both the LIV6 and the LIV12 series (lines 5–6). The latter effects seem rather strong, which contrasts sharply with the evidence of weak or no relationship between s_f and F in the ASA-NBER data (see table 17.3, lines 7–12).

17.3.6   Effects on Real Growth

Table 17.5 shows that the rate of change in real GNP (DY_t) in the years 1969–81 was positively associated with the concurrent and lagged growth rates in the M1 money supply (DM_t and DM_{t-1}) and negatively associated with the concurrent level of inflation uncertainty σ_t measured by ANB12$\bar{s}_\phi$ (though ANB6 $\bar{s}_\phi$ would do about as well). The influence of the latter factor appears to be strong but not very lasting since the negative coefficient of σ_t is to a large extent offset by a positive coefficient of σ_{t-1}. However, with only these annual series at our disposal, distributed-lag relations cannot be well assessed. Similar results are obtained when the proxy measures for uncer-

Table 17.5   Inflation Uncertainty in Equations for Real Growth, 1969–81

Variable or Statistic[a]	Regression Equations[b]					
	(5.1)	(5.2)	(5.3)	(5.4)	(5.5)	(5.6)
Constant	7.563	−2.034	1.251	−2.312	−.252	.272
	(1.40)	(−.36)	(.47)	(−.73)	(−.05)	(.08)
DM_t	10.939	9.715	10.487	6.470	10.054	8.496
	(2.59)	(2.03)	(2.64)	(1.21)	(2.47)	(1.54)
DM_{t-1}	. . .	4.051	. . .	7.807	. . .	. . .
		(1.07)		(2.02)		
ANB12 $\bar{s}_{\phi t}$	−11.578	−14.637	. . .	. . .	−11.092	
	(2.16)	(−2.75)			(−1.96)	
ANB12 $\bar{s}_{\phi t-1}$	. . .	12.176		. . .	11.681	. . .
		(2.27)			(2.36)	
LIV12 s_{ft}	. . .	. . .	−3.029	−4.474	. . .	−4.735
			(−2.58)	(−2.90)		(−2.67)
LIV12 s_{ft-1}	. . .	. . .	. . .	2.910	. . .	2.926
				(1.73)		(1.55)
TBR$_{t-1}$	. . .	. . .	. . .	. . .	−.389	. . .
					(−1.58)	
DGE$_t$	. . .	. . .	. . .	. . .	. . .	.198
						(1.52)
Standard error of estimate	1.930	1.531	1.811	1.528	1.416	1.667
R	.742	.896	.777	.896	.912	.875
$\bar{R}^2$	.461	.689	.525	.690	.734	.631
Durbin-Watson	2.07	1.42	2.27	2.23	1.49	2.19

Source: ANB: ASA-NBER surveys; LIV: Livingston surveys; *DM*, TBR, and *DGE:* Bureau of Economic Analysis *Handbook of Cyclical Indicators,* 1984.

Note: t-statistics are in parentheses.

[a]*DM* is the annual rate of change in the money supply, M1 (%); TBR is the 3-month Treasury bill rate; *DGE* is the annual rate of change in the total of real federal government expenditures and real exports (%); for the ANB and LIV variables, see the text and table 17.4.

[b]The dependent variable is the annual rate of change in real GNP (%) (*DY*).

tainty LIV12 s_f are used instead of ANB $\bar{s}_\phi$ (cf. eqs. [5.1]–[5.2] with eqs. [5.3]–[5.4]).

Reciprocal relations being ubiquitous in economics, the direction of causation is often difficult to establish: surely a prime example of this is that DY can affect DM as well as the other way around. But it makes good sense to argue that uncertainty about future inflation can influence real activity adversely in times of rapid and irregular rises in the price level (such as the 1970s), whereas the reverse causation is implausible here. (Why should low DY induce high σ?)

The t-ratios leave little doubt about the significance of the separate effects of the DM and σ variables, with a couple of possible exceptions that probably reflect collinearity problems.[18] Jointly, these variables account for about .5–.7 of the variance of DY, depending on whether their lagged terms are included (see the $\bar{R}^2$ coefficients). Real defense and other federal government purchases of goods and services are usually treated as an exogenous determinant of total output of the economy, and the same applies to real exports. However, adding the rate of change in real federal expenditures and exports (DGE) to regressions with current and lagged values of DM and $\bar{s}_\phi$ turned out to contribute very little or nothing.[19] The variable DGE_t was somewhat more effective (but at some expense of DM_t) when used along with the s_f series, as illustrated by equation (5.6). Also, there are some indications of a negative influence on DY of lagged interest rates (represented by the Treasury bill rate [TBR]), but they too are somewhat sporadic and weak (eq. [5.5]).[20]

In sum, the idea of inflation uncertainty as a short-term depressant of real activity receives substantial support from table 17.5. The Livingston s_f data provide on the whole a good proxy measure of σ in this context. These results are consistent with recent studies.[21] They seem sufficiently robust to merit cautious acceptance at this time, pending the accumulation of more evidence.

17.3.7   Effects on Interest Rates

Interest rates (i) represented by TBR_t depend positively on expected inflation Φ_t and inversely on inflation uncertainty $\bar{s}_{\phi t}$ and money growth DM_t, as seen in table 17.6, equation (6.1). The lagged terms Φ_{t-1} and $\bar{s}_{\phi t-1}$ enter with

18. The addition of ANB12$s_{\phi t-1}$ results in a low t for DM_{t-1} and reduces the Durbin-Watson statistics (which otherwise exceed 2). The addition of LIV12s_{ft-1} results in a low t for DM_t. The correlations between $s_{\phi t}$ and $s_{\phi t-1}$ is .463, that between s_{ft} and s_{ft-1} is .618, and for DM_t and DM_{t-1} the corresponding statistic is .410.

19. That is, neither DY nor the coefficients of the other variables were significantly affected. We have also tried, with similarly negative results, a series of shares of federal government purchases and exports in GNP.

20. No further search for missing variables was considered necessary or indeed desirable, given the pitfalls of data mining and our limited objectives.

21. See Levi and Makin 1980 and Makin 1982. It should be noted that this refers only to the role of ϕ_t. Our calculations were not designed to deal with the issue of anticipated versus unanticipated money growth (m^e vs. m^u); their outcome is consistent either with m^e having real effects or with m^u accounting for the largest part of total monetary change.

Table 17.6   **Inflation Expectations and Uncertainty in Equations for Interest Rates, 1969–81**

Variable or Statistic[a]	Regression Equations[b]					
	(6.1)	(6.2)	(6.3)	(6.4)	(6.5)	(6.6)
Constant	30.930	39.915	6.943	9.067	23.068	.293
	(5.07)	(4.44)	(2.14)	(3.41)	(3.25)	(.12)
DM_t	−6.871	−6.436	−8.571	−8.949	−5.106	−4.138
	(−2.26)	(−1.51)	(−1.73)	(−2.25)	(−1.75)	(−1.31)
ANB12 ϕ_t	2.558	1.883	...	...	2.717	...
	(6.47)	(2.66)			(7.38)	
ANB12 ϕ_{t-1}	...	1.382	...	...	...	...
		(1.40)				
ANB12 $\bar{s}_{\phi t}$	−40.110	−33.273	...	...	−32.956	...
	(−4.71)	(−3.43)			(−3.79)	
ANB12 $\bar{s}_{\phi t-1}$	...	−21.760	...	...	...	...
		(−1.51)				
LIV12 F_t	...	...	1.739	1.831	...	1.684
			(2.71)	(3.53)		(4.36)
LIV12 F_{t-1}	...	...	...	1.094	...	...
				(2.12)		
LIV12 s_{ft}	...	...	−4.154	−3.971	...	.184
			(−1.22)	(−1.91)		(.08)
LIV12 s_{ft-1}	...	...	...	−7.256	...	...
				(−4.34)		
GAP_t	...	...	...	...	.485	.875
					(1.75)	(4.11)
Standard error of estimate	1.346	1.268	1.826	1.068	1.213	1.098
R	.919	.952	.844	.952	.942	.953
$\bar{R}^2$	.792	.830	.617	.879	.831	.861
Durbin-Watson	2.38	2.18	1.52	2.48	2.59	1.72

Sources: See table 17.5 and Gordon 1984a, table B-1 (GAP).

Note: t-statistics are in parentheses.

[a]GAP = (actual GAP − potential real GNP)/potential real GNP (%). Other symbols are defined in the text and in tables 17.4 and 17.5

[b]The dependent variable is the 3-month Treasury bill rate (TBR).

the same signs as their current-year counterparts, but they detract from the effects of the other variables and contribute but modestly to regression (6.2).

When F_t and s_{ft} are used instead of Φ_t and $s_{\phi t}$, coefficients with the same signs are obtained, but the t, R, and Durbin-Watson statistics are all lower (cf. eqs. [6.1] and [6.3]). The lagged terms F_{t-1} and s_{ft-1}, however, make relatively strong contributions (cf. eqs. [6.2] and [6.4]).

These results suggest that the joint effects of inflation expectations and uncertainty on i have been very strong in this period. Leaving out $\bar{s}_\phi$ or s_f and including instead DGE or DY (with or without lags) reduces the correlations greatly. The influence of DM_{t-1} turns out to be weak and ambiguous in its sign.

The evidence of equations (6.1)–(6.4) supports the proposition that inflation uncertainty σ influences i negatively, which is consistent with three of the recent papers that use the Livingston s_f data for the same purpose. (Two others report positive and one reports insignificant coefficients for the current and/or lagged values of s_f; see sec. 17.1.3.) A study by Lahiri, Teigland, and Zaporowski (1986), using $\bar{s}_\phi$-type data from the ASA-NBER surveys, finds positive effects that, however, are insignificant in the presence of selected "liquidity" and "exogenous demand" variables.[22]

When the percentage divergence of actual from potential real GNP (GAP) is added to the equation with current and lagged values of the LIV measures, its impact on TRB is revealed as positive and strong.[23] The addition of GAP_t diminishes the effect of DM_t and eliminates that of s_{ft} (cf. eqs. [6.3] and [6.6]). That the impact of s_f on TRB (as observed in earlier papers written or coauthored by Makin) disappears when GAP is included has been noted by Makin and Tanzi (1984, pp. 130, 134). In contrast to s_f, however, $\bar{s}_\phi$ retains its significantly large coefficient with a negative sign in the presence of GAP (cf. eqs. [6.2] and [6.5]).

The upshot is that the balance of the evidence, with more credence given to the probabilistic than to the point forecast data, favors the view that the effect of a rise in σ is to reduce i. As noted earlier, this implies that real investment is depressed more than real savings in the process. However, this result needs to be treated with caution since it could be quite sensitive to the choice of the time period covered and other specifications.

17.4 Conclusions

We define "consensus" as the degree of agreement among corresponding point predictions by different individuals and "uncertainty" as the diffuseness of the probability distributions attached by the same individuals to their predictions. To be useful the distinction must be made operational and measurable. The quarterly ASA-NBER surveys provide data on point and probabilistic forecasts of annual percentage changes in GNP and IPD, which can be applied to this task in several ways.

---

22. The authors pool the survey data across horizons and combine them with quarterly series for other variables. They use 3- and 6-month Treasury bill rates when the forecast horizon is two quarters or less and 12-month rates when it is three quarters or more; the two situations are also distinguished by means of dummy variables. The period covered is 1969:2–1985:2. Thus their study differs from ours in several respects, and it is not clear what accounts for the discrepancy in the results.

23. GAP is a cyclical factor, which is a broad measure of capacity utilization that affects real investment positively via an accelerator-type relationship (see Tanzi 1980; Makin and Tanzi 1984).

The matched mean point forecasts (F) and mean probability forecasts (Φ) agree closely. On the whole, then, the preferred predictions coincide with the expected values of the probability distributions assessed by the survey respondents.

Standard deviations of point forecasts (s_f) tend to understate uncertainty as measured by the means of standard deviations of predictive probability distributions $(\bar{s}_\phi)$, particularly for short horizons. The s_f series show much greater variability over time than the $\bar{s}_\phi$ series, but the evidence suggests that these measures of consensus and uncertainty are for the most part positively correlated.

The s_f series derived from the semiannual Livingston survey forecasts have been widely used in recent literature as proxies for "inflation uncertainty." This practice receives direct support from our finding of substantial positive correlations between annual versions of these data and roughly consistent $\bar{s}_\phi$ series of inflation based on ASA-NBER survey forecasts. However, matching the data from the two surveys presents small-sample and other measurement problems; hence the results of this analysis must be interpreted with particular caution.

Strong positive effects of Φ on $\bar{s}_\phi$ for the rate of change in IPD (but not in GNP) provide evidence in favor of the hypothesis that expectations of higher inflation tend to generate greater uncertainty about inflation.

Real economic activity represented by the rate of change in constant-dollar GNP is adversely affected by a rise in inflation uncertainty measured by $\bar{s}_\phi$, allowing for the influence of monetary growth and exogenous demand. The Livingston s_f data produce similar results, in this study and others.

A rise in uncertainty about inflation, other things equal, can either reduce or increase interest rates, depending on whether it depresses real investment more than real savings or vice versa. Studies using the s_f data have produced mixed results, interpreted accordingly. Our results indicate that a rise in $\bar{s}_\phi$ on the average lowered the Treasury bill rate in the years 1969–81.

18   The Record and Improvability of Economic Forecasting

18.1   Questions and Problems

The question "Is better forecasting possible?" would seem to be of critical importance to both makers and users of macroeconomic predictions. Indeed, the ability to produce accurate predictions of the course of the economy in the near-term future is probably the main criterion by which the public judges the usefulness of our entire profession. It is true that this popular standard fails to discriminate between wrong specifications of economic models and wrong choices of assumptions about outside events, whereas one may argue that an economist should be held mainly responsible for the former rather than the latter source of forecast errors. But most economists would agree that the proper test of the practical aspects of their expertise consists in how well they can predict or "explain" postsample data.

Critics often assert that the economic forecasts generally are poor. However, it is not clear what standards they apply and whether such complaints represent more than casual opinions. Large errors can occur for a variety of reasons and need not be either systematic or symptomatic of forecasters' inability.

Logically, the inquiry into the improvability of forecasting should start with some prior questions: How accurate have the forecasts been on the average in the past? What are the sources and characteristics of superior forecasts? For several reasons, however, these seemingly simple questions lack unique and conclusive answers.

1. The forecasts must be explicit, verifiable, and sufficient to permit a responsible appraisal. But the recorded history of macroeconomic forecasting is of recent origin. Time series on specific, quantitative, and comparable predic-

Reprinted from *Economic Forecasts: A Worldwide Survey* 3 (December 1986): 22–30.

tions are as a rule short. Few forecasters have been active consistently over many years; many offer only small samples of observations with isolated hits or misses that could be largely due to chance.

2. Some periods are easier to forecast than others. For example, once it is clear that a recession has just ended, it is a rather safe bet that the recovery will continue in the months immediately ahead, but just when a mature expansion will end is usually quite difficult to anticipate.

3. Some variables are easier to forecast than others. In general, the trend-dominated and smooth series are better predicted than the cyclical and volatile series. Forecasting models differ greatly in size and complexity—the number and composition of endogenous and exogenous variables. It is difficult to make dependable comparisons across such models.

4. Economic agents generally use the forecasts to help formulate and improve their plans and decisions. They expect that the value of the resulting reductions in their errors will tend to exceed the effective costs to them of producing or acquiring the forecasts. However, these costs and returns are typically difficult to estimate and unknown to an outside analyst. Users have different needs, skills, and preferences ("loss functions"). The *size* of forecasting errors may not be sufficient to determine their *consequences* for the decisions based on the forecasts.

5. Different summary measures of error may lead to different appraisals of a given set of forecasts. The results will depend on whether the averages are based on absolute or squared errors; on whether the errors are computed for predictions of levels or changes; and on the importance of measurement errors and the treatment of data revisions. Absolute accuracy measures, which show deviations from the obviously unattainable state of perfection (zero errors), need to be complemented with relative accuracy measures, which compare forecasts from different sources or of different types. Here the standard is often some objective "benchmark" model, for example, low-cost extrapolations of the own history of the target series. The optimal standards vary with the properties of the time series in question.

6. Ideally, forecasts should be unbiased, that is, have random, nonautocorrelated errors averaging 0, since forecasters should use the available information to eliminate all avoidable systematic errors. But success in this endeavor requires sufficiently large samples of comparable predictions on series generated by sufficiently stable processes. If these conditions are not met, the apparent bias may be spurious. A different reason for the same result may lie in asymmetric loss functions.

7. Macroeconomic forecasts vary greatly with respect to the relative roles of model and judgment, but in practice inevitably include elements of both. There is no way to avoid judgment in the choice of the model itself and on how the modeled regularities of the sample period are to be modified in light of new and external events. Uses of objective, reproducible methods offer valuable opportunities for learning, the results of which can be recorded and

published. This advantage is not provided by those forecasters who do not disclose their assumptions and techniques or models. Experienced judgment may be the most valuable property of a forecaster but it is not something that can be readily transmitted to others.

In sum, the quality of forecasts is a relative and multidimensional concept. Forecasts vary in many ways: by source, techniques, variables and periods covered, timing, and horizon. It is generally difficult to allow for these differences so as to make meaningful comparisons across forecasters and over time, even after the event, with data on the corresponding actual values on hand.

The history of modern forecasting overlaps the "information revolution" of the last 30 years, a period of rapid expansion in the scope and content of economic data, measures, and literature. The process was (and is) the result of a number of interacting developments on both the demand side and the supply side: advances in data collection and processing, in economic theory, statistics, and econometrics; the accelerating power of the computer; the spread of modern management techniques propelled by competition; the growing size and planning requirements of governments. As usual in times of revolutionary change, great expectations were born. Some of these promised too much. This certainly applies to the notion of a road to dependable business and economic policies built by a new science of optimum forecasting.

18.2   Some Evidence and Interpretations

Is there a way to address what appears to be a complex question of *trends* in forecasting accuracy without getting bogged down in the many differences among forecasters, techniques, models, variables, horizons, and periods covered? I hope to show that the answer is a qualified yes. The problems discussed above will not be resolved but the complications they pose can be reduced by the design of the study, and some limited but pertinent results can be obtained from the available record.

18.2.1   Annual Forecasts: Comparisons across Time and Sources

Table 18.1 arrays, by common coverage in time, measures of average error without regard to sign for a large collection of annual ex ante forecasts of nominal and real growth and inflation. These are the longest authenticated time series of this kind that could be collected, but they reach back only to 1953 (for GNP) and 1959 (real GNP and the implicit price deflator).[1] There are gaps and overlaps in this compilation that one would wish away, but they reflect the availability of the data and could not be avoided. The forecasts are roughly comparable in timing, most having been made in October or November of year t for the year $t + 1$, that is, before the publication of the first official GNP estimates for the last quarter of year t.

1. See notes to table 18.1 for sources of the forecasts covered and references to related studies.

Table 18.1   Summary Measures of Error for Annual Forecasts of Percentage Changes in Aggregate Income, Output, and the Price Level, 1953–1984.

Line (1)	Period and No. of years Covered (2)	LIV[a] (3)	SPF[b] (4)	NYF[c] (5)	ERP[d] (6)	ANB[e] (7)	MIM[f] (8)	WHM[g] (9)	Mean[h] (10)	XP[i] (11)	Relative Error (10):(11) (12)
	Growth Rate of Gross National Product (GNP)										
1	1953–76 (24)	1.6	1.2						1.4	2.3	0.6
2	1956–63 (8)	1.7	1.4	1.7					1.6	1.9	0.8
3	1963–76 (14)	1.1	0.9		0.9		1.3	0.8	1.0	1.8	0.6
4	1969–76 (8)	1.0	0.6		0.8	1.0	1.0	0.9	0.9	2.0	0.5
5	1977–84 (8)				1.8	1.5	2.0	1.6	1.7	2.8	0.6
	Growth Rate of GNP in 1972 Dollars (RGNP)										
6	1959–67 (9)	1.3					1.0		1.2	1.7	0.7
7	1962–76 (15)				1.1		1.4		1.2	2.6	0.5
8	1969–76 (8)				1.2	1.0	1.6	0.9	1.2	3.6	0.3
9	1977–84 (8)				1.2	1.0	1.0	1.0	1.0	3.2	0.3
	Rate of Inflation in the GNP Implicit Price Deflator (IPD)										
10	1959–67 (9)	0.6					0.7		0.6	0.3	2.0
11	1962–76 (15)				1.0		1.0		1.0	1.3	0.8
12	1969676 (8)				1.4	1.3	1.4	1.4	1.4	2.0	0.7
13	1977–84 (8)				0.9	1.0	1.2	1.2	1.1	1.3	0.8

[a]Based on surveys conducted by Joseph A. Livingston, syndicated columnist. Published in the *Philadelphia Bulletin* and *American Banker* and, in recent years, in the *Philadelphia Inquirer*. Of the semiannual surveys, only the end-of-year ones are used here; questionnaire typically mailed in November and results published in December. Coverage 44–62 persons.

[b]Mean of end-of-year forecasts from the following sources: (1) *Fortune* magazine ("Business Roundup"); (2) Harris Bank; (3) IBM Economic Research Department; (4) National Securities and Research Corporation; (5) NICB, now Conference Board "Economic Forum"; (6) R. W. Paterson, University of Missouri; (7) Prudential Insurance Company of America; (8) UCLA Business Forecasting Project. The earliest of these predictions were made in October; the latest in January. Most of these forecasts are quarterly. For studies of these data through 1976, see Zarnowitz 1967, 1972b, 1974, and 1979 (see chapter 14, this volume).

[c]Group mean forecasts from the New York Forecasters Club. Of the semiannual forecasts, only the end-of-year ones are included. *Coverage:* 31–39 individual respondents. *Dates:* 1956–58, October; 1959–63, December. Collected through 1963 and analyzed in Zarnowitz 1967, 1972b, 1974, and 1979 (chapter 14, this volume).

[d]Annual forecasts by the Council of Economic Advisers (CEA) as stated in the *Economic Report of the President,* published as a rule in January. Often midpoints in the relatively narrow range, in a few cases interpolated and checked with the source for approximate accuracy. See Moore 1969a, 1977d, 1982; Zarnowitz 1972b, 1979 (chapter 14, this volume); Fellner 1976; McNees 1977.

[e]*Source:* Quarterly releases by the American Statistical Association (ASA) and the National Bureau of Economic Research (NBER), published by ASA in *AmStat News* and by NBER in *Explorations in Economic Research* and, more recently, *NBER Reporter*. Median forecasts from the November surveys only are used. Coverage varied between 25 and 84, but mostly 30–50. See Zarnowitz 1967, 1969b, 1972b, 1974, and 1979 (chapter 14, this volume), 1984a, 1985a; Mincer and Zarnowitz 1969; Moore 1969a; Su and Su 1975; McNees 1973, 1974, 1975, 1976.

[f]Forecasts from the Research Seminar in Quantitative Economics (RSQE) of the University of Michigan. Published quarterly (initially, three times per year). Included here are the forecasts released in connection with the University of Michigan annual "Conference on the Economic Outlook," dated as a rule in November. Based on several working models; see Suits 1962; Hymans and Shapiro 1970, 1974.

[g]*Source: Wharton Economic Newsletter,* Econometric Forecasting Unit, Wharton School of Finance and Commerce, University of Pennsylvania. Published quarterly; the forecasts used here are end-of-year, as a rule dated in November. Based on a series of Wharton models (see Evans and Klein 1967; Evans, Klein, and Saito 1972; McCarthy 1972b; Duggal et al. 1974).

[h]Mean of the entries in cols. 3–9.

Table 18.1   Continued.

[i]Extrapolative benchmark forecasts. For GNP and RGNP (lines 1–9) assumes that next year's percentage change will be the same as the average percentage change in the four previous years. For IPD (lines 10–13) assumes that next year's percentage change will be the same as that of previous year. The actual changes are based on the first official estimates following the year for which the forecast was made. See text.

Table 18.1 has a highly diversified coverage. It includes averages from regular surveys of professional forecasters (cols. 3, 5, and 7), various predictions selected for early and consistent coverage (col. 4), forecasts by the successive teams of presidential economic advisers (col. 6), and forecasts by two econometric service bureaus (cols. 8 and 9). Individual and collective judgments, informal and formal approaches, small and large models—all of these are well represented. Each line refers to a period that covers a variety of business conditions.

The mean absolute error (MAE) measures assembled in table 18.1 display no systematic upward or downward trends, as can be seen by comparing the entries within each of columns 3–9 for the individual forecast sets. The overall means in column 10 convey the same message. True, errors in the annual predictions of nominal GNP growth rates were on the average larger in the last eight complete years than in the eight previous years, for example, but the opposite applies to the predictions of real GNP growth and inflation.

To allow for any changes in the means of the predicted series across the periods covered, benchmark MAE measures were computed for selected naive models: 4-year moving-average extrapolations for the annual percentage changes in GNP and RGNP, last-year extrapolations for those in IPD.[2] Comparisons of the forecast errors (cols. 3–10) with the naive extrapolation (XP) errors (col. 11) show that the former are in all but one case (line 10) substantially smaller than the latter. Moreover, the relative errors, that is, ratios of MAE for the forecasts to the corresponding MAE-XP measures (see col. 12), show a tendency to decline between the earlier and the more recent periods. On this criterion, then, one would conclude that the annual forecasts of nominal and real GNP growth may have actually improved, at least since the late 1950s. (For inflation, the evidence is weaker, as shown in lines 10–13.)

It is also interesting to note that, consistent with several studies such as McNees 1975 and 1976 and Zarnowitz 1967, 1972b, and chapter 14, this volume, it is difficult to detect systematic differences in accuracy among the well-known professional forecasters. In general, the MAE statistics for the forecast sets included in table 18.1 do not differ much. This is well illustrated by the following tabulation:

2. These simple models perform relatively well for the respective variables, and more elaborate time-series models are neither needed nor properly applicable here. Annual data comparable to those available to the forecasters are short also; see table 18.1, n. i.

Entries in table 18.1, cols. 3–9, for

	GNP	RGNP	IPD
Mean (x)	1.2	1.1	1.0
Standard deviation (s)	0.4	0.2	0.3
Fraction within ± 1 s around x	15/20	11/12	8/12

The reasons for the similarity of the forecasts, and hence for the representativeness of the overall averages, are several. Forecasters use to a large extent the same data, receive the same news, interact, and draw upon a common pool of knowledge and techniques. The models used often differ substantially, but their outputs are adjusted to reflect the most recent changes in the economy, policies, etc., and it is known that these adjustments reduce the variation among the forecasts (Zarnowitz 1972b, Christ 1975).

Moreover, aggregation over forecasts from business outlook surveys, or other corresponding and contemporary predictions, works to reduce the effects of the outliers (see chapter 15). The aggregate (or average) forecasts are known to be more accurate over time than most of the individual forecasts from the given group.

18.2.2   Quarterly Forecasts for the Year Ahead: Cyclical Errors

Table 18.2 presents mean absolute errors and mean errors calculated over a set of quarterly 1-year-ahead forecasts from five widely used sources. The period covered, 1971:2–1985:1, is subdivided in three different ways. Of four equal (14–quarter) subperiods, it is the latest one, 1981:4–1985:1, that shows the largest MAEs. This applies to all four variables included: growth rates in GNP, RGNP, and IPD, and the unemployment rate (UR). But there is no systematic increase in the errors from one period to the next, except for GNP. The mean errors vary in sign and size irregularly across the four periods.

Each of the periods listed in section A of the table includes some especially turbulent times associated with unanticipated turning points in the level of economic activity and rates of growth in output and prices. But the last, 1981:4–1985:1, had the largest share of such events: the severe recession in late 1981 and 1982, the slowdown of mid-1984, and the surprisingly strong disinflation. It is presumably this fact that explains why forecasts for this subperiod were the least accurate.

Indeed, the breakdowns according to cyclical characteristics (sections B and C) disclose much larger and more systematic differences than the division of the period into equal parts. For each variable, the MAEs are much smaller for the predictions relating to business expansions including peaks (44 quarters) than for the predictions relating to business contractions including troughs (12 quarters). Also, the absolute values of the MEs are in each case much smaller for the first than for the second subset of the forecasts (section B).

While the dating of *business cycles* is based on the consensus of the major

Table 18.2   **Some Sources of Variability of Errors in Composite Forecasts of Nominal and Real Growth, Inflation, and the Unemployment Rate, 1971:2–1985:1**

| | Period and No. of Quarters Covered | Medians of Quarterly 1-Year-Ahead Forecasts from Five Sources[a] | | | | | | | |
| | | Mean Absolute Error | | | | Mean Error | | | |
Line (1)	(2)	GNP (3)	RGNP (4)	IP (5)	UR (6)	GNP (7)	RGNP (8)	IPD (9)	UR (10)
	A. Four Equal Subperiods[b]								
1	71:2–74:3 (14)	1.3	1.1	1.3	0.3	−1.2	0.6	−1.8	−0.1
2	74:4–78:1 (14)	1.4	1.8	1.1	0.8	0.9	1.0	−0.4	−0.5
3	78:2–81:3 (14)	2.3	1.2	1.2	0.5	−2.3	−1.0	−1.1	0.5
4	81:4–85:1 (14)	3.2	2.4	1.6	1.2	2.2	0.6	1.6	−0.3
	B. Business Cycle Phases[c]								
5	Expansions (44)	1.8	1.2	1.1	0.6	−0.8	−0.4	−0.3	0.1
6	Contractions (12)	3.0	3.0	2.5	1.0	−2.4	2.9	−0.8	−1.0
	C. Growth Cycle Phases[d]								
7	High-growth (34)	1.7	1.3	0.9	0.6	−0.3	−0.4	0.02	0.03
8	Low-growth (22)	2.7	2.1	2.2	0.8	0.3	1.3	−1.2	−0.3
	D. Total Period Covered								
9	1971:2–1985:1 (56)	2.1	1.6	1.4	0.7	−0.1	0.3	−0.5	−0.1

[a]Errors are calculated from the median forecasts by the ASA-NBER survey (ANB), Chase Econometric Associates, Inc. (CHA), Data Resources, Inc. (DRI), Wharton Econometric Forecasting Associates, Inc. (WHM), and Bureau of Economic Analysis of the U.S. Department of Commerce (BEA). On the sources of the forecasts, see notes to tables 18.1 and 18.2; also, Hirsch et al. 1974 (on BEA). For the underlying data, see McNees 1985, table 1, p. 37.

[b]See lines 1–4 col. 2, for the dates of these periods.

[c]Expansions, including peaks, cover quarters 1971:2–1973:4, 1975:2–1980:1, 1980:4–1981:3, and 1983:1–1985:1. Contractions, including troughs, cover quarters 1974:1–1975:1, 1980:2–1980:3, 1981:4–1982:4. The quarterly dates of peaks and troughs are from the NBER business cycle chronology as used in the BEA monthly publication *Business Condition Digest* (*BCD*).

[d]High-growth phases are periods during which the mean growth of real GNP exceeded the long-term trend rate (about 3% per year): 1971:2–1972:4, 1975:2–1978:4, 1980:4–1981:1, and 1983:1–1985:1. Low-growth phases are periods of below-trend growth in real GNP: 1973:2–1975:1, 1979:1–1980:3, and 1981:2–1982:4.

turning points in comprehensive economic time series, the dating of *growth cycles* is determined in a similar way from the principal turns in the *detrended values* of such series. What this means in practice here is that periods during which the economy's output grew at an average rate exceeding the long-term trend rate of about 3.3% per year are distinguished from periods during which it grew more slowly. The high-growth phases include recoveries and booms; the low-growth phases include slowdowns and recessions. For the so-defined growth cycles (section C), the contrasts between the phase forecast errors are less sharp than for business cycles but no less regular. The forecasts relating to the high-growth phases (34 quarters) have smaller MAEs than those relating to the low-growth phases (22 quarters), for each variable. The absolute values of MEs are much smaller for high-growth than low-growth phases in three cases and equal in one (GNP).

To sum up, forecasts of growth in income and output and of inflation and unemployment all tend to be both less accurate and more biased for recessions than for expansions. Similarly, the forecasts for the above-average growth phases look better than those for the below-average growth phases under both criteria. These results are consistent with the earlier ones showing that large errors tend to cluster around business cycle turns, especially peaks (Zarnowitz 1967 and chapter 14, this volume).

The statement just made is not the same as to say that forecasting failures are due to large unanticipated disturbances. Such shocks can and do occur under any economic conditions, yet they seem to cause large errors mainly during slowdowns and contractions. This may be so because it is in these phases, rather than in vigorous recoveries and strong widespread expansions, that the economy is particularly vulnerable. Various stresses and imbalances accumulate gradually as more and more industries approach high capacity operations. Costs of labor, capital goods, and credit typically rise; here and there prices and profits come under squeeze; real shortages appear, growth weakens, and investment begins to decline. Although these internal developments, if permitted to take their course, could alone bring about a downturn, it is also possible for some adverse shocks to speed up this outcome. Yet the same shocks would probably have been weathered by the economy in a less exposed state. The forecaster faces an extremely difficult problem in that (*a*) it is very difficult to anticipate just when the stresses and imbalances will do their work and (*b*) the timing of true random shocks that matter is always unpredictable, even if their consequences are not.

In addition, predicting a general downturn is always unpopular, and predicting it prematurely ahead of others may prove quite costly to the forecaster and his customers. On the other hand, most users are likely to await eagerly an upturn during a recognized recession, so forecasts of a recovery will be welcome and often accepted on the basis of early signs of improvement. In this context, it should be recalled that early cyclical indicators had in recent times much longer and more variable leads at peaks than at troughs. (However, their signals of the last recovery came relatively early in 1982, which probably induced some forecasters to err in predicting the recovery too soon.) The peak errors show up during the recession and slowdown periods; the generally smaller trough errors show up during the recovery and speedup periods.

Finally, there is the hypothesis that important macroeconomic functions which are approximately linear as long as there is substantial slack in the economy and relative price stability become nonlinear at high levels of employment and capacity utilization with rising inflation. Econometric models, it is believed, may not be capable of capturing the nonlinearities sufficiently well and hence would perform worse near the peaks of the cycle than at lower levels of macroeconomic activity (see, e.g., Evans 1974, p. 185). This argument, of course, refers to the endogenous sources of business fluctuations rather than the effects of exogenous disturbances.

18.2.3   Quarterly Multiperiod Forecasts from Econometric Services, Business Outlook Surveys, and Time-Series Models

Predicting the developments within the next year or two by quarters is far more difficult than predicting how the economy will fare from year to year. Errors of the forecasts for consecutive quarters typically offset each other to some degree within any year. Also, forecasts for the year ahead can be satisfactory when based on a good record for the first two quarters, and they tend to be more accurate than forecasts with effective spans longer than two quarters (see chapter 14).

However, there is much demand for frequent and detailed predictions, and forecasters have responded by producing quarterly or even monthly forecasts for sequences of 4–8 quarters ahead. The ambitious tendency to disaggregate forecasts over time as well as over space received much support from the falling computation costs in the 1960s and 1970s. With few exceptions, the macroeconometric models now regularly used in commercial forecasting are large, and in several well-known cases, very large.

The great expansion of the models led to expectations of dependably good forecasts, which however met with frequent disappointments. Soon the theoretical basis of the conventional macro models came under sharp attack (Lucas 1976) and some critics proceeded to challenge them with forecasts from vector autoregressive (VAR) models (Sims 1980b).

In econometric forecasting, exogenous variables are projected outside the model, and the model outputs of endogenous variables are as a rule subjected to judgmental adjustments. In contrast, there are no exogenous variables in the VAR models: each of the selected variables is predicted by regression on its own lagged values and those of the others. In the unconstrained model, the only use of economic theory and judgment is in choosing the variables. Since several lags are used for each variable in each equation, the number of variables that the model can accommodate is small. The forecasting process is mechanical and replicable, involving no judgment on the part of the model user.

In practice, this low-cost approach frequently confronts the difficulty of having to estimate many parameters from limited amounts of data with measurement errors. To avoid overfitting and improve forecasts, constraints on the coefficients are imposed in the so-called Bayesian vector autoregressions (BVAR) with the aid of the model builder's prior distributions concerning stochastic properties of the processes and lags involved (Litterman 1986).

In recent years, the autoregressive integrated moving-average (ARIMA) approach has also been used to forecast selected aggregative variables (Nelson 1972, 1984). Univariate ARIMA models require less simple statistical techniques and computer programs than VAR and more experienced judgment.

They, of course, capture neither the signals nor the noise from the multivariate interactions that are involved in the application of the VAR models.

Table 18.3 draws on recent studies (Lupoletti and Webb 1986; McNees 1986) to compare the performance of these time-series models with several econometric service bureaus and group forecasts from business outlook surveys. To concentrate on the evolution over time, the reported statistics on the root mean square errors (RMSE) are expressed at annual rates and averaged across the forecast horizons for various periods between 1970 and 1985. In addition to these absolute measures of average accuracy (part A), RMSE ratios are used to measure the accuracy of the forecasts relative to that of the corresponding VAR and BVAR projections (part B).

Comparing the periods 1970–75, 1975–80, and 1980–83 (cols. 4–6), one finds rises in the RMSEs for the econometric bureaus' forecasts of GNP, RGNP, and TBR (see lines 1–3, 8–10, and 22–24). But measures from another compilation show the forecasts for GNP and RGNP having smaller average errors in 1980–85 than in 1980–83 (cf. cols. 6 and 10). For inflation, the largest errors are found in 1970–75 and the smallest in 1975–80, but there the differences over time are comparatively small (lines 15–17). Forecasts made within two quarters from business cycle turning points show relatively large RMSEs throughout (col. 9). The large average errors of 1980:4–1983:4 reflect mainly the unexpectedly sharp and long business contraction of 1981–82.

A simple VAR model (see table 18.3, n. *b*) performed generally worse than the econometric services in the early and late 1970s but better in the early 1980s, for both GNP and RGNP.[3] However, the VAR forecasts for inflation were the best in 1970–75, among the best in 1980–83, and the worst in 1975–80. The VAR predictions of interest rates compare poorly with the others in 1970–75 and favorably with others in 1975–80. Around the turning points, and overall, VAR did on the whole not much worse than the econometricians, despite their much more complex and expensive procedures (see the corresponding entries in cols. 3–6 and 9, parts A and B).

The ARIMA and BVAR models also produce mixed results but appear to be more or less competitive with the other forecasters. Judging from the average RMSE ratios, they outperformed VAR in four out of seven cases (cols. 7 and 8).

The last column in table 18.3 sums up some accuracy comparisons of BVAR with econometric and survey forecasts, based on a study by McNees (1986). Litterman has been making BVAR predictions monthly since 1980

---

3. The VAR model was estimated for the period 1952:2–1969:4, and the obtained coefficients and predictions were then used to forecast each variable for 1970:1–1971:2; this procedure was repeated starting with each successive quarter to produce forecasts with horizons of 1–6 quarters for 1970:1–1983:4. Thus the results are postsample predictions comparable in this respect to the authentic ex ante forecasts. However, the data used in the VAR computations were the latest revised estimates available to the authors, whereas the econometric services used of course the preliminary estimates available at the time of the forecast. This could well bias the comparisons in favor of VAR, but there is some evidence that this is not the case (Lupoletti and Webb 1986, table 1 and pp. 267–69).

Table 18.3   Average Accuracy of Econometric and Other Forecasting Services versus Extrapolations from Time-Series Models, 1970–1985 and Subperiods

A. Measures of Absolute Accuracy

Root Mean Square Errors (RMSE)[a]

Line (1)	Forecaster[b] (2)	1970:4 to 1983:4[c] (3)	1970:4 to 1975:1[d] (4)	1975:2 to 1980:3 (5)	1980:4 to 1983:4 (6)	1976:2 to 1982:4[e] (7)	1980:3 to 1983:4[f] (8)	Around Turning Points[g] (9)	1980:2 to 1985:1[h] (10)
				Growth Rate of Gross National Product (GNP)					
1	Chase	4.0	2.3	4.0	5.4			4.4	4.3
2	DRI	3.5	2.3	3.0	5.0			4.0	3.9
3	Wharton	3.6	2.7	3.0	4.9			4.2	4.2
4	ANB								3.8
5	VAR	4.3	4.9	3.8	4.3	4.6	4.5	4.1	
6	ARIMA					4.8			
7	BVAR						5.0		4.3
				Growth Rate of Real GNP (RGNP)					
8	Chase	3.0	2.4	2.8	3.8			3.4	3.0
9	DRI	3.0	3.0	2.5	3.6			3.6	2.8
10	Wharton	2.8	2.7	2.5	3.2			3.3	2.7
11	ANB								3.0
12	VAR	3.6	4.3	3.2	3.4	3.5	3.5	3.9	
13	ARIMA					3.4			
14	BVAR						2.6		2.3
				Rate of Inflation in the GNP Implicit Price Deflator (IPD)					
15	Chase	2.6	2.6	1.7	2.0			2.3	1.9
16	DRI	2.1	2.8	1.6	1.8			2.3	1.8
17	Wharton	2.0	2.4	1.6	1.9			2.0	2.0
18	ANB								1.4
19	VAR	2.2	2.0	2.3	1.8	2.0	2.4	2.5	
20	ARIMA					1.8			
21	BVAR						3.5		3.3
				90-Day Treasury Bill Rate (TBR)					
22	Chase	2.5	1.6	2.4	3.3			2.7	2.6
23	DRI	2.3	1.5	1.9	3.4			2.6	3.0
24	Wharton	n.a.	n.a.	2.2	3.0			n.a.	3.0
25	VAR	2.4	2.1	1.8	3.6		3.6	2.8	
26	BVAR						3.3		3.2

B. Measures of Relative Accuracy

		RMSE Ratios (RMSE − VAR = 100)[i]							RMSE − BVAR = 100[j]
Line (1)	Forecaster (2)	1970:4 to 1983:4 (3)	1970:4 to 1975:1 (4)	1975:2 to 1980:3 (5)	1980:4 to 1983:4 (6)	1976:2 to 1982:4 (7)	1980:3 to 1983:4 (8)	Around Turning Points (9)	1980:2 to 1985:1 (10)
				GNP					
27	Chase	0.93	0.47	1.05	1.26			1.07	1.00
28	DRI	0.81	0.47	0.79	1.16			0.98	0.91
29	Wharton	0.84	0.55	0.79	1.14			1.02	0.98

(continued)

Table 18.3   Continued

B. Measures of Relative Accuracy

		RMSE Ratios (RMSE − VAR = 100)[i]							RMSE − BVAR = 100[j]
Line (1)	Forecaster (2)	1970:4 to 1983:4 (3)	1970:4 to 1975:1 (4)	1975:2 to 1980:3 (5)	1980:4 to 1983:4 (6)	1976:2 to 1982:4 (7)	1980:3 to 1983:4 (8)	Around Turning Points (9)	1980:2 to 1985:1 (10)
					GNP				
30	ANB								0.93
31	ARIMA					1.04			
32	BVAR						1.11		
					RGNP				
33	Chase	0.83	0.56	0.88	1.12			0.87	1.30
34	DRI	0.83	0.70	0.78	1.06			0.92	1.22
35	Wharton	0.78	0.63	0.78	0.94			0.85	1.17
36	ANB								1.25
17	ARIMA					0.97			
38	BVAR						0.74		
					IPD				
39	Chase	1.18	1.30	0.74	1.11			0.92	0.58
40	DRI	0.95	1.40	0.70	1.00			0.92	0.55
41	Wharton	0.91	1.20	0.70	1.06			0.80	0.61
42	ANB								0.50
43	ARIMA					0.90			
44	BVAR						1.46		
					TBR				
45	Chase	1.04	0.76	1.33	0.92			0.96	0.81
46	DRI	1.05	0.71	1.06	0.94			0.93	0.93
47	Wharton	n.a.	n.a.	1.22	0.83			n.a.	
48	BVAR						0.92		

Sources: Cols. 3–9: Lupoletti and Webb 1986, tables 2–8; col. 10: McNees 1986, tables 1, 2, 5, and 6.

[a]Averaged across forecast horizons as follows: cols. 3–6, 8, and 9, means of RMSE for horizons of 1, 2, 4, and 6 quarters; col. 7, means for horizons of 1, 2, and 4 quarters; col. 10, means for horizons of 1–8 quarters.

[b]VAR = unrestricted vector autoregressive model with six lags for each of five variables (percentage changes in the monetary base, RGNP, and IPD; the manufacturing-capacity utilization rate; and the 90-day TBR); see Webb 1984 and Lupoletti and Webb 1986. ARIMA = univariate autoregressive integrated moving-average model (Nelson 1972, 1984). BVAR = Bayesian vector autoregressive model with six lags for each of seven variables (annual growth rates of RGNP and IPD; UR; lagged levels of the money supply MI and of gross private domestic investment; 4–6 month commercial paper rate and the change in business inventories); see Litterman 1986. The BVAR model used in 1980–1983 (col. 7) consists of six variables (it does not contain the inventory series and uses real business fixed investment instead of GPDI). On the sources of the other forecasts, see references in notes to tables 18.1 and 18.2. All underlying data are authentic (postsample) forecasts measured at annual rates.

[c]The dates are for 1-quarter forecasts; 2-quarter forecasts: 1971:1–1983:4; 4-quarter forecasts: 1971:3–1983:4; 6-quarter forecasts: 1972:1–1983:4.

[d]The dates are for 1-quarter forecasts; see n. c on the starting dates for 2-; 4-; and 6-quarter forecasts.

[e]The dates are for 1-quarter forecasts; 2-quarter forecasts: 1976:3–1982:4; 4-quarter forecasts: 1977:1–1982:4.

Table 18.3   Continued

*f*The dates are for 1-quarter forecasts; 2-quarter forecasts: 1980:4–1983:4; 4-quarter forecasts: 1981:2–1983:4; 6-quarter forecasts: 1981:4–1983:4.

*g*Covers forecasts made within 2 quarters from a business cycle turning point (NBER dates). For periods covered, see n. *c*.

*h*Dates show the forecast period covered. The RMSE entries are in percentage points, cumulative growth at annual rates (GNP, RGNP, IPD) and in percentage points, cumulative changes (TBR). Chase, DRI, and Wharton are "early-quarter" forecasts; ANB are "midquarter" forecasts. BVAR are based on data available early in each quarter. The BVAR predictions based on data as of midquarter and comparable to ANB are GNP, 4.1; RGNP, 2.4; IPD, 2.8.

*i*Based on entries in part A, cols. 3–9. Ratios of RMSE of other forecasts to the corresponding RMSE of VAR.

*j*Based on entries in part A, col. 10. Ratios of RMSE of other forecasts to the corresponding RMSE of BVAR. The BVAR figures used in the ratios for Chase, DRI, and Wharton are those in lines 7, 14, 21, and 26. For the BVAR figures used in the ratios for ANB, see n. *h*.

(see table 18.3, n. *b*). Real growth was predicted much better by his model than by the other forecasters in 1980–85, but inflation was predicted much worse.

With respect to differences by forecast horizon (which are ignored in table 18.3), pairwise comparisons of the RMSEs for each VAR with each model suggest that the relative performance of VAR improved with the length of forecast. Cases in which VAR had smaller RMSEs than the other forecasts account for 24%, 25%, 42%, and 42% of all comparisons for horizons of one, two, four, and six quarters, respectively. Pairwise comparisons with BVAR show that each of the forecasters included in table 18.3 had smaller RMSEs for IPD and TRB at all horizons. The reverse obtains for RGNP, where BVAR produced the best results in half of the shortest and all of the longer forecasts. For GNP, BVAR was worst in each case over horizons of 1–4 quarters but better than the others in most of the comparisons for horizons of 6–8 quarters. When more variables and more forecasters are included, BVAR comes out ahead in most of the comparisons for the period 1980:2–1985:1 (see Granger's comment on McNees 1986). Fragmentary results for the more recent years, however, suggest some deterioration. Thus Litterman's BVAR forecasts for 1984:4–1985:4 and 1985:4–1986:4 predicted high growth rates in real GNP and such of its components as durable-goods consumption, gross private domestic investment, and residential construction. The corresponding realizations were much lower in 1985–86. Most forecasters have been much less optimistic than BVAR, and more accurate.[4]

4. The following tabulation compares some of the forecasts from Litterman 1984 with the actual percentage changes for 1985 (fourth quarter over fourth quarter):

	RGNP	C	CD	CNS	GPDI	NRFI	RFI	IPD
BVAR	3.7	4.6	10.0	3.6	6.2	6.1	12.3	3.2
Actual	2.9	3.5	6.2	3.1	0.5	6.6	7.8	3.3

18.3   Conclusion, Implications, and Further Thoughts

There is no evidence, here or elsewhere, that macroeconomic forecasts in the United States have grown systematically worse, that is, less accurate, more biased, or both. Rather this paper argues and to some extent documents that the failures of forecasting are related to the incidence of slowdowns and contractions in general economic activity. Not only the forecasts of real GNP growth and unemployment but also those of nominal GNP growth and inflation tend to go seriously wrong when such setbacks occur. This result seems strong, though qualitatively not surprising: it confirms and extends earlier indications of typically large turning-point errors.

The question that naturally arises at this point is, do such findings have useful lessons for producers and users of macroeconomic forecasts? It is clear that forecasters cannot afford to wait for long expansions to prove the usefulness of their own activities. Instead, as our results demonstrate, there is urgent need for the forecast makers to increase their ability to anticipate the retardations and declines in aggregate demand, output, and employment—and for forecast users to pay particular attention to such efforts and reward any resulting successes.

To be sure, all this is much easier said than done, but it seems highly probable that economic forecasting can be improved to some degree and that we are far from having reached the limits of this process. After all, macroforecasting as an explicit activity put to practical uses, yielding recorded and testable results, and subject to the disciplines of market and research is very young indeed. New and useful insights will not come easy here but will be achieved, and new methods and new applications of old methods are being developed continually.

The four active, broad approaches to short-term forecasting of the economy at large are time-series models, econometric models, anticipations surveys, and cyclical indicators. Each of these corresponds to a particular aspect of the entire task. Thus, time-series models are best equipped to exploit intensively the information contained in the past history of the single or several series to be predicted; macroeconometric models, to quantify the predominant relationships that the theory suggests exist among a larger (but not overly large) number of variables; anticipation surveys, to estimate aggregates of plans or intentions of economic agents for variables over which these agents exercise considerable control; and the indicators, to signal and confirm certain recurrent business cycle events. These are distinct but interrelated functions. In the present practice, none of them is performed very well because of paucity of generally agreed upon and successfully tested economic theories that would

---

C, CD, and CNS denote the percentage changes in real consumption for total, durables, and nondurables and services. GPDI, NFRI, and RFI denote percentage changes in total (gross private domestic), nonresidential fixed, and residential fixed investment.

provide strict guidance for macromodeling and because of inadequacies of the available data, estimation, and surveying techniques. Yet there are significant advantages to using each class of models or methods for the task to which it is best suited. In short, contrary to some partisan assertions and criticisms, the four approaches are essentially complements, not competitors or substitutes. They need to be refined and used in combination so as to contribute to the improvement of the forecasts.

To illustrate, the blending of time-series analytic and traditional econometric methods can result in better selection and projection of exogenous variables. The devices to be used for this purpose are tests for exogeneity and extrapolations based on full information contained in the past history of the series to be predicted and related forward-looking data (e.g., for federal government purchases, recent congressional appropriations and debates). Further, time-series models can be constructed for, and applied to, the residual errors from econometric equations as these terms are often far from being purely random. The transfer functions which thus combine regression with time-series models would be expected to have greater predictive power than either type of model alone.[5]

Similarly, consistency with the lessons from anticipated surveys and sequences of leading, coincident, and lagging indicators should enhance the usefulness of any macroforecasting model. Probably the best way to achieve this objective is to include the relationships involving the principal survey data and indicators directly in the model. To mention just one important area, promising because of strong elements of executive planning and long gestation periods, forecasting business expenditures for new plant and equipment should draw on surveys of backlogged and newly approved capital appropriations, surveys of anticipated expenditures, construction contracts for plant buildings, and new orders of nondefense capital goods industries.

The long record of leading indicators in predicting business cycle turning points is encouraging. With the aid of suitable time-series analytic transformations and decision rules, it should be possible to reach considerably better results yet in this respect. The main practical problem for this approach lies in false signals; the errors of the other type—missed turns—are rare and relatively unimportant. To reduce the risk of false warnings, a system of sequential signals from both leading and confirming indicators has been proposed and tested with generally positive results (Zarnowitz and Moore 1982 with an update in Moore 1983; Niemira 1983). Predictions with the composite index or vector of selected leading indicators can improve on autoregressive forecasts of changes in real GNP, industrial production, and the rate of unemploy-

5. On time-series analysis and econometric models, see Zellner and Palm 1974; on transfer functions, with applications, Pindyck and Rubinfeld 1981; on exogeneity tests, Granger 1969 and Sims 1972. On further developments and the more radical and controversial "index models" (using restricted VARs for business cycle analysis), see the collection of papers and comments in Sims 1977.

ment (Vaccara and Zarnowitz 1978; Auerbach 1982). Signals of cyclical downturns from the leading index can take into account estimated probability distributions of phase durations and percentage changes in the index (Neftçi 1982, Palash and Radecki 1985).

Of particular interest is a technique which combines time-series models with Monte Carlo simulations to generate repeated sample paths of the predicted series and probability distributions over the relevant turning points (Wecker 1979). This analysis has recently been extended to multivariate models for related indicator series, with explicit assessments of uncertainty in the estimates and of turning-point probabilities (Kling 1986).

To conclude, forecasters tend to rely heavily on the persistence of trends in spending, output, and the price level. To the extent that inertia prevails in the economy's movement, their predictions turn out to be roughly right, at least directionally, most of the time. But the inertia, although helpful in this sense, is only a part of the story, and such forecasts suffer from missing business cycle turns and underestimating recessions and recoveries with respect to both their real and nominal effects. These errors are only in part due to the impact of the many inevitable random disturbances to the economy that cannot be anticipated. Although variable in their observed durations and amplitudes, the expansions and contractions in the major economic aggregates, both in levels and deviations from long-term trends, show many important recurrent features. These regularities, as reflected in the relative movements of cyclical indicators, should and can be better captured in the work of macroeconomic forecasters.

References

Abel, A. B. 1980. Empirical investment equations: An integrative framework. In Brunner and Meltzer 1980.

Abel, A. B., and O. J. Blanchard. 1983. The present value of profits and cyclical movements of investment. NBER Working Paper no. 1122, May. Published in *Econometrica* 54 (1986): 249–73.

Abraham, K., and L. F. Katz. 1986. Cyclical unemployment: Sectoral shifts or aggregate disturbances? *J. Polit. Econ.* 94(June):507–22.

Abramovitz, M. 1950. *Inventories and business cycles, with special reference to manufacturers' inventories.* New York: NBER.

———. 1964. *Evidences of long swings in aggregate construction since the Civil War.* New York: NBER.

———. 1968. The passing of the Kuznets cycle. *Economica,* n.s. 35(November):349–67.

———. 1986. Comment. In Gordon 1986a.

Adams, F. G. 1986. *The business forecasting revolution: Nation-industry-firm.* New York: Oxford University Press.

Adams, F. G., and V. G. Duggal. 1974. Anticipations variables in an econometric model: Performance of the anticipations version of Wharton Mark III. *Internat. Econ. Rev.* 15(2):267–84. Reprinted in Klein and Burmeister 1976.

Adelman, I. 1965. Long cycles: Fact or artifact? *Amer. Econ. Rev.* 55:444–63.

———. 1972. Discussion. In Hickman 1972.

Adelman, I., and F. L. Adelman. 1959. The dynamic properties of the Klein-Goldberger model. *Econometrica* 27:596–625.

Aftalion, Albert. 1913. *Les crises périodiques de surproduction.* Paris: Rivière.

Aiginger, K. 1979. Empirische Informationen zur Bildung von Erwartungen. *Ifo-Studien* 25:83–135.

———. 1981. Empirical surveyed expectational data and decision theory. Paper presented at the 15th CIRET Conference, Athens. (Summary in *International research in business cycle surveys,* ed. H. Laumer and M. Ziegler. Aldershot, England: Gower Publishing, 1982.)

Akerlof, G. A., and J. L. Yellen. 1985. A near-rational model of the business cycle, with wage and price inertia. *Quart. J. Econ.* 100, suppl.: 823–38.

Alchian, A. A. 1969. Information costs, pricing, and resource unemployment. *Western Econ. J.* 7(June):109–28.

Alexander, S. S. 1958. Rate of change approaches to forecasting: Diffusion indexes and first differences. *Econ. J.* 68:288–301.

Alexander, S. S., and H. O. Stekler. 1959. Forecasting industrial production: Leading series versus autoregression. *J. Polit. Econ.* 67:402–9.

Allais, M. 1966. A restatement of the quantity theory of money. *Amer. Econ. Rev.* 56 (December): 1123–57.

————. 1972. Forgetfulness and interest. *J. Money, Credit, Banking* 4(1), pt. 1:40–73.

Almon, C. 1966. *The American economy to 1975: An interindustry forecast.* New York: Harper & Row.

Almon, S. 1965. The distributed lag between capital appropriations and expenditures. *Econometrica* 33:178–96.

Alt, J. E., and K. A. Chrystal. 1983. *Political economics.* Berkeley and Los Angeles: University of California Press.

Altonji, J. G. 1982. The intertemporal substitution model of labour market fluctuations: An empirical analysis. *Rev. Econ. Stud.* 49:783–824.

Altonji, J. G., and O. Ashenfelter. 1980. Wage movements and the labor market equilibrium hypothesis. *Economica,* n.s. 47:217–45.

Amihud, Y., and H. Mendelson. 1983. Price smoothing and inventory. *Rev. Econ. Stud.* 50(1):87–98.

Andersen, L. C., and K. M. Carlson. 1970. A monetarist model for economic stabilization. *Federal Reserve Bank of St. Louis Rev.* 52(April):7–25.

Andersen, L. C., and J. L. Jordan. 1968. Monetary and fiscal actions: A test of their relative importance in economic stabilization. *Federal Reserve Bank of St. Louis Rev.* 50(November):11–23.

————. 1969. Reply. *Federal Reserve Bank of St. Louis Rev.* 51(April):12–16.

Andersen, P. S. 1989. *Inflation and output: A review of the wage-price mechanism.* Basle: Bank for International Settlements, Monetary and Economic Department.

Ando, A., and F. Modigliani. 1963. The "life cycle" hypothesis of saving: Aggregate implications and tests. *Amer. Econ. Rev.* 53(March):55–84.

————. 1969. Econometric analysis of stabilization policies. *Amer. Econ. Rev.* 59(May):296–314.

Armstrong, J. S. 1978. *Long-range forecasting: From crystal ball to computer.* New York: Wiley & Sons.

Arrow, K. J. 1973. *Information and economic behavior.* Stockholm: Federation of Swedish Industries.

————. 1974. Limited knowledge and economic analysis. *Amer. Econ. Rev.* 64(1):1–10.

————. 1978. The future and the present in economic life. *Econ. Inquiry* 16:157–69.

Auerbach, A. 1982. The index of leading economic indicators: "Measurement without theory," thirty-five years later. *Rev. Econ. Statis.* 64(4):589–95.

Axe, E. W., and R. Houghton. 1931. Financial and business cycles, manufacturing growth, and analysis of individual industries, 1883–1930. *Annalist,* 16 January 1931, 150–51.

Ayres, L. P. 1939. *Turning points in business cycles.* New York: Macmillan.

Azariadis, C. 1975. Implicit contracts and underemployment equilibria. *J. Polit. Econ.* 83:1183–1202.

————. 1981. Self-fulfilling prophecies. *J. Econ. Theory* 25:380–96.

Backus, D. K., and P. J. Kehoe. 1988. International evidence on the historical properties of business cycles. Paper presented at McGill Macroeconomic Conference, "Approaches to the Business Cycle," March, Montreal.

Baily, M. N. 1974. Wages and employment under uncertain demand. *Rev. Econ. Stud.* 41:37–50.

————. 1978. Stabilization policy and private economic behavior. *Brookings Pap. Econ. Act.* 1:11–59.

Balke, N. S., and R. J. Gordon. 1986a. The estimation of prewar GNP volatility, 1869–1938. NBER Working Paper no. 1999, August.

———. 1986b. Historical data. In Gordon 1986a.

———. 1989. The estimation of prewar gross national product: Methodology and new evidence. *J. Polit. Econ.* 97(1):38–92.

Ball, L., N. G. Mankiw, and D. Romer. 1988. The new Keynesian economics and the output-inflation trade-off. *Brookings Pap. Econ. Act.* 1:1–82.

Barger, H., and L. R. Klein. 1954. A quarterly model for the United States economy. *J. Amer. Statis. Assoc.* 49:413–37.

Barnea, A., A. Dotan, and J. Lakonishok. 1979. The effect of price level uncertainty on the determination of nominal interest rates: Some empirical evidence. *Southern Econ. J.* 46:609–14.

Barnett, W. A., J. Geweke, and K. Shell, eds. 1989. *Economic complexity: Chaos, sunspots, bubbles, and nonlinearity.* Proceedings of the Fourth International Symposium in Economic Theory and Econometrics. Cambridge: Cambridge University Press.

Barro, R. J. 1976. Rational expectations and the role of monetary policy. *J. Monet. Econ.* 2:1–32.

———. 1977a. Long term contracting, sticky prices, and monetary policy. *J. Monet. Econ.* 3:305–16.

———. 1977b. Unanticipated money growth and unemployment in the United States. *Amer. Econ. Rev.* 67:101–15.

———. 1978. Unanticipated money, output, and the price level in the United States. *J. Polit. Econ.* 86:549–80.

———. 1980. A capital market in an equilibrium business cycle model. *Econometrica* 48:1393–1417.

———. 1981a. The equilibrium approach to business cycles. In *Money, expectations, and business cycles,* ed. R. J. Barro. New York: Academic Press.

———. 1981b. Intertemporal substitution and the business cycle. In Brunner and Meltzer 1981b.

———. 1987. *Macroeconomics.* 4th ed. New York: Wiley.

Barro, R. J., and Z. Hercovitz. 1980. Money stock revisions and unanticipated money growth. *J. Monet. Econ.* 6:257–67.

Barro, R. J., and M. Rush. 1980. Unanticipated money and economic activity. In Fischer 1980.

Barsky, R. B., N. G. Mankiw, J. A. Miron, and D. N. Weil. 1988. The worldwide change in behavior of interest rates and prices in 1914. *Europ. Econ. Rev.* 32(5):1123–47.

Bassie, V. L. 1958. *Economic forecasting.* New York: McGraw-Hill.

Batchelor, R., and P. Dua. 1990. Forecaster ideology, forecasting technique, and the accuracy of economic forecasts. *Internat. J. Forecasting* 6(1):3–10.

Bates, J. M., and C. W. J. Granger. 1969. The combination of forecasts. *Operations Res. Quart.* 20:451–68.

Becker, G. S. 1962. Irrational behavior and economic theory. *J. Polit. Econ.* 70: 1–13.

Begg, D. K. H. 1982. *The rational expectations revolution in macroeconomics: Theories and evidence.* Baltimore: Johns Hopkins University Press.

Berle, A. A., and G. Means. 1932. *The modern corporation and private property.* New York: Macmillan.

Bernanke, B. S. 1981. Bankruptcy, liquidity, and recession. *Amer. Econ. Rev.* 71(May):155–59.

———. 1982. Adjustment costs, durables, and aggregate consumption. NBER Working Paper no. 1038. Published in *J. Monet. Econ.* 15(1)(1985):41–68.

————. 1983. Nonmonetary effects of the financial crisis in the propagation of the great depression. *Amer. Econ. Rev.* 73(3):257–76.

————. 1986. Alternative explanations of the money-income correlation. In Brunner and Meltzer 1986.

Bernanke, B. S., and J. L. Powell. 1986. The cyclical behavior of industrial labor markets: A comparison of the prewar and postwar eras. In Gordon 1986a.

Beveridge, S., and C. R. Nelson. 1981. A new approach to decomposition of economic time series into permanent and transitory components with particular attention to measurement of the "business cycle." *J. Monet. Econ.* 7:151–74.

Bils, M. 1985. Real wages over the business cycle: Evidence from panel data. *J. Polit. Econ.* 93(4):666–89.

Bilson, J. F. O. 1980. The rational expectations approach to the consumption function: A multi-country study. *Europ. Econ. Rev.* 13:273–99, 301–8.

Bischoff, C. W. 1971. Business investment in the 1970s: A comparison of models. *Brookings Pap. Econ. Act.* 1:13–63.

————. 1989. The combination of macroeconomic forecasts. *J. Forecasting* 8:293–314.

Black, F. 1982. General equilibrium and business cycles. NBER Working Paper no. 950.

————. 1987. *Business cycles and equilibrium.* New York: Blackwell.

Blanchard, O. J. 1981. What is left of the multiplier-accelerator? *Amer. Econ. Rev.* 71(May):150–54.

————. 1985. Debt, deficits and finite horizons. *J. Polit. Econ.* 93(2):223–47.

————. 1986. Comment (on Hall 1986). *Brookings Pap. Econ. Act.* 2:323–28.

————. 1987a. Aggregate and individual price adjustment. *Brookings Pap. Econ. Act.* 1:57–109.

————. 1987b. Why does money affect output? A survey. NBER Working Paper no. 2285, June. Published in *Handbook of Monetary Economics,* vol. 2, eds. B. M. Friedman and F. H. Hahn. Amsterdam: North-Holland, 1990.

Blanchard, O. J., and S. Fischer, eds. 1989. *NBER macroeconomics annual 1989.* Cambridge, Mass.: MIT Press.

Blanchard, O. J., and N. Kiyotaki. 1987. Monopolistic competition and the effects of aggregate demand. *Amer. Econ. Rev.* 77(4):647–66.

Blanchard, O. J., and D. Quah. 1989. The dynamic effects of aggregate demand and supply disturbances. *Amer. Econ. Rev.* 79(4):655–73.

Blanchard, O. J., and L. H. Summers. 1986. Hysteresis and the European unemployment problem. In Fischer 1986.

————. 1987a. Fiscal increasing returns, hysteresis, real wages, and unemployment. *Europ. Econ. Rev.* 31(3):543–60.

————. 1987b. Hysteresis in unemployment. *Europ. Econ. Rev.* 31(1–2):288–95.

Blanchard, O. J., and M. W. Watson. 1982. Bubbles, rational expectations, and financial markets. In *Crises in the economic and financial structure,* ed. P. Wachtel. Lexington, Mass.: Lexington Books.

————. 1986. Are business cycles all alike? In Gordon 1986a.

Blanchard, O. J., and C. Wyplosz. 1981. An empirical structural model of aggregate demand. *J. Monet. Econ.* 7:1–28.

Blatt, J. M. 1978. On the econometric approach to business-cycle analysis. *Oxford Econ. Pap.,* n.s. 30:292–300.

————. 1980. On the Frisch model of business cycles. *Oxford Econ. Pap.,* n.s. 32:467–79.

————. 1983. *Dynamic economic systems: A post-Keynesian approach.* Armonk, N.Y.: M. E. Sharpe.

Blinder, A. S. 1979. *Economic policy and the great stagflation.* New York: Academic Press.

―――. 1986. Keynes after Lucas. *Eastern Econ. J.* 12(3):209–16.

―――. 1991. Why are prices sticky? Preliminary results from an interview study. *Amer. Econ. Rev.* 81(2):89–96.

Blinder, A. S., and S. Fischer. 1981. Inventories, rational expectations, and the business cycle. *J. Monet. Econ.* 8:277–304.

Blinder, A. S., and D. Holtz-Eakin. 1981. Temporary income taxes and consumer spending. *J. Polit. Econ.* 89(1):26–53.

―――. 1986. Inventory fluctuations in the United States since 1929. In Gordon 1986a.

Blinder, A. S., and J. E. Stiglitz. 1983. Money, credit constraints, and economic activity. *Amer. Econ. Rev.* 73:297–302.

Bober, S. 1968. *The economics of cycles and growth.* New York: Wiley.

Bodkin, R. A. 1969. Real wages and cyclical variations in employment: A reexamination of the evidence. *Canadian J. Econ.* 2:353–74.

Boehm, E. A. 1990. Understanding business cycles: A critical review of theory and fact. In P. A. Klein 1990.

Bomberger, W. A., and W. J. Frazer, Jr. 1981. Interest rates, uncertainty, and the Livingston data. *J. Finance,* June, 661–75.

Bordo, M. D. 1984. Some historical evidence, 1870–1933, on the impact and international transmission of financial crises. University of South Carolina Working Paper. Mimeo.

Boschan, C., and A. Banerji. 1990. A reassessment of composite indexes. In P. A. Klein 1990.

Boschan, C., and W. W. Ebanks. 1978. The phase-average trend: A new way of measuring growth. In *1978 proceedings of the Business and Economic Statistics Section.* Washington, D.C.: American Statistical Association.

Boschan, C., and G. H. Moore. 1990. A new monthly indicator of profit margins. In Moore 1990, chap. 5.

Boschen, J. F., and H. I. Grossman. 1982. Tests of equilibrium macroeconomics using contemporaneous monetary data. *J. Monet. Econ.* 10:309–33.

Box, G. E. P., and G. M. Jenkins. 1976. *Time series analysis, forecasting, and control.* San Francisco: Holden-Day.

Box, G. E. P., and D. A. Pierce. 1970. Distribution of residual autocorrelations in autoregressive-integrated moving average time series models. *J. Amer. Statis. Assoc.* 65(December):1509–26.

Brady, D. S., and R. D. Friedman. 1947. *Savings and the income distribution.* Studies in Income and Wealth, vol. 10. New York: NBER.

Brainard, W. 1967. Uncertainty and the effectiveness of policy. *Amer. Econ. Rev.* 57:411–25.

Branson, W., and J. Rotemberg. 1980. International adjustment with wage rigidities. *Europ. Econ. Rev.* 13(3):309–32.

Bratt, E. C. 1958. *Business forecasting.* New York: McGraw-Hill.

―――. 1961. *Business cycles and forecasting.* Homewood, Ill.: Irwin.

Braun, P., and S. Mittnik. 1985. Structural analysis with vector auto-regressive models: Some experimental evidence. Washington University in St. Louis Working Paper no. 84.

Bray, M. 1983. Convergence to rational expectations equilibrium. In Frydman and Phelps 1983.

Brenner, M., and Y. Landskroner. 1983. Inflation uncertainties and returns on bonds. *Economica* 50(November):463–68.

Britton, A. 1986. *The trade cycle in Britain, 1958–1982.* Cambridge: Cambridge University Press.

Brock, W. A. 1975. A simple perfect foresight monetary model. *J. Monet. Econ.* 1:133–50.

Bronfenbrenner, M., ed. 1969. *Is the business cycle obsolete?* New York: Wiley-Interscience.

Bronfenbrenner, M., and F. D. Holzman. 1963. Survey of inflation theory. *Amer. Econ. Rev.* 53(4):593–661.

Brooks, S., and D. Gigante. [1979] 1981. Stability in the U.S. economy: 1948 to 1978. *Data Resources Rev.*, November. Reprinted in Sanderson 1981.

Brunner, K., ed. 1981. *The Great Depression revisited.* Boston: Martinus Nijhoff.

Brunner, K., A. Cukierman, and A. H. Meltzer. 1980. Stagflation, persistent unemployment, and the permanence of economic shocks. *J. Monet. Econ.* 6:467–92.

Brunner, K., and A. H. Meltzer. 1968. Liquidity traps for money, bank credit, and interest rates. *J. Polit. Econ.* 76:1–37.

———. 1972. Friedman's monetary theory. *J. Polit. Econ.* 80:837–51.

———., eds. 1976. *The Phillips curve and labor markets.* Carnegie-Rochester Conference on Public Policy, vol. 1. Amsterdam: North-Holland.

———, eds. 1977. *Stabilization of the domestic and international economy.* Carnegie-Rochester Conference on Public Policy, vol. 5. Amsterdam: North-Holland.

———, eds. 1980. *On the state of macroeconomics.* Carnegie-Rochester Conference on Public Policy, vol. 12. Amsterdam: North-Holland.

———, eds. 1981a. *The costs and consequences of inflation.* Carnegie-Rochester Conference on Public Policy, vol. 15. Amsterdam: North-Holland.

———, eds. 1981b. *Supply shocks, incentives, and national wealth.* Carnegie-Rochester Conference on Public Policy, vol. 14. Amsterdam: North-Holland.

———, eds. 1984. *Essays on macroeconomic implications of financial and labor markets and political processes.* Carnegie-Rochester Conference on Public Policy, vol. 21. Amsterdam: North-Holland.

———, eds. 1985. *Understanding monetary regimes.* Carnegie-Rochester Conference on Public Policy, vol. 22. Amsterdam: North-Holland.

———, eds. 1986. *Real business cycles, real exchange rates, and actual policies.* Carnegie-Rochester Conference on Public Policy, vol. 25. Amsterdam: North-Holland.

Bruno, M., and J. Sachs. 1985. *Economics of worldwide stagflation.* Cambridge, Mass.: Harvard University Press.

Bry, G., and C. Boschan. 1971. *Cyclical analysis of time series: Selected procedures and computer programs.* New York: NBER.

Bullock, C. J., and H. L. Micoleau. 1931. Foreign trade and the business cycle. *Rev. Econ. Statis.* 13(4):138–60.

Bulow, J. I., and L. H. Summers. 1986. A theory of dual labor markets with application to industrial policy, discrimination, and Keynesian unemployment. *J. Labor Econ.* 4:376–414.

Burmeister, E., and L. R. Klein, eds. 1974. Econometric model performance: Comparative simulation studies of models of the U.S. economy. Symposium. *Internat. Econ. Rev.* 15:264–414, 539–653.

Burns, A. F. 1934. *Production trends in the United States since 1870.* New York: NBER.

———. 1946. Economic research and the Keynesian thinking of our times. *26th Annual Report of the NBER*, June, 3–29. Reprinted in Burns 1954.

———. 1950. New facts on business cycles. *30th Annual Report of the NBER*, May, 3–31. Reprinted in Burns 1969.

———. 1952a. Hicks and the real cycle. *J. Polit. Econ.* 60(1):1–24.

———. 1952b. The instability of consumer spending. *32d Annual Report of the NBER*, May, 3–20. Reprinted in Burns 1954.

————. 1953. Business cycle research and the needs of our times. *33d Annual Report of the NBER*, May, 3–16. Reprinted in Burns 1954.

————. 1954. *The frontiers of economic knowledge*. Princeton, N.J.: Princeton University Press for NBER.

————. 1960. Progress towards economic stability. *Amer. Econ. Rev.* 50(March):1–19. Reprinted in Burns 1969.

————. 1968. *International encyclopedia of the social sciences*, s.v. "business cycles." Reprinted in Burns 1969.

————. 1969. *The business cycle in a changing world*. New York: NBER.

Burns, A. F., and W. C. Mitchell. 1946. *Measuring business cycles*. New York: NBER.

Burnside, C., M. Eichenbaum, and S. Rebelo. 1990. Labor hoarding and the business cycle. NBER Working Paper no. 3556, December.

Butler, W. F., and R. A. Kavesh, eds. 1966. *How business economists forecast*. Englewood Cliffs, N.J.: Prentice Hall.

————. [1967] 1974. Judgmental forecasting of the gross national product. In Butler, Kavesh, and Platt 1974.

Butler, W. F., R. A. Kavesh, and R. B. Platt, eds. 1974. *Methods and techniques of business forecasting*. Englewood Cliffs, N.J.: Prentice Hall.

Cagan, P. 1956. The monetary dynamics of hyperinflation. In *Studies in the quantity theory of money*, ed. M. Friedman. Chicago: University of Chicago Press.

————. 1965. *Determinants and effects of changes in the stock of money, 1875–1960*. New York: Columbia University Press for NBER.

————. 1966. *Changes in the cyclical behavior of interest rates*. Occasional Paper no. 100. New York: NBER.

————. 1969. The influence of interest rates on the duration of business cycles. In *Essays on interest rates*, ed. J. M. Guttentag and P. Cagan. New York: Columbia University Press for NBER.

————. 1975. Changes in the recession behavior of wholesale prices in the 1920's and post-world war II. *Explorations in Econ. Res.* 2(1):54–104.

————. 1979. *Persistent inflation: Historical and policy essays*. New York: Columbia University Press.

————. 1990. The leading indicators and monetary aggregates. In P. A. Klein 1990.

Calomiris, C. W., and R. G. Hubbard. 1989. Price flexibility, credit availability, and economic fluctuations: Evidence from the U.S., 1894–1909. *Quart. J. Econ.* 104(August):429–52.

Calvo, G. A. 1978. On the time consistency of optimal policy in a monetary economy. *Econometrica* 46(6):1411–28.

Campbell, J. Y., and N. G. Mankiw. 1987a. Are output fluctuations transitory? *Quart. J. Econ.* 102(November):857–80.

————. 1987b. Permanent and transitory components in macroeconomic fluctuations. *Amer. Econ. Rev.* 77(May):111–17.

Carlson, J. A. 1977. A study of price forecasts. *Annals Econ. and Social Measurement* 6(1):27–56.

Carlton, D. W. 1979. Contracts, price rigidity, and market equilibrium. *J. Polit. Econ.* 87:1034–62.

————. 1983. Equilibrium fluctuations when price and delivery period clear the market. *Bell J. Econ.* 14(2):562–72.

————. 1986. The rigidity of prices. *Amer. Econ. Rev.* 76(4):637–58.

————. 1987. The theory and facts of how markets clear: Is industrial organization valuable for understanding macroeconomics? NBER Working Paper no. 2178, March. Published in *Handbook of industrial organization*, ed. R. Schmalensee and R. Willig. Amsterdam: North-Holland, 1989.

Caskey, J., and S. Fazzari. 1987. Aggregate demand contractions with nominal debt commitments: Is wage flexibility stabilizing? *Econ. Inquiry* 25:583–97.

Cass, D., and K. Shell. 1983. Do sunspots matter? *J. Polit. Econ.* 91:193–227.

Cecchetti, S. 1986. The frequency of price adjustments: A study of newsstand prices of magazines. *J. Econometrics* 31(August):255–74.

Central Statistical Office. 1976. Changes to the cyclical indicator system. *Econ. Trends* 271(May):67–69.

Chang, W. W., and D. J. Smyth. 1971. The existence and persistence of cycles in a non-linear model: Kaldor's 1940 model re-examined. *Rev. Econ. Stud.* 38:37–44.

Childs, G. 1967. *Unfilled orders and inventories: A structural analysis.* Amsterdam: North-Holland.

Chirinko, R. S. 1988. Will "the" neoclassical theory of investment please rise? The general structure of investment models and their implications for tax policy. In *The impact of taxation on business activity*, ed. J. M. Mintz and D. D. Purvis. Proceedings of a conference held at the Conference Centre, Ottawa, 11–13 November 1985. Kingston, Ontario: Queen's University.

Chisholm, R. K., and G. R. Whitaker, Jr. 1971. *Forecasting methods.* Homewood, Ill.: Irwin.

Chong, Y. Y., and D. F. Hendry. 1986. Econometric evaluation of linear macroeconomic models. *Rev. Econ. Stud.* 53:671–90.

Chow, G. C. 1960. Test of equality between sets of coefficients in two linear regressions. *Econometrica* 28(July):591–605.

Chow, G. C., and An-loh Lin. 1971. Best linear unbiased interpolation, distribution, and extrapolation of time series by related series. *Rev. Econ. Statis.* 53(November):372–76.

Chow, G. C., and G. H. Moore. 1972. An econometric model of business cycles. In Hickman 1972.

Christ, C. F. 1956. Aggregate econometric models: A review article. *Amer. Econ. Rev.* 46:385–408.

———. 1968. *International encyclopedia of the social sciences,* s.v. "econometric models, aggregate."

———. 1975. Judging the performance of econometric models of the U.S. economy. *Internat. Econ. Rev.* 16(1):54–74.

Clark, C. 1949. A system of equations explaining the United States trade cycle, 1921 to 1941. *Econometrica* 17:93–124.

Clark, J. J. 1969. *The management of forecasting.* New York: St. John's University Press.

Clark, J. M. 1917. Business acceleration and the law of demand: A technical factor in economic cycles. *J. Polit. Econ.* 25:217–35.

———. 1934. *Strategic factors in business cycles.* New York: NBER.

Clark, K. B., and L. H. Summers. 1979. Labor market dynamics and unemployment: A reconsideration. *Brookings Pap. Econ. Act.* 1:13–60.

———. 1982. Labor force participation: Timing and persistence. *Rev. Econ. Stud.* 49:825–44.

Clark, P. K. 1979. Investment in the 1970's: Theory, performance, and prediction. *Brookings Pap. Econ. Act.* 1:73–113.

———. 1987. The cyclical component of U.S. economic activity. *Quart. J. Econ.* 102(4):797–814.

Clemen, R. T. 1989. Combining forecasts: A review and annotated bibliography. *Internat. J. Forecasting* 5(4):559–83.

Clemen, R. T., and J. Guerard. 1989. Econometric GNP forecasts: Incremental information relative to naive extrapolation. *Internat. J. Forecasting* 5(3):417–26.

Clemen, R. T., and R. L. Winkler. 1986. Combining economic forecasts. *J. Business Econ. Statis.* 4:39–46.

Cochrane, J. H. 1988. How big is the random walk in GNP? *J. Polit. Econ.* 96(5):893–920.

Cole, A. H. 1930. Statistical background of the crisis of 1857. *Rev. Econ. Statis.* 12(4):170–80.

Cole, R. 1969a. Data errors and accuracy. In Mincer 1969a.

———. 1969b. *Errors in provisional estimates of gross national product.* New York: NBER.

Colm, G. 1955. Economic barometers and economic models. *Rev. Econ. Statis.* 37:55–62.

———. 1958. Economic projections: tools of economic analysis and decision making. *Amer. Econ. Rev.* 48(2):178–87.

Conference on Research in Income and Wealth. 1954. *Long-range economic projection.* Studies in Income and Wealth, vol. 16. Princeton, N.J.: Princeton University Press.

———. 1955. *Short-term economic forecasting.* Studies in Income and Wealth, vol. 17. Princeton, N.J.: Princeton University Press.

———. 1964. *Models of income determination.* Studies in Income and Wealth, vol. 28. Princeton, N.J.: Princeton University Press.

Conlan, D. R., and G. E. Wickersham. 1982. Highlight of the 1982 economic outlook survey. National Association of Business Economists. Mimeo.

Cooley, T. F., and S. F. LeRoy. 1981. Identification and estimation of money demand. *Amer. Econ. Rev.* 71(4):825–44.

Cooper, J. P., and C. R. Nelson. 1975. The ex ante prediction performance of the St. Louis and F.R.B.-M.I.T.-Penn. econometric models and some results on composite predictors. *J. Money, Credit, Banking* 7:1–32.

Cooper, R. L. 1972. The predictive performance of quarterly econometric models of the United States. In Hickman 1972.

Coppock, D. J. 1959. The periodicity and stability of inventory cycles in the U.S.A. *Manchester Sch. Econ. Soc. Stud.* 27(1), pt. 1: 140–74, 27(3), pt. 2:261–99.

———. 1962. Business cycles: Endogenous or stochastic? A comment. *Econ. J.* 72(June):458–68.

———. 1965. The post-war short cycle in the U.S.A. *Manchester Sch. Econ. Soc. Stud.* 33(1):17–44.

Cornfield, J., W. D. Evans, and M. Hoffenberg. 1947. Full employment patterns, 1950. *Monthly Labor Rev.* 64:163–90, 420–32.

Council of Economic Advisers. 1988. *Economic report of the president.* Appendix B. Washington, D.C.: U.S. Government Printing Office.

Courchene, T. J. 1967. Inventory behavior and the stock-order distinction. *Canadian J. Econ. Polit. Sci.* 1(August):325–27.

———. 1969. An analysis of the price-inventory nexus with empirical application to the Canadian manufacturing sector. *Internat. Econ. Rev.* 10(October):315–36.

Cox, G. V. [1929] 1930. *An appraisal of American business forecasts.* Chicago: University of Chicago Press.

Creamer, D. 1950. *Behavior of wage rates during business cycles.* New York: NBER.

Creamer, D., assisted by M. Bernstein. 1956. *Personal income during business cycles.* Princeton, N.J.: Princeton University Press for NBER.

Cukierman, A., and P. Wachtel. 1979. Differential inflationary expectations and the variability of the rate of inflation. *Amer. Econ. Rev.* 69:595–609.

Curtin, R. T. 1982. Determinants of price expectations: Evidence from a panel study. In *International research on business cycle surveys,* ed. H. Laumer and M. Ziegler. Aldershot, England: Gower Publishing.

Cyert, R. M., and M. H. DeGroot. 1974. Rational expectations and Bayesian analysis. *J. Polit. Econ.* 82:521–36.

Cyriax, G., ed. 1981. *World index of economic forecasts: Industrial tendency surveys and development plans*. 2d ed. New York: Facts on File.

Darby, M. R., J. Haltiwanger, and M. Plant. 1985. Unemployment rate dynamics and persistent unemployment under rational expectations. *Amer. Econ. Rev.* 75(September):614–37.

Darling, P. G. 1961. Inventory fluctuations and economic instability: An analysis based on the postwar economy. In Joint Economic Committee 1961–62.

Darling, P. G., M. C. Lovell, and G. Fromm. 1961–62. *Inventory fluctuations and economic stabilization*. Joint Economic Committee, 87th Cong. Washington, D.C.: U.S. Government Printing Office.

Daub, M. 1987. *Canadian economic forecasting: In a world where all's unsure*. Kingston and Montreal: McGill–Queen's University Press.

Dauten, C. A., and L. M. Valentine. 1968. *Business cycles and forecasting*. Cincinnati: South-Western Publishing.

Davidson, J. E. H., and D. F. Hendry. 1981. Interpreting econometric evidence: The behaviour of consumers' expenditure in the UK. *Europ. Econ. Rev.* 16:177–92.

Davis, R. G. 1969. Discussion. *Amer. Econ. Rev.* 59(May):316–17.

Davis, S. 1987. Allocative disturbances and specific capital in real business cycle theories. *Amer. Econ. Rev.* 72(May): 326–32.

Day, R. H. 1982. Irregular growth cycles. *Amer. Econ. Rev.* 72(June):406–14.

———. 1983. The emergence of chaos from classical economic growth. *Quart. J. Econ.* 98(2):201–13.

Day, R. H., and W. Shafer. 1985. Keynesian chaos. *J. Macroecon.* 7(3):277–95.

DeCanio, S. 1979. Rational expectations and learning experience. *Quart. J. Econ.* 93:47–57.

de Leeuw, F. 1965. A model of financial behavior. In Duesenberry et al. 1965.

———. 1987. Do expansions have memory? Bureau of Economic Analysis Discussion Paper no. 16, March.

———. 1989. Leading indicators and the "prime mover" view, *Survey of Current Business* 69(August):23–29.

———. 1991. Toward a theory of leading indicators. In Lahiri and Moore 1991.

de Leeuw, F., and E. Gramlich. 1968. The Federal Reserve–M.I.T. econometric model. *Federal Reserve Bull.*, January, 11–40.

de Leeuw, F., and T. M. Holloway. 1983. Cyclical adjustment of the federal budget and federal debt. *Survey of Current Business* 63(12):25–40.

de Leeuw, F., and J. Kalchbrenner. 1969. Monetary and fiscal actions: A test of their relative importance in economic stabilization: Comment. *Federal Reserve Bank of St. Louis Rev.*, April, 6–11.

de Leeuw, F., and M. McKelvey. 1981. Price expectations of business firms. *Brookings Pap. Econ. Act.* 1:299–314.

de Leeuw, F., A. E. Missouri, and C. S. Robinson. 1986. Predicting turning points: A progress report on the Neftçi approach. Bureau of Economic Analysis Working Paper draft, January.

De Long, J. B., and L. H. Summers. 1986a. Are business cycles symmetrical? In Gordon 1986a.

———. 1986b. The changing cyclical variability of economic activity in the United States. In Gordon 1986a.

———. 1986c. Is increased price flexibility stabilizing? *Amer. Econ. Rev.* 76(5):1031–44.

de Menil, G. 1977. Survey measures of expected inflation and their potential usefulness: Comment. In *Analysis of inflation, 1966–1974*, ed. J. Popkin. Cambridge, Mass.: Ballinger for NBER.

Denison, E. F. 1974. *Accounting for United States economic growth, 1929–1969*. Washington, D.C.: Brookings Institution.

————. 1979. *Accounting for slower economic growth: The United States in the 1970s.* Washington, D.C.: Brookings Institution.

Dhrymes, P. J., et al. 1972. Criteria for evaluation of econometric models. *Annals Econ. and Social Measurement* 1:291–324.

Dhrymes, P. J., and S. C. Perestiani. 1986. A comparison of the forecasting performance of WEFA and ARIMA time series methods. *Internat. J. Forecasting* 4(1):81–101.

Dickey, D. A., and W. A. Fuller. 1979. Distribution of the estimators for autoregressive time series with a unit root. *J. Amer. Statis. Assoc.* 74 (June):427–31.

Diebold, F. X., and P. Pauly. 1990. The use of prior information in forecast combination. *Internat. J. Forecasting* 6(4):503–8.

Diebold, F. X., and G. D. Rudebusch. 1987. Stochastic properties of revision in the index of leading indicators. In *1987 proceedings of the Business and Economic Statistics Section.* Washington, D.C.: American Statistical Association.

————. 1989. Scoring the leading indicators. *J. Business* 62(3):369–91.

————. 1990a. Forecasting output with the composite leading index: A real-time analysis. Revised July. Mimeo. Published in *J. Amer. Statis. Assoc.* 86(1991):603–10.

————. 1990b. A nonparametric investigation of duration dependence in the American business cycle. *J. Polit. Econ.* 98:596–616.

————. 1991. Turning point prediction with the composite leading index: An ex ante analysis. In Lahiri and Moore 1991.

Doeringer, P. B., and M. J. Piore. 1971. *Internal labor markets and manpower analysis.* Lexington, Mass.: Heath.

Domowitz, I., R. G. Hubbard, and B. C. Petersen. 1986. Business cycles and the relationship between concentration and price-cost margins. *Rand J. Econ.* 17(Spring):1–17.

————. 1988. Market structure and cyclical fluctuations in U.S. manufacturing. *Rev. Econ. Statis.* 70(February):55–66.

Douglas, P. H. 1930. *Real wages in the United States, 1890–1926.* Boston: Houghton Mifflin.

Drazen, A. 1980. Recent developments in macroeconomic disequilibrium theory. *Econometrica* 48(2):283–306.

Driskill, R. A., and S. M. Sheffrin. 1986. Is price flexibility destabilizing? *Amer. Econ. Rev.* 76(4):802–7.

Duesenberry, J. S. 1949. *Income, saving, and the theory of consumer behavior.* Cambridge, Mass.: Harvard University Press.

————. 1958. *Business cycles and economic growth.* New York: McGraw-Hill.

Duesenberry, J. S., O. Eckstein, and G. Fromm. 1960. A simulation of the United States economy in recession. *Econometrica* 28:749–809.

Duesenberry, J. S., et al., eds. 1965. *The Brookings quarterly econometric model of the United States.* Chicago: Rand McNally.

Duggal, V. G., L. R. Klein, and M. D. McCarthy. 1974. The Wharton model Mark III: A modern IS-LM construct. *Internat. Econ. Rev.* 15(3):572–94.

Dunlop, J. T. 1938. The movement of real and money wage rates. *Econ. J.* 48:413–34.

Dupriez, L. H. 1947. *Des mouvements économiques généraux.* Institut de Recherches Economiques et Sociales de l'Université de Louvain.

————. 1978. A downturn in the long wave? *Banca Nazionale del Lavoro Quart. Rev.* 126:199–210.

Easterlin, R. A. 1968. *Population, labor force, and long swings in economic growth.* New York: NBER.

Eckstein, O. 1968. The price equation. *Amer. Econ. Rev.* 58:1159–83.

————. 1978. Discussion. *Amer. Econ. Rev. Pap. and Proc.* 68(2):320–21.

————. [1979] 1981. Econometric models for forecasting and policy analysis: The present state of the art. Paper presented at the annual convention of the American Statistical Association, 1979. In Sanderson 1981.

———. 1983. *The DRI model of the U.S. economy.* New York: McGraw-Hill.

Eckstein, O., and G. Fromm. 1968. The price equation. *Amer. Econ. Rev.* 58(December):1159–83.

Eckstein, O., E. W. Green, and A. Sinai. 1974. The data resources model: Uses, structure, and analysis of the U.S. economy. *Internat. Econ. Rev.* 15:595–615. Reprinted in Klein and Burmeister 1976.

Eckstein, O., and A. Sinai. 1986. The mechanisms of the business cycle in the postwar era. In Gordon 1986a.

Eichenbaum, M., and K. J. Singleton. 1986. Do equilibrium real business cycle theories explain postwar business cycles? In Fischer 1986.

Einhorn, H., and R. Hogarth. 1975. Unit weighting schemes for decision making. *Organizational Behavior and Human Performance* 13(2):171–92.

Eisner, R. 1963. Investment: Fact and fancy. *Amer. Econ. Rev.* 53:237–46.

———. 1978. *Factors in business investment.* Cambridge, Mass.: Ballinger for NBER.

———. 1986. Comment. In Gordon 1986a.

Evans, M. K. 1969. *Macroeconomic activity: Theory, forecasting, and control: An econometric approach.* New York: Harper & Row.

———. 1974. Econometric models. In Butler, Kavesh, and Platt 1974.

Evans, M. K., Y. Haitovsky, and G. I. Treyz, assisted by V. Su. 1972. An analysis of the forecasting properties of U.S. econometric models. In Hickman 1972.

Evans, M. K., and L. R. Klein. 1967. *The Wharton econometric forecasting model.* Studies in Quantitative Economics no. 2. Philadelphia: Economics Research Unit, University of Pennsylvania.

Evans, M. K., L. R. Klein, and M. Saito. 1972. Short-run prediction and long-run simulation of the Wharton model. In Hickman 1972.

Fabricant, S. 1959. *Basic facts on productivity change.* New York: NBER.

———. 1972. The "Recession" of 1969–1970. In Zarnowitz 1972a.

Fair, R. C. 1969. *The short-run demand for workers and hours.* Amsterdam: North-Holland.

———. 1971. *A short-run forecasting model of the United States economy.* Lexington, Mass.: Heath.

———. 1974. An evaluation of a short-run forecasting model. *Internat. Econ. Rev.* 15(2):285–303.

———. 1978. A criticism of one class of macroeconomics models with rational expectations. *J. Money, Credit, Banking* 10:411–17.

———. 1979. An analysis of the accuracy of four macroeconometric models. *J. Polit. Econ.* 87:701–18.

———. 1988. Sources of economic fluctuations in the United States. *Quart. J. Econ.* 103(May):313–32.

Fama, E. F. 1970. Efficient capital markets: A review of theory and empirical work. *J. Finance* 25:383–417.

———. 1981. Real activity, inflation, and money. *Amer. Econ. Rev.* 71(4):545–65.

Fama, E. F., and M. R. Gibbons. 1982. Inflation, real returns, and capital investment. *J. Monet. Econ.* 9(3):297–324.

———. 1984. A comparison of inflation forecasts. *J. Monet. Econ.* 13(3):327–48.

Feige, E. L., and R. T. McGee. 1977. Money supply control and lagged reserve accounting. *J. Money, Credit, Banking* 9(November):536–56.

Feldstein, M. S. 1975. The importance of temporary layoffs: An empirical analysis. *Brookings Pap. Econ. Act.* 3.

———. 1976a. Inflation, income taxes, and the rate of interest: A theoretical analysis. *Amer. Econ. Rev.* 66:809–20.

————. 1976b. Temporary layoffs in the theory of unemployment. *J. Polit. Econ.* 8(October):937–57.

————, ed. 1980. *The American economy in transition.* Chicago: University of Chicago Press for NBER.

Fellner, W. 1976. *Towards a reconstruction of macroeconomics: Problems of theory and policy.* Washington, D.C.: American Enterprise Institute for Public Policy Research.

————. 1980. The valid core of the rationality hypothesis in the theory of expectations. *J. Money, Credit, Banking* 12:763–87.

Fels, R. 1959. *American business cycles, 1865–1897.* Chapel Hill: University of North Carolina Press.

————. 1963. The recognition-lag and semi-automatic stabilizers. *Rev. Econ. Statis.* 45:280–85.

————. 1977. What causes business cycles? *Soc. Sci. Quart.* 58:88–95.

Fels, R., and C. E. Hinshaw. 1968. *Forecasting and recognizing business cycle turning points.* New York: Columbia University Press for NBER.

Ferber, R. 1953. *A study of aggregate consumption functions.* New York: NBER.

Ferri, P. and E. Greenberg. 1989. *The labor market and business cycle theories.* Lecture Notes in Economics and Mathematical Systems, vol. 325. Berlin: Springer Verlag.

Figlewski, S., and P. Wachtel. 1981. The formation of inflationary expectations. *Rev. Econ. Statis.* 63(1):1–10.

Fildes, R. 1985. Quantitative forecasting: The state of the art: Econometric models. *J. Operations Res. Soc.* 36:549–80.

Firestone, J. M. 1960. *Federal receipts and expenditures during business cycles, 1879–1958.* Princeton, N.J.: Princeton University Press for NBER.

Fischer, S. 1977a. Long-term contracts, rational expectations, and the optimal money supply rule. *J. Polit. Econ.* 85:191–205.

————. 1977b. Long-term contracts, sticky prices, and monetary policy: A comment. *J. Monet. Econ.* 3:317–23.

————. 1977c. Wage indexation and macroeconomic stability. In Brunner and Meltzer 1977.

————, ed. 1980. *Rational expectations and economic policy.* NBER Conference Volume. Chicago: University of Chicago Press.

————, ed. 1986. *NBER macroeconomics annual 1986.* Cambridge, Mass.: MIT Press.

————, ed. 1988. *NBER macroeconomics annual 1988.* Cambridge, Mass.: MIT Press.

Fischer, S., and R. C. Merton. 1984. Macroeconomics and finance: The role of the stock market. In Brunner and Meltzer 1984.

Fischer, S., and F. Modigliani. 1978. Towards an understanding of the real effects and costs of inflation. *Weltwirtschaftliches Archiv* 114:810–83.

Fischer, S., and L. H. Summers. 1989. Should nations learn to live with inflation? NBER Working Paper no. 2815, January.

Fisher, I. 1925. Our unstable dollar and the so-called business cycle. *J. Amer. Statis. Assoc.* 20:179–202.

————. 1932. *Booms and depressions: Some first principles.* New York: Adelphi.

————. 1933. The debt-deflation theory of great depressions. *Econometrica* 1:337–57.

Flavin, M. A. 1981. The adjustment of consumption to changing expectations about future income. *J. Polit. Econ.* 89:974–1009.

Flood, R. P., and P. M. Garber. 1980. Market fundamentals versus price-level bubbles: The first tests. *J. Polit. Econ.* 88:745–70.

Foley, D. 1986. Stabilization policy in a nonlinear business cycle model. In Semmler 1986.

Foss, M. F., and V. Natrella. 1957. Ten years' experience with business investment anticipations. *Survey of Current Business* 37:16–24.

Foster, E. 1978. The variability of inflation. *Rev. Econ. Statis.* 60:346–50.

Fredman, G. T., and M. P. Niemira. 1990. An evaluation of the composite index of leading indicators for signaling turning points in business and growth cycles. Mitsubishi Bank, July. Mimeo. Published in *Business Econ.* 26, no. 4(1991):49–55.

Freeman, R. B. 1988. Contraction and expansion: The divergency of private sector and public sector unionism in the United States. *J. Econ. Persp.* 2(2):63–88.

Frenkel, J. A. 1975. Inflation and the formation of expectations. *J. Monet. Econ.* 1(October):403–21.

Frickey, E. 1942. *Economic fluctuations in the United States.* Cambridge, Mass.: Harvard University Press.

————. 1947. *Production in the United States, 1860–1914.* Cambridge, Mass.: Harvard University Press.

Friedman, B. M. 1979. Optimal expectations and the extreme information assumptions of "rational expectations" macromodels. *J. Monet. Econ.* 5:23–41.

————. 1980. Survey evidence on the "rationality" of interest rate expectations. *J. Monet. Econ.* 6:453–65.

————. 1983. The roles of money and credit in macroeconomic analysis. In Tobin 1983.

————. 1986. Money, credit, and interest rates in the business cycle. In Gordon 1986a.

Friedman, M. 1952. The economic theorist. In *Wesley Clair Mitchell, the economic scientist,* ed. A. F. Burns. New York: NBER.

————. 1957. *A theory of the consumption function.* Princeton, N.J.: Princeton University Press for NBER.

————. 1959. The demand for money: Some theoretical and empirical results. New York: NBER.

————. 1964. The monetary studies of the National Bureau. *44th Annual Report of the NBER.*

————. 1966. Interest rates and the demand for money. *J. Law Econ.* 9:71–85.

————. 1967. The monetary theory and policy of Henry Simons. *J. Law Econ.* 10(October):1–13.

————. 1968. The role of monetary policy. *Amer. Econ. Rev.* 58:1–17.

————. 1970a. Comment on Tobin. *Quart. J. Econ.* 84:318–27.

————. 1970b. A theoretical framework for monetary analysis. *J. Polit. Econ.* 78(2):193–238.

————. 1971. A monetary theory of nominal income. *J. Polit. Econ.* 79:323–37.

————. 1972. Comments on the critics. *J. Polit. Econ.* 80:906–50.

————. 1977. Nobel lecture: Inflation and unemployment. *J. Polit. Econ.* 85(3):451–72.

Friedman, M., and D. Meiselman. 1964. The relative stability of monetary velocity and the investment multiplier in the United States, 1897–1958. In *Stabilization policies,* ed. Edgar Cary Brown et al. Englewood Cliffs, N.J.: Prentice Hall for the Commission on Money and Credit.

Friedman, M., and A. J. Schwartz. 1963a. *A monetary history of the United States, 1867–1960.* Princeton, N.J.: Princeton University Press for NBER.

————. 1963b. Money and business cycles. *Rev. Econ. Statis., 45, suppl.*:32–64.

————. 1970. *Monetary statistics of the United States: Estimates, sources, methods.* New York: NBER.

————. 1982. *Monetary trends in the United States and the United Kingdom: Their relation to income, prices, and interest rates, 1867–1975.* Chicago: University of Chicago Press for NBER.

Frisch, R. 1933. Propagation problems and impulse problems in dynamic economics. *Economic essays in honor of Gustav Cassel.* London: George Allen & Unwin.

Fromm, G. 1961. Inventories, business cycles, and economic stabilization. In Joint Economic Committee 1961–62.

Fromm, G., and L. R. Klein. 1976. The NBER/NSF model comparison seminar: An analysis of results. *Annals Econ. and Social Measurement* 5:4–5.

Frydman, R., and E. S. Phelps, eds. 1983. *Individual forecasting and aggregate outcomes: "Rational expectations" examined.* Cambridge: Cambridge University Press.

Fuchs, V. R., assisted by I. F. Leveson. 1968. *The service economy.* New York: Columbia University Press for NBER.

Fuller, W. A. 1976. *Introduction to statistical time series.* New York: Wiley.

Gabisch, G., and H.-W. Lorenz. 1987. *Business cycle theory: A survey of methods and concepts.* Lecture Notes in Economics and Mathematical Systems, vol. 283. Berlin: Springer Verlag.

Gapinski, J. H. 1982. *Macroeconomic theory: Statics, dynamics, and policy.* New York: McGraw-Hill.

Garcia-Ferrer, A., R. A. Highfield, F. Palm, and A. Zellner. 1987. Macroeconomic forecasting using pooled international data. *J. Business Econ. Statis.* 5(January):53–67.

Garvy, G. 1943. Kondratieff's theory of long cycles. *Rev. Econ. Statis.* 25(November):203–20.

———. 1959. *Debits and clearings statistics and their use.* Washington, D.C.: Federal Reserve Board.

Gayer, A. D., W. W. Rostow, and A. J. Schwartz. 1953. *The growth and fluctuations of the British economy, 1790–1850.* Oxford: Clarendon Press.

Geary, P. T., and J. Kennan. 1982. The employment–real wage relationship: An international study. *J. Polit. Econ.* 90(5):854–71.

Gilbert, D. W. 1933. Business cycles and municipal expenditures. *Rev. Econ. Statis.* 15(3):135–44.

Gilbert, M. 1962. The postwar business cycle in Western Europe. *Amer. Econ. Rev., Pap. and Proc.* 52(2):93–109.

Goldfeld, S. M. 1973. The demand for money revisited. *Brookings Pap. Econ. Act.* 3:577–638.

———. 1976. The case of missing money. *Brookings Pap. Econ. Act.* 7:683–730.

Goodman, L. A., and W. H. Kruskal. 1954. Measures of association for cross classifications. *J. Amer. Statis. Assoc.* 49(December):732–64.

———. 1963. Measures of association for cross classifications, III: Approximate sampling theory. *J. Amer. Statis. Assoc.* 58(June):310–66.

Goodwin, R. M. 1951. The non-linear accelerator and the persistence of business cycles. *Econometrica* 19:1–17.

———. 1967. A growth cycle. In *Socialism, capitalism, and economic growth: Essays presented to Maurice Dobb,* ed. C. H. Feinstein. Cambridge: Cambridge University Press.

Goodwin, R. M., M. Krüger, and A. Vercelli. 1984. *Nonlinear models of fluctuating growth.* Lecture Notes in Economics and Mathematical Systems, vol. 228. Berlin: Springer Verlag.

Gordon, D. F. 1974. A neo-classical theory of Keynesian unemployment. *Econ. Inquiry* 12:431–59.

Gordon, R. A. 1951. Cyclical experience in the interwar period: The investment boom of the Twenties. In Universities–National Bureau Committee for Economic Research 1951.

———. 1961. *Business fluctuations*. 2d ed. New York: Harper Bros. First ed. 1951.

———. 1962. Alternative approaches to forecasting: The recent work of the National Bureau. *Rev. Econ. Statis.* 44:284–91.

———. 1969. The stability of the U.S. economy. In Bronfenbrenner 1969.

———. 1976. Rigor and relevance in a changing institutional setting. *Amer. Econ. Rev.* 66(1):1–14.

Gordon, R. A., and L. R. Klein, eds. 1965. *Readings in business cycles*. Homewood, Ill.: Irwin for the American Economic Association.

Gordon, R. J. 1971. Steady anticipated inflation: Mirage or oasis? *Brookings Pap. Econ. Act.* 2:499–510.

———, ed. 1974. *Milton Friedman's monetary framework: A debate with his critics.* Chicago: University of Chicago Press.

———. 1976. Recent developments in the theory of inflation and unemployment. *J. Monet. Econ.* 2(2):185–219.

———. 1980. Postwar macroeconomics: The evolution of events and ideas. In Feldstein 1980.

———. 1981. Output fluctuations and gradual price adjustment. *J. Econ. Lit.* 19:493–530.

———. 1982a. Price inertia and policy ineffectiveness in the United States, 1890–1980. *J. Polit. Econ.* 90(6):1087–1117.

———. 1982b. Why U.S. wage and employment behavior differs from that in Britain and Japan. *Econ. J.* 92(March):13–44.

———. 1983. A century of evidence on wage and price stickiness in the United States, United Kingdom, and Japan. In Tobin 1983.

———. 1984a. *Macroeconomics.* 3d ed. Boston: Little, Brown.

———. 1984b. The short-run demand for money: A reconsideration. *J. Money, Credit, Banking* 16(4), pt. 1:403–34.

———, ed. 1986a. *The American business cycle: Continuity and change.* Chicago: University of Chicago Press for NBER.

———. 1986b. Introduction: Continuity and change in theory, behavior, and methodology. In Gordon 1986a.

———. 1987. Productivity, wages, and prices inside and outside of manufacturing in the U.S., Japan, and Europe. *Europ. Econ. Rev.* 31(3):685–739.

———. 1990. What is new Keynesian economics? *J. Econ. Lit.* 28(3):1115–71.

Gordon, R. J., and J. M. Veitch. 1986. Fixed investment in the American business cycle, 1919–1983. In Gordon 1986a.

Gordon, R. J., and J. A. Wilcox. 1981. Monetarist interpretations of the Great Depression: An evaluation and critique. In Brunner 1981.

Gramlich, E. M. 1983. Models of inflation expectations formation: A comparison of household and economist forecasts. *J. Money, Credit, Banking* 15:155–73.

Grandmont, J.-M. 1985. On endogenous competitive business cycles. *Econometrica* 53(September):995–1045.

Granger, C. W. J. 1966. The typical spectral shape of an economic variable. *Econometrica* 34(1):150–61.

———. 1969. Investigating causal relations by econometric models and cross-spectral methods. *Econometrica* 37(3):424–38.

Granger, C. W. J., and M. Hatanaka. 1964. *Spectral analysis of economic time series.* Princeton, N.J.: Princeton University Press.

Granger, C. W. J., and P. Newbold. 1977. *Forecasting economic time series.* London: Academic Press.

Granger, C. W. J., and R. Ramanathan. 1984. Improved methods of combining forecasts. *J. Forecasting* 3(2):197–204.

Gray, J. 1976. Wage indexation: A macroeconomic approach. *J. Monet. Econ.* 2:221–35.

Green, E. J., and R. H. Porter. 1984. Noncooperative collusion under imperfect price information. *Econometrica* 52(1):87–100.

Green, G. R., in association with M. Liebenberg and A. A. Hirsch. 1972. Short- and long-term simulations with the OBE econometric model. In Hickman 1972.

Greenwald, B. C., and J. E. Stiglitz. 1988. Examining alternative macroeconomic theories. *Brookings Pap. Econ. Act.* 1:207–60.

———. 1989. Toward a theory of rigidities. NBER Working Paper no. 2938, April.

Greenwald, C. S. 1973. A new deflated composite index of leading indicators. *New England Econ. Rev.*, July/August, 3–17.

Griliches, Z. 1968. The Brookings model volume: A review article. *Rev. Econ. Statis.* 50(2):215–34.

Grossman, H. I. 1986. Comment. In Gordon 1986a.

Grossman, S. J. 1975. Rational expectations and the econometric modeling of markets subject to uncertainty: A Bayesian approach. *J. Econometrics* 3:255–72.

———. 1981. An introduction to the theory of rational expectations under asymmetric information. *Rev. Econ. Stud.* 48:541–59.

Grossman, S. J., and O. Hart. 1983. Implicit contracts under asymmetric information. *Quart. J. Econ.* 98, suppl.: 123–56.

Grossman, S. J., and J. E. Stiglitz. 1980. On the impossibility of informationally efficient markets. *Amer. Econ. Rev.* 70:393–408.

Grossman, S. J., and L. Weiss. 1982. Heterogeneous information and the theory of the business cycle. *J. Polit. Econ.* 90:699–727.

Grunberg, E., and F. Modigliani. 1954. The predictability of social events. *J. Polit. Econ.* 62:465–78.

Gurley, J. G., and E. S. Shaw. 1960. *Money in a theory of finance.* Washington, D.C.: Brookings Institution.

Haberler, G. [1937] 1964. *Prosperity and depression.* League of Nations. Reprint. Cambridge, Mass.: Harvard University Press.

———. 1956. Monetary and real factors affecting economic stability: A critique of certain tendencies in modern economic theory. *Banca Nazionale del Lavoro Quart. Rev.* 9:85–99.

———. 1988. Wage and price rigidities, supply restrictions, and the problem of stagflation. In Willett 1988.

Hafer, R. W., and S. E. Hein. 1985. On the accuracy of time series, interest rate, and survey forecasts of inflation. *J. Business* 58(4):377–98. Earlier version, Federal Reserve Bank of St. Louis Working Paper no. 84–022.

Haitovsky, Y., and G. Treyz. 1972. Forecasts with quarterly macroeconometric models: Equation adjustments and benchmark predictions: The U.S. experience. *Rev. Econ. Statis.* 54 (August):317–25.

Haitovsky, Y., G. L. Treyz, and V. Su. 1974. *Forecasts with quarterly macroeconometric models.* New York: NBER.

Hall, R. E. 1975. The rigidity of wages and the persistence of unemployment. *Brookings Pap. Econ. Act.* 2:301–49.

———. 1977. Investment, interest rates, and the effects of stabilization policies. *Brookings Pap. Econ. Act.* 1:61–121.

———. 1978. Stochastic implications of the life cycle–permanent income hypothesis: Theory and evidence. *J. Polit. Econ.* 86:971–87.

———. 1979. A theory of the natural unemployment rate and the duration of employment. *J. Monet. Econ.* 5:153–69.

————. 1980a. Employment fluctuations and wage rigidity. *Brookings Pap. Econ. Act.* 1:91–123.

————. 1980b. Labor supply and aggregate fluctuations. In Brunner and Meltzer 1980.

————. 1982. The importance of lifetime jobs in the U.S. economy. *Amer. Econ. Rev.* 72(4):716–24.

————. 1986. Market structure and macroeconomic fluctuations. *Brookings Pap. Econ. Act.* 2:285–338.

————. 1988. The relation between price and marginal cost in U.S. industry. *J. Polit. Econ.* 96(5):921–47.

Hamilton, J. D. 1983. Oil and the macroeconomy since World War II. *J. Polit. Econ.* 91:228–48.

————. 1987. Monetary factors in the Great Depression. *J. Monet. Econ.* 19(March):145–69.

————. 1989. A new approach to the economic analysis of nonstationary time series and the business cycle. *Econometrica* 57(March):357–84.

Hansen, A. H. 1939. Economic progress and declining population growth. *Amer. Econ. Rev.* 29(1):1–15.

————. 1964. *Business cycles and national income.* Expanded ed. New York: W. W. Norton. (First ed. 1951.)

Hansen, G. D. 1985. Indivisible labor and the business cycle. *J. Monet. Econ.* 16(November):309–28.

Hardy, G. H., J. E. Littlewood, and G. Pólya. 1964. *Inequalities.* 2d ed. Cambridge: Cambridge University Press.

Harrod, R. F. 1936. *The trade cycle.* Oxford: Clarendon Press.

Hart, A. G. 1938. *Debts and recovery.* New York: Twentieth Century Fund.

————. 1940. *Anticipations, uncertainty, and dynamic planning.* Chicago: University of Chicago Press.

————. 1965. Capital appropriations and the accelerator. *Rev. Econ. Statis.* 47:123–36.

Harvey, A. C. 1985. Trends and cycles in macroeconomic time series. *J. Business Econ. Statis.* 3(July):216–27.

Hatanaka, M. 1975. The underestimation of variations in the forecast series: A note. *Internat. Econ. Rev.* 16(1):151–60.

Hawtrey, R. G. 1913. *Good and bad trade: An inquiry into the causes of trade fluctuations.* London: Constable.

Hayek, F. A. von. 1933. *Monetary theory and the trade cycle.* New York: Harcourt, Brace.

————. 1939. *Profits, interest, and investment.* London: George Routledge & Sons.

Haywood, E. 1973. The deviation cycle: A new index of the Australian business cycle, 1950–1973. *Australian Econ. Rev.* (4):31–39.

Hertzberg, M. P., and B. A. Beckman. 1989. Business cycle indicators: Revised composite indexes. *Business Conditions Digest,* January, 97–102.

Hickman, B. G. 1960. *Growth and stability of the postwar economy.* Washington, D.C.: Brookings Institution.

————. 1969. Dynamic properties of macroeconomic models: An international comparison. In Bronfenbrenner 1969.

————. ed. 1972. *Econometric models of cyclical behavior.* 2 vols. Studies in Income and Wealth, vol. 36. New York: Columbia University Press for NBER.

Hickman, B. G., and R. M. Coen. 1976. *An annual growth model of the U.S. economy.* Amsterdam: North-Holland.

Hicks, J. R. 1935. A suggestion for simplifying the theory of money. *Economica,* n.s. 2:1–19.

————. 1937. Mr. Keynes and the "Classics": A suggested interpretation. *Econometrica* 5:147–59.

————. 1950. *A contribution to the theory of the trade cycle*. Oxford: Clarendon Press.

————. 1974. Real and monetary factors in economic fluctuations. *Scot. J. Polit. Econ.* 21:205–14.

Hillinger, C. 1966. An econometric model of mild business cycles. *Manchester Sch. Econ. Soc. Stud.* 34:269–84.

————. 1979. An empirical test of Metzler's hypothesis regarding the nature of short-run cyclical fluctuations. In *On the stability of contemporary economic systems: Proceedings of the third Reisenburg symposium*, ed. Oldrich Kýn and Wolfram Schrettl. Göttingen: Vandenhoeck & Ruprecht.

————. 1982. Business cycles are alive and well. *Econ. Letters* 9:133–37.

————. 1983. U.S. business cycles in the postwar era. Paper presented at seminar for Mathematical Economics, July, University of Munich.

————. 1986. Business cycles are periodic. Paper presented at seminar for mathematical economics, University of Munich.

Hirsch, A. A., B. T. Grimm, and G. V. L. Narasimham. 1974. Some multiplier and error characteristics of the BEA quarterly model. *Internat. Econ. Rev.* 16(3):617–31. Reprinted in Klein and Burmeister 1976.

Hirsch, A. A., and M. C. Lovell. 1969. *Sales anticipations and inventory behavior*. New York: Wiley.

Hirshleifer, J. 1973. Where are we in the theory of information? *Amer. Econ. Rev. Pap. and Proc.* 63(May):31–39.

Hobson, J. A. 1922. *The economics of unemployment*. London: George Allen & Unwin.

Hobson, J. A., and A. F. Mummery. 1889. *The physiology of industry*. London: J. Murray.

Hodrick, R. J., and E. C. Prescott. 1980. Post-war U.S. business cycles: An empirical investigation. Discussion Paper no. 451, Carnegie-Mellon University, Pittsburgh.

Hogarth, R. M. 1978. A note on aggregating opinions. *Organizational Behavior and Human Performance* 21:40–46.

Holloway, T. M. 1986. The cyclically adjusted federal budget and federal debt: Revised and updated estimates. *Survey of Current Business* 66(3):11–17.

Howitt, E. P. 1978. The limits to stability of a full-employment equilibrium. *Scand. J. Econ.* 80:265–82.

Howrey, E. P. 1968. A spectrum analysis of the long-swing hypothesis. *Internat. Econ. Rev.* 9:228–52.

————. 1972. Dynamic properties of a condensed version of the Wharton model. In Hickman 1972.

————. 1978. The use of preliminary data in econometric forecasting. *Rev. Econ. Statis.* 60:193–200.

Howrey, E. P., L. R. Klein, and M. D. McCarthy. 1976. Notes on testing the predictive performance of econometric models. In Klein and Burmeister 1976.

Hoyt, H. [1933] 1970. *One hundred years of land values in Chicago*. Chicago: University of Chicago Press. Reprint. New York: Arno Press.

Huizinga, J. P. 1980. Real wages, employment, and expectations. Ph.D. diss., Massachusetts Institute of Technology.

Hultgren, T. 1948. *American transportation in prosperity and depression*. New York: NBER.

————. 1950. *Cyclical diversities in the fortunes of industrial corporations*. Occasional Paper no. 32. New York: NBER.

————. 1960. *Changes in labor cost during cycles in production and business.* New York: NBER.

Hultgren, T., assisted by M. R. Pech. 1965. *Cost, prices, and profits: Their cyclical relations.* New York: Columbia University Press for NBER.

Hymans, S. H. 1973. On the use of leading indicators to predict cyclical turning points. *Brookings Pap. Econ. Act.* 2:339–75.

Hymans, S. H., and H. T. Shapiro. 1970. *The DHL-III quarterly econometric model of the U.S. economy.* Ann Arbor: University of Michigan, Research Seminar in Quantitative Economics.

————. 1974. The structure and properties of the Michigan quarterly model of the U.S. economy. *Internat. Econ. Rev.* 15(3):632–53. Reprinted in Klein and Burmeister 1976.

Ichimura, S. 1954. Toward a general non-linear macrodynamic theory of economic fluctuations. In Kurihara 1954.

Intriligator, M. D. 1978. *Econometric models, techniques, and applications.* Englewood Cliffs, N.J.: Prentice-Hall.

Irvine, R. O., Jr. 1981. Tests of the rationality and accuracy of manufacturers' sales expectations. Working Paper Series, Board of Governors, Federal Reserve System.

Jaffe, D. M., and E. Kleiman. 1977. The welfare implications of uneven inflation. In *Inflation theory and anti-inflation policy,* ed. E. Lundberg. London: Macmillan.

Jevons, W. S. 1884. *Investigations in currency and finance.* London: Macmillan.

Johansen, L. 1980. Parametric certainty equivalence procedures in decision making under uncertainty. *Zeitschrift für Nationalökonomie* 40(3–4):257–79.

Johnson, H. G. 1967. *Essays in monetary economics.* Cambridge, Mass.: Harvard University Press.

Johnston, J. 1960. *Statistical cost analysis.* New York: McGraw-Hill.

Jöhr, W. A. 1952. *Die Konjunkturschwankungen.* Tübingen: J. C. B. Mohr.

Joint Economic Committee. 1961–62. *Inventory fluctuations and economic stabilization.* 87th Cong., 1st sess. Washington, D.C.: U.S. Government Printing Office.

Jonung, Lars. 1981. Perceived and expected rates of inflation in Sweden. *Amer. Econ. Rev.* 71:961–68.

Jorgenson, D. W. 1963. Capital theory and investment behavior. *Amer. Econ. Rev.* 53:247–59.

————. 1971. Econometric studies of investment behavior: A survey. *J. Econ. Lit.* 9(4):1111–47.

————. 1974. Investment and production: A review. In *Frontiers of Quantitative Economics,* ed. M. D. Intriligator and D. A. Kendrick. Amsterdam: North-Holland.

Jorgenson, D. W., Z. Griliches, and E. F. Denison. 1972. *The measurement of productivity: An exchange of views.* Washington, D.C.: Brookings Institution.

Judd, J. P., and J. L. Scadding. 1982. The search for a stable money demand function: A survey of the post-1973 literature. *J. Econ. Lit.* 20(3):993–1023.

Juglar, C. [1862] 1889. *Des crises commerciales et leur retour périodique, en France, en Angleterre, et aux Etats-Unis.* Paris: Guillaumin.

Juster, F. T. 1964. *Anticipations and purchases, an analysis of consumer behavior.* New York: NBER.

————. 1979. Statement presented in hearings before the Task Force on Inflation of the Committee on the Budget. In *Impact of inflation on the economy,* House of Representatives, 96th Con. 1st sess. Washington, D.C.: U.S. Government Printing Office.

Kaldor, N. 1940. A model of the trade cycle. *Econ. J.* 50:78–92.

Kalecki, M. 1935. A macroeconomic theory of business cycles. *Econometrica* 3:327–44.

————. 1937. A theory of the business cycle. *Rev. Econ. Stud.* 4:77–97.

————. 1971. *Selected essays on the dynamics of the capitalist economy.* Cambridge: Cambridge University Press.

Kantor, B. 1979. Rational expectations and economic thought. *J. Econ. Lit.* 17:1422–41.

Kareken, J. M., and N. Wallace, eds. 1980. *Conference on models of monetary economics.* Proceedings and contributions from participants of a December 1978 conference. Minneapolis: Federal Reserve Bank of Minneapolis.

Katona, G. 1951. *Psychological analysis of economic behavior.* New York: McGraw-Hill.

Katz, L. F. 1986. Efficiency wage theories: A partial evaluation. In Fischer, 1986.

Keane, M. P., and D. E. Runkle. 1990. Testing the rationality of price forecasts: New evidence from panel data. *Amer. Econ. Rev.* 80(4):714–35.

Keen, H. 1989. The yield curve as a predictor of business cycle turning points. *Business Econ.* 24(4):37–43.

Kendall, M. G. 1948. *Rank correlation methods.* London: Griffin.

Kendrick, J. W. 1961. *Productivity trends in the United States.* Princeton, N.J.: Princeton University Press for NBER.

Kennan, J. 1988. Equilibrium interpretations of employment and real wage fluctuations. In Fischer 1988.

Kessel, R. A. 1965. *The cyclical behavior of the term structure of interest rates.* Occasional Paper no. 91. New York: NBER.

Keynes, J. M. 1923. *A tract on monetary reform.* London: Macmillan.

————. 1936. *The general theory of employment, interest, and money.* London: Macmillan.

Kiefer, N. 1988. Economic duration data and hazard functions. *J. Econ. Lit.* 26(2):646–79.

Kindleberger, C. P. 1978. *Manias, panics, and crashes: A history of financial crises.* New York: Basic Books.

King, R. G. 1981. Monetary information and monetary neutrality. *J. Monet. Econ.* 7:195–206.

————. 1983. Interest rates, aggregate information, and monetary policy. *J. Monet. Econ.* 12:299–334.

King, R. G., and C. I. Plosser. 1984. Money, credit, and prices in a real business cycle. *Amer. Econ. Rev.* 74:363–80.

King, R. G., C. I. Plosser, J. H. Stock, and M. W. Watson. 1991. Stochastic trends and economic fluctuations. *Amer. Econ. Rev.* 81(4):819–40.

King, R. G., and S. T. Rebelo. 1989. Low frequency filtering and real business cycles. Rochester Center for Economic Research Working Paper no. 205, October.

King, S. R. 1988. Is increased price flexibility stabilizing? A comment. *Amer. Econ. Rev.* 78(1):267–72.

Kitchin, J. 1923. Cycles and trends in economic factors. *Rev. Econ. Statis.* 5:10–16.

Klein, B. 1975. Our new monetary standard: The measurement and effects of price uncertainty, 1880–1973. *Econ. Inquiry* 13(December):461–84.

Klein, L. R. 1946. A post-mortem on transition predictions of national product. *J. Polit. Econ.* 54(4):289–308.

————. 1950. *Economic fluctuations in the United States, 1921–1941.* New York: Wiley & Sons.

————. 1951. Studies in investment behavior. In Universities–National Bureau Committee for Economic Research 1951.

————. 1964. A postwar quarterly model: Description and applications. In *Models of income determination,* Conference on Research in Income and Wealth. Studies in Income and Wealth, vol. 28. Princeton, N.J.: Princeton University Press for NBER.

————. 1968. *An essay on the theory of economic prediction.* Helsinki: Academic Book Store.

————. 1990. Cyclical indicators in econometric models. In P. A. Klein 1990.

Klein, L. R., and E. Burmeister, eds. 1976. *Econometric model performance: Comparative simulation studies of the U.S. economy.* Philadelphia: University of Pennsylvania Press.

Klein, L. R., et al. 1961. *An econometric model of the United Kingdom.* Oxford: Blackwell.

Klein, L. R., and A. S. Goldberger. 1955. *An econometric model of the United States, 1929–1952.* Amsterdam: North-Holland.

Klein, L. R., and R. S. Preston. 1969. Stochastic nonlinear models. *Econometrica* 37:95–106.

Klein, P. A. 1971. *The cyclical timing of consumer credit, 1920–1967.* Occasional Paper no. 113. New York: NBER.

————. 1976. *Business cycles in the postwar world: Some reflections on recent research.* Washington, D.C.: American Enterprise Institute.

————, ed. 1990. *Analyzing modern business cycles: Essays honoring Geoffrey H. Moore.* Armonk, N.Y.: M. E. Sharpe.

Klein, P. A., and G. H. Moore. 1985. *Monitoring growth cycles in market-oriented countries: Developing and using international economic indicators.* Cambridge, Mass.: Ballinger for NBER.

————. 1990. Improved measures of inventories and deliveries. In Moore 1990.

Kling, J. L. 1987. Predicting the turning points of business and economic time series. *J. Business* 60(April):201–38.

Kniesner, T. J., and A. H. Goldsmith. 1987. A survey of alternative models of the aggregate U.S. labor market. *J. Econ. Lit.* 25(3):1241–80.

Knight, F. H. 1921. *Risk, uncertainty, and profit.* Boston: Houghton Mifflin.

Kondratieff, N. D. 1926. Die langen Wellen der Konjunktur. *Archiv für Sozialwissenschaft und Sozialpolitik* 56(3):573–609. Also, translated by W. F. Stolper as "The long waves in economic life," *Rev. Econ. Statis.* 17(6)(1935):105–15.

Koopmans, T. C. 1947. Measurement without theory. *Rev. Econ. Statis.* 29(3):161–72.

————. 1949. A reply. *Rev. Econ. Statis.* 31(2):86–91.

————. 1957. Additional comment. In *Three essays on the state of economic science.* New York: McGraw-Hill. Reprinted in Gordon and Klein 1965.

Kopcke, R. W. 1977. The behavior of investment spending during the recession and recovery, 1973–1976. *New England Econ. Rev.,* November/December, 5–41.

Kosobud, R. F., and W. D. O'Neil. 1972. Stochastic implications of orbital asymptotic stability of a nonlinear trade cycle model. *Econometrica* 40:69–86.

Krelle, W. 1981. Erich Preisers Wachstums- und Konjunkturtheorie als einheitliche dynamische Theorie. In *Wirtschaftstheorie und Wirtschaftspolitik: Gedenkschrift für Erich Preiser,* ed. W. J. Mückl and A. E. Ott. Passau: Passavia Universitätsverlag.

Krueger, A. B., and L. H. Summers. 1987. Reflections on the inter-industry wage structure. In Lang and Leonard 1987.

————. 1988. Efficiency wages and the inter-industry wage structure. *Econometrica* 56(2):259–93.

Kuh, E. 1960. Profit, profit markups, and productivity. In *Employment, growth, and price levels.* Study Paper 15, prepared for the Joint Economic Committee. 86th Cong., 1st sess.

Kuran, T. 1983. Asymmetric price rigidity and inflationary bias. *Amer. Econ. Rev.* 73(3):373–82.

———. 1986. Anticipated inflation and aggregate employment: The case of costly price adjustment. *Econ. Inquiry* 24(2):293–311.

Kurihara, K., ed. 1954. *Post-Keynesian economics*. New Brunswick, N.J.: Rutgers University Press.

Kuznets, S. 1930. *Secular movements in production and prices*. Boston: Houghton Mifflin.

———. 1937. *National income and capital formation, 1919–1935*. New York: NBER.

———. 1945. *National product in wartime*. New York: NBER.

———. 1946. *National income: A summary of findings*. New York: NBER.

———. 1961. *Capital in the American economy: Its formation and financing*. Princeton, N.J.: Princeton University Press for NBER.

———. 1972. *Quantitative economic research: Trends and problems*. New York: NBER.

Kuznets, S., assisted by L. Epstein and E. Jenks. 1941. *National income and its composition, 1919–1938*. New York: NBER.

———. 1946. *National production since 1896*. New York: NBER.

Kydland, F., and E. C. Prescott. 1977. Rules rather than discretion: The inconsistency of optimal plans. *J. Polit. Econ.* 85(3):473–91.

———. 1980. A competitive theory of fluctuations and the feasibility and desirability of stabilization policy. In Fischer 1980.

———. 1982. Time to build and aggregate fluctuations. *Econometrica* 50:1345–70.

Lahiri, K., and G. H. Moore, eds. 1991. *Leading economic indicators: New approaches and forecasting records*. Cambridge: Cambridge University Press.

Lahiri, K., C. Teigland, and M. Zaporowski. 1986. Interest rates and the subjective probability distribution of inflation forecasts. State University of New York at Albany. Mimeo. Published in *J. Money, Credit, Banking* 20, no. 2 (1991):233–48.

Laidler, D. E. W. 1969. *The demand for money: Theories and evidence*. Scranton, Penn.: International Textbook.

———. 1973a. The influence of money on real income and inflation: A simple model with some empirical tests for the United States, 1953–72. *Manchester Sch. Econ. Soc. Stud.* 41:367–95. Reprinted in Laidler 1975.

———. 1973b. Simultaneous fluctuations in prices and output: A business cycle approach. *Economica*, n.s. 40:60–72. Reprinted in Laidler 1975.

———. 1975. *Essays on money and inflation*. Chicago: University of Chicago Press.

———. 1981. Monetarism: An interpretation and an assessment. *Econ. J.* 91:1–28.

Laidler, D. E. W., and M. Parkin. 1975. Inflation: A survey. *Econ. J.* 85(4):741–809.

Lang, K., and J. Leonard, eds. 1987. *Unemployment and the structure of labor markets*. Oxford: Basil Blackwell.

Latane, H. A. 1960. Income velocity and interest rates: A pragmatic approach. *Rev. Econ. Statis.* 42(4):445–49.

Lazear, E. 1981. Agency, earnings profiles, productivity, and hours restrictions. *Amer. Econ. Rev.* 71(4):606–20.

Lebergott, S. 1964. *Manpower in economic growth*. New York: McGraw-Hill.

———. 1986. Discussion. *J. Econ. Hist.* 46(2):367–71.

Lee, M. W. 1967. *Macroeconomics: Fluctuations, growth, and stability*. Homewood, Ill.: Irwin.

Leijonhufvud, A. 1968. *On Keynesian economics and the economics of Keynes: A study in monetary theory*. New York: Oxford University Press.

———. 1981. *Information and coordination: Essays in macroeconomic theory*. New York: Oxford University Press.

————. 1983. Keynesianism, monetarism, and rational expectations: Some reflections and conjectures. In Frydman and Phelps 1983.

Leontief, W. 1968. *International encyclopedia of the social sciences,* s.v. "input-output analysis."

Levi, M. D., and J. H. Makin. 1979. Fisher, Phillips, Friedman and the measured impact of inflation on interest. *J. Finance* 34(1):33–52.

————. 1980. Inflation uncertainty and the Phillips curve: Some empirical evidence. *Amer. Econ. Rev.* 70(5):1022–27.

Lewis, J. P. 1962. Short-term general business conditions forecasting: Some comments on method. *J. Business* 35:343–56.

Lewis, J. P., and R. C. Turner. 1967. *Business conditions analysis.* 2d ed. New York: McGraw-Hill.

Lewis, W., Jr. 1962. *Federal fiscal policy in the postwar recessions.* Washington, D.C.: Brookings Institution.

Liebenberg, M., A. A. Hirsch, and J. Popkin. 1966. A quarterly econometric model of the United States: A progress report. *Survey of Current Business* 46:13–39.

Lilien, D. M. 1982. Sectoral shifts and cyclical unemployment. *J. Polit. Econ.* 90(4):777–93.

Lindbeck, A. 1976. Stabilization policy in open economies with endogenous politicians. *Amer. Econ. Rev.* 66:1–19.

Lindbeck, A., and D. Snower. 1986. Explanations of unemployment. *Oxford Rev. Econ. Pol.* 1(2):34–59.

Lipsey, R. G. 1960. The relation between unemployment and the rate of change of money wage rates in the United Kingdom, 1862–1957: A further analysis. *Economica* 27:1–31.

Litterman, R. B. 1986. Forecasting with Bayesian vector autoregression: Five years of experience. *J. Business Econ. Statis.* 4:25–38.

Litterman, R. B., and L. M. Weiss. 1985. Money, real interest rates, and output: A reinterpretation of postwar U.S. data. *Econometrica* 53:129–53.

Liu, Ta-chung. 1963. An exploratory quarterly econometric model of effective demand in the postwar U.S. economy. *Econometrica* 31:301–48.

Logue, D. E., and T. D. Willett. 1976. A note on the relation between the rate and variability of inflation. *Economica,* n.s. 43:151–58.

Long, C. D. 1940. *Building cycles and the theory of investment.* Princeton, N.J.: Princeton University Press.

————. 1960. *Wages and earnings in the United States, 1860–1890.* New York: NBER.

Long, J. B., and C. I. Plosser. 1983. Real business cycles. *J. Polit. Econ.* 91(1):39–69.

Longbottom, J. A., and S. Holly. 1985. The role of time series analysis in the evaluation of econometric models. *J. Forecasting* 4:75–87.

Lorenz, E. N. 1963. Deterministic nonperiodic flow. *J. Atmosph. Sci.* 20(2):130–41.

Lovell, M. C. 1961. Factors determining manufacturing inventory investment. In Joint Economic Committee 1961–62.

————. 1964. Determinants of inventory investment. In *Models of income determination,* Conference on Research in Income and Wealth. Studies in Income and Wealth, vol. 28. Princeton, N.J.: Princeton University Press for NBER.

————. 1975. Why was the consumer feeling so sad? *Brookings Pap. Econ. Act.* 2: 473–79.

————. 1986. Tests of the rational expectations hypothesis. *Amer. Econ. Rev.* 76(1):110–24.

Lucas, R. E., Jr. 1972. Expectations and the neutrality of money. *J. Econ. Theory* 4:103–24.

————. 1973. Some international evidence on output-inflation tradeoffs. *Amer. Econ. Rev.* 63:326–34.

————. 1975. An equilibrium model of the business cycle. *J. Polit. Econ.* 83:1113–44.

————. 1976. Econometric policy evaluation: A critique. In Brunner and Meltzer 1976.

————. 1977. Understanding business cycles. In Brunner and Meltzer 1977.

————. 1980. Rules, discretion, and the role of the economic advisor. In Fischer 1980.

————. 1981. Tobin and monetarism: A review article. *J. Econ. Lit.* 19:558–67.

————. 1987. *Models of business cycles.* London: Blackwell.

Lucas, R. E., Jr., and L. A. Rapping. 1969. Real wages, employment, and inflation. *J. Polit. Econ.* 77(5):721–54.

Lucas, R. E., Jr., and T. J. Sargent. 1978. After Keynesian macroeconomics. In *After the Phillips curve: Persistence of high inflation and high unemployment.* Boston: Federal Reserve Bank of Boston.

Lundberg, E., ed. 1955. *The business cycle in the post-war world.* London: Macmillan.

————. 1958. The stability of economic growth: A critique of statistical and theoretical investigation. *Internat. Econ. Pap.* 8:45–64.

————. 1968. *Instability and economic growth.* New Haven: Yale University Press.

————. 1969. Postwar stabilization policies. In Bronfenbrenner 1969.

Lupoletti, W. M., and R. H. Webb. 1986. Defining and improving the accuracy of macroeconomic forecasts: Contributions from a VAR model. *J. Business* 59:263–85.

Lütkepohl, H. 1982. Non-causality due to omitted variables. *J. Econometrics* 19:307–78.

Macaulay, F. C. 1938. *The movements of interest rates, bond yields, and stock prices in the United States since 1856.* New York: NBER.

McCallum, B. T. 1980a. Rational expectations and macroeconomic stabilization: An overview. In McCallum 1980b.

————, ed. 1980b. Rational expectations: A seminar sponsored by the American Enterprise Institute. *J. Money, Credit, Banking,* special issue, 12(4), pt. 2.

————. 1982. Macroeconomics after a decade of rational expectations: Some critical issues. *Federal Reserve Bank of Richmond Econ. Rev.* 68:3–12.

————. 1986. On "real" and "sticky-price" theories of the business cycle. *J. Money, Credit, Banking* 18(4):397–414.

McCallum, B. T., and J. K. Whitaker. 1979. The effectiveness of fiscal feedback rules and automatic stabilizers under rational expectations. *J. Monet. Econ.* 5(2):171–86.

McCarthy, M. D. 1972a. Some notes on the generation of pseudo structural errors for use in stochastic simulation studies. Appendix to Short run prediction and long run simulation of the Wharton model, in Evans, Klein, and Saito 1972.

————. 1972b. *The Wharton quarterly econometric forecasting model: Mark III.* Philadelphia: Economics Research Unit, Wharton School, University of Pennsylvania.

Maccini, L. J. 1987. Inventories. In *The new Palgrave: A dictionary of economics,* ed. J. Eatwell, M. Milgate, and P. Newman. London: Macmillan.

McCracken, P. W., J. C. T. Mao, and C. Fricke. 1965. *Consumer installment credit and public policy.* Michigan Business Studies no. 17(1). Ann Arbor: Bureau of Business Research, Graduate School of Business Administration, University of Michigan.

McCulloch, J. H. 1975. The Monte Carlo cycle in business activity. *Econ. Inquiry* 13:303–21.

———. 1977. The cumulative unanticipated change in interest rates: Evidence on the misintermediation hypothesis. NBER Working Paper no. 222.

———. 1981. Misintermediation and macroeconomic fluctuations. *J. Monet. Econ.* 8:103–15.

McDonald, I. M., and R. M. Solow. 1981. Wage bargaining and employment. *Amer. Econ. Rev.* 71(5):896–908.

———. 1985. Wages and employment in a segmented labor market. *Quart. J. Econ.* 100(4):1115–41.

Machlup, F. 1962. *The production and distribution of knowledge in the United States.* Princeton, N.J.: Princeton University Press.

Mack, R. P. 1956. *Consumption and business fluctuations.* New York: NBER.

———. 1967. *Information, expectations, and inventory fluctuations.* New York: NBER.

McKinley, D. H., M. G. Lee, and H. Duffy. 1965. *Forecasting business conditions.* New York: American Bankers Association.

McNees, S. K. 1973. The predictive accuracy of econometric forecasts. *New England Econ. Rev.,* September/October, 3–27.

———. 1974. How accurate are economic forecasts? *New England Econ. Rev.,* November/December, 2–19.

———. 1975. An evaluation of economic forecasts. *New England Econ. Rev.,* November/December, 3–39.

———. 1976. An evaluation of economic forecasts: Extension and update. *New England Econ. Rev.,* September/October, 30–44.

———. 1977. An assessment of the Council of Economic Advisers' forecast of 1977. *New England Econ. Rev.,* March/April, 3–7.

———. 1978. The "rationality" of economic forecasts. *Amer. Econ. Rev.* 68:301–5.

———. 1979. The forecasting record for the 1970s. *New England Econ. Rev.,* September/October, 1–21 (corrected version).

———. 1981. The recent record of thirteen forecasters. *New England Econ. Rev.,* September/October, 5–21.

———. 1986. Forecasting accuracy of alternative techniques: A comparison of U.S. macroeconomic forecasts. *J. Business Econ. Statis.* 4:5–15.

———. 1988a. How accurate are macroeconomic forecasts? *New England Econ. Rev.,* July/August, 15–36.

———. 1988b. Which forecast should you use? *New England Econ. Rev.,* July/August, 36–42.

———. 1990. Man vs. model? The role of judgment in forecasting. *New England Econ. Rev.,* July/August, 41–52.

MacRae, C. D. 1977. A political model of the business cycle. *J. Polit. Econ.* 85:239–63.

Maddala, G. S. 1977. *Econometrics.* New York: McGraw-Hill.

Maddison, A. 1960. The postwar business cycle in Western Europe and the role of government policy. *Banca Nazionale del Lavoro Quart. Rev.* 13(June):99–148.

———. 1987. Growth and slowdown in advanced capitalist economies: Techniques of quantitative assessment. *J. Econ. Lit.* 25(2):649–98.

Maher, J. E. 1957. Forecasting industrial production. *J. Polit. Econ.* 65:158–65.

Maisel, S. J. 1957. *Fluctuations, growth, and forecasting: The principles of dynamic business economics.* New York: Wiley & Sons.

Makin, J. H. 1982. Anticipated money, inflation uncertainty, and real economic activity. *Rev. Econ. Statis.* 64(1):126–35.

———. 1983. Real interest, money surprises, anticipated inflation, and fiscal deficits. *Rev. Econ. Statis.* 65:374–84.

Makin, J. H., and V. Tanzi. 1984. Level and volatility of U.S. interest rates: Roles of expected inflation, real rates, and taxes. In Tanzi 1984.

Malinvaud, E. 1977. *The theory of unemployment reconsidered.* Oxford: Basil Blackwell.

Mandel, E. 1980. *Long waves of capitalist development.* Cambridge: Cambridge University Press.

Mankiw, N. G. 1985. Small menu costs and large business cycles: A macroeconomic model of monopoly. *Quart. J. Econ.* 100(2):529–39.

———. 1989. Real business cycles: A new Keynesian perspective. *J. Econ. Persp.* 3(Summer):79–90.

Mankiw, N. G., J. J. Rotemberg, and L. H. Summers. 1985. Intertemporal substitution in macro-economics. *Quart. J. Econ.* 100(1):225–251.

Mansfield, E. 1980. Technology and productivity in the United States. In Feldstein 1980.

Marquardt, W., and W. Strigel. 1959. *Der Konjunkturtest: Eine neue Methode der Wirtschaftsbeobachtung.* Berlin: Duncker & Humbolt.

Marschak, J. 1968. Economics of inquiring, communicating, deciding. *Amer. Econ. Rev. Pap. and Proc.* 58:1–18.

Marshall, A. 1923. *Money, credit, and commerce.* London: Macmillan.

Matthews, R. C. O. 1959. *The trade cycle.* Cambridge: Cambridge University Press.

———. 1969. Postwar business cycles in the United Kingdom. In Bronfenbrenner 1969.

Mayer, T. 1960. Plant and equipment lead times. *J. Business* 33:127–32.

———. 1988. The Keynesian legacy: Does countercyclical policy pay its way? In Willett 1988.

Mayer, T., et al. 1978. *The structure of monetarism.* New York: W. W. Norton.

Meltzer, A. H. 1967. Money supply revisited: A review article. *J. Polit. Econ.* 75(2):169–82.

———. 1982. Rational expectations, risk, uncertainty, and market responses. In *Crises in the economic and financial structure,* ed. P. Wachtel. Lexington, Mass.: Lexington Books.

———. 1986. Comment. In Gordon 1986a.

Melvin, M. 1982. Expected inflation, taxation and interest rates: The delusion of fiscal illusion. *Amer. Econ. Rev.* 72(September):841–45.

Metzler, L. A. 1941. The nature and stability of inventory cycles. *Rev. Econ. Statis.* 23:113–29.

———. 1946. Business cycles and the modern theory of employment. *Amer. Econ. Rev.* 36(3):278–91.

———. 1947. Factors governing the length of inventory cycles. *Rev. Econ. Statis.* 29:1–15.

Meyer, J. R., and E. Kuh. 1957. *The investment decision.* Cambridge, Mass.: Harvard University Press.

Meyer, L. H., and R. H. Rasche. 1980. Empirical evidence on the effects of stabilization policy. In *Stabilization policies: Lessons from the '70s and implications for the '80s,* proceedings of a conference, Center for the Study of American Business, Working Paper no. 53, April.

Mincer, J., ed. 1969a. *Economic forecasts and expectations: Analyses of forecasting behavior and performance.* New York: Columbia University Press for NBER.

———. 1969b. Models of adaptive forecasting. In Mincer 1969a.

Mincer, J., and V. Zarnowitz. 1969. The evaluation of economic forecasts. In Mincer 1969a.

Minsky, H. P. 1959. A linear model of cyclical growth. *Rev. Econ. Statis.* 61(May):133–45.

———. 1963. Comment on Friedman and Schwartz, Money and business cycles. *Rev. Econ. Statis., 45, suppl.:*65–66.

———. 1975. *John Maynard Keynes.* New York: Columbia University Press.

———. 1977. A theory of systemic fragility. In *Financial crises: Institutions and markets in a fragile environment,* ed. E. I. Altman and A. W. Sametz. New York: Wiley.

———. 1980. Finance and profits: The changing nature of the American business cycles. In Joint Economic Committee, *The business cycle and public policy, 1929–1980,* 96th Cong., 2d sess. Washington, D.C.: Joint Committee Print.

———. 1982. *Can "it" happen again? Essays on instability and finance.* New York: M. E. Sharpe.

Mintz, I. 1967. *Cyclical fluctuations in the exports of the United States since 1879.* New York: NBER.

———. 1969. *Dating postwar business cycles: Methods and their application to western Germany, 1950–67.* Occasional Paper no. 107. New York: NBER.

———. 1972. Dating American growth cycles. In Zarnowitz 1972a.

———. 1974. Dating United States growth cycles. *Explorations in Econ. Res.* 1(1):1–113.

Mishkin, F. S. 1981a. Are market forecasts rational? *Amer. Econ. Rev.* 71:295–306.

———. 1981b. The real interest rate: An empirical investigation. In Brunner and Meltzer 1981a.

———. 1982. Does anticipated monetary policy matter? An econometric investigation. *J. Polit. Econ.* 90:22–51.

Mitchell, D. J. B. 1980. *Unions, wages, and inflation.* Washington, D.C.: Brookings Institution.

Mitchell, W. C. 1913. *Business cycles.* Berkeley: University of California Press.

———, ed. 1922. *Income in the United States: Its amount and distribution, 1909–1919. Pt. 2, Detailed report.* New York: NBER.

———. 1927. *Business cycles: The problem and its setting.* New York: NBER.

———. 1951. *What happens during business cycles: A progress report.* New York: NBER.

Mitchell, W. C., and A. F. Burns. 1938. *Statistical indicators of cyclical revivals.* Bulletin no. 69. New York: NBER.

Mitchell, W. C., et al. 1921. *Income in the United States: Its amount and distribution, 1909–1919.* Pt. 1, Summary. New York: NBER.

Modigliani, F. 1949. *Fluctuations in the saving-income ratio: A problem in economic forecasting.* Studies in Income and Wealth, vol. 11. New York: NBER.

———. 1977. The monetarist controversy; or, Should we forsake stabilization policies? *Amer. Econ. Rev.* 67:1–19.

Modigliani, F., and R. E. Brumberg. 1954. Utility analysis and the consumption function: An interpretation of cross-section data. In Kurihara 1954.

Modigliani, F., and K. J. Cohen. 1961. *The role of anticipations and plans in economic behavior and their use in economic analysis and forecasting.* Urbana: University of Illinois.

Modigliani, F., and O. H. Sauerlander. 1955. Economic expectations and plans in relation to short-term economic forecasting. In Conference on Research in Income and Wealth 1955.

Modigliani, F., and H. M. Weingartner. 1958. Forecasting uses of anticipatory data on investment and sales. *Quart. J. Econ.* 72:23–54.

Moore, G. H. 1950. *Statistical indicators of cyclical revivals and recessions.* New York: NBER.

————, ed. 1961. *Business cycle indicators.* 2 vols. Princeton, N.J.: Princeton University Press for NBER.

————. 1962. Tested knowledge of business cycles. 42d Annual Report of the NBER.

————. 1969a. Forecasting short-term economic change. *J. Amer. Statis. Assoc.* 64(March):1–22.

————. 1969b. Generating leading indicators from lagging indicators. *Western Econ. J.* 7:135–44.

————. 1975a. Productivity, costs, and prices: New light from an old hypothesis. *Explorations in Econ. Res.* 2(1):1–17.

————. 1975b. Slowdowns, recessions, and inflation: Some issues and answers. *Explorations in Econ. Res.* 2(2):125–66.

————. 1977a. Business cycles: Partly exogenous, mostly endogenous. *Soc. Sci. Quart.* 58:96–103.

————. 1977b. Five little-known facts about inflation. In Moore 1983.

————. 1977c. Lessons of the 1973–1976 recession and recovery. In *Contemporary economic problems 1977*, ed. W. Fellner. Washington, D.C.: American Enterprise Institute.

————. 1977d. The president's economic report: A forecasting record. *NBER Reporter,* April, 4–12.

————. 1979. The forty-second anniversary of the leading indicators. In *Contemporary economic problems 1979*, ed. W. Fellner. Washington, D.C.: American Enterprise Institute. Reprinted in Moore 1983.

————. 1980. A long-run look at the business cycle. In Joint Economic Committee, *The business cycle and public policy, 1929–1980*, 96th Cong., 2d sess. Washington, D.C.: Joint Committee Print.

————. 1983. *Business cycles, inflation, and forecasting.* 2d ed. Cambridge, Mass.: Ballinger for NBER.

————, ed. 1990. *Leading indicators for the 1990s.* Homewood, Ill.: Dow Jones–Irwin.

Moore, G. H., and J. P. Cullity. 1983. Trends and cycles in productivity, unit costs, and prices: An international perspective. In Moore 1983.

————. 1990. A new layoff rate series. In Moore 1990.

Moore, G. H., and P. A. Klein. 1985. *Monitoring growth cycles in market-oriented countries: Developing and using international economic indicators.* Cambridge, Mass.: Ballinger for NBER.

Moore, G. H., and M. H. Moore. 1985. *International economic indicators: A sourcebook.* Westport, Conn.: Greenwood Press.

Moore, G. H., and J. Shiskin. 1967. *Indicators of business expansions and contractions.* New York: NBER.

Moore, G. H., and V. Zarnowitz. 1986. The development and role of the National Bureau of Economic Research's business cycle chronologies. In Gordon 1986a.

Moore, H. L. 1914. *Economic cycles: Their law and cause.* New York: Macmillan.

Morgan, J. N. 1968. *International encyclopedia of the social sciences,* s.v. "survey analysis, III, applications in economics."

Morgenstern, O. 1928. *Wirtschaftsprognose: Eine Untersuchung ihrer Voraussetzungen und Möglichkeiten.* Vienna: Springer.

————. 1959. *International financial transactions and business cycles.* Princeton, N.J.: Princeton University Press for NBER.

————. 1970. *On the accuracy of economic observations.* Rev. ed. Princeton, N.J.: Princeton University Press.

Morrison, C. J. 1988. Markups in U.S. and Japanese manufacturing: A short run econometric analysis. NBER Working Paper no. 2799, December.

Mosbaek, E. 1968. Review of *The Brookings quarterly econometric model of the United States. Econometrica* 36(1):194–96.

Mullineaux, D. J. 1978. On testing for rationality: Another look at the Livingston price expectations data. *J. Polit. Econ.* 86:319–36.

———. 1980a. Inflation expectations and money growth in the United States. *Amer. Econ. Rev.* 70:149–61.

———. 1980b. Unemployment, industrial production, and inflation uncertainty in the United States. *Rev. Econ. Statis.* 62:163–69.

Mullineux, A. W. 1984. The business cycle after Keynes: A contemporary analysis. New York: Barnes & Noble Books.

Murphy, K. M., and R. H. Topel. 1987. Unemployment, risk, and earnings: Testing for equalizing differences in the labor market. In Lang and Leonard 1987.

———. 1989. Efficiency wages reconsidered: Theory and evidence. In *Advances in the theory and measurement of unemployment,* ed. Y. Weiss and G. Fishelson. London: Macmillan.

Mussa, M. 1975. Adaptive and regressive expectations in a rational model of the inflationary process. *J. Monet. Econ.* 1:423–42.

Muth, J. F. 1960. Optimal properties of exponentially weighted forecasts. *J. Amer. Statis. Assoc.* 55:299–306.

———. 1961. Rational expectations and the theory of price movements. *Econometrica* 29:315–35.

National Planning Association. 1959. *Long-range projections for economic growth: The American economy in 1970.* Planning Pamphlet no. 107. Washington, D.C.: National Planning Association.

Neftçi, S. N. 1978. A time-series analysis of the real wages–employment relationship. *J. Polit. Econ.* 86:281–91.

———. 1979. Lead-lag relations, exogeneity, and prediction of economic time series. *Econometrica* 47(1):101–13.

———. 1982. Optimal prediction of cyclical downturns. *J. Econ. Dynam. Control* 4:225–41.

———. 1984. Are economic time-series asymmetric over the business cycle? *J. Polit. Econ.* 92(April):305–28.

———. 1986. Testing non-linearity in business cycles. In Semmler 1986.

Neisser, H. 1934. General overproduction: A study of Say's law of markets. *J. Polit. Econ.* 42(August):433–65.

Nelson, C. R. 1972. The prediction performance of the FRB-MIT-PENN model of the U.S. economy. *Amer. Econ. Rev.* 62:902–17.

———. 1975. Rational expectations and the predictive efficiency of economic models. *J. Business* 48:331–43.

———. 1981. Adjustment lags versus information lags: A test of alternative explanations of the Phillips curve phenomenon. *J. Money, Credit, Banking* 13:1–11.

———. 1984. A benchmark for the accuracy of econometric forecasts of GNP. *Business Econ.* 19(3):52–58.

Nelson, C. R., and C. I. Plosser. 1982. Trends and random walks in macroeconomic time series: Some evidence and implications. *J. Monet. Econ.* 10:139–62.

Nerlove, M. 1958. Adaptive expectations and cobweb phenomena. *Quart. J. Econ.* 73:227–40.

———. 1962. A quarterly econometric model for the United Kingdom: A review article. *Amer. Econ. Rev.* 52:154–76.

———. 1966. A tabular survey of macro-econometric models. *Internat. Econ. Rev.* 7:127–75.

Nerlove, M., and S. Wage. 1964. On the optimality of adaptive forecasting. *Management Sci.* 10:207–24.

Newbold, P., and C. W. J. Granger. 1974. Experience with forecasting univariate time series and the combination of forecasts. *J. Royal Statis. Soc. A* 137:131–46.

Newbury, F. D. 1952. *Business forecasting: Principles and practices.* New York: McGraw-Hill.

Niemira, M. P. 1983. Sequential signals of recession and recovery: Revisited. *Business Econ.*, January, 51–53.

———. 1991. An international application of Neftçi's probability approach for signaling growth recessions and recoveries using turning point indicators. In Lahiri and Moore 1991.

Nordhaus, W. D. 1975. The political business cycle. *Rev. Econ. Stud.* 42:169–90.

Nurkse, R. 1954. Period analysis and inventory cycles. *Oxford Econ. Pap.*, n.s. 6(September):203–25.

Nutter, G. W. 1951. *Extent of enterprise monopoly in the United States, 1899–1939.* Chicago: University of Chicago Press.

———. 1962. *Growth of industrial production in the Soviet Union.* Princeton, N.J.: Princeton University Press for NBER.

OECD Department of Economics and Statistics. 1987. *OECD leading indicators and business cycles in member countries, 1960–1985.* Sources and Methods no. 39. Paris: OECD.

Officer, R. R. 1973. The variability of the market factor of the New York Stock Exchange. *J. Business* 46(3):434–53.

Okun, A. M. 1959. A review of some economic forecasts for 1955–1957. *J. Business* 32:199–211.

———. 1960. On the appraisal of cyclical turning-point predictions. *J. Business* 33:101–20.

———. 1962. The predictive value of surveys of business intentions. *Amer. Econ. Rev.* 52:218–25.

———. 1971. The mirage of steady inflation. *Brookings Pap. Econ. Act.* 2:485–98.

———. 1974. Unemployment and output in 1974. *Brookings Pap. Econ. Act.* 2:495–504.

———. 1975. A postmortem of the 1974 recession. *Brookings Pap. Econ. Act.* 1:207–21.

———. 1980. Rational-expectations-with-misperceptions as a theory of business cycles. In McCallum 1980b.

———. 1981. *Prices and quantities: A macroeconomic analysis.* Washington, D.C.: Brookings Institution.

Owen, D. B. 1962. *Handbook of statistical tables.* Reading, Mass.: Addison-Wesley.

Palash, C. J., and L. J. Radecki. 1985. Using monetary and financial variables to predict cyclical downturns. *Federal Reserve Bank of New York Quart. Rev.*, Summer, 36–45.

Papadia, F. 1982. Rationality of inflationary expectations in the European Economic Community countries. EEC Working Paper. Brussels.

Parkin, M. 1986. The output-inflation trade-off when prices are costly to change. *J. Polit. Econ.* 94(1):220–24.

Parsons, D. O. 1987. The employment relationship: Job attachment, work effort, and the nature of contracts. In *Handbook of labor economics*, ed. O. Ashenfelter and R. Layard, vol. 2. Amsterdam: North-Holland.

Pashigian, B. P. 1964. The accuracy of the Commerce-S.E.C. sales anticipations. *Rev. Econ. Statis.* 46:398–405.

Patinkin, Don. 1948. Price flexibility and full employment. *Amer. Econ. Rev.* 38:543–64.

———. [1954] 1965. *Money, interest, and prices: An integration of monetary and value theory.* New York: Harper & Row.

Pearce, D. K. 1979. Comparing survey and rational measures of expected inflation: Forecast performance and interest rate effects. *J. Money, Credit, Banking* 11:447–56.

Pencavel, J. 1986. Labor supply of men: A survey. In *Handbook of Labor Economics*, ed. O. Ashenfelter and R. Layard, vol. 1. Amsterdam: North-Holland.

Persons, W. M. 1931. *Forecasting business cycles*. New York: Wiley.

Pesando, J. E. 1975. A note on the rationality of the Livingston price expectations. *J. Polit. Econ.* 83:849–58.

Phelps, E. S. 1967. Phillips curves, expectations of inflation, and optimal unemployment over time. *Economica*, n.s. 34: 254–81.

———. 1968. Money-wage dynamics and labor-market equilibrium. *J. Polit. Econ.* 76(4):678–711.

———. 1970. Introduction: The new microeconomics in employment and inflation theory. In *Microeconomic foundations of employment and inflation theory*, ed. E. S. Phelps et al. New York: Norton.

———. 1981. Okun's micro-macro system: A review article. *J. Econ. Lit.* 19:1065–73.

Phelps, E. S., and J. B. Taylor. 1977. Stabilizing powers of monetary policy under rational expectations. *J. Polit. Econ.* 85:163–90.

Phelps Brown, E. H., with H. H. Browne. 1968. *A century of pay*. London: Macmillan.

Phillips, A. W. 1958. The relation between unemployment and the rate of change of money wage rates in the United Kingdom, 1862–1957. *Economica*, n.s. 25:283–99.

———. 1981. The relation between unemployment and the rate of change of money wage rates in the United Kingdom, 1862–1957. *Economica*, n.s. 25:283–99.

Pierce, D. A., et al. 1981. *Uncertainty in the monetary aggregate: Sources, measurement, and policy effects*. Special Studies Paper no. 153. Washington, D.C.: Division of Research and Statistics, Federal Reserve Board.

Pigou, A. C. 1927. *Industrial fluctuations*. London: Macmillan.

———. 1947. Economic progress in a stable environment. *Economica*, n.s. 14:180–88.

Pindyck, R. S., and D. L. Rubinfeld. 1981. *Econometric models and economic forecasts*. New York: McGraw-Hill.

Plosser, C. I. 1989. Understanding real business cycles. *J. Econ. Persp.* 3(Summer):51–77.

Pohjola, M. T. 1981. Stable, cyclic, and chaotic growth: The dynamics of a discrete-time version of Goodwin's growth cycle model. *Zeitschrift für Nationalökonomie* 41(1–2):27–38.

Poole, W. 1970. Optimal choice of monetary policy instruments in a simple stochastic macro model. *Quart. J. Econ.* 84(2):197–221.

———. 1976. Rational expectations in the macro model. *Brookings Pap. Econ. Act.* 2:463–514.

Popkin, J. 1965. The relationship between new orders and shipments: An analysis of the machinery and equipment industries. *Survey of Current Business* 45(3):24–32.

———. 1984. The business cycle at various stages of process. *J. Business Econ. Statis.* 2:215–23.

———. 1990. Why some of the leading indicators lead. In P. A. Klein 1990.

Porter, R. H. 1985. On the incidence and duration of price wars. *J. Industrial Econ.* 33(4):415–26.

Preiser, E. 1933. *Grundzüge der Konjunkturtheorie*. Tübingen: J. C. B. Mohr (Paul Siebeck).

———. 1951. Review of Gottfried Haberler's *Prosperität und Depression*, Bern 1948. *Kyklos* 5:96–98.

————. 1959. *Nationalökonomie heute*. Munich: C. H. Beck.

————. 1961. *Bildung und Verteilung des Volkseinkommens*. 2 vols. Göttingen: Vandenhoeck & Ruprecht.

————. 1967a. Economic growth as a fetish and necessity. *German Econ. Rev.* 5(4):265–77.

————. 1967b. *Wirtschaftspolitik heute: Grundprobleme der Marktwirtschaft*. Munich: C. H. Beck.

Prescott, E. C. 1986. Theory ahead of business-cycle measurement. In Brunner and Meltzer 1986.

Prochnow, H. V., ed. 1954. *Determining the business outlook*. New York: Harper.

Rau, N. 1974. *Trade cycles: Theory and evidence*. London: Macmillan.

Reagan, P. B. 1982. Inventory and price behavior. *Rev. Econ. Stud.* 49(1):137–42.

Reder, M. W. 1988. The rise and fall of unions: The public sector and the private. *J. Econ. Persp.* 2(2):89–110.

Rees, A. 1960. *New measures of wage-earner compensation in manufacturing, 1914–1957*. New York: NBER.

————. 1973. *The economics of work and pay*. New York: Harper & Row.

Rees, A., assisted by D. P. Jacobs. 1961. *Real wages in manufacturing, 1890–1914*. Princeton, N.J.: Princeton University Press for NBER.

Rhoades, D. 1982. Statistics Canada's leading indicator system. *Current Econ. Analysis*, May, 27–35.

Robertson, D. H. [1915] 1948. *A study of industrial fluctuations*. London: Aldwych.

Romer, C. 1986a. Is the stabilization of the postwar economy a figment of the data? *Amer. Econ. Rev.* 76(2):314–34.

————. 1986b. New estimates of prewar gross national product and unemployment. *J. Econ. Hist.* 46(2):341–52.

————. 1986c. The prewar business cycle reconsidered: New estimates of gross national product, 1869–1918. NBER Working Paper no. 1969, July.

————. 1986d. Spurious volatility in historical unemployment data. *J. Polit. Econ.* 94(1):1–37.

————. 1987a. Changes in the cyclical behavior of individual product series. NBER Working Paper no. 2440, November.

————. 1987b. Gross national product, 1909–1928: Existing estimates, new estimates, and new interpretations of World War I and its aftermath. NBER Working Paper no. 2187, March.

Roos, C. F. 1955. Survey of economic forecasting techniques. *Econometrica* 23(October):363–95.

Rorty, M. C. 1923. The statistical control of business activities. *Harvard Business Rev.* 1(2):154–66.

Rose, H. 1967. On the non-linear theory of the employment cycle. *Rev. Econ. Stud.* 34:153–73.

————. 1969. Real and monetary factors in the business cycle. *J. Money, Credit, Banking* 1:138–52.

Rosen, S. 1985. Implicit contracts: A survey. *J. Econ. Lit.* 23(3):1144–75.

Rostow, W. W. 1975. Kondratieff, Schumpeter, and Kuznets: Trend periods revisited. *J. Econ. Hist.* 35(December):719–53.

————. 1978. *The world economy: History and prospect*. Austin: University of Texas Press.

————. 1980. *Why the poor get richer and the rich slow down*. Austin: University of Texas Press.

Rotemberg, J. J. 1987. The new Keynesian microfoundations. In *NBER macroeconomics annual 1987*, ed. S. Fischer. Cambridge, Mass.: MIT Press.

Rotemberg, J. J., and G. Saloner. 1986. A supergame-theoretic model of price wars during booms. *Amer. Econ. Rev.* 76(3):390–407.

Rotemberg, J. J., and L. H. Summers. 1988. Labor hoarding, inflexible prices, and procyclical productivity. NBER Working Paper no. 2591, May.

Runkle, D. E. 1987. Vector autoregressions and reality. *J. Business Econ. Statis.* 5:437–42.

Sachs, J. 1979. Wages, profits, and macroeconomic adjustment: A comparative study. *Brookings Pap. Econ. Act.* 2: 269–319.

———. 1980. The changing cyclical behavior of wages and prices, 1890–1976. *Amer. Econ. Rev.* 70(1):78–90.

Sachverständigenrat zur Begutachtung der gesamtwirtschaftlichen Entwicklung. 1968. *Alternativen aussenwirtschaftlicher Anpassung.* Jahresgutachten 1968/69. Stuttgart, Mainz: W. Kohlhammer.

Samuelson, P. A. 1939. Interactions between the multiplier analysis and the principle of acceleration. *Rev. Econ. Statis.* 21:75–78.

———. 1947. *Foundations of economic analysis.* Cambridge, Mass.: Harvard University Press.

———. 1958. An exact consumption-loan model of interest with or without the social contrivance of money. *J. Polit. Econ.* 66:467–82.

———. 1965. Economic forecasting and science. *Michigan Quart. Rev.* 4(4):274–80.

———. 1976. Optimality of sluggish predictors under ergodic probabilities. *Internat. Econ. Rev.* 17:1–7.

———. 1990. Deterministic chaos in economics: An occurrence in axiomatic utility theory. In Vellupillai 1990.

Samuelson, P. A., and R. M. Solow. 1960. Analytical aspects of anti-inflation policy. *Amer. Econ. Rev.* 50:177–94.

Sanderson, A. R., ed. 1981. *DRI readings in macroeconomics.* New York: McGraw-Hill.

Sapir, M. 1949. *Review of economic forecasts for the transition period.* Conference on Research in Income and Wealth. Studies in Income and Wealth, vol. 11. New York: NBER.

Sargent, T. J. 1976a. A classical macroeconometric model for the United States. *J. Polit. Econ.* 84:207–37.

———. 1976b. The observational equivalence of natural and unnatural rate theories of macroeconomics. *J. Polit. Econ.* 84:631–40.

———. 1978. Estimation of dynamic labor demand schedules under rational expectations. *J. Polit. Econ.* 86:1009–44.

———. 1979. *Macroeconomic theory.* New York: Academic Press.

Sargent, T. J., and C. A. Sims. 1977. Business cycle modeling without pretending to have too much a priori economic theory. In *New methods in business cycle research: Proceedings from a conference.* Minneapolis: Federal Reserve Bank of Minneapolis.

Sargent, T. J., and N. Wallace. 1975. "Rational" expectations, the optimal monetary instrument, and the optimal monetary rule. *J. Polit. Econ.* 83(2):241–54.

———. 1976. Rational expectations and the theory of economic policy. *J. Monet. Econ.* 2:169–83.

Scarfe, B. L. 1977. *Cycles, growth, and inflation: A survey of contemporary macrodynamics.* New York: McGraw-Hill.

Scherer, F. M. 1980. *Industrial market structure and economic performance.* 2d ed. Chicago: Rand McNally.

Schinasi, G. J. 1981. A nonlinear dynamic model of short run fluctuations. *Rev. Econ. Stud.* 48:649–56.

———. 1982. Fluctuations in a dynamic, intermediate-run IS-LM model: Applications of the Poincaré-Bendixon theorem. *J. Econ. Theory* 28:369–75.

Schnader, M. H., and H. O. Stekler. 1979. The existence and evaluation of economic "consensus" forecasts. In *1979 Proceedings of the Business and Economic Statistics Section*, Washington, D.C.: American Statistical Association.

Schultze, C. L. 1986. *Other times, other places: Macroeconomic lessons from U.S. and European history.* Washington, D.C.: Brookings Institution.

Schumpeter, J. A. 1934. *The theory of economic development.* Cambridge, Mass.: Harvard University Press.

———. 1935. The analysis of economic changes. *Rev. Econ. Statis.* 17:1–10.

———. 1939. *Business cycles: A theoretical, historical, and statistical analysis of the capitalist process.* 2 vols. New York: McGraw-Hill.

Schwartz, A. J. 1981. Understanding 1929–1933. In Brunner 1981.

Schwert, G. W. 1988. The causes of changing stock market volatility. University of Rochester, September. Mimeo. Published in *J. Finance* 44(5)(1989):1115–53.

Seidl, C., ed. 1983. *Lectures in Schumpeterian economics, Graz 1983.* Berlin: Springer Verlag.

Semmler, W., ed. 1986. *Competition, instability, and nonlinear cycles.* Lecture Notes in Economics and Mathematical Systems, vol. 275. Berlin: Springer Verlag.

———. 1989. *Financial dynamics and business cycles: New perspectives.* Armonk, N.Y.: M. E. Sharpe.

Shackle, G. L. S. 1949. *Expectations in economics.* Cambridge: Cambridge University Press.

Shannon, C. E. 1948. A mathematical theory of communications. *Bell System Techn. J.* 27:379–423, 523–65.

Shapiro, C., and J. E. Stiglitz. 1984. Equilibrium unemployment as a worker discipline device. *Amer. Econ. Rev.* 74:443–44.

Shapiro, M. D. 1987. Measuring market power in U.S. industry. NBER Working Paper no. 2212, April.

———. 1988. The stabilization of the U.S. economy: Evidence from the stock market. *Amer. Econ. Rev.* 78(5):1067–79.

Shaw, W. H. 1947. *Value of commodity output since 1869.* New York: NBER.

Sheffrin, S. M. 1983. *Rational expectations.* Cambridge: Cambridge University Press.

———. 1988. Have economic fluctuations been dampened? A look at the evidence outside the United States. *J. Monet. Econ.* 21(1): 73–83.

———. 1989. *The making of economic policy: History, theory, politics.* London: Basil Blackwell.

Sherman, H. J. 1976. *Stagflation: A rational theory of unemployment and inflation.* New York: Harper & Row.

———. 1991. *The business cycle: Growth and crisis under capitalism.* Princeton, N.J.: Princeton University Press.

Shiller, R. J. 1978. Rational expectations and the dynamic structure of macroeconomic models: A critical review. *J. Monet. Econ.* 4:1–44.

———. 1980. Can the Fed control real interest rates? In Fischer 1980.

———. 1981a. Do stock prices move too much to be justified by subsequent changes in dividends? *Amer. Econ. Rev.* 71:421–36.

———. 1981b. The use of volatility measures in assessing market efficiency. *J. Finance* 36:291–311.

Shinohara, M. 1969. Postwar business cycles in Japan. In Bronfenbrenner 1969.

Shiryayev, A. N. 1978. *Optimal stopping rules.* New York: Springer Verlag.

Shiskin, J. 1957. *Electronic computers and business indicators.* New York: NBER. Reprinted in Moore 1961.

———. 1961a. *Signals of recession and recovery: An experiment with monthly reporting.* New York: NBER.

————. 1961b. Statistics for short-term economic forecasting. In Moore 1961.

————. 1967. Reverse trend adjustment of leading indicators. *Rev. Econ. Statis.* 49(1):45–49.

————. 1973. Measuring current economic fluctuations. *Annals Econ. and Social Measurement* 2(1):1–15.

Shiskin, J., A. M. Young, and J. C. Musgrave. 1965. The X-11 variant of the census method II seasonal adjustment. Bureau of the Census Technical Paper 15. Washington, D.C.: U.S. Government Printing Office.

Silk, L. 1983. How to win at forecasting. *New York Times,* 27 July 1983.

Silk, L. S., and M. L. Curley. 1970. *A primer on business forecasting, with a guide to sources of business data.* New York: Random House.

Simon, H. A. 1979. On parsimonious explanations of production functions. *Scand. J. Econ.* 81(4):459–74.

Sims, C. A. 1972. Money, income, and causality. *Amer. Econ. Rev.* 62:540–52.

————, ed. 1977. *New methods in business cycle research.* Proceedings from a conference. Minneapolis: Federal Reserve Bank of Minneapolis.

————. 1980a. Comparison of interwar and postwar business cycles: Monetarism reconsidered. *Amer. Econ. Rev.* 70:250–57.

————. 1980b. Macroeconomics and reality. *Econometrica* 48:1–48.

————. 1982. Policy analysis with econometric models. *Brookings Pap. Econ. Act.* 1:107–64.

————. 1989. Comment. In Blanchard and Fischer 1989.

Sims, C. A., J. H. Stock, and M. W. Watson. 1986. Inference in linear time series models with some unit roots. Stanford University. Manuscript. Published in *Econometrica* 58(1990):113–44.

Sims, C. A., and R. M. Todd. 1991. Evaluating Bayesian vector autoregressive forecasting procedures for macroeconomic data. NSF-NBER Seminar on Bayesian Inference in Econometrics and Statistics, St. Paul, Minnesota (April).

Sinai, A. 1976. Credit crunches: An analysis of the postwar experience. In *Parameters and policies of the U.S. economy,* ed. O. Eckstein. Amsterdam: North-Holland.

Smith, W. B., and A. H. Cole. 1935. *Fluctuations in American business, 1790–1860.* Cambridge, Mass.: Harvard University Press.

Smithies, A. 1957. Economic fluctuations and growth. *Econometrica* 25(January): 1–52.

Solow, R. M. 1957. Technical change and the aggregate production function. *Rev. Econ. Statis.* 39(August):312–20.

————. 1979. Another possible source of wage stickiness. *J. Macroecon.* 1(1):79–82.

————. 1980. On theories of unemployment. *Amer. Econ. Rev.* 70:1–11.

Spencer, M. H., C. G. Clark, and P. W. Hoguet. 1961. *Business and economic forecasting: An econometric approach.* Homewood, Ill.: Irwin.

Spiethoff, A. 1953. Business cycles. *Internat. Econ. Pap.* 3:75–171. First published as "Krisen" in *Handwörterbuch der Staatswissenschaften* (1925), 6:8–91.

Spivey, W. A., and W. J. Wrobleski. 1978. An analysis of forecast performance. In *1977 Proceedings of the Business and Economic Statistics Section.* Washington, D.C.: American Statistical Association.

Sprague, O. M. W. 1910. *History of crises under the national banking system.* Washington, D.C.: U.S. Government Printing Office.

Sprinkel, B. W. 1971. *Money and markets: A monetarist view.* Homewood, Ill.: Irwin.

Stanback, Thomas M., Jr. 1962. *Postwar cycles in manufacturers' inventories.* New York: NBER.

Stein, J. L., ed. 1976. *Monetarism.* Amsterdam: North-Holland.

Stekler, H. O. 1961a. Diffusion index and first difference forecasting. *Rev. Econ. Statis.* 43:201–8.

————. 1961b. Forecasting industrial production. *J. Amer. Statis. Assoc.* 56:869–77.

————. 1962. A simulation of the forecasting performance of the diffusion index. *J. Business* 35:196–200.

————. 1970. *Economic forecasting.* New York: Praeger.

Stekler, H. O., and R. W. Thomas. 1980. Forecasts of a regional construction model: An evaluation. *Econ. Letters* 6(4):387–92.

Stigler, G. J. 1949. *Five lectures on economic problems.* London: Longmans, Green.

————. 1961. The economics of information. *J. Polit. Econ.* 69(3):213–25.

————. 1962. Information in the labor market. *J. Polit. Econ.* 70(5), suppl.: 94–105.

Stigler, G. J., and J. K. Kindahl. 1970. *The behavior of industrial prices.* New York: NBER.

Stiglitz, J. E. 1986. Theories of wage rigidity. In *Keynes' economic legacy: Contemporary economic theories,* ed. J. L. Butkiewicz, K. J. Koford, and J. B. Miller. New York: Praeger.

————. 1987. The causes and consequences of the dependence of quality on price. *J. Econ. Lit.* 25(1):1–48.

Stiglitz, J. E., and A. Weiss. 1981. Credit rationing in markets with imperfect information. *Amer. Econ. Rev.* 71:393–410.

Stock, J. H., and M. W. Watson. 1986. Testing for common trends. Harvard University. Manuscript. Published in *J. Amer. Statis. Assoc.* 83 (December 1988):1097–107.

————. 1987. Interpreting the evidence on money-income causality. Harvard University. Manuscript. Published in *J. Econometrics* 40 (1)(1989):161–81.

————. 1988a. A new approach to the leading economic indicators. Harvard University. Manuscript.

————. 1988b. A probability model of the coincident economic indicators. NBER Working Paper no. 2772, November.

————. 1989. New indexes of coincident and leading economic indicators. In Blanchard and Fischer 1989.

————. 1991a. Predicting recessions. Paper presented at the NBER conference on New Research on Business Cycles, Indicators, and Forecasting, May, Cambridge, Mass.

————. 1991b. A probability model of the coincident economic indicators. In Lahiri and Moore 1991.

Stockman, A. C. 1983. Aggregation bias and the cyclical behavior of real wages. Paper presented at the NBER Conference on Macroeconomics, July, Cambridge, Mass.

Strigel, W. H. 1981. *Business cycle surveys.* Frankfurt: Campus Verlag.

Stulz, R. M., and W. Wasserfallen. 1985. Macroeconomic time-series, business cycles, and macroeconomic policies. In Brunner and Meltzer 1985.

Su, V., and J. Su. 1975. An evaluation of the ASA/NBER business outlook survey forecasts. *Explorations in Econ. Res.* 2:588–618.

Suits, D. B. 1962. Forecasting and analysis with an econometric model. *Amer. Econ. Rev.* 52:104–32.

Summers, L. H. 1983. The nonadjustment of nominal interest rates: A study of the Fisher effect. In Tobin 1983.

————. 1988. Relative wages, efficiency wages, and Keynesian unemployment. *Amer. Econ. Rev.* 78(2):383–88.

Tanzi, V. 1980. Inflationary expectations, economic activity, taxes, and interest rates. *Amer. Econ. Rev.* 70:12–21.

————, ed. 1984. *Taxation, inflation, and interest rates.* Washington, D.C.: International Monetary Fund.

Tarshis, L. 1939. Changes in real and money wages. *Econ. J.* 49:150–54.

Taylor, J. B. 1975. Monetary policy during a transition to rational expectations. *J. Polit. Econ.* 83:1009–21.

———. 1979. Staggered wage setting in a macro model. *Amer. Econ. Rev.* 69(2):108–13.

———. 1980a. Aggregate dynamics and staggered contracts. *J. Polit. Econ.* 88: 1–23.

———. 1980b. Output and price stability: An international comparison. *J. Econ. Dynam. Control* 2:109–32.

———. 1983. Rational expectations and the invisible handshake. In Tobin 1983.

———. 1986a. Improvements in macroeconomic stability: The role of wages and prices. In Gordon 1986a.

———. 1986b. Reply. In Gordon 1986a.

———. 1988. Comment (on Kennan 1988). In Fischer 1988.

Temin, P. 1976. *Did monetary forces cause the Great Depression?* New York: Norton.

Thalberg, B. 1990. A reconsideration of Frisch's original cycle model. In Vellupillai 1990.

Theil, H. [1958] 1965. *Economic forecasts and policy.* 2d ed. Amsterdam: North-Holland.

———. 1966. *Applied economic forecasting.* Amsterdam: North-Holland; Chicago: Rand McNally.

Thorp, W. L. 1926. *Business annals.* New York: NBER.

Tichy, G. J. 1972. *Indikatoren der österreichischen Konjunktur, 1950–1970.* Vienna: Österreichisches Institut für Wirtschaftsforschung.

———. 1983. Schumpeter's business cycle theory: Its importance for our time. In Seidl 1983.

Tinbergen, J. 1938–39. *Statistical testing of business-cycle theories.* 2 vols. Geneva: League of Nations, Economic Intelligence Service.

———. 1940. Econometric business cycle research. *Rev. Econ. Stud.* 7:73–90.

Tobin, J. 1955. A dynamic aggregative model. *J. Polit. Econ.* 63:103–15.

———. 1969. A general equilibrium approach to monetary theory. *J. Money, Credit, Banking* 1:15–29.

———. 1970. Money and income: Post hoc ergo propter hoc? *Quart. J. Econ.* 84:301–17.

———. 1975. Keynesian models of recession and depression. *Amer. Econ. Rev.* 65:195–202.

———. 1977. How dead is Keynes? *Econ. Inquiry* 15:459–68.

———. 1980. *Asset accumulation and economic activity: Reflections on contemporary macroeconomic theory.* Chicago: University of Chicago Press.

———. 1981. The monetarist counter-revolution today: An appraisal. *Econ. J.* 91:29–42.

———, ed. 1983. *Macroeconomics, prices, and quantities: Essays in memory of Arthur Okun.* Oxford: Basil Blackwell.

———. 1986. The future of Keynesian economics. *Eastern Econ. J.* 13(4):347–56.

Torre, V. 1977. Existence of limit cycles and control in complete Keynesian system by theory of bifurcations. *Econometrica* 45(6):1457–66.

Townsend, R. M. 1978. Market anticipations, rational expectations, and Bayesian analysis. *Internat. Econ. Rev.* 19:481–94.

———. 1983a. Equilibrium theory with learning and disparate expectations: Some issues and methods. In Frydman and Phelps 1983.

———. 1983b. Forecasting the forecasts of others. *J. Polit. Econ.* 91:546–88.

Tsiang, S. 1947. *The variations of real wages and profit margins in relation to the trade cycle.* London: Pitman.

Tufte, E. R. 1978. *Political control of the economy.* Princeton, N.J.: Princeton University Press.

Tugan-Baranovskii, M. I. [1894] 1913. *Les crises industrielles en Angleterre.* 2d ed. Paris: Giard & Brière.

U.S. Bureau of the Census. 1966. *Long-term economic growth, 1860–1965.* Washington, D.C.: U.S. Government Printing office.

U.S. Department of Commerce. Bureau of Economic Analysis (formerly Office of Business Economics). 1921–. *Survey of current business.*

U.S. Department of Commerce. Bureau of Economic Analysis. 1977, 1984. *Handbook of cyclical indicators: A supplement to the Business Conditions Digest.* Washington, D.C.: U.S. Government Printing Office.

Universities–National Bureau Committee for Economic Research. 1951. *Conference on business cycles.* New York: NBER.

———. 1960. *The quality and economic significance of anticipations data: A conference.* Princeton, N.J.: Princeton University Press for NBER.

Vaccara, B. N., and V. Zarnowitz. 1977. How good are the leading indicators? In *1977 Proceedings of the Business and Economic Statistics Section.* Washington, D.C.: American Statistical Association.

———. 1978. Forecasting with the index of leading indicators. NBER Working Paper no. 244, May.

van Duijn, J. J. 1983. *The long wave in economic life.* London: George Allen & Unwin.

Varian, H. R. 1979. Catastrophe theory and the business cycle. *Econ. Inquiry* 17:14–28.

Vellupillai, K. 1990. *Nonlinear and multisectoral macrodynamics: Essays in honor of Richard Goodwin.* New York: New York University Press.

Vining, R. 1949a. Koopmans on the choice of variables to be studied and of methods of measurements. *Rev. Econ. Statis.* 31(2):77–86.

———. 1949b. A rejoinder. *Rev. Econ. Statis.* 31(2):91–94.

Visco, I. 1984. *Price expectations in rising inflation.* Amsterdam: North-Holland.

Volcker, P. A. 1978. *The rediscovery of the business cycle.* New York: Free Press.

Von Furstenberg, G. M. 1977. Corporate investment: Does market valuation matter in the aggregate? *Brookings Pap. Econ. Act.* 2:347–408.

Wachtel, P. 1977. Survey measures of expected inflation and their potential usefulness. In *Analysis of Inflation, 1965–1974,* ed. J. Popkin, Studies in Income and Wealth, vol. 42. Cambridge, Mass.: Ballinger for NBER.

Wallis, K. F. 1977. Multiple time series analysis and the final form of econometric models. *Econometrica* 45(6):1481–97.

———. 1989. Macroeconomic forecasting: A survey. *Econ. J.* 99(March): 28–61.

Walters, A. A. 1963. Production and cost functions: An econometric survey. *Econometrica* 31(1–2): 1–66.

Waterman, A. M. C. 1967. The timing of economic fluctuations in Australia, January 1948 to December 1964. *Australian Econ. Pap.* 5(3):77–101.

Watson, M. W. 1986. Univariate detrending methods with stochastic trends. *J. Monet. Econ.* 18(1):49–75.

Waud, R. N. 1976. Asymmetric policy marker utility functions and optimal policy under uncertainty. *Econometrica* 44:53–60.

Webb, R. H. 1984. Vector autoregressions as a tool for forecast evaluation. *Federal Reserve Bank of Richmond Econ. Rev.* 70(January/February):3–11.

Wecker, W. E. 1979. Predicting the turning points of a time series. *J. Business* 52:35–50.

Weir, D. 1986. The reliability of historical macroeconomic data for comparing cyclical stability. *J. Econ. Hist.* 46 (June):353–65.

West, K. D. 1988. Evidence from seven countries on whether inventories smooth aggregate output. NBER Working Paper no. 2664, July.

Whitman, M. V. N. 1976. International interdependence and the U.S. economy. In

AEI studies on contemporary economic problems, ed. W. Fellner. Washington, D.C.: American Enterprise Institute.

Wicksell, K. [1898] 1936. *Interest and prices: A study of the causes regulating the value of money*. London: Macmillan.

Willett, T. D. 1988. *Political business cycles: The political economy of money, inflation, and unemployment*. Durham, N.C.: Duke University Press.

Winkler, R. L. 1989. Combining forecasts: A philosophical basis and some current issues. *Internat. J. Forecasting* 5(4):605–9.

Woglom, G. 1982. Underemployment equilibria with rational expectations. *Quart. J. Econ.* 97(1):89–108.

Wojnilower, A. M. 1980. The central role of credit crunches in recent financial history. *Brookings Pap. Econ. Act.* 2:277–339.

Wold, H. 1964. Forecasting by the chain principle. In *Econometric model building: Essays on the causal chain approach*, ed. H. Wold. Amsterdam: North-Holland.

Wolfe, H. D. 1986. *Business forecasting methods*. New York: Holt, Rinehart & Winston.

Wolfson, M. H. 1986. *Financial crises: Understanding the postwar U.S. experience*. Armonk, N.Y.: M. E. Sharpe.

Yeats, A. J. 1973. An evaluation of the predictive ability of the FRB sensitive price index. *J. Amer. Statis. Assoc.* 68(December):782–87.

Young, A. H. 1974. *Reliability of the quarterly national income and product accounts of the United States, 1947–1971*. Bureau of Economic Analysis Staff Paper no. 23, U.S. Department of Commerce. Washington, D.C.: U.S. Government Printing Office.

Zarnowitz, V. 1961. The timing of manufacturers' orders during business cycles. In Moore 1961.

———. 1962. *Unfilled orders, price changes, and business fluctuations*. New York: NBER.

———. 1967. *An appraisal of short-term economic forecasts*. New York: NBER.

———. 1968a. *International encyclopedia of the social sciences*, s.v. "Mitchell, Wesley C."

———. 1968b. The record of turning point forecasts of GNP and other major aggregates. Paper presented at the Conference on Forecasting and Recognizing Turns in the Business Cycle, National Association of Business Economists and NBER, March, Long Island University.

———. 1968c. An evaluation of price-level forecasts. In *1968 proceedings of the Business and Economic Statistics Section*. Washington, D.C.: American Statistical Association.

———. 1969a. The ASA-NBER quarterly survey of the economic outlook: An early appraisal. In *1969 proceedings of the Business and Economic Statistics Section*. Washington, D.C.: American Statistical Association.

———. 1969b. The new ASA-NBER survey of forecasts by economic statisticians. *Amer. Statistician* 23:12–16.

———. 1971. New plans and results of research in economic forecasting. 51st Annual Report of the NBER.

———, ed. 1972a. *The business cycle today*. New York: NBER.

———. 1972b. Forecasting economic conditions: The record and the prospect. In Zarnowitz 1972a.

———. 1973. *Orders, production, and investment: A cyclical and structural analysis*. New York: NBER.

———. 1974. How accurate have the forecasts been? In Butler, Kavesh, and Platt 1974.

———. 1978. On the accuracy and properties of recent macroeconomic forecasts. *Amer. Econ. Rev. Pap. and Proc.* 68:313–19.

575   References

———. 1979. An analysis of annual and multiperiod quarterly forecasts of aggregate income, output, and the price level. *J. Business* 52:1–33. Now chap. 14 of this volume.

———. 1981. Business cycles and growth: Some reflections and measures. In *Wirtschaftstheorie und Wirtschaftspolitik: Gedenkschrift für Erich Preiser,* ed. W. J. Mückl and A. E. Ott. Passau: Passavia Universitätsverlag. Now chap. 7 of this volume.

———. 1982a. An analysis of predictions from business outlook surveys. In *International research on business cycle surveys,* ed. H. Laumer and M. Ziegler. Aldershot, England: Gower Publishing.

———. 1982b. Expectations and forecasts from business outlook surveys. NBER Working Paper no. 845, January.

———. 1982c. On functions, quality, and timeliness of economic information. *J. Business* 55:87–119.

———. 1983. Some lessons from research in macroeconomic forecasting. *Econ. Outlook USA* 10(4):83–86.

———. 1984a. The accuracy of individual and group forecasts from business outlook surveys. *J. Forecasting* 3:11–26. Earlier version, NBER Working Paper no. 1053, December 1982. Now chap. 15 of this volume.

———. 1984b. Business cycle analysis and expectational survey data. In *Leading indicators and business cycles surveys,* ed. K. H. Openheimer and G. Poser. Aldershot, England: Gower Publishing.

———. 1985a. Rational expectations and macroeconomic forecasts. *J. Bus. Econ. Stat.* 3:293–311. Earlier version, NBER Working Paper no. 1070, January 1983. Now chap. 16 of this volume.

———. 1985b. Recent work on business cycles in historical perspective. *J. Econ. Lit.* 23:523–80. Now chap. 2 of this volume.

———. 1986. The record and improvability of economic forecasting. *Econ. Forecasts* 3(December):22–30. Now chap. 18 of this volume.

———. 1987–88. On causes and consequences of financial instability. *Econ. Outlook USA* 14 (3):13–16.

———. 1989a. Cost and price movements in business cycles: Theories and experience. NBER Working Paper no. 3131, October.

———. 1989b. Cost and price movements in business cycle theories and experience: Causes and effects of observed changes. NBER Working Paper no. 3132, October.

———. 1989c. Facts and factors in the recent evolution of business cycles in the United States. NBER Working Paper no. 2865, February.

———. 1990. Corporate bond prices as a leading indicator. In Moore 1990.

———. 1991. What is a business cycle? NBER Working Paper no. 3863 (October). Forthcoming in *Proceedings of the 16th Annual Policy Conference,* Federal Reserve Bank of St. Louis, 1992.

Zarnowitz, V. and C. Boschan. 1975a. Cyclical indicators. *55th Annual Report of the NBER,* September.

———. 1975b. Cyclical indicators: An evaluation and new leading indexes. *Business Conditions Digest,* May v–xxii. Reprinted in U.S. Department of Commerce, Bureau of Economic Analysis 1977.

———. 1975c. New composite indexes of coincident and lagging indicators. *Business Conditions Digest,* November, v–xxiv. Reprinted in U.S. Department of Commerce, Bureau of Economic Analysis 1977.

———. 1977. Cyclical indicators. *57th Annual Report of the NBER,* September.

Zarnowitz, V., C. Boschan, and G. H. Moore, assisted by J. Su. 1972. Business cycle analysis of econometric model simulations. In Hickman 1972.

Zarnowitz, V., and P. Braun. 1989a. Comment. In Blanchard and Fischer 1989.

————. 1989b. Major macroeconomic variables and leading indexes: Some estimates of their interrelations, 1886–1982. NBER Working Paper no. 2812.

Zarnowitz, V., and L. A. Lambros. 1987. Consensus and uncertainty in economic prediction. *J. Polit. Econ.* 95(3):591–621.

Zarnowitz, V., and L. J. Lerner. 1961. Cyclical changes in business failures and corporate profits. In Moore 1961.

Zarnowitz, V., and G. H. Moore. 1977. The recession and recovery of 1973–1976. *Explorations in Econ. Res.* 4:472–557.

————. 1981. The timing and severity of the recession of 1980. *NBER Reporter.*

————. 1982. Sequential signals of recession and recovery. *J. Business* 55:57–85.

————. 1986. Major changes in cyclical behavior. In Gordon 1986a.

————. 1990. New measures of the growth of debt. In Moore 1990.

————. 1991. Forecasting recessions under the Gramm-Rudman-Hollings law. In Lahiri and Moore 1991.

Zellner, A. 1958. A statistical analysis of provisional estimates of gross national product and its components, of selected national income components, and of personal saving. *J. Amer. Statis. Assoc.* 53:54–65.

————. 1979. Statistical analysis of econometric models. *J. Amer. Statis. Assoc.* 74:628–43.

————. 1984. Posterior odds ratios for regression hypotheses: General considerations and some specific results. In *Basic issues in econometrics.* Chicago: University of Chicago Press.

————. 1985. Bayesian econometrics. *Econometrica* 53:253–69.

Zellner, A., and F. Palm. 1974. Time series analysis and simultaneous equations econometrics models. *J. Econometrics* 2:17–54.

Zellner, A., and S. C. Peck. 1973. Simulation experiments with a quarterly macroeconomic model of the U.S. economy. In *Econometric studies of macro and monetary relations,* ed. A. A. Powell and R. A. Williams. Amsterdam: North-Holland.

Author Index

Abel, A. B., 34
Abraham, K. 18n9
Abramovitz, M., 24n3, 42, 96, 166n3, 211, 239
Adams, F. G., 387n4, 425
Adelman, F. L., 45, 173, 174, 200, 266
Adelman, I., 45, 173, 174, 200, 238, 246n6, 266
Aftalion, A., 31
Aiginger, K., 64, 490
Akerlof, G. A., 120, 145
Allais, M., 189
Alt, J. E., 52n40
Altonji, J. G., 56, 57n49
Amihud, Y., 139n13
Andersen, L. C., 176, 177n24
Andersen, P. S., 126, 152n26, 154
Ando, A., 167, 175n20
Armstrong, J. S., 406n22
Arrow, K. J., 62
Ashenfelter, O., 57n49
Auerbach, A., 350, 357, 534
Axe, E. W., 225n31
Ayres, L. P., 220, 222nn24,25, 225n31
Azariadis, C. 66, 71n77, 133

Backus, D. K., 91
Baily, M. N., 71n77, 87, 123, 133, 159
Balke, N. S., 87, 89, 91, 100n16, 125n1, 362, 363
Ball, L., 127n3
Banerji, A., 338
Barnea, A., 498

Barnett, W. A., 199
Barro, R. J., 53n42, 55–57, 60, 71n77, 72n78, 101, 103n18, 161n38
Barsky, R. B., 81n1
Batchelor, R., 404, 405
Bates, J. M., 407n23, 460n17, 493n1
Becker, G. S. 463
Beckman, B. A., 322, 337nn16,17
Begg, D. K. H., 60n53
Berle, A. A., 153n27
Bernanke, B. S., 4n1, 70n74, 73n80, 111, 141, 147, 156
Bernstein, M., 166n3
Beveridge, S., 46, 185, 349n33
Bils, M., 43n25, 147
Bilson, J. F. O., 73
Bischoff, C. W., 34n10, 407n23
Black, F., 18, 71, 190
Blanchard, O. J., 4n1, 34, 65, 73n80, 127n3, 128, 134n9, 144n20, 145, 152n26, 184n3, 243, 252, 363
Blatt, J. M., 45, 257n16, 258–59
Blinder, A. S., 59–60, 66, 96, 114, 145, 250
Bober, S., 39n1
Bodkin, R. A., 43n25
Boehm, E. A., 18, 43
Bomberger, W. A., 495, 498
Bordo, M. D., 67n67
Boschan, C., 45, 173, 174n18, 185, 200, 213, 299, 316n1, 318, 329, 332, 338, 353, 356n43
Boschen, J. F., 56
Box, G. E. P. 184, 482

577

Nerlove, M., 37n16, 167n7, 173n17
Newbold, P., 246n5, 467n17, 483, 493n1
Niemira, M. P., 261, 349, 354n39, 355,
    356n45, 533
Nordhaus, W. D., 52n40
Nutter, G. W., 153

Officer, R. R., 112n26
Okun, A. M., 55–57, 71n77, 137, 145, 420,
    497
O'Neil, W. D., 39n21
Organization for Economic Cooperation and
    Development (OECD), 338

Palash, C. J., 261, 346, 534
Palm, F., 406n22, 533n5
Papadia, F., 64, 490
Parkin, M., 145
Parsons, D. O., 127n2
Pashigian, B. P., 64
Patinkin, D., 36n13, 70n73, 156n28
Pauly, P., 407n23
Pearce, D. K., 63, 463, 468, 490, 496n4
Peck, S. C., 45n30
Pencavel, J., 134
Peristiani, S. C., 406n22
Persons, W. M., 87, 224n30, 362
Pesando, J. E., 63, 490, 496n4
Petersen, B. C., 139, 143n19
Phelps, E. S., 37, 54, 60n53, 62n55, 68, 72,
    179, 465
Phelps Brown, E. H., 146
Phillips, A. W., 36, 161n38
Pierce, D. A., 324n9, 482
Pigou, A. C., 16, 31, 32n7, 36n13, 47n34
Pindyck, R. S., 487, 533n5
Piore, M. J., 131
Plant, M., 18n9
Platt, R. B., 339
Plosser, C. I., 8, 46, 70n74, 71, 184, 187n5,
    243, 365, 381
Pohjola, M. T., 197
Pólya, G., 447n8
Poole, W., 58, 60n53, 64, 115n32, 462
Popkin, J., 42, 59, 310
Porter, R. H., 143
Powell, J. L., 141, 147
Preiser, E., 43n27, 203n1
Prescott, E. C., 8, 59, 185, 243
Preston, R. S., 44n29

Quah, D., 184n3

Radecki, L. J., 261, 346, 534
Ramanathan, R., 407n23
Rapping, L., 53, 56
Rau, N., 21n2
Reagan, P. B., 139n13
Rebelo, S. T., 8, 185
Reder, M. W., 152
Rees, A., 146, 152
Rhoades, D., 338
Robertson, D. H., 31
Robinson, C. S., 261
Rodbertus, J. K., 16
Romer, C., 77–78, 89, 91, 363
Romer, D., 127n3
Rorty, M. C., 224n30
Rose, H., 39n21, 43, 196
Rosen, S., 127n2
Rostow, W. W., 24n3, 238n3
Rotemberg, J. J., 8, 57, 126, 127n3, 145
Rubinfeld, D. L., 487, 533n5
Rudebusch, G. D., 261, 325n10, 329, 338,
    346, 347n29, 348, 351–52, 357
Runkle, D. E., 324n9, 325, 359, 396n13,
    406
Rush, M., 56

Sachs, J., 125–26, 147n23, 150
Sachverständigenrat zur Begutachtung der
    gesamtwirtschaftlichen Entwicklung,
    212
Saito, M., 174n18, 522t
Samuelson, P. A., 36, 38, 66, 171, 196, 197,
    424
Sapir, M., 420
Sargent, T., 43n25, 53n42, 55, 56n47, 57,
    58n51, 62, 352n37
SAS Institute, 249n8
Scadding, J. L., 116
Scarfe, B. L., 39n21
Scherer, F. M., 138n12, 153
Schinasi, G. J., 39n21, 255
Schnader, M. H., 493
Schultze, C. L., 89
Schumpeter, J. A., xvi, 9, 24n3, 31, 32n7,
    171, 238n3, 240
Schwartz, A. J., 24n3, 47, 48n36, 49, 52,
    62, 63n58, 69n71, 106–7t, 108, 109n22,
    110, 115, 120nn37,38, 121, 157, 161,
    165, 175–76, 189, 205n6, 211, 224n29,
    228nn34,36, 229, 236n2, 254n12, 363
Schwert, G. W., 112n26
Semmler, W., 199, 255
Shafer, W., 197

Subject Index

Acceleration principle, 31, 38
Accelerator-multiplier models, 1–2, 4, 38–42, 74, 171–72, 264
AD. *See* Aggregate demand curve
Adaptive expectations (AE), 53, 62–63
AD-AS model, 253. *See also* Aggregate demand curve; Aggregate supply (AS) curve
AE. *See* Adaptive expectations
Aggregate demand (AD) curve, 155–56, 253–54
Aggregate supply (AS) curve, 155, 253
Agricultural sector, 97
Amplitudes: assessment of, 237; in cyclical movements, 220–30; standardization in composite index construction, 338; variation of phases in, 289–93
ARIMA (autoregressive integrated moving average) models and forecasts, 184, 412
AR roots. *See* Autoregressive unit roots
ARSME. *See* Average root-mean-square error
AS. *See* Aggregate supply (AS) curve
ASA-NBER median forecasts, 429, 435
ASA-NBER Quarterly Economic Outlook Survey study, 410–11
ASA-NBER survey: accuracy and consistency of participants in, 446–61; data on point and probabilistic forecasts, 517–18; forecasts, 396, 399, 401–4, 410, 429–42; properties of, 499–500; survey methods of, 444–46, 466–69
AT&T index, 224n30
Autoregressive (AR) unit roots, 184

Average root-mean-square error (ARSME), 411t, 412
Axe-Houghton index, 224n30
Ayres's index, 222n24, 225

Babson index, 224n30, 225, 229
Banks, panics and suspensions, 108
Bayesian vector autoregression (BVAR) models and forecasts, 401, 411–12
BCD. See Business Conditions Digest
BEA. *See* U.S. Department of Commerce, Bureau of Economic Analysis
Blue Chip Economic Indicators, 387n5, 404
Brookings-SSRC model, 175n20, 200, 266–68, 271, 275–76, 279
Budget, federal: components of deficit and surplus, 103–5; growth and cyclicality of, 101–2; policy for, 113–14
Business Conditions Digest (BCD), 299, 303, 305, 319
Business cycles: continuity of, 357; dating by NBER of, 283–88, 348; defined, 236–37, 283; derivation of reference chronologies for, 214–16; differences in endogenous and exogenous models of, 44; distinguished from growth cycle, 22, 30, 214–16, 242, 346; diversity in measured, 3, 17–19; equilibrium approach to, 53–60; exogenous and endogenous models of, 1–2; forces causing diversity in, 14; historical durations of, 22–23, 119–23, 125, 220–31, 233–37, 263; Keynesian theory of, 33–35; long-wave

585